THE CAMRA GUIDE TO LONDON'S BEST BEER PUBS & BARS

Des de Moor

CAMRA
BOOKS

BOOKS

Published by the Campaign for Real Ale Ltd
230 Hatfield Road, St Albans, Hertfordshire AL1 4LW
www.camra.org.uk/books
© Campaign for Real Ale 2015
Text © Des de Moor
First Edition 2011 (Reprinted with corrections 2012)
Second Edition 2015

ISBN 978-1-85249-323-3

A CIP catalogue record for this book is available from the British Library

Printed and bound in Slovenia by GPS Group Ltd.

Head of Publishing: Simon Hall
Project Editor: Julie Hudson
Design/Typography: Dale Tomlinson
Typefaces: Guardian Sans family; Veneer
Maps: James Hall
Sales & Marketing: David Birkett

Contents

WE ARE THE ONLY DEDICAT
HOUSE IN LONDON TO SELL
CIDERS FROM SMALL INDEPE

Southampton Arms (p138)

Celebrating London's beer renaissance

LONDON is once again one of the best beer cities in the world, and this book sets out to provide the complete and indispensable guide to its beery treasures. Historically a brewing colossus and long renowned for its great pubs, this great city has in a matter of years reclaimed its status as a world-class centre for making beer as well as drinking it. These pages direct both the beer beginner and the connoisseur to the best places in which to experience London's miraculous local beer renaissance alongside brewing excellence from the rest of the UK and, indeed, the world. Importantly, the book also details London's growing band of brewers and sets the contemporary beer scene in the context of the city's rich culture, history and brewing heritage.

150 years ago, London was the world's beer capital. The city's brewers pioneered industrial brewing, invented the first two international beer styles and sent their products to every inhabited continent on the planet. But London's global pre-eminence eventually declined and in the 20th century its domestic brewing dominance started to crumble too. Of course, as the capital city of one of the world's great beer countries, the city retained its pub tradition and its vibrant drinking culture. The strength of that culture owed much to the local activities of the Campaign for Real Ale (CAMRA), the organisation that from the 1970s led the fight to ensure that British brewing uniquely retained the old technique of cask conditioning, or 'real ale'. Alongside this, as a large and cosmopolitan world city, London long provided Britain's biggest market for 'world beers' from other great brewing nations like Belgium and Germany.

But until very recently London seemed to have lost its brewing credentials for good. Nearly all the big brewing groups had torn up their roots and deserted the city by the 1990s. Several of Britain's earliest microbreweries and brewpubs emerged here in the wake of the real ale revival, but they and their successors seemed unable to survive for more than a few years before closing down or moving out. Londoners could at least take pride in their two surviving independent breweries, Fuller's and Young's, both of whom played a major role in securing the future of cask beer. Then in 2006 Young's closed and merged with Wells in Bedford, bringing London's brewing fortunes to a new low with only nine commercial breweries.

2006 turned out to be a line in the sand. Over the next few years a trickle of promising startups appeared, some of them directly motivated by the determination to restore London's lost glory. This coincided with a growing consumer interest in localism and good quality, flavoursome local products from small producers, and the appearance of a younger generation of beer explorers inspired by the innovative and eclectic approach of US craft brewing. A handful of imaginative new venues latched onto this growing market, challenging received wisdom about what a good London beer pub should look and feel like. And amazingly this turnaround took place in the teeth of one of the longest and deepest economic recessions yet known, and alongside a seemingly unstoppable decimation of Britain's pub stock through closure and conversion.

The first edition of this guide, published in July 2011, recorded 14 London breweries, including seven recent newcomers, among them now-famous names like Kernel, Redemption and Sambrook's. There was already a buzz of excitement in the air, but nobody could have predicted quite how far things would go. This book details 70 London breweries and counting. It's an astonishing story that's chronicled in more detail later in this introduction.

The growth in brewing has been matched by an unprecedented surge in the range, variety and local provenance of quality beer in pubs and bars. As well as a proliferation of specialist outlets stocking a range wide enough to delight the dedicated geek, very many ordinary neighbourhood pubs have upped their game and even many of the big chains have yielded to customer demand for quality local products. The beer renaissance has undoubtedly helped many outlets buck the trend of closure: several pubs once thought beyond redemption are now prospering as beer champions, and other flourishing beer-focused venues have been converted from other uses. London beers are now appearing on London bars with a ubiquity and frequency unseen since the 1970s, and the quality and variety on offer is almost certainly the best it's ever been. I like to think this guide, appearing when it did, made a modest contribution to a truly astonishing renaissance.

One major objective of the book is to steer the beer lover to places offering something out of the ordinary. The longest section sets out 260 recommendations for great places to buy and drink beer. In 2011, my task in compiling this section was finding enough places, besides the obvious self-selecting specialists, that genuinely offered quality, choice and interest, rather than the same old handful of cask ale 'usual suspects' from breweries far outside London. In 2015, the challenge has been in deciding what to leave out. The bar has been raised so much higher that many venues that were obvious inclusions four years ago no longer make the grade if I'm to ensure you're spending your precious time and money in the very best beer venues in London.

You can read more about how the listed outlets were chosen on p 22 but the main concerns are beer choice, quality and expertise.

The selection recognises longstanding beer champions and unique places like brewery taprooms and brewpubs, and aims to be representative in including the best examples of brewery and chain outlets. Pubs are still the backbone of London's drinking scene and this book includes plenty of outstanding pubs that even teetotallers will appreciate, but this doesn't mean it's solely a pub guide. Great beer is now getting into all sorts of places, including cocktail bars, social clubs, restaurants and even public gardens, and my selection reflects this too.

Cask beer still rightly occupies central stage, for reasons explained on p 251, but it isn't the end of the story. Most London brewers bottle their beers, and many bottle condition, producing 'real ale in a bottle'. A few now package decent unpasteurised beer in cans. Many of the listed pubs and bars increase customer choice still further by stocking bottled beers from London and elsewhere,

Weights & measures

The weights and measures used should be familiar enough to most readers. I've either given metric measurements only, or both metric and non-metric measurements. The latter use the imperial system unless clearly stated otherwise: remember that an imperial pint, at 20 fl oz (568 ml), is 25% larger than a standard US pint of 16 fl oz (473 ml), and a gallon is proportionately larger too.

Rather less familiar are the measures used in the industry for bulk beer and brewery capacity. The international measure is the hectolitre (hl), equivalent to 100 l, 22 gallons or 176 pints. Many British brewers still think in terms of the old brewer's barrels, which held 36 gallons (1.64 hl, 164 l, 288 pints).

Note that British brewer's barrels are significantly more capacious than American ones: a US barrel holds only 31 US gallons (1.17 hl, 117 l, 198.5 imperial pints).

A note on the second edition

The beer scene in London has changed so much since the first edition of this book was published in July 2011 that this edition is pretty much an entirely new book. Of the 252 places to drink listed in 2011, only 100 are still listed in 2015, some of these under different names and/or new management; all have been revisited and their details checked and revised. Of the 152 that didn't make it, only 12 have actually closed, itself a remarkable statistic

given overall trends towards pub closures. The rest haven't been excluded because they dropped their standards, but simply because we want to keep the book to a reasonable length and there are now more deserving claimants to the space. Some of the places excluded by space pressures from full entries are briefly represented as ones to 'Try also'.

With the huge growth in London breweries, the individual brewery listings are of necessity

more concise, with selected brewers discussed at greater length in longer features. The previous directory of brewers from outside London has been discarded as surplus to requirements.

Readers familiar with the previous edition will notice various new features and improvements, changes to the maps and geographical layout, and a certain amount of necessary streamlining to fit it all in.

and the listings also stretch to the best places to buy beer to drink at home, including bottle shops and off-licences. Additionally, many London brewers have embraced so-called 'craft keg', producing flavoursome draught beer that isn't cask but is usually unpasteurised and often unfiltered and served without additional gas (see p 253).

Besides brewers, beers and beer outlets, this book contains a wealth of other useful detail, with summaries of pub and bar chains of interest to the beer lover, a round-up of the main festivals and events, and a guide to the beer styles brewed in London. I've included notes on beer with food, a pub user guide for visitors, and an index of places to drink by theme. For additional depth you'll find material on the history and heritage of pubs, brewing and London, and for breadth there are some alternative thoughts from some of the capital's beer movers and shakers.

Finally, as excellent as London's beer is, it would be perverse to spend all your time here in the pub. I've therefore included some context about the city, and pointed out other features of interest in the areas surrounding the listed outlets. These notes are necessarily brief and selective and I strongly recommend that to explore properly, you use this book in conjunction with a general guidebook (More information, p 318). Beer is also a cultural phenomenon and putting it in context can only enrich your appreciation of London's zythological bounty.

If you're visiting London for the first time or have just moved here, or you know the city already but aren't yet familiar with its beer scene, a very warm welcome. I hope this book will provide an excellent starting point for what I promise will be a great beer journey. If you're a longstanding Londoner and beer connoisseur, the book should steer you to new discoveries and fill in the background to things you already know, or at least provide something to argue with. Together we can all help ensure London beer remains a cause for celebration for many years to come.

Updates and feedback

A disadvantage of guidebooks is that they soon slip out of date and, given the dynamism of the current London beer scene, this one is likely to date more quickly than most. To help mitigate this, with the previous edition I provided regular updates online for some time after publication and I plan on repeating this exercise. Please check my website at http://desdemoor.co.uk/london.

Comments, updates and suggestions are all very welcome. Feedback on the previous edition helped shape this new one, for which I'm grateful. The book has a Twitter feed @LdnBestBeer and a Facebook fan page at www.facebook.com/LondonsBestBeer where comments are welcome and news is periodically posted. Likes are much appreciated. You can contact me directly at des@desdemoor.com or follow me on Twitter: @desdemoor.

The city that invented itself

London wasn't meant to exist. Those ancient urbanists, the Romans, rarely built on greenfield sites, preferring to redevelop existing settlements. When the legions crossed the Thames in 43 CE they found nothing of note on the little rise of Cornhill, on the north bank just east of the Walbrook stream. Belgic and Celtic farmers populated the wider area, but the river then was much broader, shallower and marshier than today, so settlements clung to higher ground. There may have been a farm on or close to the place where London grew, with a name later borrowed into Latin as LONDINIVM.

The Roman army originally used several crossing points, but sometime after the year 50 a decision was taken to build a permanent crossing between Southwark and Cornhill, a few metres upstream from the present London Bridge. No military emplacement was intended for the north end of the bridge, so the officer who signed off the plans couldn't have had any idea he was ushering one of the greatest cities in human history into existence.

Unsurprisingly given its strategic importance, the road junction over the bridge attracted service industries and a small settlement grew. In 60 CE the fledgling town was sacked by the Celtic Iceni tribe: their leader, Queen Boudica, is another inadvertent godparent as her actions prompted London's rebuilding as a proper planned city, with a defensive wall that can still be traced today. The centre of administration moved here from Colchester and by the end of the 1st century it was the biggest city in and the de facto capital of the province of Britannia.

It's remarkable how the earliest development of London set so much of the tone for what was to follow, driven as it was by entrepreneurs who realised there was a living to be made in hawking goods and services from the roadside. The importance of London as a port

also goes back to Roman times, the sheltered estuary and good connections to a new road network making it a more favourable entry point than the old Celtic ports on the south coast. A complex of wharves soon projected into the river, the first of many such encroachments that eventually created the narrower, deeper Thames we know today.

Three centuries later, their empire crumbling around them, the Romans abandoned Britain and their grand city began to decay, although the Germanic invaders that filled the vacuum continued to recognise it as a seat of power. The Guildhall is on the site of an Anglo-Saxon royal hall, and the Christian missionary Augustine established St Paul's cathedral nearby in 604 CE. The Anglo-Saxons developed their own trading suburb, known as Lundenwic, along the Strand, in those days the actual riverfront, but the Roman site remained in defensive use and Alfred the Great had its walls restored.

Following the unification of England in 974 CE, London's prosperity ensured its importance as a political centre and royal residence. The old city lost its political role in 1052 when Edward the Confessor moved his court upstream to Thorney Island, next to a tiny abbey which was rapidly bolstered with royal patronage. Though much altered, the palace and the abbey still stand at Westminster, and the split between economic and political centres remains a persistent feature of London's geography. This split is also behind the typographical subtlety that distinguishes the city of London – the totality of continuous development – from the City of London, occupying the original roman site.

In 1066 William the Bastard, Duke of Normandy, conquered England, building what was to become the most powerful fortress in Britain, the Tower of London, in the southeast

corner of the city. The Normans gradually abandoned the old practice of peripatetic royal courts, and by the time Magna Carta was signed in 1215, Westminster had emerged as the single administrative capital, its palace the meeting place of Parliament. The City remained the population centre and the economic powerhouse, home to the powerful guilds that controlled manufacturing and trade in the medieval world, exploiting this position to lever autonomy from cash-strapped monarchs. Today the City of London retains a structure unique in English local government and still has its own police force.

London has long been the biggest city in Britain, but as the Middle Ages ended it lagged behind Paris and even Bruges and Novgorod in the world league tables. Under the Tudors and Stuarts it began to catch up, with the population spilling over the City walls into what became the East End. Southwark, to the south of the bridge, also flourished by providing services too disreputable for the City. The theatres for which it's best known signal London's emergence as a cultural crucible, a vibrant urban environment in which talents like William Shakespeare and Christopher Marlowe could flourish.

The river was central as both barrier and lifeline, by now not only a conduit of trade but of England's growing sea power, with naval dockyards established at Deptford and Woolwich. It was busy with big ships, with watermen constantly ferrying commuters, and with royals who took to wafting in sumptuous flotillas between the string of riverside palaces from Greenwich to Windsor.

With the population rocketing, overtaking Paris by 1650, the aristocratic owners of adjoining rural estates realised the true extent of their good fortune. The Earl of Bedford got things started with the piazza at Covent Garden in the 1630s, but a pair of disasters interrupted developments. The Great Plague of 1665 killed at least 100,000 people, perhaps 20% of the population. Next year came the Great Fire, which destroyed 80% of the largely wooden buildings within the City walls over the course of four days. The wealth of London is evident from the grand rebuilding that followed, its centrepiece Christopher Wren's spectacular new home for St Paul's. But the funds didn't stretch to realising Wren's ambitious master plan to build a new system of grand boulevards – something to ponder as you wander streets and alleys that still thread between the City's office blocks on their Roman and medieval alignments.

Post-Fire, the noxious industries were exiled east, while the west saw the onward march of property development through the 18th century. The now familiar pattern of streets, squares and terraces spread into the spaces between royal hunting grounds, themselves now remade into Royal Parks. New docks boosted the city's trading capacity, and as the Industrial Revolution took hold, industry became bigger, more capital intensive and technologically advanced, feeding international markets secured by the country's growing naval might. London's famed cosmopolitan character grew as people flocked here from all over.

Better transport facilitated further expansion in the 19th century, with improved roads rapidly followed by railways that spawned commuter suburbs further and further out. 'Ribbon development' and sprawl swallowed scores of formerly separate villages and towns. Victorian London was the capital of a massive empire, dotted with sumptuous monuments to its own success, but at a cost. Beneath it was a sink of poverty, with millions packed into unhealthy slums of the sort that sparked Charles Dickens to righteous anger.

Amazingly, London had got this far without a single directing authority. It wasn't until 1855 that a Metropolitan Board of Works was set up to coordinate infrastructure such as sewers – just in time for the Great Stink of 1858 when the stench of raw sewage in the Thames even disrupted parliamentary proceedings. A fully fledged London County Council followed in 1889, but the capital's boundaries had outgrown it before it even met.

As London entered the 20th century, political pressure built to contain this relentless growth, and to protect the remaining undeveloped areas. The city emerged relatively unscathed physically, though profoundly affected economically and socially, from World War I, but the outbreak of another war in 1939 marked a watershed. German bombs rained on London for 76 consecutive nights in the Blitz of 1940–41, destroying vast areas of the

urban fabric, particularly around the docks and industrial areas. After the war a new order took hold, with an increased role for government. New planning controls locked the boundaries of the built-up area where they remain today, within a protected green belt. The slums the Luftwaffe had missed were cleared and many of their inhabitants deported to supposedly self-contained New Towns much further out.

London was now the capital of a humbler Britain, no longer a great imperial power. Its industry declined and by the 1970s, with its docks now too small for the new container ships, it had even lost its ancient role as a port. But the City clung to pre-eminence as a financial and business centre that is still only rivalled by New York City, handling the majority of the world's business in foreign exchange.

As the dowdy 1950s gave way to the 'swinging 60s', London's art and culture flourished. The evolution of British popular music from trad jazz, skiffle and rhythm & blues to the 'British invasion', psychedelia and prog can be traced through London's pubs, clubs and recording studios, and it was in London that provincial bands like the Beatles achieved their creative peak. A few years later the city was the epicentre of punk. London has nurtured leading fashion designers, photographers, architects, artists and film makers, and provided the backdrop to countless novels from Martin Amis' *London Fields* to Monica Ali's *Brick Lane*. Between them the rich heritage and the contemporary cultural buzz now attract more international tourists than any other world city; almost 17 million in 2013.

London's creativity has been informed by its ever changing complexion. From 1948 it became a new home to settlers from Britain's former colonies in the Caribbean and the Indian subcontinent, followed by significant groups from Cyprus, Vietnam, West Africa and, latterly, Eastern Europe. Currently almost a third of Londoners were born outside the UK, and over 300 languages are spoken here. While new Londoners haven't always received the warmest of welcomes, historically they're only the most recent arrivals in the flow of humanity that's converged on the city over millennia. London has also been the scene of bitter struggles – as a political and economic centre it's a focus for political protest and occasionally violent conflict, from the anti-war demonstrations of the 1960s to the anti-globalisation protests and street riots of more recent years.

In 1964 it finally gained a local authority almost commensurate with its size, though still not quite matching its true boundaries, with the creation of the Greater London Council. By 1986 this body, under its left-wing leader Ken Livingstone, became such a thorn in the side of Margaret Thatcher's Conservative government that they abolished it, leaving London balkanised between 33 boroughs. Livingstone ultimately became the first Mayor of London when a new system of governance was created in 2000, serving two terms before being ousted by eccentric Tory Boris Johnson. Now on his own second term, Johnson is also likely to be back in Parliament as an MP by the time you read this, trying to ignore criticism that he's neglecting London, with a new contest due in 2016.

Recent decades have seen large areas of the capital transformed as former docks, warehouses and industrial areas are regenerated, postwar social housing refurbished and Victorian inner city suburbs gentrified with new city and media wealth, driving up property prices to absurd and world-busting levels. The most obvious symbol of all this is the way the focus of the city has shifted eastwards, first to the new high-rise business district built around disued docks at Canary Wharf and on to other remodelled areas like the Queen Elizabeth Olympic Park at Stratford (a legacy of London's hosting the 2012 Olympic and Paralympic Games), the Greenwich Millennium Village and the vast Thames Gateway project further downriver.

London is now almost two millennia old and looks set to continue reinventing itself. It's been the first part of the UK to bounce back from the recession of 2009, though the 'age of austerity' still persists in local council spending, and the gap between rich and poor is widening again. The population, currently 8.4 million, continues to grow and is likely to hit 9 million by 2020. As always, there's not much in the way of a grand plan, and accommodating these incomers will simply add to the variegated patchwork of the city's haphazard growth.

This complex texture, although confusing to navigate, is one of London's principal delights, blissfully free of the sort of unofficial apartheid that afflicts so many US cities. When you set your sights on a great pub, don't forget to enjoy the process of reaching it – you're quite likely to pass a pompous Victorian pile, a gloomy 1960s estate, a hidden green space, a poshed-up terrace, some striking contemporary architecture and a world famous landmark all within a few minutes' walk, and you'll undoubtedly hear snatches of some of those 300 languages along the way. Perhaps there's something to be said for unplanned cities after all.

City of brewing

On Chiswell Street on the very northern edge of the City is an events and conference venue known as the Brewery, which is used, according to its website, for everything "from upscale state functions and company conferences to televised music events and discreet boardroom powwows." The biggest available option to potential hirers is the Porter Tun Room, one of the largest unobstructed indoor spaces in London. Its name might sound like a piece of quaint nonsense dreamed up by the marketing team, but is in fact an accurate reflection of the room's original purpose.

For well over a century this room housed huge wooden vats known as 'tuns' in which thousands of barrels-worth of porter beer sleepily matured. Still more beer was kept in lined cisterns in the basement, the largest of which held 6,250 hl – about 1.1 million pints. This was the heart of the Whitbread brewery, opened by Samuel Whitbread in 1750 as the first purpose-built mass production brewery in the world, and at its peak the most successful brewery in Britain.

London has many more such relics. The Truman brewery, now an entertainment, retail and business complex, is a little to the east, in Brick Lane. The Courage brewery by Tower Bridge fell early to the redevelopment of London's docklands, and is now offices and flats. The Anchor retail park in Mile End Road bears the name of Charrington's former Anchor brewery, of which a couple of key buildings survive. At Romford in London's far eastern suburbia, the Brewery shopping complex with its mattress superstores and multiplex cinema occupies the site of Ind & Smith, later Ind Coope. Between them these sites testify to London's former status as the world capital of beer.

Brewing almost certainly goes back to London's beginnings. The practice was well-established by the Middle Ages, though as elsewhere in Europe much of it took place in places like pubs and the domestic brewhouses of institutions and upper class homes. The canons of St Paul's brewed a hundred times in 1286, producing 67,800 gallons (3,082 hl, 542,400 pints) – the output of a small commercial brewery today.

The Old Truman Brewery is now an arts and media complex

The growing population created increasing opportunities for 'common brewers' – stand-alone operations making a living from supplying beer. Southwark was particularly noted for such breweries (see Southwark ale p 56). The Worshipful Company of Brewers is one of the oldest of the city trade guilds, dating back to the end of the 12th century and granted a royal charter in 1437. It still maintains a hall north of the Guildhall, just within the old City walls, though most of the breweries were elsewhere. John Stow, whose 1598 *Survey of London* mentions 26 common brewers, notes they "remaine neare to the friendly water of Thames". This was principally for transport reasons – it's a misconception that the already sewage-laden river provided the principal ingredient of London's beer. Brewers were banned in 1345 from using public water conduits, so sunk their own artesian wells, tapping the aquifers within the chalk underlying the Thames basin.

In terms of scale, these early common brewers were comparable to many of today's smaller microbreweries, producing 20–30 barrels (33–50 hl, 5,760–8,640 pints) a week with a staff of four or five people. As the city grew, so did its demand for beer which back then was a truly everyday refreshment: water, particularly in big cities, was often dangerously polluted, while beer, which had been boiled as part of the brewing process, was a much safer drink. As the modern era approached, the total number of brewers declined, some of the smaller operations failing and the surviving breweries growing to fill the gaps. How some of these modest and labour-intensive businesses grew big enough to leave the impressive legacy visible today is partly answered by the story of porter.

There are various accounts of the 'invention' of porter which are now thought to be unreliable: much more likely is that it evolved and was refined over time by several brewers from an existing style of aged dark beer, probably in the 1710s. Most authorities agree that the most likely explanation of the name is its popularity with the porters who were then an important part of the busy city's workforce: 'fellowship porters' who carried bulk goods from ships and 'ticket porters' who transported a variety of goods around the streets.

Porter was a relatively strong beer of around 7% ABV, made with brown malt that had been roasted so ferociously it was 'blown' – popped like corn (the modern technical term is 'torrefied'). This gave the fresh beer a pronounced smoky tang, so it was aged to mellow the flavour. The long maturation in wooden vessels populated by numerous wild yeasts and other microflora produced a flat beer – 'stale' was the contemporary term – with distinctive sour, vinous flavours, as still found in some traditional Belgian as well as modern wood-aged beers. Later recipes included pale malts and the 'stale' quality was eventually offset by blending aged beer with a fresher brew.

The process favoured better-resourced brewers who could afford to lock up cash and storage space with stock that might take two years to recoup its investment, sometimes accounting for over 10% of a brewery's assets. The increasing size of the porter breweries drove technological development and capital investment in mechanical equipment, steam power, coke firing and more accurate instruments like thermometers and hydrometers. Economies of scale increased profitability, and porter tuns swelled accordingly, with brewers competing to possess the biggest. Porter brewing made the most successful brewery owners into millionaires, and money bought honours and political influence to big names like the Whitbreads and the Trumans, creating a new British brewing elite since punningly referred to as the 'beerage'.

In the 19th century the porter brewers faced competition from a very different style of beer that was ultimately to change the face of brewing, and once again it emerged from London. Pale ale first appeared in the 1650s, when the invention of coke made it possible to produce paler malts, but it really grabbed attention in the hoppy variant later known as India Pale Ale, famously exported to the subcontinent from East London. In the 1830s the water of Burton upon Trent in Staffordshire was found to be particularly suited to pale ale brewing and some of the big London breweries set up branches there, though all except Ind Coope abandoned the Midlands when they discovered 'Burtonising' London water with gypsum produced comparable results.

By the mid-19th century, London tastes were turning from porter to the fresher 'running ale' long known as 'mild', now being distributed via the new railway network in sparkling form using cask conditioning. Similarly fresh but paler, hoppier beers, known in the trade as pale ale but rapidly labelled 'bitter' by drinkers, had a growing and more upmarket following. Breweries like Charrington, Courage and Watney proved adept at catering to these changing tastes. Brewers increasingly got involved in retailing, first by providing cheap finance to licensees in exchange for exclusive supply rights, then buying up their own pub estates by the end of the 19th century.

Brewing in London kept on expanding, reaching a peak around 1905. For two centuries, London had boasted the biggest brewers in the world, but after 1910 that distinction was lost. Limits on raw materials in World War I drove down the strength of all British beer, which became known almost exclusively as a low gravity, high volume product.

Mild and bitter dominated the interwar years, with porter now seen as an old man's drink. Its strength was much reduced – Whitbread's was down to 2.3% by 1930 – though its cousin Irish stout was growing in popularity and in 1933 Dublin brewer Guinness established a London plant. That same decade saw Watney's first experiments with filtered, pasteurised and artificially carbonated keg ales at the Stag brewery in Mortlake.

After World War II, the big brewers saw keg as a response to the challenge of rapidly changing markets and drinking habits, and through the 1950s and 1960s a wave of consolidation and rationalisation swept the industry as it invested in both the hardware and marketing muscle needed to launch first keg bitters, then keg lagers. Whitbread, for example, swallowed 27 smaller breweries across the country between 1948 and 1971, rapidly closing almost all of them. By the end of this period, London was home to 11 breweries, all of them except Guinness dating back to the Victorian era, and most much older.

1971 is a significant year in the history of brewing and beer appreciation as it marks the foundation of the Campaign for the Revitalisation of Ale, shortly to be renamed the Campaign for Real Ale (CAMRA). When CAMRA began campaigning it faced a situation where seven big brewery groups brewed 75% of Britain's beer and owned half its pubs. Six of these – Allied (successor to Ind Coope), Bass Charrington, Courage, Guinness, Watney and Whitbread – had significant facilities in London. The seventh, Scottish & Newcastle, owned a significant number of London pubs. These groups were now managed by people dedicated to making beer at the cheapest possible cost and sold at the greatest possible profit, with no particular loyalty to the craft and tradition of brewing or pride in the finished product. Cask conditioned ale was an unwelcome anachronism and the future as they saw it was in pasteurised, artificially carbonated keg beers of little character, including heavily promoted, shoddily made, low gravity approximations of European golden lagers.

Two smallish London breweries, Fuller's and Young's, retained their independence. Both became revered names among the growing number of dedicated real ale drinkers and grew substantially, though remained minnows compared to the big groups. The 'real ale revival' persuaded some of the big brewers to dabble with cask again, but their trajectory remained towards ever larger concentrations of production and greater efficiency. Sentiment was set aside as business logic questioned the need for capacity in a place with such high wages, property prices and traffic congestion as London.

Whitbread stopped brewing at Chiswell Street in 1976 although retained the site as a corporate headquarters until 2005. Watney's owners pulled out of brewing entirely in 1988 when its now-subsidiary Truman's closed. Courage left Southwark in 1981, Charrington shut up shop in 1985 and Allied quit Romford in 1993. Guinness – now part of global drinks combine Diageo – shut down Park Royal in 2005. Watney's Mortlake brewery, now in the hands of the world's biggest brewer, Anheuser-Busch InBev, is the only remaining fragment of old school big brewing left in London, and it too now faces eventual closure, probably at the end of 2015.

Meanwhile, growing demand for characterful beer in the wake of the real ale revival was spurring an upsurge of new UK microbreweries. London was home to one of

Fuller's brewery, Chiswick

the very first of these, Godson Freeman & Wilmot, founded in 1977. But Godson's mixed fortunes and short lifespan – it finally closed in 1986 after several suspensions of brewing – proved all too typical of similar initiatives that followed. All microbrewers faced the challenge of reinventing an industry; London microbrewers faced all the additional challenges of logistics and costs that were driving out the bigger brewers. Some of the more enduring new independent names, like Pitfield (1981), Freedom (1995) and O'Hanlon's (now Hanlon's, 1996) survived by moving out too. London also played a major role in the rebirth of the brewpub: David Bruce's Firkin chain was founded here in 1979, spreading across the country and beyond, but was shut down by new owners 20 years later.

The most significant brewery to buck the trend was Meantime, founded in 2000 by Alastair Hook, who was also involved with setting up the Freedom brewery. Meantime is still flourishing today. Significantly, it chose a very different path to what was then the typical one for a microbrewery, concentrating initially on quality lager and the bar and restaurant trade rather than pubs – a disappointment to some real ale fans, but also a demonstration that a successful modern micro could exist in the capital.

In 2006 came the grave news that Young's was abandoning six centuries of brewing history on its Wandsworth site and merging with Charles Wells in Bedford. As 2007 began, London had only nine working commercial breweries, its lowest number since 1979, and only three of these – Fuller's, Meantime and the Stag – were of any significant size. Three were small and sometimes struggling micros: Battersea, Grand Union and Twickenham. The others were brewpubs: Brew Wharf, the Horseshoe and Zerodegrees. A century of relentless decline from the absolute heights of world leader to the humiliation of total poverty seemed near complete. But events were about to take an unexpected turn.

The new city of beer

At the Great British Beer Festival at Earls Court in August 2006, Londoner Duncan Sambrook and two old friends were planning their evening's drinking when they noticed that, of all the many hundreds of breweries represented from Britain and across the world, only one — Fuller's — was from the same city in which the event took place. Mulling on this over a few pints, they concluded the only meaningful response was to start a brewery. It might just have been the beer talking, but the idea took root in Duncan's mind and, just over two years later, became reality with the opening of Sambrook's in Battersea, not far from the recently vacated site of Young's.

Sambrook's was then the most substantial dot on a line that had already begun to turn modestly upwards, despite the loss of two short-lived micros, Grand Union and Battersea, in the intervening years. In March 2007, the Capital Pub Company included a small brewhouse in its refit of the Cock and Hen pub in Fulham; a couple of months later the experiment was repeated on a slightly larger scale at the Florence in Herne Hill. The Fulham pub was sold on a year later without its brewery, but the Florence is still in action.

As Sambrook's was commissioning its kit, across the other side of London siblings James and Lizzie Brodie were busy restoring a brewery abandoned for several years at the family's pub, the William IV in Leyton. An old farm building in East London's Green Belt became the part-time Ha'penny brewery in October 2009. What is, in retrospect, one of the most significant new openings took place a couple of months later, when former cheesemonger Evin O'Riordain began brewing and selling distinctively artisanal beers from a Bermondsey railway arch under the name of Kernel.

Andy Moffat, struck by the pride local communities in Northern English cities had in their local ale, launched Redemption in Tottenham early in 2010. A few months later, the tiny vessel in the cellar of the Horseshoe at Hampstead metamorphosed into a substantial new automated brewhouse in Kentish Town railway arches under the name Camden Town. Like Meantime, it made flavoursome and unpasteurised bottled and keg beers from the start, and soon suspended regular cask production. Then there was the unexpected reappearance of the Truman's name, at first contract-brewed outside London by two young would-be brewers with a passion for history.

One of the catalysts for what followed is arguably Phil Lowry, manager of beer trader beermerchants.com. Phil and two friends took over brewing at Borough Market brewpub Brew Wharf in March 2010, junking its staid recipes in favour of internationally-inspired experiments. It was Phil who, with Evin O'Riordain, invited all the other London brewers to dinner there in May 2010. That evening, fledgling newcomers and old hands discovered a shared passion and enthusiasm for London brewing and the London Brewers' Alliance (LBA) was born.

The brewers found that consumers too were ready to drink more London beer. "It's a neglected market," Duncan Sambrook told me in 2011. "My business partner David Welsh, who was once a director at Ringwood, was amazed at the contrast with Hampshire and Wiltshire where you're always bumping into reps from other breweries. When we started selling we found there were more outlets than we originally thought – more free houses, and more opportunities to get guests in. The London market's so big, I think it could support all of us and more."

Quite how much more nobody could have foreseen. When I submitted the manuscript of the first edition of this book in March 2011, Greater London had 14 operating commercial breweries including brewpubs, the highest figure since 1981. Just before the book went to press, we heard about another soon to start, Moncada, and congratulated ourselves on being so bang up-to-date by squeezing it in. As it turned out, Moncada encountered delays and didn't finally launch until October, by which time another six breweries had appeared.

The brewery total by the end of 2011 was 22. A year later it was 36, already a higher tidemark than at the peak of the Firkin era in 1998. By the end of 2013 it was 45, and at the time of writing early in 2015 it stands at 70, almost certainly the highest figure since at least Victorian times. Neighbourhoods that hadn't smelt a whiff of boiling hops for centuries are now swimming in beer, and you can find whole bars dedicated to Hackney breweries at festivals, or shelf units reserved for southeast London beers in bottle shops.

The new Truman's brewery

There have been some casualties. LBA founders Brew Wharf and Ha'penny aren't listed in this volume, and several others have come and gone in the intervening four years. But the vast majority are not only surviving but thriving, and struggling to keep up with demand. The rest of the new breweries involved in founding the LBA have grown significantly in size and capacity, Truman's is now supplying major pub chains from its own brewery at Hackney Wick, and many more newcomers have been forced to consider expansion plans within days of first opening the books. Beavertown has perhaps the most remarkable story – from a corner of a pub kitchen in February 2012, it's expanded twice, and now has one of London's most modern and capacious microbrewing setups in Tottenham.

Brewery numbers don't equate to overall volume, of course, and many of the newcomers are still very small. Veteran brewer Derek Prentice estimates that in the days of the Big Seven, nine or ten London breweries were

Kernel Brewery

producing seven million barrels (11.5 million hl) a year between them. Today, seven times the number of breweries barely manage one million barrels (1.6 million hl), and that's including all the Bud lager currently made in Mortlake. But it's hard to argue with the claim that the overall diversity in London, and the quality from the best brewers, has never been bettered.

One of the many positive aspects of the new wave's fresh approach is the direct relationship brewers now cultivate with drinkers. The old breweries were industrial black boxes, but most of the current crop welcome the public to taprooms, open days and tours, and those that don't would love to if only they had the facilities. Establishing this practice is one of Evin O'Riordain's many achievements — taking its cue from specialist food firms and US breweries, Kernel encouraged everyone to call in and buy beer from the start. Now, it's one of a string of breweries and other beer-related enterprises that have turned Bermondsey's railway arches on Saturdays into an unlikely zythophiliac promenade.

It's also true that much of the expansion does not involve the sort of low gravity cask-conditioned beer typically enjoyed by real ale traditionalists. The craft beer culture of the USA, with its fruit-bowl hops, eclecticism and iconoclastic willingness to mix and match

Old World styles with new ideas, is undeniably now returning the favour of its own past borrowings from the British beer scene. But then London has always been a dynamic and cosmopolitan place: "The modern London style is reflective of the modern London community," Phil Lowry told me in 2011, and his comment is even more applicable today.

While names like Hackney, Moncada, Redemption, Sambrook's and Twickenham are noted for excellent cask beers, many of the newcomers have followed Camden Town, the Kernel and Meantime in concentrating on other formats, like bottles, unfiltered and unpasteurised 'craft keg' beers and — perhaps most challenging to traditionalists – 'craft cans'. These initiatives have undoubtedly widened London's beer repertoire and introduced younger and more diverse audiences, including more women, to great beer, but there's a slight danger of throwing out the baby with the bathwater. Several US beer experts have reminded me that they come to London to drink session strength cask beers, a style which is almost unique to the UK and at which British brewers excel, and not to be plied with clones of beers they could enjoy at home. And a number of licensees I spoke to when researching this book told me they wished more new London brewers did cask, as it's what many of their customers want to drink.

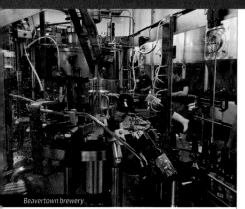
Beavertown brewery

Another issue the discerning drinker will encounter from time to time is quality. Many London brewers, including all the best-known names, are unfailingly professional, but standards aren't yet so high across the board as they are in comparable US cities and it's not unknown to encounter unintentionally sour or green flavours and gushing or flat bottles particularly from smaller producers. Several brewers and informed observers interviewed here cite quality as the one thing about the scene they'd most like to change. They're right: customers need confidence in brewers if the industry is to flourish in the long term. If you're unlucky, don't suffer in silence.

The obvious question is when and how it will all end. Jaega Wise of Wild Card is one of several professionals who told me that "beer in London is now fashionable." Indeed the archetype of the keen beer fan may even have shifted from the gent in jumper and sandals with an untidy beard pontificating over a pint of Old Crudginton's to the snappily tonsured and tattooed Hackney hipster rhapsodising over the New Zealand and Japanese hop aromas in his, or increasingly her, two-thirds of Session IPA. But it's an occupational hazard of being fashionable that you can rapidly and unexpectedly become unfashionable again at the flick of an eyebrow – is there a danger of this happening to London beer?

Peter Haydon, a fine brewer immersed in pub and beer history, says in this book that London won't re-enter the premier league of beer cities "until Londoners at large think about their city and their beer in the same way as the citizens of Munich, Brussels, Denver and Bamberg do." I'm hopeful that

we're some way there, and great beer and world class brewing are already just about firmly enough re-embedded into London's social and cultural fabric that they'll survive fickle fashionistas finding something trendier to post about on their tablets.

Meanwhile one of the best things you and I can do to ensure this happens is to continue to enjoy the fruits of all this frenetic activity. So raise your glasses, please, for a toast to London brewing. You've certainly got the widest choice ever of appropriate libations – Beavertown Smog Rocket, Brick Peckham Pils, Brixton Electric IPA, By the Horns Lambeth Walk, Hammerton N7, The Kernel London Sour, Pressure Drop Stokey Brown, Redchurch Hoxton Stout, Redemption Hopspur or Sambrook's Wandle are all possibilities that spring to mind. But perhaps the most appropriately named beer with which to wish the London brewers health, long life and prosperity is still one of the oldest-established: Fuller's London Pride.

Introduction

In the following pages you'll find details of over 270 recommended places to drink great beer, or to buy it to drink at home, with another 130 or so mentioned briefly as also worth trying in summaries at the end of each geographical section. It's a small proportion of a London pub total that, despite the toll of closures, still stands at over 6,000. Among these, I aim to direct you to the places that are most worthy of your time, money and attention.

I've looked favourably on venues that not only offer quality but also variety, particularly if they feature plenty of choice from small, independent and local brewers. In London you can drink beer from across the UK and indeed the world, and the book reflects that fact, but with so much great London-brewed beer around these days, I've inclined the selections towards venues that source at least something locally. I've also considered how the beer is presented, looking for places that take pride in their beer offer and evangelise on its behalf.

The ideal is a pub or bar with a well-chosen range that's been carefully curated to reflect a variety of styles and strengths, served by knowledgeable and enthusiastic staff able to make meaningful recommendations. While not every venue reaches the highest standards here, all of them are somewhere along the way. A pub with half a dozen handpumps offering well-known standard cask bitters from Cornwall, Suffolk and Yorkshire, served up by someone who knows nothing about them, is unlikely to qualify no matter how well-kept the beer is.

This approach naturally favours the geek-friendly 'beer exhibition' places, all of which should be present and correct. But there are plenty of other outlets with more modest but cared-for selections that provide an entry-level experience for new beer explorers while keeping both the geeks and their less obsessive partners and friends happy. I've also included a few places that serve a small range with exceptional care in a friendly and characterful setting, often longstanding traditional cask ale pubs run by genuine beer heroes.

As explained in the Brewers & Beers section (p245), cask conditioned beer has a unique character that can't be duplicated any other way, and the persistence of the cask format is almost unique to Britain. The majority of the venues listed here dispense cask beer, and can further be relied upon to do so with reliable skill and consistency, by no means always the case wherever you see a handpump on the bar. But this isn't just a cask beer guide. Some venues don't serve cask but offer at least some bottle-conditioned beer, and many provide beer in other formats which, though not cask, is unpasteurised, unfiltered and made from quality ingredients with dedication and skill.

A further criterion is that all the listed venues, in their own way, should offer a welcoming and pleasant environment for the discerning drinker. Some are very small and informal, so don't always expect lightning-fast service and four-star attention, but you should at least be able to rely on a friendly welcome and civilised company. Thankfully it seems that if they care enough to get the beer right, they almost always get the other stuff right too. If you find otherwise, I would very much like to hear about it (Updates & Feedback p7).

This isn't just a pub guide either. Most of the listed venues fit into the general pub category, but pubs are an evolving phenomenon and those that conform to the traditional 'olde worlde' stereotype of horse brasses and Toby jugs are now a rarity, especially in London. The selection includes contemporary pubs, gastropubs and micropubs, and many places that aren't pubs by any stretch of the imagination, from Spartan brewery taprooms open twice a month to fashionable bars and posh restaurants, a reflection of the way great beer is now penetrating far beyond pub culture. It also includes bottle shops and off-licences, and a few hybrids that defy categorisation.

Many of the places listed are also of considerable interest for other reasons, among them food and other speciality drinks, history, architecture, location, views or activities like music or theatre, and where appropriate these are mentioned in the text. But while such factors might have swayed the balance in one or two borderline cases, they are insufficient on their own to qualify a venue for inclusion. Some of London's most famous pubs are absent, as I didn't judge their beer offer of sufficient interest.

A SHORT HISTORY OF THE LONDON PUB

The pub, or rather the idea of the pub, holds a privileged position in British culture. People rhapsodise about its virtues, citing authorities as diverse as Samuel Johnson and George Orwell; celebrate it as a uniquely British institution that expresses something profound about the national character (a puzzle to anyone who has ever open-mindedly enjoyed the superficially different but equally convivial drinking venues of many other countries); and, increasingly, fear and sometimes prematurely mourn its loss. But pubs are not some fixed and unchanging phenomenon that reconnects us with an idyllic Merrie England now lost in the mists of time. First and foremost, they are businesses that depend on attracting customers to thrive and prosper, and have constantly reinvented themselves to achieve this more effectively, changing and evolving alongside the communities they serve.

The story of drinking houses in London stretches back to the *tabernae* of Roman times and most likely beyond, but the earliest we can usefully trace back the history of the modern London pub is the 16th century, when there were three clearly defined types of establishment. *Inns* offered accommodation as well as food and drink (a fine example, the George in Southwark (p53), survives in inner London), *taverns* concentrated on selling wine, though also stocked beer, and *ale houses* were simple places that sold only beer. During the 'gin craze' of the 1740s they were supplemented by numerous gin shops of the sort that promised to get you "drunk for a penny, dead drunk for tuppence" (see Meanwhile, on Gin Lane p314).

It was the depradations of the gin craze that began to shift respectable public opinion against the social acceptance of drunkenness,

George

eventually culminating in the temperance movement of Victorian times that gained increasing influence over public policy on the alcohol industry. Interestingly, the imperative to control alcohol sales was one of the factors that influenced the pub as we know it today, by using the licensing system to reduce the prevalence of 'public houses' – by then a catchall term for establishments where a member of the public could drink on the premises without having to eat, rent a room or become a member. Magistrates, then responsible for licensing the sale of alcohol, were discouraged from issuing new licences and prompted to find reasons to revoke existing ones, and temperance campaigners actively targeted local benches.

The other, linked, factor that shaped the modern pub was the emergence of the tied house system. Given the wealth of breweries and their obvious interest in the pub trade, it's not surprising that they began propping up landlords financially, usually through making free or low-interest loans on condition of exclusive supply rights, sometimes with the property as a guarantee. This eventually evolved into breweries taking on direct owner-ship of pubs. Interestingly most pubs in London remained nominally independent later than those elsewhere, but in the late 19th century, at a time when the industry was awash with funds from stock exchange flotations, provin-cial brewers started buying into the capital. The London brewers had no choice but to respond in kind, creating the vertically-integra-ted brewing industry that dominated most of the succeeding century. Often the pubs were then leased back to licensees, who remained small businesses in their own right, paying a reduced rent but obliged to source their beer and sometimes other stock from the brewery.

The combination of scarcity of licences and the drive towards tied houses had the effect of massively inflating the property value of pubs. And since they now needed to earn back the money spent on them, even more was invested to make them more attractive to customers, while simultaneously attempting to appease the temperance lobby. This spurred a flurry of redevelopment and refurbishment which came to a swift halt at the very end of the century when the property market inevitably crashed.

This particular collision of historical circum-stances accounts for why the vast majority of London pubs look like they do: they were pretty much all rebuilt, or extensively refitted, by a smallish handful of breweries in the 1880s and 1890s, mainly on existing sites as new licences were almost impossible to obtain. The brewer-ies adopted a grandiose style intended both to attract a wide range of customers and to demonstrate respectability and broad social appeal. The result was a riot of coloured marble, Corinthian columns, pediments and porticos, mosaic floors, engraved and painted glass and mirrors, and massive bar backs in complex classical stylings. Even small pubs were sub-divided by elaborate screens and partitions, with each compartment aimed at a different demographic, both a reflection of the stratified society of the day and an advertisement for the fact that the pub set out to cater for all of it.

Very little recognisably survives from before this period, but significant examples endure from after it, as pub development

continued in the early 20th century, but at a notably reduced rate. This was a period when London was rapidly expanding, despite the setbacks of a world war and a major recession, and all but the most ardent prohibitionists conceded the need for new pubs to serve new developments. The early 20th century also saw the emergence of self-conscious nostalgia for a more rural past in the worlds of art and design, as if to provide a comforting continuity to those whose lives were disrupted by urban-isation and change. Among pub architects this expressed itself in the style known rather dismissively as 'Brewer's Tudor' — mock half-timbered façades, interior wood panelling and fake ceiling beams.

A 'Brewer's Tudor'-style pub

The post-war period brought consolidation in the industry and a drive towards efficiency and integration that chimed well with the architectural modernism of the day. Segrega-tion and fussy Victoriana fell out of fashion: during the 1960s and 1970s much pub heritage was lost as screens and partitions were uncere-moniously ripped out to create more egalitar-ian, and more cheaply supervised, open spaces. The big brewery groups, and some of the smaller ones, subsumed their pub estates into the emerging doctrine of brand values, unsym-pathetically imposing standard decoration and, sometimes, cheesy ersatz themes. Branded chain pubs emerged, with more pubs managed directly by brewers rather than through leasehold arrangements.

There's a good argument that tied houses are one of the reasons why cask beer persisted for so long, partly because they gave the brewers more control over the way the beer was treated after it left the brewery gates. And so long as drinkers were able to walk across the street to another brewery's pub, there was still an element of competition and consumer choice. But by the early 1970s, brewery consolidation, combined with restrictions on new licences, resulted in local monopolies in many areas. The breweries could now exploit their power by foisting inferior products on a captive audience at a premium price, a situation that gave rise to the consumer revolt led by CAMRA.

The real ale movement also spawned new microbreweries, including in London (see Yeast Enders p122), but with the big breweries controlling most of the pub trade, the newcomers faced major challenges in reaching customers. CAMRA and others campaigned against this anti-competitive situation, advocating a limit on the size of estates across which the tie could be enforced. Following a number of official inquiries, in 1989 the government finally responded with regulations known as the Beer Orders, forcing breweries with large tied estates to release some of their pubs from the tie and to allow the others to stock a guest beer.

No one could have predicted quite how much this apparently modest intervention would rock the industry. The horrific prospect of allowing other brewers' beer into their pubs prompted the breweries to question the very fundamentals of vertical integration. Some of them shed all of their pubs and focused on their brewing businesses. Others, including a poignant roll call of old established independents, cashed in the property value of prime town-centre brewing sites and focused on their pubs, contracting their old brands out to others.

Anyone who thought the outcome would be a nation of free houses with newly liberated landlords beaming a hearty welcome from behind an array of exotic pumpclips soon had those illusions shattered. A whole new wave of consolidation followed, and the old Big Seven have since been succeeded by five global giants, all but one of whom don't own pubs. A similar process swept the retailing side of the industry, with a handful of big pub-owning companies or 'pubcos' eventually emerging, often streamlined around a limited range of beer.

Although they no longer brewed, pubcos retained their rights to enforce the tie on their leaseholders, placing the biggest ones in a powerful position. They negotiated aggressively for substantial discounts from the brewer, while selling on to the licensee at an eye-watering markup, as much as double the price charged on the open market, progressively hiking up rents at the same time. Such practices have made it difficult for some leaseholders to stay competitive, and there are numerous stories of pubcos deliberately running down sites because they see more value in selling them off for non-pub use.

Today, about half the UK's pubs remain tied in one way or another, though in retrospect, the shake-up has resulted in an overall widening of choice, and made the pub owners more susceptible to consumer demand. One effect has been a notable increase in the number of 'free houses' where the owners have no link to brewing interests. Historically, these were a small minority, including among their number several important specialist beer champions. Following the Beer Orders, chains of managed free houses emerged, again often with a limited range but more open to approaches from new brewers.

The opportunities for brewers were further boosted in 2002 with the introduction of Progressive Beer Duty, reducing the duty payable by the smallest breweries by as much as half. The number of British breweries has increased more than tenfold since the early 1970s, with many newcomers selling significant quantities through big national pub estates that once would have been completely off-limits. Access to pubs has been increased by initiatives like small brewers' organisation SIBA's Direct Delivery Scheme, which enables breweries to supply beer direct to tied houses near them, though the pubs are still invoiced through the pubco at an inevitable mark-up.

Despite these improvements for drinkers, the beginning of the 21st century has been an unprecedented era of pub closure. You don't have to spend long walking London's streets to spot ex-pubs: within a few minutes' walk of my flat in Deptford there are a good 15 examples, now converted to flats, convenience stores or betting shops. Depending on whose figures you use, at the time of writing the UK is still losing between 13 and 29 pubs a week. The finger of blame for this is pointed in various directions – high taxation, greedy pubcos, undercutting by supermarkets, property inflation, the smoking ban, and the failure of licensees to offer a good enough service. But there are broader social changes at work too, including reduced overall alcohol consumption, increased home comforts and new home-based distractions, and increased mobility and heterogeneity of local communities, that have helped ensure pubgoing is no longer the everyday habit it once was.

With pubs now having to work much harder to win customers, they've become more diverse. The phenomenon of gastropubs focusing on good food began in London in the early 1990s and continues apace. It's influenced not only pub menus but their interior decoration. Many now have a self-consciously casual stripped-back feel, with bare floorboards, warm wood, clean pastel colours and mismatched reclaimed furniture including an obligatory corner with saggy old sofas and armchairs.

Once-despised Victorian features are these days proudly exhibited, though our ancestors' taste for subdividing the space is only rarely honoured.

Another little-remarked-upon phenomenon is the appearance of pubs and bars in places that weren't originally built to accommodate them. Chains like J D Wetherspoon and some breweries have been converting old department stores, banks, post offices, public halls, cinemas and other buildings into big town centre pubs since the 1990s, and recent years have seen independent initiatives in more modestly-sized places, including railway arches and smaller shops. It's not enough to compensate for the loss of traditional buildings, but it's certainly increased variety.

Typical of this last trend are micropubs, which began in Kent in 2005 and have now spread all over Britain, with over 100 at the time of writing, including a number in the

PUB USER GUIDE

If you're familiar with British pub culture, you'll know all this already, but visitors and new arrivals might find the following guidelines useful.

The general rule in Britain is to **order drinks at the bar** and pay for them immediately. You'll only find table service in restaurants, a few posh bars, and areas set aside for eating in certain pubs. If you're **unsure what to order**, ask the bar staff: some pubs might offer a free taster.

Quantities for serving draught beer (and cider and perry) are set by law and are still in imperial measurements. The legal measures are a third-pint (197 ml, 6.67 fl oz), two-thirds (394 ml, 13.33 fl oz) or multiples of a half pint (284 ml, 10 fl oz). Half and full pints (567 ml, 20 fl oz) are offered everywhere; the other measurements are more likely to be found in the places listed here than elsewhere.

Glasses have an official stamp showing the measure. Traditional glassware in London is designed to be filled to the brim, with very little head, though you'll occasionally find oversized lined glasses. Licensees are legally allowed to fill brim glasses only 95% full, but if you're unhappy with the measure you've been served, you're within your rights to ask for a top-up, and all the places listed here should be happy to oblige.

Bottled and canned beer and all other drinks are sold in metric measures. British-brewed beers usually come in bottles (and cans) of 330 ml (11.2 fl oz) or 500 ml (16.9 fl oz), and occasionally in bigger sizes like 750 ml (25.4 oz) or US-style 'bombers' (650 ml, 22 fl oz).

At the time of writing, a typical pint of draught cask beer in a London pub **costs** around £4 (€5.20, $6), but

could vary by up to 50p either way. 'Craft keg' is significantly more expensive, particularly if strong: since 2011, a misguided duty regulation has disproportionately penalised beer that's stronger than 7.5% ABV. A decent 500 ml British bottle might cost £2 (€2.60, $3) in a supermarket, but £5 (€6.50, $7.50) in a pub; again, stronger and rarer beers will cost more. (Currency conversions are based on an exchange rate of €1.30 or $1.50 to £1 but this is highly likely to change.)

Most pubs take **credit and debit cards**, though some make an additional charge for transactions below a certain amount, often £10 (€13, $15). Some run a tab for card users and may well want you to leave your card behind the bar – make sure you reclaim it before leaving. A few pubs are still cash-only so check before ordering if necessary.

Kent-facing suburbs of London. Almost all in small shopfront sites, micropubs focus on selling a small range of often locally-brewed cask beers in an atmosphere that encourages conversation, usually with a ban on recorded music, TVs, games machines and mobile phones. With a décor typically inspired by the public bars of the post-war period, they see themselves as a return to tradition, and could be viewed as a revival of the old-fashioned ale house, but in other respects they're thoroughly modern. They would have been unthinkable in the days before microbreweries and more liberal attitudes to licensing.

As I write, another shakeup is underway. In November 2014, following extensive lobbying, Westminster MPs defied the government to pass a new law forcing companies that own 500 or more pubs to offer their leaseholders a 'market rent only' option. This would give licensees the right to negotiate a higher rent in return for being able to buy their beer from whomever they wish on the open market. Such arrangements already exist in limited circumstances – some of the pubs with the widest selections of beer in this book are leased free-of-tie from breweries and pubcos – but are about to become much more common than before. As with the Beer Orders there will likely be unforeseen consequences, perhaps presaging a new generation of managed branded chains, the pub equivalent of fast food chains. But it should also make things easier for more specialist concerns targeting a niche market.

Whatever happens, it's clear that reports of the death of the pub are grossly exaggerated. Pub culture is undoubtedly changing and those changes might not be to everyone's taste, but as recent innovations demonstrate, our desire to enjoy our drinks in a communal, social space certainly hasn't gone away.

If there's something genuinely **wrong with the beer** – and things do go wrong, especially with cask beer, even in the most scrupulous pubs – tell the bar staff before drinking a substantial amount. Places in this guide should change it without question.

Tipping isn't customary when ordering drinks at a bar. It won't offend but no-one will think the less of you if you don't. Customers are more likely to offer to buy staff a drink, in which case the equivalent in cash will usually go in a jar, but this also isn't obligatory. If there's table service and you're presented with a bill, particularly if you've also eaten, this may well include the automatic addition of a 10–15% optional service charge, and the menu should forewarn you of this. If not, the bill will very likely state prominently that service is not included, in which case 10–15% is the usual rate. You can refuse to pay a service charge if you think the service provided doesn't merit it, but this is a power to be used with discretion.

Once you've got your drink, you're generally free to occupy any unoccupied space, unless there's a **reserved** sign or other indication you shouldn't be there (areas reserved for diners when you're only drinking, for example). Unlike in some countries, prices aren't cheaper at the bar. At busy times it's usually fine to ask if you can share a table. Some pubs will reserve tables for large groups.

The **legal drinking age** in the UK is 18. The only exception is for 16–17 year olds dining in the company of adults, who are permitted to drink, but not buy, beer, wine and cider with their meal.

Some licensees have a policy of asking everyone who looks under 21, or even 25, to show proof of age, though evidence of identity is otherwise rarely required. Note they're under no obligation to serve you even if you are over 18, so long as they don't break equal opportunity laws by discriminating against you on the grounds of race, religion, gender, sexuality or disability. Accompanied children are allowed to eat and to drink soft drinks in most pubs: see listings for more details.

Smoking in enclosed public places has been banned since 2007. Some places have sheltered and heated outdoor smoking areas, but if one of these isn't available and you want to smoke in the street, ask before taking your drink outside with you as local licensing rules sometimes prohibit this.

Beer & food

While the majority of places listed in this book serve decent homemade food in which they take great pride, and a few offer fine cuisine of quality and distinction (see the list under Exceptional food p323), only a handful seriously explore the gastronomic possibilities of serving beer *with* food. London is the home of the gastropub, but for the first wave of these, the 'pub' bit of the designation was more about the informality than the beer, which was usually relegated to a couple of well-known cask ale brands and mass market lagers and stouts.

Beer advocates have been arguing for decades that beer is at least as worthy of a place on the dining table as wine. Indeed, the grain offers a wider range of flavours than the grape – beer can be fruity, floral, rich, tannic and even sour just like wine, but it can also be biscuity, roasty and bitter in a way wine cannot. Even the most ardent oenophiles admit that wine struggles with certain foods, like chocolate and curries, while beer copes admirably. Diners usually agree too, if you can persuade them to experiment, but old habits and wine's sophisticated image go a long way, and progress in the trade has been slow. It's not helped by the fact that wine is generally more expensive and its retail mark-ups are more generous, so restaurateurs do better from wine than beer.

This is particularly true at the upper end of the market. London now has one of the most interesting and varied fine dining scenes in the world, but you'll still struggle to find a serious gourmet restaurant with a good beer list, of the sort that are increasingly appearing in many US cities. At one point I considered listing Michel Roux Jr's celebrated and dual Michelin-starred Gavroche in this book, as it commissions its own beer and stocks several others, including aged Fuller's Vintage Ale. But I concluded that, given the beer

list is a single page at the end of a weighty tome that lists many hundreds of rare and fabulous wines, this was being thankful for very small mercies. More noteworthy is South Indian-themed Quilon (p98), which for years has had a beer tasting menu.

There's better news on the less formal catering scene, where local beer in particular is making significant inroads. In 2011, a talented young chef called Becky Davey opened an imaginative and very laid-back café-restaurant close to me, on New Cross Road, not a location previously known for its culinary excellence. When she got her drinks licence, the first alcohol to appear was a small but well-chosen range of bottle-conditioned beer, including some from Kernel. The business has since expanded into neighbouring units with a cocktail bar and an upmarket chippie, both stocking locally-brewed beer (the former, the LP Bar, is a try-also in the Greenwich and Lewisham section p175).

At the time, Becky's choice was courageous, but today it's less surprising, as London beer has become almost ubiquitous among a certain class of independent London eateries and bars, like a badge of how imaginative, open-minded and locally focused they are. Also in 2011, the ambitious gourmet burger chain, Byron, added a 'craft beer' menu as a summer experiment, curated by beer writer and PR man Mark Dredge, including both London and US choices. It's now a permanent feature, and has expanded to include draught keykeg beers in some locations. Several similarly US-inspired operators have followed suit.

Indeed it's often transatlantic culinary inspirations that prompt beer matching, perhaps partly because US culture, including craft beer culture, is even trendier than usual at the moment, but also because of beer's ability to match the roasty flavours and fattiness

Adam and Eve (p 105)

of grilled and barbecued meat and the smoke and spice of Southern-style cooking. Such food matches even sparked the creation of a brewery, Beavertown (p 149), and the pub where it originated, Dukes Brew and Que, is still doing great things (p 142). Several other places push the pairing of smoke and suds, notably the Smokehouse (p 145), which also delves into Korean-style barbecue cuisine.

Then there's the Old World combination of beer and shellfish. Belgian bars lubricating *moules frites* with tasty golden ales are well-established in London; they're now rivalled by champions of the more indigenous pairing of oysters with porter or stout. These were once everyday victuals in the capital and deserve to increase in popularity again. Wright Brothers Oyster and Porter House (p 61, a branch of a Cornish oyster fishery at Borough Market, has been sailing on this tack for a while, but there are now others. Harrild and Sons (p70) in the City is particularly adept: its manager says they see promoting a combination at least some customers will already have heard about as an entry point into exploring other beer and food combinations.

Even if matching isn't emphasised, there's the obvious opportunity to create your own combinations in a pub with a good range of both beer and food. British pub food has improved immeasurably in the past 25 years

and London standards are generally high, especially in the independently-run sector – unfortunately and inevitably, so are prices. 'Pub grub' has evolved under the influence of Modern British cookery, usually focusing on modern versions of comfort food classics – sausage and mash, fish and chips, pies, steaks, lamb chops, burgers – made with high quality ingredients. For fish, think ethical sourcing and beer batter, for sausage think free-range rare-breed organic, for herbs think the local allotment. All good stuff, though sometimes a little predictable, and prone to 'me-too' trends. At the time of researching this book, pork was definitely in – slow roast pork belly and American-style pulled pork were everywhere. If you're a vegetarian and want a change from a veggieburger, expect to eat a lot of butternut squash and wild mushrooms.

Wright Brothers Oyster and Porter House (p 61)

The conquest of pulled pork is also evident in the fashion for 'dirty meat' – fat-dripping politically incorrect burger and sandwich horrors to make a dietician weep. This sort of stuff is lapped up, preferably with a deep-fried battered pickle on top, by much the same demographic now discovering 'craft' beer, so has inevitably penetrated several beer venues. Like strong beer, it's fine in moderation, as long as the quality justifies the negative health impact.

At the other extreme, more and more places are now pursuing a less-is-more food policy, serving only a small range of substantial snacks that don't require cooking, again often upmarket spins on retro favourites. The Scotch egg and the sausage roll, long debased by unappetising mass-market versions, now boast their own gourmet competitions, held, of course, in pubs. Both match extraordinarily well with beer. Cheese and charcuterie tasting plates have also become a mainstay – the former is particularly welcome as, contrary to received wisdom, beer easily trumps wine in getting friendly with *fromage*. Venues adopting such minimalist policies often do so out of necessity due to restricted space, but increasingly it's out of choice too. And while the slow advance of beer and food together is something to applaud, it's reassuring to know that licensees no longer feel compelled to boost their public appeal with a full meal service when the beer speaks for itself.

Mitch's matches

Publican and sometime beer and cider writer Mitchell Adams is famed for the beer dinners he hosted when running the Thatchers Arms on the Essex/Suffolk boundary. He made the leap back to London in July 2014 to take on the Bull at Highgate (p151), home of the London Brewing Company. "I've followed the scene since 2011 when we held a London beer festival at the Thatchers," says Mitch. "Then there were less than 15 breweries to choose from. Now our little plant sits proudly among over 70 breweries in the capital. It truly is a great time for London beer." Here are his top five London beer and food pairings: *bon appetit!*

Peruvian ceviche of gilthead bream with Kernel London Sour (3.5%)
"The sharp acidity of a Berliner Weisse-style adds a final squeeze of lemon to this clean and fresh South American dish. Not everyone gets on with sours, but paired with the right food they can steal the show."

Meat or veggie chilli with Camden Town Wheat (5%)
"A favourite pairing from my 2011 event. German wheats are great with spice and this occasional Camden Town brew does a splendid job. Malt sweetness cools the heat and the beer's own spiciness helps lift the more complex flavours. The more jalapeño and tomato the better!"

Spicy buffalo wings and blue cheese dip with London Brewing Skyline (5%)
"Hops fire up hot sauce, but as the blue cheese is already cooling things down, this dry-hopped American-style pale ale is perfect with a big punch of fruity US hops."

Beetroot-infused Scotch egg, hollandaise and bacon dust with Beavertown The Gose Strikes Black (4.8%)
"I enjoyed this impressive blackberry-infused twist on a German-style Gose, a collaboration between Beavertown and Lervig brewery, at the Re-evolution

beer dinner at Duke's Brew and Que (p142). The egg was stunning too, but beer and Scotch eggs are the holy grail of food pairing and the whole is always far greater than the sum of its parts."

Christmas pudding with Fuller's Vintage Ale (8.5%)
"This rich, dark and raisiny beer is slightly different every year, and if you can bear to keep any in your cupboard it ages beautifully. Break open a bottle or two at Christmas and try with traditional pud: some vintages will undoubtedly work better, or worse, than others, but the fundamental flavours happily unite as well as turkey and stuffing."

How to use the listings

Note that all the information given in the listings can, and some of it certainly will, change during the currency of this book. See Updates and feedback p 7 for details of how to keep up to date. While I've made every effort to make sure details are accurate at the time of going to press, I strongly advise that, if the success of your trip depends on a place being open at a certain time, or being able to obtain particular beers, food or services, you contact them in advance to check.

Navigation

The listings cover Greater London, as administered by the Greater London Authority, the Mayor of London and the 33 London Boroughs. It stretches out beyond the London postal district to include places like Barnet, Bromley, Croydon, Twickenham and Woodford which some people still insist are in Hertfordshire, Kent, Surrey, Middlesex and Essex even though they've been part of London since 1964. This is a large area of 1,572 square kilometres (607 square miles) and there's no universally-agreed way of subdividing it, so I've been pragmatic, taking account of postcodes, local authorities, local practice and the distribution of venues. The maps on the inside front cover and in the listings, and the introductions to each geographical section, should make things clear.

The maps are intended only to give a general idea of the spread of venues and aren't in themselves enough to ensure foolproof navigation. Use them alongside electronic mapping or a street atlas (see More information p 318 for recommendations).

Names

Within each section, venue names are listed alphabetically, ignoring initial 'the' (and 'ye'). Punctuation of pub names is often inconsistent so has been regularised by dropping apostrophes.

Top 25 or **Top 5** after the name indicates a venue listed in the Top 25 places to drink or the Top 5 bottle shops respectively: see pp 36–38.

Venue category

The term 'pub' historically refers to a particular kind of licence – a 'public house' is licensed to sell alcohol to the public at large, rather than just diners, hotel residents or club members. But for most people today it raises expectations of a certain kind of venue in terms of décor and atmosphere too, and I've tried to reflect this here so people know what to expect, as well as identifying venues with different kinds of licences.

A **traditional pub** is the closest thing to the romantic stereotype of the pub, usually in purpose-built premises dating from at least before World War II, with old-fashioned fittings, perhaps a significant amount of preserved Victoriana, and in some cases even a proper old-style public bar.

A **contemporary pub** still feels very much like a pub and is often in the same kind of building as a traditional pub. But it has a more modern interior, refitted in the past couple of decades, often in a contemporary stripped-back or more modernist style.

A **micropub** is a new category of very small pub, often in a former shop or restaurant and usually with a focus on real ale and quiet conversation, with no TV, music or machines.

A **gastropub** implies at least as much a focus on food as drink. I've reserved it for pubs that genuinely aspire to be a dining destination in their own right, not just a pub with good food. But gastropubs are still pubs, and non-dining drinkers should be welcome too.

A **bar** is any other venue where you can call in just for a drink, but doesn't really look or feel like a pub (though it might well have a similar licence). Sometimes these are inspired by other countries' drinking traditions.

A **brewpub** is a pub or bar that sells beer brewed on the premises. These vary in style so I've usually used the term in conjunction with another.

A **taproom** is a bar at a brewery or close by, primarily intended as a shop window for that brewery's beer, though it may sell other products too. They can overlap with brewpubs but in my view, if it's primarily a bar or pub that happens to brew, it's a brewpub; if it's primarily a brewery with a bar, it's a taproom.

A **specialist** is a place where an extensive range of quality beer really is the primary attraction. I've used the term in conjunction with others.

A **club** is a bar reserved for members and their guests. The few included here welcome CAMRA and EBCU members, and sometimes people carrying CAMRA guides, as guests.

A **restaurant** is somewhere that's primarily about serving food, and where you'll normally have to eat a meal in order to drink. Where a restaurant has an area that welcomes people just for a drink, I've added the word 'bar' – but they may prefer to give priority to diners waiting for tables at busy times.

A **shop** is somewhere that primarily sells alcohol for consumption off the premises, also known as an off-licence. The category has become slightly muddied recently as some of the new breed of bottle shops also have an on-licence with a modest amount of accommodation for people drinking in, but this isn't their main business and they likely won't welcome groups of people installing themselves for a session.

Where a pub belongs to a group or chain and this isn't otherwise obvious, I've shown its name in brackets after the category.

Heritage pubs

★ identifies pubs listed on the National and Regional Inventories of Historic Pub Interiors maintained by CAMRA and English Heritage. These record pubs with significant interior features dating from before 1945 or, in some exceptional cases, before 1970.

A full list of these is under Places to drink by theme (p 321). Note that there are many more pubs on the inventories in London than those in this book, as I've only included heritage pubs if they're noteworthy from a beer point of view. For more information and a complete listing see www.heritagepubs.org.uk.

The exteriors of pubs are also often of architectural and historic interest and these can also be protected by English Heritage listings, but they're more likely to have survived than interiors: it's not unknown for a pub with a magnificent late Victorian façade to have been completely stripped of all its internal heritage features. Places not on the inventories but otherwise of architectural interest, contemporary as well as historic, are also shown under Places to drink by theme (p 321). For context, see 'A short history of the London pub' p 23.

Contact details

The street address includes a full **postcode**. I've left out the word 'London' for places in the London Postal Districts (postcodes beginning E, EC, N, NW, SE, SW, W and WC).

T Phone numbers are shown with the area code in brackets, usually 020.

Web addresses occasionally cover a group of venues but with an obvious way of searching for the correct place. I haven't listed emails as these can usually be found on websites, or there will be a contact form. In my experience phoning pubs is often a more reliable method of making sure you get an answer.

f indicates a Facebook page: type www.facebook.com followed by the name shown, or if it contains hyphens, find it using the Facebook search facility.

🐦 indicates a Twitter username; type **www.twitter.com** followed by the name shown. To tweet or message the venue you'll need to prefix it with @.

Opening times

🕐 Shown using the 24-hour clock, with days indicated as *Mo*, *Tu*, *We*, *Th*, *Fr*, *Sa* and *Su*.

Pay attention to these: the days when most pubs kept the same hours are long gone. Most places open daily, but many listed here no longer bother with opening on weekday daytimes. Pubs in business areas, particularly the City of London, often don't open at weekends. Micropubs have revived the practice of closing for a few hours in the afternoon, and several taprooms are open only on Saturday daytimes. Hours can easily change at short notice, and places are occasionally closed for refurbishment, private parties or holidays or may even go out of business, so call ahead to check if making a special trip.

Policy on children

Most places now allow well-behaved children if accompanied by adults, though usually with an early evening curfew and sometimes only in certain parts of the premises. Children are never allowed at the bar itself. I've summarised this policy after the opening times, and said 'Children very welcome' if the venue makes a special effort (and see the list on p322) — some even have play areas and child-friendly activities. If nothing about children is shown, assume they're not permitted inside the venue, although they will usually be welcome in outdoor areas – some places still have adults-only licences or prefer to maintain an adult environment.

Drink

I've shown how many different **Cask beers** are stocked, and how many **Other beers** – the latter includes quality bottles, including bottle-conditioned beer, and 'craft keg' but not mainstream industrial brands. Notes in brackets give a bit more detail, including regularly stocked breweries if any: most places listed regularly rotate guest beers. 'Unusual' indicates beers from smaller breweries and/or in more unusual styles. 'Local' means beers from London or other close-by breweries.

Like everything else, these details can change and, as cask beers in particular have a short shelf life, some places offer more variety towards the weekend when they're busier than earlier in the week. For more about the different 'formats' see p251.

Most of us appreciate other quality drinks too, so where a venue offers a particularly noteworthy selection of something else that I happened to notice, it's mentioned under **Also**. 'Cider' and 'perry' indicate the 'real' versions, naturally fermented and served without gas pressure. More and more London bars are stocking single malts and other specialist whiskies and bourbons, and artisanal spirits including some made locally in craft distilleries (see Meanwhile, on Gin Lane p314), so notes about 'malts' and 'specialist spirits' usually indicate much more than the odd bottle of Glenfiddich or Absolut. Pretty much every venue in this book manages a few drinkable wines, aside from a few brewery taprooms, so a note of 'wine' acknowledges an exceptional effort.

Take it as read that most places have a selection of soft drinks – some of these are now locally made. Most offer hot drinks like tea and coffee too, though they might not thank you for asking for them late on a busy weekend night.

Food

🍴 indicates the food on offer, beyond packets of crisps and nuts, with an indication of the style and price range. More detail on food, with example dishes, is often given in the text below. It's now very rare not to have at least one vegetarian option on the menu, and where places do notably better than this I've mentioned it. Kitchens are also now more open to dealing with food allergies and other dietary requirements but I strongly advise you to call them first to discuss your needs.

As it's perfectly normal not to eat a formal three course meal in nearly all the places listed, I've based the price categories on the cost of a main course, or the most substantial items on the menu if the venue doesn't do conventional plated meals.

> **£** Mostly less than £8 (€10.50, $12)
> **££** Mostly £8–15 (€19.50, $22.50)
> **£££** Mostly above £15

This is a rough guide: different lunchtime and evening menus are common, with lunches often cheaper, and a few places serve cheaper and more limited dishes in the bar and more sophisticated and expensive meals in a separate restaurant.

Space precludes listing food service times so if you're relying on food, always ring ahead to check. Most places serve food lunchtimes and evenings daily, but the kitchen could well be closed in the afternoon. I've tried to note when food is only sold at lunchtimes, or not on certain days of the week. On Sundays, everything could change: many places chuck out the regular menu in favour of a limited choice of roast dinners (usually with a veggie option) from midday until stocks run out, which might well be before dinnertime.

¶⊀¶ indicates somewhere offering outstandingly good food, to the extent you'd consider visiting it for this alone. A list of all these places is under Places to drink by theme (p 321).

For general notes on beer and food, see p 28.

Outdoor space

⊼ precedes a brief description of available outdoor space, from standing space on the street to extensive gardens. If nothing is shown here, assume licensing or space restrictions preclude you taking drinks outside. Smoking is legal outdoors but some places with outdoor dining terraces ban it from these too.

❀ indicates the venue has a particularly noteworthy outdoor area. This is a purely subjective judgement on my behalf – it could be because of extent, or facilities, or design, or seclusion, or obvious levels of pride and tender loving care.

Disabled toilet

♿ indicates an accessible disabled toilet adapted for wheelchair users, and by implication level access to the venue itself, although it's always advisable to call in advance, as this might be through a side door that's usually kept locked. If nothing is listed, assume there isn't one, although the venue may still have flat access. Sadly this is one area in which London certainly doesn't lead the world. Most places in this book will be as helpful as they can, but disabled facilities are only obligatory with new builds and major refurbishments, and retrofitting them to historic buildings can be a financial, design and heritage challenge.

Activities

These are listed in italics just before the reviews: they're mostly self-explanatory and include things like beer-related events, live entertainment and pub games, with regular days if applicable. 'Functions' indicates that a separate room or a part of the venue can be set aside for private parties, meetings and other such activities.

Transport

Relevant transport information is given as follows:

- ≠ National Rail station
- ⊖ London Overground station (note the Overground is a specific rail network operated by Transport for London and largely integrated with the Underground: confusingly some Londoners still use the term to mean National Rail)
- ⊖ London Underground (Tube) station
- ⊖ Docklands Light Railway station
- ⊖ Croydon Tramlink stop
- ⊷ River pier or canal mooring with regular boat service.
- 🚌 Bus stop, with brief details of services and key destinations in brackets. All bus stops in London now have their own names.
- ⚲⚲ Principal cycling route
- ⚡ Principal walking route

Despite what many Londoners appear to believe, their city has comparatively excellent public transport and everywhere listed in this book is easily accessible by it. Yes, it's expensive (eye-wateringly so if you buy single tickets), overcrowded in peak hours, and prone to closures for engineering works at weekends. But driving in London is far worse and I advise you very strongly against it, particularly as a means of accessing opportunities to drink. Don't be discouraged if some places aren't on the Tube – this is a habit that visitors and some Londoners should get over. There are many places the Tube doesn't reach, but there are other modes of transport which are much more user-friendly than they used to be, and you'll see much more of the city from the top deck of a bus. Do investigate payment options like Oyster cards and contactless payments as they're much cheaper than buying tickets for every journey and cash is no longer accepted on the buses.

For full transport information, including tickets and fares, an excellent journey planner and walking and cycling details, see the Transport for London (TfL) website at **www.tfl.gov.uk**.

For all the places listed, I've shown the nearest, or occasionally the most convenient, Tube, rail or Tramlink stop. Where this is some distance away, I've given bus details – I've erred on the side of caution with distances so it's worth checking how far the venue is from the station as you may find it quicker to walk.

Travelling by boat is not only a great way to see London but also a reaffirmation of the Thames' historic role in the city's development, so I've shown river piers where they're convenient. Thames Clippers offer a fast, frequent and reasonably priced service on the main stretch of the river. The more touristy, summer-only services between Richmond and Kingston and on the Regents Canal are referenced too.

Walking and cycling will help you work off the calories from all that beer, and facilities are improving all the time, though still some way behind international best practice. Note though that while there's no specific blood alcohol limit for cyclists, it's illegal and also highly irresponsible to cycle when drunk. Central, inner east and southwest London are

Beehive (p 148)

covered by a short-term cycle hire scheme, the so-called 'Boris bikes', after the Mayor who presided over their launch. You pay an access fee for a period of at least a day and can then use any bike without further charge so long as you don't hang onto it for longer than half an hour.

You can walk and cycle anywhere in London so I've only mentioned these modes when venues are close to principal routes. For cyclists, these are the Sustrans National Cycle Network (NCN), TfL's Cycle Superhighways (CS) and some others like the international Avenue Verte from London to Paris. There are other London-wide and local numbered routes but the network is dense and specific routes aren't always identified on the ground. For walkers I've shown TfL's signed strategic long distance walking routes and some others. A route listed on its own is only a few minutes away; 'Link to' means a straightforward bit of extra legwork is required to reach it. If you can't find more information on the TfL site, check the route name/number online.

Try also

There are now so many great beer places in London that this book could easily have been twice the length. I've given many of those that aren't featured honourable mentions at the end of each geographical section. They include places that do a more limited range, and numerous particularly worthy branches of chains. By the standards of the last edition, they would all have likely merited a full listing: indeed many of them had one, but we're now in a different world. I've given the full address and the website for each, so you can check online for opening times and other details.

London's Top 25 places to drink

Visiting every place in this book on consecutive nights will take you the best part of nine months and undoubtedly contravene the Chief Medical Officers' guidelines on alcohol consumption. Those who would prefer to prioritise are referred to the list below of 25 outstanding venues (or in one case a group of venues) which together offer an incomparable beer experience. Most are specialist pubs and bars offering a notably wide range of unusual beers but there are beer champions with a more modest range and a couple are excellent brewery pubs. A **Top 5** list of outstanding bottle shops is appended. All the places are listed in alphabetical order with no further priority intended.

Bohemia

Beer Rebellion Peckham
Central South London (p 158)
The most expansive of Late Knights' hip but friendly micropub-goes-cool venues.

Bermondsey Breweries
Borough & Southbank (p 64–67)
Individually these brewery taprooms might not make this list but collectively on a Saturday they're a crucial London beer experience.

BrewDog Clapham

Bohemia
Outer North London (p 150)
London Brewing's vast brewpub rhapsodises in the wilds of North Finchley.

BrewDog Clapham Junction
Battersea, Brixton & Clapham (p 183)
No cask sadly but all the BrewDogs have stunning bottle selections, and this one is more homely than most.

Carpenters Arms
Shoreditch & Hoxton (p 86)
Old school class and a warm welcome in this pretty and civilised East End local.

Cask Pub and Kitchen
Westminster to Notting Hill (p 97)
The original failing local reborn as a beer specialist, and still the connoisseur's choice.

Cock Tavern
Hackney (p 107)
As fabulous as its older sister the Southampton Arms, but often less crowded and with a brewery in the cellar.

Craft Beer Co Islington

Craft Beer Co Islington
Angel Islington (p 43)
Hard not to include all the Crafts here but this has the edge for its comfy, pubby setting.

Crown and Anchor
Battersea, Brixton and Clapham (p 185)
Friendly and accessible rescued pub on the Brixton fringes with a fine range.

Dog and Bell
Greenwich & Lewisham (p 169)
Hidden gem supplementing fine local cask with Belgian bottles and community warmth.

Door Hinge
Outer Southeast London (p 176)
London's first micropub with top CAMRA London honours in 2014, a character-driven cask haven.

Draft House Seething
City of London (p 69)
The best and most central of this improving chain, in an intriguing and unexpected setting.

Draft House Seething

Earl of Essex
Angel Islington (p 43)
Picturesque Barworks brewpub with an exemplary list and expert staff.

Hope
Outer Southwest London (p 198)
Saved by the community, and since evolved into a spot-on blend of traditional and contemporary.

Magpie and Crown
Outer West London (p 220)
Consistently improving cask and contemporary excellence in a Brentford Brewer's Tudor shell.

Mother Kellys
Tower Hamlets (p 120)
Heaven in Bethnal Green's Paradise Row: London's first bottle shop-bar fusion.

Mother Kellys

Priory Arms
Battersea, Brixton & Clapham (p 189)
Longstanding Stockwell specialist beer champion back on top under new and ambitious management.

Rake
Borough & Southbank (p 58)
London's international beer geek drop-in centre remains an essential Borough Market call.

Red Lion
Outer East London (p 127)
Antic's master of dispense in Hitchcock country, with fine casks and bottles galore.

Royal Oak
Borough & Southbank (p 59)
Harvey's London flagship is close to perfection for a traditional pub.

Star Tavern
Westminster to Notting Hill (p 100)
Top Fuller's cask is a London must, and where better than this permanent *Good Beer Guide* entry and serial Cellarman of the Year finalist?

Stormbird
Central South London (p 165)
A Camberwell beauty with expanding cask choices and rich pickings in a haphazardly presented bottled range.

Sussex Arms
Outer West London (p 223)
More than a rugby team's worth of draught choice and well-selected bottles in this Twickenham champion.

Sussex Arms

Wanstead Tap
Outer East London (p 127)
A beer- and activity-packed railway arch that's all the better for being so unexpected.

White Horse
Fulham, Hammersmith & Chiswick (p 214)
This smart specialist has been in the race since the 1980s and is still ahead of the field.

White Horse

Top 5 bottle shops

Craft Beer Shop (Kris Wines)
Islington (p 141)
Succour for the true obsessive in this rarity-packed high street offie-turned-beer-geek paradise.

Dr.Ink of Fulham
Fulham, Hammersmith & Chiswick (p 209)
A distinguished selection, a sunny sampling terrace, and samosas on Saturdays.

Hop Burns and Black
Central South London (p 163)
Shelf loads from south London, New Zealand rarities, hot sauces and cool vinyl in designer East Dulwich.

Utobeer
Borough & Southbank (p 61)
Pioneer beer champion amid Borough Market's gourmet heaven, still tops for trailblazing imports.

We Brought Beer
Wandsworth (p 195)
Balham newcomer winning prizes within weeks of opening, great for London and UK beers and carefully chosen visitors.

CENTRAL
LONDON

CENTRAL LONDON

There is no official definition of Central London, so I've based mine on Transport for London's Fare Zone 1, which includes all the mainline rail terminals and the area within the Circle Line, with extensions northeast to Angel and Hoxton, east to Shoreditch High Street and Aldgate East, southwest to Earl's Court and south to Vauxhall and Elephant & Castle. All the venues listed below are within a few minutes' walk of a Zone 1 station (with the exception of some of the Bermondsey breweries: see below).

Beer options tend to be more plentiful in the east and south of this area. The 'square mile' of the **City** is the site of the original settlement that developed into the Roman provincial capital and gave the whole of London its name. The City is now London's most prominent financial district, throbbing to the thrum of international capital on weekdays and much quieter at other times. It's not as deathly as it once used to be at weekends, thanks to flexible working, tourism and a modest growth in residential property, but many pubs are still closed, particularly on Sundays. There are numerous classic pubs in the City: many serve a limited range of better-known brands, but recently there has been a notable increase in more specialist places.

To the northeast, **Shoreditch & Hoxton** were once refuges for less respectable activities not permitted in the City, including industry and the performing arts – William Shakespeare worked in Shoreditch when he first moved to London. Once impoverished despite its proximity to a sizeable slice of the world's wealth, since the 1990s much of the district has become painfully fashionable, with former industrial units remade as galleries and bars, and several great beer outlets have opened in recent years. My definition takes in a bit of Bethnal Green too – for the rest see Tower Hamlets (p118).

The area around **Angel** Tube in southern Islington, one of London's first examples of gentrification in the 1970s and the spiritual home of New Labour in the 1990s, is still lively, even preserving remnants of its working class roots in Chapel Market. A few years ago, good beer outlets were remarkably sparse round here but some serious contenders have opened recently. Venues further away from Angel are dealt with under Islington to Stoke Newington (p140).

Clerkenwell & Farringdon, immediately northeast of the City, were among London's first suburbs, once home to religious

Belsize Park

Dalston

Angel Islington p42		
Bloomsbury, Euston & St. Pancras p46		Shoreditch & Hoxton p85
	Clerkenwell & Farringdon p73	

Regent's Park

Maida Hill

Westminster to Notting Hill p96

| Soho & Fitzrovia p92 | Holborn & Covent Garden p78 | City of London p68 |

| Borough & Southbank p51 | Bermondsey p67 |

Chelsea

Pimlico

Kennington

institutions like the Knights Hospitallers of St John of Jerusalem, and later associated with printing, watchmaking and revolutionary socialism. This is a fascinating area to explore, perhaps following the pavement plaques of the Clerkenwell Historic Trail, with several fine beer outlets tucked away in historic streets and alleys, and a food culture shaped by the presence (for now) of the wholesale meat market at Smithfield.

The built-up area first spread west, across the now-covered river Fleet and along the Strand, in Anglo-Saxon times. The Knights Templar built their London base, the Temple, here in the 12th century, with lawyers moving in when the Knights were suppressed. The area is still associated with the legal profession, as well as journalists, who are often known to like a drink or two. Most of the latter are now gone but the area still boasts some classic backstreet pubs and interesting newcomers.

Covent Garden, west of Kingsway, became the site of London's first modern property development in 1630 when the Dukes of Bedford commissioned Inigo Jones to build a church and three terraces around an Italianate piazza. Soon afterwards it became a fruit and vegetable market, then was redeveloped again in 1980 as a successful leisure and retail destination – a model for many subsequent transformations of historic urban space. With its various theatres and other attractions, the neighbourhood is functionally an eastern extension of the West End. This whole area is easily walkable and I've dealt with it in a single section, including the streets around Charing Cross, as **Holborn & Covent Garden** – though note that while the latter hums all week, the former is quieter at weekends and some pubs close.

Northwards, the Georgian terraces and squares of Bloomsbury, with their early 20th century literary associations, stretch to Euston Road – originally known as the New Road when it was built in 1756 as London's first bypass, marking the northern edge of the central area. Thanks to the presence of numerous educational institutions including University College and a string of main line stations along the north side of Euston Road, there are rich pickings for beer lovers here, as detailed under **Bloomsbury, Euston & St Pancras**.

The West End proper is dealt with under **Soho & Fitzrovia**, which includes everywhere from Leicester Square through Soho north to Marylebone and Euston Roads. This is the liveliest part of one of the world's liveliest cities, encompassing Chinatown, Piccadilly Circus, Theatreland, the shopping nexus of Oxford Circus, the gay village around Old Compton Street, the media industry strip along Charlotte Street and the closest thing London has to a red light district in southern Soho. Property premiums here mean that most pubs are owned by big groups but I've highlighted the best of these along with a few independents.

West of here, recommendable outlets become so sparse that I've grouped together the rest of the central area north of the river Thames as **Westminster to Notting Hill**. It's a mix of Royal Parks and palaces, government offices around the Houses of Parliament and along Whitehall, grand 18th century developments now occupied by embassies, hotels and very rich individuals in Mayfair and Belgravia, luxury shopping streets and more modest but now largely gentrified residential areas in eastern Kensington and Notting Hill. Places a little further away from Earls Court Tube are covered under Inner West London (p 205).

Things get much more interesting on the other side of the river. Southwark, also known as the Borough, immediately to the south of London Bridge, is London's third historic core. The area was long associated with brewing, and the reinvention of Borough Market as a foodie honeypot has helped good beer thrive again, notably in a string of new breweries along the railway line into Bermondsey. London's liveliest promenade stretches from Tower Bridge and City Hall upriver past Bankside, with Shakespeare's Globe and the Tate Modern, to the cultural quarter of the Southbank Centre with its theatres and arts venues, and on to overgrown ferris wheel the London Eye and Lambeth Bridge. There are several more beery gems along this stretch, including one off the beaten track in old Lambeth. You'll find them all under **Borough & Southbank**, including a section dealing with the Bermondsey breweries – even though some of these are technically well outside Zone 1 it made sense to treat them all together.

Angel Islington

1. Brewhouse and Kitchen Islington · 2. Charles Lamb · 3. Craft Beer Co · 4. Earl of Essex · 5. Three Johns · 6. Wenlock Arms

Brewhouse and Kitchen Islington (1)

Brewpub, bar
Torrens Street EC1V 1NG　**T** (020) 7837 9421
www.brewhouseandkitchen.com/islington
f ✔ BKIslington
⊕ *Mo-Th* 11.00-23.00, *Fr* 11.00-24.00, *Sa* 09.00-24.00, *Su* 09.00-21.00. Children welcome.
Cask beers 7 (Brewhouse & Kitchen),
Other beers 11 keg, 30 bottles, ***Also*** 1 cider
🍴 Burgers, steaks, enhanced pub grub **££**,
🌳 Small front terrace, ♿
Brewing sessions, monthly beer events, tastings, occasional quiz, live music, functions

⊖ Angel　🚴 Regents Canal towpath
🚶 Jubilee Greenway, New River Path

The first London branch of a new brewpub chain (p 281) poured its first pints in October 2014 in a spacious and smartly refurbished former bar just round the corner from Angel Tube. Old school polished wood and copper, post-industrial bare brick and exposed ducting pick up the look of the small brewhouse at the back. Cask beers are usually all brewed in-house, with interesting changing seasonals and specials. Bottles are mainly world beer classics like Little Creatures and Westmalle Dubbel, with US imports like Fordham.

Brewhouse and Kitchen Islington

The menu admirably suggests beer style matching for its internationally-inspired food: wheat beer for the house speciality *tartiflette*, English ale for slow-roasted pork belly, American ale for the wild mushroom and spinach penne. There's a children's menu too. A second branch should now be open up the road at Highbury (2a Corsica Street N5 1JJ), brewing mainly lager-style and keg beers.

Charles Lamb (2)

Gastropub
16 Elia Street N1 8DE　**T** (020) 7837 5040
www.thecharleslambpub.com
f The-Charles-Lamb　**✔** thecharleslamb
⊕ *Mo-Tu* 16.00-23.00, *We-Sa* 12.00-23.00, *Su* 1200-22.30. Children welcome.
Cask beers 4 (Dark Star, Windsor & Eton, 2 unusual guests), ***Other beers*** 5 keg, 15 bottles,
Also 1 cider, wines, malts
🍴 Modern European menu **££**,
🌳 Tables on street
Quiz (Mo), seasonal events

🚊 Essex Road　⊖ Angel　🚴 Regents Canal towpath
🚶 Jubilee Greenway, New River Path

This small and welcoming place tucked away near the Regent's Canal gets pretty much everything right. A 2005 refurbishment has preserved some pleasingly well-worn spaces in pastel green with original brown tiling. The pub's former name, the Prince Albert, is still visible on the bar back clock, and there's a tiny snug commemorating its current namesake.

The beer range isn't vast but is conscientiously selected, with Hophead and Windsor Knot regularly on, and guests, often including darker choices, from Londoners like Head in a Hat or Late Knights, or from Hobsons, Mayfields or Otley. Munich's Hacker-Pschorr is on keg, with a guest IPA from the US or a London brewer like Beavertown, while Flensburger, Kernel, Odell and Rogue are among the bottles.
The daily changing French-influenced menu has been widely praised – pork *rilette* with cornichons, four cheese frittata or beef ragu might be on offer.

Pub trivia *The French flavour extends to a bilingual website ("Pub londonien traditionnel à la cuisine familiale"), a listing in* Les Routiers *and a big do for Bastille Day.*

Craft Beer Co Islington (3)
Specialist, contemporary pub   **Top 25**
55 White Lion Street N1 9PP
www.thecraftbeerco.com/pubs/islington
 craftbeercon1
 Mo-We 16.00-23.00, *Th* 16.00-24.00, *Fr-Sa* 12.00-01.00, *Su* 12.00-22.30. Children until 19.00.
Cask beers 10 (Kent, unusual guests),
Other beers 22 keg, 75+ bottles,
Also Specialist spirits
 Gourmet burgers **££**,
 Front terrace, side beer garden
Occasional meet the brewer/tap takeover, home brewing club, live piano (Tu), live music (We), board games, functions

 Angel   Link to Regents Canal towpath
 Jubilee Greenway

Previously an underachieving local known as the Lord Wolseley, this generously proportioned pub became the third of the London Crafts late in 2012 and rapidly claimed a place among the capital's top beer venues, with its combination of a phenomenal beer range and a spacious, comfortable, more traditionally pub-like environment. It's done out in dark green and scarlet, with exposed pillars and a wooden corner bar, while an extra space at the back, reservable for functions and events, has murals illustrating the brewing process. The guest casks often feature several beers from the same brewer: perhaps Dark Star, Hackney, Oakham, Redemption, Siren or

Tiny Rebel. Two ranks of keg taps regularly dispense Londoners like Beavertown, Five Points, Kernel or Weird Beard, with other prized UK brewers and always interesting imports (draught Tilquin Gueuze when I last called). The bottled list combines Belgian classics like Rochefort and St Bernardus with more Londoners, hard-to-find US imports (Crooked Stave, Green Flash, Hoppin' Frog) and rarely seen Scandinavians like Hornbeer and Omnipollo. As always at Craft, well-educated staff guide customers through the dazzling choice, and bottles are also sold to take away. Food is simple but tasty stuff supplied by Forty Burgers.

Craft Beer Co, Islington

Earl of Essex **Top 25** (4)
Brewpub, contemporary pub (Barworks)
25 Danbury Street N1 8LE
T (020) 7424 5828
www.earlofessex.net   theearlofessex1
 Mo 13.00-23.30, *Tu* 14.00-23.30, *We-Th* 12.00-23.30, *Fr-Sa* 12.00-24.00, *Su* 12.00-23.00. Children until 20.00.
Cask beers 5 (usually local guests),
Other beers 13 keg, 50 bottles (including Earls),
Also Specialist spirits
 Cooked bar snacks, enhanced pub grub **££**,
 Beer garden
Beer launches, meet the brewer/tap takeover

 Angel   Regents Canal towpath
 Jubilee Greenway, New River Path

This pub in pleasantly-terraced back streets reopened in July 2012, recalling its past with a vintage bar back behind an island bar. But otherwise the space is clean and modern, with a delightful walled garden at the back.

Wood-handled handpumps and keg taps are unlabelled so you need to look at the list on the wall, which always includes a few items from in-house brewery Earls. Other casks are from brewers like Brew by Numbers, East London, Redwillow, Summer Wine or Windsor & Eton. Kegs tend towards London and the UK with a few Belgians, Americans and Scandinavians. An impressive bottle list covers numerous styles and countries, stretching from Boon lambics and Estrella Inedit to Lervig and Lost Abbey. Thirds are served and the 'beer of the day' on the website is another nice touch. A shortish menu with a touch of flair offers cooked bar snacks, sharing plates, burgers, beer battered coley and chips, steaks, and exotica like smoked duck, watermelon and peashoot salad.

Three Johns (5)

Contemporary pub (Barworks)
73 White Lion Street N1 9PF
T (020) 7837 1892   www.three-johns.com
f thethreejohns   **y** thethree_johns
🕐 *Mo-Th* 12.00-24.00, *Fr-Sa* 12.00-01.00,
   Su 12.00-22.30. Children until 19.00.
Cask beers 3 (London and unusual guests),
Other beers 12 keg, 60 bottles,
Also Specialist spirits
🍴 Pizzas **££**, 🪑 Benches on street, ♿
Monthly meet the brewer/tap takeover

⊖ Angel ♿ Link to Regents Canal towpath
🏃 Jubilee Greenway

This famous Chapel Market boozer finally got over a longstanding identity crisis in May 2014 by reclaiming its real name and become something like a proper pub again. A spacious, funky but civilised interior with a dazzling beaten copper ceiling is lit through massive picture windows. There's usually at least one cask from a London brewer – Crate, Hackney, London Fields and Redchurch are likely – while others could be from Grain or Siren. Keg taps dispense proper German lagers and keykegs from the UK and US (Odell or Wild, for example), and the bottle list is serious stuff, enabling you to compare, say, the Bruery's Oude Tart with classic Rodenbach Grand Cru. Big bottles and third measures complete a beer-friendly

picture. Food is gourmet pizzas served whole or in slices, with toppings like fennel sausage, chilli and roasted sprouting broccoli.

Pub trivia *The name recalls radical John Wilkes (1727–97), from just down the road in Clerkenwell, and two of his campaigning colleagues. Look out for him in a portrait, disrespectfully depicted as blowing a gum bubble.*

Wenlock Arms (6)

Traditional pub
26 Wenlock Road N1 7TA **T** (020) 7608 3406
www.wenlockarms.com **y** wenlockarms
🕐 *Su-We* 12.00-23.00, *Th* 12.00-24.00,
   Fr-Sa 12.00-01.00. Children until 20.00.
Cask beers 10 (Local and unusual guests),
Other beers 6 keg, 6 cans, **Also** 6 ciders/perries,
some malts and gins
🍴 Salt beef bagels, stews, hot bar snacks **£**,
🪑 Tables on street, ♿
Occasional tastings, live music, darts, cricket team

⇌ Old Street ⊖ Old Street, Angel 🚌 Windsor Terrace
(numerous Angel, Old Street) ♿ Link to Regents Canal towpath
🏃 Link to Jubilee Greenway

I'm particularly pleased to be able to list the Wenlock Arms once again: last time around the future of this legendary backstreet venue was uncertain, but it's since become a pub rescue success story. Despite the Wenlock brewery mirrors, this was originally a Courage pub: both brewery and pub took their names from a local property-owning family. Previous landlords Steve and Will, who had operated the pub as a real ale free house since 1994 when

LONDON DRINKERS
Andreas Akerlund

Andreas, born in Sweden though educated in London, founded the Barworks group with compatriot Patrik Franzen in 1995 by opening the Two Floors bar in Soho, still open today after 20 years. Originally they ran spirit-focused bars aimed at a youthful audience, but then both their staff and their customers started demanding better beer. "I'm one of those people," says Andreas. "I love good beer but struggled to find it, and was very impressed and inspired by places like the Euston Tap (p47). So with every new venue we've pushed it a little bit more, aiming at a good range, not just the beers we know will be big sellers." They share friendship, office space, trading links and an investment interest with Camden Town Brewery, and now operate some of London's most imaginative and interesting beer venues, including brewpub the Earl of Essex (p43).

How do you rate London as a beer city, on a world scale?
We've come a very long way in the last four years. Brussels and other traditional beer cities are hard to compete with, and American cities are taking things further but are 10 or more years ahead.

What's the single most exciting thing about beer in London at the moment?
Londoners' thirst for better beer. It pushes pubs and brewers to get better and better.

What single thing would make things even better?
More of the same! Fortunately the trend is in the right direction so pubs and breweries should just get better still.

What are your top London beers right now?
Beers from Beavertown and One Mile End. I'd say Camden Town too but we have an interest.

What's your top great beer night out (other than in your own venues)?
It's so hard not to mention Barworks venues as they're as good as anyone! But among the others, the Cock (p107), the White Hart (p121), the Bull (p151), any of the Crafts or BrewDog bars.

Who's your London beer hero?
Jasper Cuppaidge of Camden Town.

Who will we be hearing a lot more from in future?
Logan Plant at Beavertown.

Which are your other top beer cities?
Brussels and Munich are classic places. But I'm really looking forward to going to Chicago in a few weeks.

---

such venues were rare in London, sold it in late 2011 to a developer who aimed to demolish it and build flats. But thanks to a local campaign, the council declared the pub part of a conservation area. A less destructive refurbishment saw the ground floor retained for pub use and it reopened under new management in June 2013. The sympathetic work has preserved the essence of the old place, in a way that won't disturb longstanding beer pilgrims who continue to visit from across the country and the world, while giving it a well-deserved polish. It's even revealed a long-covered mosaic of the pub name on the floor of one of the porches. The horseshoe bar counter still hosts a line of handpumps dispensing a range of styles, including milds and porters, with Burning Sky, Crouch Vale, Dark Star, Hobsons and Mighty Oak regularly appearing. A new rotating keykeg IPA features alongside Camden Town beers, and the fridge has a small range of 'craft cans'

from people like BrewDog and Fourpure. The ever-popular salt beef sandwiches remain on sale, alongside a few other food offerings like toasties, but the Wenlock is an honest alehouse at heart, and once again one of London's best.

TRY ALSO

The **Lexington** (96–98 Pentonville Road N1 9JB, www.thelexington.co.uk) is best known for its gigs and massive selection of US bourbons and whiskies, but also has a fair choice of US craft beers and a few casks from the Heineken list. Gastropub the **Pig and Butcher** (80 Liverpool Road N1 0QD, www.thepigandbutcher.co.uk) offers a good choice of better-known Londoners and imports plus a few casks to accompany an impressive menu. The big, brash and busy **Wenlock and Essex** (18–26 Essex Road N1 8LN, www.wenlockandessex.com) is another Barworks venue with plenty of beer, though a little less than some others in the group.

Bloomsbury, Euston & St Pancras

Bree Louise (7)

Specialist, contemporary pub
69 Cobourg Street NW1 2HH
T (020) 7681 4930
www.breelouise.pub 🐦 TheBreeLouise
🕐 *Mo-Sa* 11.30-23.00, *Su* 12.00-22.30.
   Children welcome.
Cask beers 18 (various, unusual guests), ***Other beers***
5 keg, ***Also*** 10 ciders/perries, 20–30 whiskies
🍴 Pies, pub grub **£**, 🪑 Benches on street
Themed beer festivals, seasonal events,
major big screen sport, board games

🚆🚇 Euston   🚇 Euston, Euston Square   🚶 Jubilee Walkway

7. Bree Louise · 8. Euston Tap · 9. Lamb · 10. Museum Tavern · 11. Parcel Yard · 12. Queens Head · 13. Sourced Market · A. Bloomsbury Brewery

This smallish and ordinary-looking pub, just round the corner from Euston station and the South Indian food outlets in Drummond Street, dispenses what's likely London's widest selection of independently brewed cask beer. Originally the Jolly Gardeners, it's been under the stewardship of current landlords Craig and Karen Douglas since 2003, and in 2008 they bought out the tie from building owners Enterprise for a considerable annual fee so they could stock what they liked. Seven beers are handpumped, the rest are on a cooled stillage and poured straight from the cask. Dark Star Hophead and beers from Brains, Sambrook's, Stod Fold, Tiny Rebel, Titanic and Windsor & Eton are always on, with guests from far and wide: the policy is not to stock anything too mainstream so when better-known brewers crop up it's with their lesser-known brands. Good value unpretentious food includes award-winning pies, ploughman's, burgers, various pastas and specialist cheese plates. The single, sparsely decorated room is frequently crowded and the tables favour group drinking, so you often end up sharing, though groups can reserve in advance. The commitment to promoting cask beer and supporting small producers is beyond question, but the pub is not without its detractors for its unflattering interior and the alleged variable serving quality particularly of the beers on stillage, which tend to have an even lower carbonation than handpumped cask. I've always found it basic but comfortable, with polite and informed staff and decent beer quality, but if you're unsure you can request a taster first. The pub may be demolished if the HS2 rail project goes ahead, but that's still several years away.

Bree Louise

Euston Tap (8)
Specialist, bar
West Lodge, 190 Euston Road NW1 2EF
T (020) 3137 8837   🐦 eustontap
www.eustontap.com   f Euston Tap
🕐 *Mo-Sa* 12.00-23.00, *Su* 12.00-22.00.
   Children until early evening.
Cask beers 8 (unusual guests)
Other beers 18 keg, 80 bottles
🍴 Pizzas to order in, cooked bar snacks **£-££**,
🌳 Side terrace

⇄ ⊖ Euston   ⊖ Euston, Euston Square   🏃 Jubilee Walkway

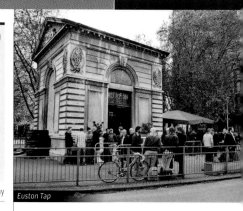
Euston Tap

This historic lodge in front of Euston station was reborn in 2010 as one of the first of London's new wave of beer venues. Space is cramped: a rectangular ground floor area has a bar with taps mounted American-style on the copper bar back. A precarious spiral staircase winds to a mezzanine level where there's an equally small sofa-strewn lounge, while benches and umbrellas on Euston Square Gardens expand the space on fine days. Instead of a kitchen, there's an arrangement with a local pizza delivery business. Cask beers, served using a siphon method by friendly and helpful staff, are typically supplied by brewers like Brass Castle, Magic Rock, Moor, Summer Wine, Thornbridge and Tiny Rebel. They're supplemented by unpasteurised Czech lagers and 'craft kegs' from the likes of Beavertown, Beerd and Marble. Bottles, in fridges flanking the bar, include numerous Belgian classics, some good lambics, Londoners like Partizan and Pressure Drop and a few big and special Americans like Brooklyn Local 1. Beer ranges like this are no longer as remarkable in London as when the Tap first opened, and its own sister venues the Holborn Whippet (p80) and the Pelt Trader (p71) are among the competition. But it also boasts the advantage of a unique building in a very convenient location.

Visitor note *This unusual building and its opposite number, home to a dedicated cider and perry bar since 2011, once flanked the largest Doric arch ever built, demolished in 1961 but potentially to be restored if the station is redeveloped to accommodate the new HS2 rail line. The lodges were originally used as parcels and administrative offices.*

Lamb (9)
Traditional pub (Young's) ★
94 Lambs Conduit Street WC1N 3LZ
T (020) 7405 0713
www.thelamblondon.com   🐦 lambWC1
🕐 *Mo-We* 12.00-23.00, *Th-Sa* 12.00-24.00,
   Su 12.00-22.30. Children until 17.00.
Cask beers 8 (Wells & Young's, 3 often local guests), **Other beers** 4 keg, 4 bottles,
Also 3 ciders/perries, wines
🍴 Enhanced pub grub, sandwiches, sharing platters **££**, 🌳 Rear patio
Quiz (Su), seasonal events, board games, functions

⇄ Kings Cross, St Pancras International
⊖ Russell Square, Holborn   🏃 Jubilee Walkway

A rare original pub from the late 18th century development of Bloomsbury, the Lamb is now one of Young's most reliable beer pubs. Bitter, Special, Gold and Courage Directors are the regulars, with a Young's seasonal (it's a reliable source of Winter Warmer at the right time of year) and guests often from London brewers: Redemption brews Bloomsbury Blend especially for the pub. A broad menu includes dishes like minted lamb pie, Cumberland ring with autumn mash or grilled stuffed mushrooms. It's charming and comfortable, with wood panelling, engraved glass, interesting prints and the star heritage feature: twin rows of swivelling opaque glass "snob screens" on each side of the horseshoe bar, originally designed to obscure eye contact between well-heeled customers and lowly staff.

Pub trivia *There's no piped music, unless you count the polyphon, a giant Victorian music box that can be set working in exchange for a donation to charity.*

Museum Tavern (10)

Traditional pub (Taylor Walker) ★
49 Great Russell Street WC1B 3BA
T (020) 7242 8987 🐦 MuseumTavernPub
www.taylor-walker.co.uk
🕐 *Mo-Th* 11.00-23.30, *Fr-Sa* 11.00-24.00,
Su 12.00-22.00. Children welcome.
Cask beers 6 (Fuller's, Theakston, Westerham,
3 often unusual guests), ***Other beers*** 5 keg,
3 bottles, ***Also*** 1-2 ciders
🍴 Sandwiches, pub grub **££**, 🪑 Tables on street
*Occasional meet the brewer events, tastings,
board games*

🚇 Tottenham Court Road 🚶 Jubilee Walkway

Despite its tourist-friendly location right
opposite the British Museum, this welcoming
and attractive venue is helped enormously by
a mellowed heritage interior. The pub was
here first, opening as the Dog and Duck in the
18th century, but cannily rebranded when one
of the capital's top attractions landed on its
doorstep in 1823. The distinctive panelled
ceiling, heavy wood bar back, counter and
Watney's Imperial Stout mirror survive from a
major refit in 1889. Amazingly, considering its
relatively small size, it was originally divided
into five smaller areas, as evidenced by the
various outside doors and labelling in the glass.
It's long been a rare permanent outlet in London
for cask Theakston Old Peculier, alongside
London Pride, Westerham's 1730 and guests
that tend to come from Cottage, Thwaites,
Truman's or Woodforde's. Preprinted standard
menus outline classic pub grub – bangers, pies,
fish & chips and changing veggie options.

Parcel Yard (11)

Contemporary pub (Fuller's)
8 Shared Service Yard, Goods Way N1 9AH
T (020) 7713 7258 🐦 TheParcelYard
www.parcelyard.co.uk
🕐 *Mo-Sa* 08.00-23.00, *Su* 09.00-22.30.
Children until early evening.
Cask beers 11 (Fuller's, 4 often London guests),
Other beers 6 keg, 15 bottles, ***Also*** Wines, whiskies
🍴 British food and upmarket pub grub,
breakfasts **££**, ♿
*Occasional drink festivals, major big screen sport,
functions*

🚆 Kings Cross, St Pancras International
🚇 Kings Cross St Pancras 🚴 Link to Regents Canal towpath
🚶 Link to Jubilee Greenway, Jubilee Walkway

Accessed via escalators from the the new
Kings Cross concourse, the Parcel Yard challenges preconceptions about the station pub
experience. A previously derelict but Grade I
listed parcels office has been lavishly transformed into a huge pub with a mix of spaces
around a rectangular courtyard that's now a
delightful glass-covered atrium, scattered
with reminders of the golden age of rail. It
claims to offer the widest range of Fuller's
beers in London: Chiswick, Discovery, ESB,
HSB, London Pride and Seafarers are all regularly stocked on cask, plus a seasonal and at
least two guests, usually locals like Hackney
or Moncada or from places served by rail from
the station, all poured to Master Cellarman
standards. A full range of Fuller's bottles and
kegs provides further choice. The impressive
menu reaches beyond pub grub classics to
dishes like cassava and cheese croquettes,
steamed mussels, pot roast hake or roast
guinea fowl with puy lentils.

Visitor note *Harry Potter fans should look out for
Platform 9¾ near the steps to the pub.*

Museum Tavern

Queens Head (12)

Contemporary pub
66 Acton Street WC1X 9NB
T (020) 7713 5772 🐦 TheQueens_Head
www.queensheadlondon.com
🕐 *Su-Mo* 12.00-23.00, *Tu-Sa* 12.00-24.00.
   Children until 19.00.
Cask beers 3 (Redemption, 2 unusual guests),
Other beers 7 keg, 40 bottles
🍴 Cheese, ham, pork pies, with some beer
matching **£-££**, ⊼ Small rear patio
Jazz (Tu&Su), board games, pub for hire

Queens Head

🚆 Kings Cross, St Pancras International
🚇 Kings Cross St Pancras 🚶 Link to Jubilee Walkway

Down a side street off Grays Inn Road, a short walk from Kings Cross, this handsome pub benefits from fine original features, happily preserved thanks to decades of underinvestment before its June 2010 refurb, including extensive ceramic tiling, engraved glass, mirrors and light fittings from the gaslight era. Redemption Trinity is the regular cask, alongside beers from locals like Five Points and Hammerton, or Milton and Tiny Rebel from further afield. Most bottles are from London and the UK – Buxton, Kernel, Harbour, Siren, Weird Beard, Wiper & True – while La Chouffe might pop up on keg alongside British 'craft keg' purveyors. Food is limited to cold plates and sharing boards of cheese and cold meat, some helpfully provided with matching beer suggestions. This friendly pub shares ownership with Simon the Tanner (p 60) and has the same knack of interesting dedicated geeks without scaring off everyone else.

Sourced Market (13)

Shop, bar
St Pancras International, Pancras Road NW1 2QP
T (020) 7833 9352 🐦 sourcedmarket
www.sourcedmarket.com
🕐 *Mo-Fr* 07.00-21.00, *Sa* 08.00-20.00,
Su 09.00-20.00. Children welcome.
Cask beers None, **Other beers** 2–3 keg, 100+ bottles
(mainly London), **Also** Wines
🍴 Deli platters, sandwiches, salads,
specialist food **£-££**, ♿ on station
Tastings (most Fr)

🚆 St Pancras International, Kings Cross
🚇 Kings Cross St Pancras 🚲 Link to Regents Canal towpath
🚶 Jubilee Walkway, link to Jubilee Greenway

Fronted by the gobsmacking Gothic Revival Grand Midland Hotel, St Pancras station is one of the great monuments to the railway age, restored to its former glory in 2007 as the terminus for Channel Tunnel trains. The vaults

Sourced Market

below platform level, used until the 1960s to store beer arriving from Burton upon Trent, have been repurposed as retail space, and this delectable deli, which began as a music festival popup, occupies a long strip at the north end, facing the National Rail ticket office. It stocks an impressive range of London brewers — Beavertown, Five Points, Hammerton, Kernel, Partizan, Sambrook's, Weird Beard, Wild Card — and other English producers. You can drink in for a modest corkage and people-watch from a high stool while nibbling on artisanal cheese. Popular with departing Londoners as well as homebound visitors, it's an offer to equal anything at the Brussels end of the line.

TRY ALSO

Near the British Museum, **Royal Mile Whiskies** (3 Bloomsbury Street WC1B 3QE, www. royalmilewhiskies.com) stocks a good range of Scottish bottled beers, including some rarely seen south of the border, alongside London beers and single malts. Between Euston and St Pancras stations, the **Somers Town Coffee House** (60 Charlton Street NW1 1HS, www. thesomerstowncoffeehouse.co.uk) has up to 10 cask beers, mainly from Wells & Young's, in a pleasant wood-panelled setting. Near the Lamb (p47), independent pub **The Perseverance** (63 Lambs Conduit Street WC1N 3NB, www. the-perseverance.moonfruit.com) added its own brewery late in 2014.

HOP HISTORIES The Great Beer Flood

One of the most notorious brewing disasters in history happened on 17 October 1814 at Meux's Horse Shoe brewery, at the junction of Tottenham Court Road and Oxford Street. At about 16.30, one of the iron hoops fell from a giant 6.7 m-high wooden vat containing 3,550 barrels (5,800 hl) of 10-month-old porter. Brewery staff thought little of the incident as this was a relatively common occurrence, usually easily fixed, but about an hour later, the whole vat collapsed, the force of its exploding staves knocking out several other vats and barrels nearby. A flood of porter and debris weighing several hundred tonnes poured out of the brewery in a wave at least 4.5 m high, inundating cellars, knocking down walls and washing people from first floor rooms in the slum housing of St Giles 'rookery' opposite.

Eight people died, not, as is sometimes supposed, from drowning in beer or intoxication but from injuries caused by debris and the force of the flood. All were women and children: five from poor Irish families who were, tragically, holding a wake in a cellar, and three young children in the St Giles workhouse. The death toll would undoubtedly have been higher but for the time of day, as most people were out at work. And the vat that burst wasn't even the biggest in the brewery - it may have been one of the smallest. Astonishingly, the firm avoided paying compensation and even managed to reclaim the duty it had already paid on the lost beer, though the disaster made porter brewers rethink their policy of building ever-bigger vats and might ultimately have helped turn fashions away from aged 'stale' porter towards fresher, 'running' beers.

Brewery owner Sir Henry Meux had been a partner in Meux Reid's Griffin brewery in Clerkenwell, built in 1763, which pioneered the use of giant vats in porter production. In 1807, following a dispute, Meux set up on his own by buying the Horse Shoe, which had been around since (probably) before 1764. In 1914 Meux's took over Thorne Brothers' Nine Elms brewery in Vauxhall and transferred brewing there seven years later: the original Horse Shoe was demolished in 1922 and the Dominion Theatre (268 Tottenham Court Road W1T 7AQ) now occupies the site. Eventually merged as Friary Meux, the company became part of Ind Coope in 1961 and stopped brewing at Nine Elms in 1964.

Reid & Co, meanwhile, merged into Watney Combe Reid in 1898 (see Roll out the red barrel p100) and the Clerkenwell plant was closed a year later. Some of the brewery buildings still stand, including former tap the Griffin pub (125 Clerkenwell Road EC1R 5DB), which survives rather ignominiously as a strip club.

Borough & Southbank

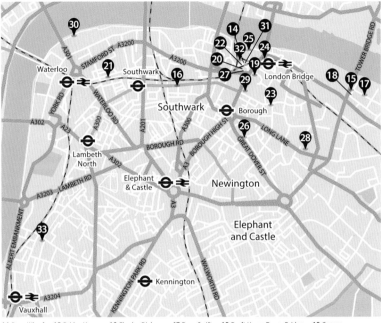

14. Brew Wharf · 15. Bridge House · 16. Charles Dickens · 17. Dean Swift · 18. Draft House Tower Bridge · 19. George ·
20. Katzenjammers · 21. Kings Arms · 22. Market Porter · 23. Miller · 24. Oddbins London Bridge · 25. Rake ·
26. Royal Oak · 27. Sheaf · 28. Simon the Tanner · 29. St Christophers Inn · 30. Understudy (National Theatre) ·
31. Utobeer · 32. Wright Brothers Oyster and Porter House · 33. Zeitgeist (Jolly Gardeners)

Brew Wharf (14)

Bar, restaurant
14–16 Stoney Street SE1 9AD
T (020) 7378 6601
www.brewwharf.com ⬛ Brew-Wharf
🕐 Mo-Fr 11.00-23.00, Sa 10.00-23.00,
Su 11.00-21.00. Children welcome.
Cask beers 2 (Truman's), **Other beers** 9 keg,
45 bottles **Also** Wines, cocktails
🍴 Gastro and enhanced pub grub menu
££-£££, ⛱ Front patio, ♿
Tastings, seasonal events, functions

⇌ ⊖ London Bridge ⛴ London Bridge City ♿ NCN4,
link to CS7 🚶 Jubilee Greenway, Jubilee Walkway, Thames Path

Created in 2005 as the beer department of
Vinopolis, an exhibition and 'tasting experience'
in the arches of a former railway viaduct,

this upmarket Borough Market haunt was
originally a sporadically creative brewpub
co-founded by Trevor Gulliver of St John
fame (p 77). A short-sighted decision by new
owners in mid-2014 saw brewing suspended,
but there's still a decent list to match the
beer-themed decorations, with third-pint
tasting flights on offer. You'll find casks
from Truman's, Meantime unfiltered tank
lager, imported wheat beer, big bottles of
St Feuillien and Boon Mariage Parfait and
even some decent fruit flavoured options
like Meantime Raspberry Wheat and St
Germain rhurbarb saison from France.
Meals are essentially upmarket pub grub:
pies, braised pork belly, or exotica like
beetroot and ricotta tortelloni or teriyaki
steak salad. Brew Wharf may be closed for
major refurbishment in 2016: please check.

Bridge House (15)

Contemporary pub (Adnams)
218 Tower Bridge Road SE1 2UP
T (020) 7407 5818
www.bridgehousebar.co.uk
◼ thebridgehousebar 🐦 BridgeHouseBar
🕐 *Mo-We* 11.30-23.00, *Th-Sa* 11.30-24.00,
  Su 12.00-23.00. Children welcome.
Cask beers 7 (Adnams), **Other beers** 3 keg,
2-3 bottles, **Also** Wines, specialist spirits
🍴 Enhanced pub grub **££**,
⍭ Bench on street, ♿
Monthly book club, functions

🚆 London Bridge 🔵 Tower Hill, London Bridge
🔵 Tower Gateway 🚢 Tower Millennium 🚲 NCN4
🚶 Jubilee Greenway, Jubilee Walkway, Thames Path

Adnams beers are now widely sold in the
capital, but this is the only London pub actually
owned by the well-loved Southwold independent. Appropriately given the brewery's coastal
location, this leasehold pub enjoys a prime
waterside site on the southern approach to
Tower Bridge. It's bright, cheerful and friendly
despite the touristy surroundings, and though
operated as mainly table service with a focus
on food, you can still just pop in for a pint. It
serves Adnams casks including Explorer, Ghost
Ship, seasonals and specials, also sold in thirds
– this was the first Adnams pub to offer the
measure. Bottles include the odd Jack Brand
beer and Tally Ho in season, while food takes
in shepherd's pie, jackets, beef chilli and
halloumi kebabs. The brewery's second life
as a wine importer and specialist distiller is
also well represented.

Pub trivia *The building housed one of London's earliest
microbreweries in the 1980s (see Southwark Ale p 56).*

Charles Dickens (16)

Traditional pub
160 Union Street SE1 0LH
T (020) 7401 3744
www.thecharlesdickens.co.uk
🕐 *Mo-Sa* 12.00-23.00, *Su* 12.00-21.00.
  Children welcome.
Cask beers 12 (unusual guests),
Other beers 2 keg, 1 bottle, **Also** A few malts
🍴 Pub grub **£**, ⍭ Rear terrace
Quiz (We), big screen sport, functions

🚆 Waterloo 🔵 Borough, Southwark 🚢 Bankside
🚲 NCN4, CS7 🚶 Link to Jubilee Greenway, Jubilee Walkway,
Thames Path

A warm and welcome bolthole in the rapidly
changing area between Blackfriars and
Southwark bridges, this is a longstanding
and reliable real ale free house relatively
close to Tate Modern. The cask handpumps
have recently doubled to a dozen, largely
dispensing beers from established
microbrewers like Cottage, Hogs Back,
Nelson and Nethergate, with the occasional
Adnams and locals from Brentwood,
Portobello and Twickenham. Food is well-
priced, home-made fare like meat or veggie
sausage and mash, liver and bacon, pies and
ploughman's. It's a pleasant, basic, bright
place decorated with numerous prints related
to the author whose name it has borrowed,
with a secluded wooden terrace at the back.

Dean Swift (17)

Contemporary pub (Pubs of Distinction)
32 Lafone Street SE1 2LX
T (020) 7357 0748
www.thedeanswift.com 🐦 DeanSwiftSe1
🕐 *Mo-Sa* 12.00-24.00, *Su* 12.00-23.00.
  Children until 22.00.
Cask beers 4 (unusual guests),
Other beers 10 keg, 60 bottles
🍴 Enhanced pub grub/gastroish menu,
cooked bar snacks **££**
*Beer and food matching, meet the brewer/tap
takeover, quiz (Su), big screen sport, board games,
functions*

🚆 London Bridge 🔵 Tower Hill, London Bridge, Bermondsey
🔵 Tower Gateway 🚢 Tower Millennium, London Bridge City
🚲 NCN4 🚶 Jubilee Greenway, Jubilee Walkway, Thames Path

Dean Swift

Just around the corner from Shad Thames, this "Local Beer House" opened in 2010 as the first of three Pubs of Distinction venues, and remains pleasant and inviting. Dancing Duck, Magic Rock, Moor, Redemption and Siren are among daily changing brewers featured on the cask pumps. Bermondsey breweries like Brew by Numbers, Bullfinch and Kernel are in bottle and sometimes keg, alongside Buxton, Summer Wine, Titanic and imported classics from Belgium, Germany and the USA. The menu runs from fish and chips to spiced venison and stout stew and Jerusalem artichoke and wild mushroom pie, with snacks like anchovy crostini served amid clean and elegant décor. For all this, when there's a big match on the Dean proves it's still a Bermondsey local at heart by rolling down the big screen.

Pub trivia *The name commemorates Irish satirist and political commentator Jonathan Swift: the fictitious title character of his most famous work,* Gulliver's Travels, *was a local man.*

Draft House Tower Bridge (18)

Specialist, contemporary pub
206 Tower Bridge Road SE1 2UP
T (020) 7378 9995
www.drafthouse.co.uk   🅵 🐦 DraftHouseTB
🕐 *Mo-Sa* 12.00-23.00, *Su* 12.00-22.30.
    Children welcome.
Cask beers 4 (Sambrook's, unusual guests),
Other beers 16 keg, 65 bottles,
Also Specialist spirits
🍴 Diner-style menu **££**
Occasional beer events, tastings, functions

🚆 London Bridge   🔵 Tower Hill, London Bridge
🔵 Tower Gateway   🚢 Tower Millennium   🚲 NCN4
🚶 Jubilee Greenway, Jubilee Walkway, Thames Path

Opened in 2010 on the southern approach to Tower Bridge, this most fortuitously located of the Draft Houses inevitably attracts sightseers but also soaks up weary walkers recuperating from a trudge around the Bermondsey breweries. They won't be disappointed with a range that includes brewers like Beerd, Celt. Cottage or Red Squirrel on cask (with a changing 'cask of the day' at bargain price), 'craft kegs' that may well come from Arbor, Beavertown, Hardknott, Titanic or Pressure Drop, and a rounded bottled list touching on Belgian classics (Orval, Timmermans Oude Gueuze),

Draft House Tower Bridge

Londoners and international craft brewers like Founders, Odell and Mikkeller. Thirds are served, and a short and light-hearted diner-style menu matches the bright colours and cheerful décor, in this case enlarged album covers and Ghostbusters wallpaper on the stairs. More spacious than some branches, it's nonetheless often busy, with a separate cocktail bar downstairs.

George (19)

Traditional pub (Greene King) ★
77 Borough High Street SE1 1NH
T (020) 7407 2056   www.gkpubs.co.uk/
pubs-in-london/the-george-inn-pub
🅵 georgeinnlondonbridge   🐦 georgeinn1677
🕐 *Daily* 11.00-23.00. Children until 21.00.
Cask beers 8 (Greene King, 1–2 guests),
Other beers 4 keg, 8 bottles
🍴 Enhanced pub grub **££**, 🪑 Large courtyard
*Occasional outdoor jazz, theatre,
hog roasts in summer*

🚆🔵 London Bridge   🚢 London Bridge City
🚲 NCN4, link to CS7   🚶 Link to Jubilee Greenway, Jubilee
Walkway, Thames Path

London's only remaining example of a 17th century galleried coaching inn has stood in its yard off Borough High Street since at least 1598, but what you see today is a mere 339 years old, dating from a rebuilding after a serious fire that consumed most of mediaeval Southwark. You could write a whole book about the history of this place: indeed beer writer Pete Brown has done exactly that, with *Shakespeare's Local* (2012). Only one of the original three wings endures, but even this fragment is surprisingly extensive with numerous rooms on several floors. Admire the courtyard from one of the galleries and you'll be reliving an experience familiar to Samuel Pepys, Samuel Johnson and Charles Dickens. The most authentically

George

fitted downstairs room is the first on the right as you enter the courtyard, with a glassed-in bar including an unusual (disused) Victorian cash register-style beer engine and woodwork likely installed in the 1676 rebuild. It's now owned by the National Trust and leased to Greene King. Cask Abbot, IPA, Old Speckled Hen and a standard session bitter rebadged for the pub are always on sale, alongside seasonals (XX Mild has even been known to appear) and guests from breweries like Brains and Oakham, plus some of GK's more interesting bottled beers like Suffolk Strong. Don't expect to feast on larks and blackbirds: food is standard up-market pub grub, though cheeseboards stocked by nearby Neal's Yard Dairy add interest.

Katzenjammers (20)

Bar (Red Car)
24 Southwark Street SE1 1TY
T (020) 3417 0196
www.katzenjammers.co.uk
🕐 *Mo-Th* 12.00-23.00, *Fr-Sa* 12.00-24.00,
Su 12.00-22.30. Children until 19.00.
Cask beers None, ***Other beers*** 9 keg, 25 bottles
(German), ***Also*** Schnapps
🍴 Bavarian-style menu **£-££**
Oompah band (Fr-Sa), major big screen sport

🚈 ⊖ London Bridge 🚢 London Bridge City 🚲 NCN4, link
to CS7 🚶 Jubilee Greenway, Jubilee Walkway, Thames Path

The vaulted storage cellars of the Hop Exchange (see Southwark ale p 56) may no longer be stacked with hop 'pockets' but since 2009 they've housed two bars, both under the same ownership, that amply showcase the

principal use of the resinous plant: the Sheaf (p 59) and this German-themed joint. As often is the case with such places, it trades partly on caricatures of hearty Bavarian partying but there's a respectable choice of beer. Most of the draughts are from Paulaner in Munich but Hopf and König Ludwig feature too. Flensburger, Schlösser Alt, Schlenkerla and Schneider Aventinus add depth to a bottled list that, oddly, includes a Belgian fruit beer section. Food is predictably big on sausages and schnitzel. Daytimes are quieter for beer sampling, but the plain benches are more atmospheric when packed by merry folk swaying to an oompah band that includes Queen covers in its repertoire.

Kings Arms (21)

Traditional pub (Windmill)
25 Roupell Street SE1 8TB
T (020) 7207 0784
🕐 *Mo-Sa* 11.00-23.00, *Su* 12.00-22.30.
Children until 17.00.
Cask beers 9 (Adnams, 8 often local guests),
Other beers 2 keg, 10 bottles/cans (mainly London)
🍴 Thai menu **£-££**
Meet the brewer/tap takeover, board games (Su)

🚈 ⊖ Waterloo 🚢 London Eye 🚲 NCN4
🚶 Link to Jubilee Greenway, Jubilee Walkway, Thames Path

If the unspoilt terraces of early 20th century workers' cottages between the river and Waterloo East look like a set from a BBC period drama, it's because you've seen them featured in several such productions. Halfway along one of the terraces is this fine pub, retaining smallish, partitioned public and saloon bars, lettered in an incongruous 1960s font that recalls a past life as an Ind Coope house. A backyard converted to a conservatory is now a Thai restaurant. The improving beer range features largely local casks: Gipsy Hill, Late Knights, Moncada, Redemption and Windsor & Eton are regularly offered alongside visitors like Beerd and Brains. A changing 'craft keg' line is often from Beavertown, and Fourpure, Kernel and Redchurch beers are in the fridges. While it's often busy with well-informed commuters and visitors to nearby attractions, it stands sufficiently apart from all of these to retain a community feel.

Kings Arms

discoveries are unlikely to return. There's no list, so making a considered choice means perusing the pump clips, not always easy when the crowd at the bar is three deep, and the staff are too rushed to advise. The warm and woody main bar is optimised for vertical drinking, while the homely upstairs lunchtime restaurant is usually an oasis of calm, offering the likes of steak and ale pie, veggie pasta and mixed grill, with a smaller selection sold downstairs.

Pub trivia *If you fancy sampling obscure microbrews as Radio 4's Today programme hits the airwaves, this is one of the few London pubs still making use of its early morning market licence.*

Market Porter (22)

Specialist, traditional pub
9 Stoney Street SE1 9AA
T (020) 7407 2495
www.markettaverns.co.uk/The-Market-Porter
🐦 TheMarketPorter
🕐 *Mo-Fr* 06.00-09.30, 11.00-23.00, *Sa* 12.00-23.00, *Su* 12.00-22.30. Children until early evening.
Cask beers 12 (Harvey's, Marston's, 10 unusual guests), **Other beers** 5 keg, **Also** 3 ciders/perries
🍴 Enhanced pub grub, sandwiches, lunchtimes only **££**, 🪑 Standing on street, ♿
Major big screen sport, functions

🚆 ⊖ London Bridge ⛴ London Bridge City
🚲 NCN4, iink to CS7 🚶 Jubilee Greenway, Jubilee Walkway, Thames Path

This Borough Market fixture has been attracting a crowd that frequently spills out onto surrounding streets since well before the current beer renaissance and was even once one of London's first new generation brewpubs (see Southwark ale p 56). Aside from the permanent presence of Sussex Bitter, the policy is to buy in beers new to the pub from right across Britain, sell them quickly and put something different on, sometimes as often as nine times a day, with around 50 different cask beers in a wide variety of styles offered every week. Beers from Boggart, Firebrand, Hambleton, Highland, London Beer Factory, Milestone, Mordue, Roosters, Sunny Republic and Weltons were on when I called. The advantage is that there's always something new to try, often from very small outfits that otherwise rarely appear in London. The disadvantages are that you never know what to expect, the experience can be a little hit-and-miss and

Miller (23)

Contemporary pub
96 Snowsfields SE1 3SS
T (020) 7407 2690
www.themiller.co.uk 📘 🐦 themillerpub
🕐 *Mo-We* 12.00-23.00, *Th* 12.00-24.00,
   Fr 12.00-01.00, *Sa* 18.00-01.00, *Su* closed.
   Children until early evening.
Cask beers 4 (guests), **Other beers** 1 keg, 36 bottles (London), **Also** Cocktails, specialist spirits
🍴 Burgers, sharing boards, lunchtime sandwiches
£-££, 🪑 Benches on street, side terrace
Comedy or music in upstairs venue most days, DJs, table tennis, pool

🚆 London Bridge ⊖ Borough, London Bridge 🚲 Link to NCN4

A big pub just south of the Guy's Hospital campus, the Miller is now in the same hands as the Sebright Arms (p 120), and just as friendly, funky and beer-aware, with a quirky interior hung with film posters and psychedelic artwork. Like its sister it also functions as an entertainment venue, hosting regular comedy in a 100-seat theatre upstairs. The draught lines are tied to Greene King and do their best with guest ales – Brains, Brighton and York are regular visitors. It's a different story in the bottle fridges, with a long London beer list arranged under style headings above the bar. The work of less widely-distributed brewers like Belleville, Brick, Honest Brew and Rocky Head features alongside firm favourites like Beavertown, Kernel, Pressure Drop and Weird Beard. Food is simple stuff like pizzas and burgers, with panini refuelling local medics at lunchtimes.

SOUTHWARK ALE

SOUTHWARK owes its unique character to its strategic location, on the main road route to Kent and mainland Europe and at the foot of what was until 1750 the only bridge across the Thames in central London. In the past the bridge was lined with houses and shops and was regularly congested, so transport terminated in Borough High Street. Travellers arriving outside daylight hours, when the bridge was closed, could take refuge in one of the numerous large inns in courtyards off the High Street, of which the George (p53) is the only survivor. Southwark also escaped much of the City's regulation, making it a haven for more disreputable activities. Bankside, just upriver of the bridge, was famously the site of several theatres in Elizabethan and Jacobean times, as well as bull- and bear-baiting venues and London's largest concentration of brothels.

All this created a healthy market for brewers. Southwark ale was famous enough by 1390 that the Miller in Geoffrey Chaucer's *Canterbury Tales* could apologise in advance for the potential effects of alcohol on his storytelling abilities with the words: "and therfore if that I mysspeke or seye, / Wyte it [blame it on] the ale of southwerk, I you preye." Originally most brewing took place in inns, ale houses and institutions like nearby Bermondsey Abbey, but as standalone 'common brewers' emerged, Southwark remained a favoured location. The more cosmopolitan and liberal atmosphere would also have appealed to migrants who couldn't always rely on the warmest of welcomes in London. From the 15th century onwards, brewers from the Low Countries and Germany met an increasing demand for continental-style

hopped beer in London, as opposed to old-fashioned English unhopped ale, from breweries in Southwark.

The district was also well-placed for the delivery of raw materials from Kent and other parts of southern England. Its role in the hop trade was confirmed by the building in 1867 of the magnificent Hop Exchange on Southwark Street, now the last surviving purpose-built trade exchange building in the capital. And of course there was the activity on the river itself: London Bridge marked the upper limit of the stretch known as the Pool of London, once the busiest port in the world.

Brewing spread down the Pool to Bermondsey where the Anchor Brewhouse occupied the riverside at Horselydown, immediately to the east of where Tower Bridge now stands, perhaps from the 16th century. It was once owned by a Flemish brewer, and in 1787 sold to a consortium led by John Courage, an ambitious shipping agent born in Aberdeen of French Huguenot descent. Most big London brewers back then specialised in porter, but Courage promoted fresher 'running ale' styles, and by 1895 when the now-expanded site was rebuilt, it was one of the most successful brewers in the capital.

Another Anchor, this time known as a brewery rather than a brewhouse, was built by James Monger in 1616 a little upriver on Park Street, on the site of William Shakespeare's Globe theatre, which had burned down three years previously (the current Globe, on the riverside 230 m to the north, is a 1997 replica).

SOUTHWARK ALE

In the 18th century the Thrale family turned this Anchor into one of London's best-known porter breweries, and in 1781, diarist Samuel Johnson helped sell it on behalf of his friend Henry Thrale's widow Hester, describing it as "not just a parcel of boilers and vats, but the potentiality of growing rich beyond the dreams of avarice". The new Quaker owners, Barclay and Perkins (the former from the same family as the founders of Barclays Bank), turned it into what was once the biggest brewery in the world, a technological marvel of its day, and a mid-19th century visitor attraction. Its most famous beer was the potent Imperial Russian Stout, brewed originally for export from the end of the 18th century.

In 1921, Barclay became the first large and established British brewer to adopt lager brewing, which caught the attention of Courage, and in 1955 the latter bought out its near neighbour, soon turning it entirely over to lager production. By the beginning of the 1970s brewing had ceased, through storage and distribution continued on the site. By this time Courage had expanded into one of Britain's Big Seven national brewers, and in 1981 it ceased all London production including at Horsely-down, selling off both sites. The Horselydown brewery still stands, now converted to luxury flats and offices, an early example of Docklands regeneration. There's a plaque on the wall at 50 Shad Thames SE1 2LY but the best view is from across the other side of Tower Bridge.

The Park Street site was completely demolished and replaced by modern housing, though there are two plaques visible from Park Street (SE1 9DZ). One of these commemorates a curious incident in 1850 when General Julius Haynau, known as the 'Austrian butcher' for his role in brutally suppressing rebellions, was recognised and beaten up by draymen while visiting the brewery. Both brewery taps survive - the Anchor Tap (20A Horselydown Lane SE1 2LN) is now a Sam Smith pub which retains an unspoilt interior, while the Anchor Bankside (34 Park Street SE1 9EF) is part of the Taylor Walker chain and popular with tourists. Wells & Young's bought the brands from eventual owner Heineken and now brew some of the beers in Bedford, including, occasionally, Imperial Russian Stout.

Brewing also spread upriver to Lambeth. The large Godings Brewery opened in 1837 between Belvedere Road and the river, surmounted by two large lion sculptures in artificial Coade stone, which became such familiar landmarks that the company later renamed itself the Lion brewery. Taken over by Hoare & Co (see Yeast Enders p122) in 1923, the Lion closed shortly afterwards, and lay derelict for years. It was finally demolished in 1949, and the Royal Festival Hall was built on the site for the 1951 Festival of Britain. One of the lions now stands a little further upriver, guarding the steps from the Thames Path to Westminster Bridge by County Hall.

The area immediately south of the river later played its part in the real ale revival. In 1979, unemployed young would-be entrepreneur David Bruce was out running when he spotted a large derelict former Truman's pub, the Duke of York, not far from Borough Tube. Minimally renovated and renamed the Goose and Firkin, it became Britain's first modern brewpub, with a 5-barrel kit (8 hl) initially brewing from malt extract. The Goose provided the model for a whole chain of Firkin brewpubs across London, and ultimately the UK and abroad. Bruce sold the company in 1988, later founding several other pub chains, and eventual owner Bass closed all the breweries in 1995. The Goose is now a Shepherd Neame pub known once again as the Duke of York (47 Borough Road SE1 1DR).

Other early microbreweries in the area included Simon's Tower Bridge Brewery, set up with the help of investment from CAMRA in 1980, which brewed intermittently under several owners until 1983 in the building on Tower Bridge that's now the Bridge House pub (p52); and a small brewhouse which operated between 1981-88 in the Market Porter on Borough Market (p55), and again as the Bishop's Brewery between 1993-98 in the building opposite that now houses Monmouth Coffee (2 Park Street SE1 9AB). Now Brew Wharf (p51) has decommissioned its brewhouse, there are currently no commercial breweries in Southwark proper – but the Bermondsey brewers (p 64) are continuing a distinguished tradition nearby.

Oddbins London Bridge (24)

Shop
7 Borough High Street SE1 9SU
T (020) 7407 5957   www.oddbins.com/
ourstores/oddbins-london-bridge
OddbinsLondonBridge   OddbinsLBridge
Mo-Tu 09.00-20.00, *We-Fr* 09.00-20.30,
Sa 11.00-19.00, *Su* 12.00-19.00.
Cask beers None, **Other beers** 75+ bottles,
Also Wines, malts, gins
Occasional tastings

London Bridge   London Bridge City   NCN4,
link to CS7   Jubilee Greenway, Jubilee Walkway, Thames Path

Oddbins was instrumental in developing the British public's taste in wine in the 1980s, and even sold some of the earliest US craft beers seen in the UK in the 1990s. It's now a rare survivor of the devastation wrought by supermarkets on high street off-licences, and once again growing, helped by a wholehearted embrace of local beer. This branch, neatly sited under the London Bridge railway tracks, has more than most – appropriately, given its proximity to Borough Market and the Bermondsey breweries. Over half the bottles are from London brewers like Beavertown, Brixton, By the Horns, Five Points, Fuller's, Kernel, Moncada, Redchurch, Twickenham and several others. Have fun finding these on the London beer map displayed on the wall beside a helpful style guide. They'll deliver bigger orders for free if you're lucky enough to live nearby.

Rake   Top 25 (25)

Specialist, bar (Utobeer)
14 Winchester Walk SE1 9AG
T (020) 7407 0557   The-Rake   Rakebar
www.utobeer.co.uk/the-rake
Mo-Th 12.00-23.00, *Fr* 11.00-23.00, *Sa* 10.00-23.00,
Su 12.00-22.00. Children on terrace only.
Cask beers 3 (unusual guests),
Other beers 7 keg, 150+ bottles, **Also** Cider
Pork pies, sausage rolls, Scotch eggs **£**,
Front terrace,
4 annual beer festivals, meet the brewer/tap takeover, tastings

London Bridge   London Bridge City   NCN4,
link to CS7   Jubilee Greenway, Jubilee Walkway, Thames Path

The people behind Utobeer (p61) turned a Borough Market greasy spoon café into the avant-garde of a new wave of London beer bars back in 2006. Other venues now compete with it in terms of beer range, but discerning palates and worldwide connections ensure the Rake retains its place as an essential stop on the international craft beer circuit, as attested by the various brewer autographs on the wall. The cask handpumps favour beers from associated brewpub Tap East (p117), alongside Dark Star, Hardknott,

Oakham, Thornbridge and many others, with over 20 different choices served in a week. Kegs and bottles stretch from London (Beavertown, Fourpure, Kernel, Partizan) across the world – this is one of the places in the capital you're most likely to find the latest imports from the US, exclusive Belgians like Bzart, and British rarities like Burning Sky specials and English 'lambic' Elgood's Coolship. Space is restricted ("the size of a minicab office" comments one reviewer) and basic, but boosted by a pleasant wooden-decked and heated terrace that also hosts extra stillages during special events like the well-established Welsh beer festival in early March.

Royal Oak

Royal Oak   Top 25   (26)

Traditional pub (Harveys)
44 Tabard Street SE1 4JU
T (020) 7357 7173   www.harveys.org.uk
🕐 *Mo-Sa* 12.00-23.00, *Su* 12.00-21.00.
   Children welcome.
Cask beers 7 (Harveys, 1 guest),
Other beers 10+ bottles, **Also** 1 cider
🍴 Enhanced pub grub, sandwiches **£-££**,
🎋 Tables on street
Occasional live music, functions

🚊 London Bridge   ⊖ Borough

The Royal Oak is well loved with good reason
as it's pretty much the perfect traditional pub
– clean, bright and civilised but unpretentious
and friendly, with a genuine community feel,
no recorded music nor bleeping machines, in
a Victorian building with some surviving
heritage features, and top quality beers on
sale. It's one of only two London pubs tied to
respected family brewer Harveys of Lewes,
stocking a comprehensive range besides the
famed Sussex Bitter: the rather fine dark mild,
new Wild Hop beer, big Armada Ale, traditional
and unusual bottled specialities including
benchmark-setting Imperial Russian Stout and
cask guests, often seasonals from Fuller's. Food
includes cooked sandwiches, wholesome pies,
veggie specials and unusual options like roast
partridge or haggis and mash. The space around
the island counter is divided in two, still distinguished by the greater amounts of soft furnish-
ings on the 'saloon' side, with an old-style
hatchway in the lobby once used for off sales.

Visitor note. *Tabard Street is the original route of Watling
Street, the road to Canterbury used by Geoffrey Chaucer's
fictitious pilgrims; its modern name commemorates the
now-vanished inn where they assembled.*

Sheaf   (27)

Contemporary pub (Red Car)
24 Southwark Street SE1 1TY
T (020) 7407 9934
www.redcarpubs.com/The-Wheatsheaf
🕐 *Mo-Th* 11.00-23.00, *Fr-Sa* 11.00-24.00,
   Su 12.00-22.30. Children until 21.00.
Cask beers 10 (Fuller's, Nethergate, Wells & Young's,
7 unusual guests), **Other beers** 4 keg, 9 bottles
🍴 Enhanced pub grub, sandwiches, sharing
boards **££**
*Occasional live music, big screen sport, darts,
board games, functions*

🚊⊖ London Bridge   🚢 London Bridge City   🚲 NCN4, link
to CS7   🚶 Jubilee Greenway, Jubilee Walkway, Thames Path

A companion piece to Katzenjammers (p 54) in
the vaults of the Hop Exchange, this originated
as a temporary replacement for well-loved
Young's pub the Wheatsheaf, on Borough
Market, while a new rail viaduct was slotted in
above it. Now the original Wheatsheaf has
reopened, its offshoot continues as a freehouse
with a shortened name, occupying a surprisingly big, bright and pleasant space decorated
with poignant monochrome photos of past
regulars. Young's Bitter is still stocked, but this
is also a great place to find beers from an array
of small brewers rarely spotted in London:

59

Atomic, Elgood, Frog Island, Goffs, Lodestar and Malmesbury were on offer when I called. Food encompasses tapas-sized tempura vegetables and mini-burgers, roasted salmon burger and comfort stodge like roast beef and mash or pies.

Pub trivia. From 1954 this vault housed the eccentric Becky's Dive Bar, one of the first specialist beer pubs in Britain, literally an underground refuge for some of the enthusiasts who would influence the emergence of CAMRA and the microbrewing movement. Becky's was always noted more for its range than its hygiene: it was the dodgy sausage sandwiches which, by all accounts, triggered its final demise in 1975.

Simon the Tanner (28)

Contemporary pub
231 Long Lane SE1 4PR **T** (020) 7357 8740
www.simonthetanner.co.uk
Simon-the-Tanner   Simon_theTanner
Mo 17.00-23.00, Tu-Sa 12.00-23.00, Su 12.00-22.00. Children welcome.
Cask beers 4 (Adnams, 3 often local guests), **Other beers** 9 keg, 17 bottles, **Also** Some wine
Sharing boards, cooked sandwiches, enhanced pub grub **£-££**,
Quiz (Tu), meet the brewer/tap takeover

London Bridge   Borough   London Bridge City
Link to NCN4, CS7   Link to Jubilee Greenway, Jubilee Walkway, Thames Path

Bermondsey remains a patchwork of gentrification (*Vogue* dubbed Bermondsey Street the coolest street in London) and unregenerated social housing once populated by dockers or workers in the leather trade. That occupation is recalled in the unusual name of this 200-year-old gem, which lay derelict for six years before being reopened in 2011 by the same group that runs the lovely Queens Head (p 49). Like that pub, it's a community venue with a considered beer choice, with casks often from locals like Crate, Five Points, Hackney, Gipsy Hill and Redemption, and a dedicated keykeg line for Kernel. Crate, Orbit, Fourpure, Pressure Drop and Weird Beard enliven the fridges alongside a few Trappists and strong Scottish ales. A shortish menu exhibits the same care: sharing plates of charcuterie and British cheeses, salt beef sandwiches and dishes like chilli con carne and cheese-topped puy lentil casserole.

St Christophers Inn (29)

Traditional pub (Interpub)
121 Borough High Street SE1 1NP
T (020) 7407 2392
www.stchristopherspub.co.uk
stchristopherspub   StChrisInn
Su-We 11.00-01.00, Th-Sa 11.00-02.00. Children until 21.00.
Cask beers 5 (unusual sometimes local guests), **Other beers** 5 keg, 35+ bottles
Sharing plates, brunch, enhanced pub grub **££**, Benches in side alley
Live music (Tu-Sa), major big screen sport, functions

London Bridge   Borough, London Bridge
London Bridge City   Link to NCN4, CS7
Link to Jubilee Greenway, Jubilee Walkway, Thames Path

Owned by an international backpackers' hostel group and with accommodation above, this long, narrow old pub on the corner of an inn yard was once run as a youth-oriented bar, but a few years back returned to a more traditional feel of dark wood and bare floorboards, with more loungey seating at the back. An improving beer range has casks from Londoners like Truman's and Twickenham besides Caledonian, Hogs Back and Vale, and bottles and kegs which, though hardly out of the ordinary, cover a variety of bases: among the highlights are bottled Hacker-Pschorr Kellerbier, Harviestoun Old Engine Oil, Redchurch and Rochefort 6 and Delirium Tremens on tap. The menu features ingredients sourced from nearby Borough Market – cheese and meat boards, baked sea bass, chicken korma, burgers and veggie pies.

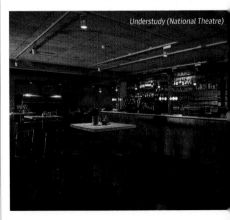
Understudy (National Theatre)

Understudy (National Theatre) (30)

Bar
Southbank SE1 9PX   🐦 ntUnderstudy
www.nationaltheatre.org.uk/your-visit/
food-and-drink/the-understudy
🕐 *Mo-Th* 12.00-24.00, *Fr-Sa* 12.00-01.00,
   Su 12.00-23.00. Children until early evening.
Cask beers None, **Other beers** 11 keg, 40+ bottles
(mainly London & SE England), **Also** Specialist
spirits, cocktails
🍴 Cooked bar snacks, pizzas in good weather
£, 🪑 Large riverside terrace, ♿
*Beer events, live music, interactive projections,
adjoining theatre*

🚆🚇 Waterloo   ⛴ London Eye   🚲 NCN4
🚶 Jubilee Greenway, Jubilee Walkway, Thames Path

Today the Southbank is one of London's
busiest and most vibrant promenades, so it's
surprising to note that when the National
Theatre was built in the mid-1970s, it turned
its back on the river as unworthy of interest.
In October 2014 the National finally gained a
riverfront bar in former storage space in the
northeast corner, commanding a large and
popular terrace. Even more impressively, it
has a beer theme – there's no cask as cellar
space is restricted, but there's unfiltered
Meantime tank lager and 'craft kegs' mainly
from Londoners like Brew by Numbers,
Brixton, Five Points, Redchurch and interlopers
like Siren. More Londoners feature on the
bottled list alongside Belgian lambics and good
stuff from Germany and the USA. Clever interior
design makes the best of the *béton brut* architecture to create a cosy space that recycles
theatre lighting and part of a drum revolve.

Utobeer   Top5   (31)

Shop
Borough Market, Borough High Street SE1 1TL
☎ (020) 7378 6617
www.utobeer.co.uk   📘🐦 utobeer
🕐 *Tu* 10.30-17.30, *We-Fr* 11.00-18.00, *Sa* 09.00-
17.00, *Su-Mo* closed.
Cask beers None, **Other beers** 700+ bottles
🍴 Specialist and gourmet food from
surrounding stalls £-££, ♿ on market

🚆🚇 London Bridge   ⛴ London Bridge City   🚲 NCN4,
link to C57   🚶 Jubilee Greenway, Jubilee Walkway, Thames Path

Utobeer has flown the flag for fine beer among
all the other fine food and drink at Borough
Market since 1999, and by educating the taste-
buds of a generation of drinkers and brewers
it undoubtedly helped lay the foundations for
London's current flourishing beer culture. It
still has one of the biggest and best chosen
selections, often carrying stuff nobody else
does thanks to its ear-to-the-ground buyers
and importing and distribution activities.
London and UK brewers are well represented,
including rare bottlings from associated brew-
pubTap East (p117). And as a longstanding
champion of US craft brewing it regularly features rarely-seen producers like Moylans,
North Coast, Ruhstaller and Shmaltz besides
limited edition specials like Anchor, Brooklyn
and Stone. Dutch and Belgian high performers
like De Dochter van de Korenaar and De Molen,
rarities from revered names like Schneider and
seasonal collections make it easy to forgive
them their painfully punning name.

Wright Brothers Oyster and Porter House   (32)

Restaurant
11 Stoney Street SE1 9AB
☎ (020) 7403 9554   🐦 wrightbroslondon
www.thewrightbrothers.co.uk
📘 WrightBrothersOysters
🕐 *Mo-Sa* 12.00-23.00, *Su* 12.00-22.00.
   Children welcome.
Cask beers None, **Other beers** 2 keg, 16 bottles,
Also 40+ wines
🍴 Oysters, seafood, fish ££-£££,
🪑 Tables on street

🚆🚇 London Bridge   ⛴ London Bridge City   🚲 NCN4, link
to C57   🚶 Jubilee Greenway, Jubilee Walkway, Thames Path

Pleasingly, this Borough Market shopfront for
Cornish oyster fisher Wright Brothers foregrounds porter and stout as the ideal accompaniment. Half the bottle list focuses on the
dark stuff, appropriately enough for an outlet
a stone's throw from the former site of one of
the greatest porter brewers in the world.
Suppliers include Kernel as well as Anchor,
Harviestoun, Meantime, St Peter's and
Whitstable. Adnams and Pressure Drop feature
among paler choices, and then there's the

Wright Brothers Oyster and Porter House

more expensive but equally traditional matching option of champagne. At least six varieties of oysters are served, as well as mussels, shrimps, crab and Guinness and oyster pie: vegetarians will find themselves rather at sea. Non-diners might be able to squeeze onto a stool at the bar, but this is a small, intimate place with table space reserved for diners and pre-booking is advised.

Zeitgeist (Jolly Gardeners) (33)
Bar
49 Black Prince Road SE11 6AB
T (020) 7840 0426   **f** Zeitgeist-Pub-London
www.zeitgeist-london.com
🕐 *Su-Mo* 12.00-23.00, *Tu-Th* 12.00-24.00, *Fr-Sa* 12.00-01.00. Children until 17.00.
Cask beers None, **Other beers** 13 keg, 35 bottled (German), **Also** Schnapps
🍴 German menu **£-££**, 🌳 Beer garden, tables on street
Big screen sport including Bundesliga, functions

🚇🚆 Vauxhall   🚢 St George Wharf   🚲 Link to Avenue Verte, NCN4, CS8   🚶 Link to Jubilee Greenway, Jubilee Walkway, Thames Path

In 2008 this then-decaying venue in the oldest part of Lambeth was given a makeover by new German owners and turned into a decent *Gaststätte*, mercifully free of accordions and fake Bavarian kitsch. The Victorian shell is obvious from the big and heavy island bar and the high ceilings; the current décor offers stools and giant high banquettes in a friendly and cheerful atmosphere. German expats come to watch the Bundesliga and to sample a range of beers they'd be lucky to find in one

place at home: Ettal Benediktiner wheat beer, Flensburger, König Pils and Paulaner Dunkel are among the kegs, while bottles include Augustiner Edelstoff, Eifel unfiltered Landbier, Jever, König Ludwig Dunkel, Mühlen Kölsch, Schlenkerla and Schneider. The menu includes lesser-seen Germanic specialities like *Flammkuchen* and veggie platters besides *Leberkäse*, *Schweinebraten* and enough sausages and schnitzels to fuel another World Cup win.

Pub trivia *Charlie Chaplin may well have known the Jolly Gardeners from the days when his father played piano here.*

TRY ALSO

At Borough Market, the old **Wheatsheaf** (6 Stoney Street SE1 9AA, **www. wheatsheafborough.co.uk**) has reopened with the new rail viaduct directly overhead. It's now a spacious and comfortable Young's pub with a slightly bigger beer range than usual. On a prime riverside site in a historic tea warehouse adjoining Hays Galleria on the Thames Path, the **Horniman at Hays** (26 Hays Galleria SE1 2HD, www.nicholsonspubs.co.uk/ thehornimanathayslondonbridge) is a big and better-than-average Nicholson's. The Victorian-styled but trendy **Rose** (123 Snowsfields SE1 3ST, **www.therosepublichouse.co.uk**), in back-streets behind Guy's Hospital, has good guest casks and 'craft keg' besides food.

Station caterer SSP's **Beer House** bars are generally disappointing, though the one on Waterloo station (opposite platforms 1–4, SE1 7ND) is worth a look for its comfortably pub-like environment, cask beers mainly from Greene King and Wells & Young's and better-known 'crafty' brands in keg and bottle.

LONDON'S BREWING

Kernel

"We've just gone with the flow," responds founder Evin O'Riordain when asked about the remarkable growth of Kernel, now one of the most significant and most revered breweries in London. When the last edition of this book was published in 2011, he was brewing twice a week on a small four barrel (6.5 hl) kit in a Bermondsey arch shared with two other businesses, and making his own deliveries by tricycle, helped out by the occasional friend: "You always need friends," he remarks. But already his unselfconsciously artisanal and often-changing range of hoppy US-inspired pale ales alongside strong stouts and porters from historic London recipes were winning devoted admiration from the cognoscenti.

From Waterford in Ireland, Evin studied English Literature as a postgraduate, but ended up working for well-known specialist cheesemonger Neal's Yard Dairy on Borough Market. His beer epiphany happened when his employers sent him to New York City and he encountered people who took beer as seriously as he took cheese. On his return, he took up homebrewing and began researching historic recipes as well as working in the fresh, hoppy styles he'd encountered in the US. He sold his first beers under the Kernel name late in 2009, taking what was then an unusual step for a British brewer by focusing on bottle conditioning rather than cask. The results provoked excitement among connoisseurs almost immediately.

In April 2012, the Kernel expanded to two capacious arches of its own about a kilometre down the railway line at Bermondsey Spa, quintupling its brewlength to 20 barrels (33 hl) (the old kit went to Partizan). Brewing now takes place four or five times a week, and the fermentation capacity has increased several times over. At the end of 2014 the brewery became the first in London to install *foeders*, big Flemish-style wooden maturation vessels similar to those once used in the capital to mature porter, though these ones are currently filled with saison. The range has diversified to incorporate delightful low gravity beers and sours, and a handful of regular beers has emerged, but the spirit of innovation and creative expression remains, and the name stamped onto the minimalist brown paper labels is still more like an artist's signature than a brand.

The Kernel has also been influential in embedding the idea of regular brewery openings and taprooms into London's beer culture. Evin followed the example of his cheesemaking and other foodie friends in selling direct from his arch from the start, later adding a bar. This was the founding moment of what's now the bustling Saturday Bermondsey beer scene. Such face-to-face contact with the engaged beer drinker remains an important part of the brewery's philosophy but the unforeseen popularity hasn't always been easy to deal with and there are no plans to extend the current facilities or limited hours.

Evin is a quiet, thoughtful and modest man who points out the brewery benefited from being in the right place at the right time, just as the beer scene in London began to take off. He's also generous to the people who work with him: there's now a team of 11, with a head brewer, Toby Munn, though everyone works on the basis of covering the process from start to finish, taking turns at brewing, bottling, driving the forklift and answering the phone. But it's undoubtedly his own flair for brewing, and his attention to quality, that have enabled his brewery to ride the wave so successfully. And you can't help thinking his business sense is sharper than it might at first appear. The co-founder of another admired London brewery once told me: "If we need to make a difficult decision, we always ask ourselves, 'What would Evin do?'"

BERMONDSEY BREWERIES `Top 25`

ONCE only mechanics, builders' merchants and other such prosaic small businesses operated from the railway arches southeast of London Bridge, but today they've found a new purpose. Wander alongside the Victorian brickwork on a Saturday daytime and you'll encounter an assortment of keen beer drinkers passing and repassing: tattooed young hipsters of both genders; cheery families; groups of older middle-class couples clutching gourmet food carrier bags; dapper lone gentlemen with notebooks; international beer tourists; garrulous delegations from CAMRA branches; and the occasional misplaced stag party who assumed this was some kind of drinking game. All are attracted by the string of breweries, bottle shops and sundry specialist food retailers now occupying the inner catacombs of one of the oldest such viaducts in the world, built in 1836 for the London and Greenwich Railway, the first public steam railway in London. Over the past couple of years, this unlikely promenade has become one of the most interesting and immersive beer experiences in Britain.

The story begins at the London Bridge end of the railway in the mid-2000s when the traders of 'foodie heaven' Borough Market discovered the railway arches along Druid Street provided convenient and cool warehouse space. Some then started opening their warehouses to the public on Saturdays, and in 2010, following friction with the market trustees, a second gourmet market appeared on the Ropewalk side of the line

off Maltby Street, supported in part by the patchwork gentrification of what was once one of London's poorest areas.

The first brewery to join this community was Kernel in 2009, at first sharing an arch on Druid Street with a cheesemaker and an importer. Like its foodie neighbours, Kernel opened its Ropewalk doors on Saturdays, and soon developed into a must-visit beer destination, all the more compelling for its short opening hours and the excellence of its produce.

In March 2012 Kernel, along with several other former Maltby Street businesses, moved about a kilometre southeast along the line to become part of a new cluster of food and drink businesses at Spa Terminus, once briefly the London end of the railway before it was extended to London Bridge. Kernel's old kit went to the Partizan brewery, which launched that November in another arch in Almond Street even further southeast, also open on Saturdays. Then in June 2013, Brew by Numbers expanded from its basement near Elephant and Castle to an arch in Enid Street, just round the corner from the Ropewalk. Since then the brewing strip has reached further in both directions: Fourpure opened at South Bermondsey late in 2013, and in March 2014 Anspach and Hobday, who also host Bullfinch, restored a Saturday taproom to Druid Street. In August 2014 Southwark Brewing opened closer to Tower Bridge Road.

It didn't take long for someone to coin the phrase 'Bermondsey

Beer Mile', a label disliked by the breweries for its suggestion of a drinking challenge. The ever-popular Kernel has even shifted to earlier hours to avoid being the final call for overindulged promenaders. It's a minor, if irritating, problem: most customers are appreciative, responsible and respectful, though overcrowding is an issue at times.

Exploring the Bermondsey breweries has become an essential London beer experience, with a unique and sociable atmosphere. The brewers themselves are usually around and keen to talk, and there's a chance to taste beers at their best and freshest, with rare and exclusive specials on sale. Somehow even the basic accommodation – typically temporary communal tables, sometimes improvised from kegs and pallets, occupying what's normally workspace – adds to the sense of being up close and personal.

The best advice is not to attempt to cover all the breweries in one day - there are now too many, and the times too restricted to do this comfortably while giving each the attention it deserves. And if you hurry, you're more likely to drink quickly and consume more than you intended.

If you really do only have a day, treat it as more of a sightseeing and shopping expedition than a drinking one. Resist the obvious option of working outwards and start instead at South Bermondsey National Rail station: Tower Bridge is a much better place to finish, and this way Kernel is the third brewery along, so if you start as early as possible and stay disciplined you should easily get

Top 25 BERMONDSEY BREWERIES

Fourpure taproom

there before it closes. Alternatively, avoid the worst of the crowds at Kernel with an early start there, work your way on foot southeast via Partizan to Fourpure, then catch the number 1 bus back up to Caledonian Market to cover the northwest breweries. End-to-end, the 'mile' is actually almost exactly 2 km (1¼ miles) and easily walkable, though the southeastern breweries are more dispersed.

At South Bermondsey, your first stop will be **Fourpure**, the only brewery not in an arch but an industrial unit wedged between viaducts. This has one of the most expansive drinking spaces and a long bar which alongside easy-drinking core beers offers numerous specials from a pilot brewery, including experimental and Belgian-style brews.

Partizan is just off Southwark Park Road Market in the former Cockney heartland of the Bermondsey Blue. When I last visited, the retail space here was just a few metres at the front of the arch but expansion into a neighbouring unit has since created a bigger taproom. There's a rare opportunity to try the brewery's beers on tap, including limited-availability specials,

while admiring some of the original artwork for its striking label designs framed on the walls.

Kernel itself now has long experience of Saturday crowds, and copes with efficiency while retaining a warm welcome. It occupies two tall and spacious arches accessed from Dockley Road, with a decent-sized drinking area that soon fills up, and a children's sandpit. Draught beers are often decanted straight from the conditioning tanks and sold only in two-thirds measures, while bottles from a separate stall are likely to include exclusives and one-offs as well as core lines. The only disappointment is that the yard around the arches, with its patches of grass and trees, is strictly off limits to drinkers due to licensing restrictions.

Brew by Numbers, opposite residential flats in Enid Street, has a narrow space equipped with a basic but oddly charming little bar area. Choosing between sometimes over 20 beers is made easier by the helpful tasting cards on the wall, grouped as Belgian, Dark, Hoppy and Sour. Pallets outside function as improvised seating in good weather.

The next arches of interest face north onto Druid Street. The **Bottle Shop** isn't a brewery but an arch-based trade warehouse that also opens to the public on Saturdays, with a massive range of bottles from the UK and all over the world. Lovers of sour beers in particular will find much of interest, and a handful of draught beers on keg and cask is usually offered, with Weird Beard often providing a pop-up

bar. A mezzanine floor provides extra seating and event space.

Only a couple of doors along is **Anspach and Hobday**, with a small but well-presented drinking space at the front of its arch, which is likely to remain the taproom when the brewery expands. The occasional cask on stillage, usually containing a one-off rarity like a dry-hopped version of a regular line, supplements keykeg taps and bottles that encompass the rarely-seen Bullfinch brands brewed independently and intermittently on the kit here. Tasting flights of thirds are an option.

Dodge to the south of the lines again to the Ropewalk market, a great place to refuel on anything from Spanish charcuterie and English pies to French patisserie and falafel. You could even treat yourself to oysters, and wash them down with a stout or porter from a well-chosen selection of mainly London and UK bottled beers at the **Modern Beer Co**, a Bottle Shop offshoot.

Back on Druid Street, **Southwark Brewing** focuses on session strength cask beers served at their peak, including specials from a pilot kit, with four-pint takeaway containers too and even a few Belgian bottled classics. Comfort here even stretches to a sofa or two. A few steps further along, a fine view of Tower Bridge provides a fitting end to your expedition, and nearby venues like the Bridge House (p52), the Dean Swift (p52) or the Draft House Tower Bridge (p53) offer an opportunity to rest your weary legs in a proper pub.

BERMONDSEY BREWERIES `Top 25`

Anspach and Hobday (34)

Taproom
118 Druid Street SE1 2HH
www.anspachandhobday.com
🅕 AnspachandHobday 🐦 AnspachHobday
🕐 *Sa* 11.00-18.00, *Su* 12.00-17.00,
    closed other days. Children welcome.
Cask beers Occasional, *Other beers* 8 keg,
10 bottles (Anspach & Hobday, Bullfinch)
🍴 Pies, occasional BBQ £, 🪑 Tables on street
Seasonal events

🚲 London Bridge 🚇 Bermondsey 🚌 Maltby Street (C10
Bermondsey, Borough), Dockhead (47 381 Bermondsey, London
Bridge) 🚴 Link to NCN4

Bottle Shop (35)

Shop, bar
128 Druid Street SE1 2HH
T (01227) 656280   www.bottle-shop.co.uk
🅕 BottleShop.UK 🐦 bottle_shop
🕐 *Sa* 10.00-18.00, closed other days.
    Children welcome.
Cask beers Occasional, *Other beers* At least 2 keg,
around 350 bottles 🪑 Benches at front
Meet the brewer/tap takeover

🚲 London Bridge 🚇 Bermondsey 🚌 Maltby Street (C10
Bermondsey, Borough), Dockhead (47 381 Bermondsey, London
Bridge) 🚴 Link to NCN4

Brew by Numbers (36)

Taproom
79 Enid Street SE16 3RA
T (020) 7237 9794   www.brewbynumbers.com
🅕 Brew-By-Numbers 🐦 brewbynumbers
🕐 *Sa* 10.00-17.00, closed other days.
    Children welcome.
Cask beers None, *Other beers* 6 keg, 20+ bottles
(Brew by Numbers)
🍴 Scotch eggs £, 🪑 Benches at front, ♿
Functions

🚲 London Bridge 🚇 Bermondsey
🚌 Maltby Street (C10 Bermondsey, Borough),
Dockhead (47 381 Bermondsey, London Bridge)

Fourpure Brewing Co (37)

Taproom
22 Bermondsey Trading Estate,
Rotherhithe New Road SE16 3LL
www.fourpure.com
🅕 fourpure 🐦 fourpurebrewing
🕐 *Sa* 11.00-17.00, closed other days. Children welcome.
Cask beers None, *Other beers* 11-13 keg, 7+ cans/bottles
(Fourpure), *Also* Local soft drinks
🍴 Pies, Scotch eggs, sausage rolls £,
🪑 Benches at front
Occasional special events

🚲 South Bermondsey 🚇 Surrey Quays
🚌 Beamish House, Rotherhithe New Road (1 381 Surrey Quays)

Kernel Brewery (38)

Taproom
11 Dockley Road Industrial Estate SE16 3SF
T 0775 755 2636
www.thekernelbrewery.com
🅕 The-Kernel-Brewery 🐦 kernelbrewery
🕐 *Sa* 09.00-14.00, closed other days.
    Children very welcome.
Cask beers None,
Other beers 8 keg, 12+ bottles (Kernel)
🍴 None but adjacent arches sell cheese,
charcuterie, baked goods, ♿
Informal brewery tours

🚇 Bermondsey

Modern Beer Co (39)

Shop, bar
41 Maltby Street SE1 3PA
www.maltby.st 🐦 ModernBeerCo
🕐 *Sa* 09.00-18.00, closed other days.
    Children welcome.
Cask beers None, *Other beers* 30 bottles
🍴 Variety of food stalls in market £-££,
🪑 All outdoor, ♿ in market

🚲 London Bridge 🚇 London Bridge, Bermondsey
🚌 Maltby Street (C10 Bermondsey, Borough),
Dockhead (47 381 Bermondsey, London Bridge)

`Top 25` BERMONDSEY BREWERIES

Partizan Brewing (40)

Taproom
8 Almond Road SE16 3LR
www.partizanbrewing.co.uk
◼ ▾ PartizanBrewing
🕒 *Sa* 11.00-17.00, closed other days.
Cask beers None,
Other beers 6 keg, 10 bottles (Partizan)
☷ Standing on street, ♿
Occasional special events

⊖ Canada Water   ⊖ Canada Water, Bermondsey
🚌 Anchor Street (1 381 Canada Water)

Southwark Brewing Co (41)

Taproom
46 Druid Street SE1 2EZ
www.southwarkbrewing.co.uk
◼ southwarkbrewing ▾ southwarkbeer
🕒 *Sa* 11.00-18.00, closed other days.
   Children welcome.
Cask beers 4 (Southwark), ***Other beers*** 5 bottles
♿
Functions

⇌ London Bridge ⊖ London Bridge, Tower Hill
⊖ Tower Gateway 🚌 Boss Street (47 381 London Bridge)
🚲 Link to NCN4 🚶 Link to Jubilee Greenway, Jubilee Walkway, Thames Path

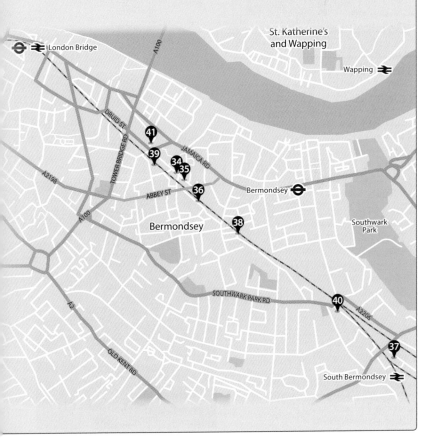

City of London

42. Blackfriar · 43. Crosse Keys · 44. Draft House Seething · 45. Harrild and Sons ·
46. Magpie · 47. Pelt Trader · 48. Williams Ale and Cider House · A. Still & Star

Blackfriar (42)

Traditional pub (Nicholson's) ★
174 Queen Victoria Street EC4V 4EG
T (020) 7236 5474 www.nicholsonspubs.
co.uk/theblackfriarblackfriarslondon
🕐 *Mo-Sa* 10.00-23.00, Su 10.00-22.30.
   Children until 20.00.
Cask beers 8 (Fuller's, Sharp's, St Austell,
Truman's, 5 guests), ***Other beers*** 4 bottles
🍴 Enhanced pub grub **££**, 🪑 Front terrace

🚆🚇 Blackfriars 🚲 Link to NCN4 🚶 Jubilee Walkway,
Thames Path, link to Jubilee Greenway

One of London's most extraordinary heritage
pubs, this flatiron-shaped 1875 building was
remodelled in 1905 into a unique British
art nouveau extravaganza, inspired by the
Dominican friary that once stood nearby.
From the street the glittering mosaic name-
plate, statuary and plaques are intriguing
enough, but inside is overwhelming. Every
surface is sumptuous, with layers of multi-
coloured marble, stained glass, mirrors and
richly polished wood, lavishly illustrated with
fanciful scenes of monastic life in dramatic
handmade bas-relief. It's all a marvellous
challenge to the English reputation for reserve,

but we can only speculate on what its supposed
subjects the Dominicans, mendicant preachers
who helped found the Inquisition, would make
of it. This is one of the better Nicholson's pubs:
guests from the seasonal list could include
locals from By the Horns or more unusual
choices from Exmoor, Hopdaemon, Rooster's,
Sunny Republic or Wold Top, and there are
Redchurch beers in bottle.

Crosse Keys

Crosse Keys (43)

Contemporary pub (Wetherspoon)
9 Gracechurch Street EC3V 0DR
T (020) 7623 4824   🐦 TheCrosseKeys
www.jdwetherspoon.co.uk
🕐 *Mo-Th* 08.00-23.00, *Fr* 08.00-24.00,
   Sa 09.00-23.00, *Su* 09.30-19.00.
   Children until 20.00.
Cask beers Up to 23 (Adnams, Greene King,
Sharp's, up to 20 unusual guests), ***Other beers***
11 keg, 8 bottles, ***Also*** 1–2 ciders/perries
🍴 Wetherspoon menu **£-££**, ♿
*Beer festivals, food promotions, occasional meet
the brewer, functions*

🚆 Cannon Street, Liverpool Street   🚇 Liverpool Street
🚇 Bank   🚴 Link to CS7   🚶 Link to Jubilee Walkway, Thames Path

Despite the low prices, standard furniture and curry nights, this is not your average local Wetherspoon. It's housed in the palatial former London headquarters of HSBC, with massive pillars rising between green and grey marble walls, and a grand staircase climbing to a balcony with Chinese-style sculptures. Then there's the beer range, one of the biggest in the chain, with at least 16 casks listed on the monitors above the big island bar and some-times the full complement of 23 – a 24th handpump is reserved for cider. Extra stillages go up during Wetherspoon festivals, raising the cask choice to as much as 100. On a midweek afternoon I spotted Cameron's, Mauldons, Nottingham, Inveralmond, Otter, Rhymney, Weltons and Wharfe Bank among others, with a good mix of styles including milds and porters. There are a few more bottles and 'craft kegs' than usual too, including Belgian and US favourites.

Pub trivia The pub revives the name of a coaching inn that once stood on the site, adopting the emblem of St Peter after neighbouring St Peter upon Cornhill church, a Wren rebuild which claims to stand on the site of the oldest Christian church in Britain.

Draft House Seething (44)

Specialist, bar   **Top 25**
14 Seething Lane EC3N 4AX
T (020) 7097 5140
www.drafthouse.co.uk   🐦 drafthousesl
🕐 *Mo-Sa* 12.00-23.00, *Su* closed.
   Children welcome.
Cask beers 4–5 (Sambrook's, up to 4 unusual
often local guests), ***Other beers*** 12 keg, 45 bottles
🍴 Burgers, hot dogs, salads **££**, ☂ Perching on
street, ♿
Occasional tastings, major big screen sport

🚆 Fenchurch Street   🚇 Tower Hill   🚇 Tower Gateway
🚢 Tower Millennium   🚴 CS2, CS3, link to NCN13
🚶 Jubilee Walkway, Thames Path

At the bottom of an office block just round the corner from both the Tower of London and Fenchurch Street station, this former post office became the latest and arguably the best Draft House in July 2013, its exposed concrete set off strikingly by several big bold neon signs flashing beer-related messages. There are more cask beers than usual, from locals like Late Knights, Sambrook's or Windsor & Eton and others like Rooster's, Red Squirrel or Waen, sometimes on the 'cask of the day' offer. And it's one of the few London outlets for unfiltered *tankovna* Pilsner Urquell, the copper tanks clearly on display above the door. Other options could be Buxton, Green Flash, St Bernardus or

Weird Beard in bottle, and keg taps lining up Camden Town and London Fields beside rarities like Quantum from Stockport or Australia's Stone and Wood.

Harrild and Sons (45)

Bar (Barworks)
26 Farringdon Street EC4A 4AB
T (020) 3714 2497　🅵 🅨 HarrildandSons
www.harrildandsons.com
🕐 *Mo-We* 12.00-24.00, *Th* 12.00-01.00,
　　Fr 12.00-02.00, *Sa* 17.00-24.00, *Su* closed.
　　Children until early evening.
Cask beers 3-4 (unusual often local guests),
Other beers 10 keg, 120 bottles, **Also** Occasional cider, some fine wines, specialist spirits, cocktails
🍴 Seafood, meat **££**, 🌴 Rear sheltered terrace, ♿
Occasional meet the brewer/tap takeover

🚆 City Thameslink　🚇 Farringdon　🚇 Blackfriars
🚶 Jubilee Walkway, link to Thames Path

Educating consumers to think more about beer with food in easy steps since February 2014, this bright, smart post-industrial bar near Holborn Viaduct pushes the simple message of porters and stouts with oysters. The menu boasts a wide choice of bivalves and an excellent selection of the dark stuff, ranging from Buxton's approachable Dark Knights to hefty imperials like Molen Rasputin, with not a mass-produced Dubliner in sight. Among other beers are changing casks from people like Brixton, Hackney, Great Heck or Thornbridge, British

keykegs and bottles galore, mainly from the UK (a wide range of Wild beers when I looked), Belgium and the USA. The kitchen offers other seafood options alongside steak, veal and duck dishes, though with thin pickings for vegetarians.

Pub trivia *The big space once housed a printshop, accounting for the glass-roofed rear section which was designed to make the best of natural light.*

Magpie (46)

Traditional pub (Nicholson's)
12 New Street EC2M 4TP
T (020) 7929 3889　🅨 MagpieThe
www.nicholsonspubs.co.uk/
themagpiebishopsgatelondon
🕐 *Mo-Fr* 10.00-23.00, *Sa* 11.00-23.00, *Su* closed.
　　Children welcome.
Cask beers 8 (Sharp's, St Austell, Truman's, 5 unusual guests), *Other beers* 2 keg, 2-3 bottles
🍴 Enhanced pub grub **££**, 🌴 Standing on street, ♿
Meet the brewer, tastings, functions

🚆 🚇 🚇 Liverpool Street

In a narrow alley just off Bishopsgate and on the site of a former ambulance station, the Magpie looks ordinary as Nicholson's pubs go but is favoured both for location and for beer choice. Enthusiastic 'cask master' Anna now looks after the cellar, picking the work of brewers like Bath, By the Horns, Roosters or Sadlers for the seasonal guest list partly as a result of customer consultation, partly to

Magpie

achieve a range of styles. A few more options in the fridge might include Duvel or Norwich's Redwell, just down the line from Liverpool Street nearby. Unsurprisingly given its location it's very much a city boy pub but, even if you're the only customer not wearing a suit, you'll be made welcome.

Pelt Trader (47)
Bar
3 Dowgate Hill EC4N 6AP   **T** (020) 7160 0253
www.pelttrader.co.uk   🐦 PeltTrader
🕐 *Mo-Fr* 12.00-23.00, *Sa-Su* closed.
   Children welcome.
Cask beers 6 (unusual guests),
Other beers 12 keg, **Also** A few specialist spirits
🍴 Pizzas **££**, 🪑 Standing on street
Pub for hire

⇌ ⊖ Cannon Street   🚲 Link to CS7   🚶 Thames Path, link to Jubilee Walkway

In a spacious arch under the platforms of Cannon Street station, this city counterpart to the Holborn Whippet (p 80) uses a similar system of pumping cask beer to taps on the back bar using an air compressor. The high tables and half-panelled brick walls with shelves are functionally designed for efficient consumption. Six changing casks from brewers like Arbor, Bristol, Burning Sky, Dark Star, Oakham and Redemption check several style categories. Expect UK, German, US and the occasional Belgian or Scandinavian beer on the keg lines – Kernel, Siren and Kirkstall's Framboise are current favourites. There were no bottled beers at the time I visited but these may be added.

Pub trivia *The name reflects the fact that the City livery companies at Skinners Hall and Dyers Hall are near neighbours and if you're wondering, the boat hull hanging from the ceiling was originally intended to house the beer taps.*

Williams Ale and Cider House
Contemporary pub (Metro)   (48)
22 Artillery Lane E1 7LS
T (020) 7247 5163   🐦 alencider
www.williamsspitalfields.com
📘 The-Williams-Ale-&-cider-house
🕐 *Mo-We* 11.00-23.00, *Th-Fr* 11.00-24.00, *Sa* 16.00-24.00, *Su* closed. Children welcome.
Cask beers 9 (Greene King, Truman's, 7 often local guests), **Other beers** 5 keg, 2 bottles,
Also 3 ciders/perries
🍴 Enhanced pub grub, cooked bar snacks **££**,
🪑 Standing on street
Live music (Th), occasional beer events, board games

⇌ ⊖ Liverpool Street   ⊖ Shoreditch High Street

The Williams was an ordinary Greene King pub until September 2013, when it relaunched as the brewery's most centrally sited 'craft beer' venture. Like several other pubs given this treatment, it stocks very little of its owner's beer: the house ale is Spitalfields Brew, actually a generic bitter specifically brewed for such rebadgings, and there's the keg stout from GK's Scottish subsidiary Belhaven. But otherwise the beers are more likely to come from Londoners like Hackney, Sambrook's, Signature or Truman's, or in keg or bottle from Lagunitas or Camden Town. Burgers and other hot sandwiches are on the menu alongside dishes like *fattoush* salad with halloumi, smoked haddock fishcakes or merguez sausages. If the brick arches and low ceilings in the cavernous main space make you feel claustrophobic, try to claim a diner-style booth in the side room.

TRY ALSO

German-themed **Bierschenke** (4 London Wall Buildings, Blomfield Street EC2M 5NT, www. bierschenke.co.uk) moved in 2014 to a much bigger space between Liverpool Street and Moorgate, selling solid if traditional German beers including several house brews commissioned from Müllerbräu in Neuötting, Bavaria. Nearby is one of the City's better Nicholson's pubs, **The Globe** (83 Moorgate EC2M 6SA, www.nicholsonspubs.co.uk/ theglobemoorgatelondon). Famous Young's pub the **Lamb** (10 Leadenhall Market EC3V 1LR, www.lambtavernleadenhall.com) now has self-proclaimed "craft beer" outlet **Old Toms Bar** in its cellar, with casks from London brewers and numerous Meantime kegs and bottles to wash down deli boards.

Further east near Fenchurch Street station, the small and handsome **East India Arms** (67 Fenchurch Street EC3M 4BR, www.eastindiaarms.co.uk) is one of London's best Shepherd Neame pubs, with reliable cask quality. Nearby, the unpretentious **Still and Star** (1 Little Somerset Street E1 8AH, www.stillandstar.co.uk) has operated a picobrewery since late in 2014. Near the Tower of London and Draft House Seething (p 69), the **Liberty Bounds** (15 Trinity Square EC3N 4AA, www.jdwetherspoon.co.uk) is a big Wetherspoon with a wider beer range than usual. The **Dispensary** (19a Leman Street E1 8EN, www.thedispensarylondon.co.uk), just beyond the eastern edge of the City near Aldgate, offers several unusual and well-kept guest casks in an interesting historic building.

HOP HISTORIES — The second biggest room in London

Bedfordshire-born Samuel Whitbread was only 16 when in 1736 he apprenticed himself to a Clerkenwell brewer. Six years later he went into partnership with brothers Thomas and George Shewell at the Goat brewhouse in Old Street, at its junction with Whitecross Street. At first they brewed porter here, and ales at a brewhouse on the other side of Old Street in what's now Central Street. But it was porter that everyone wanted, prompting Whitbread to create, in partnership with Thomas Shewell, what was likely the world's first purpose-built porter brewery, a complete rebuild and expansion of a brewhouse called the Kings Head on Chiswell Street, a short walk south on the edge of the City.

Opened in 1750, the Chiswell Street brewery was by 1758 the biggest porter producer in Britain, with an output of 64,600 barrels (105,700 hl) a year. By Whitbread's death in 1796 it was turning out 200,000 barrels (327,300 hl). The famous Porter Tun Room was built between 1776–84 after fire destroyed its predecessor, at a scale sufficient to house the increasingly large vats used for maturing the beer. With a floor area of 778 square metres and the exposed timbers of a king-post roof over 18 m above, it had the widest unsupported timber span in London after Westminster Hall. Even more remarkable were the vaults below, conceived by Whitbread as a more efficient and oxygen-proof alternative to the tuns: vast watertight cisterns lined with a special cement capable of resisting the beer's acidity, applied by ship's caulkers, with a total capacity of 12,000 barrels (19,650 hl or almost 3.4 million pints!).

Inevitably tastes moved on and Whitbread diversified into other styles of beer. The last of the famous tuns was removed in 1900, though porter production – now by different methods and at declining strengths – continued into the 1950s. It was around this time that the brewery launched the so-called 'Whitbread Umbrella' in response to the wave of mergers then sweeping the industy, buying shares in smaller regional breweries and obtaining favourable trading agreements on the promise of protecting them from hostile takover. The umbrella might have shielded them from other brewers but not from Whitbread itself, as by the early 1970s most of these regionals had been absorbed, turning the City brewer into a major national presence with an estate of around almost 8,000 pubs and a portfolio of nationally-marketed brands, including European lager brands brewed under licence in the UK like Heineken and Stella Artois.

Brewing ceased at Chiswell Street in 1976, though the building continued in use as the corporate headquarters until 2005. By then Whitbread had already sold its brewing interests to Stella brewer Interbrew in Belgium so it could concentrate on being a "branded leisure retailer", operating among others the Premier Inn hotel chain. Interbrew is now part of the world's biggest brewing group, Anheuser Busch InBev. The brewery still stands, now converted into the luxury Montcalm hotel and the Brewery conference and events venue (52 Chiswell Street EC1Y 4SD) – you can step inside the yard to admire the clock and other features. Whitbread tap the St Pauls Tavern is now a restaurant, the Chiswell Street Dining Rooms, but the Porter Tun Room still has one of the biggest uninterrupted roof spans in London.

Clerkenwell & Farringdon

49. Ask for Janice · 50. BottleDog Kings Cross ·
51. Craft Beer Co Clerkenwell · 52. Dovetail ·
53. Exmouth Arms · 54. Jerusalem Tavern ·
55. Old Red Cow · 56. Slaughtered Lamb · 57. St John

Ask for Janice (49)

Bar, restaurant (Urban Leisure)
50 Long Lane EC1A 9EJ
T (020) 7600 2255
www.askforjanice.co.uk ♥ askfor_janice
⊕ *Mo-Fr* 07.30-00.30, *Sa* 10.30-17.00, *Su* closed.
     Children until early evening.
Cask beers None, **Other beers** 8 keg, 45 bottles,
Also 40 gins, whiskies, wines
¶ Modern British/sharing menu ££
Meet the brewer/tap takeover, gin club, functions

⇌ Farringdon   ⊖ Barbican, Farringdon

This cool café-bar named after a Beastie Boys track, a sister venue to the **Elgin** (p205), opened in May 2014 just down from the **Old Red Cow** (p76). Whitewashed walls, a white-tiled bar, an original Damien Hirst spot painting, a Chris Bracey neon (see Wild Card p128) and a Kid Acne hiphop mural downstairs provide the ambience; London brewers like Beavertown, Camden Town, Crate, Fourpure, Fuller's, London Fields, Meantime, Pressure Drop and Redchurch provide much of the beer, though all in bottle and keg. Contributions from Brewers & Union, Thornbridge and Two Cocks round things out. Imaginative food fuels both

lunchtime and evening diners: clams with cider, burnt aubergine soup, wild mushroom and fennel hotpot, goose curry or smokehouse salmon hash might be among the offerings. Janice also has a thing for gin, some of it from new London craft distillers.

BottleDog Kings Cross (50)

Shop (BrewDog)
69 Grays Inn Road WC1X 8TP
T (020) 7241 7808
www.brewdog.com/bars ♥ bottledogkingsx
⊕ *Mo-Fr* 12.00-21.00, *Sa* 12.00-20.00,
     Su 12.00-18.00.
Cask beers None, **Other beers** 4 keg, around 250 bottles, **Also** Homebrew supplies, bottled ciders
Meet the brewer, homebrew classes, public and private tastings

⇌ Kings Cross, St Pancras International
⊖ Chancery Lane, Farringdon, Russell Square
🚌 Clerkenwell Road/Rosebery Avenue (45 46 Kings Cross,
Chancery Lane) 🏃 Link to Jubilee Walkway

BrewDog's first off-licence, BottleDog, is a bit of a walk down Grays Inn Road from Kings Cross but well worth it for the broad beer selection, curated by typically knowledgeable and enthusiastic staff. There's lots of BrewDog of course, including rarities and specials like the Abstrakt series, but also lots from Danish eccentric Mikkeller and London brewers.

73

BottleDog Kings Cross

Belgian and German imports tend towards classics like Boon, Schlenkerla and Trappists. North Americans include some rarely seen in London, like California's Cismontane and Ruhstaller, with a focus on obtaining the freshest possible stock. The four keg beers are dispensed using oxygen-purging growler fills, and a comprehensive range of homebrew supplies encourages a new generation of brewers, with grains milled to order.

Craft Beer Co Clerkenwell (51)

Specialist, contemporary pub
82 Leather Lane EC1N 7TR
www.thecraftbeerco.com
 craftbeercoec1
 Mo-Sa 11.00-23.00, Su 12.00-22.30.
   Children until 18.00.
Cask beers 16 (Kent, 15 unusual guests),
Other beers 21 keg, 200 bottles,
Also Cider/perry, whiskies, specialist spirits
 Pork pies, Scotch eggs **£**
Meet the brewer/tap takeover

 Farringdon   Chancery Lane, Farringdon

This first Craft Beer Co set the template for its successors when it opened in June 2011 – a previously failing and decaying pub spruced up and stocked with a dazzling beer range. Cask remains central, sourced from far and wide, including Burning Sky, Dark Star, Magic Rock, Mallinsons, Stewart near Edinburgh, Thornbridge and Londoners Weird Beard. The bottled selection is strong on IPAs from London and the US alongside fine lambics like Cantillon and Tilquin, while Thornbridge's

Kölsch-style Tzara often pops up on keg besides British, US and Scandinavian innovations. As with other Crafts, it's worth seeking advice from informed bar staff about bottles as not all are shown on the list. The smallish corner pub boasts a pleasing mix of traditional heavy wood fittings, spectacular wall and ceiling mirrors, chandeliers and designer radiators, and benefits from an interesting location on a historic market street.

Dovetail (52)

Bar
9 Jerusalem Passage EC1V 4JP
T (020) 7490 7321   www.dovepubs.com
 The-Dove   DovePubs
 Mo-Sa 12.00-23.00, Su 14.00-22.00.
   Children welcome.
Cask beers None, **Other beers** 13 keg,
100+ bottles (Belgian), **Also** Genever
 Belgian bistro and British pub grub **££**,
 A few tables in alleyway,
Monthly tastings

 Farringdon   Clerkenwell Historic Trail

The name of this alleyway off Clerkenwell Green recalls the city where the order of St John was founded, and the Dovetail claims to be built on stones brought back from Palestine. The bar is the little sister of the Dove (p 110) but concentrates exclusively on Belgian beers: the smart pewter and marble bar counter is a rare outlet for draught Rodenbach and De Koninck alongside Chimay Triple, Brugse Zot and a changing guest. A comprehensive Belgian and Dutch Trappist selection leads a strong bottled list that stretches to Boon Mariage Parfait, Saison Dupont, the odd younger name like Belgoo and perhaps a few too many fruity options. Food has a Belgian twist with mussels, *carbonnade flamande*, *waterzooi* and veggie and meaty croquettes and sausages. Poster-sized reproductions of one of Belgium's other famous cultural exports, Hergé's *Tintin* graphic novels, complete an attractive picture.

Jerusalem Tavern

Exmouth Arms (53)

Contemporary pub (Barworks)
23 Exmouth Market EC1R 4QL
T (020) 3551 4772
www.exmoutharms.com ☐ ☑ exmoutharms
🕐 *Mo-Th* 11.00-24.00, *Fr-Sa* 11.00-01.30, *Su* 11.00-
22.30. Children very welcome until 21.00.
Cask beers 4 (unusual often local guests),
Other beers 14 keg, 70 bottles, **Also** Cocktails,
mezcal, whiskies
🍴 Sliders, US-style menu **£-££**,
🌲 Tables on street, ♿
Functions

⇌ Farringdon   ⬦ Angel, Farringdon
🏃 Clerkenwell Historic Trail, link to New River Path

A 2011 refurbishment of this commandingly-
sited pub stripped away black cladding to
reveal striking green Courage tiling and stained
glass leaded windows. A simply but tastefully
furnished interior is enlivened by some truly
bizarre art, with a chichi cocktail bar upstairs.
Four handpumps rotate a changing array
including at least one London option like
Redemption; Roosters, Thornbridge or Titanic
might also show up. Three Camden Town kegs
are joined by other London guests, at least
one US import and several Europeans, while
Buxton, Crate, De Molen, Kaapse, Rochefort
and Ska are among the bottles and cans.
Imaginative tapas-style sliders (Catfish and
pickled cucumber, BBQ aubergine, pulled

pork) mix on the menu with Camden Town-
battered fish and chips and lobster roll, with
good Sunday roasts.

Pub trivia *Exmouth Market, now one of London's trendiest
shopping streets, owes its name to the pub, which was already
established when the street market started in the 1890s.*

Jerusalem Tavern (54)

Traditional pub (St Peter's)
55 Britton Street EC1M 5UQ
T (020) 7490 4281 www.stpetersbrewery.
co.uk/london-pub ☑ Jerusalemtavern
🕐 *Mo-Fr* 11.00-23.00, *Sa-Su* closed.
Children lunchtimes only.
Cask beers 6 (St Peters),
Other beers 3 keg, 17 bottles (St Peters),
Also 2 ciders, a few whiskies
🍴 Imaginative home-cooked lunches, sand-
wiches **£-££**, 🌲 Benches on street

⇌ ⬦ Farringdon   🏃 Clerkenwell Historic Trail

In 1996, Suffolk-based St Peter's Brewery
appropriated the name of a pub that once
stood next to St John's Priory gateway for its
London shopfront, in a former coffee house
and watchmaker's dating from 1720. The glass
partition that once separated public counter
from workshop still stands, creating a front
area with tiles copied from those discovered
behind panelling during the renovation.
Six cask ales are siphoned under air pressure

75

through fake barrel heads behind the bar: best bitter, golden ale and changing specialities that usually include a fruit beer, a mild or stout and something stronger. Two of the brewery's own lagers and another ale, usually an IPA, are on keg, and there's a comprehensive bottled range. Home-cooked lunchtime food could include stew made with cream stout or gnocchi and mussels. This unusual pub is understandably popular, so you'll need to time your visit to avoid the crowds.

Old Red Cow (55)

Contemporary pub (Pubs of Distinction)
71 Long Lane EC1A 9EJ
T (020) 7726 2595
www.theoldredcow.com oldredcow
⏱ *Mo-We* 12.00-23.00, *Th-Sa* 12.00-24.00,
  Su 12.00-22.30. Children until early evening.
Cask beers 4 (London and unusual guests),
Other beers 11 keg, 90 bottles, *Also* Wines
🍴 Enhanced pub grub/gastroish menu **££**
Meet the brewer/tap takeover, women's beer group, home brewing club, functions

⇌ Farringdon ⊖ Barbican

The second "local ale house" from the team behind the Dean Swift (p 52), this Smithfield Market venue, within sight of the Barbican, reopened in April 2011. The small downstairs bar boasts handpumps and high stools around tall communal tables; upstairs has a keg-only bar and more space. Casks are from local brewers like Gipsy Hill, Redemption, Southwark and Windsor & Eton, or the likes of Fyne and Waen. Keykegs could come from Kernel, Celt or Firebrand, bottles are mainly London beers or Belgian classics, and the 'brewer of the month' enjoys exposure across formats. Sunday roasts are a local legend and you're advised to book; on other days you might enjoy confit duck leg and white bean cassoulet, coley (coalfish) and chips or roast squash tart alongside burgers, steaks and cooked bar snacks. Larger parties can reserve whole suckling pigs and other choices from the bespoke menu.

Pub trivia *The pub hosts women's beer club the Red Cowgirls.*

Slaughtered Lamb (56)

Bar (Barworks)
34 Great Sutton Street EC1V 0DX
T (020) 7253 1516 slaughteredlam
www.theslaughteredlambpub.com
 theslaughteredlambpub
⏱ *Mo-Th* 11.30-24.00, *Fr* 11.30-01.00, *Sa* 12.00-01.00, *Su* 12.00-22.30. Children until 19.00.
Cask beers 4 (unusual guests), ***Other beers*** 10 keg, 45+ bottles, *Also* Specialist spirits
🍴 Sliders, salads, burgers **£-££**,
🪑 Benches on street, ♿
DJs (Fr-Sa), live music, occasional comedy, functions

⇌ Farringdon ⊖ Barbican, Farringdon
🏃 Link to Clerkenwell Historic Trail

This big, black, brash and party-minded back-street dive, borrowing its name from the fictitious pub in 1981 film *An American Werewolf in London*, has cranked up its beer awareness several notches in recent years. Changing casks are from brewers like Arbor, Brass Castle, Grain and Tiny Rebel, with numerous keykegs from similar suppliers. There's a good bottle list too, including too-rarely seen classics like Rodenbach and Courage Imperial Stout besides 'craft' heroes like De Molen, Redwillow, Ska, Stone and Thornbridge. Foodwise, you can order a selection of small sliders – barbecued aubergine, blackened catfish – or burgers, salads and pulled pork sarnies. There's one big room upstairs, and another sizeable space downstairs where musicians and comedians perform in front of a neon pentagram. Not the place for a quiet drink, but you might get bitten by its charms.

St John (57)

Bar, restaurant (St John)
26 St John Street EC1M 4AY
T (020) 7251 0848   🐦 SJRestaurant
www.stjohnrestaurant.com   ⓕ St-JOHN
🕑 *Mo-Sa* 11.00-23.00, *Su* 12.00-17.00.
    Children welcome.
Cask beers 3 (Black Sheep, Wadworth, often
local guest), *Other beers* 4 keg, 6 bottles, *Also*
Wines, a few malts, cocktails, bottled ciders
🍴 Modern British, substantial cooked snacks,
bar **£-££**, restaurant **£££**, ♿
Occasional tastings, functions

🚉 Farringdon   ⊖ Farringdon, Barbican
🚶 Clerkenwell Historic Trail

Good beer has been an essential part of
restaurateur Trevor Gulliver's vision for revital-
ising traditional British cuisine since his first
venture, the Fire Station in Waterloo (now long
since in other hands), was Young's biggest
free trade account back in the early 1990s.
Upmarket St John, opened in 1994 in a former
smokehouse near Smithfield Market, which
once housed the offices of *Marxism Today*,
is one of Britain's most influential eateries – it
famously champions eating animal parts more
squeamish diners avoid (an upmarket spin on
tripe and chips is a mainstay), but also treats
vegetables with respect and has a fabulous
in-house bakery. A separate stone-floored
bar has simpler dishes at affordable prices.
A well-chosen beer selection includes cask
Black Sheep Bitter, Wadworth 6X and
Redemption, several Meantime beers on
keg and Kernel and Tim Taylor in bottle.
"Beer is like food to us," comments Trevor.

LONDON DRINKERS   Martin Hayes

Beer-loving entrepreneur Martin Hayes was brave enough (some would then have said foolhardy) to take on an apparently termin-ally failing Pimlico pub, free of tie from Greene King, in 2009. He converted it into trailblazing contemporary beer champion the Cask Pub and Kitchen (p97). The initiative was such a success it provided the blueprint for the first Craft Beer Co in Clerkenwell (p74) two years later, created in partnership with Peter Slezak. It's since been joined by three other outstanding London beer venues, all of them listed in this book.

How do you rate London as a beer city, on a world scale?
To use football terminology, when I opened Cask it was in the Confer-ence but in a very short space of time it's joined the Premier League. It's now a world class destination for the beer lover.

What's the single most exciting thing about beer in London at the moment?
The speed at which it's growing not just in size but in confidence, with breweries pushing boundaries and consumers willing to buy all sorts of weird and wonderful beers.

What single thing would make things even better?
No more new bars without cask ale! Cask should sit proudly alongside keg and bottled beers in any good beer outlet.

What are your top London beers right now?
Kernel India Pale Ale, Beavertown Bob Barley, Hammerton N7 Pale.

What's your top great beer night out (other than in your own pubs)?
A visit to Bermondsey and its many breweries is a great way to spend a few hours.

Who's your London beer hero?
One has to be inspired by Evin O'Riordain's success with the Kernel (p63). He's grown it into one of the finest breweries in the world.

Who will we be hearing a lot more from in future?
I would expect Beavertown to keep growing rapidly.

Which are your other top beer cities?
Rome and Barcelona are both greatly underappreciated.

Holborn & Covent Garden

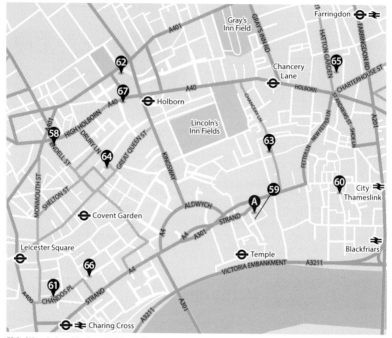

58. Craft Beer Co Covent Garden · 59. Edgar Wallace · 60. Hack and Hop · 61. Harp · 62. Holborn Whippet · 63. Knights Templar · 64. Lowlander Grand Café · 65. Olde Mitre · 66. Porterhouse · 67. Princess Louise · A. Essex Street Brewing

Craft Beer Co Covent Garden
Specialist, bar (58)
168 High Holborn WC1V 7AA
www.thecraftbeerco.com/pubs/
coventgarden ⬜ 🐦 craftbeercowc1
🕐 *Su-We* 12.00-24.00, *Th-Sa* 12.00-01.00.
Children until 18.00.
Cask beers 14 (Kent, 13 unusual guests),
Other beers 25 keg, 60 bottles,
Also 1 cider, specialist spirits
🍴 Gourmet burgers, pies **££**,
🚭 Standing on street
Occasional beer launches, tastings

⊖ Tottenham Court Road

Opened in May 2014, this is the most centrally-located Craft Beer Co branch, in a prime position on the edge of Theatreland and Covent Garden. It's smartly and simply turned out with wood finishes and gleaming pipework, and staffed by helpful experts. Relief from the crowds often clogging the long and narrow ground floor bar is provided by a more spacious, if windowless, basement in crimson and dark wood. Casks from brewers like Acorn, Magic Rock, Salamander, Siren and Tiny Rebel are featured, often with several beers from the same source, while kegs draw on imports (Dogfish Head, Highwater and Tilquin, for example), UK 'craft' brewers and Londoners like Five Points, Kernel and Weird Beard. A slightly smaller bottled range than some Crafts is particularly strong on stouts and sours. A menu fulfilled by Forty Burgers includes a forbidding-sounding Elvis Burger with peanut butter.

Edgar Wallace (59)

Traditional pub
40 Essex Street WC2R 3JF
T (020) 7353 3120
🕐 *Mo-Fr* 11.00-23.00, *Sa-Su* closed.
Cask beers 8 (Colchester, Crouch Vale,
6 unusual guests)
🍴 Sandwiches, pub grub **££**
Functions

⊖ Temple   🏃 Link to Jubilee Walkway

Edgar Wallace

Behind this rather defensive exterior, at the end
of an alley that twists round the Middle Temple,
is a bright single bar clad promisingly with pump
clips and, more unexpectedly, now-forbidden
vintage cigarette ads. It's undisturbed by piped
music or TV but massively popular with post-
work lawyers. A line of stylish metal pump
handles dispenses a house beer from
Colchester Brewery and Crouch Vale Brewers
Gold alongside often more unusual changing
selections from breweries like Dark Star,
Oakham, Red Squirrel, Rudgate or Woodforde's,
sourced through Enterprise's direct delivery
scheme. Sandwiches, burgers, ploughman's
lunches and specials like mushroom
stroganoff are on the menu.

Pub trivia *The pub was originally the Essex Head,*
after local landowner the Earl of Essex, but since 1977
has preferred to honour crime writer Edgar Wallace,
author of the original treatment of King Kong and over
175 novels. A library of his books and a memorabilia
collection can be viewed in the upstairs room.

Hack and Hop (60)

Specialist, bar (Pubs of Distinction)
35 Whitefriars Street EC4Y 8BH
T (020) 7583 8117   🅵 🆈 HackandHop
www.thehackandhop.com
🕐 *Mo-Fr* 11.00-23.00, *Sa* 12.00-23.00,
    Su 12.00-18.00. Children until early evening.
Cask beers 4 (unusual guests), ***Other beers*** 11 keg,
90 bottles, ***Also*** Specialist spirits
🍴 Enhanced pub grub/gastro menu, cooked
bar snacks **££**
Tastings, meet the brewer/tap takeover,
major big screen sport, functions

🚆 City Thameslink ⊖ Blackfriars, Chancery Lane
🏃 Jubilee Walkway

The people behind the Old Red Cow (p 76)
ventured further into central London in
November 2013 with this smart but smallish
place just off Fleet Street. Previously the Coach

and Horses, an unremarkable Greene King house, it's now a modern and minimalist beer specialist in an area more normally associated with classic traditional pubs. Imaginative beer choices could include casks from Buxton, Magic Rock, Hop Studio, Redemption, Redwillow or Windsor & Eton and 'craft kegs' from Beavertown, Firebrand, Titanic and Wild. The bottled range favours fewer brewers and more beers from each, with Londoners, lambics and saisons featured heavily in a well-presented and informative menu. Changing food options could include burgers with bone marrow and rauchbier, pan-seared scallops, pumpkin, sage and blue cheese tart or various deli boards, best enjoyed in the more relaxed space upstairs.

Harp (61)

Traditional pub (Fuller's)
47 Chandos Place WC2N 4HS
T (020) 7836 0291
www.harpcoventgarden.com
Harp London harppub
Mo-Th 10.30-23.30, Fr-Sa 10.30-24.00, Su 12.00-22.30.
Cask beers 9 (Dark Star, Fuller's, Harvey's, 5 unusual often local guests), **Other beers** 2 keg, 4 bottles, **Also** 6-8 ciders/perries, malts
Sausage baguettes **£**, Standing on street

Charing Cross Charing Cross, Leicester Square Embankment Links to Jubilee Walkway, Thames Path

So far the only London entrant to win CAMRA's National Pub of the Year (in 2010),

the Harp is still a magnet for beer lovers following management changes. Former owner Bridget Walsh retired in summer 2014, selling to Fuller's for a rumoured £7 million. The Chiswick brewery has wisely changed little, keeping the bare floorboards, chandeliers, mirrors, faded period portraits and celebrated home-cooked sausage baguettes. Most importantly, bar staff continue to pour well-chosen guest ales in flawless condition, including milds and stouts, from brewers like Arbor, Crouch Vale, Dark Star, Thornbridge, Sambrook's, Twickenham, Weird Beard and Windsor & Eton, with Kernel in keg and bottle. Such a fine pub, blissfully free of music and TV, is a rare find just a stone's throw from Leicester and Trafalgar Squares, so it's unsurprisingly often crowded, though there are usually seats in the cosy and more loungey upstairs room.

Pub trivia *Contrary to most people's assumptions, the name does not reflect the long-standing Irish influence on London's licensed trade: the pub was actually known as the Welsh Harp when it opened in the 1930s.*

Holborn Whippet (62)

Bar (Euston Tap)
25 Sicilian Avenue WC1A 2QH
T (020) 3137 9937 holbornwhippet
www.holbornwhippet.com
Mo-Sa 12.00-23.30, Su 12.00-22.30. Children until 18.00.
Cask beers 6 (unusual guests), **Other beers** 10 keg, **Also** Some wines and specialist spirits
Pizzas, bratwurst, burgers **£-££**, Some tables on street

Holborn Jubilee Walkway

The owners of the Euston Tap expanded to this more central location in June 2012. While not as characterful as the Tap's repurposed gatehouse, it has an unusual location on Sicilian Avenue, a small and elegant Italian-inspired 1910 shopping development that provides a pleasant surprise in businesslike Holborn. Indoors is breezily but stylishly minimalist, centred on a brick pillar from which cask and keg taps sprout, the former running on air pressure. It's often packed with drinkers seeking great beers served

Holborn Whippet

Knights Templar (63)
Contemporary pub (Wetherspoon)
95 Chancery Lane WC2A 1DT
T (020) 7831 2660
www.jdwetherspoon.co.uk
🕐 *Mo-Fr* 09.00-24.00, *Sa* 09.00-22.00
(sometimes closed for private hire),
Su closed. Children until early evening.
Cask beers 10 (Adnams, Greene King, Sharp's,
7 often local or unusual guests), ***Other beers*** 3
keg, 6 bottles, ***Also*** 2 ciders/perries
🍴 Wetherspoon menu, ♿
*Beer festivals, food promotions, functions,
pub for hire*

➤ Chancery Lane   🚶 Jubilee Walkway

by very knowledgeable staff. Cask beers
from top performers like Bristol, Mallinsons,
Moor, Oakham, Redemption and Siren
are likely to be on sale, with Adnams,
Kernel and Magic Rock on keg alongside
decent German lagers and wheats and
occasional Americans. There's no room
for a bottle fridge but it's hardly missed.

One of London's most impressive Wetherspoon
conversions, the former Union Bank retains its
opulent decoration, with slender black marble
pillars reaching up to an airy ceiling. A modern
sculpture of a Knight Templar dominates the
bar back, setting the theme for other Templar
memorabilia scattered around, which no doubt
helped qualify the pub for its cameo appearance in the film version of Dan Brown's silly
potboiler *The Da Vinci Code*. Even more importantly, it's one of the most beer-focused
outlets in the chain, thanks to managers
Jan and Jerry Swords, in post since the 1989
conversion, and keen cellarman Ian, who

Knights Templar

"avoids stocking samey stuff". Local beers from Hop Stuff, Sambrook's, Truman's and Twickenham are regularly featured alongside Dark Star, Itchen Valley and Kelham Island, and there's even a modestly more interesting range of bottled and keg beers than usual.

Lowlander Grand Café (64)

Bar

36 Drury Lane WC2B 5RR

T (020) 7379 7446   www.lowlander.com

 LowlanderGrandCafe LowlanderLondon

 Mo-We 10.00-23.00, *Th* 09.00-23.30, *Fr-Sa* 09.00-24.00, *Su* 09.00-22.30. Children until early evening.

Cask beers None, **Other beers** 11 keg, 95 bottles, **Also** Genever

 Breakfasts, deli platters, hot specials **££**,

 Tables on street

Tutored tastings for groups, occasional beer events

 Charing Cross   Covent Garden   Jubilee Walkway

Declaring itself a grand café in Low Countries style when it opened in 2001, the Lowlander is rather less grand in dimensions, so visit off-peak to grab a good seat on the upstairs balcony or the big ground floor tables. It remains a Belgian specialist at heart, still offering a broad choice of Trappists (including Achel, Orval, Rochefort and Dutch options from La Trappe) and plenty of secular brews, mainly solid choices from established family brewers: I've drunk the freshest draught De Koninck in London here. Recently the list has expanded to encompass US beers from Kona, Germans from Hopf and Paulaner, and even Brits like Beavertown and Tiny Rebel. Food starts at breakfast then moves on to a menu that includes Belgian staples like mussels and *carbonnade flamande*, with options like fish pie, vegetable hot pot and sharing boards, all listed with beer suggestions.

Lowlander

Olde Mitre

Olde Mitre (65)

Traditional pub (Fuller's) ★

1 Ely Court EC1N 6SJ

T (020) 7405 4751

www.yeoldmitre.co.uk   Ye-Olde-Mitre

 Mo-Fr 11.00-23.00, *Sa-Su* closed.

Cask beers 7 (Fuller's, 5 sometimes unusual guests), **Other beers** 1 keg, 5 bottles, **Also** 1 cider, malts

 Sandwiches, snacks **£**,

 Standing in courtyard

Themed beer festivals

 Farringdon   Chancery Lane

London guidebook writers are fond of recounting that this little pub hidden down a tiny alley off Holborn Circus was built in 1546, though it's been much rebuilt since, and the current Tudor-style interior is largely a 1930s pastiche. They'll also point out that the lump of wood behind glass near the entrance is from a cherry tree which may have been danced around by Elizabeth I and once marked the boundary of the Bishop of Ely's garden. The pub was built on the Bishop's land to serve his staff, so you might even read that it's really in Cambridgeshire, which is clearly nonsense, though the licence was indeed issued in

Cambridgeshire until the 1950s. A long-standing real ale champion, it's now a Fuller's house, but stocks numerous guests from breweries like Dark Star, Hackney, Kelham Island, Redemption, Sambrook's or Wooden Hand, with around 30 different beers served in a week, and even more at a mini-festival coinciding with the Great British Beer Festival, the only weekend the pub opens. Some decent German lagers and Fuller's bottles add extra variety. Food is minimal, and the three small and often crowded rooms are free of piped music and TV.

Porterhouse (66)

Contemporary pub
21 Maiden Lane WC2E 7NA
T (020) 7379 7917　　**f** porterhouselondon
www.porterhousebrewco.com
⏱ *Mo-Th* 12.00-23.00, *Fr* 12.00-23.30,
　Sa 12.00-24.00, *Su* 12.00-22.30.
Cask beers 4 (Porterhouse, 3 guests),
Other beers 11 keg,100+ bottles, **Also** Cocktails
🍴 Burgers, pizza, pub grub **££**, 🪑 Front patio, ♿
At least 4 annual beer festivals, live bands (Th-Sa), seasonal events

🚆 Charing Cross　　◉ Covent Garden　　🚢 Embankment
🏃 Link to Jubilee Walkway

Since the dawn of the millennium, this vast, brash and busy 'superpub' in a converted warehouse has provided the English outpost of one of Ireland's most persistently successful microbrewers, based near Dublin. The orange-lit and labyrinthine multi-level interior, with spaceship-like post-industrial tubing and a massive beer bottle collection displayed on every spare surface, is often heaving despite the size. Cask beers include Porterhouse's own TSB, created for the venue, and guests from people like Moorhouses, Purity and Sambrook's. The best choices among the kegs are undoubtedly and unsurprisingly the porters and stouts, including a genuine oyster stout and tasty historical revival Wrasslers XXXX. The bottled range includes British, US and Belgian classics and a few too many mediocre lagers from exotic places. Food is pizza, burgers, steaks, fry-ups and salads. Look out in particular for the stout festival in March and Czech festival in late autumn.

Princess Louise (67)

Traditional pub (Samuel Smith) ★
208 High Holborn WC1V 7BW
T (020) 7405 8816
⏱ *Mo-Sa* 12.00-23.00, *Su* 12.00-22.30.
　Children until early evening.
Cask beers 1 (Samuel Smith), **Other beers** 6 keg,
14 bottles (Samuel Smith), **Also** Gins
🍴 Sandwiches, pub grub **£**

◉ Holborn　🏃 Jubilee Walkway

The elegant but relatively modest 1872 exterior conceals one of London's pub heritage treasures: a stunning confection of mosaic tiles, mirrors, carved wood and glass, with an elaborate original bar back and moulded ceiling, all created during a radical remodelling in 1891. Timber and etched glass screens project from a horseshoe bar to divide the space into a number of smaller rooms, with connecting corridors down both sides, and the gentlemen's lavatories are among the most sumptous in Britain. The original partitioning was dismantled in the 1960s and restored in 2008 by current owner, taciturn Yorkshire brewer Samuel Smith. This is a great environment in which to sample the brewery's one cask beer and rather better bottled specialities, alongside hearty pub grub like steak and ale pie, lamb's liver and onions or mushroom and Brie Wellington.

Pub trivia *The pub is named after Queen Victoria's wayward fourth daughter.*

Princess Louise

TRY ALSO

Besides the **Princess Louise** (p 83) two other pubs of major historic interest offer a similar beer range from Samuel Smith: the **Cittie of York ★** (22 High Holborn WC1V 6BS), with its 1920s vision of a Tudor banqueting hall complete with massive wooden vats, a huge stove and Gothic-styled side booths; and the dark and warren-like **Olde Cheshire Cheese ★** (Wine Office Court, 145 Fleet Street EC4A 2BU), one of London's few genuinely old pubs, including some 18th century remnants.
City Pubs' first London brewpub venture the **Temple Brew House** (46 Essex Street WC2R 3JF, www.templebrewhouse.com) opened close to the **Edgar Wallace** (p 79) in November 2014, with a good range of beer.

In an alley behind Holborn Tube, tiny **Bar Polski** (11 Little Turnstile WC1V 7DX) does mainly vodka and lagers from big Polish brewers but has some dark and honey beers plus a few from the more specialist Amber brewery in Bielkówko near Gdansk. Just to the south,

Belgo Kingsway (67 Kingsway WC2B 6TD, www.belgo-restaurants.co.uk) has a decent-sized drinking space, while a few minutes' walk away beneath an old Covent Garden warehouse, **Belgo Centraal** (50 Earlham Street WC2H 9LJ) boasts a big post-industrial restaurant as well as a small bar. Both stock a similar range to Belgo Noord (p 133), mainly sourced from more established Belgian brewers.

Nearby, the pretty **Cross Keys** (31 Endell Street WC2H 9EB, www.crosskeyscoventgarden.com) is the other West End Brodies pub (see also the Old Coffee House p 93), a proper boozer with several of the owners' beers on handpump. The **White Swan** (14 New Row WC2N 4LF, www. nicholsonspubs.co.uk/thewhiteswanlondon), converted to a Nicholson's in 2012, has some interesting casks and enthusiastic cellar staff. In the arches under Charing Cross station and uniquely split in two by a public walkway, the **Ship and Shovell** (2 Craven Passage WC2N 5PH, www.hall-woodhouse.co.uk) is another central option besides the St Stephens Tavern (p 99) for sampling Badger beers.

LONDON DRINKERS Jane Peyton

Jane, crowned Britain's Beer Sommelier of the Year 2014, is the author of several books including *Beer o'Clock*, and the driving force behind the annual Beer Day Britain on 15 June. She lives and works in London as a sommelier, event organiser and tour guide, including leading award-winning tours of historic pubs (www.school-of-booze.com).

How do you rate London as a beer city, on a world scale?
Number 1, without a doubt. A city that has an enthusiastic market for beers brewed in a pub through to international pilsner brands is special indeed. And its brewing heritage as well as its current dynamism cannot be ignored.

What's the single most exciting thing about beer in London at the moment?
The splendid choice.

What single thing would make things even better?
If tax was slashed to reduce the price of beer, people would go to the pub more often and help to maintain the growth of small breweries.

What are your top London beers right now?
Fuller's Bengal Lancer, Kernel Table Beer, Sambrook's Battersea Rye.

What's your top great beer night out?
A crawl of several Craft Beer Co pubs. A diverse selection of cask, keg and bottles and enthusiastic customers.

Who's your London beer hero?
Helen Wilson, licensee of the Mad Bishop and Bear (p98), the first woman to win Fuller's Master Cellarman of the Year and a great supporter of the London Brewers Alliance who takes care to train her staff in beer knowledge.

Who will we be hearing a lot more from in future?
Wild Card: they brew highly drinkable beers and they have a brilliant tap room where food and music feature strongly.

Which are your other top beer cities?
Brussels and Munich for heritage and beer infrastructure, and Portland, Oregon, for the fact that residents drink more craft beer than mainstream brands.

Shoreditch & Hoxton

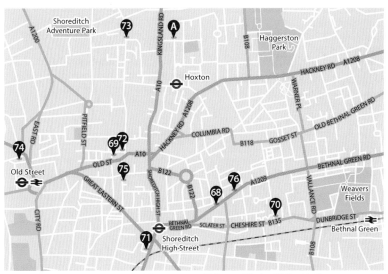

68.BrewDog Shoreditch · 69.Byron Hoxton · 70.Carpenters Arms · 71.Crown and Shuttle · 72.Electricity Showrooms ·
73.Howl at the Moon · 74.Old Fountain · 75.Strongroom · 76.Well and Bucket · A.Hackney Brewery

BrewDog Shoreditch (68)

Specialist, bar
51 Bethnal Green Road E1 6LA
T (020) 7749 9670
www.brewdog.com/bars 🐦 brewdogshored
🕐 *Su-Th* 12.00-24.00, *Fr-Sa* 12.00-01.00.
  Children until 22.00.
Cask beers None, ***Other beers*** 20 keg, 130 bottles,
Also Beer cocktails
🍴 Gourmet burgers, wings, cooked snacks
£-££, 🎋 Front terrace
Meet the brewer/tap takeover, weekly live music/
DJs, board games

🚆 Bethnal Green, Old Street 🚇 Shoreditch High Street

First opened in 2010 as beer bar Mason and
Taylor, this glass-walled space below a residential block was bought out by BrewDog in 2012
as its second London venue. The interior is
funky but functional, retaining its dignity in an
area known for hipsterish pretension, with
industrial lampshades and canine grafitti art.
As customary, draughts are all 'craft keg', half

BrewDog, half other UK brewers and imports:
it's good to see Five Points, set up by the
previous owners, among the taps. The bottled
range is particularly strong, with rarities like
BD's Abstrakt series, big barley wines, wild
beers from Beavertown and Mikkeller, and
New Zealanders like 8 Wired. Food is gourmet
burgers and Southern US-inspired fare, while
the basement space serves up beer cocktails
under the self-deprecating label Underdog.
As with all BrewDog bars, the absence of cask
disappoints in what is otherwise a very
rounded offer.

85

Byron Hoxton (69)

Restaurant
46 Hoxton Square N1 6PB
T (020) 3487 1230
www.byronhamburgers.com/locations/hoxton
🕐 *Mo-Th* 12.00-23.00, *Fr-Sa* 12.00-23.30,
    Su 12.00-22.30. Children welcome.
Cask beers None,
Other beers 5 keg, 9 bottles/cans
🍴 Gourmet burgers, salads **££**, &

≋ ⊖ Old Street ⊖ Hoxton

In a prime location on Hoxton Square, this
pleasantly woody restaurant is one of the
older branches of rapidly expanding beer-
friendly gourmet burger chain Byron. It's
modest compared to some of their more
recent post-industrial conversions, but
regularly boasts the biggest beer sales, and is
also one of a small but growing number of
Byrons offering draught beer – 'craft keg' of
course – alongside the bottles, including in
three third-pint tasting flights. Beavertown,
Camden Town (who supply the house beers
as well as their own brands) and Kernel are
among regular London suppliers, with US
imports from the likes of Founders, Lagunitas,
Odell and Oskar Blues. Like all branches it's a
restaurant so you'll have to eat to drink, but
that's hardly an imposition with a choice of
quality burgers, veggieburgers, salads and
fries served with flair at reasonable prices.

Byron Hoxton

Carpenters Arms Top25 (70)

Traditional pub
73 Cheshire Street E2 6EG
T (020) 7739 6342
www.carpentersarmsfreehouse.com
🕐 *Mo-We* 16.00-23.00, *Th&Su* 12.00-23.00,
    Fr-Sa 12.00-00.30. Children until 20.30.
Cask beers 3 (Adnams, Timothy Taylor, 1 some-
times local guest), **Other beers** 7 keg, 40 bottles,
Also Malts, wines
🍴 Good value gastro menu **£-££**,
🌳 Small beer garden 🐾

≋ Bethnal Green, Cambridge Heath ⊖ Shoreditch High Street
⊖ Bethnal Green

This treasure, just south of Bethnal Green Road,
was the place gangland bosses Ronnie and
Reggie Kray bought for their mother. These
days it pursues a more honest living under
the watchful eyes of landlords Eric and Nigel,
enlivened by fresh flowers and displays of
carpenter's tools, with greenery and sculptures
in a pretty backyard. The beer range includes
Taylor Landlord, a changing Adnams product
and a guest from St Peter's or Truman's on
handpump, wheat beer from Ettal Benedictine
abbey in Bavaria on tap, and a bottled list that
includes Harviestoun Ola Dubh, Orval, Schneider
Weisse and guilty pleasure Pelforth Brune.
The good value French-shaded blackboard
menu stretches to slow-roasted lamb shank and
honey-roast goat cheese salad, which I doubt
were a familiar sight in Mrs Kray's kitchen, and
there can't be many places in London you can
get *escargots au beurre à l'ail* for £6.

Crown and Shuttle (71)

Contemporary pub
226 Shoreditch High Street E1 6PJ
T (020) 7375 2905
www.crownandshuttle.co.uk
📘 The-Crown-and-Shuttle 🐦 CrownShuttle
🕐 *Mo-We* 11.00-23.00, *Th* 11.00-24.00,
    Fr 11.00-01.00, *Sa* 12.00-01.00, *Su* 12.00-22.30.
    Children until 18.00.
Cask beers 6 (London and unusual guests), **Other
beers** 9 keg, 22 bottles
🍴 Gourmet cooked sandwiches, seafood, salads
££, 🌳 Beer garden 🐾
Occasional beer events

≋ ⊖ ⊖ Liverpool Street ⊖ Shoreditch High Street

Located midway between the besuited industriousness of the City and the hipster hedonism of Hoxton, this youthful laid-back place might just appeal to both sides. The 1885 building was derelict for over a decade before reopening early in 2013. The interior is still just recognisable as an old pub, but the exposed brickwork, distressed wood, open rafters and reclaimed furniture are unapologetically post-modern. A magnificent back garden, a rarity round here, has verdant planters, picturesque trellises and sheltered seating. Besides admired suppliers from elsewhere like Arbor and Anarchy, London brewers are regularly supported, with Crate, Five Points, Hackney, London Beer Factory, Signature and Truman's appearing on cask and Meantime's unfiltered tank lager among the kegs. A neat bottled list extends to Pressure Drop and Redchurch besides Rochefort and Weihenstephan. Food is cooked sandwiches (blackened chicken breast brioche, veggie meatball ciabatta), salads and simple seafood like shrimps or whitebait.

Pub trivia *The name is a reminder of the Huguenot weavers who once dominated the industrial scene in this part of town.*

Electricity Showrooms (72)

Bar (Barworks)
39A Hoxton Square N1 6NN
T (020) 7739 3939
www.electricityshowrooms.com
electricityshowrooms electricityshow
Su-Th 12.00-24.00, Fr-Sa 12.00-01.00. Children until 19.00.
Cask beers 2 (unusual or London guests), **Other beers** 10 keg, 52 bottles, **Also** Cocktails and specialist spirits
Sliders, wings, salads **£-££**,
Benches on street
DJs (Fr-Sa)

Old Street Hoxton

This big bar commanding the entrance to Hoxton Square was indeed once an electricity showroom before succumbing early to reinvention in the Cool Britannia era. Since then it's aged with its customer base into a more relaxed place, though still popular and busy. Along the way it's evolved an impressive beer list, including cask offerings from the likes

of Firebrand, Moor or various London breweries, with US imports and beers from brewers like Burning Sky and Tempest on keg. Bottles stretch from Mikkeller, Rodenbach and Stone to Ilkley's excellent Siberia and locals from Brew by Numbers and Rocky Head. Food includes intriguing slider dishes like crispy squid, honey and thyme sweet potato wedges or mini-burgers. The ironically kitsch decor, including a big gaudy neon peacock that lures customers to the cocktail bar downstairs, is smart enough not to be tiresome.

Howl at the Moon (73)

Contemporary pub
178 Hoxton Street N1 5LH **T** (020) 3341 2525
www.hoxtoncrafthouse.com hoxtonhowl
Su-Th 12.00-23.00, Fr-Sa 12.00-01.00. Children until 19.00.
Cask beers 4 (London), **Other beers** 8 keg, 60 bottles, **Also** 2 ciders
Burgers, pop-up gourmet sandwiches **£**,
Benches on street
Occasional live bands/DJs, food promotions, major big screen sport

Liverpool Street, Old Street Hoxton Old Street
St Leonards Hospital (243 Old Street, numerous Liverpool Street) Link to Regents Canal towpath Link to Jubilee Greenway

Lengthy Hoxton Street with its traditional market endures as a slice of the old East End: walk north along it and you'll leave most of the fashion victims and dot-com entrepreneurs behind. Next to the Community Garden with its incongruous clock is this pleasant single-room pub, remade in 2009 in contemporary style but retaining a friendly local feel. Beers include changing casks from Hackney and Redemption and keykegs from Brodie's, whose Hoxton IPA is brewed for the pub. Guinness's historical revival Dublin Porter acknowledges the venue's Irish connection, with more Londoners among the bottles alongside the likes of Celt Experience and Thornbridge Hall specials. Burgers and hot dogs are supplemented on some days by visits from a pop-up gourmet sandwich maker, and the role of the pub as the headquarters of the Old Street Rugby Club sets the tone for its sporting loyalties.

Old Fountain (74)

Traditional pub
3 Baldwin Street EC1V 9NU
T (020) 7253 2970
www.oldfountain.co.uk 🐦 OldFountainAles
🕐 *Mo-Fr* 11.00-23.00, *Sa-Su* 12.00-22.30. Children until early evening.
Cask beers 8 (Fuller's, 7 unusual guests),
Other beers 8 keg, 10 bottles, **Also** 1 cider
🍴 Enhanced pub grub **££**,
🌳 Tables on street, roof terrace
Live music/DJs (Sa-Su), darts

🚆 ⊖ Old Street

Between Baldwin Street and Peerless Street with entrances both sides, this beer haven of a free house has been in the Durrant family since 1964. It's a smallish, friendly old pub with padded benches, stained glass, a recently opened and very pretty roof terrace and a tasty home-cooked menu that could include smoked pork belly and apple sausages or ratatouille with grilled halloumi. London Pride is the only regular cask; other brewers might include Arbor, Hawkshead, Magic Rock and Oakham or locals like Hammerton. Stouts and porters are a feature including among the 'craft keg' options, often those from Kernel, London Fields or Pressure Drop or US suppliers like Rogue. And there's some serious stuff in the fridges too – De Molen Amarillo DIPA and BrewDog Cocoa Psycho were on sale when I looked.

Strongroom

Shoreditch's current reputation owes much to the Strongroom, a recording studio established in 1985 in a former furniture warehouse off Curtain Road, originally sharing space with punk iconographer Jamie Reid. A bar added in 1997 became a mainstay of the burgeoning local scene. Recently refurbished and extended, it's a friendly place that's less painfully trendy than some of its neighbours, with a leafy yard that intermittently hosts London beer festivals. A good choice of casks, often from locals Signature Brew as well as Alechemy, Copper Dragon, Hop Studio, Purple Moose, Siren or Thornbridge, is supplemented by unfiltered Pilsner Urquell from tanks, 'craft kegs' that might come from Hackney or London Beer Factory, and bottles that include Tailgate from the US, Londoners Beavertown and Redchurch and some Belgian mainstays. Food is suitable for hungry musicians, with good vegetarian options and Mediterranean-shaded specials like lamb with lemon and herb tabbouleh.

Pub trivia. *Clients of the adjacent studio have included John Cale, Nick Cave, Dido, Kasabian, Moby, Olivia Newton John, Orbital, Placebo, Santana, the Ting Tings and the Who. Imagine all of that lot on stage at once.*

Strongroom (75)

Bar
120 Curtain Road EC2A 3SQ
T (020) 7426 5103 📘🐦 strongroombar
www.strongroombar.com
🕐 *Mo* 09.00-23.00, *Tu-We* 09.00-24.00, *Th* 09.00-01.00, *Fr* 09.00-02.00, *Sa* 12.00-02.00, *Su* 12.00-22.00. Children until 20.00.
Cask beers 4-5 (unusual guests), **Other beers** 7 keg, 35+ bottles, **Also** Specialist spirits
🍴 Burgers, wraps, sharing boards, specials **£-££**, 🌳 Beer garden in yard 🐾, ♿
Beer festivals, films (Mo), live music (We), DJs (Th-Sa), seasonal events, table football, functions

🚆 ⊖ Old Street ⊖ Shoreditch High Street

Well and Bucket (76)

Bar (Barworks)
143 Bethnal Green Road E2 7DG
T (020) 3664 6454 📘🐦 WellandBucket
www.wellandbucket.com
🕐 *Mo-Th* 12.00-24.00, *Fr-Sa* 12.00-00.30, *Su* 12.00-23.00. Children until 19.00.
Cask beers 3-4 (unusual guests),
Other beers 12 keg, 80+ bottles, **Also** Specialist spirits, cocktails, occasional cider
🍴 Oysters, seafood, salads **££**,
🌳 Beer garden, ♿
60s soul DJs (Su)

⊖ Shoreditch High Street ⊖ Bethnal Green

Well and Bucket

Originally built in 1818 by nearby Truman's to serve the Club Row live animal market, this one-room pub was sumptuously decorated with painted tiles depicting scenes from local life as well as abstract patterns. Following closure in the late 1980s the building became a leather warehouse, with much of the tilework and fittings cumulatively dismantled and sold to collectors. The painted scenes have been lost but what remains is now listed by English Heritage and was lovingly buffed up for a welcome reopening in 2013. There's a wide choice of oysters, once an East End delicacy, and an even wider choice of stouts and porters in a variety of strengths from brewers local and far-flung, like Beavertown, Flying Dog, Goose Island, Green Flash, Hammerton, Kernel and Rogue. Lighter cask options could come from East London, Marble or Siren and the bottles also include genuine lambics and rare surprises from Italy and Scandinavia. Interesting salads (french beans, pomegranate and giant couscous, for example) and slider-style snacks provide other dining possibilities.

TRY ALSO

The spotless **Pride of Spitalfields** (3 Heneage Street E1 5LJ) offers a slice of the old East End, serving new Truman's cask beers as well as more traditional styles from other brewers just off Brick Lane and within the shadow of the old Truman's. In contrast, contemporary café-bar the **Beagle** (397 Geffrye Street E2 8HZ, www.beaglelondon.co.uk), in arches under Hoxton Overground round the back of the Geffrye Museum, has London beers in bottle and keg. Classic East End boozer the **Birdcage** (80 Columbia Road E2 7QB, www.drafthouse.co.uk), on a famous flower market, became a Draft House late in 2014, though preserves its pubby character.

On Old Street, **City Beverage** (303 Old Street EC1V 9LA, www.citybeverage.co.uk) has a good range of local beers as well as wines, teas and coffees, while cycling-themed café **Look Mum No Hands** (49 Old Street EC1V 9HX, www.lookmumnohands.com) has London beers in bottle, though no draught, unlike its Hackney sister venue (p 112).

HOP HISTORIES — From Black Eagle to Dark Star

BRICK LANE was a country track through open fields in the mid-17th century when Thomas Bucknall chose it as the location of his small Black Eagle brewery. Sometime in the 1660s one Joseph Truman joined the team, and by 1697 had bought Bucknall out. Truman's shrewd and ambitious grandson Benjamin took a seat on the board in 1722, and began the process of turning the brewery into one of London's biggest and most successful by concentrating on porter brewing.

Porter has a long association with this part of London. A widely repeated account dating from the early 19th century credits Ralph Harwood, of the Blue Last pub in Curtain Road, Shoreditch, with the invention of the style in 1730. The story that he devised it as a labour-saving single-cask replacement for 'three threads', a popular blend of mature, mild and pale ale that had to be mixed to order by bar staff, has now been discredited, but porter was certainly once hugely popular in the East End.

By the 1830s, Truman Hanbury & Buxton was producing 200,000 barrels (330,000 hl) of porter a year. Its philanthropic links are mentioned by Charles Dickens in *David Copperfield*: partner Thomas Buxton, who joined in 1809, was an anti-slavery campaigner and prison reformer, and both he and his uncle and fellow partner, tobacco importer Sampson Hanbury, were Quakers, related to the Barclays who part-owned Barclay Perkins (see Southwark Ale, p56). The brewery was rebuilt extensively in 1929, with a new boiler house sprouting a 49 metre-high brick chimney

that dominated the local roofscape. Truman clung doggedly to independence as consolidation swept the industry in the 1950s and 1960s, but finally fell in 1971 to the Grand Metropolitan hotel group who used it as leverage to buy out Watney the following year, creating Watney Mann Truman (see Roll out the red barrel, p101). It was finally closed in 1988 after years of neglect, but as we shall see was never quite forgotten.

Meanwhile one of the UK's most influential early microbreweries was reaching its peak just up the road. In August 1981, beer fan Rob Jones became the manager of a pioneering specialist beer shop in Pitfield Street, Hoxton, then an impoverished and neglected backwater very different from the fashionable district of today. Jones began brewing in the basement in 1982 under the name Pitfield's, and soon afterwards got together with friend and customer Martin Kemp and others to buy the business, renaming it The Beer Shop.

In 1984 Pitfield's expanded to its own site around the corner in Hoxton Square where a year later it brewed a new and unusual dark, strong ale called Dark Star.

This proved a surprise success, becoming the first microbrew to win the title of CAMRA's Supreme Champion Beer of Britain. In 1989 the brewery had to leave its site due to redevelopment, and its owners disagreed on what to do next. So Kemp hung on to the shop, while Jones and Canadian head brewer Andy Skene moved brewing to Staffordshire, merging with another micro which later collapsed.

The Beer Shop went on to introduce a generation of London drinkers to then-rare imports from Belgium and Germany as well as a variety of British brews. In 1996 it moved to bigger premises a few doors away at 14 Pitfield Street N1 6EY, where Kemp began brewing Pitfield's beers again, leaning towards organic beers and historical recreations. In 1998 Skene returned as head brewer, but as the new millennium began, Hoxton's newfound desirability drove up rents to unaffordable levels, and in 2005 the shop and brewery relocated to rural Essex. Kemp went into semi-retirement in 2012 and Skene took over, adding his own Dominion brands to the range.

Rob Jones, meanwhile, moved to Brighton where in 1994 he started brewing in the cellar of the Evening Star pub, adopting the name of his greatest previous success, Dark Star. This brewery went on to become one of the most lauded and loved in Britain, thanks in part to exceptional former head brewer Mark Tranter (who later set up Burning Sky), and now operates from a much bigger standalone site in Partridge Green, West Sussex. The award-winning beer that made it all possible has two successors: Dark Star Original and Pitfield's Black Eagle, the latter a nod to a famous near-neighbour.

Back on Brick Lane, the original Black Eagle re-emerged as an arts, shopping and leisure complex in the late 1990s, the focus of an increasingly trendy local scene that gave yet another new face to one of London's most frequently reinvented streets. Head for that chimney and you'll find many of the original buildings still standing, giving a feel for the vastness of the site (91 Brick Lane E1 6QL).

Two beer and pub enthusiasts who fell for the place's sense of history were local workers James Morgan and Michael-George Hemus, who conceived what seemed like the wild idea of resurrecting the beer. Truman had always retained its cachet, particularly in east London, and retained a visible presence thanks to the brewery's policy of building large, lavish, landmark pubs, many of which still proudly bore its name. After a year of persistent phone calls, current brand owners Heineken agreed first to licence then to sell them the rights.

Lacking capital for new kit and premises, the pair initially opted to contract-brew outside London, originally at Nethergate near Bungay and later at Everards in Leicester. Best bitter Runner, the first Truman's beer for 22 years, appeared in 2010: it wasn't an historical recreation but a new beer created in the spirit of the old, with some help from former Truman's brewer Derek Prentice.

The new owners were insistent that contracting was only a stepping stone, helping them make a case for investment in their own plant. They'd considered, and dismissed, the romantic but expensive and impractical notion of a micro-brewery at the Black Eagle itself but were determined to stay in east London.

As it happened, Truman's reappeared at just the right time, as demand for London beer was growing, and was able to stay true to its word: the new brewery, the Eyrie, opened in an industrial estate on Fish Island near Hackney Wick in summer 2013 (p306). Around the same time, a sample of the original Truman yeast, deposited at the National Collection of Yeast Cultures in 1958, was recovered and put to good use by talented German-born head brewer Ben Ott, formerly of London Fields. The brewery is due to expand significantly in 2015, and, quite unexpectedly, the pleasure of sitting in a proper old East End Truman's boozer and drinking local Truman's beer now seems assured for the next generation of London drinkers.

Soho & Fitzrovia

De Hems (77)

Bar (Nicholson's)
11 Macclesfield Street W1D 5BW
T (020) 7437 2494 www.nicholsonspubs.
co.uk/dehemsdutchcafebarsoholondon
⊕ *Mo-Sa* 11.00-24.00, *Su* 11.00-22.30.
Children until 20.00.
Cask beers 2 (St Austell, guest),
Other beers 8 keg, 40+ bottles, **Also** Genever
⑪ Dutch and British snacks and pub grub **££**,
⊼ Standing on street, &
DJs (Fr-Sa), monthly acoustic music, Dutch nights

⊖ Piccadilly Circus   🏃 Link to Jubilee Walkway

77.De Hems · **78**.Draft House Charlotte · **79**.Lyric ·
80.Old Coffee House · **81**.Queens Head · **82**.Whyte and Brown

De Hems is just about what you'd expect if you crossed a Central London pub with the more boisterous kind of urban Dutch *bruin café*, and popular with expats: you may occasionally encounter bouts of arm swaying and communal singing in the guttural mother tongue. It sports bilingual signing and a menu of authentically unhealthy Dutch street food like *patatje oorlog* (chips with satay sauce) alongside British pub grub. Nicholson's pale ale is joined by an often-seasonal guest on cask, but most beers are keg and bottled: Lindeboom pils, Dutch trappist La Trappe Dubbel and Delirium Tremens on tap and UK beers from Beavertown, Redchurch and Siren besides Belgian classics in bottle. It's a shame they don't stock more stuff from Dutch micros, though. Upstairs is usually quieter than downstairs, but if you're after a quiet drink on Koningsdag (King's Day) on 27 April, avoid at all costs.

Pub trivia *Captain De Hem was a retired Dutch sailor who ran the pub, then called the Macclesfield, as an oyster bar in the early 1900s, and during World War II the place was used as an unofficial headquarters of the exiled Dutch resistance. Renamed De Hems in 1959, it was once popular with musos like Georgie Fame and Alan Price.*

Draft House Charlotte

Lyric   (79)

Contemporary pub (Leisure & Catering)
37 Great Windmil Street W1D 7LU
T (020) 7434 0604
www.lyricsoho.co.uk   🐦 lyricsoho
🕐 *Mo-Th* 11.00-23.30, *Fr-Sa* 11.00-24.00,
     Su 12.00-22.30. Children until 19.00.
Cask beers 6 (unusual guests), ***Other beers*** 9 keg,
16 bottles, ***Also*** Wines, some malts
🍴 Enhanced pub grub **£-££**
Major big screen sport

🚇 Piccadilly Circus   🚶 Link to Jubilee Walkway

This pretty little boozer just off Piccadilly Circus was revamped in May 2013, by the forces behind the Sussex Arms (p 223), into a rare beer-friendly free house in an area dominated by chains and pubcos. Beyond the unusual bowed wood frontage with its etched windows and decorative tiles is a homely bar serving up six casks, including dark and unusual styles from brewers like Dark Star, Otley, Magic Rock, Tiny Rebel and Wild Weather. Camden Town, Harbour and Wild could be on keykeg, with Cooper's, Kernel and Orval in the fridges. Another attractive room upstairs provides overspill for diners, who can choose from good value lunchtime specials like pork roast or salmon and potato salad, with cooked sharing plates, pie and mash, steaks and veggie stir fry also likely to be on the menu. An unexpectedly decent package in the heart of Theatreland.

Draft House Charlotte   (78)

Specialist, bar (Draft House)
43 Goodge Street W1T 1TA
T (020) 7323 9361
www.drafthouse.co.uk   🐦 drafthousecs
🕐 *Mo-Sa* 12.00-23.00, *Su* closed.
     Children until early evening.
Cask beers 3 (Sambrook's, 2 unusual often
local guests), ***Other beers*** 8 keg, 100+ bottles,
Also A few bourbons
🍴 Pie and mash **£**, 🎎 Standing on street
*Meet the brewer/tap takeover, occasional beer and
food tastings*

🚇 Goodge Street

The smallest of the Draft Houses is this little corner pub among a strip of fashionable eateries in Fitzrovia's media quarter. Formerly named the Northumberland Arms and dating back to the 18th century development of the area, it reopened in its current guise in August 2012. A single bar that's often crowded, it retains a late Victorian decorated ceiling and surviving fragments of engraved glass. Besides Wandle, casks are typically sourced from southern England or Yorkshire, with Brighton, Great Heck, Hastings, Mallinsons, Roosters and Twickenham among the favourites. London brewers like Beavertown, Brew by Numbers, Kernel, Orbit and Redchurch are among the bottles and keykegs, with a changing Lagunitas line and a wide range of bottles stretching to imported German Gose, Belgian sours and Scandinavians like To Øl. In these cramped conditions, food is limited to pie, mash and parsley liquor, with veggie options.

Old Coffee House   (80)

Traditional pub (Brodie's)
49 Beak Street W1F 9SF
T (020) 7437 2197
🕐 *Mo-Sa* 11.00-23.00, *Su* 12.00-22.30.
     Children until early evening.
Cask beers 6 (Brodies), ***Other beers*** 5 keg (Brodies)
🍴 Daytime sandwiches and pub grub **£**
Major big screen sport, board games, functions

🚇 Oxford Circus, Piccadilly Circus   🚶 Link to Jubilee Walkway

This corner site did indeed once host a genuine coffee house, though the current 1850s building is now one of the more straightforward pubs in Soho. An ample bar is decorated with bric-a-brac such as old musical instruments, stuffed animals and, for some unexplained reason, a signed photo of Kiss. It's one of two West End pubs operated by the Brodie family, and has been directly run by Brodie's Brewery co-founder Lizzie since long-standing managers retired in 2013. Though partially tied to Heineken's Star group, it stocks Brodie's beers on cask and keg, with Bethnal Green Bitter, London Fields Pale and Kiwi as regulars and numerous specials and oddities at low prices for the area. Wholesome unreconstructed pub grub like steak & Brodie's ale pie, scampi and chips and veggie lasagne offers top value, eaten either in the bar or upstairs in a pretty room decorated with equestrian prints.

Queens Head (81)

Traditional pub
15 Denman Street W1D 7HN
T (020) 7437 1540
www.queensheadpiccadilly.com
QueensHeadPiccadilly queensheadw1d
Mo-Th 11.00-23.30, Fr-Sa 11.00-24.00,
  Su 12.00-22.30. Children in restaurant only.
Cask beers 5 (Fuller's, Robinson's, Sambrook's, 2 London guests), **Other beers** 2 keg, 12 bottles,
Also A few wines
Cheeseboards, enhanced pub grub ££
Comedy (Su), monthly DJs

Piccadilly Circus Link to Jubilee Walkway

The pleasant late Victorian styling and decorated mirrors of this rare West End free house are partly a legacy of the building's stint both as a fake Irish pub and a Nicholson's. Robinsons Trooper is a popular cask regular, alongside guests usually from Dark Star or London brewers like Gypsy Hill, London Beer Factory and Moncada. A smallish but well-chosen bottle selection encompasses BrewDog, Partizan, Goose Island and Meantime. Downstairs you can graze on artisanal cheeseboards and cooked bar snacks, while upstairs does a good trade in pre-theatre dining with dishes like confit duck leg and flageolet beans, Trooper meat pie and mash, butternut squash risotto and indulgent desserts. A welcome retreat with notably friendly and enthusiastic staff.

Pub trivia *The first pub to open on this site, in 1736, occupied a much bigger space including the site of the Piccadilly Theatre next door. The current narrow building dates from the rebuilding of the theatre in 1928.*

Whyte and Brown (82)

Restaurant, bar
Kingly Court W1B 5PW
T (020) 3747 9820 www.whyteandbrown.com
Whyte-Brown whyteandbrown
Mo-Fr 09.00-22.00, Sa 10.00-22.00,
  Su 12.00-18.00. Children very welcome.
Cask beers None, **Other beers** 2 keg, 13 bottles,
Also Cocktails, specialist spirits
Chicken, egg, US-style menu ££
Covered courtyard,
Occasional functions

Oxford Circus, Piccadilly Circus

50 years on from its Swinging London heyday, youth fashion hub Carnaby Street is still welcoming the world, though it's rather less welcoming to lovers of good beer. One surprising exception is this informal restaurant splendidly sited with a big terrace set in a galleried courtyard. The theme is free range chicken and beer, which the branding insists is the perfect combination – the signature dish is beer can-roasted chicken, but there's also chicken in pies, kebabs, burgers and other dishes. A few non-avian ingredients also feature, including excellent veggie halloumi souvlaki. Menus encourage matching with an imaginative range of keg and packaged beers from small London and UK brewers like Bad Seed, Fourpure, Hardknott, Rocky Head and Wild alongside imports from Goose Island, Little Creatures and Schneider. This is currently the only branch, opened in July 2013, but it looks like a successful chain in the making.

TRY ALSO

Several Nicholson's heritage pubs are also notable for beer choice and quality, including the large and impressive **Argyll Arms** ★ (18 Argyll Street W1F 7TP, www.nicholsonspubs.co.uk/theargyllarmsoxfordcircuslondon) opposite the London Palladium near Oxford Circus. This retains its 1890s partitioned spaces, carved wood, glass and mirrors and an even earlier textured ceiling. The much smaller **Dog and Duck ★** (18 Bateman Street W10 3AJ, www.nicholsonspubs.co.uk/thedogand-ducksoholondon), with its striking tilework, is many people's favourite Soho pub, including, apparently, Madonna's. Just off the north end of Carnaby Street, the friendly **Clachan** (34 Kingly Street W1B 5QH, www.nicholsonspubs.co.uk/theclachankinglystreetlondon) has a wider-than-usual beer range and partially-obscured floor mosaics.

The wood-panelled **Coach and Horses (Normans) ★** (29 Greek Street W1F 7HG, www.coachandhorsessoho.co.uk) is one of Soho's most famous pubs, once home to the self-proclaimed rudest landlord in London, haunt of literati and old soak actors and still the editorial base for satirical magazine *Private Eye*. It's now a Fuller's leasehold and regularly serves their beers as well as Redemption. Round the corner on Cambridge

Circus, the expansive **Spice of Life** (6 Moor Street W1D 5NA, www.spiceoflifesoho.com) has McMullen beers and a downstairs music and comedy venue.

Glitzy and pricey award-winning basement cocktail joint **Marks Bar** (66–70 Brewer Street W1F 9UP, www.marksbar.co.uk) improbably features a bar billiards table, alongside a small but well-chosen beer list including own labels commissioned from Palmers in Dorset by restaurateur Mark Hix. The bustling Soho branch of "BBQ Smokehouse" diner chain **Bodeans** (10 Poland Street W1F 8PZ, www.bodeansbbq.com) is as good a place as any to peruse a list of US and UK bottled and canned beers that includes few surprises but a number of goodies. **Whole Foods Market Piccadilly Circus** (20 Glasshouse Street W1B 5AR, www.wholefoodsmarket.com/stores/piccadilly), London's second biggest branch of the upmarket US grocery chain, has around 80 local, UK and international bottles.

LONDON DRINKERS **Derek Prentice**

If anyone personifies London brewing, it's Derek. He began his brewing career at the old Truman's in Brick Lane at the age of 18, worked for many years at Young's and became brewing manager at Fuller's in 2006. He retired in 2014 but is now back with a microbrewery project, the Wimbledon Brewery. He's also sharing his vast knowledge and experience by training apprentices and offering advice and support to London's multitude of new brewers.

How do you rate London as a beer city, on a world scale?
If you'd asked me six years ago I would have said pretty dire, but now it's one of the most vibrant and exciting places, leading the UK in expanding the variety of beer.

What's the single most exciting thing about beer in London at the moment?
The drinkers. They're much more diverse, receptive, appreciative and knowledgeable than they've ever been before.

What single thing would make things even better?
We've done great things with innovation but we could now do with catching up a bit on consistency and quality. Good training for brewers is an important part of that.

What are your top London beers right now (other than your own)?
There are too many to mention! Fuller's, Kernel and Redemption stand out but there are so many others.

What's your top great beer night out?
I tend to go out locally but I've been impressed by the way some

of the chain pubs, like Young's and Wetherspoon, have improved beer choice and quality. And I had a great time in the Aeronaut (p217) the other night – it's really buzzing.

Who's your London beer hero?
Alan Mayfield, the brewer I worked for at Truman's, taught me so much. He had an inspiring attitude, always open-minded and willing to learn. And John Young, of course. And Ken Don at Young's, Reg Drury and John Keeling at Fuller's.

Who will we be hearing a lot more from in future?
Fourpure and Five Points are doing great things. And By the Horns, where my son works.

Which are your other top beer cities?
Portland, Oregon, and San Francisco for US West Coast craft beer, Brussels for tradition, and Stockholm for innovation.

Westminster to Notting Hill

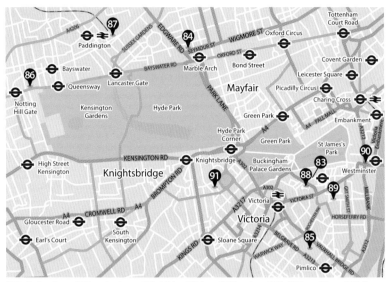

83.Buckingham Arms · 84.Carpenters Arms · 85.Cask Pub and Kitchen · 86.Champion · 87.Mad Bishop and Bear · 88.Quilon ·
89.Speaker · 90.St Stephens Tavern · 91.Star Tavern

Buckingham Arms (83)

Traditional pub (Young's)
62 Petty France SW1H 9EU
T (020) 7222 3386   🐦buckinghamarms
www.youngs.co.uk/pubs/buckingham-arms
🕐 *Mo-Fr* 11.00-23.00, *Sa-Su* 11.00-18.00.
    Children until 17.00.
Cask beers 5 (Wells & Young's, 1 often London
guest), ***Other beers*** 3 keg, 5 bottles,
Also Some wines
🍴 Enhanced pub grub/gastroish menu,
sandwiches **£-££**, ♿
Major big screen sport, pub for hire

⇌ Victoria   ⊖ St James's Park   🏃Link to Jubilee
Greenway, Jubilee Walkway

This fine Victorian Young's house not far
from Buckingham Palace is one of only two

London pubs listed in every single edition
of the *Good Beer Guide* (the other is the
Star p100). It is still one of the top places
to enjoy a pint of cask 'Ordinary' Bitter or
Special, plus Bombardier, seasonals and a
guest that might come from London Fields
or Sambrook's. A few other Meantime and
Wells & Young's specialities in bottle and
keg widen the choice. There's even a few
beer matching suggestions on a menu that
encompasses gourmet sausage and mash,
lemon and black pepper sea bass, grilled
chicken and cashew salad, grilled veg platter,
posh sandwiches and traditional stodgy
puds. It's a handsome place with a skylight
picking out stained glass and a mirrored
bar back, while a former side corridor
provides unusual extra drinking space.

Carpenters Arms (84)
Traditional pub (Market Taverns)
12 Seymour Place W1H 7NE   **T** (020) 7723 1050
**www.markettaverns.co.uk/
the_carpenters_arms.html**
🕐 *Mo-Sa* 11.00-23.00, *Su* 12.00-22.30.
   Children welcome.
Cask beers 6 (Harveys, 5 unusual often local
guests), **Other beers** 1 keg, 2 bottles
🍴 Pork pies, Scotch eggs **£**, 🎍 Tables on street
*Darts (Tu), occasional quiz, chess club,
big screen sport, functions*

🚇 Marble Arch   🚲 Link to Hyde Park routes   🏃 Link to
Jubileee Greenway, Princesss Diana Memorial Walk

Cask Pub and Kitchen

Under the same management as the Market
Porter (p 55), this cosy back-street free house
retains the feel of a traditional local despite
being only a few steps from Edgware Road
and Marble Arch, with preserved mosaics,
tiling and pillars and a big wooden bar. Harveys
Sussex Best is the only regular; guests aren't
quite the same ever-changing mix as at the
Borough pub but might include beers from
Cotleigh, Cottage, Sambrook's, Slaters, Truman's,
Twickenham, Weltons and more, plus rotating
'craft kegs' supplied by Marston's. A rare gem
in the West End.

Cask Pub and Kitchen (85)
Specialist, bar   **Top 25**
6 Charlwood Street SW1V 2EE
T (020) 7630 7225
www.caskpubandkitchen.com
📘 Cask Pubandkitchen   🐦 CASK_PUB_SW1
🕐 *Mo-Sa* 12.00-23.00, *Su* 12.00-22.30.
   Children until early evening.
Cask beers 10 (unusual guests), **Other beers** 14 keg,
300+ bottles, **Also** Whiskies, specialist spirits
🍴 Gourmet burgers, Sunday roast **££**,
🎍 Tables on street
Tap takeover/meet the brewer, acoustic music (Su)

🚃 Victoria   🚇 Pimlico, Victoria   🚲 Link to Avenue Verte,
NCN4, CS8   🏃 Link to Thames Path

Once a decaying local on the corner of a
housing block, in 2009 the former Pimlico
Tram was leased free of tie from Greene King
and transformed into a groundbreaking new
beer bar that became one of the flagships of

London's beer renaissance, spawning the Craft
Beer Co chain. It's still a great place for serious
beer exploration in a cheeful, amenable and
modern, if slightly basic, setting. Acorn,
Anarchy, Dark Star, Fyne and Magic Rock are
among favoured cask suppliers, but if there's
a buzz about a small brewery in an obscure
part of the country, its beers will likely pop up
here. Beavertown and Kernel have regular keg
lines; others are from top British producers with
the occasional Belgian, US or Scandinavian
import. The vast and impeccably curated
bottled beer list is a treasure house, particularly strong on lambics and sours (3 Fonteinen,
Cantillon, Hanssens, Tilquin, with Crooked
Stave and Lost Abbey from the US), bombers
from the likes of AleSmith, Green Flash,
Hoppin' Frog and Stone, and Londoners like
tiny Bullfinch – ask staff as the printed list isn't
comprehensive. Both draught and bottled
beer are sold to take away; food is from Forty
Burgers, plus a popular Sunday roast.

Champion (86)
Contemporary pub (Castle)
1 Wellington Terrace W2 4LW
T (020) 7792 4527   🐦 thechampionpub
www.thechampionpub.co.uk
🕐 *Mo-Th* 12.00-23.00, *Fr-Sa* 12.00-24.00,
   Su 12.00-22.30. Children welcome.
Cask beers 5 (Adnams, Windsor & Eton, 3 often
local guests), **Other beers** 7 keg, 10 bottles,
Also Some wines
🍴 Enhanced pub grub/gastroish menu **££**,
🎍 Tables on street, beer garden, ♿
*Quiz (Tu), live music (Sa), DJs, beer festivals,
food promotions*

🚇 Notting Hill Gate, Queensway   🏃 Link to Jubilee
Greenway, Princess Diana Memorial Walk

Manager Josh started here in April 2014 after a stint at the famous White Horse (p 214), which explains the obvious beer focus of this main road pub close to Kensington Gardens and Notting Hill Gate. The cask pumps regularly feature very local brewers Moncada and Portobello, besides Adnams, Bath, Oakham, Sambrook's, Sunny Republic and Windsor & Eton. Other draught options could include Adnams 'craft keg' or seasonal beers from Brooklyn, while London brewers like Beavertown and Redchurch line up alongside Delirium Tremens, Sly Fox and Newport's Tiny Rebel in the fridge. Food includes options like mushroom and butternut squash farro risotto and cottage pie alongside pub grub staples like steaks and fish and chips. It's a pretty place with some surviving original tiling and flower murals at the back that lead you down-stairs to a quiet space done out with beer enamels and an ivy-clad 'secret garden'.

three-thirds tasting paddles. And in prominent view alongside the wines is a wide range of Fuller's bottled beers, including 1845, Bengal Lancer, Brewers Reserve and Vintage Ale, with decent lagers on keg too. Food starts with breakfast and continues with ploughmans, sausage and mash, salads with beer dressing or maybe a sweet potato curry.

Pub trivia. *The bishop was the Bishop of London, who sold the land to the Great Western Railway at a knockdown price, and the bear you can work out for yourself.*

Mad Bishop and Bear (87)

Traditional pub (Fuller's)
Upper Level Paddington Station W2 1HB
T (020) 7402 2441
www.madbishopandbear.co.uk
 madbishopandbear MadBishopBearW2
 Mo-Sa 08.00-23.00, Su 10.00-22.30.
   Children very welcome until 21.30.
Cask beers 8 (Fuller's, 2–3 often local guests),
Other beers 3 keg, 20 bottles
 Breakfast, sandwiches, pub grub **£-££**,
Occasional beer tastings, major big screen sport

 Paddington NCN6, Regents Canal towpath
 Jubilee Greenway, Grand Union Canal Walk

Fuller's pioneering quality station pub and undoubtedly the inspiration for the more spectacular Parcel Yard at Kings Cross (p 48), the Mad Bishop is on the top floor of the Lawns food and shopping court that now occupies Paddington station's former front concourse. The interior is surprisingly ornate with pillars, mirrors, and a five-tier chandelier. Besides Chiswick, ESB, London Pride and St Austell Tribute, the place stocks seasonals and numer-ous cask guests, with other London brewers like Redemption regular visitors, all sold in

Quilon (88)

Restaurant, bar
41 Buckingham Gate SW1E 6AF
T (020) 7821 1899   www.quilon.co.uk
 TheQuilon
 Mo-Fr 12.00-14.30, 17.30-23.00, Sa 12.30-15.00,
   17.30-23.00, Su 12.30-15.00, 23.00-22.30.
   Children in restaurant only.
Cask beers None, **Other beers** 20+ bottles,
Also 180+ wines, 60 whiskies, specialist spirits
and cocktails
 Michelin-starred south Indian **£££**,
 in hotel

 Victoria St James's Park, Victoria Link to Jubilee
Greenway, Jubilee Walkway

Stylish Quilon, opened in 1999, is one of a tiny subset of London's numerous world class fine-dining restaurants to make any kind of effort with the beer list. It currently lists Anchor Liberty Ale, Camden Town Hells, Pietra from Corsica, Sam Smith's rarely seen Yorkshire Stingo, Sharp's Chalky's Bark, Williams Brothers Ceilidh Lager and several examples of aged Fuller's Vintage Ale to enjoy alongside exquisite cooking derived from coastal southwest Indian traditions, with plenty of veggie options. You can even request a tasting menu matching beers to such delicacies as lotus stem chop, grilled scallops with mango and chilli, cauliflower fry with yoghurt, lamb biryani and coconut with asparagus and snow peas. Prices are pitched at luxury levels and you'll inevitably pay a premium on the beer, but the set lunches are some of the best bargains in London given the quality on offer.

Speaker   (89)

Traditional pub (Pleisure)
46 Great Peter Street SW1P 2HA
T (020) 7222 1749
www.pleisure.com   ☐ The-Speaker
🕐 *Mo-Fr* 12.00-23.00, *Sa-Su* closed.
Cask beers 5 (Taylor, Wells & Young's, 3 often unusual guests), **Other beers** 16 bottles,
Also Some malts
🍴 Sandwiches, pub grub **£**
Regular themed beer events

⇌ Victoria   ⊖ St James's Park

As the chair of debates in the House of Commons, the Speaker is strictly non-political and impartial – appropriate, perhaps, also for a small pub among government offices within heckling distance of Parliament. Taylor Landlord and a house beer sourced from Wells and Young's are regulars, while guests are from brewers like Harveys, Hogs Back, Hop Back, Sambrook's, Woodforde's and York. Monthly themes trigger rapid rotation through guests sourced from far and wide: autumn ales, Hallowe'en beers and at least 20 milds in May, immaculately served by Dennis, manager of 14 years standing. Bottles run from Sussex's Long Man Brewery to Flying Dog and Westmalle. Food, very good value for the

area, includes Thai curry on Thursdays and a celebrated chicken liver pâté, enjoyed in an atmosphere of civilised conversation unhindered by background music and games machines. There's a fine collection of political caricatures on the walls – impartial, of course.

St Stephens Tavern   (90)

Traditional pub (Hall & Woodhouse) ★
10 Bridge Street SW1A 2JR
T (020) 7295 2286
www.ststephenstavern.co.uk
☐ ststephenstavern
🕐 *Mo-Sa* 10.00-23.30, *Su* 10.00-22.30.
    Children welcome.
Cask beers 4 (Badger), **Other beers** 5 bottles (Badger)
🍴 Enhanced pub grub **££**,
☷ Benches on street, ♿
Functions

⊖🚆 Westminster   🚲 Link to Avenue Verte, NCN4
🚶 Jubilee Greenway, Jubilee Walkway, Thames Path

On the immediate approach to Westminster Bridge, this 1875 building takes its name from the public entrance to the Houses of Parliament opposite. Standing on Parliamentary land and inevitably busy with tourists, it's well worth investigating partly for its lofty rooms and impressive Victorian bar fittings – exotic etched mirrors and glass, a coffered ceiling, and upholstered leather benches in House of Lords green. Dorset brewer Hall & Woodhouse restored the pub sensitively in 2003 and it now showcases their beers: First Gold, Tanglefoot, K&B Sussex and a seasonal are well kept on cask, and there's a few others in bottle too. Food includes quite a few veggie options like squash, blue cheese and sage quiche alongside pub grub staples and 'Our Famous Sussex Smokey', a smoked fish crumble.

99

Star Tavern Top 25 (91)

Traditional pub (Fuller's)
6 Belgrave Mews West SW1X 8HT
T (020) 7235 3019
www.star-tavern-belgravia.co.uk
🕒 *Mo-Fr* 11.00-23.00, *Sa* 12.00-23.00,
  Su 12.00-22.30. Children welcome.
Cask beers 5 (Fuller's, 1 London guest),
Other beers 1 keg, 5 bottles, *Also* 30+ whiskies
🍴 Enhanced pub grub, lunchtime
sandwiches **£-££**
*2 annual beer festivals, seasonal events,
board games, functions*

🚃 Victoria 🚇 Hyde Park Corner, Knightsbridge

Tucked away in elegant Belgravia, down an alley that runs between the Austrian and German embassies, the Star is the other London pub to appear in every edition of the *Good Beer Guide* (see also Buckingham Arms p 96). It was probably intended for domestic staff in the big houses hereabouts, and is still a relaxed and informal place centred on an old horseshoe bar, shabbily genteel but spotlessly clean. It's a Fuller's house that offers impeccable Chiswick, changing seasonals, guests from London breweries, and a few bottles that include Vintage Ale and 1845. Food includes pies, steaks, broccoli quiche and cooked snacks like chicken goujons.

Pub trivia *The Great Train Robbery was planned here (now commemorated by occasional events) and stars like Peter O'Toole and Diana Dors would once come to rub shoulders with gang bosses. You can spot the pub in Carol Reed's classic 1948 film* The Fallen Idol.

HOP HISTORIES | Roll out the red barrel

When James Watney bought the Stag brewery at the west end of Victoria Street in 1858 he couldn't have guessed that his name would one day become one of brewing's few irredeemably toxic brands. Back then, the Stag was a medium-sized ale brewery to the south of the Royal Parks and Buckingham Palace, which had only relatively recently become Queen Victoria's official residence. Before Victoria station opened in 1860, the neighbourhood was known as Pimlico, a label now usually restricted to the area south of the station. Palaces once had their own domestic breweries, and it's likely the Stag originated as a brewhouse attached to St James's on the other side of the park. Commercial brewing on the site started under William Greene in 1641.

Watney pursued a vigorous policy of expansion, eventually adding a second plant up the river at Mortlake, bought from More & Co in 1889. The brewing tradition on this riverside site stretched back to a mediaeval monastery and a 15th-century manor house with a domestic brewery. By 1765 there were two small commercial outfits that later merged as the Star brewery. In 1898 Watney became a major London force by taking on and closing Combe & Co in Long Acre, Covent Garden, and Reid's Griffin brewery in Clerkenwell (see The Great Beer Flood p 50) to form Watney Combe Reid. It continued to develop both its sites in the 20th century and in 1931 became one of the first UK brewers to experiment with pasteurised keg ale, producing the first versions of a beer called Red Barrel at Mortlake for the export market. Through the 1950s and 1960s Watney grew into a national brewer through a ruthless programme of buying up and closing regional breweries, acquiring an estate of around 6,000 pubs through which it increasingly pushed its own generic keg products.

In 1959 Watney closed its historic Victoria site so a new gyratory traffic system could be built at the now-busy junction, and concentrated London production at Mann's brewery in Whitechapel (see Yeast Enders, p 122), which it had bought the previous year, and at Mortlake, which inherited the Stag name. Red Barrel soon became the core brand, originally promoted as a premium product which was even sold aboard luxury liners like the Queen Elizabeth II. But it gradually came to symbolise all that had gone wrong with British brewing in the era of the Big Seven and, in particular, the replacement of local distinctiveness and character with homogenous, bland, mass-produced, overpriced and heavily promoted national brands.

The brewery reformulated and relaunched the beer in 1971 as Watneys Red, with an unlikely campaign exhorting drinkers to

TRY ALSO

This area is home to numerous classic pubs that don't quite qualify for a full entry, several of them good Fuller's options. The little **Red Lion ★** (2 Duke of York Street SW1Y 6JP, www.redlionmayfair.co.uk) near St James's, Piccadilly, is one of the capital's most beautiful pubs, with a dazzling display of late Victorian etched glass mirrors across two walls. Another **Red Lion ★** (48 Parliament Street SW1A 2NH, www.redlionwestminster.co.uk), close to the Palace of Westminster and popular with MPs and civil servants, has glazed screens and a carved Renaissance-style bar back. Across from Westminster Abbey in an early 20th-century office block, **Sanctuary House** (33 Tothill Street SW1H 9LA, www.sanctuaryhousehotel.co.uk) is more modern

"join the Red Revolution" under images of Fidel Castro and Mao Zedong. But the damage was done: Red Barrel was famously pilloried on television in *Monty Python's Flying Circus* in 1972, and Watney itself was written up in the first edition of CAMRA's *Good Beer Guide* in 1974 with the simple sentence "Avoid like the plague", hastily amended to the only slightly more flattering "Avoid at all costs" at the insistence of the printer, who feared legal action. By the end of the 1970s, Red and other national keg bitters were fading from view as big brewers switched to promoting equally feeble lager-style beers.

By then Watney itself had fallen to bigger predators. In the early 1970s it was the subject of a bitterly-fought hostile takeover bid by the Grand Metropolitan hotel group, and tried to strengthen and protect itself by attempting to buy London's last surviving major independent, Truman's

(see From Black Eagle to Dark Star p 90). But instead Grand Met took Truman's and, in 1972, Watney as well, merging them to create Watney Mann Truman. Mann was closed in 1979, and Truman's in 1989, as Grand Met gradually withdrew from brewing, sellings its remaining plants to Courage, which in turn was ultimately absorbed by Heineken.

In 1991, Courage leased the Stag in Mortlake to US giant Anheuser Busch as the main European production plant for Budweiser lager, a function it continues to fulfil today. The site isn't open to the public but can be viewed from the street (Lower Richmond Road SW14 7ET). AB is now part of the world's biggest brewing group AB InBev, which has other breweries in the UK and has been talking about closing the Stag since 2008. It's been reprieved several times and is currently expected to go offline at the end of 2015. Though its current

output may hold little appeal for readers of this book, its final demise will be something of a sad end for what's now likely London's oldest continuous commercial brewing site and the last remnant of big brewing in the capital.

Back at Victoria, all trace of the original Stag has long since been obliterated. A new Stag pub in brutalist concrete was part of the late 1950s redevelopment scheme but has since been demolished as the site is being rebuilt yet again under the name Nova Victoria – it remains to be seen whether any reminders of its past will be incorporated. The hind statue that once stood in front of the brewery offices now graces a Maidenhead shopping centre. And you'll have to look hard to find a beer brave enough to carry the Watney name, though Watneys Scotch Ale is still occasionally brewed by Heineken's Belgian subsidary Alken-Maes.

in style, with a boutique hotel upstairs often used to billet visiting brewers.

Further out, the elegant but cheerful **Victoria ★** (10a Strathearn Place W2 2NH, www.victoriapaddington.co.uk), in Bayswater just north of Hyde Park, is noteworthy for preserving earlier Victorian fittings than most heritage pubs, including a Regency-style fireplace and a tiled and mirrored side wall dating from the 1860s. More 1930s in style is the **Churchill Arms ★** (119 Kensington Church Street W8 7LN, www.churchillarmskensington. co.uk), a local institution known for its collection of Churchill memorabilia and astounding exterior floral displays in season. Very different and definitely not Fuller's is the **Electric Diner** (191 Portobello Road W11 2ED, www. electricdiner.com), the informal restaurant next to Portobello Road's celebrated Electric Cinema, which has a handful of well-chosen London, Belgian and US beers in bottle and keg.

One of central London's better Young's pubs is the **Windmill** (6 Mill Street W1S 2AZ, www.windmillmayfair.co.uk), off Regent Street near Savile Row, which prides itself on its pies as well as a good range of beer. Round the corner, behind West End Central police station, the independent **Burlington Arms** (21 Old Burlington Street W1S 2JL, www. burlingtonarms.com) is posh but relaxed, with its own picobrewery and a few good bottles too.

On Whitehall despite its name, the **Lord Moon of the Mall** (16 Whitehall SW1A 2DY, www.jdwetherspoon.co.uk) has 11 well-served cask beers in an otherwise typical Wetherspoon bank conversion: the character on the pub sign turns out to be company founder Tim Martin. Another Wetherspoon worth knowing about, with up to 10 casks, is in a raised atrium between the Kent and Sussex sides of Victoria station: it's simply known as **Wetherspoons** (5 Main Concourse SW1V 1JT).

Closer to Buckingham Palace, the tiny **Cask and Glass** (39–41 Palace Street SW1E 5HN, www.shepherd-neame.co.uk) is a charmingly unspoilt purveyor of top nick Shepherd Neame cask beers and not much else. South of Hyde Park, in a picturesque mews near the Albert Hall, the **Queens Arms** (30 Queens Gate Mews SW7 5QL, www.thequeensarmskensington.co.uk) has more interesting beers than many of its fellow Castle pubs, and is one

Churchill Arms

of the prettiest in the chain. Further west, the smartly turned-out **Kings Head** (17 Hogarth Road SW5 0QT, www.faucetinn.com/the-kings-head) offers a reasonable range of London beers in an alleyway near Earls Court.

Daniel Boulud's **Bar Boulud** (66 Knightsbridge SW1X 7LA, www.barboulud.com), in the Mandarin Oriental Hyde Park Hotel on Knightsbridge, is one of the few swanky hotel bars in London to make an effort with the beer list, with around 14 keg and bottled options and tasting paddles too, along with gourmet cheese and charcuterie – but don't expect pub prices. Among Oxford Street department stores, **Selfridges Food Hall** (400 Oxford Street W1A 1AB, www.selfridges.com) stocks around 60 beers. In the same building, by the wine shop on the lower ground floor, tiny **Harry Gordons Bar** offers 10 decent keg and bottled beers alongside wines and cocktails – if you can get a seat.

Kensington High Street's retail therapy options include **Whole Foods Market Kensington** (63 Kensington High Street W8 5SE, www.wholefoodsmarket.com/stores/kensington), the UK flagship branch of the US grocery chain, which has around 150 bottles in its main beer section in the basement, a selection of takeaway draughts and a more limited bottled range on the ground floor, and four changing bottled beers to sample at the wine tasting bar nearby.

EAST
LONDON

EAST LONDON

East London in this book covers all the E postcodes outside the central area, and the rest of London east of these and north of the Thames to the Essex boundary. Though there's precious little to write about in the far reaches of the area, the inner districts boast some of the most exciting venues in this book.

Hackney covers not only Hackney itself but the Borough of Hackney, including Clapton, Dalston and Homerton – though not Stoke Newington which has an N postcode and is dealt with elsewhere (under Islington to Stoke Newington p140). Hackney is emblematic of the rapid growth of London's beer culture, which has seen a number of failing old pubs happily rescued and reinvented for a new audience. The area has long had its population of arty types and alternative lifestylers, but I struggled to find places to list round here for the previous edition of this guide. Since then gentrification has proceeded apace and this time round I was trying hard to find reasons for leaving venues out. Note that most of Hackney Wick is actually in the Borough of Tower Hamlets and is dealt with in Around the Olympic Park.

Following the 2012 Olympic and Paralympic Games, the Queen Elizabeth Olympic Park finally reopened in 2014 as a combination of new residential and business developments, major venues and extensive and magnificent public space and parkland. With new walking, cycling and bus links, it's knitted together Victoria Park, Hackney Wick, Leyton and Stratford in a way that fully justifies keeping a separate **Around the Olympic Park** section in this guide.

Tower Hamlets covers much of the classic East End: all the Borough of Tower Hamlets except the central bits listed under the City (p68) and Shoreditch (p85) and the areas immediately adjacent to the Olympic Park. There are some great new places here too, notably around Bethnal Green, including some good brewery taprooms.

Outer East London deals with the rest, though most of the listings are around Walthamstow, northern Leyton and Leytonstone, areas also undergoing significant demographic change.

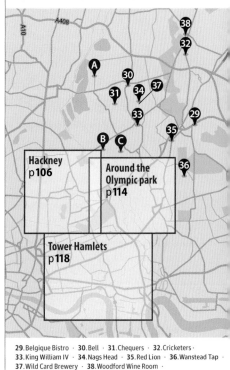

29. Belgique Bistro · **30.** Bell · **31.** Chequers · **32.** Cricketers ·
33. King William IV · **34.** Nags Head · **35.** Red Lion · **36.** Wanstead Tap ·
37. Wild Card Brewery · **38.** Woodford Wine Room ·
A. Left Bank Brewery · **B.** East London Brewing · **C.** Signature Brew

Hackney

Adam and Eve (1)

Contemporary pub (Lanzarote)
155 Homerton High Street E9 6AS
T (020) 8985 1494
www.adamandevepub.com
☐ theadamandevee9   ☐ adamandevee9
⏲ *Mo-Th* 16.00-23.00, *Fr-Sa* 12.00-01.00, *Su* 12.00-23.00. Children very welcome until 21.00.
Cask beers 6 (unusual often local & Cornish guests), **Other beers** 2 keg, 12+ bottles,
Also A few wines
🍴 Enhanced pub grub/Cornish menu **££**,
🌳 Courtyard with edible garden ✿
Beer and food festivals, tap takeover/meet the brewer, home brew events, bingo (We&Su), DJs (Fr-Sa), film club, floristry class, art & craft fairs, pool, table tennis (summer), board games, functions

⊖ Homerton

An architecturally important but long-neglected Homerton pub reopened in June 2014, this big place is now a buzzing local. Among the fine features is a large rear courtyard where an old stable houses the Home Brew Depot, offering brewing supplies, demonstrations and courses (www.homebrewdepot.co.uk) to those inspired by the quality local beer on offer. Cask lines rotate through brewers like Hackney, Truman's and Wild Card, with occasional Cornish interlopers like Tintagel resonating with food from a kitchen run by the Cornwall Project – rare breed beef, lobster, braised celery with blue cheese and Sunday roasts are typical. Five Points beer is sold in bottle alongside several international classics, with other locals including Meantime on keg.

Pub trivia *The handsome Edwardian façade - cream terracotta, purple-glazed tiles and a relief of the eponymous biblical couple - dates from 1915, on a site that's been a pub since at least 1735. In the 1970s this was a Teddy Boy haunt, an era recaptured in some of the decoration.*

Café OTO (2)

Bar
18 Ashwin Street E8 3DL
T (020) 7923 1231
www.cafeoto.co.uk   ☐ Cafeoto
⏲ *Mo-Fr* 08.30-17.30, *Sa* 09.30-17.30, *Su* 10.30-17.30, bar open later if no evening event. Children welcome.
Cask beers None, **Other beers** 4 keg, 15+ bottles,
Also Tea, coffee, shochu, sake, plum wine, malts
🍴 Breakfasts, wraps, salads, lunches, cakes and pastries **£-££**, 🌳 Tables on street, ♿
Experimental, jazz, folk, rock music most evenings, jukebox

⊖ Dalston Junction, Dalston Kingsland

Dalston's arty and alternative edge predates current redevelopment and gentrification. In the former Hackney Gazette building and next to the Arcola Theatre is the Printworks, where one of London's more unusual music venues, Café OTO, operates beneath solar-powered workspaces for creative enterprises. In the daytime it's a chilled out café offering salads, Persian-inspired flatbread wraps, delicious cakes and pastries and a surprisingly good range of beers. There's a long-standing relationship with Kernel, with numerous beers served from keykeg and bottle, bottles from East London and several good Belgians like Orval and Westmalle. Ticketed performances by avant-garde and left-field musicians follow most evenings – *oto* is Japanese for 'sound', and the national origin of a co-founder also explains the wide choice of Yamazaki whiskies, shochu and plum wine.

Visitor note *Nearby Fassett Square was the model for Albert Square in long running BBC soap EastEnders.*

Clapton Craft (3)

Shop
97 Lower Clapton Road E5 0NP
www.claptoncraft.co.uk 🏳️🐦claptoncraft
🕐 *Mo-Sa* 11.00-21.00, *Su* 12.00-20.00.

Cask beers None, **Other beers** 7-8 keg, 300+
bottles, **Also** Some bottled ciders, local and
US spirits
Occasional tastings, meet the brewer/tap takeover

🚇Hackney Downs, Hackney Central 🚌Glenarm Road
(numerous Hackney Central, Hackney Downs, Clapton)

Opened in April 2014 in a derelict shop unit
that was once a photography studio, this was
London's first off-licence selling takeaway
keykeg beer with a hygienic oxygen-beating
filler system. There are separate lines for filling
1 l plastic bottles, usually used for more sessionable, everyday beers and occasional ciders,
and 1.89 l (just over 3 pint) growlers, the format
of choice for more serious stuff. London
brewers like Brodie's, Crate, Kernel and Weird
Beard are favoured, though non-London and
overseas suppliers also appear. An expertly-
chosen pre-packaged range is led by a pile of
US and London canned beers, and bottle
shelves that divide four ways between London,
the rest of the UK, the US and the rest of the
world: founder William Jack works hard to
find stuff other places don't stock, including
imports from his native New Zealand.

Visitor note. *The shop is right opposite the Round Chapel,
regular venue for the local CAMRA branch's Pig's Ear beer
festival in December.*

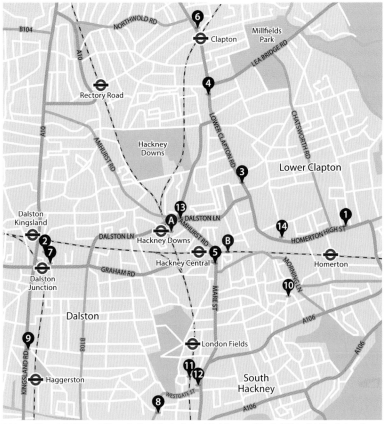

1.Adam and Eve · 2.Café OTO · 3.Clapton Craft · 4.Clapton Hart · 5.Cock Tavern · 6.Crooked Billet · 7.Dalston Eastern Curve
Garden Café · 8.Dove · 9.Fox · 10.Gun · 11.London Fields Brewery · 12.Look Mum No Hands · 13.Pembury Tavern ·
14.Plough · A.Five Points Brewing · B.Pressure Drop Brewing

Clapton Craft

Clapton Hart (4)

Contemporary pub (Antic)
231 Lower Clapton Road E5 8EG
T (020) 8985 8124
www.claptonhart.com ☐ ☑ claptonhart
🕐 *Mo-Th* 16.00-23.00, *Fr* 16.00-01.00, *Sa* 12.00-
   01.00, *Su* 12.00-23.00. Children until 21.00.
Cask beers 7-8 (London and unusual guests),
Other beers 2 keg, 40 bottles,
Also Cider, home made spirit infusions
🍴 Shortish gastroish menu, dishes cooked with
beer **£-££**, 🏕 Benches on street, beer garden, ♿
Quiz (Tu), VHS film nights, food promotions,
table football, board games

🚇 Clapton 🚉 Lea Bridge Roundabout (numerous Hackney
Central, Clapton) 🚴 Link to NCN1 🚶 Link to Capital Ring,
Lea Valley Path

This vast place by Lea Bridge Road roundabout
was once the sumptuous White Hart Hotel,
but more recently had a grim reputation as a
landmark on 'murder mile' and spent the best
part of a decade derelict and boarded. Ongoing
makeovers since reopening in May 2012 have
left it still distressed but appealingly atmospheric, its elaborate exterior mouldings eroded
like old gravestones. Cask beers often include
milds, stouts and contemporary pale ales from
locals like East London, Hackney and others
like Arbor, Otley, Redwillow and Summer Wine.
An expanding bottle range has Beavertown,

Kernel plus Odell, Rogue and Sly Fox from
the USA, while guest kegs could come from
Pressure Drop or Siren. Beer is used in the
kitchen for rarebit, chutney, fish batter and
even mushy peas and the shortish menu has
more than the usual share of vegetarian
options alongside steaks, burgers and fish.

Cock Tavern Top 25 (5)

Brewpub, traditional pub
315 Mare Street E8 1EJ
T (020) 8533 6369   www.thecocktavern.co.uk
☐ Cock-Tavern ☑ TheCockTavernE8
🕐 *Su-Th* 12.00-23.00, *Fr-Sa* 12.00-01.00.
   Children welcome.
Cask beers 10 (6+ Howling Hops, London),
Other beers 8 keg, 30 bottles, **Also** Ciders/perries
🍴 Pies, Scotch eggs **£**, 🏕 Tiny beer garden
Occasional live piano

🚇 Hackney Central, Hackney Downs

The reopening of this fine old pub in July 2012
brought a much needed source of great beer
to Hackney town centre, a few steps from the
famous Empire music hall and 'cultural quarter'.
It offers a similarly appealing package to sister
pub the Southampton Arms (p138) but it's often
less crowded, has an ever wider choice and,
most importantly, its own brewery, Howling
Hops, in the cellar. This now accounts for most
of the draught range; the rest has a London

focus, with breweries like nearby Five Points and Beavertown, Brew by Numbers, Fourpure, Kernel, Partizan, Pressure Drop and Weird Beard featuring across the formats. It's a solid red brick corner pub that's scrubbed up well with an attractively old-fashioned public bar feel, restored half height dark panelling, ceramic tiles and floorboards. A Hackney classic that's also helped inspire the rehabilitation of several other local pubs.

Crooked Billet (6)

Contemporary pub
84 Upper Clapton Road E5 9JP
T (020) 8291 8649
www.e5crookedbillet.co.uk
f y e5crookedbillet
🕑 *Mo-Th* 16.00-23.00, *Fr-Sa* 12.00-24.00, *Su* 12.00-23.00. Children until 19.30.
Cask beers 5 cask (London guests), **Other beers** 4 keg, 9 bottles, **Also** Rum bar weekends in summer, specialist spirits
🍴 Gastroish menu **££**,
🍺 Large sheltered beer garden
Meet the brewer/tap takeover, quiz (Mo), cycle surgery (Th), big screen football (Sa), seasonal events, board games

🚇 Clapton 🚲 Link to NCN1 🥾 Link to Capital Ring, Lea Valley Path

There's a whole history of social change in the fact that most of the large car park, provided when this roadside pub near Clapton station was rebuilt in the 1950s, was reclaimed as an extension to the beer garden when the place reopened in Autumn 2013 with regular cycle

surgeries among the attractions. The makeover has thankfully managed the trick of appealing to the area's prosperous new incomers without entirely alienating the old regulars. All casks and some keykegs are from London brewers including By the Horns, Hackney, Five Points, Signature and Truman's, while numerous Pressure Drop bottles line up beside Duvel and Goose Island in the fridges. Food has a gastro flourish – heritage tomatoes, pan-fried gnocchi and merguez sausages – but there are steaks and burgers too, served in a bright and uncluttered interior replete with plenty of warm wood and sofas.

Dalston Eastern Curve Garden Café (7)

Bar
13 Dalston Lane E8 3DF
www.dalstongarden.org
f dalstongarden y easterncurve
🕑 *Daily* 11.00-dusk. Children very welcome.
Cask beers 5 cask (ELB, bag in box), **Other beers** 1 keg, 1 bottle, **Also** 1 cider, local soft drinks
🍴 Soup and sandwiches, summer clay-baked pizzas (*TuSa&Su*) **£-££**, 🍺 All outdoor 🐾, ♿
Summer live music (Tu), children's workshops, garden volunteering

🚇 Dalston Junction, Dalston Kingsland

Perhaps London's most unexpectedly beautiful setting in which to enjoy great beer is this hidden treasure opposite Dalston Junction station: an exquisite enclosed public garden created in 2010 on a short stretch of abandoned railway. A sheltered verandah scattered with bean bags and festooned with paper lanterns overlooks a glade of silver birches amid wild flower beds and vigorous growths of tomatoes and herbs. Operated as a community enterprise supported by volunteers, the project sustains itself by running events, activities, and a tiny café. The café miraculously serves up five bag-in-the-box ales in a range of styles from nearby East London brewery and a Whitstable beer on keg alongside sarnies, tea and cakes. But visit soon, as a plan to run a public path through as part of surrounding redevelopments has raised fears the site will lose its intimate character.

LONDON'S BREWING — Pressure Drop/Five Points

Hackney is one of the places most changed by the London beer renaissance, and not just by its new crop of pubs and bars. Once a brewery-free borough, it now boasts more than most, including three in the heart of the town centre itself.

"I live in Hackney, my kids were born in Hackney, and of course I wanted to brew here," says Ed Mason, founder of the Five Points brewery by Hackney Downs station. Long involved in the pub trade in Leeds and London, and with a keen insight into customers' tastes, Ed got his chance while running pioneering Shoreditch beer bar Mason & Taylor, thanks to headline-grabbing Scottish brewery BrewDog. "They visited us a few times for events," recounts Ed, "and then James Watt asked me if I was interested in selling, as it would be the perfect site for the second BrewDog bar in London. I told him it wasn't for sale, but then he made me a serious offer." Mason & Taylor duly became BrewDog Shoreditch (p85), and Hackney gained another fine brewery, named after the five-way junction nearby.

Head brewer Greg Hobbs, formerly at East London, joined the project and beer from a 10-barrel (16 hl) installation was first sold in September 2012. "We decided to do cask, keg and bottles from the start, as few London breweries were then doing all three," says Ed. "We wanted strong core brands, and spent the first 18 months brewing just three beers – our pale ale, porter and red ale." All three are brewed at session strengths, but there are now stronger beers too, including an annual vintage barley wine and a smoked porter.

The strategy has paid off, and by the time you read this, Five Points should have doubled its brewlength with a new kit from OAL, who number Burning Sky, Magic Rock and fellow Londoners Beavertown among their customers. In 2014 it became the first brewery to sign up to the London Living Wage scheme, and if growth continues it might have to find a new site – in Hackney of course.

A stone's throw away, Pressure Drop makes equally delicious beers but with a rather different approach. The three original founders still run the whole show, with occasional part-time help. Graham O'Brien and Sam Smith (no relation to the famous Yorkshire brewing family) are old school friends, and Graham met the third partner, Ben Freeman, on an internship at London Fields. They developed their first recipes on a Braumeister pilot brewery in Graham's garden shed in Stoke Newington in the summer of 2012, but lack of space meant much of the work was done outside – which they quickly realised wasn't a viable option with winter on its way. The first commercial brews emerged from a small industrial unit nearby, but in March 2013 they moved to their current Hackney location, where a five barrel (8 hl) kit from ABUK is now fired up twice every weekday.

The trio brews mainly bottle-conditioned and keykeg beers in imaginative and unusual styles: Pale Fire, for example, contains a new and distinctive Kent hop variety currently known only as Hop X, while Wu Gang Chops the Tree is a Hefeweisse flavoured with locally foraged herbs which Graham picks himself. "It's mainly bay, actually," he says, "and we need quite a bit for each brew, but I know a few good parks and gardens." They sell everything they brew, mainly in London and other big UK cities, and sometimes have to turn down orders. "We've discussed expansion," Graham continues, "but it's a sustainable business as it is. We've never rushed anything, we've always taken small steps, and that's the way we plan to go on."

Dove (8)

Specialist, contemporary pub
24 Broadway Market E8 4QJ
T (020) 7275 7617   **www.dovepubs.com**
TheDove   dovepubs
Sn-Fr 12.00-23.00, *Sa* 11.00-23.00.
    Children until 18.00 or 20.00 if dining.
Cask beers 6 (Crouch Vale, East London,
Timothy Taylor, 3 unusual guests), **Other beers**
14 keg, 160 bottles (Belgian, international),
Also Wines, genever
Belgian and British menu **££**,
Tables on street, small balcony,
Jazz (Su), quiz (We), seasonal events, board games

London Fields, Hackney Central, Shoreditch High Street
Broadway Market (236 Canonbury-Hackney, 394 Shoreditch
-Hackney)   Regents Canal towpath   Jubilee Greenway

With its extensive specialist beer selection,
good food and quirky but relaxed vibe, the
Dove sits well on arty-crafty Broadway Market,
though this current iteration of the former
Goring Arms dates from the 1990s, long before
the street's recent facelift. The Leffe corner
complete with Gothic pews is a reminder of
the original beer policy, and this muzak-free
pub is still a great place to enjoy Belgian beer,
with a long list of Trappists, classics from Boon,
Dupont and Rodenbach, and newer names
like Belgoo, Gaverhopke and Hof ten Dormaal.

Dove

But there's a growing range of British and
international beers, including London-brewed
casks and US imports, with tasting planks
on offer. Bottles include St Peter's and
Westerham alongside rarely-seen imports
from France, Italy and Mexico. The kitchen
still serves up Belgian classics – *carbonnade
flamande* made with beer, *waterzooi*,
mussels and chips – alongside veggie lasagnes,
gourmet burgers and English cheese plates.

Fox (9)

Specialist, contemporary pub
372 Kingsland Road E8 4DA
T 07807 217734 **www.thefoxe8.com**
thefoxe8
Mo-Fr 16.00-24.00, *Sa* 12.00-24.00,
    Su 12.00-23.30. Children until 20.00.
Cask beers 5–6 (unusual guests),
Other beers 14 keg, 150 bottles,
Also 3 ciders/perries, specialist spirits
Sharing plates, enhanced pub grub **££**,
Sheltered roof terrace, benches on street
Monthly tap takeovers, photo booth, functions

Haggerston   Middleton Road (various Liverpool Street,
Dalston)   Link to Regents Canal towpath   Link to
Jubilee Greenway

Some way from Shoreditch and not quite in
Dalston, this big Victorian roadside pub struggled through several unsuccessful makeovers
before relaunching in February 2012 as a
self-proclaimed "Craft Beer House" under the
same ownership as Howl at the Moon (p 87).
The large open interior has been rigorously
stripped back to bare brick and exposed
girders, where friendly and informed staff serve
guest casks from brewers like Burning Sky,
Buxton, Dark Star, Magic Rock, Redemption,
Siren, and Weird Beard. There are several more
Londoners on 'craft keg' lines and an impressive
bottled list that encompasses Belgian classics
like Cantillon and Westmalle and international
craft choices from Mikkeller, Ska and To Øl.
Food includes meat and veggie pies, and
sharing plates of pork belly bites and blue
cheese croquettes. A splendid roof terrace
and station-style photo machine complete an
interesting package.

Gun   (10)

Bar

235 Well Street E9 6RG   **T** (020) 8985 6296

www.thegunwellstreet.com   ◨ thegunwellst

🕐 *Mo-Fr* 17.00-23.00, *Sa* 12.00-23.00,
    Su 12.00-22.30. Children until early evening.

Cask beers 1 (usually local), **Other beers** 9 keg,
17 bottles, **Also** Local and international
specialist spirits, cocktails

🍴 Toasties, small plates **£**,

⊼ Tables on street, roof terrace

*DJs (Fr-Sa), quiz, occasional tap takeovers, board
games*

⊖ Homerton

Gun

London bottles from Kernel and Weird Beard
share fridge space with Buxton, Siren and
California's Bear Republic on a considered list.
A new roof garden should be completed by
the time you read this.

"Secret plans and clever tricks," reads the
enigmatic neon sign in the snug. Perhaps the
cleverest trick was finessing this small and
previously undistinguished old boozer into a
viable beer-focused venue, welcoming
Hackney's newly upwardly-mobile without
completely abandoning its old-school feel.
The old Whitbread signing on the distinctive
single storey projecting frontage has been
restored to view since reopening in July 2014,
but indoors is stylishly minimalist. The single
cask is usually from Redemption or Sambrook's,
the changing kegs are likely to be from
Beavertown, Brew by Numbers or Camden
Town, or US imports like Lagunitas. All draughts
are for sale in 1½ pint takeaway containers.

London Fields Brewery   (11)

Bar

365 Warburton Street E8 3RR

T (020) 7241 5983

www.londonfieldsbrewery.co.uk/tap-room

◨ londonfieldsbrewery   🐦 LdnFldsBrewery

🕐 *Daily* 11.00-23.30. Children until 21.00.

Cask beers 6 (London Fields, occasional
guests), **Other beers** 12 keg, 9 bottles,
Also 2 ciders/perries

🍴 Burgers, hot dogs, cooked snacks **£-££**, ♿

Jazz (Su), live music (alternate We), tastings

⊖ London Fields

London Fields Brewery tap room

This smallish but pleasant and ever-popular hop-bedecked bar has continued in use despite recent troubles at London Fields, though all the beers are now contract-brewed elsewhere. There's a wide range of own-branded beers from cask, keg and bottle, with one or two guests from the likes of Magic Rock and Siren. Food consists of guilty pleasures like gourmet burgers, pulled pork sarnies and "beery cheese on toast".

Look Mum No Hands (12)

Bar
125 Mare Street E8 3RH   **T** 07985 200472
www.lookmumnohands.com
☐ ☑ lookmumnohands
🕐 *Mo-Fr* 08.00-23.00, *Sa* 09.00-23.00,
   Su 09.00-22.00. Children very welcome.
Cask beers None, **Other beers** 7 keg, 15 bottles (mainly London)
🍴 Pies, salads, light meals, cakes **£-££**,
🪑 Tables at front overlooking square, ♿
Cycling event screenings, films, knitting, cycle speed dating, food promotions

🚇 London Fields

A cycling themed café-bar with superfast WiFi, serving up 'craft' beer with organic salads on stripped pine benches? It could only be Hackney, or perhaps Hoxton, where the original branch of this mini-(bike) chain is sited. Both have bottled beers, but Hackney also has keykegs

from London brewers like Five Points, Hackney, Kernel, Redchurch and Weird Beard and occasional visitors like Celt and Quantum. Fresh café food includes filling breakfasts, imaginative salad bowls, meat and veggie pies, delectable cakes and evening specials like kimchi-loka vegan rice or sticky chicken wings. Cycling-related films and events are shown on the big screen and bike accessories are on sale. On the ground floor of a former community college otherwise occupied by fashion designers, it's not too boisterous at night and wonderfully quiet during the day when pretty much all the customers are glued to laptops and tablets.

Pembury Tavern (13)

Contemporary pub (Individual/Milton)
90 Amhurst Road E8 1JH
T (020) 8986 8597   ☑ Pembury Tavern
www.individualpubs.co.uk
🕐 *Mo-Th* 12.00-24.00, *Fr-Sa* 12.00-01.00,
   Su 12.00-23.00. Children until 20.00.
Cask beers 8-10 (5 Milton, unusual guests),
Other beers 2 keg, 10+ bottles, **Also** Specialist whiskies
🍴 Pizzas, pasta, imaginative pub grub **£-££**,
🪑 Tables on street, ♿
Occasional beer festivals, quiz (Mo), seasonal events, board games, bar billiards, pool

🚇 Hackney Central, Hackney Downs

This big and imposing pub dominating the busy junction at the top of Amhurst Road was reopened in 2006 following a fire to become what's now the only London pub owned by Cambridgeshire's Milton brewery. The full complement of 16 handpumps is rarely deployed but there's usually a respectable choice of Milton beers, plus guests like locals Brentwood and Redemption or Banks & Taylor and Purbeck from further afield. Czech and German draughts and bottles from London brewers including the very local Five Points and East London widen the offer, while food is wood-fired pizzas and pub grub with several veggie choices and exotica like merguez sausages. With the basic but comfortable air of a community arts centre, and occasional events to match, it's somethng of a local institution.

Look Mum No Hands

Plough (14)

Contemporary pub
23 Homerton High Street E9 6JP
T (020) 8525 0203   🅕 🅨 hackneyplough
www.hackneyplough.co.uk
⊕ *Mo-Th* 17.00-23.30, *Fr* 16.00-24.00, *Sa* 13.00-
    24.00, *Su* 13.00-23.30. Children until 19.30.
Cask beers 3 (Hackney, local guests),
Other beers 5 keg, 20 bottles, *Also* Cocktails
made with own infusions
🍴 Short unusual menu **££**,
🪑 Standing on street
DJs (Fr-Sa), seasonal events, food promotions

⊖ Hackney Central, Homerton, Hackney Downs

Much of the heritage of this rescued pub near
Homerton Hospital was obliterated during
recent stints as a wine bar and kebab shop,
but a plain and simple September 2013 refurbishment now subtly frames the original carved
bar back and what's left of the elaborately
decorated porch with floor mosaics and a tile
painting of a ploughman at work. Casks are
locally sourced from Five Points, Hackney,
One Mile End or Redemption; more London
beers like Bear Hug, Beavertown, Pressure
Drop and Wild Card are in keykeg and bottle
alongside less obvious selections from New
York City's Brooklyn, and there are no macro
brands. A shortish but interesting food choice
could include wild mushroom pilaf, soft shell
crab with samphire or pork chops with cavolo
nero. I'm not sure what the bloke in the
painting would make of it all, but today's
locals should be well pleased.

*Pub trivia. Records of a pub on the site go back to 1704,
when scenes like the one on the tile painting would have
been familiar locally. The current building, with embedded
octagonal tower, copper dome, gables and friezes, is an
1898 Truman's rebuild.*

TRY ALSO

Good beer has become astonishingly easy to
find in Hackney, and many of the places listed
below would have breezed into a full entry
in the first edition of this book. In an arty
industrial estate by the northwest corner
of Hackney Downs, the **Russet** is a *very*
Hackneyesque family-friendly bar-restaurant
and "creative space" that serves up several
local beers in keykeg and bottle, plus bag-in-box
cider, with wholesome sustainably-sourced
food. On the way to Clapton, the beautifully
refurbished **Windsor Castle** (135 Lower Clapton
Road E5 8EQ, **www.thewindsorcastleclapton.
com**) stocks six often local casks and a generous
handful of international bottles. At Homerton
near the hospital and Chats Palace arts centre,
Eat17 (64 Brooksbys Walk E9 6DA, **www.eat17.
co.uk**) is a Spar supermarket built for hipsters,
with around 70 bottles including Londoners
and unusual imports, and Crate beers on keg
to drink in with imaginative fast food.

Dalston options include the cheerfully regenerated **Three Compasses** (99 Dalston Lane E8 1NH,
www.threecompasses.com) at the eastern
end of Ridley Road Market, with a couple of
cask beers and a neat range of Londoners in
keg and bottle; and a typically distressed Antic
pub, **Farrs School of Dancing** (17 Dalston Lane
E8 3DF, **www.farrsschoolofdancing.com**), next
door to the Dalston Eastern Curve Garden (p108).

Besides the Dove (p110), Broadway Market also
boasts **Off Broadway** (63 Broadway Market
E8 4PH, **www.offbroadway.org.uk**), a tiny
but cool US-inspired cocktail bar that was
once linked to the Beavertown brewery and
still stocks a range of US and London bottles.
Nearby, boutique wine shop **Noble Fine
Liquor** (27 Broadway Market E8 4PH, **www.
noblefineliquor.co.uk**) has around 20 bottled
beers and four growler-fill keykeg lines
supplied by London and other UK brewers.
South of the Regents Canal is the **Albion in
Goldsmiths Row** (94 Goldsmiths Row E2 8QY,
www.thealbioningoldsmithsrow.co.uk), a
memorabilia-crammed football-themed pub
(the Albion is of the West Bromwich variety)
that prides itself on its civilised, tolerant
atmosphere and its four well-kept cask ales,
with some interesting bottles on sale too.

Around the Olympic Park

15. Brew Testament (Bottle Apostle) · 16. Crate · 17. Cygnet ·
18. Eleanor Arms · 19. Leyton Orient Supporters Club ·
20. Peoples Park Tavern · 21. Tap East · A. Truman's Beer

Brew Testament (Bottle Apostle)

Shop (15)
95 Lauriston Road E9 7HJ
T (020) 8985 1549
www.brewtestament.com
🅵 thebrewtestament 🐦 brewtestament
🕐 *Mo-Fr* 12.00-21.00, *Sa* 10.00-20.00,
   Su 10.00-20.00.

Cask beers None, **Other beers** 100+ bottles, **Also**
World boutique wines, sake, specialist spirits
Tastings (Fr), occasional meet the brewer

🚇 Cambridge Heath · 🚌 Victoria Park Road (277 London
Fields, Mile End) · 🚲 Link to NCN1 · 🚶 Victoria Park paths,
link to Jubilee Greenway

Boutique wine sellers Bottle Apostle are
so keen on expanding their beer business
they've dreamt up a second brand with a

suitably evangelical ring. Brew Testament
occupies its own space at the rear of the
company's flagship store among the chichi
shops of what estate agents call Victoria
Park Village, and though the Clapham and
Crouch End branches also sell decent beer,
this is the mother lode. It's all British and
nearly all London, with less obvious choices
like Anspach & Hobday, Brixton, Hammerton
and Strawman alongside well known stars
like Beavertown, Kernel (filling nearly a whole
shelf unit) and Partizan. Interlopers might
include Siren and Two Cocks. A collection
of beer reference books and a chalked up
list of hop varieties and their flavour profiles
strengthen the educational mission.

Crate (16)

Brewpub, bar
Queens Yard, White Post Lane E9 5EN
T 07834 275687
www.cratebrewery.com 🅵 🐦 CrateBrewery
🕐 *Su-Th* 12.00-23.00, *Fr-Sa* 12.00-24.00.
   Children welcome.

Cask beers 5 (Crate), **Other beers** 5 keg, 30 bottles
🍴 Gourmet pizzas **££**, 🌳 Canalside terrace, ♿
Occasional beer festivals, DJs (Fr-Su), arts events

🚇 Hackney Wick · 🚲 NCN1, Lee Navigation towpath,
Olympic Park paths · 🚶 Capital Ring, Jubilee Greenway,
Lee Valley Path, Olympic Park paths

Launched in late July 2012 just days before the
Olympic opening ceremony, this place fits in
perfectly to the artily repurposed post-industrial surrounds of Hackney Wick. In a big white
former printworks and sweet factory, it has
furniture made from reclaimed pallets and a
lovely waterside terrace with a view of the
Olympic stadium. Since summer 2014 the beer
has been produced in the Brewshed across the
yard, which doubles as an additional bar at busy

Crate

times and an events venue – including during the wittily-named Hackney WickED art festival in early August which Crate co-sponsors. The full range of house-brewed beers is on draught, with occasional London and other guests; bottles contain good stuff from locals like Five Points and more far-flung contributors like Bear Republic and Rogue. Stone-baked pizzas, deploying unconventional toppings like sweet potato, stilton and walnut or lemon chicken tagine, are of notable quality too.

Cygnet (17)

Bar (Truman's)
60 Dace Road E3 2NQ   **T** (020) 8525 9541
www.swanwharf.org 🐦 TheCygnetBar
🕒 *Su-Th* 09.00-23.00, *Fr-Sa* 09.00-01.00.
   Children welcome.
Cask beers 5 (Truman's), **Other beers** 3 keg,
8 bottles, **Also** Specialist spirits
🍴 Breakfasts, gourmet burgers, local ice
cream **££**, 🪑 Riverside terrace 🐾, ♿
*Swing night (Tu), quiz (We), magic (Fr), pool,
table football, regular arts, performance,
music events in Swan Wharf*

🚇 Hackney Wick   🚌 Wansbeck Road (276 Hackney Wick,
339 Stratford)   🚴 Greenway, Lee Navigation towpath, link to
NCN1, Olympic Park paths   🚶 Capital Ring, Jubilee Greenway,
Lee Valley Path, link to Olympic Park paths

The reborn Truman's gained a splendid tap in April 2014 when it opened this bar, in partnership with the owners of the Swan Wharf arts complex, in a former warehouse close to the

brewery. Four Truman's beers, both core and seasonal, are always on cask, usually supplemented by London guests from brewers like Five Points or Redemption. The regular keg pale ale is joined by beers from Beavertown, which was the brewery's next door neighbour for a time, while the bottles include some world classics like Cooper's. Indoors is all reclaimed wood, event flyers and classic rock; outdoors is a front yard with elevated terrace overlooking Old Ford Lock on the River Lee Navigation. Food options include cooked breakfasts and generously stuffed gourmet burgers, while community spirit is suitably flattered by the provision of discount cards to those with proof of local residence.

Eleanor Arms (18)

Traditional pub (Shepherd Neame)
460 Old Ford Road E3 5JP   **T** (020) 8980 6992
www.eleanorarms.co.uk 🐦 EleanorArmsPub
🕒 *Mo-Th* 16.00-23.00, *Fr* 12.00-24.00, *Sa* 12.00-
   01.00, *Su* 12.00-22.30. Children until 19.00.
Cask beers 4 (Shepherd Neame, occasional
guest), **Other beers** 8 bottles (Shepherd Neame),
Also 25 malts
🍴 Filled baguettes **£**, 🪑 Beer garden, ♿
*Monthly quiz, jazz (Su), major big screen sport,
board games, shove ha'penny, pool*

🚇 Bow Road, Bethnal Green   🚇 Bow Church   🚌 Old Ford
Road (8 Bethnal Green – Bow Church)   🚴 NCN1, Regents Canal
and Hertford Union canal towpaths, Hackney Parks Olympic
Greenway   🚶 Jubilee Greenway, Regents Canal towpath,
link to Capital Ring and Lea Valley Path, Victoria Park paths

Only a few steps across the Hertford Union Canal from Gunmaker's Gate on the southern edge of Victoria Park, this is one of the most inviting pubs in the area. Once a Fuller's house, it was one of a batch in London bought by Kent brewer Shepherd Neame in the late 1980s and as a recurring *Good Beer Guide* entry is a great showcase for their beers. Kent's Best and Whitstable Bay are cask regulars, with other core beers and seasonals on rotation with guests that might come from Inveralmond or St Austell. The comprehensive range of Shep's bottled beers includes historical recreations like Brilliant Ale and IPA. Long-standing music-loving landlords Frankie and Lesley have decorated the place with classic rock posters, old advertising and quirky art and strewn it with a comfortable mix of tables and sofas to create a welcoming community space.

Leyton Orient may currently only play in League One, in fact the third rung of English football, but its supporters' club has worked its way into the Premier League of beer venues. Changing Mighty Oak beers are always on, with guests from locals like East London and Hackney or others like Brighton or Slaters, at keen prices. It's open immediately before and after matches – they get through 14 nine-gallon (41 l) casks on a typical Saturday – as well as for two annual beer festivals where additional stillages are installed, and for several smaller themed festivals and special events like screenings of international games: check the website for times. Visitors carrying CAMRA membership cards or guides are welcome, as are well-behaved away supporters. Lauded with numerous awards proudly displayed beside the footie memorabilia and staffed by friendly volunteers, this is one of London's most delightfully unexpected beer champions.

Leyton Orient Supporters Club (19)

Club
Matchroom Stadium, Oliver Road E10 5NF
T (020) 8988 8288   🐦lofcsupporters
www.orientsupporters.org
🕐 See following text.
Cask beers 8 (Mighty Oak, 7 unusual often local guests), ***Other beers*** 3 bottles (including gluten-free), **Also** 4 ciders/perries, 8 malts
🍴 Filled rolls **£**, 🪑 Standing on front terrace, ♿
Beer festivals, occasional quiz, major big screen football, functions, football matches in adjoining stadium

🚇Leyton   🚌 Buckingham Road (various Leyton)

Peoples Park Tavern (20)

Brewpub, contemporary pub (Laines)
360 Victoria Park Road E9 7BT
T (020) 8533 0040   📘🐦peoplestavern
www.peoplesparktavern.pub
🕐 *Su-Th* 12.00-24.00, *Fr* 12.00-01.00, *Sa* 12.00-02.00.
   Children very welcome until 19.00.
Cask beers 8 (Laines), ***Other beers*** 5-6 bottles,
Also 2 ciders
🍴 Enhanced pub grub/gastroish menu **££**,
🪑 Terrace, big garden, tables on street🐾, ♿
Quiz (We), DJs (Fr-Sa), monthly comedy, swing night, summer barbecues, functions

🚇Homerton, Hackney Wick   🚌 Gascoyne Road (388 Stratford, Cambridge Heath)   🚲 Link to NCN1   🚶 Victoria Park paths, link to Jubilee Greenway

Peoples Park Tavern

Splendidly sited with a huge garden adjoining much-loved Victoria Park and a frontage overlooking Wick Common, this substantial pub became the second of three London brewpubs in the Laine's chain in December 2013. Most casks are brewed in-house under the name People's Pint, in a diverse and changing range of styles, with a few Monteith's New Zealand beers in the fridge. Food includes nods to past and present like cockles with lemongrass, and some decidedly untraditional options like taleggio and beetroot tart with celeriac puree. There's an old carved bar back and heritage ceiling cornices to admire, and the place is as family friendly as you'd expect given its location.

Visitor note. *The park opened in the 1840s as the capital's first such purpose-designed amenity, to improve the environment of the increasingly overcrowded and industrialised East End. Thus the 'People's Park' name now borrowed by the pub, though when built in 1865 it was named the Queens Hotel as it sat beside the park's Queen's Gate. It's been a brewpub before, as the Falcon and Firkin, the sixth in the pioneering Firkin chain (see Southwark ale p56), between 1986–95.*

Tap East   (21)

Brewpub, bar
The Great Eastern Market, Westfield
Stratford City E20 1ET   **T** (020) 8555 4467
www.tapeast.co.uk 🔲 Tap-East 🐦 TapEast
🕐 *Mo-Sa* 11.00-23.00, *Su* 12.00-22.00.
   Children welcome.
Cask beers 6 (Tap East, 3 unusual guests),
Other beers 10 keg, 100+ bottles
🍴 Cooked bar snacks, sausages, burgers **££**,
🪑 Tables on piazza, ♿
2 annual beer festivals, tap takeover

🚆🚇 Stratford International, Stratford 🚇🚇 Stratford
🚲 Link to NCN1, CS2, Olympic Park paths 🏃 Olympic Park paths

When Westfield opened its massive Stratford City mall adjoining the Olympic Park in September 2011, it invited the Utobeer (p61) team to create a brewpub at short notice for the Great Eastern Market, the requisite ghetto of specialists nestling amid the globalised brands. After a shaky start, this has matured into a very good beer venue indeed, in a space that's as comfy as it can be for an open-fronted shopping centre box. Besides in-house brews, often including mild and coffee stout, casks could come from Burning Sky, Dark Star, Roosters, Siren and Thornbridge, while the bottled list is particularly strong on London brewers like Partizan, Trappists, and German classics, with the occasional rarity from New Zealand or Italy. All the beers are also available to take away and there are gift packs too. Things step up a notch at the annual Open Brewhouse festival featuring exclusive collaborations with guest brewers.

TRY ALSO

One of the most spectacular Antic conversions is the **Leyton Technical** (265B High Road E10 5QH, **www.leytontechnical.com**) in part of Leyton's massive and fancifully neoclassical 1896 town hall and technical institute. Opened as a pop-up during the 2012 Olympics but now permanent, it stocks eight cask beers and a decent selection of bottles and kegs.

Tower Hamlets

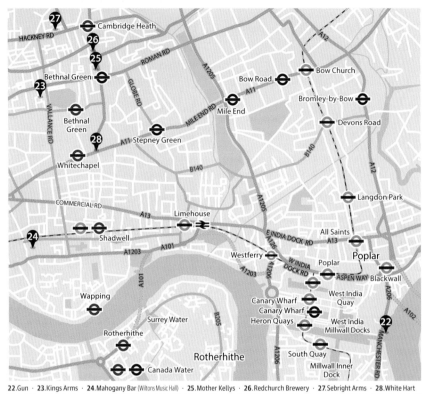

22.Gun · 23.Kings Arms · 24.Mahogany Bar (Wiltons Music Hall) · 25.Mother Kellys · 26.Redchurch Brewery · 27.Sebright Arms · 28.White Hart

Gun (22)

Gastropub (ETM)
27 Coldharbour E14 9NS
T (020) 7215 5222 🐦 thegundocklands
www.thegundocklands.com
🕐 *Mo-Sa* 11.00-24.00, *Su* 11.00-23.00.
   Children welcome.
Cask beers 4 (Adnams, Sambrook's, 2 sometimes
local guests), **Other beers** 4 keg, 14 bottles,
Also Wines, specialist spirits, cocktails
🍴 Cooked bar snacks, gourmet restaurant
menu with fish specialities **££-£££**,
🌲 Riverside and side terraces 🌿, ♿
4 annual beer festivals, seasonal events

⊖ Canary Wharf ⊖ Blackwall 🚆 Crossharbour (D6 Blackwall, D7 Canary Wharf) ♿ Link to CS3 🏃 Lea Valley Path

Among a pretty enclave of historic housing where
Admiral Nelson once lived, backing onto the river
a short walk from the economic powerhouse of
Canary Wharf, it's not surprising that this former
dockers' local is rather posher than it once was.
Smartly dressed waiters dish up oysters, lobster
and roast whole grouse at fine dining prices in the
front restaurant area, though drinkers at the bar can
order bar snacks cooked to the same standards for
less than you might expect. A sheltered riverside
terrace has breathtaking views across the Thames
to the O$_2$. Adnams and Sambrook's are always
on cask, with guests from people like Anarchy,
Butcombe, Burning Sky, Great Heck and Waen,
and a well-chosen choice of kegs, bottles and cans
including several Beavertown and Camden Town
options, Kernel, Late Knights, Tiny Rebel, West
and imports from Rogue and Hacker-Pschorr.

I called) and Uncommon. Food is upmarket snacking on gourmet Scotch eggs and artisanal cheese plates. The place has been tastefully and comfortably done out, with an original porch that once led to a separate off-licence, and unexplained lepidoptery displays on the walls.

Mahogany Bar (Wiltons Music Hall)

Bar   (24)
Graces Alley E1 8JB
T (020) 7702 2789   www.wiltons.org.uk
🆗 wiltonsmusichall 🐦 WiltonMusicHall
🕐 *Mo-Fr* 12.00-23.00, *Sa* 17.00-23.00, *Su* closed.
   Children welcome.
Cask beers 2 (Adnams), **Other beers** 4 keg,
12 bottles, **Also** Some specialist spirits
♿
Occasional tastings, acoustic music (Mo),
full theatre programme, building tours

🚇 Shadwell 🚇 Tower Hill 🚇 Tower Gateway
🚌 The Highway (100 Tower Gateway) 🚲 CS3, lnk to CS2, NCN13

Wiltons is one of the most remarkable survivors in London, a complete Victorian music hall attached to a row of 18th century houses on a picturesque alley off Cable Street. One of the houses was a pub since at least 1743, known as the Mahogany Bar from 1826, and 1850s landlord John Wilton built the music hall behind. Rescued from dereliction in 1997, it's being incrementally restored as a performance venue. Pleasingly, the original pub is once again open even to casual visitors as a theatre bar. Even more pleasingly, it stocks some great beers, with Adnams and occasionally Truman's on cask, decent German imports, and a largely London-based bottle range including Brixton, Hackney, Kernel and Meantime. The current look is cosy but distressed: the mahogany is long gone and the bar is actually recycled scenery from a past production, but the place still oozes history.

Kings Arms

Specialist, contemporary pub (Barworks) (23)
11A Buckfast Street E2 6EY **T** (020) 7729 2627
www.thekingsarmspub.com 🐦 kingsarmse2
🕐 *Su-We* 15.00-23.30, *Th* 12.00-23.30,
   Fr-Sa 12.00-24.00. Children until 21.00.
Cask beers 4 (Earls, unusual often local guests),
Other beers 13 keg, 70+ bottles, **Also** Specialist
spirits
🍴 Gourmet cheese and meat boards, snacks ££,
🪑 Tables on street, ♿
Meet the brewer, beer launches

🚇 Bethnal Green, Shoreditch High Street 🚇 Bethnal Green
🚌 Barnet Grove (8 388 Shoreditch High Street, Bethnal Green)

A rescued backstreet Bethnal Green pub that was once a spirits house, this reopened in December 2013 as a sister to the top notch Earl of Essex (p 43). Earl's beers are regularly on the handpumps, perhaps besides offerings from Magic Rock, Moor, Redemption, Rooster's, Wild or Windsor & Eton. Kegs stretch further afield to Boon lambics, Scandinavians like Beer Here and US imports like Westbrook, with a pressurised growler filler too. There's a fridge full of big bottles for sharing, with rare treats from Italy's Borgo and less commonly found Americans like the Bruery, Lost Abbey (the sublime Cuvée de Tomme was in stock when

Mahogany Bar (Wiltons Music Hall)

119

Mother Kellys Top 25 (25)

Specialist, bar, shop
251 Paradise Row E2 9LE
www.motherkellys.co.uk 🐦 mother_kellys
🕐 Mo-Th 12.00-23.00, Fr-Sa 12.00-24.00,
   Su 12.00-23.30. Children welcome.
Cask beers None, **Other beers** 19 keg, 250+ bottles
🍴 Gourmet cheese and meat boards, snacks
£-££, 🎍 Front terrace, ♿
*Beer launches, themed weekends,
murder mystery nights*

🚇 Bethnal Green 🚇 Bethnal Green

A genuine innovation for London, this combination bottle shop-bar from the people behind Simon the Tanner (p 60) opened in April 2014. Though occasional cask stillages may appear, the regular draught is all 'craft keg', with Brits like Brew by Numbers, Buxton, Kernel, Tiny Rebel and Wild plus US and Scandinavian imports. Bottles from the fridges filling one wall are sold to drink in or take away at a discount and could include London stars like Partizan and Weird Beard; Italians like Amarcord; Founders and Smuttynose from the US; and Belgians like 3 Fonteinen, Senne and Cazeau. They've even experimented with selling beer from big bottles by the glass. Drinking water is provided by default, still too rare a practice in UK bars. It's only a big brick railway arch with graffiti art and communal tables, but suddenly the name of the once-neglected alleyway on which it stands sounds more appropriate.

Visitor note *The bar is more-or-less opposite the Bethnal Green Museum of Childhood and next door to the Craft Cocktail Company.*

Mother Kellys

Redchurch Brewery (26)

Taproom
275 Poyser Street E2 9RL
☎ 07968 173097 🐦 redchurchbrewer
www.theredchurchbrewery.com
📘 The-Redchurch-Brewery
🕐 Th-Fr 18.00-023.00, Sa 12.00-23.00,
   Su-We closed. Children until 20.00.
Cask beers None, **Other beers** 9-10 keg,
8 bottles (Redchurch), **Also** Whisky, gin
🍴 Cheese and charcuterie plates **£**,
🎍 Standing on street, ♿
Occasional tastings, DJs (Fr-Sa), live music

🚇 Cambridge Heath 🚇 Bethnal Green 🚲 Link to
Regents Canal towpath 🚶 Link to Jubilee Greenway

Just behind Cambridge Heath Road, this is one of the most comfortable of the new breed of railway arch taprooms. It's a biggish space on a mezzanine above the brewhouse, where saggy sofas and the sounds of vintage vinyl from a small bar create a cosy effect under the bowed ceiling. All Redchurch's characterful core beers are on sale in bottles (to take away if required) and on keg, with a growing number of specials and one-offs: a delicious strong barrel-aged stout when I called, proving an excellent match for an artisanal cheese grazing plate.

Sebright Arms (27)

Traditional pub
34 Coate Street E2 9AG ☎ (020) 7729 0937
www.sebrightarms.co.uk 📘🐦 SebrightArms
🕐 Mo-Fr 17.00-24.00, Sa 12.00-24.00, Su 12.00-
   22.30. Children until 20.00.
Cask beers 4 (London), **Other beers** 4 keg, 40
bottles, **Also** 2 ciders, wines, some specialist
spirits
🍴 Gourmet burgers **££**, 🎍 Benches on alleyway
DJs (Fr-Sa), nightly live music in basement venue

🚇 Cambridge Heath, Bethnal Green, Hoxton 🚇 Bethnal
Green 🚆 Warner Place (numerous Hackney, Cambridge Heath,
Liverpool Street) 🚲 Link to Regents Canal towpath
🚶 Link to Jubilee Greenway

Don't be put off by the forbidding frontage on Coate Street – glance instead down Sebright Passage where stained glass windows and picnic benches form a prettier picture. Long known as a music venue, the Sebright was saved from demolition by a local campaign and reopened in November 2011. It's since established a reputation as a funky, friendly place with an attractive panelled interior and regular gigs from bands like the Vaccines and Maximo Park in a big cellar space where, it's rumoured, bare knuckle boxing once took place. Draught lines and half the bottles are devoted to London brewers like Brick, Crate, East London, Five Points, Hackney, Hammerton, Rocky Head and Weird Beard; bottles from Wild and US imports like Green Flash and Port may also pop-up. At the time of writing, acclaimed gourmet burger flippers Lucky Chip were in residence in the kitchen but this may change.

Visitor note. *Lovely Haggerston Park and Hackney City Farm are only a few steps away.*

White Hart (28)

Brewpub, gastropub
1 Mile End Road E1 4TP **T** (020) 7790 2894
www.thewhitehartbrewpub.com
🅵 🆈 TheWHBrewPub
🕐 *Mo-Th* 11.00-00.30, *Fr-Su* 09.00-00.30.
   Children until early evening.
Cask beers 6 (One Mile End, London guests),
Other beers 9 keg, 10+ bottles, **Also** 25 gins, wines, local soft drinks
🍴 Gastroish menu **££**, 🪑 Front terrace, ♿
Quiz (Th), live jazz (Su)

🚇 🚇 Whitechapel   🚲 CS2

The appearance of a smart brewpub at the main Whitechapel junction may have revived a local brewing tradition (see Yeast Enders p 122)

but is also a sure sign of the way the East End is changing, presenting a contrast not only to the Cockney gangland of legend but to the contemporary street scene of Bangladeshi shops and stalls (the East London Mosque, one of the largest in Europe, is just up the road). The comfortable interior has warm wood, restored Corinthian columns and a long mirrored bar back. Cask and keykeg beers in numerous styles emerge from the cellar under the One Mile End name, with occasional guests from suppliers like Redemption, and bottles from other London brewers. A comprehensive menu offers small plates (pigs in blankets, whitebait), cheese and Spanish charcuterie platters, and more unusual dishes like harissa roast rump of lamb or brie and spring veg tortilla.

TRY ALSO

Resembling a Dutch *bruin café*, the small and often-overlooked **Indo** (133 Whitechapel Road E1 1DT) by Whitechapel Tube is a rare survivor in an area where most pubs have closed, with three relatively unusual cask beers and a surprisingly wide bottle collection. Tucked away on elegant Tredegar Square at Mile End is Metro's well-refurbished gastropub the **Morgan Arms** (43 Morgan Street E3 5AA, www.morganarmsbow.com), with five often local cask beers, some decent bottles and locally renowned food. The best bet around the business centre of Canary Wharf is a reasonable Nicholson's pub, the **Henry Addington** (22 Mackenzie Walk E14 4PH, www.nicholsons.co.uk) overlooking Middle Dock.

White Hart

HOP HISTORIES **Yeast Enders**

ALONGSIDE Southwark, the industrial powerhouse of the East End was one of London's most important brewing centres, the home not only of Truman's (see From Black Eagle to Dark Star p90) but of several long-vanished businesses whose contributions to global beer culture still echo down the ages.

According to brewing historian Martyn Cornell, the mass production of porter was perfected in Lower East Smithfield, just downstream from the Tower. At the time of its closure in the 1930s, the Red Lion brewery, at the junction of what's now St Katherines Way and Burr Close, was said to be the oldest brewery in Britain and one of the oldest businesses in London. A brewhouse on the site had Flemish owners in 1492 and by the 17th century the Parsons family were in control. Humphrey Parsons, who took over in 1705, was later twice Lord Mayor of London, a knight, a Tory MP and, allegedly, a hunting companion of Louis XV of France. Parsons likely first had the idea of maturing porter in tall vats rather than casks, installing several 1,500-barrel (2,450 hl) vats in 1736. His investment paid off, and by 1748, seven years after his death, his brewery was the fourth biggest in London, its products toasted in verse by poet Oliver Goldsmith as "Parsons' black Champagne."

The brewery, later known as Hoare & Co, just escaped demolition during the construction of St Katherine Docks, and was finally taken over and closed by Charrington in 1934, with the new owners continuing to use its Toby jug logo. The Dickens Inn pub (Marble Quay E1W 1UH), actually an 18th century timber-framed warehouse which was relocated 70 m away from its original site when the docks were redeveloped in the 1970s, may be the only surviving remnant of this crucible of modern brewing.

George Hodgson began brewing further northeast in 1752, in what was probably an existing brewhouse on the western approach to Bow Bridge over the river Lee, then the boundary between Middlesex and Essex. Hodgson took advantage of good access by boat to the East India Company's moorings at Blackwall by offering preferential credit terms to the Company's captains. Among the products he shipped to India was October beer, a strongish, long-maturing, well-hopped pale ale of a type popular among the landed gentry, who often laid it down in wooden casks in their own cellars.

As it turned out, the temperature changes and movement of an often-rough four-month sea voyage accelerated this beer's maturation so it arrived in India in top condition. Hodgson's was not the only such exporter but by the end of the 18th century its beers had built an enviable reputation among expatriates and in 1802 it was shipping 4,000 barrels (6,550 hl) a year to the subcontinent.

In the 1820s, the brewery's management made a misjudged attempt to cut out the middleman by shipping the beer themselves, infuriating the Company so much it approached Allsopp, of Burton-upon-Trent in Staffordshire, to brew a similar beer in direct competition. Burton water turned out to be particularly suited to pale ale, and as the style's popularity grew in domestic and other markets in the 1830s, under the name India Pale Ale or East India Pale Ale, it became associated more with Burton than London.

The Bow Bridge brewery subsequently enjoyed mixed fortunes, though it survived until 1927 when, now known as Smith Garrett, it was taken over by Taylor Walker (see below). Council flats were built on the site in 1933, and still stand next to the modern replacement for historic Bow Bridge – the tangle of concrete known as the Bow Flyover.

Richard Ivory built the Albion brewery next door to his Whitechapel pub, the Blind Beggar, in 1808. In the early 20th century, the much-expanded firm, now known as Mann Crossman Paulin, developed a sweet bottled brown ale once regarded as something of an East End speciality. In 1958 Watney took over the brewery (see Roll out the red barrel p100), eventually closing it in 1979. Some of the buildings still stand, including the Blind Beggar itself, now notorious as the place where Ronnie Kray murdered George Cornell in 1966 (337 Whitechapel Road E1 1BU). Mann's Brown is still around though brewed some way outside London, at Banks's in Wolverhampton.

Other famous East End brewing names include Taylor Walker, now recycled to label an almost entirely unconnected pub chain, which began as Hare & Salmon in Stepney in 1730 and relocated to Limehouse in 1823. It was bought by Ind Coope and demolished in the mid-1960s. Charrington originated in Bethnal Green in the 1750s, transferring to the purpose-built Anchor

Charrington's brewery, Mile End, 1957

Brewery on Mile End Road in 1770. In 1963, it became a key component of the combine generally regarded as kicking off the 'merger mania' of the day, United Breweries, created by colourful Canadian entrepreneur Eddie Taylor. The Anchor ceased brewing in 1975 and most of the site became a retail park, but the offices were retained for a while by its successor, Big Seven brewer Bass Charrington, as its London HQ and still stand today (129 Mile End Road E1 4BF).

East London also played a role in more recent brewing history as home to arguably Britain's second-ever modern standalone microbrewery, and the first new brewing company launched in the capital since the beginning of the 20th century. In 1977, Patrick Fitzpatrick,

who'd first become interested in beer by reading about London's remaining family brewers, began supplementing his real ale distribution business by brewing his own. He found a key collaborator in ex-Whitbread veteran John Wilmot, who went on to help set up several other microbreweries. The operation was first based in an old sweet factory in Clapton, relocating to Bow in 1978 and the following year to a former veneer factory near Victoria Park. On the basis that breweries should sound like solid Victorian partnerships, it was initially named Godson Freeman & Wilmot. At its peak it produced 150 barrels (245 hl) a week and was even stocked by pioneering beer bar Café Gollem in Amsterdam.

Like many microbrewing

pioneers, Fitzpatrick faced an uphill struggle with unsuitable premises, quality control and financial issues and in 1982 production was suspended. It was briefly revived in 1982 under the name Godson Chudley following a merger with another struggling London startup, but closed for good two years later. The building is now an art and performance studio and gallery complex known as Chisenhale Art Place (64 Chisenhale Road E3 5QZ). A disillusioned Fitzpatrick broke ties with the beer world: "I was so devastated by what happened to the brewery," he told beer writers Jessica Boak and Ray Bailey in 2013. It's about time he was better acknowledged as a modern hero of East End brewing heritage.

123

Outer East London

Belgique Bistro (29)

Restaurant, bar
29 Cambridge Park E11 2PU
T (020) 8532 2255
www.belgique.co.uk/locations/wanstead
 BelgiqueUK BelgiqueLondon
 Mo-Sa 07.30-19.30, *Su* 07.30-17.00.
   Children very welcome.
Cask beers None, ***Other beers*** 16 bottles (Belgian),
Also Belgian spirits and liqueurs, tea and coffee
 Belgian menu, breakfasts, cheese,
charcuterie, patisserie **£-££**, Large front
terrace overlooking green,
Fortnightly jazz (Fr), functions

 Wanstead   Link to Roding Valley Greenway
 Link to Roding Valley Greenway

Leafy Wanstead is an unexpected
setting to stumble on this outpost of
Low Countries culture, the only licensed
outlet in a small Belgian-owned patisserie
chain. A decent range of bottled beer (if
a little weak in the lambic department)
doesn't just stick to the well distributed
likes of Leffe and Hoegaarden but runs
to Brugse Zot, Troubadour, Verhaeghe
Duchesse de Bourgogne and Trappists from
Orval, Rochefort and Westmalle. Though
you're welcome to call in just for a beer,
this is also a food venue with a slightly
transient feel to its comfortable orange
and slate interior and extensive outdoor
terrace. The comprehensive menu ranges
from breakfasts, brunches, lunches and
afternoon tea and cakes to sharing boards,
hotpots and (of course) mussels; Belgian
cheese, chocolate, patisserie, beers and
other specialities are sold to take away
from the shop section at the front.

Bell (30)

Contemporary pub
6 Forest Road E17 4NE
T (020) 8523 2277 **www.belle17.com**
 thebelle17 Bell_E17
 Su-Mo 12.00-23.00, *Tu-Th* 12.00-24.00, *Fr-Sa*
   12.00-0100. Children until 20.00.
Cask beers 8 (Timothy Taylor, unusual often local
guests), ***Other beers*** 1 keg, 8 bottles, ***Also*** 1 cider
 Interesting enhanced pub grub menu **£-££**,
 Large beer garden,
*Quiz (Tu), bluegrass (We), monthly live jazz (Su), DJs,
pinball, board games*

  Walthamstow Central   Bell Corner (numerous
Walthamstow Central)

This pub is a true landmark as the busy crossroads on which it stands has long been known
as Bell Corner. The current pub is a roomy
building in gabled red brick, rebuilt for Mann's
early in the 20th century and refurbished and
reopened in November 2012, scattering red
plush sofas among splendid old fireplaces and
surviving patches of panelling. Guest casks,
sourced through Enterprise's direct delivery
scheme, could come from London brewers

Bell

Bell

like ELB, Five Points, Hackney, Redemption or Wildcard, and often include darker styles. A few bottles of interest take in the better known US craft brewers and German lager. A changing and imaginative menu could include spiced aubergine dal, maple syrup gravlax or pork and pineapple chilli. The pub has become such a valued community asset that local estate agents use it as an excuse to bump up house prices.

Chequers (31)

Contemporary pub (Camden)
145 High Street E17 7BX
T (020) 8503 6401
www.chequerse17.com   🖪 🐦 chequerse17
🕓 *Mo-Th* 17.00-23.00, *Fr* 17.00-24.00, *Sa* 12.00-24.00, *Su* 12.00-22.30. Children until 19.00.
Cask beers 6 (unusual often local guests),
Other beers 3 keg, 15+ bottles, *Also* 1 cider
🍴 Burgers, enhanced pub grub **££**,
🪑 Beer garden, ♿
DJs (Fr-Sa), seasonal events, film nights, major big screen sport, table football

➤ Walthamstow Queens Road, Walthamstow Central
➤ Walthamstow Central

This site right on historic and bustling Walthamstow Market has hosted a pub since at least 1757, though the current building with its unusual mix of single and multistorey sections looks late Victorian. Closed in 2012 following a troubled period, it was reopened by Antic in March 2013, who uncovered the old Meux brewery branding on the façade. Sold on to Camden Bars a few months later, it now has a firm following among E17's influx of young(ish) professionals, their families and dogs. Cask beers usually include Londoners like Five Points, Hackney, Late

Knights or Wild Card or others from brewers like Saltaire or Ticketybrew. A Five Points keg beer is always on, alongside imported Lagunitas, while Redhook, Westmalle and Whistable add class to the fridges. Food is posh pub grub: steaks, burgers, beer battered haddock and chips, salads or barbecued halloumi and vegetable skewers.

Pub trivia *In 1967 the Kray twins allegedly unwound over a drink here after murdering Jack 'The Hat' McVitie.*

Cricketers (32)

Traditional pub (McMullen)
299 High Road, Woodford Green IG8 9HQ
T (020) 8504 2734
www.mcmullens.co.uk/cricketerswoodford
🖪 The-Cricketers-Woodford
🕓 *Mo-Sa* 11.00-23.00, *Fr-Sa* 11.00-24.00, *Su* 12.00-22.30. Children lunchtimes only if dining, no pushchairs.
Cask beers 3 (McMullen), *Other beers* 3 bottles
🍴 Pub grub, baguettes at lunchtimes only **£**,
🪑 Benches in side yard, ♿
Magic (Mo), quiz (Su), occasional live music, darts, golf society

➤ Woodford, South Woodford   🚌 Woodford Cricketers (179 W13 South Woodford) 🥾 Link to Epping Forest Centenary Walk

Although refurbished as recently as 2009, this roadside 'brewers' Tudor' pub in villagey surroundings close to a swathe of Epping Forest happily retains the sort of traditional décor that would have been recognised by pubgoers in the 1950s. A plain public bar with lino floor and dartboard and a posher carpeted saloon help preserve the ambience of a community local, alongside decently priced lunch offerings like steak and ale pie and veggie lasagne, a popular quiz and a golf society. It's my top recommendation in London for sampling McMullen beers from Hertford, with well-kept AK, Cask Ale and Country Bitter on the handpumps and old-fashioned bottled beers like Stronghart.

Pub trivia *A corner of the saloon bar commemorates Winston Churchill, who among many other things was MP for Woodford from 1945 until he retired from politics in 1964. A little to the north, an imposing statue of Churchill commands the open space of Woodford Green.*

King William IV (33)

Brewpub, traditional pub (Brodie's)
816 High Road E10 6AE **T** (020) 8556 2460
www.williamthefourth.net

🕔 *Su-Th* 11.00-24.00, *Fr-Sa* 11.00-01.00.
Children until 21.00.
Cask beers 7–8 (Brodies, occasional guests),
Other beers 8 keg, 6+ bottles (Brodies)
🍴 Pub grub, pizzas £, 🪑 Tables on street,
rear patio
*Beer festivals, live music/karaoke (Sa), monthly jazz
(Th), big screen sport, darts, bar billiards*

🚆 Stratford 🚇 Leyton Midland Road, Stratford Leyton
🚇 Stratford 🚌 Leyton Green (69, 97 Leyton, Walthamstow
Central; 257 Stratford)

This big high street pub, reconstructed in 1891,
is most notable today as the home of the
Brodie's brewery (p282): the brewhouse is in an
old stables across the back yard though there's
now a plan to find a bigger location for it. The
interior is liberally dotted with old musical
instruments, copper kitchen equipment and
other curiosities, with ample space in both a
banquette-lined front bar and a more relaxing
back room with an open fire. Most of the handpumps are only used for festivals, though there
are always several Brodie's beers from cask
and keykeg at keen prices, including unusual
styles. Even more own brands are available
bottle conditioned. Guests from other London
brewers and interlopers like Hop Craft and
Milestone also pop up. Basic food includes
pizzas, burgers, homemade lasagnes and
casseroles. Good value B&B rooms are sometimes occupied by visiting beer tourists.

King William IV

Nags Head

Nags Head (34)

Contemporary pub
9 Orford Road E17 9LP
T (020) 8520 9709 🐦 Thenagshead_E17
www.thenagsheade17.com
📘 The-Nags-Head-Pub-Walthamstow-village
🕔 *Mo-Sa* 12.00-23.00, *Su* 12.00-22.30.
Children in outside areas until 19.30 only.
Cask beers 8 (St Austell, Timothy Taylor, 6 often
local guests), **Other beers** 3 keg, 25+ bottles,
Also Wines, bottled cider, whiskies
🍴 Italian/mediterranean menu **££**,
🪑 Large rear garden, benches at front 🐾
*Beer festivals, life drawing (Mo), pilates (Tu-We), jazz (Su),
music quiz, fortnightly bring your own vinyl, monthly
wine tastings, book exchange, board games, functions*

🚇 🚇 Walthamstow Central 🚌 Beulah Road (W12
Walthamstow Central)

Just east of busy Hoe Street, and seemingly a
world away, is the historic centre of
Walthamstow Village, where the 15th-century
half-timbered Ancient House, several old
cottages and a pretty church form a picturesque cluster offset by a Victorian post box.
Nearby is this charming pub, with a distinctive
but tasteful and homely interior dating from a
2002 rescue by current landlady Flossie, who
famously flushed out the dodgier clientele by
playing jazz and putting down tablecloths.
Aside from Tribute and Landlord, the beer is
sourced from London and Essex through the
Enterprise direct delivery scheme: Crate, East
London and Redemption are regular visitors,
and Mighty Oak Oscar Wilde is often featured
alongside other dark choices. Beavertown,
Meantime, Whitstable and various Belgian
fruit beers lurk in the fridges. A busy diary of
events and classes underlines the community
spirit, under the watchful eye of two self-
satisfied pub cats.

Red Lion Top25   (35)

Specialist, contemporary pub (Antic)
640 High Road E11 3AA **T** (020) 8988 2929
www.theredlionleytonstone.com
🅵 leytonstonelion   🐦 red_lion_e11
🕐 *Su-We* 12.00-23.00, *Th* 12.00-24.00, *Fr-Sa* 12.00-
   02.00. Children very welcome until 21.00.
Cask beers 10 (unusual guests), **Other beers** 7 keg,
60 bottles, **Also** 2 ciders, 20+ wines
🍴 Short imaginative pub grub/gastro menu,
summer barbecues **££**, 🪑 Sheltered rear
garden, tables on street 🐾, ♿
DJs (Fr-Sa), acoustic music (Su), monthly open mic,
deckchair cinema, clothes exchange, seasonal
events, art exhibitions

🚇 Leytonstone   🚶 Link to Epping Forest Centenary Walk

This big street-corner pub reopened in June
2011 with the biggest beer range in the Antic
chain, served amid standard lamps and peel-
ing iron pillars ("it's meant to look that way,"
they once told me). The handpumps feature
locals like Beavertown, Redemption or
Sambrook's, with an effort made to hunt out
happening newcomers from elsewhere. A
wide UK-biased bottle range includes

Londoners like Brew by Numbers, Kernel and
Partizan besides Oakham, Siren, Thornbridge
or Wild; a few US brewers like Elysian and
Odell creep in and the 'craft kegs' are equally
eclectic. Imaginative food from a shortish
menu has a seaside slant – whole brown crab,
barbecued salmon – alongside steaks and
veggie choices, a very English dessert list, and
pies and Scotch eggs on the bar. A big back
garden and outhouse are decorated with
giant grafitti art, and canine friendliness extends to dog bowls and water.

Wanstead Tap Top25   (36)

Specialist, bar, shop
352 Winchelsea Road E7 0AQ
T 07976 787419   🐦 thewansteadtap
www.thewansteadtap.co.uk
🕐 *MoTuWe&Sa* 10.00-18.00, *Th* 10.00-22.00,
   Fr 10.00-23.00, *Su* 10.00-16.00.
   Children very welcome until 19.30.
Cask beers 1 (unusual guest),
Other beers 1 guest keg, 100+ bottles,
Also Local soft drinks, bottled cider
🍴 Pies, quiches and soup *(Fr-Sa)*; other times
cakes and snacks only **£**, ♿
Tastings, films, fortnightly supper club,
book launches, comedy nights, live music

🚆 Forest Gate 🚇 Wanstead Park 🚌 Sidney Road/
Pevensey Road (58 308 Wanstead Park, Forest Gate)
🚶 Link to Epping Forest Centenary Walk

One of London's new breed of bottle shop-bars
opened in March 2014 in the unlikely location of
a railway arch a few steps from Wanstead Flats,
in a dead end street otherwise populated by
car repairers. Over half the studiedly artisanal
bottle range is from London breweries like
Beavertown, Brixton, Crate, ELB, Hackney,
Pressure Drop or Wild Card; the rest are from
other young and interesting UK producers like
Bad Seed, Hardknott, Ticketybrew or Wild,
with guest casks and kegs from similar suppliers.
"If it pops up in the supermarket, we take it off
the shelves" says owner Dan, a reliable source
of advice for undecided customers. The bar is
proud to be cyclist-, walker- and dog-friendly,
and it's about as cosy as a railway arch can be,
offering not only great beer but a children's play
area, big screen films and a regular supper club.

Red Lion

Wanstead Tap

Wild Card Brewery (37)

Taproom
7 Ravenswood Industrial Estate,
Shernhall Street E17 9HQ
T 0798 240 2650   ⓕ ⓨ wildcardbrewery
www.wildcardbrewery.co.uk
🕐 Fr 17.00-23.30, Sa 10.00-23.30, Su 10.00-22.00,
Mo-Th closed. Children welcome.
Cask beers 6 (Wild Card, guests),
Other beers 20 bottles (mainly London)
🍴 Food cart **£**, 🪑 Picnic tables at front.
Beer festivals, live music, seasonal events

🚆 Walthamstow Central, Leytonstone
🚇 Wood Street   🚇 Walthamstow Central
🚌 Addison Road (W16 Walthamstow Central, Leytonstone)

This yardful of undistinguished breezeblock
sheds behind Walthamstow Village is home
to the late Chris Bracey's neon art specialist
God's Own Junkyard, a purveyor of liqueurs
flavoured with locally grown fruit called

Wild Card Brewery

Mother's Ruin, and E17's own Wild Card
Brewery, all welcoming a mix of locals
and obsessives at weekends. Wild Card
has a few tables in the brewhouse
itself and picnic benches outside in
good weather. The brewery's three
core beers and current specials are
pulled from handpump at a petite bar,
alongside occasional London guests.
More own brews are in the fridge, with well-
chosen local alternatives like Five Points,
Partizan and Strawman, plus wines and soft
drinks for those who remain unconvinced.

Woodford Wine Room (38)

Shop
17 Mill Lane, Woodford Green IG8 0UN
T (020) 8504 2440
www.woodfordwineroom.co.uk
ⓕ Woodford-Wine-Room
🕐 We-Th 14.00-19.30, Fr 12.00-20.00,
Sa 10.00-19.30, Su-Tu closed.
Cask beers None, ***Other beers*** 30+ bottles
(London, Italian), ***Also*** Unusual Italian wines
🪑 Small terrace at front overlooking green
Regular tastings

🚇 Woodford   🚌 Mill Lane (275 Woodford)
🏃 Link to Epping Forest Centenary Walk

In a picturesque cottage overlooking a dappled
green in deepest Woodford, this is, as its name
suggests, mainly a wine retailer and importer,
specialising in small Italian vineyards. But owner

Alessandro is equally enthusiastic about Italian beer. He's the UK importer of Birrone, from Vicenza, and stocks several other reliable names like Amiata. Alongside these are well chosen bottles from London brewers including locals East London and Wild Card as well as Brew by Numbers and Kernel. The relatively limited selection wouldn't otherwise merit a listing here, but the rarity and quality of the products and the tender loving care on display make this little shop worth seeking out.

TRY ALSO

Still going strong in Walthamstow is the very welcoming **Olde Rose and Crown** (53 Hoe Street E17 4SA, yeolderoseandcrowntheatrepub.

co.uk), with six handpumps that rotate through direct delivery-sourced guests, including locals, and a busy programme of theatre and events. Out in the residential area of Higham Hill, the **Warrant Officer** (318 Higham Hill Road E17 5RG, www.the-wo.co.uk) is a decent community pub with five cask beers that briefly hosted Wild Card and Solvay Society breweries in its cellar and may yet become a brewpub a third time. To the south, the **Drum** (557–559 Lea Bridge Road E10 7EQ, www.jdwetherspoon. co.uk) is a rare small Wetherspoon and was actually one of the first in the chain. Customers help choose a well-kept guest beer selection, making this worth a look if visiting the King William IV (p126) nearby.

LONDON DRINKERS **Christine Cryne**

Long-standing CAMRA campaigner Christine was the first woman to organise the Great British Beer Festival and has also organised the smaller London Drinker festival. An expert taster, she's worked hard to raise awareness of beer flavour and quality among CAMRA's membership, running tasting training and chairing the London Tasting Panel. The latter provides notes for the *Good Beer Guide* and selects entrants for the Champion Beer of Britain competition.

How do you rate London as a beer city, on a world scale?
In the top ten now. There are few cities that could boast over 70 breweries and London gets beer from all over Britain.

What's the single most exciting thing about beer in London at the moment?
Breweries producing very good bottled beer, and more beer in

delis and restaurants. At last you might get a decent beer when you eat.

What single thing would make things even better?
Better distribution. Even now drinkers often find it hard to get beer from a smaller London brewer. The SIBA Direct Delivery Scheme has helped but it's still a drop in the ocean.

What are your top London beers right now?
Brick Blenheim Black, Portobello Porter (although I think it's a stout!), and Sambrook's Lavender Pale. I could have chosen all porters, there are so many good ones now.

What's your top great beer night out?
Everyone knows about places like Crate (p114), the Old Fountain (p88) and the Wenlock (p44), which all are great pubs, but I'd go for the Snooty Fox (p146), which deserves to be better-known.

Who's your London beer hero?
So many people are doing great things but I think it's got to be John Keeling, one of the founders of the London Brewers Alliance as well as a great brewer, who took over from the great Reg Drury at Fuller's.

Who will we be hearing a lot more from in future?
Hammerton in Islington. They have a dream to go places.

Which are your other top beer cities?
Antwerp has as good a range as Brussels and is a bit cheaper, Copenhagen has a growing scene and a top beer festival, Manchester has great pubs with prices that make Londoners envious, but keep an eye too on Dublin, where the beer scene is blossoming.

HOP HISTORIES **Beyond the marshes**

The swathe of London east of the marshy Lee Valley has its own brewing history. Before it was dissolved by Henry VIII in 1538, Stratford Langthorne Abbey owed much of its prosperity to controlling the regional trade in one of the key ingredients of beer. Grain from Essex and Hertfordshire was shipped down the Lee to be milled at Stratford, mainly for baking but also for brewing, including in the abbey's own brewhouse. It was monks seeking power for watermills who first divided the watercourse into the multiple strands of the Bow Back Rivers that are now a much-admired landscape feature of the Queen Elizabeth Olympic Park. To the south, several historic 18th and 19th century mill buildings survive next to the busy film and TV studio at the aptly named Three Mills – though these mainly served gin distilleries rather than breweries.

Romford was a rural Essex market town in 1708 when George Cardon started brewing at the Star Inn. In 1799 the business was bought by Edward Ind in partnership with John Grosvenor, who later sold his share to John Smith. It was Smith's son Henry who, along with his brother-in-law, head brewer John Turner, quit the firm in 1845 to take over the Griffin brewery in Chiswick, creating Fuller Smith & Turner (see p289). In 1856, like several other London breweries, Ind Coope, as it was now known, created a Burton-upon-Trent subsidiary, and in 1934 merged with Allsopp, the brewery responsible for bringing India Pale Ale to Burton in direct

Ind Coope brewery, Romford, 1889

competition with Hodgson's in Bow (see Yeast Enders p122).

In 1961 Ind Coope became the heart of one of the Big Seven breweries by merging with Tetley Walker in Leeds and Ansells in Birmingham to create what was then the biggest drinks company in Europe, Allied Breweries. By now Burton was the main plant but Romford continued in use until 1993. Most of the brewery has been demolished and the site rebuilt as a shopping centre, but a chimney and façades are preserved and one of the buildings is now the Havering Museum (19 High Street RM1 1JU). Displays about the brewery will interest heritage buffs but good beer options nearby are thin on the ground: you're probably best off at the Moon and Stars, a Wetherspoon near the station (103 South Street RM1 1NX). The rest of Ind Coope ended up in the hands of Carlsberg in 1997, and beers bearing the brand are occasionally commissioned from other brewers.

Tolly was a well-known brewing name in East Anglia into the early 21st century, but you may be puzzled why some London pubs are also still nicknamed 'Tollys', including the Richard I in Greenwich (p173). The answer lies in E17, where William Hawes opened the Walthamstow Brewery in St James's Street in 1859. In 1920 it was bought by Tollemache in Ipswich, later Tolly Cobbold, as a foothold in the London market. But Tolly's regional and national ambitions weren't realised: in 1972 the brewery was closed and production centred in Ipswich. Tolly's subsequent history was chequered: the London pubs were eventually sold to other brewers and, after passing through several different hands, the Ipswich parent, now reduced to microbrewery status, finally closed in 2003. The brand is now owned by Greene King and occasionally resurrected for seasonals. All trace of the Walthamstow brewery has vanished except the tap, which is still recognisable on Markhouse Road, though converted to flats in 2009.

NORTH
LONDON

NORTH LONDON

North London in this book includes all the N and NW postcodes outside the central area, apart from a couple of places in Kensal Green and Queens Park which are further west than some of the W postcodes and can be found under Inner West London (p 205).

Camden means not just Camden Town but the Borough of Camden, except for those bits in the central area such as Bloomsbury and parts of Holborn and Covent Garden. Major centres like Hampstead and Camden itself have several good beer outlets, but there's a surprisingly rich cluster in the western part of Kentish Town.

Outlets in the southern part of Islington around Angel and Clerkenwell are listed under Central London but the rest of the borough, including Archway, Barnsbury, Canonbury and Holloway, plus an adjoining bit of Hackney with an N postcode, is here under **Islington to Stoke Newington**. Numerous fine new places to drink have opened in the neighbourhood recently and more are to be expected.

Outer North London covers the rest, up to the Hertfordshire boundary, including the taproom of one of the capital's best new breweries and several notable brewpubs.

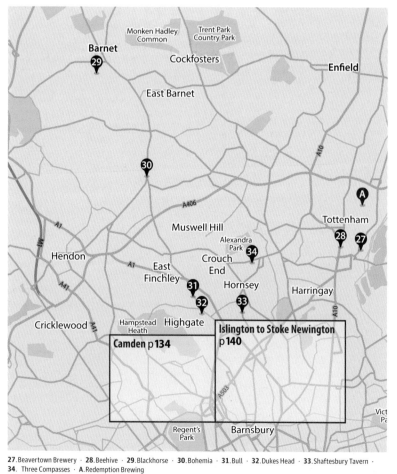

27. Beavertown Brewery · 28. Beehive · 29. Blackhorse · 30. Bohemia · 31. Bull · 32. Dukes Head · 33. Shaftesbury Tavern · 34. Three Compasses · A. Redemption Brewing

Camden

Belgo Noord (1)

Restaurant, bar
72 Chalk Farm Road NW1 8AN
T (020) 7267 0718
www.belgo-restaurants.co.uk ☐ ☑ belgobill
🕘 *Mo-Sa* 12.00-23.00, *Su* 12.00-22.30.
　Children very welcome.
Cask beers None, *Other beers* 4 keg, 50+ bottles
(mainly Belgian), *Also* Genever
🍴 Belgian/British menu ££, ⛱ Small front
terrace

☻ Chalk Farm　🚋 Camden Lock　🚲 Link to Regents
Canal towpath　🚶 Link to Jubilee Greenway

The original Belgo, opened in 1992, got a new
lease of life in 2012 when its street level bar was
refurbished to create a more substantial open
frontage and started to be staffed regularly
rather than just at weekends. A pleasant interior
has wood panelling painted with beer brands,
while outdoor tables contribute to the Chalk
Farm ambience. Sadly the beer list hasn't really
moved with the times, relying heavily on bigger
and multinational-owned breweries and
sweetened fruit beers, so don't hope for rarities
from innovative newcomers. Nonetheless
there are plenty of traditional high scorers like
Boon Mariage Parfait, Bush, Duchesse de

Bourgogne, Saison Dupont, Grottenbier and
beers from five Trappists. The mussels-and-
pub-grub menu is served upstairs as well as in
the adjoining refectory-styled cellar restaurant.

Black Heart (2)

Bar (Barworks)
3 Greenland Place NW1 0AP
T (020) 7428 9730　www.ourblackheart.com
☐ blackheartcamden　☑ ourblackheart
🕘 *Mo-Tu* 12.00-23.30, *We-Th* 12.00-24.00,
　Fr-Sa 12.00-02.00, *Su* 12.00-23.00.
Cask beers 1-2 (often unusual guests), *Other beers*
9 keg, 60 bottles, *Also* Bourbons, cocktails
🍴 Hot meat/veggie sandwiches and sides
£-££, ⛱ Standing on street
Meet the brewer/tap takeover, DJs most nights,
seasonal events, pool, live music/comedy in
adjoining venue

☻ Camden Road　☻ Camden Town　🚋 Camden Lock
🚲 Link to Regents Canal towpath　🚶 Link to Jubilee Greenway

In an old warehouse in an alley near Camden
Town Tube, the catholic tat-bedecked Black
Heart has got both beerier and grungier, and
is now one of the closest places in London to
a US craft beer dive bar, complete with a small
forest of oversized branded tap handles. Gigs
in the upstairs venue bring in a partying crowd
spotted with black-clad Camden types, but
the beer range is an attraction in its own right.
Casks could come from East London, Elgood's,
Fyne, Pope's or Tiny Rebel while bottles run
to top Londoners, a spectrum of US imports
from easygoing pale ales to extreme beers in
big bottles from Rogue and Southern Tier; and
some rare Belgians like Rodenbach Vintage
and St Feuillien Saison. It's not made easier to
spot on a dark night by the big black heart that
serves as a pub sign, but it's worth the effort.

1.Belgo Noord · 2.Black Heart · 3.BrewDog Camden · 4.Bull and Last · 5.Camden Town Brewery · 6.Duke of Hamilton ·
7.Grafton · 8.Horseshoe · 9.One Sixty · 10.Pineapple · 11.Southampton Arms · 12.Tapping the Admiral

BrewDog Camden (3)

Specialist, bar
113 Bayham Street NW1 0AG
T (020) 7284 0453 **www.brewdog.com/bars**
BrewDog-Bar-Camden
BrewDogCamden
Mo-Th 12.00-23.30, Fr-Sa 12.00-24.00, Su 12.00-22.30. Children welcome until 2000.
Cask beers None, **Other beers** 19 keg, 90+ bottles
Gourmet burgers, bar snacks **£-££**
*Homebrew demos, beer dinners, meet the brewer/
tap takeover, board games, functions*

Camden Road · Camden Town · Camden Lock
Link to Regents Canal towpath · Link to Jubilee Greenway

In December 2011 BrewDog's always provocative founders rolled through Camden Town in
a tank to open the Scottish brewery's fourth
pub, and first in London, in the former Laurel
Tree. It's since been joined by several more,
but remains typically lively and evangelical,
stylishly done out with walls clad in gym-style
parquet tiles and bar top and drinking shelves
made of slabs of grey stone in a suggestion of
'granite' Aberdeen. There's the usual line-up
of BrewDog core beers and rare, often strong
specials, joined by Londoners from Beavertown,
Brew by Numbers, Kernel and Pressure Drop,
lots of Mikkeller bottles and others from
brewers like Anchor, Québec's Dieu du Ciel, Evil
Twin, Magic Rock, Stone and Weihenstephaner,
though no cask. Food includes rather decent
gourmet burgers and dogs, US-style tots and
fried green tomatoes, and intriguing beer sorbets
co-created with artisanal gelateria Gelupo.

Bull and Last (4)

Gastropub
168 Highgate Road NW5 1QS
T (020) 7267 3641
www.thebullandlast.co.uk 🐦 thebullandlast
🕐 *Mo-Th* 12.00-23.00, *Fr-Sa* 09.00-24.00,
    Su 09.00-22.30. Children welcome.
Cask beers 4 (unusual often local guests),
Other beers 4 keg, 6 bottles, **Also** 1 cider, wines,
gin, whisky
🍴 Daily changing gastro menu **££-£££**,
🍺 Benches on street
Quiz (Su)

🚆 ⭕ Kentish Town   ⭕ Gospel Oak   🚌 William Ellis
School (214 C2 Kentish Town)   🚲 Link to Hampstead Heath
paths   🚶 Link to Belsize Walk, Hampstead Heath paths

A staff member once explained to me why this
celebrated gastropub decided to evolve its
beer range: "We're proud of the care we put
into our food and wine, and we realised our
beer simply wasn't standing up." In truth there's
a little way to go to match the impressive fine
wine list, but it's great to see local beers like
East London and Redemption on cask, including darker options, a regular keykeg house
pale made in collaboration with Five Points,
and some little jewels among the bottles like
Weird Beard and Wiper & True. You're welcome
to call in for a pint with some seating around
the bar kept unreserved, but food is the main
focus, with dishes like roast venison, ricotta
and black cabbage ravioli, aged *côte de bœuf*
and fine cheese. Much is home made, even
the ice cream and oatcakes, and advanced
booking is advisable.

Camden Town Brewery (5)

Taproom
55 Wilkin Street Mews NW5 3NN
T (020) 7485 1671
www.camdentownbrewery.com/brewery-bar
📘🐦 CamdenBrewery
🕐 *Tu-We* 12.00-18.00, *Th-Sa* 12.00-23.00,
    Su-Mo closed. Children until early evening.
Cask beers None, **Other beers** 15 keg, 10+ bottles
(mainly Camden Town)
🍴 Rotating pop-up street food **£**,
🍺 Front terrace
*Beer festivals, meet the brewer, tastings,
brewery tours, seasonal events, functions*

🚆 ⭕ Kentish Town   ⭕ Kentish Town West

As befits one of London's
biggest and most ambi-
tious new breweries,
Camden Town boasts one
of its best appointed taprooms, added in April 2012
in one of the brewery's
arches under Kentish Town
West Overground. There's
a comprehensive range of
the core beers in keg and
bottle, alongside season-
als, specials and rarities
such as the Versus series
and contributions from US
soulmates like Ska, sold to
drink in and take away, with
oxygen-free growler fills. It's
an attractive space with a

glass front looking out onto a courtyard
where rotating pop-up food providers ply
their trade, and a park beyond, perfectly
aligned to catch the sun on fine afternoons.

Duke of Hamilton (6)

Traditional pub
23 New End NW3 1JD **T** (020) 7794 0258
www.thedukeofhamilton.com
🐦 dukeofhamilton
🕐 Daily 12.00-23.30. Children welcome.
Cask beers 6 (Dark Star, Fuller's, Sharp's,
2 unusual sometimes local guests),
Other beers 1 keg, 8 bottles
🍽 Small front terrace, rear beer garden
*Darts, functions, live music, comedy, theatre in
downstairs venue*

🚇 Hampstead Heath 🚇 Hampstead
🚶 Link to Hampstead Heath paths

A veteran real ale stalwart with a lengthy roll
call of arty celebrity regulars, including Oliver
Reed who often overindulged here, the Duke
should have featured in the last edition of this
book but its future was then uncertain.
Happily new owners have retained it as that
rarity in modern Hampstead, a proper pub,
traditionally furnished and with unusual
stained glass and tiles advertising long obsolete
cleaning products. It's curiously sited on a
raised platform which, given its popularity
with actors and the proximity of the New End
Theatre, might remind you of a stage, and has
its own performance venue in the cellar.
London Pride, HSB, Hophead and Doom Bar
are always on, with guests sometimes from
London brewers or Adnams, and Schneider
Weisse, McChouffe and Jever Pils might be
spotted in a small but intriguing range of
bottled beers.

Duke of Hamilton

Grafton (7)

Contemporary pub
20 Prince of Wales Road NW5 3LG
T (020) 7482 4466   🅕 🐦 thegraftonnw5
www.thegraftonnw5.co.uk
🕐 Mo-Th 12.00-23.00, Fr 12.00-24.00,
 Sa 10.00-24.00, Su 10.00-22.30.
 Children very welcome until 19.00.
Cask beers 8 (Hogs Back, Timothy Taylor, 6
usually local guests), **Other beers** 4 keg, 8 bottles
🍽 Enhanced pub grub/street food £-££,
🍽 Tables on street
*Beer festival, meet the brewer, quiz (Tu), piano
singalong (Su), clothing swap, seasonal events,
occasional DJ, live music, theatre, craft events,
board games, functions*

🚆🚇 Kentish Town 🚇 Kentish Town West

Since this handsome Victorian pub close to
the impressively-restored St Pancras Baths reopened in September 2012, it's made good use
of Enterprise's direct delivery scheme to source
mainly local beers, including Brodies, By the
Horns, East London, Hackney, Portobello,
Redemption, Sambrook's, Truman's, Twickenham, and Windsor & Eton. Even more local is
Camden Town, just a few steps away, sold in
keg and bottle; other bottle suppliers of note
are Beavertown, Founders and Flying Dog.
Originally food was provided by pop-ups and
the permanent kitchen honours that legacy
by combining street food with pub grub,
sometimes employing local ingredients in
dishes like reuben sandwiches, neck of lamb
stew and buttermilk chicken pieces. A fine first
floor roof terrace adds interest to this well-
refurbished contemporary twist on a
community boozer.

Horseshoe (8)

Gastropub (Camden Town)
28 Heath Street NW3 6TE
T (020) 7431 6206   🐦 LuckyHampstead
www.thehorseshoehampstead.com
🅕 TheHorseshoeHampstead
🕐 Mo-Th 10.00-23.00, Fr-Sa 10.00-24.00,
 Su 10.00-22.30. Children welcome.
Cask beers 3 (unusual sometimes local guests),
Other beers 8 keg (Camden Town, 1 guest),
20 bottles, **Also** Wines
🍽 Gastro menu ££, 🍽 Benches on street
Theatre upstairs

✈ Hampstead Heath   ✈ Hampstead   ✚ Link to LCN+50 and Hampstead Heath cycle routes   🏃 Belsize Walk, Hampstead Heath footpaths

Camden Town Brewery was founded in the cellar of this bright and cheerful Hampstead favourite and even though it's long since moved to much bigger premises (p 284), the pub remains its showcase. Camden rarely brews cask beers but when it does they pop up here, sharing the handpumps with brewers like Burning Sky, Crate or Windsor & Eton. Besides the owners' beers, bottled choices include Londoners like Beavertown, Brew by Numbers and Pressure Drop, with imports from reliable names like Augustiner, Goose Island, Orval and Schneider. It's also much admired by its generally youngish clientele for its short but stylish menu, which might include sole with samphire and capers, pearl barley with summer veg or seared sirloin steak salad, with good value lunch deals.

Visitor note. The pub was built in the 1880s originally as the Three Horseshoes and was a Wetherspoon for a time before its 2006 refurbishment. The independently owned Pentameters theatre above dates from the heady days of 1968, when it was well known for improvised poetry and jazz events. More recently, your author is among the luminaries to have trodden its boards.

One Sixty   (9)

Bar, restaurant
291 West End Lane NW6 1RD
T (020) 7794 9786   www.one-sixty.co.uk
🅕 🐦 onesixtylondon
🕑 *Mo-Th* 17.00-23.00, *Fr* 17.00-24.00, *Sa* 10.00-24.00, *Su* 10.00-22.30. Children until 19.30, later in restaurant.
Cask beers None, **Other beers** 13 keg, 55 bottles, **Also** Specialist spirits, wines
🍴 US-style barbecue and smokehouse food
££-£££, ⅂ Sheltered front terrace, ♿
Occasional DJs, big screen rugby (Sa)

⇌ ✈ ✈ West Hampstead

Easy to miss among the shops and eateries of West End Lane, this laid-back bar and diner, opened in March 2014, turns out to be less food-led than it first might appear. There's a big bar area fronted by an alluring

sheltered terrace, with lighthearted beer-themed murals and a small restaurant area with canteen-style seating. US-style smoked stuff dominates a menu that includes smoked ribs and ox cheek, pulled pork, burgers, mac and cheese, one pound lobster rolls and indulgent desserts like jarfuls of banoffee. The closest thing to cask is Meantime unfiltered tank beer, with several other Meantime offerings, Beavertown and Delirium Tremens on tap. A large bottled selection has lots from London (Five Points, Orbit, Partizan, Redchurch) and solid but thoughtful choices from elsewhere, like Tiny Rebel, Rochefort, Hopf and Brooklyn chocolate stout.

Pineapple   (10)

Traditional pub (McGrath Davies) ★
51 Leverton Street NW5 2NX
T (020) 7284 4631   🅕 🐦 thepineapplepub
🕑 *Mo-Sa* 12.00-23.00, *Su* 12.00-22.30.
    Children until 19.00.
Cask beers 5 (Sharp's, 4 unusual sometimes local guests), **Other beers** 4 keg, 5+ bottles
🍴 Thai menu **£-££**, ⅂ Beer garden ❀
2 annual beer festivals, quiz (Mo), cheese night (Th), charity events

⇌ ✈ Kentish Town

This handsome little place is only a short stroll from Kentish Town tube but seems a world away in its quiet terraced street. Saved from closure by a local campaign in the early 2000s, it retains community loyalties. The front drinking area is arranged around a small central bar dominated by a Grade II-listed bar back with etched glass mirrors, and at the back, beyond an impressive red marble fireplace, is an elegant conservatory decorated with illustrations of wild birds that looks out onto a pleasant beer garden. The window glass indicates this was once an Ind Coope house, but today the only regular cask beer is Doom Bar, while the other pumps rotate through locals like Redemption and Truman's, or maybe Firebrand or Oxfordshire. Kegs include German König Pilsner and new beers from Marston's Revisionist range, and Camden Town and Moncada are among the bottles.

Pub trivia *The name may seem unlikely for a backstreet North London pub but, as a traditional symbol of hospitality, it's more than apt.*

Southampton Arms (11)
Specialist, traditional pub
139 Highgate Road NW5 1LE
T 07958 780073   🐦 SouthamptonNW5
www.thesouthamptonarms.co.uk
🕐 *Mo-Sa* 12.00-24.00, *Su* 12.00-23.30.
   Children welcome.
Cask beers 10 (unusual often local guests),
Other beers 2 keg, **Also** 8 ciders/perries
🍴 Substantial cheese and meat snacks **£**,
🎋 Rear sheltered beer garden
Quiz (Mo), live piano (We&Su)

🚇 Gospel Oak   🚇 Kentish Town   🚌 Lady Somerset Road
(214, C2 Kentish Town / Highgate)   🚴 Link to Hampstead
Heath paths   🥾 Link to Belsize Walk, Hampstead Heath paths

Transformed in 2009 into an unpretentious but perfectly judged purveyor of, as the sign says, 'Ale, Cider and Meat', this pioneer of the London beer renaissance has profoundly influenced many of the new beer-focused venues that followed, including some shameless copycats, right down to the white tiles, floorboards and recycled church hall furniture. But the original remains at least one of the best, as proved by the crowds of everyone from local celebs to bearded geeks that pack this small, narrow pub every night of the week (afternoons are best for a quiet drink). Expect a well chosen and varied range, with Londoners Howling Hops, from sister pub the Cock Tavern (p107) and Redemption and others from Buxton, Magic Rock or Summer Wine on the handpumps, and kegs from Camden Town and changing guests, enjoyed to the sounds of live piano or classic jazz on vinyl.

Tapping the Admiral (12)
Contemporary pub (McGrath Davies)
77 Castle Road NW1 8SU
T (020) 7267 6118
www.tappingtheadmiral.co.uk
📘 Tapping-the-Admiral   🐦 TappingAdmiral
🕐 *Su-Tu* 12.00-23.00, *We-Sa* 12.00-24.00.
   Children welcome.
Cask beers 6-8 (Dark Star, 5-7 unusual often London guests), **Other beers** 5 keg, 1 bottle,
Also 4 ciders/perries, cocktails & home-blended spirits
🍴 Pies, burgers, enhanced pub grub **£-££**,
🎋 Beer garden, ♿
Quiz (We), Irish music (Th), food promotions

🚇 Kentish Town West
🚇 Chalk Farm, Camden Town, Kentish Town

Pineapple owner Kirk McGrath (p137) opened two new pubs in 2011 along broadly similar lines: the Railway Tavern (p145) and this delightful place near Kentish Town West station, where legendary pub cat Nelson presides over a clean, cosy and characterful interior. Dark Star Hophead is permanent and the remaining cask pumps favour locals – Gypsy Hill, Hammerton, Portobello, Redemption, Twickenham – and Welsh and Yorkshire breweries like Barnsley, Kingstone and Otley. Camden Town and Bavarian abbey wheat beer Benediktiner add interest to the kegs. Tasty Spicer's Pies and mash, including veggie options, are a major focus of a menu that also includes dishes like baked salmon supreme or gnocchi with blue cheese and spinach, and there's a top value £6 lunch deal.

Pub trivia *Originally known as the Trafalgar, the pub was derelict for years and once threatened with demolition. The current name refers to the story that Admiral Nelson's body was returned from Trafalgar preserved in a brandy barrel, from which sailors surreptitiously sipped by drilling holes and inserting macaroni straws.*

TRY ALSO

Of the two well-known music pubs operated by Camden Bars in Camden Town itself, the best beer choice is to be found in the pleasantly worn and chilled out **Lock Tavern** (35 Chalk Farm Road NW1 8AJ, www.lock-tavern.com), with four often local casks and a shelf of

London and US bottles to enjoy alongside acts that have included the Dandy Warhols and Kate Nash (sister pub the Monarch has a much more standard offer).

At Kentish Town West, almost opposite the Grafton (p136) and near Camden Town Brewery, corner off-licence **Drinkers Paradise** (129 Castlehaven Road NW1 8SJ, ⚑ DrinkersParadise) stocks up to 250 surprisingly varied bottled beers. At Kentish Town proper, close to the station, 1898 Flemish Renaissance landmark the **Assembly House ★** (292 Kentish Town Road NW5 2TG, www.assemblyhouse.co.uk) is now a Metropolitan pub, with some unusual guests as well as a whole wall full of sumptuous original engraved mirrored panels. North of Tufnell Park towards Archway, **Theatre of Wine** (124 Junction Road N19 5LB, www.theatreofwine.com) offers a well-curated beer selection, with around 90 bottles from London and the UK complete with tasting notes.

Two heritage pubs in central Hampstead are good representatives of their respective owning groups. Fuller's **Holly Bush ★** (22 Holly Mount NW3 6SG, www.hollybushhampstead.co.uk), hidden in narrow hilly streets to the north, retains numerous late Victorian features and a brown-stained lived-in feel. Commemorating in its name Hampstead's former life as a mineral spa, Young's **Flask ★** (14 Flask Walk NW3 1HG, www.theflaskhampstead.co.uk), in an alleyway round the corner from the Tube, has a panelled screen with five fine original chromolithographs of sentimental Flemish paintings.

Near the Royal Free Hospital, the **Stag** has up to five sometimes local guest casks and a decent international bottle range, as well as an extensive garden. Finally, although the beer range is restricted to (always well-kept) keg Pilsner Urquell and Budweiser Budvar plus a few very mainstream Czech and Slovak bottles including Budvar Dark, the **Czechoslovak National House** (74 West End Lane NW6 2LX, www.czechandslovakclub.co.uk) at West Hampstead is a unique London drinking experience. It's an expat club now open to all in a big villa that doesn't look like it's changed much since the 1950s, with an extensive and authentic food menu.

LONDON DRINKERS | Jane Jephcote

Veteran pubs campaigner and pub heritage expert Jane is chair of CAMRA's London Pubs Group and active in the Campaign's South West London branch. Her top three London heritage pubs are:

1. **Forester** (2 Leighton Road W13 9EP, www.foresterealing.co.uk, not included in this book but selling good Fuller's beer). "This was designed by architect Thomas Henry Nowell Parr: it's a wonderful building with a fantastic interior."

2. **Blackfriar** (p68): "Superb *Art Nouveau* design by Herbert Fuller-Clark with interior decoration by Henry Poole."

3. **Ivy House** (p 163): "Originally the Stuart Arms, this is a fantastic inter-war Truman's pub with most of its interior features intact, saved from redevelopment by a community buy-out."

How do you rate London as a beer city, on a world scale?
Pretty highly nowadays, except that it's lost nearly all of its traditional breweries.

What's the single most exciting thing about beer in London at the moment?
The number of new microbreweries. It seems we hear of a new one almost every week.

What single thing would make things even better?
Pub companies lifting the restrictions on beer choice that they put on licensees.

What are your top London beers right now?
Sambrook's Powerhouse Porter, By the Horns Stiff Upper Lip, Dragonfly Early Doors. I've been enjoying beers from the Brockley Brewery too, in the wonderful Ivy House.

What's your top great beer night out?
Craft Beer Co Clerkenwell (p74).

Who's your London beer hero?
Duncan Sambrook.

Which are your other top beer cities?
Brussels would get my vote.

Islington to Stoke Newington

13. Charlotte Despard · 14. Craft Beer Shop (Kris Wines) · 15. Duke of Wellington · 16. Dukes Brew and Que · 17. Hop and Berry ·
18. Hops and Glory · 19. Jolly Butchers · 20. Lamb · 21. North Pole · 22. Prince · 23 Railway Tavern · 24. Smokehouse ·
25. Snooty Fox · 26. Taproom · A. Hamerton · B. Brewhouse and Kitchen Highbury

Charlotte Despard (13)

Contemporary pub
17 Archway Road N19 3TX **T** (020) 7272 7872
www.thecharlottedespard.co.uk
 The Charlotte Despard
 TheDespard, bar_bint
 Mo-Th 17.00-01.00, *Fr-Sa* 16.00-01.00,
 Su 16.00-24.00. Children until 22.00.
Cask beers 4 (London guests), **Other beers** 4 keg,
45 bottles, **Also** Wines, specialist spirits
 Only for pre-booked events
*Meet the brewer, quiz (Tu), pool, darts, table
football, board games, major big screen sport*

 Archway

Just round the corner from the tangle of traffic
around Archway Tube, this smallish local has
further improved its beer range since new
owners Chris and Amber took over in

September 2011. Much is made of London suppliers with changing cask beers from nearby Hammerton as well as Brew by Numbers, East London, Redemption or Sambrook's, and a guest 'craft keg' from people like Beavertown and Kernel. Some of these also line up in the bottle fridge alongside decent international contributors like Cooper's, Goose Island and Belgium's Troubadour. Warm wood and sofas create a relaxing atmosphere in which to read the freely supplied papers.

Pub trivia *Back in the 1980s, when it was called the Dog, this was one of the earliest Wetherspoon pubs and the company itself was run from an office upstairs. It was renamed to match the street it corners: Charlotte Despard was a novelist, socialist, feminist and Irish republican campaigner (1844–1939).*

Craft Beer Shop (Kris Wines) (14)
Shop   **Top 5**
394 York Way N7 9LW   **T** (020) 7607 4871
www.kriswines.com 🐦 KrisWinesLtd
🕐 *Mo-Sa* 13.00-23.00, *Su* 13.00-21.30.
Cask beers None, **Other beers** 800+ bottles,
Also Wines

🚆 Kentish Town, Kings Cross, St Pancras   🚇 Camden Road
🚇 Caledonian Road, Camden, Kentish Town   🚌 York Way
(390 Kings Cross, Tufnell Park, 29 253 Camden Town)

Krishna Menan is not the only local off-licence owner to move into speciality beer, but he's taken things much further than most. The range began growing in the mid-2000s, meticulously researched through online rating sites and beer books, and is now probably the biggest and most comprehensive collection in London. In 2014 the changing focus was made explicit when the sign above the door changed from 'Kris Wines' to 'The Craft Beer Shop'. It's a great place to look for geek-friendly stuff like Crooked Stave, Jolly Pumpkin and Lost Abbey from the US, Dutch mavericks like Rooie Dop and Uiltje, Scandinavian eccentrics and new Belgian startups. The UK shelves often include smaller London outfits like Strawman and rarely-seen goodies from Hopshackle and Tempest besides the usual suspects. Bottles are crammed into every available space so take your time looking or you could easily miss a gem.

Duke of Wellington   (15)
Contemporary pub
119 Balls Pond Road N1 4BL   **T** (020) 7275 7640
www.thedukeofwellingtonn1.com
📘 thedukeofwellingtonn1   🐦 TheDukeN1
🕐 *Mo-We* 16.00-24.00, *Th-Fr* 16.00-01.00, *Sa* 12.00-01.00, *Su* 12.00-23.30. Children until 20.00.
Cask beers 5 (Sambrook's, 4 unusual guests),
Other beers 1 keg, 17 bottles, **Also** 2 real ciders/perries, specialist whiskies
🍴 Gourmet hot sandwiches and sides **£-££**,
🪑 Tables on street, ♿
3 annual beer festivals, monthly film club, fine dining night, occasional live folk/jazz, big screen sport

🚇 Dalston Kingsland, Dalston Junction

Officially in Islington though closer to Dalston, the Duke has stood here since 1842. A contemporary makeover in 2008 polished its heart as a comfortable, sprawling community boozer, and an ownership reshuffle in 2012 changed little. Sambrook's Wandle remains the only regular cask while guests ordered through Enterprise's direct delivery scheme could encompass Kent, Otley, Otter, Redemption or Salopian. An increased and interesting bottle selection lines up locals like Beavertown, Five Points and Pressure Drop with imports from Augustiner, Odell and Schneider. The kitchen is leased to Sub Cult and produces US-style cooked sandwiches with fillings like pulled pork, seared scallops and calamari or roasted broccoli. The main drinking area retains its handsome island bar, etched glass, tiled fireplace and pillars while one of the mosaic floored porches has been converted into a tiny snug; the screening room at the back offers saggy sofas.

Dukes Brew and Que (16)

Restaurant, bar (Beavertown)
33 Downham Road N1 5AA **T** (020) 3006 0795
www.dukesbrewandque.com
🅵 Dukes-Brew-Que 🐦 dukesjoint
🕐 *Mo-We* 16.00-23.00, *Th-Fr* 16.00-23.30,
Sa 11.00-23.30, *Su* 11.00-22.30.
Children very welcome until 19.30.
Cask beers 1 (local guest), *Other beers* 9 keg, 35 bottles (including Beavertown), **Also** Tequilas and tequila cocktails, some specialist spirits
🍴 US-style barbecues and burgers **££-£££**,
🪑 Tables on street, ♿
Beer matching dinners

🚇 Haggerston 🚣 Regents Canal towpath 🏃 Jubilee Greenway

The Beavertown brewery began in this transatlantic beer and barbecue joint in the shell of the Duke of York in De Beauvoir Town, occupying a corner of the kitchen when it first opened in February 2012. The brewery has moved on to much bigger things (p 279) but Dukes remains a key showcase. A good two

thirds of the quirkily-decorated floor area (old prams, antlers) is given over to dining but drinkers are always welcome at the cheerful bar. The single immaculately-served cask could well be a Beavertown, otherwise very rare in this form, or from Dark Star or London Beer Factory. A well-curated and wide-ranging selection of guests is sourced from people like Brew by Numbers, Kernel, Partizan or Thornbridge alongside US, Italian and Japanese imports. The mainly meat-focused cuisine – ribs, pulled pork, steaks, burgers and specials like veggie gumbo – pairs well to beer, but pre-booking is advisable.

Hop and Berry (17)

Specialist, contemporary pub
209 Liverpool Road N1 1LX **T** (020) 7607 5519
www.thebarnsbury.co.uk 🐦 thebarnsburypub
🕐 *Mo-Th* 16.30-23.00, *Fr-Sa* 12.00-23.00,
Su 12.00-22.30. Children until early evening.
Cask beers 4-6 (London guests), *Other beers* 12 keg, 30+ bottles (London), **Also** Local soft drinks
🍴 Gastroish/pub grub menu **££**, 🪑 Benches on street, rear terrace
Meet the brewer/tap takeover, live music, board games

🚉🚇 Highbury & Islington 🚇 Highbury & Islington, Angel
🚌 Islington Town Hall (numerous Angel)

Listed in the previous edition as the Barnsbury, this handy retreat from the bustle of Upper Street upped the ante still further in the late summer of 2014 by mutating into a "London craft" venue under the tutelage of Tony Lennon, ex-Euston Tap (p 47). Casks could be from Hop Stuff or Late Knights, while kegs, bottles and cans stretch to Anspach & Hobday, Brodie's, Crate, Hammerton, Partizan and Weird Beard. A full list of London brewers complete with map is proudly displayed on the wall. An evolving menu could include sirloin steak with baked bone marrow, quinoa and kidney bean kiev or snacks like chilli squid or marinated anchovies. The front drinking area has been decluttered back to wood panelling and a few tall benches, with industrial lampshades hanging over the old horseshoe bar; the rear area with its tables remains more comfortable and intimate.

Hops and Glory

Hops and Glory (18)

Brewpub, contemporary pub

382 Essex Road N1 3PF

T (020) 7226 2277　www.hopsandglory.co.uk

🅕 🅨 thehopsandglory

🕘 *Mo-We* 16.30-23.00, *Th* 16.30-24.00, *Fr* 16.30-02.00, *Sa* 12.00-02.00, *Su* 12.00-22.30. Children until early evening.

Cask beers 3-4 (unusual often local guests), *Other beers* 15 keg, 45 bottles, *Also* Specialist whiskies

🍴 Burgers, hot dogs, cheese, pop-ups **£-££**, 🪑 Small beer garden

3 annual beer festivals, occasional quiz

🚃 Essex Road　↔ Canonbury　↔ Angel, Highbury & Islington　🚌 Ockenden Road (numerous Angel)　🚶 Link to New River Path

This corner pub near the top of Essex Road has been through numerous recent incarnations, though its December 2012 reconfiguration into a "craft beer pub and bottle shop" should prove more sustainable, especially with Solvay Society brewery now installed in the cellar. The handpulls feature a range of styles from Londoners like Five Points or Truman's alongside Dark Star, Langham or Magic Rock. House-brewed beers are on keykeg alongside other locally-sourced choices and US brews from Lagunitas and Rogue. Similar breweries feature on the bottle shelves, alongside a small Belgian selection that pleasingly includes lambics from 3 Fonteinen and Cantillon. The "bottle shop" bit in the strapline reflects the fact that all these are sold to take away too, with a 25% discount if you buy four or more bottles.

Jolly Butchers (19)

Specialist, contemporary pub (London Village Inns)

204 Stoke Newington High Street N16 7HU

T (020) 7249 9471　www.jollybutchers.co.uk

🅕 thejollybutchers　🅨 jollybutchers

🕘 *Mo-Fr* 16.00-24.00, *Sa* 12.00-01.00, *Su* 12.00-23.00. Children welcome.

Cask beers 6 (unusual guests), *Other beers* 12 keg, 80 bottles, *Also* 2-3 ciders/perries

🍴 Gastroish menu **££**, 🪑 Benches on street, ♿ *Meet the brewer/tap takeover*

↔ Stoke Newington　🚌 Stoke Newington station (numerous Dalston)　🚶 Capital Ring

Once this was a fearsome place where customers entertained themselves by throwing bottles at the bar: current owner Martin Harley confesses he felt nervous on site inspections. In 2010, Martin propelled it into ranks of contemporary London beer venues, done out in deep red and dark green with art wallpaper and bright new glazing in the big arched windows, and the troublemakers melted away. It's still holding its own against much-increased competition thanks to a strong offer, an expansive vibe and informed staff. Casks from brewers like Anarchy, Redwillow and Summer Wine appear alongside more local choices like Hop Stuff, Kent or Redemption while the fridges yield several big US 'bomber' bottles, Londoners and Belgians like Ellezelloise and Orval. Unlike some beer-forward pubs, there's a comprehensive menu with dishes like pan-fried salmon, asparagus risotto, slow-cooked pork ribs and cheese and charcuterie boards.

Lamb (20)
Contemporary pub
54 Holloway Road N7 8JL
T (020) 7619 9187   www.thelambn7.co.uk
🅵 thelambn7   🆇 thelambpub
🕐 *Su-Th* 16.00-24.00, *Fr-Sa* 16.00-00.30 (*opens earlier for Arsenal home games*). Children welcome.
Cask beers 3 (Fuller's, 2 usually London guests),
Other beers 5 keg, 5 bottles, ***Also*** Specialist spirits, cider/perry in summer
🍴 Cheese and meat boards, local gourmet pizzas delivered **££**, ⛲ Small rear yard
Beer festivals, Irish sessions/acoustic music (TuWe&Su), occasional live music other days, functions

⇌ ⊖ ⊖ Highbury & Islington   🚊 St Mary Magdalene Church (numerous Highbury & Islington, Holloway Road)

Just up from Highbury Corner, the Lamb has built a loyal following since relaunching in 2012 as a local that happens to do good beer, culminating in its recognition as Holloway's best pub in *Time Out*'s 2014 Love London Awards. New owners took it on soon afterwards but plan to change little. There's a Fuller's seasonal and cask guests usually from London brewers like Hackney or Hammerton but sometimes an ale brewed for the pub by the rarely-seen Marshall's Hermitage brewery in Berkshire. More Hermitage beers are in bottles alongside Kernel and a couple of well-known Americans, while Camden Town, Harviestoun or Partizan might be on keg. It's an atmospheric place with dark wood panelling and a slightly studenty feel, unsurprisingly as it's just down the road from London Metropolitan University, but it's also close to Arsenal FC's Emirates Stadium and becomes rather more earthy on match days.

North Pole (21)
Contemporary pub (Leisure & Catering)
188 New North Road N1 7BJ
T (020) 7354 5400   🅵 🆇 thenorthpolepub
www.thenorthpolepub.co.uk
🕐 *Su-Th* 12.00-23.00, *Fr-Sa* 12.00-24.00. Children until 20.00.
Cask beers 6-7 (unusual often local guests),
Other beers 12 keg, 20+ cans/bottles,
Also 3-4 ciders/perries, wines
🍴 US-influenced pub grub **££**, ⛲ Beer garden
Tastings, meet the brewer/tap takeover, food promotions, bar billiards, retro video games, board games

⇌ Essex Road   ⊖ Angel, Old Street   🚊 Baring Street (271 Essex Road, numerous Old Street)   🚲 Regents Canal towpath   🚶 Jubilee Greenway, link to New River Path

In a slightly out-of-the-way corner of Islington near the Regent's Canal, the former North Star was reopened as the North Pole in July 2012 following a lavish refurbishment – the oddly shaped bar area is now clean, bright and cheerful with light wood and pot plants, and there's a wood-decked terrace at the back. Casks are likely to hail from brewers like Beerd, Dark Star, Malt, the local Hammerton or Big Smoke, the last based in sister pub the Antelope (p197). A non-mainstream keg offer with guests like Arbor, Harbour, Moor and Tiny Rebel and a succint bottle selection mixing Beavertown and Fourpure, several from Flying Dog and Belgian standbys like Rochefort rounds things out. The kitchen turns out a varied burger selection alongside barbecue ribs, jerk chicken and vegan superfood salad. A friendly, civilised place that feels a bit more grown-up than some venues with similar lists.

Lamb

Prince (22)

Gastropub
59 Kynaston Road N16 0EB **T** (020) 7043 5210
www.theprincen16.com 🐦 ThePrinceN16
🕐 *Mo-Th* 12.00-23.00, *Fr* 12.00-24.00, *Sa* 11.00-
24.00, *Su* 12.00-22.30. Children until 19.30.
Cask beers 3 (St Peter's, 2 often local guests),
Other beers 7 keg, 30 bottles, **Also** 1 cider,
seasonal cocktails, wines, specialist spirits
🍴 Gastro menu, cooked bar snacks **££**,
🪑 Side courtyard, ♿
Beer events, quiz (Mo), food assembly (Tu),
food pickups, occasional live music, functions

⊖ Stoke Newington 🚌 Brooke Road/Stoke Newington High
Street (numerous Dalston)

This backstreet local reopened in June 2014
with more than a hint of designer gastropub,
mixing traditional pub elements like big mirrors
and red banquettes with marquetry tables and
retro flourescent lighting. The suggestion is
confirmed by a menu that includes roast hake
with grilled escarole and gremolata, upmarket
liver and bacon, and potato terrine with roast
onion and duck egg, not to mention oysters as
a bar snack. But it's also a friendly place with a
beer range that includes a cask St Peter's choice
and guests likely from Five Points, Hackney,
Ilkley, Saltaire, Signature or Tiny Rebel, usually
with a dark option. Beavertown and Pressure
Drop feature in the fridges along with a few
Americans and Belgians (Founders, Rochefort),
while Firebrand, London Fields and Siren could
appear on keykeg. The pub also hosts local
produce distributor Stoke Newington Food
Assembly.

Railway Tavern (23)

Contemporary pub (McGrath Davies)
2 St Jude Street N16 8JT
T (020) 0011 1195 📘 RailwayTavernAleHouse
🕐 *Mo-Th* 16.00-23.00, *Fr-Sa* 12.00-24.00,
Su 12.00-22.30. Children until 21.00.
Cask beers 6 (Adnams, 5 unusual often local
guests), **Other beers** 5 keg, 16 bottles, **Also**
Occasional cider
🍴 Thai, Sunday roasts **£-££**, 🪑 Benches at front
Quiz (Tu), monthly live music, board games

⊖ Dalston Junction, Dalston Kingsland

With a Stoke Newington postcode but closer
to Dalston's various arts venues and the well-
known Duke of Wellington (p141), this was
another failing backstreet pub rejuvenated in
2011 as a companion piece to the Pineapple
(p137). The L-shaped space preserves some
original Victorian features like multiple street
doors, a carved fireplace with floral tiling and
pillars with elaborate gilt capitals, now supplemented by a wood burning stove and floppy
sofas. Guest casks might be from locals
Redemption or Upstairs, or from various
Marston's subsidiaries, with an Adnams beer
always on. There are two Pressure Drop
keykeg lines and Kernel in bottles alongside
other London and Belgian options. Decent
good value Thai food includes massaman lamb
and various iterations of rice, noodles and
curry, with traditional roasts on Sundays.

Visitor note *Take care - this is a different Railway Tavern*
to the one next to Dalston Kingsland station. A former owner
tried to mitigate confusion by renaming this one the Old
Henry, but have a look high up on the blank wall at the back
of the pub and you'll see why the decision to revive the
original name was a wise one.

Smokehouse (24)

Gastropub (Noble)
63 Canonbury Road N1 2DG
T (020) 7354 1144 🐦 smokehouseN1
www.smokehouseislington.co.uk
🕐 *Mo-Th* 16.30-23.00, *Fr* 16.30-24.00, *Sa* 11.00-
24.00, *Su* 12.00-22.30. Children until 21.00.
Cask beers 2-3 (unusual sometimes local
guests), **Other beers** 15 keg, 60 bottles,
Also Cider in summer, wines, specialist spirits
🍴 Specialist home-smoked and barbecued
menu **££-£££**, 🪑 Tables on street, beer
garden 🐾, ♿
Occasional tastings, meet the brewer

🚇 Essex Road ⊖⊖ Highbury & Islington 🏃 New River Path

This is one of the few places in London seriously
to promote beer alongside fine dining, with
staff trained accordingly, spurred by star chef
Neil Rankin's conviction that beer stands up
best to the robust flavours of his smoked
specialities. Since reopening in August 2013,
it's sourced casks from brewers like Bath,
Firebrand, Magic Rock, Truman's or Vale, with

other draughts from Kernel, Hopf and Rogue. An intelligent bottled list has little flab, listing Odell, Orval, Partizan, Rochefort, Siren and, of course, Schlenkerla Rauchbier. There really is an on-site smokehouse as well as a butchery, and dishes might include Korean kimchi, Cornish hake with smoked mussels, smoked ham hock with pig cheek and chilli squid, or a delicious Mexican-style veggie *masa* with duck egg. A decently sized unreserved area complements crisp tables for diners, including several slotted into a patch of maze-like topiary at the front of this wedge-shaped site.

Snooty Fox

Snooty Fox (25)
Contemporary pub
75 Grosvenor Avenue N5 2NN
T (020) 7354 0094   🄵 🅈 snootyfoxlondon
www.snootyfoxlondon.co.uk
🕐 *Mo-Th* 16.00-23.00, *Fr* 16.00-01.00, *Sa* 12.00-01.00, *Su* 12.00-23.30. Children until 21.00.
Cask beers 4 (Otter, 3 unusual and local guests), ***Other beers*** 3 keg, 2 bottles, ***Also*** 1 cider
🍴 Rotisserie chicken, smoked meats, roasts
££, 🪑 Front terrace
2 annual beer festivals, quiz (Tu), DJs (Fr-Sa), jukebox, board games

🚇 Canonbury   🚶 New River Path

A modern, comfortable and not at all snooty place just across from Canonbury Overground station, this is a very musical Fox, with a great collection of classic rock and pop pics and a well-stocked jukebox. The beer range, largely sourced through site owners Enterprise, is small but perfectly formed: Otter Ale from Devon, a changing London handpump likely to feature By the Horns, Five Points,

Hammerton, Redemption or Weird Beard, a beer from an established brewery like Adnams or Hook Norton, and newer beers from further afield like Hop Craft or Revolutions, plus Meantime and Czech classics in keg and bottle. Imaginatively themed beer festivals, often with a musical link, boost the range. Grilled chicken, home-smoked ribs and wild boar sausages, fish of the day, salads and Sunday roasts complete an attractive picture.

Taproom (26)
Specialist, contemporary pub
163 Upper Street N1 1US
T (020) 7288 1606   🄵 🅈 TaproomN1
www.thetaprooms.co.uk
🕐 *Mo-Fr* 16.00-23.00, *Sa* 12.00-23.00, *Su* 12.00-22.30. Children until early evening.
Cask beers 10 (unusual guests), ***Other beers*** 4 keg, 20 bottles, ***Also*** At least 2 ciders, bottled cider, 10 single malts
🍴 Substantial bar snacks **£**, 🪑 Rear yard, tables on street, ♿
Meet the brewer/tap takeover, occasional live music, comedy

🚆 🚇 🚇 Highbury & Islington

"London's first cask to glass ale house" brought much needed beer interest to Upper Street as a pop-up over Christmas 2012, and from June 2013 has been a permanent fixture on a narrow site formerly used as council offices: you can still see the ghostly shadows of vanished sinks among the bare brick. Casks line up in a refrigerated glass-fronted stillage with protruding

Taproom

copper taps, an arrangement that the owners have apparently patented. Those taps, and more conventional handpumps, typically dispense beers from Brighton, Burning Sky, Grain, Ledbury, Oakham or Otley, or locals like Crate, Hammerton or Gipsy Hill, all available in tasting flights of three thirds. Kegs are from Camden Town and Kernel, complemented by bottles of less obvious beers from better-known US craft brewers. Food is restricted to toasties and huge Scotch eggs; company is convivial, and copious when live musicians strike up in the basement space.

TRY ALSO

Just a few steps from Highbury & Islington station, small supermarket **Budgens of Islington** (213 Upper Street N1 1RL, www. budgens.co.uk/store-locator/89-Islington)

has a range of local beers from By the Horns, Hammerton, Moncada and others and lots from bigger UK breweries. Another convenience store, the **Fountayne Road Londis** (76 Fountayne Road N16 7DT, www.supermarket. londis.co.uk/38471-kj-supermarket) on Stoke Newington Common, stocks around 70 bottles with a good East London selection. Smart Church Street wine shop **Borough Wines** (163 Stoke Newington Church Street N16 0UL, www.boroughwines.co.uk), an offshoot of Utobeer's neighbours in Borough Market's Drinks Cage, has around 90 bottles, mainly from London brewers with some Belgians. Gourmet burger and beer joint **Stokey Bears** (129 Stoke Newington High Street N16 0PH, www.burgerbearuk.com) opened late in 2014 as a collaboration between the Bear Hug beer firm and sometime brewer BurgerBear Tom.

LONDON'S BREWING   Hammerton

When Lee Hammerton first conceived the idea of becoming a brewer, he didn't realise he had beer in his blood. Originally from Colchester but now living in Islington, he was fed up with his job as an IT business analyst in the City. An occasional homebrewer, he'd already started to develop plans for a brewery in a part of London where there was an obvious gap in the market. Serendipitously, he then discovered there had already been a Hammerton brewery in the capital, and further digging in the family history unearthed the fact that he was distantly related to its owners. So the project changed from the launch of a new brewery to the re-establishment of an old one.

The sizeable Stockwell Brewery, on the other side of the river near Brixton, was founded in 1730 on what was then a prime brewing site on Stockwell Green, close to local springs. In the late

19th century it was run by Charles Hammerton, and in 1938 became likely the first brewery in the world to put real oysters into stout (there's an earlier claim from New Zealand, but so far no supporting evidence). Watney bought it out in 1951, primarily for its lucrative off-licence chain rather than its pubs, which were sold on to Charrington. Brewing ceased, although the site remained in use as a bottling plant for a while before being redeveloped as housing. The brands eventually passed to Heineken, and Lee had to reclaim his own name by applying to revoke the trademark on the grounds of non-use.

Lee recruited head brewer Sam Dickinson, previously at Moncada, and moved into a sizeable industrial unit near Caledonian Road & Barnsbury station in January 2014, installing a 15-barrel (26 hl) kit from Malrex. Naturally enough,

one of the first brews was an oyster stout, with real fresh Maldon oysters added to the boil, shells and all. "We couldn't find the original recipe," says Lee, "and we probably would have wanted to do something more contemporary anyway, but it's in the spirit of the original."

Several people I've spoken to have used the phrase "hit the ground running" when talking about Hammerton: within only a few months it seemed like their beer was everywhere, and with good reason. Sam is now moving on, but output is still set to increase, and they're adding a pilot kit to develop more unusual styles, such as a Peruvian-themed beer inspired by Lee's Peruvian wife. They're experimenting with open days too, and might move to opening more regularly. "It's all down to hard work, research and thorough planning," says Lee, but maybe there's an element of genetic predisposition too.

Outer North London

Beavertown Brewery

Beavertown Brewery (27)

Taproom (Beavertown)
17 Lockwood Industrial Park,
Mill Mead Road N17 9QP

T (020) 3696 1441 🐦 beavertownbeer
www.beavertownbrewery.co.uk
🕐 *Sa* 14.00-20.00, closed other days.
   Children welcome.
Cask beers Occasional, **Other beers** 10 keg,
15 bottles (Beavertown, occasional guests)
🍴 Pop-up food carts **£**, 🪑 Benches at front
Table tennis, cornhole & cricket outside

🚆 ➔ Tottenham Hale 🚲 NCN1 🏃 Lea Valley Path

Beavertown's gleaming new brewery was
installed in summer 2014 in a spacious industrial unit behind newly redeveloped Hale
Village, only a step from Tottenham Hale
station and Lee Valley Park. It accommodates
one of London's most expansive weekly
taprooms – appropriately given the growing
reputation and popularity of the beers.
A decent-sized bar within sight of the brewhouse dispenses house beers, and sometimes
guests and collaborations, from keykeg (in half
and two-thirds measures), bottle and can,
including plenty of rarities from the pilot kit.
The view from the front yard isn't London's
prettiest but it sure catches the sun.

Beehive (28)

Contemporary pub (Camden) ★
Stoneleigh Road N17 9BQ

T (020) 8808 3567   **www.beehiven17.com**
📘 TheBeehivePub 🐦 Beehiven17
🕐 *Mo-Th* 17.00-23.00, *Fr* 16.00-23.00,
   Sa 12.00-23.00, *Su* 12.00-22.30.
   Children very welcome until 20.30.
Cask beers 4-6 (Greene King, Redemption, local
guests), **Other beers** 5 keg, 3–4 bottles, **Also**
Some specialist whiskies/spirits
🍴 Gourmet hot sandwiches, salads, pub grub
£-££, 🪑 Large beer garden 🐾
*Quiz (We), summer barbecues, major big screen
sport, pool, table tennis, functions*

➔ Bruce Grove 🏃 Better Haringey Trail, Moselle River Walk

Good pubs are a rarity in Tottenham, so it's not
surprising the rejuvenated Beehive immediately
attracted a loyal following when it reopened in
March 2014. An expansive and comfortable
interior preserving numerous 1920s features
overlooks a leafy garden complete with
statuary and a children's play area, appreciated
by numerous local young families. The pub has
become something of a tap for the nearby
Redemption brewery, alongside other
Londoners like Beavertown and Signature
Brew, with some Greene King lines and imports
from Anchor, Goose Island and Lagunitas in
bottle and keg. The kitchen, branded Phileas
Hog, dispenses dishes like pork shoulder or salt
beef sandwiches, veggie sweet potato burgers
and lentil and aubergine salad. The pub has a
patchy recent history, so it's heartening to see
it treated with such evident care.

Pub trivia *This Grade II listed building, built in 1927 on the
site of an 1870s predecessor, is a splendid example of a big
Brewers' Tudor pub of its era, finished with copious amounts
of plywood-based fake wood panelling. Elaborate stained
glass is used among other things to name the various rooms,
some of which, uniquely, are also numbered in brass. The
former off-licence, now a daytime coffee shop, retains its
original serving hatch.*

LONDON'S BREWING

Beavertown

Though his father is Robert Plant of Led Zeppelin, a true rock'n'roll colossus, Logan Plant enjoyed a down-to-earth upbringing in the Black Country of the English West Midlands, a region awash with great beer where, as he puts it, "the pub was like an extension to your house." By his early 20s he was obsessively seeking out classic local cask ales from Bathams, Enville and Holden's. At first he followed in the family tradition by becoming a singer and musician, but one night in New York City, on tour with his alt-rock band Sons of Albion, he ate barbecued food washed down with US craft beer, and the combination struck him as sublime. The idea sparked that night finally took shape in February 2012 when he opened an innovative London brewpub, Dukes Brew and Que (p142), in De Beauvoir Town on the western fringe of Hackney.

A little four barrel (6.5 hl) brewing kit was squeezed into a corner of the pub kitchen, where twice a week Logan brewed smoked porter Smog Rocket to serve with beef ribs and 8-Ball rye IPA for the pork. But the beers were so good that demand for them beyond the pub rapidly grew, so he moved the fermenters into a small unit a mile away, transporting the hopped wort by car. In May 2013, brewing transferred to a bigger site in Hackney Wick, next door to the new Truman's, but the operation soon outgrew that too. "We were really pushing ourselves," says Logan. "We'd expanded from four to 14 fermenters, but we still had the same little kit, and had to brew seven or eight times a week on it."

		1/3	1/2	2/3
1. NECK OIL 4.3% SESSION IPA		1.5	2	2.5
2. GAMMA RAY 5.4% APA		1.5	2	2.5
3. 8 BALL 6.2% RYE IPA		1.5	2	2.5
4. BLACK BETTY 7.4% BLACK IPA		1.5	2	2.5
5. SMOG ROCKET 5.4% SMOKED PORTER		1.5	2	2.5
6. LEMON PHANTOM 3% 'BERLINER WEISSE	1.5	2	2.5
7. 'SPRESSO 9% BEAVER/CARAVAN/PRAIRIE COFFEE STOUT		2.5	3	3.5
8. QUELLE 4.2% DRY HOPPED SAISON		1.5	2	2.5

Inspired by what he'd since seen of craft breweries in the US — he cites Matt Brynildson, head brewer at California's outstanding Firestone Walker, as a particular influence — he decided a more serious upgrade was needed. So in April 2014, Beavertown relocated to a bigger industrial unit further out, in the Lee Valley at Tottenham Hale, with good rail and road links to central London. Here, a new 50 hl brewhouse fabricated in Bulgaria feeds 1,200 hl of fermentation tanks, though the old kit has been retained for pilot brews and small runs of specials. Expert head brewster Jen Merrick, a Salt Lake City native formerly at Dark Star and Meantime, ensures it's all put to good use.

Perhaps the aspect of the new operation that's drawn the most attention is the shiny new range of canned beer, well-presented with the brewery's eye for striking graphic design. "We invested in a small canning line as well as a bigger bottling line, because we weren't sure how the cans would go," recounts Logan. "But now I wish we'd gone the other way. 95% of the beer we sell in small packs is now in cans."

The next big thing is a wood-ageing programme, something the brewery has experimented with in the past but which is about to get very serious indeed. When I spoke to Logan, they had 30 wooden barrels of various kinds on the go, and were awaiting delivery of two big Flemish-style vats or *foeders*, making Beavertown the second London brewery after Kernel to install these. They've rented the unit opposite to house it all, and will probably move the taproom there too.

"I love the thought of drinking great beer surrounded by all that wood," says Logan.

Besides all these exotica, the more everyday beers will remain the mainstay - like Neck Oil, the brewery's popular session IPA. "It began back at Dukes as an attempt to replicate Bathams Bitter," recalls Logan. "It was hopeless." Funny how things go.

Black Horse (29)

Brewpub, contemporary pub (Oak)
92 Wood Street, Barnet EN5 4HY
T (020) 8449 2230
www.blackhorsebarnet.co.uk
🅵 The-Black-Horse-Barnet
🐦 theblackhorseph
🕓 *Daily* 12.00-24.00. Children welcome.
Cask beers 8 (Barnet, 6 often unusual guests),
Other beers 1-2 bottles (Barnet), **Also** 1 cider
🍴 Gastroish menu **££**, 🍴 Front terrace, front
garden, ♿
*Tastings, meet the brewer, quiz (We), live music
(most Sa), occasional soul nights, ladies' nights,
food promotions*

🚇 High Barnet 🚌 Union Street (various High Barnet)
🏃 Link to London Loop

This sprawling Victorian pub just outside
Barnet town centre was relaunched late in
2012 by a group that runs several brewpubs
outside London. Previously something of a
laddish Sky Sports place, it has since earned
praise for being female-friendly and a social
club for over-40s women now regularly meets
here. The brewery, in an outhouse at the side,
usually provides two of the cask beers and
some bottles, supplemented on handpumps by
suppliers like Adnams, Ilkley and Red Squirrel,
including some unusual styles (Itchen Valley
Blackberry Mild when I called) sourced through
Punch's direct delivery scheme. The tasteful
light grey interior is part-pub, part-restaurant,
serving dishes like pan-fried chicken and
chorizo, salmon and horseradish fishcakes or
marinated vegetable and halloumi kebab, but
the division isn't enforced: "locals wanted
good food, but they also begged us not to turn
it into a restaurant," says area manager Alex.

Bohemia Top 25 (30)

Brewpub, contemporary pub (London Brewing)
762 High Road N12 9QH
T (020) 8446 0294 **www.thebohemia.co.uk**
🅵 Bohemia-N12 🐦 Bohemia_N12
🕓 *Mo-We* 12.00-23.00, *Th* 12.00-24.00, *Fr-Sa* 12.00-
01.00, *Su* 12.00-22.30. Children until 21.30.
Cask beers 5 (London Brewing, 2 local guests),
Other beers 12 keg, 36 bottles, **Also** 5 ciders/
perries, wines
🍴 Enhanced pub grub, burgers, salads **££**,
🍴 Front terrace, ♿
*Quiz (Tu), singalong (Su), food promotions, photo
booth, table tennis, table football, pinball*

🚇 Woodside Park, East Finchley 🚌 Tally Ho Corner (263 East
Finchley, High Barnet) 🏃 Link to Dollis Valley Greenway

Out beyond the North Circular and close to
the artsdepot performance venue, this huge
building has been an O'Neill's, a furniture shop
and a supermarket. For almost a year from
August 2012 it was an Antic pub, which closed
unexpectedly when lease negotiations failed,
sparking a local outcry and a brief occupation
by squatters. In May 2014 it was reopened by
the owners of the Bull in Highgate (p 151) and
like the Bull it now boasts its own brewery at

Bohemia

the back, though focusing on keg beers and lagers. Casks from Highgate are supplemented by suppliers like Five Points or Redemption, with other top UK and imported choices on keg besides own brews. Bottled highlights include specials from Brooklyn and Goose Island, Kernel pale ales and Belgian classics from Boon and St Bernardus. Food stretches to Cromer crab cakes, spiced feta and spinach filo pie or Welsh rarebit made with own-brewed beer as well as gourmet burgers. Clever design makes the best of the cavernous space and prettily tiled floor. Despite its size and remote location, it's regularly buzzing throughout, and more than likely to send you into rhapsodies.

with a meal feature on a list that mixes Belgian classics like Boon and Rochefort, cutting-edge Brits like Wild and reliable Americans like Bear Republic, Brooklyn and Odell. There are many longer and more obscure beer menus now in London, but few as well-presented and civilised.

Bull (31)

Brewpub, gastropub (London Brewing)
13 North Hill N6 4BX
T (020) 8341 0510
www.thebullhighgate.co.uk
 The-Bull-Highgate Bull_Highgate
 Mo-Th 12.00-23.00, Fr 12.00-24.00,
    Sa 09.30-24.00, Su 09.30-22.30.
    Children very welcome.
Cask beers 4-6 (London Brewing, occasional unusual guests), **Other beers** 10 keg, 35+ bottles, **Also** Wines, local spirits
 Gastro menu **££**, Front terrace,
Beer festivals, beer dinners, quiz (Mo), knitting (Tu), occasional opera and theatre events, board games, functions

 Highgate   Hillcrest Estate (143 Archway, East Finchley)
 Link to Parkland Walk   Link to Capital Ring

This long-neglected roadside Highgate pub reopened in August 2011 under the steward-ship of Dan Fox, former manager of the famous White Horse (p214). It's now managed by some-time beer writer Mitch Adams, while Dan looks after sister pub the Bohemia (p150). Staff can advise what to drink alongside dishes like spiced cauliflower fritters with beer cheese fondue, pancetta-wrapped hake, or confit duck with wild mushrooms, with private dining for groups. In-house beers branded London Brewing are always on cask, with occasional visitors, kegs from the Bohemia and changing draughts from brewers like Beavertown and Burning Sky. Several big bottles for sharing

Dukes Head (32)

Specialist, contemporary pub
16 High Street N6 5JG
T (020) 8341 1310   dukeshighgate
www.thedukesheadhighgate.co.uk
 Mo-We 12.00-24.00, Th-Sa 12.00-01.00,
    Su 12.00-23.30. Children welcome.
Cask beers 8 (unusual sometimes local guests), **Other beers** 9 keg, 16 bottles, **Also** Specialist spirits
 Gourmet meat & veggie sandwiches **£-££**
 Standing on street/yard
Meet the brewer, tastings, mini-festivals, DJs (Fr), seasonal events, major big screen sport, darts, board games

 Highgate, Archway   Link to Hampstead Heath paths

This long, thin pub near the top of Highgate Hill was reopened in September 2013 by two industry newcomers as a stripped-back, grey-painted, flagstone-floored ale and cider house, exhibiting every sign of keen and knowledgeable stewardship. Local casks from Hammerton and Brodies share the handpumps with beers from contemporary favourites like Bristol, Burning Sky, Siren and Waen, while a bank of bar back taps dispenses Beavertown, Fourpure, Kernel ,Magic Rock and Redwell. Bottles and cans are entirely London-sourced and might include Brixton or Redchurch beers. The small kitchen is separately managed by street food specialists Bell & Brisket, serving up salt beef, cheese and home made pickles in

bagels and rye bread rolls that match the place well. There's no garden, sadly, but standing room extends into an ancient sheltered side passage named after the pub.

Shaftesbury Tavern (33)

Traditional pub (Remarkable)
534 Hornsey Road N19 3QN
T (020) 7272 7950   ⬛ 🐦 ShaftesburyT
www.remarkablerestaurants.co.uk
🕐 *Mo-Th* 16.00-23.00, *Fr* 15.30-00.30,
   Sa 12.00-00.30, *Su* 12.00-22.30.
   Children very welcome until 18.30.
Cask beers 4 (Fuller's, Dragonfly, 2 often London guests), **Other beers** 12 keg, 25+ bottles,
Also Cocktails, specialist spirits
🍴 Enhanced pub grub, some Thai **£-££**,
🌴 Front terrace, ♿
Quiz (Tu), live music (Sa), vinyl DJs (Su), jukebox, functions

⊖ Crouch Hill   🚲 Link to Parkland Walk
🏃 Link to Capital Ring

This big corner boozer opposite Elthorne Park was reopened in October 2014 in fine and friendly form: rich dark wood and tiles, engraved mirrors, a massive elaborate bar back surmounted by grand broken pediments and a cosy back room with booths and a skylight. Seafarers from Fuller's is regularly stocked along with a Dragonfly beer from sister pub the George and Dragon in Acton (p 218) and two guests that might come from Hammerton, Pope's, Redemption, Weird Beard or Windswept. Some of the same, along with

Beavertown, are on the keg taps and there are more Londoners in the fridges (Fourpure, Pressure Drop), except for the one reserved for Belgians like Orval and St Feuillien. An interesting menu mixes pub grub with steamed seabass and Thai treats like massaman curry and pad thai, with children's options too.

Three Compasses (34)

Contemporary pub
62 High Street N8 7NX   **T** (020) 8340 2729
www.threecompasses.com
⬛ ThreeCompassesPub.Hornsey.N8
🐦 Three_Compasses
🕐 *Mo-Th* 11.00-23.00, *Fr* 11.00-24.00, *Sa* 11.00-24.00 unusual and local, *Su* 12.00-23.00.
   Over 14s only, over 18 after 21.00.
Cask beers 6 (Fuller's, Redemption, Timothy Taylor, guests), **Other beers** 1 keg, 5-6 bottles,
Also Wines, cocktails
🍴 Pub grub *(Fr-Mo only)* **£-££**, ♿
3 annual beer festivals, quiz (Mo), pool league (Tu), jazz/blues (Th), live music (monthly Sa), seasonal events, major big screen sport, board games, pool, darts

🚉 Hornsey   ⊖ Turnpike Lane   🚌 Hornsey Myddleton Road (144 Turnpike Lane)   🏃 Link to New River Path

A hardworking and very friendly community local under the long-standing direction of licensee Alison, this local cask champion regularly pours Redemption Pale alongside guests from the likes of Cottage, Red Squirrel or locals like East London, sourced through SIBA and the Punch list and available in thirds and lined glasses. Goose Island and Theakston's Old Peculier in bottle widen the options. Home-cooked grub includes pies, fish and chips or pork belly, with vegetarian options like spinach filo parcels, though note the kitchen is closed Tuesday to Thursday. There's plenty of comfortable seating in a relaxed and informal environment, with a rear space used for beer festivals and offbeat events including, of all things, an annual celebration of Elvis Presley's birthday.

Pub trivia *The pub is a late Victorian rebuild of a coaching inn on Hornsey's original village street. Though today it sadly lacks a garden, at one point its grounds extended to the New River, a 17th century aqueduct that's since been diverted to the other side of the road.*

Shaftesbury Tavern

LONDON'S BREWING | Redemption

In an industry full of decent people, Andy Moffat stands out as, well, even nicer than usual - dedicated to the work he does, genuinely delighted that it brings pleasure to others, and generous with his time and expertise. Originally from Glasgow, Andy was a banker who'd lived in London for 18 years, but was keen to start his own business, preferably doing something he felt passionate about and enjoyed. And like an increasing number of young European brewers, he found his inspiration not at home but across the Atlantic, reading *Brewing up a Business*, a how-to book by influential US craft brewer and Dogfish Head founder Sam Calagione.

Andy was determined to create a genuinely local North London brewery at a time when brewing in the capital seemed in irreversible decline. Following a course at BrewLab he installed himself on a Tottenham industrial estate early in 2010 – and

started to hear about all the other new breweries launching in London. "I thought, fine," he recalls. "Other people think this is a good idea too." But quite how good an idea it was, no-one could have guessed.

REDEMPTION
L O N D O N

Redemption still has the same 12-barrel (20hl) plant bought second-hand from Slater's brewery in Stafford, but the fermentation capacity has increased several times. A team of eight, including four brewers who all take turns, now produces up to 80 barrels (130 hl) a week, 95% of it in cask, with a sideline in bottle conditioning since January 2012. The brewery has also become a London Living Wage employer. The beer is as affable as its creator, with smart but not too challenging branding

and distinctive but approachable flavours that appeal to newbie craft kids and dyed-in-the-wool real ale drinkers alike.

The best seller is hoppy pale ale, Hopspur, the name a nod to a certain local football team, but the minor miracle is the 3% Trinity, surely one of the most drinkable beers in the UK. Unusually among London's newer brewers, one yeast has always been used across the range, a culture originally from Scottish and Newcastle in Edinburgh that's now bedded down enough to lend a house character.

"It's been going well," says Andy, "but we've no great ambitions. We'll be happy if we double in size over the next five years and we'll likely upgrade the kit at some point. We'd need to expand our space, though. We've never really had the space for a taproom here so it would be good to add one. But we've certainly no plans to leave Tottenham." The genuinely local brewery is here to stay.

153

TRY ALSO

The **Salisbury Hotel ★** (1 Grand Parade, Green Lanes N4 1JX, www.remarkablerestaurants.co.uk) is one of London's most impressive and important heritage pubs, an 1890s three-storey hulk ringed with black larvikite pillars and surmounted by a crown, richly fitted out inside with floor mosaics, etched *art nouveau* mirrors, carved wood screens and marble floors. Well managed by Remarkable Restaurants, it offers a decent choice of beers from Fuller's, Redemption and the group's own Dragonfly brewery, plus a few good imports. Another corner off-licence worth a look is **Jacks** (178A

Stroud Green Road N4 3RS) at Crouch Hill right by the Albert Road bus stop: despite the unpromising Heineken branding this has over 200 British and imported bottles.

LONDON DRINKERS Joe Stange

Beer blogger and co-author of CAMRA's *Good Beer Guide Belgium*, Joe Stange is originally from Springfield, Missouri. Married to a diplomat, he's lived in Brussels and San José, Costa Rica, and now Berlin. He visits London at least twice a year, missing out on too many museums and great historical sites in favour of atmospheric pubs and low-strength cask ale in great condition, "my favourite drink in the world for an evening out," he says. Read more at www.thirstypilgrim.com.

How do you rate London as a beer city, on a world scale?
It's the world's greatest drinking city, as cosmopolitan as a world city ought to be, but still with a sense of its own identity. To foreign eyes, it's still very English, while New York, in contrast, has never been especially American. The public transit is excellent too. The high prices aren't so good, but that's always a problem in places where everyone wants to be.

What's the single most exciting thing about beer in London at the moment?
Neighbourhoods and villages getting their own breweries again. And railway arches are cool – they provide instant atmosphere. As a tourist, I'm not personally excited about finding American-style IPAs, even if I can see why a local might be. Britain's great contribution to the world of beer is cask ale, and some of it from new London brewers is excellent, packing hop aroma and flavour into a more elegant, drinkable frame, without excessive bitterness.

What single thing would make things even better?
Quality control. At the moment, variety is king. We can only hope that quality comes later. In the meantime we vote in the usual way.

What are your top London beers right now?
Southwark Gold from real handpulls at the end of the Bermondsey run. Kernel Table Beer is a synthesis of all the things that I love about American, Belgian and British ale. And I have a long-running and affectionate friendship with Fuller's Chiswick Bitter.

What's your top great beer night out?
It's not my top recommendation but Bermondsey (p64) is a must-do. But I'd rather spend the whole evening in a comfortable pub with good cask, like the Finborough Arms (p206).

Who's your London beer hero?
I really admire John Keeling at Fuller's, for his knowledge, perspective, and being an ambassador for the practical side of beer making.

Who will we be hearing a lot more from in future?
The folks running Mother Kelly's (p120), the Queen's Head (p49) and Simon the Tanner (p60) appear really formidable.

Which are your other top beer cities?
Brussels, my personal favourite, for the lambic, the atmosphere, and hedonistic attitude to food and drink. Bamberg, the world capital of full-flavoured lagers. Portland, Oregon lives up to its hype. But it's not all about variety: I love Düsseldorf for the Altstadt, Altbier, and its brewpubs.

SOUTHEAST
LONDON

SOUTHEAST LONDON

This section covers the SE postcodes outside the central area and further south and southeast.

Central South London is mainly the Borough of Southwark, except for the places covered under Borough and Southbank (p 51). It includes Camberwell, Dulwich and Peckham, and parts of Lambeth with SE postcodes like Herne Hill and Kennington. It also covers all the listings around Gipsy Hill and Crystal Palace, some of which are on the edges of Bromley and Croydon. This is another part of London that's witnessed major growth in both breweries and beer outlets in recent years, particularly around Nunhead and Dulwich, and now provides one of the longest sections in the book.

Greenwich & Lewisham covers those boroughs, including Blackheath, Brockley, Catford, Deptford, Eltham and Woolwich as well as the towns of Greenwich and Lewisham themselves. With the Maritime Greenwich

World Heritage Site, the Royal Park and numerous other attractions, Greenwich is London's most popular tourist destination outside the centre, and is also home to one of its largest breweries, so you'd expect it to have a few good beer options. More surprising is quite how many once-dowdier neighbour Lewisham now has too.

The big story in **Outer Southeast London** is the recent appearance of several micropubs – small, simple but convivial places focusing on good local beer and sometimes cider. The concept began and still flourishes largely in Kent, and has now spread to parts of London that historically belonged to the county, such as Bexley and Bromley boroughs. The section also includes a few places of note in the borough of Croydon.

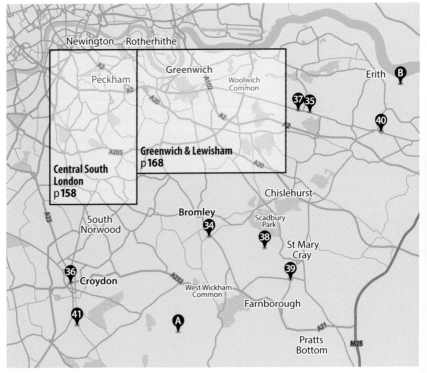

34. Bitter End · 35. Door Hinge · 36. Green Dragon · 37. New Cross Turnpike · 38. One inn the Wood · 39. Orpington Liberal Club · 40. Penny Farthing · 41. Wine Cellar · A. The Cronx Brewery · B. Bexley Brewery

Central South London

Bambuni (1)

Shop, bar
143 Evelina Road SE15 3HB
T (020) 7732 4150
www.bambuni.co.uk 🐦 BambuniNunhead
🕐 *MoTuWeTh&Sa* 09.00-17.30, *Fr* 09.00-19.00,
  Su 10.00-16.00, *Mo* closed. Children welcome.
Cask beers None, **Other beers** 150+ bottles,
Also Fine wines, tea, coffee
🍴 Light lunches, sandwiches, cheese,
charcuterie, deli goods **£**, 🪑 A few tables on
street, ♿
*Occasional tastings, monthly bar nights,
masterclasses, functions*

🚃 Nunhead   🚶 Link to Green Chain Walk

The appearance of a specialist deli among a
parade of bookies, convenience stores and
launderettes is a sure sign of gentrification
hitting a suburb. In Bambuni's case, there's the
added bonus of numerous shelves full of top
notch bottled beer, and a drink-in policy that
means this small and tidy shop and sandwich
seller doubles as a miniature daytime bar.
Opening hours are extended into the evening
on occasional "bar nights". The range is a roll
call of fine locals like Bear Hug, Belleville,
Brew by Numbers, Brockley, Brick, Fourpure
and Kernel, and British brewers of the moment
like Arbor, Buxton, Great Heck, Mallinsons,
Tempest, Thornbridge and Wiper and True.
Owner Huey, who opened up next door to
locally celebrated fishmonger Sopers in
September 2011, allowed himself only one
imported line: the fact he picked Rochefort 10
demonstrates his impeccable taste.

Beer Rebellion Gipsy Hill (2)

Specialist, bar (Late Knights)
126 Gipsy Hill SE19 1PL
www.lateknightsbrewery.co.uk
🐦 beerrebellion
🕐 *Mo-Fr* 17.00-23.00, *Sa-Su* 12.00-23.00.
  Children until early evening.
Cask beers 8 (Late Knights, local and unusual
guests), **Other beers** 4 keg, 45+ bottles,
Also 4 ciders/perries
🍴 Burgers, substantial bar snacks **££**,
🪑 Tables at front, ♿
*Live brewing, meet the brewer/tap takeover,
occasional quiz, board games*

🚃 Gipsy Hill   🔵 Crystal Palace

Late Knights brewery's first pub first popped
up opposite Gipsy Hill station in March 2013,
and now has a permanent site in the next-door
unit, reclaimed from a betting shop. The place
still has the intimate, hidden treasure feel of a
micropub, but with a big range of a spot-on
contemporary craft beer bar, with casks
dispensed using an air pressure system.
Besides Late Knights beers expect to find
other Londoners like Five Points, Fourpure and
nearby Head in a Hat, and beers from further
afield rarely seen in London, including Bad
Seed, Big Rabbit and Truefitt, supplied as part of
brewery swaps. The bottled selection is mainly
local – very much so in the case of Gipsy Hill
and Brockley – with a few visiting Americans
like Founders. Brewery owner Steve Keegan
began his beer career in pubs, helping Fuller's
create the Union (p 208), and it shows.

1. Bambuni · **2.** Beer Rebellion Gipsy Hill · **3.** Beer Rebellion Peckham ·
4. Beer Shop London · **5.** Brick Brewery · **6.** Florence · **7.** Flying Pig ·
8. Four Quarters · **9.** Fox on the Hill · **10.** Gipsy Hill Brewery ·
11. Good Taste · **12.** Grape and Grain · **13.** Hop Burns and Black ·
14. Ivy House · **15.** London Beer Factory · **16.** Oaka (Mansion House) ·
17. Orbit Beers · **18.** Stormbird · **19.** Westow House ·
A. Clarkshaws Brewing & London Beer Lab · **B.** Canopy Beer Co ·
C. Strawman brewery

Beer Shop London

Beer Rebellion Peckham (3)
Specialist, bar (Late Knights)　　　**Top 25**
129 Queens Road SE15 2ND
www.lateknightsbrewery.co.uk
🐦 PeckhamBR
🕑 Daily 12.00-23.00. Children until 19.00.
Cask beers 4 (Late Knights, 2 unusual often local
guests), **Other beers** 10 keg, 48 bottles (mainly
London), **Also** 4 ciders/perries, a few whiskies
🍴 Pork pies, sausage rolls **£**, 🪑 Tables on street, ♿
*Live brewing, meet the brewer/tap takeover,
quiz (Mo), occasional DJs*
🚆⊖ Queens Road Peckham

In August 2014 Late Knights brewery converted
a former betting shop on a unlikely stretch of
main road by Queens Road Peckham station
into one of the best beer dives south of the
river: a particularly pleasing outcome as round
here the change of use is usually in the other
direction. A good range of casks arrives via
vertical dispense from a glass-fronted coldroom,
with guests from people like Celt, Five Points,
Head in a Hat and Truefitt besides Late Knights
beers, also served in thirds or to take away.
There's a similar London theme among the
keykegs, though with occasional US and
Scandinavian imports. The bottled range is
entirely sourced from the capital – this is a rare
outlet for Bullfinch beers alongside Brockley,
By the Horns, Partizan, Rocky Head and
others. High wooden tables provide adequate
drinking space, while vaguely disturbing
murals illustrate the brewing process.

Beer Shop London (4)
Micropub, shop
42 Nunhead Green SE15 3QF
T (020) 7723 5555　📘🐦 beershoplondon
www.thebeershoplondon.co.uk
🕑 Tu-Th 16.00-23.00, *Fr* 16.00-23.30,
　Sa 12.00-23.30, *Su* 12.00-20.00, *Mo* closed.
　Children until 19.00.
Cask beers 4 (South London), **Other beers** 40+
bottles, minicasks (London, mainly south),
Also 4 ciders/perries
🍴 Pork pies, sausage rolls **£**, ♿
Meet the brewer, tastings, occasional acoustic music
🚆 Nunhead　🚶 Link to Green Chain Walk

In a former haberdasher's on Nunhead Green that's more recently been used as council offices and a rehearsal studio, this is despite its name more bar than shop. It's a living room-sized space scattered with cushions and sporting a primary-coloured mountain landscape mural, with casks on stillage behind a small bar counter. The stocking policy is ultra-local, with nearly everything sourced from south London. Brew by Numbers, Brick, Brixton, Brockley, By the Horns, Canopy, Clarkshaws, Gipsy Hill, Kernel, Head in a Hat, Hop Stuff and Orbit all feature regularly, among a few long distance visitors from Tottenham and Ealing. Rotating guest bottles exemplify other regions, styles and themes. Ex-Antic manager Lee Gentry and partner Lauren Willis, who opened the place in December 2014, are effusive and informative with advice and recommendations, and also do a brisk takeaway trade in bottles, gift packs, minicasks and cartons filled from cask.

Brick Brewery (5)

Taproom
209 Blenheim Grove SE15 4QL
T 07747 787636   **www.brickbrewery.co.uk**
🐦 brick_brewery
🕐 *Fr (&Th in summer)* 17.00-21.00, *Sa* 12.00-21.00, closed other days. Children welcome.
Cask beers 3 (Brick), *Other beers* 4 keg, 3 bottles (Brick, occasional London guests), *Also* 2 ciders, bottled local mead
🍴 Pop-up street food £-££, 🌳 Front terrace
Seasonal events

🚆 ⊖ Peckham Rye   🚲 🚶 Link to Surrey Canal path

Few places expose London's social mix more nakedly than Peckham, for many decades one of the most impoverished and multiethnic of neighbourhoods until the council pursued a deliberate policy of encouraging artists to move in, with young professionals soon following. Brick Brewery, in a railway arch behind Peckham Rye station, has stood among this curious jigsaw of trendy coffee bars and pound shops since November 2013. The brewery's beers are dispensed in a variety of formats from a little bar in one corner, and there's an outdoor yard furnished with recycled pallets that buzzes in warmer weather. Further redevelopment around the surprisingly

handsome station building is planned so the brewery might have to close temporarily during the currency of this book.

Florence (6)

Contemporary pub, brewpub (Metro)
131 Dulwich Road SE24 0NG
T (020) 7326 4987   📘 🐦 theflorencepub
www.florenceherneill.com
🕐 *Su-Th* 11.30-24.00, *Fr* 11.30-01.00, *Sa* 11.00-01.00. Children very welcome until 20.00.
Cask beers 4 (Florence, guests),
Other beers 5 keg, 10 bottles
🍴 Eclectic pub grub ££, 🌳 Extensive beer garden, tables at front 🐾, ♿
Seasonal events, table football

🚆 Herne Hill   ⊖ Brixton   🚌 Herne Hill (3, 196 Brixton)
🚲 🚶 Brockwell Park paths

Home to what's now known as the Head in a Hat brewery since a refit by previous owners in 2007 (p 290), the generously proportioned Florence is perfectly placed round the corner from the station and right opposite Brockwell Park. It's a natural destination for families enjoying the green space, and even provides a kids playroom across the other side of the pretty garden with its palm trees in illuminated pots. A long and eclectic menu stretches from sandwiches to meals like paprika squid and chickpea salad or couscous with goat cheese and roast red pepper. House brewed Beaver, Bonobo and Weasel are the regulars, alongside beers from ultimate owners Greene King and others like Sambrook's and Sharp's. London brewers Camden Town, and Truman's are on keg and some of the same names occur among the bottles, alongside classic imports like Duvel and Erdinger.

Florence

Flying Pig

Four Quarters (8)

Bar

187 Rye Lane SE15 4TP

T (020) 3754 7622 **f** **y** fourquartersbar

🕐 *Mo-We* 17.30-01.00, *Th* 17.30-01.30, *Fr* 17.00-02.00, *Sa* 14.00-02.00, *Su* 14.30-00.30. Children very welcome until 19.00.

Cask beers 2 (Purity, 1 unusual guest), **Other beers** 9 keg, 43 bottles, **Also** Cocktails
🍴 Hot dogs **£**, 🪑 Standing on street, ♿ *Vintage games machines, pinball, tournaments, themed events*

🚃 🚇 Peckham Rye 🚲 🚶 Link to Surrey Canal path

Flying Pig (7)

Specialist, bar (Centrale)

58 East Dulwich Road SE22 9AX

T (020) 7732 7575

www.theflyingpiglondon.com

f EDFlyingPig **y** ED_FlyingPig

🕐 *Su-Th* 12.00-23.00, *Fr-Sa* 12.00-24.00. Children until 19.00.

Cask beers 4 (unusual often local guests), **Other beers** 11 keg, 130+ bottles, **Also** 2 ciders, bourbon, gin
🍴 Burgers, diner-style menu **££**, 🪑 Front terrace, ♿ *Meet the brewer/tap takeover, quiz (We), food promotions*

🚃 East Dulwich 🚇 Peckham Rye

Having visited New York City's celebrated Barcade venues, which serve craft beer among retro arcade games, I certainly wasn't expecting to find something similar in a former butcher's shop on Peckham's Rye Lane. Opened by a group of collectors and beer fans in April 2014, Four Quarters boasts 15 vintage video games, the earliest a monochrome Asteroids game from 1979, all activated by US 25¢ coins available from a change machine (thus the name). Upstairs gets even weirder, with trippy lighting, cushions and obsolete tabletop games consoles. Purity is the regular cask beer, with a changing guest that might come from Moor, while Londoners like nearby Brick, Bear Hug, Brew by Numbers, Hop Stuff, Kernel, Orbit and Partizan are among the bottles, with the odd US import from people like Ska, and Beavertown, Camden Town and Meantime on keg. An extraordinary melding of genuine enthusiasms.

Formerly one of a small chain of Italian restaurants, this venue on a smart East Dulwich parade was farsightedly and unexpectedly converted by its owners to a cracking "craft beer pub and BBQ" in August 2013. It's bigger than it looks from the outside, stretching back to a comfortable rear seating area decorated with pump clips. Prominent among the regular cask suppliers are locals Brick, Brockley and Head in a Hat, with Brewster's, Dark Star, Raw and Roosters from further afield. Londoners also account for subtantial swathes of the bottled list (Beavertown, Camden Town, Fuller's, Kernel, Late Knights, Partizan, Wild Card), alongside Durham, Wild and classy US imports. A lighthearted menu covers home-smoked chicken, salads, pulled pork buns and cooked bar snacks, ideally enjoyed in fine weather on the pretty front terrace.

Visitor note *The black and pink spiral bollards outside were designed by Zandra Rhodes, and the Pig is only a short step from Goose Green, where a mural commemorates William Blake's vision of angels on nearby Peckham Rye Common.*

Fox on the Hill (9)

Contemporary pub (Wetherspoon)

149 Denmark Hill SE5 8EH

T (020) 7738 4756 **y** TheFoxontheHil1

www.jdwetherspoon.co.uk

🕐 *Su-Th* 08.00-24.00, *Fr-Sa* 08.00-00.30. Children very welcome until 22.00.

Cask beers 7-10 (Fuller's, Greene King, up to 7 often local guests), **Other beers** 2 keg, 8+ bottles, **Also** 2 ciders/perries
🍴 Full Wetherspoon menu **£-££**, 🪑 Very large front and rear gardens, ♿ *Beer festivals, local beer events, food promotions*

🚃 🚇 Denmark Hill

This red brick pile, built in the 1930s for Charrington's, glowers on a hilltop round the corner from the Salvation Army training college with its landmark tower; it's also close to Kings College and Maudsley hospitals and pretty Ruskin Park. The pub's own outdoor space is the size of a small public park, while the labyrinth of spaces indoors affords seating capacity of German beer hall proportions. Since 1993 the place has been that rarity, a Wetherspoon that was actually built as a pub, and it's one of the better examples of the chain, with its own local beer festivals as well as the national ones. Guest beers regularly include locals like By the Horns, Portobello, Redemption and Sambrook's as well as King and Weltons and there's a larger than usual range of keg and bottled beers of interest too.

Gipsy Hill Brewery

sofa-strewn marquee goes up in the yard at the front. A small bar in the brewery itself dispenses the three Gipsy Hill regulars and specials, sometimes from keg as well as cask, or as single bottles and gift packs to take away. A few bottles and kegs from other Londoners like Five Points and Late Knights add variety.

Good Taste   (11)

Shop

28 Westow Hill SE19 1RX   **T** (020) 8761 7455
www.goodtaste-fd.co.uk
🆕 goodtastefd   🐦 GoodTasteFood
🕐 Mo-We 09.00-18.00, Th-Fr 09.00-20.00,
   Sa 09.00-22.00, Su 11.00-18.00.
   Children welcome.
Cask beers None, **Other beers** 200+ bottles,
Also Boutique wines, specialist spirits
🍴 Cheese, charcuterie, pickles
Tastings

🚆 Gyspy Hill, Crystal Palace   ⬥ Crystal Palace
🏃 Link to Capital Ring, Green Chain Walk

Fox on the Hill

Gipsy Hill Brewery   (10)

Taproom

11 Hamilton Road Industrial Estate SE27 9SF
T (020) 8761 9061
www.gipsyhillbrewing.com
🆕 gipsyhillbrewing   🐦 gipsyhillbrew
🕐 1st & 4th Sa of month 12.00-18.00.
   Children welcome.
Cask beers 1-2 (Gipsy Hill), **Other beers** 6 keg,
4 bottles (Gipsy Hill, London)
🍴 Special events only, 🪑 Tables at front
Occasional bands/DJs, seasonal events

🚆 Gipsy Hill

A session ale specialist opened in July 2014 amid residential streets on the same small industrial estate as London Beer Factory (p 164), this gets quite cosy twice a month when a

Ebullient young owner Manish Utton-Mishra's passion for beer as the perfect accompaniment to the fine cheeses he first set out to sell has driven his small deli into the forefront of great London bottle shops since it opened in March 2011. Displayed tastefully in stacked wooden boxes, products from small local breweries abound: Clarkshaw's, Cronx, Gipsy Hill, Inkspot and Rocky Head line up alongside better-known London names like Weird Beard, high performers from elsewhere in England like Summer Wine and Wild, and delicious obscurities personally hunted out by Manish himself like Norfolk's Poppyland. On Saturday nights they clear the counter and open as a "cheese bar" for a drink-in session with a modest corkage charge.

Grape and Grain (12)

Contemporary pub (Independent, small group)
2 Anerley Hill SE19 2TF
T (020) 8778 9688   🐦 TheGrapeandGrain
www.thegrapeandgrainse19.co.uk
🕐 *Mo-Th* 12.00-23.00, *Fr-Sa* 12.00-24.00,
  Su 12.00-22.30. Children until 18.00.
Cask beers 11 (Adnams, By the Horns, Hogs
Back, unusual guests), ***Other beers*** 2 keg,
18 bottles, ***Also*** Some wine and malts
🍴 Enhanced pub grub, ⛱ Large front terrace, ♿
2 annual beer festivals, jazz big band (Mo),
folk (Tu), swing dance (We), quiz (Th), blues (Fr-Sa),
afternoon live jazz (Su), monthly open mic,
book club, board games

≠ ⊖ Crystal Palace   🏃 Link to Capital Ring, Green Chain Walk

Commanding the hilltop road junction at the northwest corner of Crystal Palace Park, this big pub went by many names including the Crystal Palace Tavern until refurbished and much improved by a new owner in 2009. Manager John, formerly of the sadly closed Brewery Tap in Wimbledon, has increased the beer appeal still further since taking over in May 2013. A wide cask range always features locals, with guests in varied strengths and colours from people like Ilkley, Oakleaf, Slaters and Windsor & Eton. Bottles stretch to Westerham and the now rarely-seen Worthington White Shield as well as imports from Achouffe and Point. It's a comfortable space with an impressive art nouveau fireplace and an extensive front terrace, but make the best of it while you can: it's due to become a Wetherspoon after the current lease expires in 2016.

LONDON'S BREWING Gipsy Hill

It sometimes seems there are more escapees from the City of London among the brewing community than on the average Friday evening train from Cannon Street. "I really wanted to get out of the City," recalls one of them, Sam McNee. "I was just starting a family and all I could see was the time I could spend with them shrinking. I'd done a bit of homebrewing, and I saw brewing as the ideal lifestyle." Sam started researching potential customers and making plans, but things then started moving faster than he'd expected. "I'd known Charlie Shaw for 12 years as a friend of a friend," he continues. "And I was talking about my brewery plans to this friend and he said, 'You need to talk to Charlie'."

Charlie, it turned out, was a lot further along the journey than Sam. As well as extensive homebrewing, he'd been working at Five Points to learn his way around professional equipment, and had already registered a business, found a site and ordered a 15-barrel (24.5 hl) kit from Burton upon Trent supplier

Malrex. Working in partnership made sense, with Sam bringing his business and financial skills and some additional capital. "I quit my job three years ahead of schedule, which was scary," Sam says, "but I thought, it's now or never."

The pair decided they needed an experienced brewer, and found Simon Wood, previously with the Piddle brewery in Dorset (and yes, everyone sniggers at the name, but it's taken from the brewery's home village, Piddlehinton). Simon had taken a break from brewing but was keen to return. "He'd done some interesting stuff, had the right attitude and energy, and an engineering background, which was very useful," says Sam.

The site was close to both of them in Gipsy Hill, and it made sense simply to name the brewery after the place, tapping into the local community spirit. The primary aim has been to establish a core range of good, reliable but contemporary beers at session strengths. "At the time we started, if you wanted

to drink an interesting craft beer it was usually at a high ABV," explains Sam. "We wanted to brew beer so that you can have a few pints with your friends, but with plenty of hoppiness and character." They've certainly achieved this with beers like 3.6% Beatnik, which is proving more than a local hit.

75% of the beer is cask. "We see cask as a really important part of being in the beer market," says Sam. "It suits the more delicate beers. But keykeg and bottle are growing too." The response has been excellent, and since selling their first beers in July 2014 they're already planning on increasing their fermentation capacity and brewing more often than anticipated.

And has Sam yet achieved his ideal lifestyle? He hesitates just a little. "Well, I thought I'd be working less than I actually am," he concludes. "It's probably a bit less than previously, but only just. There's still the weekends and the late evenings. But I'm a lot more physically active, and I'm enjoying it so much more."

Hop Burns and Black Top5 (13)
Shop, bar
38 East Dulwich Road SE22 9AX
T (020) 7450 0284   ⬛🇫 🐦 hopburnsblack
www.hopburnsblack.co.uk
🕑 *Tu-We* 12.00-20.00, *Th-Fr* 12.00-22.00,
   Sa 10.00-22.00, *Su* 10.00-17.00, *Mo* closed.
Cask beers None, **Other beers** 4 keg, 850+ bottles,
Also Some wine, specialist cider
🍴 100+ hot sauces, pies, Scotch eggs **£**,
🪑 Tables at front, rear yard
Fortnightly tastings, meet the brewer/
tap takeover, occasional music

≋ East Dulwich, Peckham Rye   ⊖ Peckham Rye

A shelf label in this stylish bottle shop reads
Southeast London. Four years ago, only two
breweries would qualify – today at least 14
jointly fill a section with the highest turnover
in the shop. Anspach & Hobday, Bear Hug,
Brew by Numbers, Brick, Kernel, Late Knights
and Partizan are among the highlights, with
numerous other Londoners alongside other UK
brewers like Buxton, Ilkley, Tempest, Wiper &
True and Williams Brothers, some American,
Belgian and German beers and – a rare sight in
London – New Zealanders Tuatara and Yeastie
Boys. These last acknowledge the origins of
proprietors Jen and Glenn, who opened in a
former launderette a few doors down from the
Flying Pig (p160) in November 2014. Their other
passion is hot chilli sauces, and the range
includes some made with beer. Oxygen-free
growler fills, a few seats for drinking in and a
collection of classic vinyl add to the attractions.

Ivy House

Ivy House (14)
Traditional pub ★
40 Stuart Road SE15 3BE
T (020) 7277 8233   🐦 Save_Ivy_House
www.ivyhousenunhead.com
🕑 *Mo-Th* 12.00-23.00, *Fr-Sa* 12.00-24.00, *Su* 12.00-
   22.30. Children very welcome until 20.00.
Cask beers 7 cask (Brockley, Dark Star, Hobson's,
Truman's, unusual often local guests),
Other beers 9 keg, 3 cans (London), **Also** 1 cider
🍴 Quality pub grub **££**, 🪑 Tables at front,
beer garden
Beer events, live music (TuFr&Su, sometimes other
nights), children's workshops, cookery, art, yoga,
knitting, functions

≋ ⊖ Brockley, Peckham Rye   🚍 Stuart Road (343 Peckham
Rye)   🚶 Link to Green Chain Walk

In Nunhead backstreets close to the famous
cemetery and Peckham Rye Common, this
well-preserved big Truman's pub is one of
London's happiest preservation success stories.
Rebuilt in 1937 in vaguely Tudor style, it still has
multiple rooms, wood panelling, original bar
counters, tiled spitoons, a big ferny garden and
a back room decorated with mock-heraldic
emblems. In 2012 it was saved from demolition
and redevelopment by a vigorous local
campaign, becoming the first pub listed as
an Asset of Community Value, and the first
building bought under the 'community right to
buy' provisions of the 2011 Localism Act, with
Grade II heritage protection. It's owned and
run by a community interest company with
371 shareholders, including several London
breweries, and stocks a great range of local
casks, keykegs and 'craft' cans, alongside
outsiders like Burning Sky, Buxton or Siren,

also sold in takeaway containers. Food is good quality pub grub – Pieminister pies, burgers, pasta, steak, fish and chips, with lots of veggie choices. A packed programme of events underlines the pub's function as a community hub, and makes good use of space which is shortly to increase still further when a long-abandoned additional bar is brought back into use.

Pub trivia *The pub is so big because the street was once a lively local centre, but the adjoining shops were destroyed by a V1 during World War II and never replaced. In the 1970s, as the Newlands Tavern, this was a key venue on the pub rock circuit, hosting performances by Ian Dury, Dr Feelgood and Joe Strummer's pre-Clash band the 101ers.*

London Beer Factory (15)

Taproom
160 Hamilton Road SE27 9SF
T (020) 8670 7054
www.thelondonbeerfactory.com
🄵 londonbeerfactory 🐦 ldnbeerfactory
🕐 Check for times.
Cask beers 4 (3 London Beer Factory, unusual guests), **Other beers** 4 keg (London Beer Factory, unusual guests)
🍴 Pop-up stands for events £,
🍺 Beer garden at front
Tastings, tours by arrangement, seasonal events, major big screen sport, table football, table tennis

🚆 Gipsy Hill

With its distinctive sawtooth roof, this ambitious brewery, opened in July 2014 in a residential backstreet, does indeed look like a proper factory, and the generously proportioned interior and outdoor yard are perfect for barbecues and events, with rugby screenings particularly popular. A proper bar dispenses cask beers on keg and handpump, mainly brewed in-house but with occasional London guests. Check the website as at the time of writing they hadn't settled into a regular opening pattern – hopefully you'll be able to visit Gipsy Hill (p161), just across the yard, at the same time.

Oaka (Mansion House) (16)

Restaurant, bar (Oakham)
46 Kennington Park Road SE11 4RS
www.oakalondon.com 🄵 🐦 oakalondon
🕐 *Mo-Th* 12.00-23.30, *Fr-Sa* 12.00-24.00, *Su* 12.00-22.30. Children welcome.
Cask beers 6-8 (Oakham), **Other beers** 5 keg, 50 bottles, **Also** Wines, cocktails
🍴 Pan-asian menu ££, 🍺 Tables on street, ♿ *Seasonal events, functions*

🚇 Kennington 🚲 CS7

Peterborough's Oakham brewery, a pioneer of contemporary hoppy beers in the UK, established a London presence in March 2013 by converting Kennington's Mansion House pub into a branch of its Oaka pub-restaurant chain. The vibe here leans more towards the restaurant side, and much of the smart modern space with its Thai-style carving is reserved for sit-down dining. Food is pan-Asian fusion, with dishes including tamarind duck, sambal pork belly or *pad graprow*, with various set menus including numerous veggie options. You're welcome just to call in for a drink, though the atmosphere doesn't quite encourage settling in for the evening. Oakham core beers like the ever-popular Citra are well-served on cask, and there are more house beers on a decent bottled list where they rub shoulders with Londoners like Partizan, old school classics like Saison Dupont, Orval and Worthington White Shield, and interesting imports from Emelisse and Left Hand.

Oaka (Mansion House)

Orbit Beers   (17)

Taproom
225 Fielding Street SE17 3HD
www.orbitbeers.com   📘 🐦 OrbitBeers
🕒 *Sa* 12.00-18.00 (22.00 for special events),
   closed other days. Children welcome.
Cask beers Occasional, **Other beers** 4 keg,
4+ bottles (Orbit)
🍴 Food cart for special events,
🪑 Benches at front
Seasonal events, DJs, occasional tours

🚉 Elephant & Castle   ⊖ Kennington, Elephant & Castle
🚲 🚶 Link to Surrey Canal path

The Scottish-owned, German-leaning Orbit
brewery first opened its railway arch to the
public in October 2014. It's a friendly but basic
operation: a foldaway table with keg taps at
the front of a smallish brewhouse, with
bench-style seating and the blessing of a
secluded outdoor yard in good weather.
Core beers and specials are for sale in keg and
bottle, with the occasional casking for special
events, and food trucks roll up on busier days.
The location off an unpromising stretch of
Walworth Road is better than it looks, with
the pretty Grosvenor Park conservation area
on one side and rapidly regenerating Elephant
& Castle only a short walk away.

Stormbird   Top 25   (18)

Specialist, bar
25 Camberwell Church Street SE5 8TR
📞 (020) 7277 1806   🐦 StormbirdSE5
www.thestormbirdpub.co.uk
🕒 *Mo-Th* 16.00-24.00, *Fr* 16.00-01.00, *Sa* 12.00-
   01.00, *Su* 12.00-24.00. Children until 18.00.
Cask beers 6 (Dark Star, 5 unusual often local
guests), **Other beers** 16 keg, 100+ bottles,
Also A few malts and specialist spirits
🍴 None but customers welcome to bring in
takeaways, 🪑 Tables on street

🚉 ⊖ Denmark Hill   ⊖ Oval, Elephant & Castle
🚌 Camberwell Green (numerous Oval, Elephant & Castle)

This corner site reopened as an unexpectedly
impressive beer bar late in 2011 under the same
ownership as the Hermits Cave opposite.
The simple, smallish, tastefully decorated and
friendly venue tempts both Camberwell's arty
young things and visiting connoisseurs to enjoy
a well-chosen range, with further handpumps
recently added to accommodate guests from
people like East London, Magic Rock, Salopian,
Saltaire and nearby Brick. Beavertown, Kernel,
Schneider and a changing Belgian choice are
on keg alongside a mix of Brits like Moor and
Siren and imports. You'll have to lean over the
bar to peruse a large but chaotic bottle collection that includes some surprising rarities like
BrewDog Tactical Nuclear Penguin, Cantillon
Iris, Mikkeller 黑, Rogue Voodoo Bacon, and a
good range of Partizan saisons. The one thing
that would most improve the place is an
up-to-date printed list.

Westow House   (19)

Contemporary pub (Antic)
79 Westow Hill SE19 1TX
📞 (020) 8670 0654   www.westowhouse.com
📘 Westow-House   🐦 westow_house
🕒 *Su-Th* 12.00-24.00, *Fr-Sa* 12.00-02.00.
   Children welcome until 21.00.
Cask beers 8 (Adnams, Dark Star, Sharp's,
5 unusual often local guests),
Other beers 7 keg, 35+ bottles
🍴 Gastroish menu **££**, 🪑 Front terrace, ♿
*4 annual beer festivals, meet the brewer/tap
takeover, quiz (Tu), live music (Fr/Su), DJ (Sa), pinball,
table football, table tennis, board games*

🚉 ⊖ Crystal Palace   🚶 Link to Capital Ring, Green Chain Walk

This big place looks slightly dark and forbidding
behind its busy terrace on the corner opposite
the Grape and Grain (p 162), but turns out to

Westow House

have a playful, curiously embellished and Chesterfield-strewn interior. Manager Justin Hutton is one of the keenest beer advocates in the Antic group, and the range reflects his taste and enthusiasm. Casks are likely to be from Bristol, Magic Rock, Siren, Weird Beard, Wild and nearby Gipsy Hill and Late Knights. A rotating US keg tap features the likes of Brooklyn and Odell alongside domestic 'craft keg' like Camden Town, Fourpure, Harbour and Wiper & True, well-priced big bottles from Burning Sky, Meantime, Rogue and Savour, and rarely-seen Australian imports from Stone & Wood, besides more familiar bottled names. An imaginative but accessible daily changing food menu might include salmon, barley and leek Wellington or haunch of venison besides pub grub staples.

TRY ALSO

Next door to Oaka (p164) at Kennington is the Brewers' Tudor **Old Red Lion** (42 Kennington Park Road SE11 4RS, www.theoldredlion.com), now in the capable hands of Antic, offering four unusual cask beers and a good range of bottles.

Close to the Flying Pig (p160) and Hop Burns and Black (p163), Antic's first ever pub, the landmark **East Dulwich Tavern** (1 Lordship Lane SE22 8EW, www.eastdulwichtavern.com), is still going strong, with five good casks and a small bottled range. In residential streets to the south is spacious neighbourhood pub the **Great Exhbition** (193 Crystal Palace Road SE22 9EP, www.drinkinlondon.co.uk/great-exhibition), newly refurbished by Laines and with some of their beers on sale.

LONDON DRINKERS | Jen Ferguson

From Nelson, New Zealand, home of some of the world's best hops, Jen has beer in her DNA. After a stint doing PR for Moa Beer back home, she opened beer, hot sauce and vinyl shop Hop Burns and Black (p163) with her partner Glenn Williams in London in October 2014.

How do you rate London as a beer city, on a world scale?
One of the most exciting on the planet. We have more than 50 different beers in our shop's Southeast London section alone. As Johnson might have said, if you're tired of beer in London, you're tired of life.

What's the single most exciting thing about beer in London at the moment?
The passion, creativity and enthusiasm of everyone involved, and the willingness to push the boundaries. Not everything works, of course, but fortune favours the brave...

What single thing would make things even better?
More people getting over their phobia of cans.

What are your top London beers right now?
Weird Beard Mariana Trench and Beavertown Black Betty are favourite go-to beers, and I loved Brew by Numbers 12|05 Barrel Aged Mosaic Tripel that we got as a Christmas treat from the brewery.

What's your top great beer night out?
I'm biased because we're based here, but you can't go wrong in Peckham, with so many great beer places. There's the Brick Brewery taproom (p159), our neighbour the Flying Pig (p160) and then Beer Rebellion Peckham (p158).

Who's your London beer hero?
Andrew Morgan from the Bottle Shop – a top bloke who really knows his beer. He was enormously helpful to us in the planning stages

for our shop, and a Bermondsey trip isn't complete without a few weird and wonderful brews in his taproom (p66).

Who will we be hearing a lot more from in future?
Hammerton and Orbit Brewing are recent arrivals but already making great beers, and Weird Beard are on the top of their game right now.

Which are your other top beer cities?
Wellington has some hugely exciting breweries, Yeastie Boys, Tuatara and Garage Project among them: the Kiwi craft scene is definitely one to watch. Tokyo is also packed with amazing places: it's only a matter of time before Japan does with beer what it's done with whisky. And we love Bristol, home of terrific beer bars and two of our favourite breweries, Moor and Wiper & True, with Wild Beer not far away.

Greenwich & Lewisham

Blythe Hill Tavern (20)

Traditional pub ★
319 Stansted Road SE23 1JB
T (020) 8690 5176
www.blythehilltavern.co.uk
🕐 *Su-We* 11.00-23.30, *Th-Sa* 11.00-24.00.
   Children very welcome until 19.00.
Cask beers 6 (Harveys, Wells & Young's,
4 sometimes local guests), **Other beers** 10
bottles, **Also** 5 ciders/perries
🍴 Summer weekend barbecues only,
🍻 Large garden, tables at front ♿
*Quiz (Mo), Irish session (Th), big screen sport,
board games*

🚆 Catford, Catford Bridge ⊖ Forest Hill 🚌 Blythe Vale
(171 185 Catford) ⚲ Link to NCN21 🏃 Link to Waterlink Way

"Perhaps I've been here too long, it just seems
old to me," says leaseholder Con Riordan of the
pub he's presided over for 27 years. "But everyone else loves it." The multi-room layout and
'olde worlde' style of this former Courage pub,
including fake ceiling beams and fine tiled
fireplaces, have changed little since a refit in
the 1920s. Decorations have Irish and sporting
themes: golf at the front, racing at the back.
Staff in shirts and ties serve up traditional ales
like Courage Best alongside more contemporary or local beers from people like Brockley,
Dark Star, Sambrook's and Westerham, some
of them fetched from the cellar, and there's a
selection of UK and imported bottles too.
Obscurely sited on the South Circular between
Catford and Forest Hill, it's worth seeking out
as an outstanding old school local of a type
now rare in London.

Brockley Brewery (21)

Shop
31 Harcourt Road SE4 2AJ
T 07950 304387 ❚f 🐦 brockleybrewery
www.brockleybrewery.co.uk
🕐 *Fr* 17.30-19.30, *Sa* 10.00-17.00, closed other days.
Cask beers 4 (Brockley),
Other beers 4 bottles (Brockley)
🍴 At special events only.
*Occasional ticketed food, film, beer and music
events, brew school, tours by arrangement*

🚆 ⊖ Brockley 🏃 Link to Green Chain Walk

This decent and decidedly local brewery
occupies a space not much more than a big
shed in a residential street near Brockley
station. Since October 2013, a stall within the
brewhouse has sold beer to take away in
bottles, cartons filled to order from cask, or
polypins if ordered in advance, and the brewers
are often around for a chat. It's also used as a
venue for prebooked activities and events –
including training enthusiasts to brew at home.

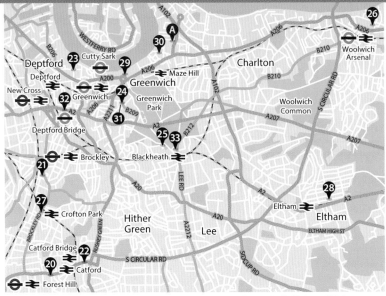

20. Blythe Hill Tavern · **21.** Brockley Brewery · **22.** Catford Constitutional Club · **23.** Dog and Bell · **24.** Greenwich Union ·
25. Hare and Billet · **26.** Hop Stuff Brewery · **27.** London Beer Dispensary · **28.** Long Pond · **29.** Old Brewery · **30.** Pelton Arms ·
31. Richard I · **32.** Royal Albert · **33.** Zerodegrees · **A.** Meantime Brewing

Catford Constitutional Club

Contemporary pub (Antic)   (22)
Catford Broadway SE6 4SP
T (020) 8613 7188
www.catfordconstitutionalclub.com
🄵 CatfordConstitutionalClub 🐦 CatfordCClub
🕘 *Mo-Th* 16.00-23.00, *Fr* 16.00-01.00, *Sa* 12.00-
24.00, *Su* 12.00-23.00. Children until 21.00.
Cask beers 6 (Adnams, Brains, Caledonian, 3
unusual often local guests), **Other beers** 2 keg,
18 bottles, **Also** Specialist spirits
🍴 Gastroish menu **£-££**, 🪑 Front courtyard, ♿
*Quiz (Tu), monthly comedy, film nights, oocasional
acoustic music, functions*

🚃 Catford, Catford Bridge 🚲 NCN21 🚶 Waterlink Way

On a pretty courtyard off Catford Broadway,
this unusual boozer opened in November 2013
in a former Conservative club abandoned in
1996, and initailly so decayed it had a tree
growing out of the bar. It still looks notably
distressed ("heavy on the shabby, light on the
chic," comments manager Alex) with displays
of *Private Eye* covers and fading portraits of
Churchill and the Queen. Guest casks usually
include beers from London (Head in a Hat,

Sambrook's) and Yorkshire (Ilkley, Rooster's),
with unfined examples regularly favoured,
while a well-curated bottled list includes
Beavertown, Pitfield's, Rogue and Schneider.
Dishes like duck leg confit, grilled smoked
haddock, pappardelle with butternut squash
and chestnuts and exquisite devilled mushrooms on toast no doubt give the ghosts of
the Tory ladies that once presided here a
right turn. Enjoy it while you can, as the whole
area is eventually due for redevelopment.

Dog and Bell Top 25 (23)

Traditional pub
116 Prince Street SE8 3JD
T (020) 8692 5664 **f** Dog-Bell-SE8
⊕ *Su-Th 12.00-23.30, Fr-Sa 12.00-24.00.*
Cask beers 5-6 (Fuller's, 4-5 unusual often local guests), **Other beers** 20+ bottles (mainly Belgian), **Also** 20 malts
🍴 Pub grub, sandwiches £,
🪑 Beer garden at back, ♿
Quiz (Su), annual pickles festival, bar billiards, board games

🚉 Deptford 🚇 Cutty Sark 🚌 Abinger Grove (188 Canada Water, Surrey Quays, Cutty Sark) ⛴ Greenwich 🚲 NCN4, link to NCN21 🚶 Jubilee Greenway, Thames Path, link to Waterlink Way

Charlie and Eileen Gallagher took on this fine backstreet free house in 1988 and have significantly expanded both its size and its reputation, doing a magnificent job of keeping it contemporary, comfortable and welcoming to a diverse crowd while ensuring it remains at heart a genuine community local with an always reliable range of quality beers. Guests are often local, with Brockley, Clarkshaw's, East London and Head in a Hat featured besides brewers like Dark Star, Slaters and Westerham, in a range of strengths and colours. Bottles are mainly beefy Belgians from Boon, Dupont, Orval, St Bernardus, St Feuillien and Troubadour, with the odd German wheat beer. Food is home cooked and well priced – sandwiches, shepherd's pie, curries and veggie

specials – while the pickles festival in late autumn must be unique in the capital. A pleasant shaded yard decked with colourful planters supplements the homely interior.

Pub trivia *Opened in 1823 and rebuilt in the late 1860s opposite the site of Henry VIII's naval dockyard, the pub was once owned by the now-closed Wenlock brewery in Islington, later by Bass and briefly by Fuller's in the late 1970s – it has stocked London Pride ever since. The unusual name may derive from the fact that Prince Street was once called Dock Street and known locally as Dog Street.*

Greenwich Union (24)

Specialist, contemporary pub (Meantime)
56 Royal Hill SE10 8RT
T (020) 8692 6258 **f** **y** greenwichunion
www.greenwichunion.com
⊕ *Mo-Th 12.00-23.00, Fr-Sa 10.00-23.00, Su 10.00-22.30.* Children welcome.
Cask beers None, **Other beers** 17 keg, 150 bottles (including Meantime)
🍴 Sandwiches, gastroish menu, weekend breakfasts **££**, 🪑 Front terrace, beer garden
Occasional tastings, beer course, food events

🚉 🚇 Greenwich ⛴ Greenwich 🚲 Links to NCN4, NCN21

Opened in 2001 as Meantime's first pub, the Union was almost upstaged by the impressive Old Brewery (p171), but has fought back with a bigger and smarter beer range. It has warm wood and padded benches, a popular garden at the back and plenty of sockets for laptop tappers. A comprehensive range of Meantime and other British beers on keg is boosted by a long bottle list, complete with detailed notes, foregrounding traditional European styles – lambics, a comprehensive Trappist selection including newish Austrian entrant Stift-Engelszell, plenty from Schlenkerla and Schneider – alongside US names like Brooklyn and Rogue. Food includes imaginative starters (black pudding Scotch eggs, homemade beetroot hummus) and dishes like mixed vegetable tart with blue cheese sauce or mussels in white wine with samphire besides burgers and steaks. Next door to another classic Greenwich pub, the Richard I (p 173), the Union marches on.

Hare and Billet (25)

Specialist, contemporary pub (Metro)
1a Hare and Billet Road SE3 0QJ
T (020) 8852 2352 🇫 🐦hareandbillet
www.hareandbillet.com
🕐 *Mo-We* 12.00-23.00, *Th-Fr* 12.00-24.00, *Sa* 11.00-24.00, *Su* 11.00-22.30. Children until 19.00.
Cask beers 8 (Greene King, 6 unusual often local guests), **Other beers** 8 keg, 35 bottles, **Also** Wines, a few malts, digestifs and sweet wine
🍴 Imaginative British/international menu **££**
🍺 Plastic cups on the heath, ♿
Tastings, food matching, meet the brewer, quiz (Mo), board games

🚆 Blackheath 🚌 Vale Eliot Place (380 Lewisham, 386 Blackheath) 🚲🚶Blackheath paths

In February 2013 this rustic Blackheath landmark was transformed from a very ordinary Greene King pub into a top notch beer specialist in the company's Metropolitan chain, with a tasteful new interior in white tiles and wood. It now stocks casks from locals like Brockley, Hop Stuff and Late Nights as well as Caveman, Celt, Kent, Otley or Wild besides its owner's more interesting lines: customers taste beers and vote on those to stock in a monthly 'beer council'. A profusion of London bottles includes rare specials like Camden Town's Versus series, alongside suppliers like Hardknott, Ilkley and Tiny Rebel and a few imports from Fordham, Rodenbach and Rogue. The imaginative menu could include *imam bayıldı*, roast cod with borlotti beans or pressed pork belly with celeriac puree, and a tempting list of puds. Plastic glasses and takeaway containers facilitate *al fresco* enjoyment on the Heath.

Pub trivia *This is one of the few pubs in London to have a pond named after it, and overlooks the tree-ringed pool in question. It was originally built in the 17th century to serve travellers on nearby Watling Street, the old Roman road to Dover, now the A2, though has been rebuilt several times.*

Hop Stuff Brewery

Hop Stuff Brewery (26)

Taproom
7 Gunnery Terrace SE18 6SW
T (020) 8854 9509
www.hopstuffbrewery.com
🇫 hopstufflondon 🐦Hopstuffbrewery
🕐 *1st Fr of month* 18.00-22.30, *1st Sa of month* 11.00-15.00, closed other days. Children welcome on Saturday.
Cask beers 4 (Hop Stuff), **Other beers** 1 keg, 2-3 bottles (Hop Stuff)
🍴 Sausage rolls, pies **£**
Prebooked group tastings

🚆🚇 Woolwich Arsenal 🚲NCN1 🚶Thames Path, link to Capital Ring

The Royal Arsenal at Woolwich now has its own brewery, opened in an industrial unit in November 2013. The taproom is cosier than some, with carpets, sofas and malt sacks on a gantry overlooking the fermenters. Five core beers and additional specials are served from cask and bottle and occasionally keykeg and polypin, with growlers and polypins happily filled to take away. Delicious table sauces made with the brewery's beer are also on sale, just the thing to pep up gourmet backed savouries supplied by Flicks Fancies in Horton Kirby.

Visitor note *The Royal Arsenal grew from an ordnance depot established in 1671 into what was once Britain's biggest producer of armaments, not to mention the original home of Arsenal FC. The vast Thameside site was finally demilitarised in 1994 and redeveloped on a grand scale from the 2000s.*

London Beer Dispensary (27)

Specialist, bar (Late Knights)
389 Brockley Road SE4 2PH
T (020) 8692 1550   ■ ▼ LDNDispensary
www.lateknightsbrewery.co.uk/bars
🕓 *Su-Th* 12.00-23.00, *Fr-Sa* 12.00-24.00.
 Children welcome.
Cask beers 8 (Late Knights, usually local guests),
Other beers 3 keg (Late Knights, 2 mystery beers),
45 bottles, **Also** 5 ciders/perries, whiskies
🍴 Gourmet burgers, salads **£-££**,
🪑 Rear patio, shared with wine bar
Live brewing, meet the brewer/tap takeover

⇌ Crofton Park   ⊖ Brockley   🚌 Crofton Park Station (171,
172 New Cross, Brockley)   🏃 Link to Green Chain Walk

Since long-standing Brockley bottle shop and
wine bar Mr Lawrence appeared in the last
edition, a partnership with Late Knights brewery has seen the bottle business moving online
and the wine bar moving into the shop, creating space for the London Beer Dispensary.
With its wood panelling and rear snug supervised by a stuffed stag's head, the place has a
surprisingly old fashioned and lived-in feel for
somewhere opened only in May 2014, though
the beer range is bang up-to-date. There's no
bar counter, just a central servery with casks
on stillage, including brewers like Anspach &
Hobday, Brick, Bullfinch, Crate, Kernel, Partizan
and Rocky Head besides Late Knights in cask,
keykeg or bottle, with visitors like Bristol or
Celt Experience and occasional imports. Two
of the kegs are "mystery beers" in both dark
and light styles. The charming little patio at
the back is shared with the wine bar.

Visitor note *Just down the road is one of the area's quirkier
attractions, the red velvet and crystal-bedecked Rivoli,
London's only remaining 1950s ballroom.*

Old Brewery

Long Pond (28)

Micropub
110 Westmount Road SE9 1UT
www.thelongpond.co.uk   ▼ thelongpond
🕓 *Mo* 17.30-22.00, *Tu-We* 11.30-14.30, 17.00-22.00,
 Th-Fr 11.30-14.30, 17.00-23.00, *Sa* 11.00-15.00,
 18.30-23.00, *Su* 12.00-14.30.
Cask beers 6 (Tonbridge, 5 local guests),
Also 4 ciders
🍴 Sausage rolls, pies, cheese **£**, ♿
*Beer and food matching (Mo), tastings, meet the
brewer, occasional acoustic music, seasonal events*

⇌ Eltham   🏃 Capital Ring, Green Chain Walk

Named after a landmark in nearby Eltham Park
South, this former plumbers' merchant became
London's fourth micropub in mid-December
2014 thanks to ex-money broker and local man
Mike Wren. It's a friendly, chatty place that's
just a little bigger than average, with a plain but
comfortable main drinking area of the half-
panelled and high stools variety, collections
of framed music-themed beermats, and a
walled-off snug with tables and chairs. Eltham
hasn't been in Kent since 1889 but the place
still celebrates old regional loyalties, with a
house beer supplied by Tonbridge brewery and
guests from Gadds, Old Dairy and Whitstable
as well as locals like Bexley, Brockley and Hop
Stuff, all poured from the cask in a cool room
behind the bar and sold at good value prices.

Pub trivia Older readers will be reassured to hear that
the vintage Watneys Red bar mount is only there as an
ironic talking point.

Old Brewery (29)

Brewpub, restaurant (Meantime)
Pepys Building, Old Royal Naval College SE10
9LM   **T** (020) 3327 1280
www.oldbrewerygreenwich.com
■ OldBreweryGreenwich   ▼ OldBrewery
🕓 *Daily* 10.00-24.00. Children very welcome.
Cask beers 2 (unusual guests), **Other beers** 8 keg
(Meantime), 80 bottles, **Also** Wines
🍴 Modern British **££-£££**, 🪑 Front patio, ♿
Brewery tours, tastings, seasonal events

⇌ Greenwich, Maze Hill   ⊖ Cutty Sark   ⛴ Greenwich
🚲 NCN1, NCN4, Greenwich Park paths   🏃 Thames Path,
Jubilee Greenway, Greenwich Park paths

The gleaming microbrewery towering above diners in Meantime's upmarket showcase venue hasn't been used as much as originally planned since opening in 2010, but should be back in action by the time you read this, turning out specials to serve alongside the brewery's keg beers and unfiltered lager, cask ales from Dark Star and others, and an encyclo-paedically-documented bottle list of fine London porters and textbook classics like Anchor Old Foghorn, Cantillon Gueuze and Schneider Aventinus. You can enjoy these at the small red-curtained bar, outside on the sunny patio, or alongside a meal in the glitzy restaurant, where sausages are dosed with raspberry wheat beer and chicken legs braised with pale ale. There's a children's menu too.

Pub trivia. *This is one of London's most spectacularly-sited beer outlets, near the riverfront in the grounds of Christopher Wren and Nicholas Hawksmoor's masterpiece the Old Royal Naval College. The building was indeed a brewery when the complex first opened in 1712 as the Royal Hospital, actually a veterans' hostel. It's on the site of the Tudor Palace of Placentia, birthplace of Mary I and Elizabeth I.*

LONDON'S BREWING **Meantime**

IT'S not too fanciful to suggest that Alastair Hook changed the face of British brewing. Back in the early 1990s, he already had a much more international background than the typical aspirant microbrewer. Born in Greenwich, he trained at Heriot-Watt in Edinburgh, but regularly spent summers in California witnessing and modestly assisting in the early days of the craft beer movement. Then he learned German so he could pursue postgraduate studies at the famous Weihenstephan brewing school near Munich.

Despite an early love of good real ale, he wasn't about to start brewing best bitters, but in Britain back then there wasn't really a model for much else. And 'quality lager' was almost a contradiction in terms: lager was a near-flavourless industrial beer that you either drank uncritically or avoided like the plague.

In 1991 Alastair became the brewer at a pioneering brewpub, the Packhorse, in Ashford, Kent, specialising in German-style beers. Four years later he was back in London as the major force in the creation of Freedom in Fulham, which turned out to be the first successful UK 'craft' lager brewery, still in operation today, although in Staffordshire under different ownership. He then helped set up two of Britain's earliest US-style upmarket brewpub-restaurants, before launching Meantime in 2000, in Charlton near the Thames Barrier, named for its location near Greenwich and its commitment to properly matured beers.

The brewery originally earned its keep by contract brewing and marketing to restaurants and bars rather than the pub trade, but soon gained confidence to launch its own brands, including an authentic bottle-conditioned IPA and porter. And finally public tastes caught up with Alastair's vision. In 2010 Meantime not only launched a spectacular new bar-restaurant, the Old Brewery, in the Greenwich World Heritage Site (p171), but finally achieved its ambition to move brewing to the town, with a new site not far from the O₂, boasting an auto-mated 100 hl kit and, since 2015, a smart taproom and visitor centre.

Until very recently, Meantime was the second oldest and second biggest of London's independent breweries, with an output of around 100,000 hl a year. Chief Executive Nick Miller, recruited in 2011 with a remit to turn it into a national brand, oversaw the sale of the company to his former em-ployers, multinational SABMiller, as a 'craft' subsidiary in May 2015. How much the brewery will remain rooted in quality beer and brew-ing tradition, with initiatives like its pioneering unfiltered and un-pasteurised 'tank' lager and its urban hop garden on the Greenwich peninsula, remains to be seen.

Alastair remains unapologetic about an approach that's never endeared him to real ale purists. "I'm a passionate believer in brewery conditioning," he once told me, "because you can't trust the distribution chain. What I learned in Germany was that the most important factor is giving beer enough time to mature, which too few brewers do, including cask brewers – too many of them rush beer out when it's too young. But to spend six or eight weeks lovingly making a beer, so it's properly matured with a nice structure, only to have it ruined by an untrained and uncaring cellarman is just awful." His decision to plough his own furrow 25 years ago now seems more far-sighted by the day.

Pelton Arms   (30)

Traditional pub
23-25 Pelton Road SE10 9PQ
T (020) 8858 0572   www.peltonarms.com
The-Pelton-Arms-Pub peltonarms
Mo-Th 12.00-24.00, *Fr-Sa* 12.00-01.00,
  Su 12.00-23.00. Children until 19.00.
Cask beers 9 (Greene King, St Austell, Wells &
Young's, up to 6 often unusual guests), *Other*
beers 1 keg, **Also** 1 cider, some whiskies and wines
Sandwiches, quality pub grub *(not Mo)* **£-££**,
Beer garden ,
Live music (acoustic/bands) (Th-Su), darts (Mo),
quiz (Tu), knitting night/Northern Soul DJ (We),
major big screen sport, bar billiards, board games

Maze Hill   Cutty Sark   Tyler Street (numerous,
Greenwich)   Greenwich   NCN1, link to NCN4
Thames Path, Jubilee Greenway

Follow the Thames Path downstream from
Greenwich pier and turn off into a side street
of modest Victorian terraces to reach this
busy local, run with traditional style and a
modern sensibility since a refresh in 2009 and
also used as a base by the Pearly Queen of
Greenwich. There's a bar with deep red walls
and deep red armchairs, and a lovely garden
lined with well-tended planters and equipped
with its own big screen. Guests ales sourced
through Punch's direct delivery scheme could
include Brentwood, Hop Stuff, Red Squirrel,
Westerham or Truman's. Food is wholesome,
well-priced stuff, from fish and chips and
whitebait to butternut squash risotto and
slow cooked pork belly.

Pub trivia. *Don't get confused by a second name, The Nags*
Head, over the door – in 2010 the pub was used as a location
for Rock & Chips, the Only Fools and Horses prequel, with
Greenwich standing in for Peckham.

Richard I

Richard I   (31)

Contemporary pub (Young's)
52 Royal Hill SE10 8RT   **T** (020) 8692 2996
www.richardthefirst.co.uk
Richard-I RichardFirstPub
Mo-Sa 12.00-23.00, *Su* 12.00-22.30.
  Children until 20.00.
Cask beers 6 (3 Wells & Young's, London guests),
Other beers 6 keg (Camden Town, Meantime,
Wells & Young's), 16 bottles, **Also** Wines
Enhanced pub grub/gastro **££**, Front
terrace, beer garden,
Tastings, food matching, quiz (Tu), acoustic music
(Su), molly dancing visits

Greenwich   Ashburnham Grove (numerous,
Greenwich)   Greenwich   Links to NCN4, NCN21

Two adjoining bow-windowed Georgian
cottages were at some stage fused together
to create this pub next door to the Greenwich
Union (p 169), now a Young's house but still
known locally as Tollys from a previous tie. A
major refurb in 2014 added a rear conservatory, boosted the beer range and integrated
the space still further, though the quiet front
bar on the left, still the bolthole of choice for
discerning locals, retains its own character.
Young's Bitter, Special and seasonals are
supplemented on handpump by beers from
London brewers like By the Horns, East
London, Hackney, London Fields, Portobello
or Sambrook's. Elsewhere there are choices
from Camden Town, Meantime and Hop Stuff.
Dishes like smoked lamb and burned leek
shepherd's pie and various twists on macaroni
cheese feature on the menu besides steaks,
burgers, sharing plates and a good cheeseboard.

THE PELTON ARMS

Zerodegrees (33)

Brewpub, bar
29 Montpelier Vale SE3 0TJ
T (020) 8852 5619 www.zerodegrees.co.uk
 zerodegreesrestaurant Zerodegreesbeer
 Su-Th 12.00-24.00, *Fr-Sa* 12.00-00.30.
   Children in restaurant only.
Cask beers None, **Other beers** 6 keg, minicasks
(Zerodegrees), **Also** Wines
 Pizzas, mussels, salads, pasta,
 Front and rear terraces,
Brewery tours, tastings, occasional DJs

 Blackheath   Blackheath paths

Opened in 2001 and now the capital's longest serving brewpub, this spacecraft-like space behind an unassuming Blackheath Village frontage was one of the UK's earliest venues directly inspired by the US craft beer scene. A major refurbishment early in 2014 expanded the floor space and toned down the brash post-modern decor, though it's still determinedly contemporary, with views of the gleaming brewhouse from a warren of mezzanine floors. Only house brews, all unfiltered and served by air pressure, are on sale, by the glass or take-away minikeg. Continuing the transatlantic theme, stonebaked pizzas with unusual toppings feature heavily on the menu, alongside pasta, mussels and sausage and mash.

Pub trivia. The name refers to the proximity of the Greenwich Meridian at 0° longitude, but has been retained for subsequent daughter venues in Bristol, Cardiff and Reading.

Royal Albert (32)

Contemporary pub (Antic)
460 New Cross Road SE14 6TJ
T (020) 8692 3737 www.royalalbertpub.com
 The Royal Albert theroyalalbert
 Mo-Th 16.00-24.00, *Fr* 16.00-01.00, *Sa* 12.00-
01.00, *Su* 12.00-24.00. Children until 20.00.
Cask beers 7 (Adnams, Dark Star, Sharp's, 4 local
guests), **Other beers** 3 keg, 20 bottles, **Also** 1 cider,
specialist spirits
 Gastroish menu, cooked bar snacks **£-££**,
 Front terrace,
*Beer festival, meet the brewer/tap takeover,
quiz (Mo), DJ (Fr), live music (Su)*

 New Cross   Deptford Bridge   Link to NCN21
 Link to Waterlink Way

This roadside pub spent years hiding much of its Victorian splendour under the guise of a music venue, until an Antic takeover in 2007 jettisoned the music but restored much else, including the original name, some chunky carved wood and a splendid skylight at the back. Since then it's continuously improved its beer offer, and still celebrates the day it doubled its handpump count with the Octopump festival in September. Regulars are Lighthouse, Hophead and Doom Bar, while guests are usually sourced locally from brewers like Brockley, Crate, Cronx, East London, Five Points or Whitstable, with London 'craft keg' too. Bottles could stretch to Beavertown, Firebrand and Ticketybrew, besides Adnams, Duvel and Kernel. An imaginative daily chang-ing menu includes old fashioned cooked bar snacks, cheese plates, pub grub staples and dishes like roast salmon or cep and goat cheese risotto.

TRY ALSO

This part of London is particularly dense with good Antic pubs. Besides those with full listings it's worth looking in at **Jam Circus** (330 Brockley Road SE4 2BT, www.jamcircus.com), close to the London Beer Dispensary (p171) and Rivoli ballroom; the **Job Centre** (120 Deptford High Street SE8 4NS, www.jobcentredeptford. com), indeed in the former Deptford Job Centre and fairly close to the Dog and Bell (p169); and big Ladywell roadhouse the **Ravensbourne Arms** (323 Lewisham High Street SE13 6NR, www.ravensbournearms.com).

Another good Antic is the **Sylvan Post** (24 Dartmouth Road SE23 3XU, www.sylvanpost. com) in the old Forest Hill Post Office, with two curious snugs in former walk-in safes. Just round the corner is a more spectacular conversion to pub use: Wetherspoon's **Capitol** (11 London Road SE23 3TW, www.jdwetherspoon. co.uk) in a lavish former cinema, one of the best of the chain's south London outlets for interesting guest beers. Both pubs are handy for the Horniman Museum and Gardens, a little further up London Road. Just beyond Lewisham among a pretty parade of shops by Hither Green station, the newly refurbished **Station Hotel** (14 Staplehurst Road SE13 5NB, www.stationhotelhithergreen.co.uk) has eight mainly local cask beers.

The big **Montague Arms** (289 Queens Road SE15 2PA, www.montaguearms.co.uk) between Queens Road Peckham (see Beer Rebellion Peckham p158) and New Cross Gate was happily rescued from threatened closure in 2014, and now offers four unusual casks and some interesting kegs and bottles alongside its regular music programme. Further on near New Cross station, the little **LP Bar** 401 New Cross Road SE14 6LA, www.thelpbar.co.uk) has a small but well-chosen range of local bottled beers including Kernel: the adjoining London Particular café and upmarket chippy Maddy's Fish Bar are under linked ownership and also offer local beer. Top Antic recommendation the Royal Albert (p174) is close by.

The sizeable **Meantime Tasting Rooms** (Lawrence Trading Estate, Blackwall Lane SE10 0AR, www.meantimebrewing.com/ tasting-rooms) at this Greenwich brewery near the Blackwall Tunnel Approach just missed the deadline for review here – they're open daily, with a full food menu and brewery tours too (best pre-booked). Not far away, the now-bustling area around the O₂ at North Greenwich boasts open-air pop-up brewery bar the **Meantime Beer Box** (Peninsula Square SE10 0DX), with cable car as well as Tube connections.

Nearby is the **Pilot** (68 River Way SE10 0BE, www.pilotgreenwich.co.uk), one of the few historic buildings in a rapidly developing area: much refurbished and expanded inside, it's now an upmarket but welcoming Fuller's pub. On the way back to Greenwich town centre, the original branch of **Theatre of Wine** (75 Trafalgar Road SE10 9TS, www.theatreofwine. com), stocks a decent range of local and UK bottles, though not quite so many as its Tufnell Park sister. **Oddbins'** Blackheath branch (26 Tranquil Vale SE3 0AX, www. oddbins.com) reopened in March 2015 as a dedicated beer shop.

In a historic and admirably converted building on the Woolwich Arsenal site, overlooking the original ground of Arsenal FC and not far from Hop Stuff brewery (p292), is an expansive Young's pub, the **Dial Arch** (The Warren, Royal Arsenal Riverside SE18 6GW, www.dialarch.com), serving a wide range of Wells & Young's beers and occasional London guests. You'll likely find Hop Stuff beers right by Woolwich Arsenal station among the six casks at another impressive conversion, Antic's **Woolwich Equitable** (General Gordon Square SE18 6AB, www.woolwichpub.com) in a former building society headquarters. Between the town centre and the ferry terminal is veteran unpretentious real ale free house **Roses** (Prince Albert) (49 Hare Street SE18 6NE) with up to six guest casks including very local brews.

Not far from the Long Pond (p171), the **Park Tavern** (45 Passey Place SE9 5DA, www. parktaverneltham.co.uk), just off Eltham town centre is handy for English Heritage's Eltham Palace. It serves up eight cask beers mainly from small brewers in a civilised setting more like a chintzy English tea shop than a pub.

Outer Southeast London

Bitter End (34)

Shop
139 Masons Hill, Bromley BR2 9HW
T (020) 8466 6083
www.beerbarrels2u.co.uk 🐦 beerbarrels2u
🕐 Mo-Fr 12.00-21.00, Sa 11.00-21.00,
  Su 17.00-21.00.
Cask beers 8-12 (Sharp's, Timothy Taylor, often
local guests), ***Other beers*** 200 bottles, up to
200 bulk cask beers to order, ***Also*** 8 ciders/
perries, French wines
Occasional tastings

🚆 Bromley South

The cask ale stillage first went up in this pioneering specialist off-licence in 1983. It's since
become the nerve centre of a flourishing online
business, BeerBarrels2U, serving a growing
market for draught beer at home in quantities
from 5 l minicasks to full 9-gallon (41 l) firkins.
Takeaway measures in the shop start more
modestly at two pints, for about a third less
than you'd pay in a pub; beers from Dark Star,
Harvey's, Oakham, Timothy Taylor (often
including other brands besides Landlord),
Tonbridge and Westerham are stocked, with
even more to order online. The bottle selection
now focuses on the UK and tends slightly
towards the traditional with plenty of Harvey's
and Sam Smith's, as well as Bristol, Hepworth,
Redemption and Rooster's among others and
a handful of solid Belgian and German classics.

Door Hinge Top 25 (35)

Micropub
11 High Street, Welling DA16 1TR
T 07956 845509
www.thedoorhinge.co.uk 🐦 HurleyRapnd
🕐 Tu-Th 15.00-21.00, Fr-Sa 12.00-22.00, Su 12.00-
  .15.00, Mo closed. Children on football days only.
Cask beers 4-6 (unusual often Kent guests),
Also Cider/perry
🍴 Cheese and roasties on Sundays

🚆 Welling

The first permanent outpost of the micropub
movement to creep from Kent into southeast
London, the Door Hinge was deservedly
named as CAMRA's London Pub of the Year in
2014: an impressive accolade for a place in the
farflung suburbs that seats a mere 22 people
and only opened in March 2013. The shopfront
site has been refitted in traditional but basic
pub style with benches and half-panelling,
with beer poured from the cask in a glass-
fronted cool room at the back. Keenly-priced
ales in a range of styles are often from Kent
and London brewers like Gadds, Old Dairy,
Portobello, Redemption and Tonbridge, though
with others like Dark Star, Marble and Oakleaf
also appearing. The small space, mobile phone
ban (there's a sacrificial display of the things
nailed to the wall) and absence of TVs and
music encourage conversation between
strangers, with takeaway containers filled too.
But what really makes the place is landlord
Ray Hurley, a garrulous but no-nonsense
ale-loving southeast Londoner who drove a
cab for 20 years before opening his "oasis",
labelling it with an old family nickhame.

Visitor note *Just down the road is the ground of
non-league but well-supported Welling FC, the 'Wings',
who play in the Conference Premier, so expect the
pub to be busy on match days.*

Green Dragon (36)

Contemporary pub (Stonegate)
58 High Street, Croydon CR0 1NA
T (020) 8667 0684   🐦 thegreen_dragon
www.thegreendragoncroydon.co.uk
🕓 *Mo-Tu* 10.00-23.00, *We-Th* 10.00-24.00,
Fr-Sa 10.00-01.00, *Su* 12.00-22.30.
Children until 21.00.
Cask beers 8 (Dark Star, 6 often local guests),
Other beers 4 keg, 4 bottles, **Also** 2 ciders
🍴 Breakfasts, enhanced pub grub **££**, ♿
*Beer festivals, meet the brewer, tastings, quiz (Mo),
DJ (Th-Sa), acoustic music (Su), food promotions,
book swap, pool, functions*

⇌ East Croydon, West Croydon   ⇌ West Croydon
⊖ George Street   🚶 Links to Vanguard Way, Wandle Trail

Regenerated in 2006 and now given
considerable freedom by its owning chain,
this big pub has long combined a strong
beer offer with a lively, youthful vibe.
Beneath a banner proclaiming "Hail the
Ale," six handpumped and two gravity
dispensed casks are headed by Cottage,
Dorking, Hogs Back, King and Westerham
making regular appearances. 'Specimen
jars' on the bar display the beer colours
and tastings are offered. Beers from
BrewDog, Erdinger, Goose Island and
Meantime feature among the expanding
keg and bottled range. A comprehensive
menu starts with breakfast, moving on to
sandwiches and pub grub like aubergine
bake, steaks, fish and chips, pies. Still easily
the best Croydon town centre choice.

New Cross Turnpike (37)

Contemporary pub (Wetherspoon)
55 Bellegrove Road, Welling DA16 3PB
T (020) 8304 1600   🐦 Nturnpike
www.jdwetherspoon.co.uk
🕓 *Daily* 09.00-24.00.
Children very welcome in family area.
Cask beers 8-12 (Greene King, up to 10 often
local guests), **Other beers** 3 keg, 5 bottles/cans
🍴 Wetherspoon menu **£**,
🌳 Small beer garden, ♿
Beer festivals, food promotions

⇌ Welling

Don't be misled: this place is a long way east
of New Cross. At first sight a typical suburban
town centre Wetherspoon with a few attractive
touches like mosaics and a pretty garden, it's
actually one of the chain's genuine beer champions and a recurring *Good Beer Guide* entry.
Keen cellar manager Scott sources guests
directly, often from local suppliers: Hop Stuff
in nearby Woolwich is regularly featured,
alongside By the Horns, Gypsy Hill and Kent
brewers like Kent, Nelson and Westerham.
Traditional tastes are met by rotating beers
from Fuller's, Marstons and Wells and Young's.
The chain's growing 'craft' range goes down
well here too. Well worth a look, particularly if
visiting the nearby Door Hinge (p 176).

Pub trivia. *The pub stands on Watling Street, the Roman
road from London to the Kent coast. This section was once
known as the New Cross Turnpike because the 'turnpike trust'
that improved it in 1718 had a toll gate at the New Cross end.
The pub opened only in 1998, in a former shop, taking a
suitably historic, if rather geographically confusing, name.*

One Inn the Wood   (38)
Micropub
209 Petts Wood Road, Petts Wood BR5 1LA
T 07799 535982   www.oneinnthewood.co.uk
 Oneinnthewoodmicropub   oneinthewood
 Tu-Th 12.00-14.30, 17.00-21.30, Fr 12.00-14.30,
   17.00-23.00, Sa 11.00-23.00, Su 12.00-15.00,
   Mo closed. Children until 19.00.
Cask beers 6 (local/unusual guests), **Other beers**
1 bottle, **Also** 4 Kent ciders, Kent wine
 Pork pies, sausage rolls, Kent cheeseboards
£, Tables on street
Beer school, board games

 Petts Wood   Link to London Loop

Former money broker Barry Bridge's micropub,
opened in May 2014 in a quiet cul-de-sac just
round the corner from the station, proudly
reclaims local Kentish heritage by stocking
beers, ciders, wines, pies and cheeses from
within the traditional county boundaries.
Gadds, Old Dairy and Westerham products
usually appear among the cask beers served
from gravity in a room at the back, alongside
interlopers like Cronx and Hogs Back. At least
one dark beer is usually on, and the only lager,
bottled Curious Brew, is from Sussex but
commissioned by Kent's Chapel Down
vineyard. A bright, simple and contemporary
design makes good use of the limited space in
this former wine bar, overlooked by a mural-
sized photo of the nearby National Trust
woodland (famous for its monument to Wiliam
Willett, the inventor of daylight saving time)
which gives the town its name.

Orpington Liberal Club (39)
Club
7 Station Road, Orpington BR6 0RZ
www.orpingtonliberalclub.co.uk
 OrpingtonLiberalClub   OrpLibClub
 Mo-Th 20.00-23.00, Fr 18.00-23.00,
   Sa 12.00-15.00, 19.00-23.00, Su 12.00-15.00,
   20.00-22.30. Children very welcome.
Cask beers 3-6 (unusual often local guests),
Other beers 1 bottle, **Also** 6 ciders/perries
including Kent
 Occasional barbecues and event food,
 Patio and back garden
Beer festivals, blues/folk (Tu&Fr & some other nights),
German speaking group, quiz, darts functions

 Orpington   Link to Cray Riverway

You don't have to be a Liberal Democrat to
appreciate this friendly little place in a house on
the edge of Orpington town centre – indeed
some of the keen volunteers who run the bar
here have put their own party loyalties aside
to celebate a common interest in great beer
which has won the club regional awards. Cask
beers are predominantly from London – Hop
Stuff, Twickenham – or Kent, with Kissingate,
Millis, Tonbridge and Westerham particular
favourites, although beers from more far-flung
parts of the UK feature too. All are sold at keen
prices, in thirds or takeaway cartons if required.
The regular drinking space is a homely bar with
pub furniture and sofas, expanding to the
adjoining hall and the extensive garden during
regular beer festivals. For licensing reasons
you'll need to show a CAMRA or other EBCU
membership card to be admitted as a guest.

Penny Farthing   (40)
Micropub
3 Waterside, Crayford DA1 4JJ
T 07772 866645   Penny-Farthing
 Tu-Th 12.00-15.00, 17.00-21.30, Fr-Sa 12.00-22.30,
   Su 12.00-15.00, Mo closed.
Cask beers 3-5 (unusual often local guests),
Also 4 Kent ciders/perries
 Tables on street may be added

 Crayford   Cray Riverway, London Loop

London's third micropub, opened in September
2014 by Bob Baldwin, overlooks a little park

along a stretch of the river Cray near the old ford that gives Crayford its name. Although the last tenant sold pottery, this address was a well-known cycle shop, thus the name. The simple square room is painted in relaxing pastel shades, festooned with hops and equipped with tall benches and tables, while a quiet policy encourages civilised conversation. Cask beers, dispensed into oversized glasses or takeaway cartons from a glass-fronted stillage in one corner, change so rapidly that they'd already got through 100 different beers within three months of opening. As often, Kent brewers like Canterbury, Kent, Gadds, Tonbridge, Wantsum and Westerham appear alongside Londoners like Bexley, East London and Hop Stuff and the likes of Adnams, Brentwood and Oakham. There's no food other than packet snacks and free roast potatoes on Sundays.

Wine Cellar (41)
Shop
9 Station Parade, Sanderstead Road, South Croydon CR2 0PH
T (020) 8657 6936
www.winecellared.com   🆕 🐦 winecellared
🕐 *Daily* 06.00-23.00.
Cask beers 3 (often local guests), ***Other beers***
400 bottles, ***Also*** 1,200 wines, specialist spirits
🍴 Groceries, US sweets
Daily beer tastings

🚆 Sanderstead, Purley Oaks

Don't be deceived by the name or the display of fresh fruit and veg outside: this convenience store just round the corner from Sanderstead station turns out to be a beer emporium. Owner Ben has built the range over a decade, and in 2014 added cask beer to take away, from Croydon brewers and Cronx as well as brewers like Dark Star, Dorking, Harveys, Portobello, Rudgate, Surrey Hills or Westerham. Labels with tasting notes highlight particular bottles in a mainly British range that is likely to include Beavertown, Box Steam, Late Knights, Hobsons, Hoggleys, Thornbridge and Wye Valley among others. A few US imports (Anchor, Fordham, Flying Dog) and Belgian and German classics round things out. A sister store in central Croydon stocking 1,000 beers with more casks and keg growler fillers should open in 2015.

TRY ALSO

Right by West Norwood station is pleasantly refurbished gastropub the **Great North Wood** (3 Knights Hill SE27 0HS, 🆕 TheGreatNorthWoodWestNorwood) with four cask beers and a small but well-chosen range of bottles from Crate, Brixton, Pressure Drop and other Londoners.

Just off Croydon town centre and within a short walk of the Green Dragon (p177), unspoilt Fuller's leasehold the **Royal Standard** (1 Sheldon Street, Croydon CR0 1SS, www.royalstandard-croydon.co.uk) applies royal standards to cask quality too. Wine bar turned long-standing cask champion the **Claret** (4a Bingham Corner CR0 7AA) is a short ride west by Addiscombe tram stop, offering six casks including from Dorset independent Palmer's.

Options in central Bromley include the

Barrel and Horn

Barrel and Horn (206 High Street, Bromley BR1 1PW, www.barrelandhorn.com), Fuller's first venture into contemporary 'craft beer' territory with a good range of London and imported kegs and bottles amid designer décor; and **Belgo Bromley** (242 Intu Bromley BR1 1DN, www.belgo-restaurants.co.uk), serving a range similar to the other Belgos (see Belgo Noord p133) in a surprisingly pleasant and leafy setting at the back of the Intu shopping mall (formerly the Glades).

The outer fringes of southeast London, especially in Bromley borough, encompass extensive green space and genuine country-side on the edge of the Surrey Hills and Kent Downs Areas of Outstanding Natural Beauty, with some great walks and pretty village pubs. None offers enough beer interest to merit a full entry, but one near-miss is long-standing *Good Beer Guide* entry and previous local CAMRA

Pub of the Year the **Five Bells** (Church Road BR6 7RE, www.thefivebells-chelsfieldvillage.co.uk) at Chelsfield, a rustic weatherboarded Kentish pub with a big garden, well-priced home-cooked food, an old-fashioned public bar and a choice of four flawless cask beers often of a darker hue. Also worth a look for quality guest casks is the smart **Queens Head** (25 High Street BR6 7US, www.queensheaddowne.com) next to Downe church and not far from Charles Darwin's former home at Down House, now a National Trust property. Buses from Orpington station serve both pubs.

Yet another Bexley micropub, the **Broken Drum** (308 Westwood Lane DA15 9PT, www.thebrokendrum.co.uk) at Blackfen between Welling and Sidcup, should have opened by the time you read this.

LONDON'S BREWING **Late Knights**

Among the less-remarked aspects of Britain's brewing boom has been a modest return to the old-school business model of vertical integration – breweries that have their own estates of pubs. London's most prominent example is Late Knights, which now has five pubs, including in Brighton and Ramsgate, with more on the way. Most of its output is now sold this way, with the pub estate getting through 40 casks and 20 kegs a week, and a deliberate policy to slim down the external sales. "It's mainly about sustainability," explains founder Steve Keegan. "At one point we were selling lots to particular pub companies, and I thought, it only takes a change of management or ownership and we're in trouble."

But I suspect it's also about the fact that Steve knows and loves pubs first and foremost. Originally from Middlesbrough, he's worked in them since he was 14, and worked his way up through the hierarchy at Mitchells & Butlers before becoming an operations manager for Fuller's, assigned to turning around unperforming sites. It was Steve who created the Union Tavern (p208), an expression of his passion both for London-brewed

beer and pubs with distinctive identities. That led to an interest in brewing – never a homebrewer, his first ever brewing experience was on a professional kit as a 'cuckoo' brewer back in Middlesbrough, working with Matt Power at Truefitt to create the first Late Knights beer. The results sold surprisingly well, and he started to make plans to quit his job.

He found a business partner in Brockley wine importer and retailer Graham Lawrence, who owned a warehouse in Penge. The first London-brewed Late Knights beers emerged from here in April 2013, produced on a seven-barrel (11.5hl) kit lashed up from old dairy equipment. A few months later, keen homebrewer Sam Barber joined as head brewer.

While they were working on the brewery, an opportunity arose to open a pop-up pub in Gipsy Hill – so the first Beer Rebellion was launched the week after the first brew. This has now moved to a permanent site next door (p157), with a sister pub in Peckham (p158) and the London Beer Dispensary in Graham's old shop (p171), alongside the two outside London. "Opening five pubs in less than two years has made me go a bit grey, to be honest," comments Steve.

Each pub has evolved its own identify. "I hadn't really heard of micropubs when I started," Steve says. "As the Gipsy Hill site was temporary we couldn't do any major decoration so we had to work with what we had, and we learned a lot from that. Then people starting coming in and saying, 'oh, this is a micropub.' We don't want to do branded pubs, we're not a pub company with an ego problem. That's what we mean by Beer Rebellion. The rebellion is very quiet and polite but it's there."

Now there are some big plans in the pipeline. They're taking over the Alexandra in Penge, but even more exciting is a scheme for the long-neglected Fellowship Inn in Bellingham, a huge place with its own ballroom and theatre, for which they've secured £3.9 million in regeneration funding. The theatre will become a cinema (amazingly, the only one in Lewisham borough), the ballroom an events space, with room left for a bakery and a new brewery downstairs, likely with a bottling and canning line, opening some time in 2016. In the meantime, it looks like Steve's in for a few more grey hairs, and a few more late (k)nights.

SOUTHWEST LONDON

SOUTHWEST LONDON

In this book, Southwest London covers all the SW postcodes outside the central area and south of the Thames. This is potentially slightly confusing as there are also SW postcodes to the north of the Thames, but these are included under West London.

I've pulled the more central listings together under the heading **Battersea, Brixton & Clapham**, which accounts for most of Lambeth borough and a bit of Wandsworth, around Battersea (parts of Lambeth with SE postcodes are dealt with under Central South London on p157 or Borough and Southbank p51). These are some of the liveliest and most characterful neighbourhoods in inner London, with some great beer venues to match, including several newly-opened outlets.

The rest of Wandsworth borough is discussed under **Wandsworth**, which encompasses Balham, Putney and Tooting as well as Wandsworth Town. The Young's brewery once dominated the beer scene here and its successor pubco retains numerous local pubs, though there are some excellent independents too.

Outer Southwest London covers the rest, including Wimbledon which boasts a cluster of recommendable outlets, alongside scattered gems in suburban centres like Carshalton, Kingston and Surbiton and the borough of Richmond south of the Thames (Twickenham and Teddington on the opposite bank are listed under Outer West London p217).

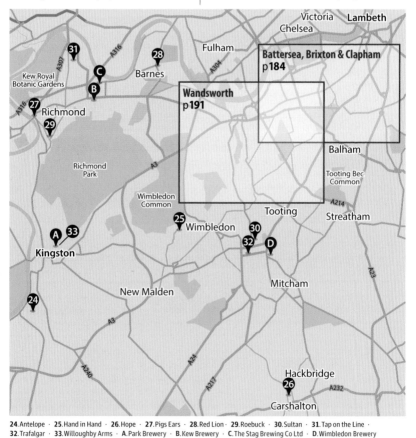

24. Antelope · **25.** Hand in Hand · **26.** Hope · **27.** Pigs Ears · **28.** Red Lion · **29.** Roebuck · **30.** Sultan · **31.** Tap on the Line · **32.** Trafalgar · **33.** Willoughby Arms · **A.** Park Brewery · **B.** Kew Brewery · **C.** The Stag Brewing Co Ltd · **D.** Wimbledon Brewery

182

Battersea, Brixton & Clapham

BrewDog Clapham Junction

Specialist, bar **Top 25** (1)

11 Battersea Rise SW11 1HG

T (020) 7223 6346 **www.brewdog.com/bars**

 brewdogclapham BrewDogClaphamJ

Mo-Sa 12.00-24.00, Su 12.00-23.30.

Children until mid-evening.

Cask beers None, **Other beers** 24 keg, 75+ bottles,
Also Beer cocktails

 Deli plates, toasties, Scotch eggs **£-££**,

 Sheltered front terrace,

Meet the brewer/tap takeover

 Clapham Junction Clapham Common
 Eccles Road (35 37 Clapham Common, Clapham Junction)
 Link to Avenue Verte Clapham Common paths

Actually just off the northwest corner of
Clapham Common, this former restaurant
became the fourth and possibly the best of
London's BrewDog bars in August 2014. Like
its sister outlets it boasts an extensive range
of cutting-edge beers and handsome post-
modern design, with exposed girders, chip-
board and bare brick, but feels more spacious
and intimate, with a pretty front terrace and
inviting sofas and booths. Draught beers are
all keg, of course, half BrewDog regulars and
specials and half guests from brewers like
Beavertown, Brodies, Evil Twin, Mikkeller and
Victory, served in thirds and tasting flights if
required. A particularly well-chosen bottle list
is conveniently arranged by style, with London
beers from Beavertown, Brew by Numbers,
Kernel and Redchurch, lots of contemporary
IPAs, real lambics and Belgian oddities like
Fantôme. Food is hassle-free stuff prepared
at the bar, like cheese plates and gourmet
Scotch eggs, including veggie options.

BrewDog Clapham Junction

Brixton Brewery (2)

Taproom

547 Brixton Station Road SW9 8PF

T 07761 436757 **www.brixtonbrewery.com**

  brixtonbrewery

Sa 12.00-16.00, closed other days.

Children welcome.

Cask beers Occasional, **Other beers** 6 bottles,
occasional keg (Brixton)

 Sausage rolls, pies **£**

Quarterly open days, tastings

 Brixton

Only a short step along the railway viaduct
from Brixton's famous and still vibrant markets,
its eponymous brewery, opened in October
2013, is very much rooted in the local community. The public face is a foldaway table and a
few picnic benches laid out for a few hours a
week at the front of one of its two adjoining
arches. Most of the beer is bottled, and served
that way, to take away or, since September
2014, to drink in. This is also the place to catch
small runs and specials, the occasional keykeg
or casks, and intermittent guests from other
London brewers, as well as talk to the people
behind the beer.

1. BrewDog Clapham Junction · 2. Brixton Brewery · 3. Craft Beer Co Brixton · 4. Craft Beer Co Clapham · 5. Crown and Anchor ·
6. Draft House Northcote · 7. Draft House Westbridge · 8. Eagle Ale House · 9. Falcon · 10. Four Thieves · 11. Lighthouse ·
12. Powder Keg Diplomacy · 13. Priory Arms · 14. Sambrook's Brewery · A. Mondo Brewing

Craft Beer Co Brixton (3)

Specialist, bar
11 Brixton Station Road SW9 8PD
T (020) 7274 8383
www.thecraftbeerco.com/location/
brixton-london
🄵 craftbeercosw9 🐦 thecraftbeerco
🕘 *Mo-We* 16.30-23.00, *Th* 16.30-24.00, *Fr* 16.30-
01.00, *Sa* 12.00-01.00, *Su* 12.00-22.30.
Cask beers 9 (Kent, 9 unusual guests),
Other beers 18 keg, 70+ bottles, **Also** Rums,
bourbons, malts
🍴 Pork pies, Scotch eggs **£**, 🪑 Front terrace
Tastings, occasional open mic nights, functions

🚆 ⊖ Brixton

London's second Craft branch brought a
welcome infusion of contemporary beer
culture to central Brixton in September 2012.
It's small but neatly designed with drinking
room upstairs and down. A proscenium arch of
copper tubing studded with keg taps frames
the bar, while fridges beneath the counter
face invitingly outwards. Guest casks are from
breweries like Dark Star, Durham, Glastonbury,
Northern Monk, Siren, Summer Wine and
Thornbridge. There are permanent keykeg lines
for nearby Brixton as well as Beavertown,
Hammerton and Kernel, with other UK and

Scandinavian visitors. Brixton is also represented among the bottles alongside Anspach and
Hobday, Europeans like Rooie Dop, fine lambics
from 3 Fonteinen and Tilquin and sharing
bottles from solid US names like Alesmith,
Cigar City and Jester King, all sold to take away
too with a buy-five-get-one-free offer. It's
handy for the Tube , Academy music venue,
markets and Brixton Recreation Centre.

Craft Beer Co Clapham (4)

Specialist, contemporary pub
128 Clapham Manor Street SW4 6ED
T (020) 7498 9633 🄵 🐦 craftbeercosw4
www.thecraftbeerco.com
🕘 *Mo-Th* 16.00-23.00, *Fr* 16.00-24.00, *Sa* 12.00-
24.00, *Su* 12.00-23.00. Children until 18.00.
Cask beers 10 (Kent, 9 unusual guests), **Other
beers** 18 keg, 70 bottles (UK & international),
Also Specialist gins and whiskies
🍴 Gourmet burgers **££**,
🪑 Beer garden, front terrace
Beer festivals, tastings, meet the brewer

⊖ Clapham High Street · ⊖ Clapham Common · 🚴 Link to
CS7, Avenue Verte · 🚶 Link to Clapham Common paths

Listed in the previous edition as the Manor Arms,
this backstreet pub near Clapham Common
metamorphosed in December 2013 into

London's fourth Craft Beer Co and the beer range multiplied mightily. It retains a genuine pub feel, with a heated terrace sporting huge vintage brewery enamels and carpeted with fake grass, and attracts a more local crowd than the geek-friendly central branches. Aside from the regular house cask pale ale, the names on the pumps regularly change, favouring out-of-town brewers like Dark Star, Fyne, Mallinsons, Magic Rock and Tiny Rebel. Thornbridge and Rothaus are on keg alongside guests from locals like Five Points and Kernel and rare imports like Highwater and Saugutuck. A strong selection of bottled lambics lines up alongside US sours and Gose and Londoners like Anspach & Hobday, Brew by Numbers and Partizan.

Crown and Anchor Top 25 (5)

Specialist, contemporary pub (London Village Inns)
246 Brixton Road SW9 6AQ
☎ (020) 7737 0060   🐦 crown_anchorsw9
www.crownandanchorbrixton.co.uk
🕐 *Mo-Th* 16.30-24.00, *Fr* 16.30-01.00, *Sa* 12.00-01.00, *Su* 12.00-23.00. Children welcome until early evening.
Cask beers 8 (local and unusual guests), ***Other beers*** 14 keg, 70 bottles, ***Also*** 2 ciders/perries
🍴 Enhanced pub grub, sharing plates **££**,
🍴 Tables on street
Meet the brewer/tap takeover, food events, quiz (Tu), fortnightly comedy (Th), live music (Su), board games

🚆 Brixton   ⊖ Stockwell, Brixton   🚌 Loughborough Road
(numerous Brixton, Oval)   🚲 Link to CS7

A southern sister to the Jolly Butchers (p143), and similarly decayed before reopening in April 2012, this big boozer is now an attractive contemporary space with plain glass windows and bare brick offset by arty light fittings, but the old bar counter and some unusual arches at the back have been preserved. The pedestrianised street alongside leads to Slade Gardens, creating a pretty outdoor space. Handpumped beers always include locals like Belleville, Brixton and Gipsy Hill, with rare casks from Beavertown sometimes appearing. Kegs could be imported from brewers like Flying Dog, Sierra Nevada and Ska, while there are more Americans and locals in the fridges, alongside

Brains Craft Brewery beers and good Belgians like Ellezelloise Hercule. If a street food pop-up hasn't been invited to occupy the kitchen temporarily, food is likely to include well-priced mezze platters, veggie stacks, bangers and mash and pan-fried salmon.

Draft House Northcote (6)

Specialist, bar
94 Northcote Road SW11 6QW
☎ (020) 7924 1814   🐦 DraftHouseNC
www.drafthouse.co.uk
🕐 *Mo-We* 12.00-23.00, *Th-Fr* 12.00-24.00, *Sa* 10.00-24.00, *Su* 10.00-22.30. Children welcome.
Cask beers 3 (1 Sambrooks, unusual guests),
Other beers 15 keg, 60 bottles, ***Also*** Specialist spirits, some wines
🍴 Diner-style menu **£-££**, 🍴 Front terrace
Meet the brewer/tap takeover

🚆⊖ Clapham Junction   ⊖ Clapham South   🚌 Salcott Road
(319 Clapham Junction, Streatham)   🚲 Link to Avenue Verte
🚶 Link to Capital Ring

Opened in 2009 as the second Draft House and now perhaps boasting the best beer range, this place fits well among the independent restaurants and foodie-oriented specialist shops of Northcote Road. Cheerful bright green stools around the bar facilitate informal drinking, while a sit-down restaurant area decked out with classic rock and pop posters serves gourmet burgers and hot dogs, pulled pork buns and mac and cheese. Changing 'casks of the day' are sold at keen prices, perhaps from Arbor, Celt, Cottage, Firebrand or Thornbridge. Kegs include a lager brewed for the chain by Portobello, and changing guests that are increasingly British

Draft House Northcote

(Bristol, Burning Sky, Camden, Magic Rock), all sold in thirds if required. Londoners like Beavertown, Rocky Head and Weird Beard, are in the bottle fridges alongside US craft beers and Belgian classics Dupont and Orval, a well curated list that shows beverage manager Laurence knows what he's doing.

King, Thornbridge or Windsor & Eton. Most other beers are now from the UK or US, with Londoners Beavertown and Kernel often in evidence besides Odell, Rogue, Siren, Tiny Rebel and Williams Brothers. The group's Northcote branch on the other side of Battersea has a sharper beer focus but there's still much to detain you here.

Draft House Westbridge (7)

Bar, specialist
74 Battersea Bridge Road SW11 3AG
T (020) 7228 6482   🐦 DraftHouseWB
www.drafthouse.co.uk
🕓 *Mo-Th* 12.00-23.00, *Fr-Sa* 12.00-24.00,
  Su 12.00-22.00. Children welcome.
Cask beers 3 (Sambrook's, 2 unusual and local guests), **Other beers** 15 keg, 50+ bottles,
Also Specialist spirits, some wines
🍴 Diner-style menu **£-££**, 🪑 Sheltered front terrace, beer garden, ♿
Films (Su), seasonal events, functions

🚆 Battersea Park, Queenstown Road   🚌 Parkgate Road (49, 319 Clapham Junction) 🚲 Link to NCN4, CS8
🚶 Link to Thames Path

This was the first Draft House, opened in 2007 as an early glimmer of new excitement on London's beer scene. In a decently-sized, rounded-corner building, it has a pleasant front bar, a fern-strewn terrace, a red ceilinged restaurant decorated with Sex Pistols and Billy Bragg posters, He-Man and the Masters of the Universe wallpaper on the way to the toilets and two rooms for hire upstairs. On offer is a similar food menu and beer range as the other branches, including a bargain Cask of the Day that might come from Belleville,

Draft House Westbridge

Eagle Ale House (8)

Traditional pub
104 Chatham Road SW11 6HG
T (020) 7228 2328
www.theeaglealehouse.co.uk
📘 The Eagle Ale House   🐦 eaglealehouse
🕓 *Mo-Fr* 15.00-23.00, *Sa* 12.00-23.00,
  Su 12.00-22.30. Children until early evening.
Cask beers 6-8 (unusual often local guests),
Also Malts, wines
🍴 Scotch eggs, sausage rolls, sausages ,
🪑 Beer garden with sliding roof, front terrace
Beer festivals (May, August), occasional live music, summer barbecues, major big screen sport, board games

🚆 🚇 Clapham Junction   🚌 Darley Road (319 Clapham Junction, Streatham) 🚲 Link to Avenue Verte
🚶 Link to Capital Ring

Licensees Simon Clarke and David Law, now well into their second decade at this real ale stalwart just off Northcote Road, make full use of Enterprises's direct delivery scheme to serve an always-interesting range of casks, usually including a mild or other dark beer. Belleville brewery, a few streets away, regularly supplies its appropriately named Northcote Blonde and other favoured locals and near-locals are Cronx, Hackney, Pilgrim and Surrey Hills. Beer festivals in the sheltered garden provide further choice. The exterior is modestly handsome, with a fine terracotta frieze above the entrance, while the well-worn interior is a pleasingly jumbled mix of benches and cosy cubby holes replete with clubby red leather armchairs and dusty books.

Pub trivia *It's believed the real life model for Sherlock Holmes' fictitious nemesis Moriarty was a regular and you can just about imagine the arch fiend plotting his misdeeds in the snug.*

Falcon

Falcon (9)

Traditional pub (Nicholson's) ★
2 St Johns Hill SW11 1RU
T (020) 7228 2076   www.nicholsonspubs.
co.uk/thefalconclaphamjunctionlondon
🖪 The-Falcon 🔽 falconclapjunct
🕐 *Su-We* 10.00-23.00, *Th-Sa* 10.00-24.00.
    Children welcome.
Cask beers 13-16 (Fuller's, Sambrook's, Sharp's,
St Austell, Truman's, 8+ sometimes local guests),
Other beers 2 keg (Meantime), 3-4 bottles,
Also Some wines and specialist spirits
🍽 Nicholson's pub grub menu **££**, 🍴 Standing
on street, ♿
*Beer festivals, occasional tastings, beer library,
board games*

🚊 🚇 Clapham Junction   🚲 Link to CS8

This big heritage gem close to Clapham
Junction station boasts the longest continuous
bar in England, and puts it to good use as
housing for an impressive bank of handpumps:
a keen previous manager built a reputation
for the beer range, and his successors have
wisely retained the policy. Guests from the
pub chain's list err towards traditional producers like Adnams, Brains and Butcombe but
also embrace modern pale ales from smaller
brewers, with tasters offered to the undecided.

*Pub trivia A pub called the Falcon, a name derived from
the crest of a former local landowner, has welcomed
travellers at this busy crossroads on the old Guildford coach
road since at least 1801. The current pub, built in 1898 to
capitalise on the closeness of what was already London's
busiest station, boasts numerous unique original features
besides the celebrated bar counter, including decorated
alcoves and fireplaces and exquisite stained and painted
glass. A glass triptych at the back depicts past incarnations
of the pub, the panel with funeral carriages recalling a
former landlord called Mr Death.*

Four Thieves (10)

Brewpub, contemporary pub (Laines)
51 Lavender Gardens SW11 1DJ
T (020) 7223 6927   🖪 🔽 FourThievesPub
www.fourthieves.pub
🕐 *Mo-Th* 12.00-24.00, *Fr-Sa* 12.00-02.00,
    Su 12.00-22.30. Children until 20.00.
Cask beers 8 (5 Laines, unusual guests), **Other
beers** 2 keg, 8 bottles, **Also** Gins (local and own)
🍽 Burgers, salads, enhanced pub grub **££**,
🍴 Beer garden 🐾, ♿
*Quiz (Tu), comedy (We), live music (Th&Su), DJs/
cabaret (Fr-Sa), photo booth, functions*

🚊 🚇 Clapham Junction   🚌 Lavender Hill Police Station/
Battersea Arts Centre (numerous Clapham Junction)

Reopened in September 2014, this enormous
former music hall is now not only the third
London brewpub in the Laines group but the
first pub distillery too. A big main bar is decked

Four Thieves

out in patterned tiles, textured wallpaper and eccentric tat, with another large space at the side used for entertainment – not to mention the auditorium upstairs, which had not yet been reopened at the time of writing. Most casks are brewed here or at other Laines pubs, with guests from suppliers like Ticketybrew, though the house brand unfiltered tank lager that appears to be fed direct from the brew-house through a copper pipe actually comes from Hepworth in Sussex. Food includes salads and dishes like mussels and bacon in cider or slow-braised baby back ribs as well as pub grub stables and several vegetarian choices like aubergine and cashew nut paella.

Pub trivia *The name recalls a gruesome European legend about four grave robbers who saved themselves from execution by sharing the secret recipe for a herb-infused vinegar that stopped them catching the plague. One of the ingredients was lavender, which once grew profusely in this part of London, and now perfumes the trellises of the large and delightful 'gin yard' outside. It's used as a botanical in the house gin.*

Lighthouse (11)
Contemporary pub (City)
414 Battersea Park Road SW11 4LR
T (020) 7223 7721 lighthousesw11
www.thelighthousebattersea.com
Mo-Th 12.00-23.00, Fr-Sa 12.00-24.00, Su 12.00-22.30. Children very welcome.
Cask beers 3 cask (often Adnams and local guests), **Other beers** 6 keg, 15+ bottles, **Also** "Whisky wall and gin window", some wines
Gastroish/enhanced pub grub menu **££**,
Beer garden, tables at front,
Beer festivals, occasional tastings, fortnightly live music (Fr&Su), fortnightly films (Su), board games

 Clapham Junction Battersea Park School (44, 344 Battersea Park, 344 Clapham Junction) CS8 Link to Battersea Park paths, Thames Path

It might not really look like a lighthouse, but the fairy lights and flowers of this largish pub shine like a reassuring beacon on a busy junction near Battersea Park. Inside is spacious and cheerful, with a splendid covered terrace at the back. Thanks to a succession of keen managers, including current incumbent and "craft beer convert" Sue, it boasts one of the strongest

beer offers in its small group. Understandably, Adnams Lighthouse is a near regular on cask, with other guests from locals like Belleville, By the Horns, Head in a Hat or Sambrook's and interlopers like Sunny Republic or Tiny Rebel. 'Craft keg' from Burning Sky, Firebrand or Wild and bottles from Brewers & Union, Fordham, Kernel and Pressure Drop are among the other options. Food includes a 'build your own burger' system with venison and veggie options, or choices like grilled swordfish, blue cheese and apple salad.

Powder Keg Diplomacy (12)
Bar (Lost & Co)
147 St Johns Hill SW11 1TQ
T (020) 7450 6457
www.powderkegdiplomacy.co.uk
 Powderkegdiplomacy BaronPowderKeg
Mo-Th 16.00-23.00, Fr 16.00-24.00, Sa 10.00-24.00, Su 10.00-23.00. Children welcome until 19.30.
Cask beers 3 (unusual often local guests), **Other beers** 5 keg, 30+ bottles, **Also** Cocktails, wines, home made soft drinks & spirit infusions
Modern British menu, cooked bar snacks **££-£££**, Tables on street
Tastings, seasonal events

 Clapham Junction

Priory Arms

The idea of installing handpumps in a hip cocktail bar would once have seemed ridiculous, but PKD is a sign of how times have changed. Opened late in 2011, it has a well-groomed *fin de siècle* colonial theme – a ceiling map of the British Empire at its height, hatstands, a lovely rear conservatory with a ceiling fan. Besides cocktails, a beer selection dispensed by attentive, informative and occasionally uncomfortably overpolite staff shows all the right signs of tender loving care. Breweries like Bristol, Dark Star, Ilkley, Magic Rock and Windsor & Eton supply the cask beers, including dark options. Numerous Londoners rattle in the fridges including Beavertown, Belleville, Brixton, By the Horns, Redchurch, Rocky Head and Weird Beard, alongside other top UK producers. Food could include roast pheasant, pan fried hake or grilled polenta cake with smoked goats cheese, or substantial bar snacks like oysters and braised haggis balls.

(Achel, Boon, Jever, Rochefort, Schlenkerla, Schneider) and a few Americans (Brooklyn, Founders). Kegs avoid macrobrews in favour of Camden Town, Redwell and Thornbridge. Food is basic: burgers, chicken wings and chilli with several veggie options. The place has a subtle and appropriately tasteful continental feel with big windows shedding light on a raised seating area.

Priory Arms Top 25 (13)
Specialist, contemporary pub
83 Lansdowne Way SW8 2PB
T (020) 7622 1884 prioryarms83
www.theprioryarms.com
Mo-Fr 17.00-23.00, Sa-Su 12.00-23.00.
 Children until early evening.
Cask beers 5 (unusual guests),
Other beers 11 keg, 60 bottles
 Burgers, pub grub **££**, Front terrace
Beer festivals, meet the brewer/tap takeover, quiz (Su), occasional comedy, cabaret, live music, board games, functions

 Wandsworth Road Stockwell Link to CS7

This long-standing free house, just down the road from Stockwell's impressive and architecturally important 1950s bus garage, was likely the first UK pub offering draught imported wheat beer in the 1990s. Under the able stewardship of ex-Craft Beer Co manager Tom since 2013, it's now upped its game further. Cask beers are from brewers like Crouch Vale, Dark Star, Firebrand, Kent, Red Squirrel or Thornbridge while the bottled selection includes several choices each from Beavertown, Kernel, Partizan and Wild, alongside Belgian and German classics

Sambrook's Brewery (14)
Shop
1 Yelverton Road SW11 3QG
T (020) 7228 0598 www.sambrooksbrewery.co.uk sambrookale
Shop Mo-Fr 10.00-18.00, Sa 10.00-13.00,
 Su closed; bar open for special events only.
Cask beers Only in bulk or when bar is open,
Other beers 8 bottles, minikegs
Ticketed open evenings (3rd We of month), prebooked brewery tours, functions

 Clapham Junction Badric Court (44 Battersea Park, Wandsworth) CS8, link to NCN4 Link to Thames Path

Now one of London's most established and successful new brewers, Sambrook's sells direct to the public from the reception area of its substantial Battersea premises. You're guaranteed to find all the core beers plus seasonals and one-offs in bottle, with minikegs, minipins, polypins and whole firkins available to pre-order: they even hire out dispensing equipment if you need it. There are various books and gift packs too. The pleasant bar upstairs, with a view of the brewery, only opens for ticketed events and pre-booked groups and tours.

TRY ALSO

Celebrated gastropub the **Canton Arms** (177 South Lambeth Road SW8 1XP, **www. cantonarms.com**), between Vauxhall and Stockwell, offers four good casks, often including, unusually, Timothy Taylor Golden Best, alongside top notch modern British food in an appropriately pubby and dressed-down environment. On the other side of Brixton, in residential streets between

Brixton Hill and Tulse Hill, is the very amenable **Elm Park Tavern** (76 Elm Park SW2 2UB, **www.elmparktavern.com**) which regularly stocks beers from nearby Belleville brewery. **Pratts and Payne** (103 Streatham High Road SW16 1HJ, **www.prattsandpayne.com**), behind the impressive art deco façade of a former menswear shop near Streatham station, is a good Antic pub with up to seven cask beers and a handful of interesting bottles.

LONDON'S BREWING — Sambrook's

When accountant Duncan Sambrook and two university friends combed the beer list at the Great British Beer Festival in 2006, they realised that, aside from Fuller's, not a single London brewery appeared. The obvious solution to Duncan was to start a brewery of his own. There's a certain juicy irony in the fact that, a few years later, Sambrook's became one of the first new London brewers whose beers appeared in Young's pubs, as it was that brewery's departure from the capital that tore the biggest hole in the city's brewing fabric. Today, sales to Young's remain a healthy source of business.

Duncan's first attempts foundered on lack of experience. Then he met David Welsh, a veteran brewer and former director of Ringwood brewery. Duncan grew up in Salisbury and his formative drinking years had been fuelled by Ringwood beers – when he got over being star-struck he asked David to join him as a business partner. The new brewery, in a modern industrial building in Battersea, came on stream in November 2008 as the first new freestanding brewery in London since 2004. Many more would follow.

They're still using the Canadian-built 20 barrel (33 hl)

kit, but have now expanded to occupy all three units in their block, with much-increased fermentation and storage. The head brewer is now Sean Knight, a former chemical engineer ("the best brewers are good engineers," opines Duncan), and there's a rigorous training programme. Since 2013 they've also had a share, along with Kent breweries Gadd's and Westerham, in a specialist bottling line, where several other brewers contract their bottling. But the ethos remains the same, including a dedication to British ingredients. "We get pretty much everything from within 100 miles (160 km)," says Duncan proudly. "The hops are mainly from Kent, the malt from Hampshire and Wiltshire, sourced through Warminster maltings."

Cask ale remains a vital part of the business, with now well-known core brands like Wandle and Junction. "I'd say we've pretty much cemented

ourselves as London's second cask ale brewery, after Fuller's," reflects Duncan. "In 2014 we added our craft range, with beers in keykeg and bottle conditioned in 330 ml bottles to appeal to more contemporary tastes, but the idea is the same: English beers with a modern twist. The Rye IPA is a US recipe, but uses English hops. The keg pale ale is English too, but we condition in keg, using German-style kräusening [adding unfermented wort to spark a secondary fermentation] to create a natural carbonation."

Further expansion is possible. "We want to keep the business the same, but bigger, and stay part of the community," Duncan adds. "We'll keep brewing here, though we're considering moving the distribution offsite. But it's already expanded beyond expectations. When we started, I never dreamt we'd be selling beer to Tesco and Waitrose, let alone Fuller's and Young's."

Wandsworth

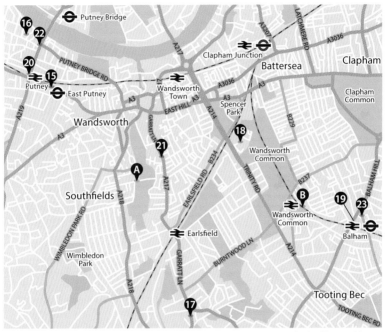

15. Beer Boutique · 16. Bricklayers Arms · 17. By the Horns Brewing Co· 18. Gothique · 19. Hagen and Hyde · 20. Lost and Co ·
21. Old Sergeant · 22. Swift · 23. We Brought Beer · A. Rocky Head Brewery · B. Belleville Brewing

Beer Boutique   (15)
Shop
134 Upper Richmond Road SW15 2SP
T (020) 8780 3168
www.thebeerboutique.co.uk
 The-Beer-Boutique thebeerboutique
 Su-We 12.00-20.00, Th 12.00-21.00,
Fr-Sa 11.00-21.30.
Cask beers None, ***Other beers*** 2 keg, 400 bottles
Monthly tastings, themed beer events, functions

 Putney East Putney Link to NCN4
 Link to Thames Path

Opened in August 2011 just as the beer scene
in London went ballistic, this stylishly under-
stated shop brought boutique wine style to
beer retailing. Since then its range has
expanded substantially, and now invites you
to drink in while you're browsing, either from
bottles, with a minimal corkage charge, or
from two keykeg lines supplied with beers
from Beavertown, Kernel, Siren or US brewers. Stock is grouped by broad style, making
connections that cross national divides, so
Schneider Aventinus might appear next to a
strong, dark abbey ale, or Saison Dupont
neighbour contemporary interpretations
from Brew by Numbers, Burning Sky or
Partizan. Besides Londoners and modern
IPAs, the range is particularly strong on
porters and stouts – Orkney Dark Island
Reserve is a favourite – and quality Belgians,
with lambics from 3 Fonteinen, Boon and
Cantillon. They can also organise private
tastings either in the shop or at other venues.

Bricklayers Arms (16)

Traditional pub
32 Waterman Street SW15 1DD
T (020) 8789 0222   🐦 brickybecky
www.bricklayers-arms.co.uk
🕐 *Mo-Sa* 12.00-23.00, *Su* 12.00-22.30.
   Children until 21.00.
Cask beers 6-11 (changing guests, often local),
Other beers 5 keg, **Also** 1-2 ciders/perries
🍴 Only for prebooked events, 🌳 Beer garden
Beer festivals (Feb, Sep), cider festival (Oct), occasional charity events, skittles, shove ha'penny, functions

🚃 🚤 Putney   🚇 Putney Bridge   🚲 NCN4
🚶 Thames Path, link to Beverley Brook Walk

Set back a little from the river but within cheering distance of the start of the annual Oxford–Cambridge University Boat Race, this is likely the oldest pub in Putney, dating from 1826. A real ale champion since 2005, it's best known for its annual Yorkshire Beer Festival in February, offering over a hundred beers; a second regional festival is held in September. At other times the handpumps rotate beers from breweries like Dark Star, Downton, Isle of Purbeck, Sambrook's, Twickenham and Windsor & Eton, often featuring several from the same source. The interior is basic but comfortable, with fragments of a snob screen on the bar, a pretty garden and open fire. As well as scooping numerous CAMRA awards, this "compact Victorian gem" was selected as one of the Top 10 traditional English pubs by *National Geographic* magazine in 2012.

By the Horns Brewing Co (17)

Taproom, shop
25 Summerstown SW17 0BQ
T (020) 3417 7338   📘 🐦 ByTheHornsBrew
www.bythehorns.co.uk
🕐 Shop *Mo-We* 12.00-17.00, *Th-Fr* 12.00-22.00,
   Sa 12.00-18.00, *Su* closed; bar *Th-Fr* 17.00-
   22.00, *Sa* 12.00-18.00, closed other days.
   Children welcome.
Cask beers 4 (By the Horns, 1 local guest), **Other beers** 9 keg, 10 bottles (mainly By the Horns)
🍴 Pork pies, Scotch eggs, pop-up food for events **£**, 🌳 Picnic tables at front
Tastings, monthly comedy, acoustic music, films, seasonal events, major big screen sport, table football, functions

🚃 Earlsfield   🚌 Summerstown/Huntspill Street (numerous Earlsfield, Tooting)   🚲 Link to Avenue Verte, NCN20
🚶 Link to Wandle Trail

The busy brewers of By the Horns have created a surprisingly atmospheric taproom in their industrial unit in Summerstown, in the hinterland between Wandsworth and Tooting. Much of it is made from recycled pallets, but old bar stools and a piano add a homely touch. During the week it's open as a bottle shop, with core beers, specials and one-offs regularly available, but towards the weekend the bar springs to life with numerous own-brewed beers on cask and keg, plus guests from other London breweries. Things get even livelier with special events like parties, gigs and films, when a food cart usually rolls up.

Bricklayers Arms

Signature. "Sometimes I get a cask of something strange at 8% just because I want to try it," he says. The courtyard, winner of a Wandsworth in Bloom award, provides space for weddings and popular beer festivals, including one at Hallowe'en making the best of the spooky setting.

Pub trivia *Constructed in 1859 as a curious hybrid of Scottish baronial castle and Gothic French château, the building was originally a girls' orphanage. It was taken over by the military in World War II and used among other things to interrogate Rudolf Hess.*

Gothique

By the Horns

Visitor note The brewery is more-or-less opposite Wimbledon Stadium, London's last surviving greyhound racing venue, though there's currently a plan to convert it into a new home for cult League Two football team AFC Wimbledon.

Gothique (18)
Bar, restaurant
Royal Victoria Patriotic Building,
John Archer Way SW18 3SX
T (020) 8870 6567   www.legothique.co.uk
legothiquelondon   gothique_le
Mo-Th 12.00-15.00, 17.00-23.00,
    Fr-Sa 12.00-15.00, 17.00-24.00 (check on
    Sa as sometimes closed for weddings),
    Su 12.00-15.00. Children very welcome.
Cask beers 3 (London guests), ***Other beers*** 2 keg,
10+ bottles, ***Also*** 1 cider, French wines
French restaurant menu, pub grub **£** (bar),
££-£££ (restaurant), Large courtyard
garden
Beer festivals (March, Hallowe'en), functions, weddings

Wandsworth Town, Clapham Junction   Clapham Junction
Windmill Road (77 Clapham Junction, 219 Wandsworth)
Link to Avenue Verte   Link to Capital Ring

Mark Justin has been running this bar-restaurant in the Royal Victoria Patriotic Building, with its pulpit and looming angel sculpure, ever since the vast and forbidding Gothic pile overlooking Wandsworth Common was redeveloped 30 years ago. Full service of French dishes like *salade de poulet fumé et mangue* or *feuilleté des legumes* is offered at the upstairs restaurant while the bar has bargain grub like pasta dishes and burgers. Mark has long stocked real ale and keenly supports London brewers, regularly offering Sambrook's, Twickenham or Fuller's seasonals, with bottles perhaps from Brew by Numbers, Kernel, Pressure Drop or

Hagen and Hyde (19)
Bar (Antic)
157 Balham High Road SW12 9AU
T (020) 8772 0016
www.hagenandhyde.com   hagenhyde
Mo-We 16.00-23.00, *Th* 16.00-24.00, *Fr-Sa* 12.00-
    02.00, *Su* 12.00-23.00. Children until 20.00.
Cask beers 10 (Adnams, Castle Rock,
Thornbridge, 7 local/unusual guests), ***Other
beers*** 8 keg, 9 bottles, ***Also*** 2 ciders/perries,
specialist spirits, home made spirit infusions
Gastroish menu **££**, Split level garden/
patio,
Quiz (Mo), DJ (Fr), live music (Sa), functions

Balham   CS7   Link to Capital Ring

A typically cavernous but curiously cosy Antic venue in former shop premises, Hagen & Hyde announces it trades in 'Liquors' and 'Victuals' on the Edwardian-style frontage, a helpful clarification in case you were confused by the dressmaker's dummy and haberdashery drawers in the big front windows. On two levels with terraces and gardens, it stretches a long way back from the street. Guest casks aim to cover diverse styles including hoppy pale ales and dark beers, with a good showing for Londoners like Belleville, Late Knights and Twickenham. Camden Town, Meantime and Sambrook's supply the kegs, while Norwich's Redwell lines up alongside Chimay in the fridge. Fresh food from a changing menu might well include tempting salads (halloumi, roast aubergine and tabbouleh; pan-fried salmon niçoise) or substantial fare like baby back pork ribs, with cooked snacks like piri-piri chicken skewers to distract you at the bar.

Lost and Co (20)

Bar (Lost & Co)
160 Putney High Street SW15 1RS
T (020) 8780 2235   www.lostputney.co.uk
 lostandco   lostputney
 Su-Th 12.00-24.00, Fr-Sa 12.00-02.00.
   Children until 18.00.
Cask beers 2 (often local guests),
Other beers 8 keg, 20+ bottles, **Also** Cocktails
 Pizzas, hot dogs, wraps, salads, sharing
plates £-££
Live music (Su&We), DJ (Fr-Sa), food promotions

 Putney East Putney Link to NCN4
 Link to Thames Path, Beverley Brook Walk

Once this place opposite Putney station was dressed-down cocktail bar Citizen Smith, which gradually evolved its beer range thanks to the personal interest of the owners.It was revamped in March 2013 as an airier, even less pretentious rendezvous for "urban drinking and dining". It remains youthful, garrulous and big on playful comfort food – pizza choices include truffle or Moroccan lamb with yoghurt and mint leaf, while variants on hot dogs go by names like Twerkin Gherkin and Kevin Bacon. The beer range regularly changes with only the chain's own brand Belgian lager a permanent fixture – you might find Londoners Fourpure or Late Knights alongside Purple Moose, Titanic or US imports, with Alechemy, Arbor, Brewers & Union, Emelisse, Marble, Orval or Rooster's in the fridge and a featured Brewery of the Month. Try to grab the comfy snug at the back.

Old Sergeant (21)

Brewpub, contemporary pub (Young's)
104 Garratt Lane SW18 4DJ
T (020) 8874 4099   oldsergeantpub
www.rampubcompany.co.uk
 Sa-We 12.00-23.00, Th-Fr 12.00-24.00.
   Children until 21.00.
Cask beers 4 (Wells & Young's, 2 London guests),
Other beers 1 keg, 6 bottles (London, UK)
 Sandwiches, wings, burgers, pub grub £-££,
 Large beer garden,
Quiz (Mo), occasional live music, darts, board games, functions

 Wandsworth Town, Earlsfield Old Sergeant (44 270 Wandsworth-Earlsfield-Tooting) Link to NCN20
 Link to Wandle Trail

This 1780 former coaching inn on the main road south from Wandsworth towards Tooting got an award-winning boost in May 2011 when Lee and Keris, formerly of the well-loved Nightingale in Balham, took over. They've created a contemporary feel indoors, a sheltered and delightfully soft-furnished beer garden, and a John Young room upstairs, commemorating the late London brewing colossus with an engrossing collection of souvenirs and ephemera (see The Wandle Ram p196). This is still a good place to try Young's Bitter and Special alongside more locally sourced guests from Sambrook's or Twickenham and bottles from Brixton, By the Horns and Rocky Head. The menu is big on spiced wings and given added interest by South African specialities like bobotie, alongside good pub grub staples and cooked sandwiches. The pub also sponsors an annual charity walk along the Thames Path.

Swift (22)

Bar (Fuller's)
46 High Street SW15 1SQ
T (020) 8780 5437   swiftputney
www.theswiftputney.co.uk
 Mo-Th 10.00-23.00, Fr-Sa 10.00-01.00,
   Su 10.00-22.30. Children until early evening.
Cask beers 2 (Fuller's, London guests), **Other beers** 8 keg, 30+ bottles, **Also** Gins (including local)
 Sandwiches, cheese, charcuterie ££,
Meet the brewer/tap takeovers, food events, bring your own vinyl, board games, functions

 Putney Putney Bridge NCN4
 Thames Path, link to Beverley Brook Walk

This contemporary café-bar on the approach to Putney Bridge sparked protests from local CAMRA members when it opened in August 2013 without any plans to serve cask beer. Owners Fuller's relented and now two hand-pumps flank the keg taps on one of London's few US-style back bars. They dispense London Pride and a guest London beer, while the taps, bottles and cans also feature Londoners like Beavertown, Crate, Fourpure, Kernel and Sambrook's alongside Fuller's beers and imports like Achel Trappist and Oskar Blues. Deli-style food could include porter-smoked salmon sandwiches, reuben burgers, gourmet macaroni cheese and sharing plates featuring rare English cheeses or air dried mutton, and during the day you'll find most people are drinking quality tea and coffee. A worn Guinness entrance mosaic hints at a pubby past, but in fact the building was a bank until 1995 when it was initially converted to an Irish bar.

We Brought Beer Top5   (23)

Shop, bar

28 Hildreth Street SW12 9RQ

T (020) 8673 9324

www.webroughtbeer.co.uk

f webroughtbeeronline　**y** webroughtbeer

⏲ *Mo-Tu* 16.00-20.00, *We-Fr* 14.00-21.00,
　Sa 10.00-20.00, *Su* 11.00-20.00.

Cask beers None, **Other beers** 4 keg, 350+ bottles,
Also Homebrew supplies

☂ Tables on street

Fortnightly tastings/meet the brewer, live brewing

⇌⊖ Balham　☍CS7　⚹ Link to Capital Ring

This bright, smart and smartly-named bottle shop opened near Balham station in August 2014, in an attractive pedestrianised side street alongside other specialist retailers and market stalls. Only three months later, *Time Out* named it the best shop in Balham in the Love London awards. The growler-filling keg lines feature largely London and UK brewers – Brew by Numbers, Buxton, Ilkley, Kernel, Magic Rock, Partizan, Siren and Weird Beard are among the favourites. The bottle shelves include unusual Italian imports like Brewfist and Borgo, rarer Belgians like Belgoo, new English favourites like Arbor, Burning Sky and Ticketybrew, big US bottles and lots of Londoners. The shop also stocks Brooklyn Brewshop brew-your-own kits, with everything needed to create a full mash picobrew at home. And though it's not really a bar atmosphere, you're welcome to crack a bottle open and drink while you're browsing.

TRY ALSO

One of the few old buildings left in Wandsworth's redeveloped Riverside Quarter by the confluence of the rivers Wandle and Thames, the **Cats Back** (86–88 Point Pleasant SW18 1NN, www.thecatsback.com) became London's second Harveys pub (after the Royal Oak p 59) in May 2012, and has a good range of the famed Sussex independent's beers in cask and bottle served in tastefully refurbished surroundings.

Close to **Hagen and Hyde** (p 193) and **We Brought Beer** (p 195), bar-restaurant **Firefly**

We Brought Beer

(3 Station Parade, Balham High Road SW12 9AZ, www.fireflybar.co.uk) pours a single changing cask beer and several London keykegs and bottles, plus international options, alongside good value, well-reputed Thai food. One stop further along the Northern Line at Tooting Bec, street corner Antic the **Wheatsheaf** (2 Upper Tooting Road SW17 7PG, www.wheatsheaftootingbec.com), has up to seven cask beers in cheerfully distressed surroundings.

There's another good Antic one stop further again at Tooting Broadway: the **Antelope** (76 Mitcham Road SW17 9NG, www.theantelopepub.com), with six casks often including unusual guests. A little further along Mitcham Road is independent cocktail specialist **Little Bar** (145 Mitcham Road SW17 9PE, www.littlebarsw17.wordpress.com), which lives up to its name on size but not on welcome, and offers around ten well-chosen bottles including some from Kernel and from By the Horns nearby.

HOP HISTORIES | The Wandle Ram

There's a good case to be made that the Ram site, at Wandsworth near the mouth of Thames tributary the river Wandle (Wandsworth High Street SW18 4JT), has the longest documented continuous history of brewing in Britain, and certainly in London. Nobody is quite sure when brewing began but an inn with the sign of a ram stood here at least as far back as 1533. Inns in those days often had breweries, though the first written records of commercial brewing date from 1581, when the landlord, Humphrey Langridge, sold beer not only to his guests but to other pubs and private houses. The Young family bought the brewery in 1831, gradually shifting its focus from porter towards the lighter, more sparkling beers for which the Young's name would become famous.

The beer consumer movement of the 1970s and 1980s knew the brewery as a fiercely independent fortress of brewing tradition. Young's always kept the faith with traditional cask ales, retained wooden casks years after most of the industry had converted to aluminium, kept a ram in the brewery yard and still delivered locally using horse-drawn drays.

It only finally retired the steam engines in 1976, and even invited the Queen Mother to pull its pints.

So it came as a shock to many when, in 2006, chairman John Young admitted he'd let his head rule his heart as he announced Young's was partnering with Charles Wells and relocating all production to the latter's big 1970s plant in Bedford. Rocketing property values and the challenges of modernising the cramped old site had finally undermined the case against change. In a poignant twist, Young, a great-great-grandson of the firm's founder, died aged 85 the very week his company brewed its last beer at the Ram.

Young's employee John Hatch and some of his colleagues were determined that the lengthy record of continuous brewing should not be broken. Hatch became site manager for the new owners, and as the buildings were stripped, scraped together a workable kit from bits and pieces, including tea urns and rubbish bins. He's continued to brew non-commercially once a week pending the potential launch of a small brewery on the redeveloped site.

The redevelopment plans were long mired in local contro-

versy, planning disputes and funding troubles, but construction of the Ram Quarter, as it's now known, eventually started in autumn 2014. The design preserves several historic buildings and includes new public space so future generations should still get some idea of how the Ram looked in its heyday.

Meanwhile, as the brewery chimneys continue to dominate the townscape, the Young's name still shouts from practically every pub within walking distance. The pub estate was retained by the existing shareholders who in August 2011 sold their remaining shares in the merged brewery, Wells & Young's, to partner Charles Wells. So Young's today is just a pub chain, though for the time being Wells still brews its former brands.

There's no doubt that Young's retreat from the capital was one of the triggers for the emergence of new London brewers. Ironically, some of those newly-inspired brewers now sell guest beers to Young's pubs, catering to customers who prefer to drink local products. Who can guess what would have happened if John Young had instead let his heart rule his head, and kept the ram on the Wandle?

Outer Southwest London

Antelope (24)

Brewpub, contemporary pub
87 Maple Road, Surbiton KT6 4AW
T (020) 8399 5565   🅕 🅨 theantelpekt6
www.theantelope.co.uk
🕐 *Mo-Th* 12.00-23.00, *Fr-Sa* 12.00-24.00,
  Su 12.00-22.30. Children until 19.00.
Cask beers 10 (Big Smoke, unusual sometimes
local guests), ***Other beers*** 6 keg, 50+ bottles,
Also 5 ciders/perries, specialist whiskies
🍴 Imaginative comfort food **££**, 🪑 Front
terrace, beer garden
Live music (Th)

🚆 Surbiton   🚶 Link to Thames Path

Revamped in February 2014 by the team behind
the Sussex Arms (p223) on a generous Greene
King tie, this friendly and pretty pub on a leafy
street now offers easily the best beer choice
in the area, since enhanced by the in-house
brewery across the yard. Visiting casks in a
range of styles are likely to be from Arbor,
Binghams, Cronx, Dark Star, Late Knights, Titanic
and Tiny Rebel, while the helpfully catego-
rised bottled beer list numbers Londoners
Brew by Numbers and Rocky Head alongside
Oakham, Odell, Oskar Blues and Rochefort.
A menu divides into small plates like smoked
aubergine dip or real ale chipolatas, and large

plates like seared cod cheeks or gourmet hot
dogs (including a veggie option). Wood panelling, cool grey paint, floorboards and candle
wax dripping from mantlepieces make for
pleasant surroundings. Loyalty cards are
interchangeable with other pubs in the group.

Hand in Hand (25)

Traditional pub (Young's)
6 Crooked Billet SW19 4RQ
T (020) 8946 5720   🅨 HandWimbledon
www.thehandinhandwimbledon.co.uk
🕐 *Mo-Th* 11.00-23.00, *Fr* 11.00-24.00,
  Sa 11.00-24.00, *Su* 12.00-23.00. Children
  very welcome in family room and outdoors.
Cask beers 6–7 (Wells & Young's, local guests),
Other beers 2 keg, 2 bottles,
Also Cider in summer, some wines
🍴 Enhanced pub grub **££**,
🪑 Front terrace, adjacent common
*2 annual beer festivals, monthly cellar workshop,
tastings, poker night (Mo), "really very hard" quiz (Tu),
occasional acoustic music and Morris dancing*

🚆 Raynes Park, Wimbledon   🚇 Wimbledon   🚌 Edge Hill
(200 Raynes Park, Wimbledon) 🚶 Wimbledon Common paths

Andrew Ford, long-standing landlord of this
picturesque Young's pub with its poignant sign
on the edge of Wimbledon Common, was the
first licensee in London to invite the public into
his cellar for regular cask ale workshops. His
handpumped beers – Young's Bitter, Special,
Bombardier, seasonals and guests from locals
Sambrook's and Twickenham – are reliably
immaculate. Other choices include bottled
German lagers and wheat beers. Food is mainly
traditional fare like pie and mash, steaks and
ploughman's lunches, but might include sweet
potato chilli or summer salads. Three armchairs
around an open fire at the front provide a
perfect place to ensconce oneself with a pint of

Antelope

Hand in Hand

Winter Warmer and a good book after a stride across the common on a foggy January afternoon, while on warmer days drinkers can request plastic glasses and drink on the grass outside.

Pub trivia *The core of this low-beamed pub was built as a bakehouse in 1831. It's been a Young's pub since 1974.*

Hope Top25 (26)

Specialist, traditional pub
48 West Street, Carshalton SM5 2PR
T (020) 8240 1255
www.hopecarshalton.co.uk
🅕 hopecarshalton 🐦 pubcathope
🕐 *Mo-Sa* 12.00-23.00, *Su* 12.00-22.30. Children very welcome until 19.00 in back room only.
Cask beers 7 (Downton, Windsor & Eton, 5 unusual/often local guests), **Other beers** 8 keg, 40+ bottles, **Also** 3 ciders/perries, mead, English country wines
🍴 Pub grub, pot meals and snacks **£**, 🪑 Large beer garden, ♿
Near-monthly beer festivals, monthly folk workshop, occasional other live music, pagan events, bar billiards, board games

🚆 Carshalton 🚲 Link to Avenue Verte, NCN20
🏃 Link to Wandle Trail

When, in 2010, the regulars here heard that landlords Punch were intent on selling the pub off as a restaurant, they literally didn't give up

Hope

Hope. A group of them formed a community company and negotiated a 20-year lease as a beer-friendly free house. Downton New Forest Ale and Windsor & Eton Knight of the Garter are regulars, with breweries like Arbor, Beavertown, Bristol, Brodie's, Hop Craft, Kent, Magic Rock, Redemption and Siren providing further casks, always including both hoppier and darker styles. Some of these also supply keykeg beers, tapped alongside decent imported lagers, while the changing bottled range could include Kernel and Siren alongside Belgium's Fantôme and Bavaria's Tegernsee. Food is uncomplicated but hearty, cooked fresh at lunchtimes and pot-based in the evenings: sausage and mash, tagliatelle with meatballs or ploughman's, for example. The front section is woody and traditional, while an airy conservatory at the back looks out on a fine garden complete with permanent marquee for the regular beer festivals, which include one dedicated to black and dark beers. Only a short walk from Carshalton station, this ever improving venue is now an essential trip.

Pigs Ears (27)

Bar, restaurant
5 Hill Street, Richmond TW9 1SX
T (020) 8332 0055
www.pigs-ears.co.uk 🐦 pigsearsrichmon
🕐 *Mo* 17.00-22.00, *Tu-Th* 17.00-23.00, *Fr* 16.00-01.00, *Sa* 12.00-01.00, *Su* 12.00-22.00. Children until 20.00 in bar, later in restaurant.
Cask beers 1 (unusual guest), **Other beers** 10 keg, 90+ bottles
🍴 International menu **££**
Beer festivals, tutored tastings, food promotions

🚆🚇 Richmond 🚢 Richmond St Helens 🚲 Link to Richmond Park paths, NCN4 🏃 Capital Ring, Thames Path

Originally a Belgian-themed spinoff from Brouge in Twickenham (p217), this was reinvented in 2011 as a "craft beer cellar" showcasing new British breweries alongside imports. These days you'll find the likes of Williams Brothers, Bristol Beer Factory, Hardknott and London newcomers Fourpure and Rocky Head alongside Boon, Rodenbach and De Ranke. The cask beer is often something special, Ilkley's 7.8% Dutch collaboration *De Passie* when I last called, with a further refurb and more cask lines planned. A selection of mussel pots on a seafood-leaning menu is a reminder of the former Burgundian focus, alongside fish pies, pork chops, burgers and sharing platters, with numerous deals and offers throughout the week. Décor is intimate, with dimmed lights and candles making the best of the vaulted setting, though the atmosphere is occasionally undermined by overloud music.

Red Lion

Red Lion (28)

Contemporary pub (Fuller's)
2 Castelnau SW13 9RU   **T** (020) 8748 2984
www.red-lion-barnes.co.uk 🐦 RedLionBarnes
🕐 *Mo-Sa* 11.00-23.00, *Su* 12.00-22.30.
   Children very welcome until 18.00.
Cask beers 4 (Fuller's), ***Other beers*** 3 keg,
4 bottles, ***Also*** Wines
🍴 Enhanced pub grub, sandwiches **££**,
🌳 Sheltered non-smoking terrace, beer garden, ♿
Beer and food events, cellar tours, functions

🚉 Barnes Bridge   🚌 Barnes Red Lion (209 Barnes Bridge, Hammersmith; others Hammersmith, Wandsworth)   🚲 NCN4
🚶 Barnes Trail, Beverley Brook Walk, link to Thames Path

Co-manager Angus McKean's perfectionism has ensured him multiple awards in Fuller's Cellarman of the Year competition. As well as enjoying the results of his tender loving care at this handsome 1830s building right by the London Wetlands Centre, you can also find out how he does it on an occasional cellar tour. Cask Chiswick, Pride and ESB are permanent here as well as a seasonal, served as flawlessly as you're likely to find in London, and there's the odd bottle and keg of interest, including Frontier. Angus is a chef by training so the food is serious but straightforward – smoked salmon in London porter, a legendary chicken and leek pie, butternut squash red curry, plus a children's menu – while the annual sausage roll bakeoff is now a fixture in the capital's gourmet calendar.

Pub trivia *Before the studio closed in 2009, numerous Olympic recording artists popped out between takes for a quick pint at the Red Lion, including Jimi Hendrix who allegedly wrote two songs here while working on* Are You Experienced *in 1967. Look hard at the wooden fixtures at the back and you'll see motifs of crabs, seahorses and scallops - apparently a previous landlord bought them as a job lot from a demolished seamans' mission in Grimsby.*

Roebuck (29)

Traditional pub (Taylor Walker)
130 Richmond Hill, Richmond TW10 6RN
T (020) 8948 2329   **www.taylor-walker.co.uk**
📘 The-Roebuck   🐦 roebuckrichmond
🕐 *Mo-Th* 12.00-23.00, *Fr* 12.00-24.00,
   Sa 11.00-24.00, *Su* 12.00-22.30.
Cask beers 8 (Fuller's, 7 often local guests),
Other beers 1 keg, 3 bottles, ***Also*** 1 cider
🍴 Enhanced pub grub menu **££**,
🌳 Park opposite, ♿
Morris dancers, occasional quiz, major big screen sport

🚉🚇🚇 Richmond   🚌 American University (371 Richmond-Kingston), Nightingale Lane (65 Richmond-Kingston)   🚤 Richmond St Helens   🚲 Link to Richmond Park paths, NCN4   🚶 Capital Ring, Thames Path, Richmond Park paths

This historic pub is perched atop Richmond Hill, a sustained but gentle climb from the town centre that rewards you with breathtaking views west across Petersham meadow with its grazing cows and the Thames valley to Windsor Castle. Over their impressive 16 years in office, friendly managers Paul and Marie Weymouth have pushed the boundaries of possibility for a chain pub, building up the cask beer range using the SIBA Direct Delivery Scheme. Current favourite suppliers include Dark Star, Surrey Hills, Westerham and London brewers By the Horns and Redemption, with a smattering of bottles and kegs from BrewDog, Duvel and Goose Island. Sadly the interior feels a little ersatz, not helped by the pre-printed pub grub menus, but there are some cosy spaces and the view is as good as it was when Wordsworth and Turner admired it. Richmond Park is just around the corner.

Pub trivia *In the 19th century this was also a hotel, and a well-known destination for day trippers on pleasure boats from central London.*

Sultan (30)

Brewpub, traditional pub (Hop Back)
78 Norman Road SW19 1BT
T (020) 8542 4532
www.hopback.co.uk 🐦 sultansw19
🕐 *Su-Th* 12.00-23.00, *Fr-Sa* 12.00-24.00.
Children until 19.30.
Cask beers 8 (Sultan, Hop Back, unusual and local guests), ***Other beers*** 4 keg, 5 bottles,
Also A few malts
🍴 Hot bar snacks, Sunday roasts,
🌳 Beer garden, ♿
Beer festival (end Sep), beer club (We&Fr), quiz (Th), occasional barbecues, morris dancing, darts, rugby/cricket teams

🚇 Colliers Wood, South Wimbledon 🚲 Link to Avenue Verte, NCN20, CS7 🚶 Link to Wandle Trail

Times changed at London's only Hop Back pub in 2014 when, following the departure of leaseholder Angela after 18 years, the Salisbury-based brewery began managing the place directly. Since then the beer range has expanded, most notably through the addition of a microbrewery in an outhouse in the beer garden, commissioned early in 2015. Besides own brews and established Hop Back favourites in cask and bottle, you'll find locals like By the Horns, Sambrook's and Signature or more distant but adventurous brewers like Red Squirrel and Siren. The pub, named after a racehorse rather than a middle eastern potentate, has a rather plain and bulky 1950s

red brick exterior that looks like it really belongs on a main road rather than a South Wimbledon back street, but inside is bright and cosy, with two bars, open fires, stripped wood tables and an attractive outdoor patio.

Tap on the Line (31)

Contemporary pub (Fuller's)
Station Approach, Richmond TW9 3PZ
T (020) 8332 1162 📘 🐦 tapontheline
www.tapontheline.co.uk
🕐 *Mo-Fr* 08.00-23.00, *Sa* 09.00-23.00,
Su 10.00-22.30. Children welcome.
Cask beers 6 (Fuller's, 1 London guest), ***Other beers*** 9 keg, 25+ bottles, ***Also*** Whiskies and specialist spirits (including local), wines
🍴 Gastroish menu ££, 🌳 Leafy front terrace, ♿ in station
Occasional live music

🚇 🚇 Kew Gardens 🚶 Link to Thames Path

The only remaining pub on a London Underground platform, this abuts the eastbound District Line at Kew Gardens station, well placed for the eponymous botanical gardens. It was reopened in September 2013 with an unfussy interior – cream and green tiles, a tall back bar topped by an authentic vintage railway clock – that fits in perfectly with the Victorian country ambience of the station. There's a changing choice of Fuller's seasonals and guests from other London brewers, available in thirds and

Tap on the Line

taster paddles, classic keg imports like Budvar Dark and Chimay, and fridges stocked with a generous handful of mainly US and British beers. Food could include dressed Devon crab with tiger prawn and cracked wheat, chicken thigh with courgette and quinoa, or warm broccoli, chestnut mushroom and feta cheese salad, with a sticky toffee pudding made from Vintage Ale to follow.

Pub trivia *The building, originally a timber steaming hall, dates from around the time the station opened in 1868, and served as a buffet before first becoming a pub in the 1980s as the Flower and Firkin, later renamed the Railway. The delightful glass conservatory might look authentically Victorian but dates from Firkin days.*

Trafalgar   (32)
Traditional pub
23 High Path SW19 2JY   **T** (020) 8542 5342
www.thetraf.com
⌚ *Mo-Th* 16.00-23.00, *Fr-Su* 12.00-23.00.
   Over-12s only, over-18 from early evening
Cask beers 6 (unusual often local guests), *Other beers* 3 keg, 15 bottles, *Also* 2 ciders/perries
🍴 Pot meals **£**, 🪑 Sheltered standing room
Beer festivals, live jazz/acoustic music (Fr&Su), darts, pub games

⊖ South Wimbledon   ᪣ Link to Avenue Verte, NCN20, CS7
🏃 Link to Wandle Trail

This small pub amid looming tower blocks has long stood as a shining example of how to sustain a community local in a challenging location. Fears for its fate when the long-standing owners retired were assuaged when a team led by Rodger Molyneux from the Hope moved in (p 198). knocking through and brightening up the place for reopening in June 2014. Downton Quadhop and Surrey Hills Shere Drop are regular casks, with guests from all over the country, usually including something dark, often from Binghams. The bottle range focuses on Belgium, with lesser known brands like De Maeght van Gottem. Amazingly, they manage to squeeze in live bands twice a week and an occasional beer festival. The long term future is still in question as the surrounding estate is due for redevelopment, but Merton Council is keen to protect the pub as a community asset.

Willoughby Arms   (33)
Traditional pub
47 Willoughby Road, Kingston upon Thames
KT2 6LN   **T** (020) 8546 4236
www.thewilloughbyarms.com
𝐟 Willoughby-Arms
⌚ *Mo-Sa* 10.30-24.00, *Su* 12.00-24.00.
   Children until early evening.
Cask beers 7 (Fuller's, Sharp's, Timothy Taylor, Twickenham, 3 local guests)
🍴 Pizzas, pies **£**, 🪑 Beer garden, front seating, ♿
3 annual beer festivals, monthly acoustic open mic, SPBW meetings, big screen sports, darts, pool, table football

⇌ Kingston   ᪣ Shortlands Road (K5 Kingston)
🚤 Kingston Turks   ᪣ Link to NCN4   🏃 Link to Thames Path

This big and rather clunky-looking 1892 street corner pub was in apparently terminal decline in 1997 when Rick and Lysa Robinson turned it round not by going gastro but by concentrating on old-fashioned community appeal, sport and cask ale. Rick has links to the Society for the Preservation of Beers from the Wood, an organisation that predates CAMRA, so it's no surprise that the regular offerings are solidly traditional: London Pride, Doom Bar, Taylor Landlord and others from the likes of Black Sheep, Weltons or Twickenham. Three annual beer festivals widen the choice. Check out the free film and sport exhibition on the walls, with a still from *Escape to Victory* to mark the transition, or avoid the big screen TVs in the unspoilt, wood-panelled saloon bar.

TRY ALSO

Close to the Sultan (p 200) and the Trafalgar (p 201) in South Wimbledon, off-licence **Nelson Wines** (168A Merton High Street SW19 1AZ) has one of London's longest-standing ranges of specialist bottled beer. Although a little eclipsed by newcomers in terms of expertise and presentation, it can still muster 600 beers on a good day, at keen prices.

If you're visiting the Hope (p 198), the **Sun** on the other side of Carshalton station (4 North Street SM5 2HU, **www.thesuncarshalton.com**) is worth a look: it's a loungey place with a family room, a busy events programme and five decent cask beers plus a few bottles.

At Surbiton, the family-friendly **Lamb** (73 Brighton Road KT6 5NF, www.lambsurbiton. co.uk) has a much narrower range than the nearby Antelope (p 197), but boasts a great atmosphere, an extensive garden, fine British cheeses and a few immaculately kept local cask beers.

In Kingston town centre, the large and historic **Druids Head** (2 Market Place KT1 1JT, www.gkpubs.co.uk) is a Greene King pub with an expanding range of guest beers from small breweries and a small, quiet and easily-missed public bar. Along the Thames Path, Metro's **Boaters Inn** (Lower Ham Road KT2 5AU, www. boaterskingston.com) doesn't need to try very hard given its idyllic riverside location in

Canbury Gardens (book moorings in advance if arriving by boat), but tries nonetheless with a good range of local casks from Portobello, Truman's and Twickenham. It's also a well-established venue on the jazz circuit, and a brisk stroll from the Willoughby Arms (p 201).

Tat-bedecked **Woodies Freehouse** (The Sportsground, Thetford Road KT3 5DX, www. woodiesfreehouse.co.uk) is one of London's quirkiest and hardest-to-find beer venues, a former cricket pavilion with a splendid veranda hidden away in the Hogsmill valley in deepest New Malden, and handy for the London Loop walk. Seven cask beers include guests from southwest English breweries rarely seen in the capital.

LONDON DRINKERS **Martyn Cornell**

Historian and beer writer Martyn is a Londoner born and bred, with a family history in the capital going back at least 200 years, and a fascination with London's historic beer styles and its vanished breweries. His book *Amber Gold & Black*, the first history of British beer styles, has chapters on the roots of porter, stout, brown ale and IPA in London. Read more at www.zythophile.wordpress.com.

How do you rate London as a beer city, on a world scale?
London is one of the greatest beer cities in the world. For probably two centuries it was home to the biggest breweries. Without London there would be no porter, no stout and no IPA.

What's the single most exciting thing about beer in London at the moment?
It's a hard call between the explosion of new breweries and the explosion of choice on the bar top.

What single thing would make things even better?
Better quality cask beer across the board: it's still a sad fact that in too many pubs, cask ale quality is a lottery.

What are your top London beers right now?
Twickenham Naked Ladies is always a favourite, and I drink Redemption Fellowship Porter whenever I see it, but right now I'm enjoying Fuller's Imperial Stout as it matures in bottle.

What's your top great beer night out?
A crawl around the Holborn/Fleet Street area: if you plan it well, and start early, you can take in some unique pubs, like the Blackfriar (p68) and the Princess Louise (p83), and get in some tremendous beer choices as well, in bars like the Holborn Whippet (p80).

Who's your London beer hero?
Derek Prentice (p95): there isn't a man in London with more experience in making marvellous

beers. I've never had a conversation with him without learning something new.

Who will we be hearing a lot more from in future?
Ed and Tom Martin: I think their ETM Group of pubs, like the Gun (p118), is going to be doing some very interesting things now that they're opening a brewpub in Ealing.

Which are your other top beer cities?
I'll avoid the obvious and nominate Hong Kong as an up-and-coming place to watch. Lots of young people there have found out about great beer in places like New York City and London, and are now demanding the same choice at home. Bars have responded by boosting the beers available, from all over the world, Japan to Norway, and there's been a surge in new brewery openings too.

WEST
LONDON

WEST LONDON

This section covers the W and SW postcodes outside the central area and north of the Thames, with a couple of exceptions.

A handful of listings immediately west and northwest of Central London, on the fringes of the City of Westminster and the borough of Kensington and Chelsea, including some with NW postcodes, didn't fit neatly anywhere else so I've grouped them together here under **Inner West London**.

Fulham to Chiswick covers a number of places west along the Thames and the District Line in the borough of Hammersmith & Fulham and the eastern part of the borough of Hounslow. This is Fuller's country, but the listings here are surprisingly diverse.

Outer West London wraps up the rest, including a notable cluster of top recommendations around Twickenham, with some of the richest pickings in West London (for the southern part of Richmond borough, see Outer Southwest London p197).

The section also highlights scattered jewels at Acton, Brentford, Ealing, Hanwell and Mortlake, and points you in the direction of decent ale at Heathrow Airport.

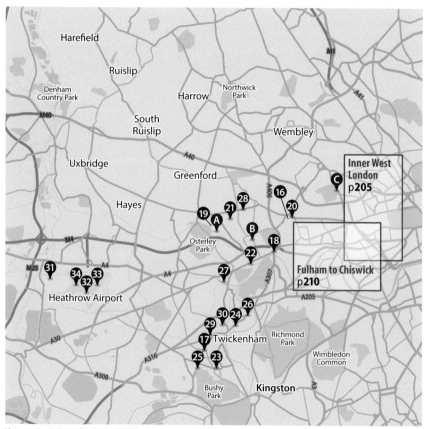

16. Aeronaut · 17. Brouge (Old Goat) · 18. Express · 19. Fox · 20. George and Dragon · 21. Grosvenor · 22. Magpie and Crown · 23. Masons Arms · 24. Mulberry Tree · 25. Noble Green Wines · 26. Real Ale · 27. Red Lion · 28. Star and Anchor · 29. Sussex Arms · 30. Twickenham Fine Ales · 31. Crown Rivers · 32. Flying Chariot · 33. London's Pride · 34. Three Bells · A. Weird Beard Brew Co · B. Ealing Park Tavern · C. Portobello Brewing

Inner West London

Elgin (1)

Bar, restaurant (Urban Leisure)
255 Elgin Avenue W9 1NJ   **T** (020) 7625 5511
www.theelgin.com   🐦 the_elgin
🕐 *Mo-Th* 08.00-23.00, *Fr* 08.00-24.00, *Sa* 09.00-
24.00, *Su* 09.30-23.00. Children until 21.00.
Cask beers None, **Other beers** 9 keg, 35 bottles,
Also Wines, specialist spirits, coffee
🍴 Brunch, sharing plates, gastro menu
££-£££, 🪑 Benches on street, ♿
Meet the brewer/tap takeover, board games, functions

🚇 Maida Vale   🚴 Link to NCN6, Regents Canal towpath
🚶 Link to Grand Union Canal Walk, Jubilee Greenway

1. Elgin · 2. Finborough Arms · 3. Parlour · 4. Salusbury Wine Store ·
5. Truscott Arms · 5. Union Tavern · 6. · A. Moncada Brewery

A stylish mix of contemporary eatery, beer dispensary and coffee bar in the shell of an old pub right by Maida Vale Tube, the Elgin has successfully defied categorisation since reopening in November 2012. Traditionalists will bemoan the lack of cask, but there's a neat bottle range listed on a tearoff menu. Numerous Londoners like Brew by Numbers, Kernel, Partizan and Weird Beard line up alongside unusual UK visitors like Scotland's Tempest and a few imports from Brewers & Union and others, with Beavertown and occasional imports on keykeg. Food is good enough to please the local French expat community: brunch choices include classics (salmon, various eggs) and exotica like avocado, chilli and lime toast; later you might enjoy fish stew, longhorn steaks or baked aubergine and chickpea tagine. A wall of rich green tiles provides a reminder of a more pubby past.

Finborough Arms

Finborough Arms (2)
Contemporary pub
118 Finborough Road SW10 9ED
www.finborougharms.co.uk
🐦 FinboroughArms
🕐 *Mo-Fr* 17.00-23.00, *Fr-Sa* 12.00-24.00,
Su 12.00-23.00. Children until early evening.
Cask beers 4 (local or northeast England),
Other beers 5 keg, 10+ bottles, **Also** 2-3 ciders/
perries, a few specialist spirits
🍴 Cooked bar snacks, platters **£-££**,
🌳 Benches on street, ♿
*Beer festivals, monthly comedy, big screen sport,
theatre upstairs*

🚇 West Brompton 🚇 West Brompton, Earls Court

Pioneer beer blogger turned publican Jeff Bell
took on the Finborough in February 2014,
stretching his wings in a free house after
several years of working wonders at the Punch-
tied Gunmakers in Clerkenwell. Jeff sold the
pub in May 2015 to an equally enthusiastic
successor. Locals Moncada, Portobello and
Twickenham are regulars on cask; other choices
could be from brewers like Anarchy. Keg beers
include the sublime unfiltered Tipopils from
Borgo in Italy, alongside Schneider Weisse and
other solid German selections, and there's
more Borgo in bottle alongside the likes of
Orval and Schlenkerla. On a slightly awkward
wedge-shaped site with a quiet street on one
side and a busy road on the other, the place
has a pleasantly open feel, extending to the
glass-fronted cellar which can be viewed from
a comfortable drinking space downstairs.

Visitor note *Above is one of London's leading pub theatres,
with an enviable track record of transferring successful
shows to the West End. Chelsea FC's Stamford Bridge ground
is just down the road so the pub can get busy on match days.*

Parlour (3)
Bar, restaurant
5 Regent Street NW10 5LG
T (020) 8969 2184　www.parlourkensal.com
📘 Parlour 🐦 ParlourUK
🕐 *Tu-Su* 10.00-24.00, *Mo* closed.
Children until early evening.
Cask beers None, **Other beers** 8 keg, 16 bottles,
Also Cocktails, specialist spirits, wines
🍴 Modern British food, cooked bar snacks
££-£££, 🌳 Rear garden
Tastings

🚇 Kensal Rise 🚇 Kensal Green 🚃 Kilburn Lane
(numerous Kensal Rise) 🚲 Link to NCN6 🚶 Link to Grand
Union Canal Walk

Originally a Truman's pub called the Grey Horse,
this long-neglected building was thoughtfully
refitted in November 2012 as a relaxed bar-
restaurant, adding extra interest with a leafy
little garden centred on a tree, and Cocteausque
ironwork sculptures wrought by a relative of
one of the owners. The management plans to
add cask beer eventually; meanwhile there's
a rotating Beavertown keykeg line, draughts
from Camden Town, Meantime and Paulaner,
and bottles that include the very local Moncada
besides Harviestoun, Kernel and Wild, with top
Belgians like Duchesse de Bourgogne and Orval.
A varied menu offers breakfast and brunch, a
range of snacks and tapas (chestnut hummus,
duck live pâté, home made sodabread with
beer), main courses like wild duck with black-
berries or grilled mackerel with broccoli, and
retro desserts like Arctic roll. It's also a pickup
point for a local organic veg box scheme.

Parlour

Salusbury Wine Store (4)

Shop, bar
54 Salusbury Road NW6 6NN
T (020) 7372 6664   🐦 SalusburyWine
www.thesalusburywinestore.com
🕐 *Mo-Sa* 10.00-21.00, *Su* 10.00-18.00.
Cask beers None, **Other beers** 100 bottles,
Also Wines including Puglian, specialist
whiskies and spirits
🍴 Cheese, charcuterie, chocolate **£-££**,
🪑 Front terrace
Tastings, meet the brewer

🚇 Queens Park

Sandwiched between a pub-restaurant and a
bakery under the same ownership, this
efficiently white-tiled venue near Queens
Park station was the first off-licence to sell
Beavertown beers and they're still very much
a feature, alongside other Londoners like
Brew by Numbers, Fourpure, Kernel, Pressure
Drop and Weird Beard and interlopers like
Arbor, Hardknott, Magic Rock, Siren and Wild.
A minority of well chosen international beers
like North Coast and Orval round things out.
For a modest corkage, you can drink any beer
at the scattering of tables on the small terrace,
alongside plates of fine cheese and charcuterie
from the UK, France and Italy and very good
wines by the glass. It's all very civilised, and
the popular pub next door is worth a look too,
with good food and a few fine bottled beers
supplementing the Greene King tie.

Truscott Arms (5)

Gastropub
55 Shirland Road W9 2JD
T (020) 7266 9198   🔵🐦 TheTruscottArms
www.thetruscottarms.com
🕐 *Mo-Th* 10.00-23.30, *Fr-Sa* 10.00-24.00,
Su 10.00-22.30. Children until 19.30.
Cask beers 4 (London), **Other beers** 9 keg,
6 bottles, **Also** Fine wines, specialist spirits,
cocktails
🍴 Breakfasts, enhanced pub grub, gastro
menu **££-£££**, 🪑 Front terrace, beer garden
*Beer festivals, quiz (Mo), films (Tu), wine club,
seasonal events, art displays, functions*

🚇 Warwick Avenue   🚤 Little Venice   🚲 Link to NCN6,
Regents Canal towpath   🚶 Link to Grand Union Canal Walk,
Jubilee Greenway

Highly rated for its Modern British cooking,
this smart but relaxed place in well-to-do
Maida Vale just a short stroll from Little Venice
gets much else right too, including the beer.
Draughts are sourced from London brewers –
Sambrook's, Hackney, Moncada, Redemption
and Truman's are regularly on cask. A few
other Londoners, including Kernel, share the
bottle fridges with a small range of gluten-free
beers. Formerly the Shirland Hotel, the pub
was tastefully restored and reopened in March
2013 by theatre director Andrew Fisher, with
an expansive bar downstairs and a crisply

Truscott Arms

laid-out restaurant above. The latter does fixed-price menus with all the trimmings (roast Cornish cod, guinea fowl, glazed beef cheek or herb gnocchi are typical); the pub food is more informal but with some overlap and equal quality. Art is another feature: hung works and murals change intermittently and are as well chosen as everything else.

Union Tavern Top25 (6)

Specialist, contemporary pub (Fuller's)
45 Woodfield Road W9 2BA
T (020) 7286 1886 🐦union_tavern
www.union-tavern.co.uk
🕐 *Mo-Th* 12.00-23.00, *Fr-Sa* 12.00-24.00,
Su 12.00-22.30. Children until 19.30.
Cask beers 5 (London), ***Other beers*** 12 keg,
60 bottles, ***Also*** Some specialist spirits
🍴 BBQ meat, sandwiches, salads **£-££**,
🍹 Canalside terrace
*Meet the brewer, quiz (We), live music (Th),
summer outdoor barbecues*

🚇Westbourne Park 🚤 Little Venice 🚴NCN6
🚶Grand Union Canal Walk

In June 2012, surviving established London independent Fuller's further confirmed its embrace of London's beer renaissance by reconfiguring one of its best sited pubs as a showcase for capital brews. Although the owning brewery has some presence, you're as likely to find East London, Hackney, Moncada, Redemption, Sambrook's, Weird Beard or Windsor & Eton on the cask pumps and Brew by Numbers, Camden Town, Fourpure and Redemption on keg. Several other London brewers stack up in a tall fridge besides quality imports mainly from the USA, like Anderson Valley, Bear Republic and Founders. US-inspired meals like burgers, pulled pork and Philly steak sandwiches, are sold along with the odd fish dish and interesting salads, with daily changing deals, in a clean and contemporary space. Then there's the considerable bonus of a lower level that opens on to a terrace right beside the Grand Union Canal.

Visitor note. *If you're lucky enough to own your own boat, ring ahead to book a free guest mooring.*

Fulham to Chiswick

BrewDog Shepherds Bush (7)
Specialist, bar
15 Goldhawk Road W12 8QQ
www.brewdog.com/bars/shepherds-bush
🐦 BrewDog ShepBush
🕐 Mo-Sa 12.00-24.00, Su 12.00-22.30.
  Children until 22.00.
Cask beers None, **Other beers** 40 keg (20
BrewDog, 20 London and international),50
bottles (international), **Also** Specialist whiskies
🍴 Meat platters, burgers, hot dogs ££,
🪑 Tables on street, ♿
*Meet the brewer/tap takeover, occasional acoustic
music, pinball, board games*

🚇 Shepherds Bush   🚇 Goldhawk Road, Shepherds Bush

London's third BrewDog bar is also its biggest,
opened late in 2013 just off the southwestern
tip of Shepherds Bush Green. There's seating
on squishy banquettes and street views
through the big picture windows, though
something of a fast food bar feel. No less than
40 keg lines sprout from the corrugated
concrete bar. Half are BrewDog, the rest
dispense beers from a variety of sources,
including Londoners like Beavertown, Brodie's
and Weird Beard, always including a black IPA,
a sour and an Imperial stout. Bottles and cans
are restricted by BD standards but still stretch
to Partizan alongside the likes of Clown Shoes,
Mikkeller, Oskar Blues and Stronzo. Food is
mainly dirty meat, branded Texas Joe's, with
beef brisket, pork shoulder and hot link
sausages by the pound. Staff are evangelical,
dispensing tasters and third pint measures
and, unusually for the chain, providing table
service on Wednesdays to Saturdays.

Dr. Ink of Fulham Top5 (8)
Shop
349 Fulham Palace Road SW6 6TB
☎ (020) 7610 6795 www.drinkoffulham.com
📘 Drinks of Fulham 🐦 drinkoffulham
🕐 Tu-Fr 14.00-20.00, Sa 11.30-20.00, Su 12.00-
16.00 *(closed Su Jan-Apr)*, Mo closed.
Cask beers None, **Other beers** 500 bottles/cans,
Also Specialist ciders, some wines
🍴 Curry sauce and spice mixes; vegetarian
farsan snacks *(Sa)* £, 🪑 Small front terrace
Occasional Indian food and beer tastings

🚇 Parsons Green, Putney Bridge   🚌 Bishops Park Road
(numerous Putney Bridge)   🚶 Thames Path

Shrila Amin opened this smallish but well-or-
ganised shop opposite Bishop's Park early
in 2010, fusing world beer culture with her
own Gujerati background by dishing out spice
mixes and curry pastes and, on Saturdays,
some of the most delicious samosas and
kachoris in London alongside a dazzling
range of beer. There are lots of Londoners –
Belleville, Brew by Numbers, Brodies, Canopy,
Clarkshaw's, Moncada, Pressure Drop and
Twickenham to name a few – besides solid
English choices like Box Steam, Mallinson's

BrewDog Shepherds Bush

209

Dr.Ink of Fulham

Fest (Octoberfest) (9)

Bar
678 Fulham Road SW6 5SA
T (020) 7736 5293 www.octoberfestpub.com
 Octoberfest-Pub octoberfestpub
 Su-Th 12.00-23.00, *Fr-Sa* 12.00-24.00.
Cask beers None, **Other beers** 12 keg , 45+ bottles
(mainly German), **Also** Schnapps
 German pub menu, sausages, snacks **E-££**,
Oompah band (Fr-Sa), big screen sport (UK/German),
seasonal events, pool, functions

 Parsons Green   Fulham Road (220 Hammersmith)

and Two Cocks, a whole section of Scottish
beers, Dutch specialities from Kaapse and
De Molen, Belgian essentials from Boon
and Rochefort, and up-to-the-minute US
West Coast imports like Cismontane, Mike
Hess and Mission, rarely seen in the UK. To
top it all, an on-licence and a few wooden
seats at the front create a beautiful space
to enjoy a fine beer when the sun shines.

This friendly outpost of the Bundesrepublik in
deepest Fulham is also known as Octoberfest,
in curiously Anglo-German spelling, but is listed
here under the name it proclaims in suitably
Gothic script above the door. Like several other
German-themed venues, it marches to the
oompah tune, but with a better beer offer than
most, though still strictly traditional. König
Ludwig and Weihenstephan wheat beers and
Köstrizter Schwarzbier are on draught; the
bottled selection reaches to Augustiner, Jever,
Mühlen Kölsch, Schlenkerla, Schlösser Alt,

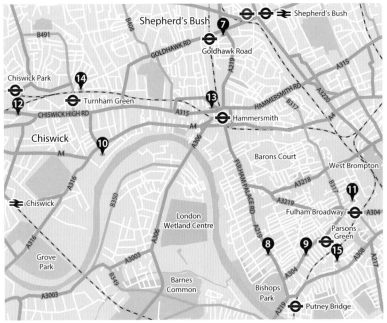

7. BrewDog Shepherds Bush · 8. Dr.Ink of Fulham · 9. Fest (Octoberfest) · 10. Fuller's Brewery Shop · 11. Lazy Fox ·
12. Old Packhorse · 13. Swan · 14. Tabard · 15. White Horse

Tegernsee and others, with Bockbier from Andechs and Ayinger and annually replenished stocks of all six bottled Oktoberfest brews. Wurst platters, schnitzels and *Schweinebraten* are on offer at quite moderate prices given the area. TV sport dominates a little, as you'd expect at the London base of the FC Bayern München supporters' club.

Fuller's Brewery Shop (10)

Shop
Chiswick Lane South W4 2QB
T (020) 8996 2000
www.fullersbreweryshop.co.uk
⊕ *Mo-Fr* 10.00-20.00, *Sa* 10.00-15.00, *Su* closed.
Cask beers None, **Other beers** 30+ (mainly Fuller's),
minicasks, bulk casks to order, **Also** Wines
Brewery tours

⇌ Chiswick   ⊖ Turnham Green   🚃 Hogarth Roundabout
(190 Richmond, Stamford Brook, Hammersmith)
🏃 Thames Path

This biggish, helpful shop is on the brewery site just round the corner from the famous wisteria. Alongside the core Fuller's range, it's a reliable source of hard-to-find specialities, stocking several beers from the limited edition Past Masters and Brewer's Reserve series and numerous aged Vintage Ales, plus Chimay and Sierra Nevada seasonals which the brewery imports. For serious devotees there are glasses, bar towels and an extensive range of branded merchandise. You can buy tickets here too for the excellent brewery tour, which always starts a few steps away at the dual-named Mawson Arms/Fox and Hounds (Mawson Lane W4 2QD, www.mawsonarmschiswick.co.uk). The pub is also worth a look for cask beers that are as fresh as you'd expect given the location, but note it closes early in the evening and all day at weekends.

Lazy Fox (11)

Contemporary pub (Robot Pub Group)
18 Farm Lane SW6 1PP
T (020) 7386 3783   ⓕ ⓨ lazyfoxfulham
www.thelazyfox.rpgpubs.com
⊕ *Mo* 16.00-24.00, *Tu-Sa* 12.00-24.00,
Su 12.00-22.30. Children welcome.
Cask beers 2–3 (Windsor & Eton, unusual often local guests), **Other beers** 15 keg, 25 bottles
🍴 Enhanced pub grub, desserts **££**,
🪑 Benches on street, ♿

⊖ Fulham Broadway

A self-service pub sounds unpromisingly gimmicky, and indeed when this red brick place was first reopened in its new guise late in 2012, it stocked only big brands, but struggled to find customers. Buying out the tie and going 'craft' has changed all that. The 'wall of beer' invites you to help yourself to keg beers from Beavertown, Kernel, Windsor & Eton, other UK guests and imports from Paulaner, Schremser and Stiegl, supplemented on the bar by the likes of Burning Sky. Some tables even have their own taps, with requests for specific beers accepted from pre-booked parties. Casks could be from Marble, Roosters, Tiny Rebel or Windsor & Eton, while bottles include Beavertown and Kernel – "what we like to drink," says manager James. Pub grub runs to wild boar and apple sausage and mash, macaroni cheese rarebits, ribeye steaks and burgers, with artisanal ice cream to follow.

Lazy Fox

LONDON'S BREWING Fuller's

When current brewing director John Keeling first joined Fuller's in 1981, the brewery was a well-respected London independent with a modest regional estate, making 70,000 barrels (115,000 hl) of beer a year. Today it's the only surviving historic independent brewery in London, and one of the best known brewers in Britain. Its best bitter, London Pride, is a national brand, its estate of almost 400 pubs stretches to Somerset and Birmingham, and its annual output has more than tripled to 220,000 barrels (360,000 hl). Beers like ESB have found worldwide fame and helped inspire a new generation of brewers in North America.

Yet at heart Fuller's is still very much a brewer-led and quality-focused business, mixing innovation with a dedication to traditional methods. Though the high volume cask brands are its bread and butter, John still finds time to produce the annual Vintage Ale, a world class bottle-conditioned barley wine, as well as ageing beer in spirit casks and scouring the archives for historic styles to recreate. Recently, the brewery has successfully courted more contemporary-minded drinkers with a creditable American-style pale ale, Wild River, and a popular keg 'craft' lager-style beer, Frontier, also with US hops, which could yet end up as Fuller's first 'tank' beer.

"I firmly believe," says John, "that popular beer doesn't have to be bland. The only reason bland beers are popular is that they're propped up with massive marketing campaigns. But I grew up drinking Draught Bass and Boddingtons, which in those days were flavourful, distinctive beers – and everybody drank them."

Things could so easily have been different. In the early 1970s the brewery was poised to ditch cask production and convert entirely to keg beers, but the growing interest in real ale influenced management to drop the plans. Had they been pursued, the brewery would almost certainly have failed to compete with larger competitors and ended up bought out for its pubs and closed.

Brewing on the site is claimed to date back to a brewhouse in the gardens of Bedford House on Chiswick Mall in the 1650s. Thomas Mawson started the first commercial brewery there in 1701 and a Fuller first became involved in 1829. The founding date of 1845 shown on the brewery logo was when John Bird Fuller got together with Henry Smith (formerly of Ind & Smith – see Brewing beyond the marshes p130) and his brother-in-law John Turner to take over the site. Descendants of the founding partners remain involved, including chairman Michael Turner and corporate affairs director Richard Fuller.

Most of the red brick brewery buildings date from the 1870s but parts are older: the wisteria carpeting some of the walls may be the oldest in England, from a Chinese cutting planted in 1816. Perhaps the beer helped it flourish as another cutting from the same batch that went to Kew Gardens later died. The brewery still makes use of the old practice of 'parti-gyling' – making beers of various strengths from the same basic mash depending on the dilution of the 'runnings' from the mash tun, with some tweaks to the hop additions. The brewery's signature beers – Chiswick, London Pride and ESB – are related in this way. The first new parti-gyle recipe in 50 years has just been developed to create a family of golden ales in celebration of this year's 170th anniversary.

A less confident company might have seen the rapid expansion of new breweries as a threat, but instead Fuller's has slipped into the role of elder statesman and mentor. John, a sparkling Mancunian with a wicked taste in music, was a founder of the London Brewers Alliance, offering his encyclopaedic knowledge and reliable advice to awestruck young microbrewers. Former brewing manager Derek Prentice (p95) and his successor Georgina Young are also deeply engaged with the capital's brewing community. The current abundance of great beer in London would have been so much more difficult, if not impossible, to achieve without the continued presence of this international treasure, still producing world class beers by the side of the Thames.

Swan (13)

Traditional pub (Nicholson's)
46 Hammersmith Broadway W6 0DZ
T (020) 8748 1043   www.nicholsonspubs.
co.uk/theswanhammersmithlondon
🐦 swanhammersmith
🕐 *Mo-Th* 10.00-23.00, *Fr-Sa* 10.00-24.00, *Su* 10.00-
    22.30. Children until 19.00, later in restaurant.
Cask beers 10 (Fuller's, St Austell, Windsor & Eton,
7 guests), **Other beers** 4 bottles, **Also** Some wines
🍴 Enhanced pub grub menu
Occasional beer events

🚇 Hammersmith   🏃 Link to Thames Path

Old Pack Horse (12)

Contemporary pub (Fuller's) ★
434 Chiswick High Road W4 5TF
T (020) 8994 2872   🔲 oldpackhorse
www.oldpackhorsechiswick.co.uk   🐦 OPHW4
🕐 *Mo-We* 11.00-24.00, *Th* 11.00-01.00, *Fr-Sa* 11.00-
    02.00, *Su* 12.00-24.00. Children until 21.00.
Cask beers 6 (Fuller's, 1 often local guest),
Other beers 7 keg, 25 bottles (Fuller's, inter-
national), **Also** 1 cider, 20 whiskies, other
specialist spirits, 25 wines
🍴 Thai menu **£**, 🪑 Front terrace, courtyard
*Fortnightly live music (Sa), retro DJs, art gallery,
board games, functions*

🚇 Chiswick Park

This landmark pub opposite Hammersmith
shopping centre and a short step from the
Apollo began life as an 18th century coaching
inn, though what you see today is an early 20th
century rebuild necessitated after the District
Line was routed beneath. It was splendidly
refurbished as a Nicholson's late in 2009,
reclaiming its early Edwardian opulence –
elaborate ceilings, big plaster arches, pillars,
tiling, stained glass, mirrors, wooden partitions,
a marble bar top and a distinctive double
staircase leading up to the dining rooms. Beer
options are good too, with a varied cask choice
from the chain's seasonal list, usually including
dark beers: Butcombe, Leeds, Peerless and
Truman's were on when I visited. Redchurch
beers from Hackney were a welcome sight in
the fridge. Easily the standout choice in a
busy town centre.

This big pub overlooking Turnham Green
reopened in November 2012 following a refurbishment that successfully combines heritage
elements with a more contemporary, funky
feel, functioning both as a youthful late night
venue and as a fine town centre showcase for
nearby owning brewery Fuller's. Chiswick,
ESB, London Pride, Seafarers, Fuller's
seasonals and the occasional third party
guest occupy the handpumps, while bottles
of 1845 and Bengal Lancer line up alongside
Delirium Tremens and Singha. A bright and
cheerful Thai restaurant at the back has
notably better food than many such places.

*Pub trivia A long-standing part of the brewery estate,
the pub was rebuilt in 1910 to the designs of celebrated
Edwardian pub architect T H Nowell Parr and well
exemplifies his exuberant style - glazed faience finishes,
elaborate arched doorways, Ionic columns and first
floor bay windows. Indoors, there's an Arts and Crafts
fireplace framed by a Tudor arch, an original bar back
and counter and fragments of art deco stained glass. A
collage of playbills, a lightbox and a few tipup seats recall
the Empire Theatre, which stood nearby until 1959.*

Swan

Tabard

White Horse Top 25 (15)

Specialist, contemporary pub (Castle)
1 Parsons Green SW6 4UL
T (020) 7736 2115 🐦 WhiteHorseSW6
www.whitehorsesw6.com
🕐 *Su-We* 09.30-23.30, *Th-Sa* 09.30-24.00.
  Children welcome.
Cask beers 8 (Adnams, Harveys, Timothy
Taylor, 5 unusual often local guests), ***Other
beers*** 12 keg, 120 bottles, ***Also*** Malts, gins, wine
🍴 Gastro/enhanced pub grub menu **££-£££**,
🪑 Front terrace, ♿
*4 annual beer festivals, monthly Beer Academy
tastings, meet the brewer/tap takeover, functions*

⊖ Parsons Green

Tabard (14)

Traditional pub (Taylor Walker) ★
2 Bath Road W4 1LN **T** (020) 3582 2479
www.taylor-walker.co.uk
📘 thetabardpub 🐦 chiswicktabard
🕐 *Su-Th* 12.00-23.00, *Fr-Sa* 12.00-24.00.
  Children until 21.00.
Cask beers 9 (often unusual and local guests),
Other beers 7 keg, 7 bottles, ***Also*** 1 cider, a few
malts
🍴 Pub grub **££**, 🪑 Front/side terrace, ♿
*Beer festivals, food promotions, occasional live music,
quiz, functions, theatre/comedy venue upstairs*

⊖ Turnham Green

This famous former coaching inn overlooking
dappled Parsons Green is now part of the
Castle chain, though uniquely retains its
specialist focus. Casks are sourced by style,

The White Horse

"We're the best real ale pub in west London,"
a staff member once told me with admirable
loyalty: perhaps a little overstated, but it's quite
likely the best London pub in the Taylor Walker
chain. The beer range is a testimony to the
enthusiasm and persistence of manager Tim
Rider: there are no regular cask ales, though
names like By the Horns, Plain, Sambrook's,
West Berkshire, White Horse, Windsor & Eton
and XT often turn up, providing a range of
styles. Bottled Black Sheep, Duvel, Maisels
Weisse, Westerham and a few London 'craft
kegs' add further choice. The absence of piped
music, proximity to Acton Green and Chiswick
commons and a separately managed upstairs
theatre that's played host to Russell Brand
and Al Murray all help make the case too.

Pub trivia *On the southwest corner of 1880s garden
suburb Bedford Park and dating from the same period, this
is a big pub in the Arts and Crafts sytle, with a handsome
rustic exterior and some exquisite tiling, including an
original fireplace surround depicting Little Bo Peep.*

with strong, dark and hoppy beers always on offer, from breweries like Binghams, Caveman, Hammerton, Hastings, Moor and West Berkshire. Keykegs tend to be British and American, with unfiltered Czech Pilsner Urquell tank beer – this was the first UK pub to offer it. Bottled beers are still by far the biggest section of the hefty drinks list, with sharers from AleSmith, Rogue, Southern Tier and Thornbridge, numerous Trappists and abbey beers including Achel and St Bernardus, several fine lambics as well as Mikkeller 'spontane' beers, and British bottled classics like Harveys Russian Stout and White Shield. Upmarket pub grub could include free range sausages, ox cheek and kidney pie and caramelised onion tart. Thanks to its prize location in an area of Chelsea overspill, it's known rather unkindly as the 'Sloaney Pony' for its popularity with wax-jacketed types and there's a

certain slightly colonial poshness about the place. But the customers are generally a genial mix and the staff remain welcoming, polite and informative even when, as often, they're run off their feet.

Pub trivia *This is the oldest surviving pub with a claim to being London's 'beer central'. In 1981, postgraduate student Mark Dorber took a holiday job here and soon found himself intrigued both with the specifics of running a good cellar and with beer in general. Inspired by the writings of Michael Jackson, he set out on his own beer hunts, personally dry-hopped the Draught Bass, ran festivals celebrating rare styles, and eventually became manager, presiding until 2007. By the 1990s the pub was renowned for its lengthy bottled list, including aged beers, and celebrated beer and food dinners sometimes presided over by Jackson himself. Wisely, current owners Mitchells & Butlers have granted subsequent managers, including current incumbent Jez Manterfield, similar freedoms, though the dry-hopped Bass and vintage bottles are no longer.*

LONDON DRINKERS   Jeremy aka @bonvoeux1

Jeremy, better-known on Twitter as Jezza @bonvoeux1, is the co-creator of *A London Beer and Pub Guide* at www.beerguidelondon.com, recommending 150 of the best places to drink good beer as well as keeping track of current and future breweries, with regular updates tweeted from @beerguidelondon. "For me beer remains a hobby," he says, "but it's a hugely enjoyable one as we strive to meet the challenge of keeping our guide up to date."

How do you rate London as a beer city, on a world scale?
With the explosion of breweries, new pubs, bars, brewpubs and taprooms, and with the diversity of beer styles and dispense methods all happily co-existing, it's now undoubtedly a world class city for residents and tourist alike.

What's the single most exciting thing about beer in London at the moment?

The rebirth of the brewery tap. Until recently I'd never have considered spending my Saturdays under railway arches or on industrial estates in Bermondsey or Tottenham, and I definitely would not have expected to find excellent beer there.

What single thing would make things even better?
An overall increase in beer quality.

What are your top London beers right now?
I love my hops. Three of my favourites are the outstanding Beavertown Gamma Ray, Rocky Head Imitera IPA and Fourpure IPA.

What's your top great beer night out?
Take your pick from the many pub crawls that didn't exist only two or three years ago. How about starting with beer and barbecue at Dukes (p142), calling in to the nearby Fox (p110), then a wander towards the Angel for the great places there? Gospel Oak to

Camden is another possibility, while Shoreditch to Bethnal Green could be the best in town.

Who's your London beer hero?
It's hard to look much beyond Evin O'Riordan of the Kernel. He demonstrated the art of the possible, and remains an incredibly grounded, decent and down-to-earth guy.

Who will we be hearing a lot more from in future?
The person who finally nails a truly great, world class venue pairing food with beer and showcasing both. I could do without seeing pulled pork on offer in every beer bar.

Which are your other top beer cities?
My favourite three are Bruges, Bamberg (and around) and New York City. If San Diego had better public transport it would also be on the list, as it's home to an incredible concentration of some of the world's best breweries.

This is Fuller's country, and one of the Chiswick brewer's loveliest and most idyllically sited pubs is the **Dove ★** (19 Upper Mall W6 9TA, www.dovehammersmith.co.uk) on the riverside at Hammersmith Mall, with a view both of the brewery and of Hammersmith Bridge. One of late beer writer Michael Jackson's favourites, it boasts officially the smallest public bar in Britain. In Chiswick itself, the huge **George IV** (185 High Road W4 2DR, www.georgeiv.co.uk) is a lavishly refurbished alternative showcase to the nearby Old Pack Horse (p 213), and also does a range of bottled beers including from other London brewers. Revered Italian craft brewers **Baladin** and **Ducato** opened a London shop window in Chiswick, **The Italian Job** (13 Devonshire Road W4 2EU, www.theitalianjobpub.co.uk) in February 2015.

HOP HISTORIES Toucan gestures

Accounts of the dark days of big brewing in the early 1970s often mention the Big Six, but a more accurate term would be the Big Seven. The seventh brewer was Guinness, which from 1937–2005 operated a subsidiary brewery at Park Royal in West London. The reason for the discrepancy is that, although Guinness and the other six breweries between them were responsible for the vast majority of beer drunk in the UK, the Irish giant uniquely owned no pubs, instead using its strong brand and a network of wholesaling and bottling deals to ensure its ubiquity in almost every pub.

Even before it built Park Royal, Guinness's history, and the history of Irish brewing in general, was intertwined with London brewing. Back in 1759, when Arthur Guinness first set up on his own at St James's Gate in Dublin, the whole of Ireland was ruled from London. Guinness first brewed ales in the local style but in 1778 brewed porter for the first time, copying the London-brewed beers which by then were becoming increasing fashionable in the Irish capital. His was likely not the first Irish brewery to do this but ultimately the most successful.

By the mid-19th century Guinness was one of the biggest brewers in the British Isles, successfully transforming porter and stout (the latter originally simply a stronger porter), into something characteristically Irish. The fame of Irish stout, and of Guinness in particular, spread across the world with the Irish diaspora, making it one of the first global brands, and by 1914 St James's Gate was producing an astonishing 4.34 million hl a year.

Quite why Irish porter and stout retained their popularity while their English parent styles declined has not yet been satisfactorily explained but by the 1930s, with Dublin now the capital of an independent state and English porter heading inexorably towards extinction, mainland Britain was one of Guinness's most important export markets. The beer's appeal spread far beyond the Irish community thanks in part to the brewery's well-known flair for clever advertising, with still-quoted tag lines like "Guinness is good for you" and memorable characters such as the iconic toucans. While important markets in the north-west and Scotland were easily reached by sea from Dublin, the south of England was less accessible, so Guinness decided to build a satellite brewery in London.

The site chosen was Park Royal in Willesden, a former Royal Agricultural Society showground in the western suburbs on the A40 trunk road which was then being redeveloped as an industrial zone. Guinness built a massive state-of-the-art facility, designed in *art deco* style by George Gilbert Scott, which when it opened in 1937 for a while restored to London the long-lost distinction of being home to the biggest brewery in the world. It turned out to be last new brewery in the capital before the arrival of modern microbrewing in the late 1970s (see Yeast Enders p122). Park Royal was pasteurising and pressurising its draught beer by the 1950s but its standard bottled stout was bottle conditioned until 1994.

In 1997 Guinness merged with former Watney owner Grand Metropolitan to form Diageo, one of the biggest drinks companies in the world. In 2005, following an increase in capacity in Dublin, the London plant was deemed surplus to requirements and closed down. Despite its importance, the brewery building was rejected for listing by English Heritage and was demolished, among some controversy, in 2006. Diageo's offices are still based on part of the site (Lakeside Drive NW10 7HQ), while the rest is being redeveloped for business use.

Outer West London

Aeronaut (16)

Brewpub, contemporary pub (Laines)
264 High Street W3 9BH
T (020) 8993 4242
www.aeronaut.pub   🅕 🅨 AeronautActon
🕐 *Su-We* 12.00-24.00, *Th* 12.00-01.00,
   Fr-Sa 12.00-01.30. Children until 20.00.
Cask beers 6 (Laines, occasional guests), **Other beers** 2 keg, 2 bottles/cans, **Also** 2 ciders, wines
🍴 Modern pub grub and platters **££**,
🪑 Beer garden ✿, ♿
Circus cabaret (Fr-Sa), live music (Su-Mo), swing dancing (Tu), quiz (We)

🚇 Acton Central   🚇 Ealing Common   🚌 Denehurst Gardens (numerous Acton Central, Ealing Common)

In November 2013 this big pub with a troubled recent history became the first of Laine's London brewpubs in a makeover accomplished with youthful flair and humour. The brewery vessels overlook a long main bar with a wooden glider suspended from the ceiling, while at the side a mock big top marks out a large perfor-mance space and dance floor where circus and cabaret performers entertain eager crowds at weekends. The spectacular back garden is equipped with fake carnival booths, and plenty of greenery and shade. Nearly all the cask beer is brewed in-house, in a range of styles from hoppy pales to porters, amply washing down food that includes mediterranean veggie platters, steaks, burgers and choices like prawn and crayfish salad or mushroom risotto. Not quite the greatest beer show on earth, but they're certainly not clowning around.

Brouge (Old Goat) (17)

Comtemporary pub, restaurant
241 Hampton Road, Twickenham TW2 5NG
T (020) 8977 2698   www.brouge.co.uk
🕐 *Su-Th* 12.00-23.00, *Fr-Sa* 12.00-23.30.
   Children very welcome.
Cask beers 2-3 (Twickenham, unusual sometimes local guests), **Other beers** 7 keg, 50 bottles,
Also Cocktails, 30 wines
🍴 Belgian/international menu **££**,
🪑 Beer garden
Beer tastings by arrangement, quiz (Mo), family carvery (Su), food promotions, occasional live music

🚌 Fulwell   🚌 Sixth Cross Road (various Twickenham)
🚶 Link to London Loop

Created in 2003 by beer importer and distributor Pig's Ear, though independent since 2014, the surprisingly beer-savvy Brouge achieves a pleasing fusion between a rural Belgian café and a suburban London boozer. Beer choice has become more internationalised over the years but still retains its Belgian core: Palm supplies most of the keg beers though there's Schneider from Bavaria too. Cask is sourced from nearby Twickenham and guests like Truman's or Williams Brothers; bottles include Lindemans Oude Gueuze, Orval and Rochefort Trappists, Saison Dupont and Van Steenberge Gulden Draak alongside UK

Aeronaut

producers Bristol Beer Factory and Dark Star and some better known Americans. Belgian staples like *waterzooi*, sausages with *stoemp* and several variants of mussels and chips mix on the menu with fajitas and butternut squash risotto. Numerous bargain offers are available throughout the week and staff can advise on beer and food matching.

Express (18)

Traditional pub (Leisure & Catering) ★
56 Kew Bridge Road, Brentford TW8 0EW
T (020) 8560 8484   🐦 expresstavern
www.expresstavern.co.uk
🕐 *Mo-We* 11.00-23.00, *Th-Sa* 11.00-24.00,
Su 12.00-23.00. Children until 20.00.
Cask beers 10 (Haresfoot, Marston's), **Other beers** 8 keg, 44 bottles, **Also** 5 ciders/perries, some specialist spirits
🍴 Enhanced pub grub, lunchtime sandwiches
£-££, 🪑 Beer garden 🐾, ♿
Meet the brewer/tap takeovers, quiz (Mo), seasonal events, function

� Kew Bridge   🏃 Thames Path

Since a September 2014 refurbishment by the people behind the Sussex Arms (p 223), the vintage red neon sign advertising Draught Bass once more illuminates this landmark pub in line of sight of Kew Bridge. Pleasingly, the beer, now brewed by Marston's, is still on sale, though most of the other breweries supported were unheard of when the sign last shone 21 years ago, with Anarchy, Big Smoke, East London, Oakham, Turners and Windsor & Eton often among the guests. The bottle list combines Londoners Beavertown and Brew by Numbers with Oakham, Siren, Früh, Rochefort and North American imports. The menu mixes pies and pub grub with baby back pork ribs, rabbit terrine and veggie risotto. An old bowling green at the back is now a pretty garden lit by coachlights.

Pub trivia *Rebuilt in the 1870s, the pub preserves numerous Victorian and 1930s mock-Tudor features, most notably a beautiful double-sided clock above the old door to the landlord's parlour behind the bar.*

Fox (19)

Traditional pub ★
Green Lane W7 2PJ
T (020) 8567 3912   www.thefoxpub.co.uk
🕐 *Su-Th* 11.00-23.00, *Fr-Sa* 11.00-23.30.
   Children very welcome until 21.30.
Cask beers 5 (Fuller's, Sharp's, Taylor, 2 guests),
Other beers 4 keg, 1 bottle, **Also** A few malts
🍴 Pub grub ££, 🪑 Beer garden
2 annual beer festivals, quiz (Th), monthly open mic, outdoor music in summer, monthly craft market, weekend craft barn

� Hanwell   🚌 Half Acre Road (numerous Ealing Broadway)
🚲 Grand Union Canal towpath 🏃 Capital Ring, Grand Union Canal Walk

At Hanwell, the Grand Union Canal climbs 18 m through a flight of five locks. Operating these is still thirsty work and boaters have long been glad of the proximity of this 1848 pub set just back from the waterway, a charming place preserving a rural quality among allotments at the end of a former drove route. A serial winner of the local CAMRA branch's Pub of the Year, it offers three flawlessly kept regular cask beers – London Pride, Cornish Coaster and Landlord – and draws its guests from small and often local breweries, like Sambrook's, Twickenham and West Berkshire. 'Craft' lagers from Fuller's and Sharp's add interest, and there's bottled BrewDog Punk for dedicated hopheads. Food is honest home cooking, like minted lamb chops, fish pie and Sunday roasts.

Visitor note *A barn in the garden opens to sell arts and crafts at weekends, expanding to a popular outdoor market with food as well as crafts on the first Saturday of the month.*

George and Dragon (20)

Brewpub, traditional pub (Remarkable)
183 High Street W3 9DJ
T (020) 8992 3712   🅵 🐦 dragonflyacton
www.dragonflybrewery.co.uk
🕐 *Su-Th* 12.00-23.00, *Fr-Sa* 12.00-24.00.
   Children in front area only.
Cask beers 5 (Dragonfly), **Other beers** 8 keg,
10 bottles, **Also** 1 cider
🍴 Cooked bar snacks, burgers, rolls, salads ££,
🪑 Side yard, ♿
Tastings, food promotions

🚇 Acton Central   🚇 Ealing Common   🚌 King Street
(various Acton Central, Ealing Common)

In May 2014, Acton's oldest building became its newest brewpub. There's no longer a bar at the front, so you'll need to walk through some attractively panelled spaces to reach an airy hall dominated at one end by the gleaming brewhouse, and order from an island bar supporting looming art nouveau lamp standards in the shape of female nudes. All the casks and some of the keykegs are usually house beers, with guest kegs and bottles from other London breweries and no macro brands. Food such as sage and onion Scotch eggs and veggie Shepherds Pie are as reassuringly English as the pub's name, though other dishes, like burgers and "New Yorker dogs", lean across the Atlantic.

Pub trivia *Former Courage pub the George, to use its original name, began as one of several inns in what was once a bustling market town alongside the road from London to Oxford. The building was likely created by knocking together two early 17th century houses, one behind the other, and became one of the few pubs in London to escape the rebuilding mania of late Victorian times, though the interior was refitted more recently. Look out for the embossed list of landlords stretching back to 1759, in the solemn style usually reserved for Rectors of this Parish.*

LONDON'S BREWING Weird Beard

Weird Beard is one of those brands that shouldn't work but does: it somehow sounds both self-assured and self-deprecating, and raises expectations of something out of the ordinary. And if it hadn't been for the brand, then the brewery might not have happened. Co-founder Gregg Irwin was starting to get frustrated at the lack of progress in getting ideas together, when collaborator Bryan Spooner showed him some initial ideas for the visual identity and suddenly everything seemed to fall into place. "It looked so good I was tempted back," says Gregg.

Gregg and Bryan were both keen homebrewers who met at a BrewDog IPA event at the Euston Tap in 2010: "It was the same night I fell in love with Japanese Sorachi Ace hops," Gregg recalls. Back then he was running his own photography business taking graduation photos: financially rewarding but hardly creatively inspiring. The brewery plans got more realistic when the pair met another would-be professional, Mike Ellenberg, at a London Amateur Brewers meeting. They agreed to pool their resources to create London's first shared brewery. Ellenberg's bought the 10-barrel (16 hl) brewhouse, Weird Beard bought the bottling kit and the forklift, and both owned their own fermenters. Following a further succession of frustrating experiences with site-hunting, they finally found their current premises in Hanwell, West London, and sold their first beer in March 2013.

As it happened things didn't work out for Ellenberg's – a clear demonstration that brewing good beer, which Mike certainly did, isn't enough if the marketing and, yes, the branding isn't there. Meanwhile Gregg and Bryan quickly became recognised as two of the most interesting new brewers in London, with a range of intriguing and well-presented beers that soon started winning awards, hoppy contemporary IPAs among them, but also a luscious stout and an unusual dark and hoppy session ale. "In the first year we brewed 60 times and Mike brewed about six times," recalls Gregg. "So in early 2014 we offered to buy him out. We're still on good terms – he works for us, not as a brewer, but he's really good at fixing stuff." That summer they expanded to a neighbouring unit as warehouse and office space, and bought new fermenters too.

Half the brewery's output is bottle conditioned, the rest is cask and keykeg. A quarter is now exported, as far afield as the USA and Australia, and even to Belgium. "It's massively exceeded expectations," says Gregg. "Our business plan was based on growing to three times the size in five years – we've actually grown five times the size in two." They now have an eight-strong team, though several are part-time. Bryan handles most of the brewing, while Gregg looks after the business side as the 'faithless spreadsheet ninja' celebrated in the name of their lager. "I've now got a nice warm office to work in, and not a freezing cold brewery," he comments with obvious relish. Future plans include more regular public opening, and a canning or bottling line - trial cans from a mobile line are expected in 2015.

And yes, both founders go some way to living up to the brand by sporting lush facial hair – but while both the beards and the beer are impeccably turned out, the latter is more extraordinarily good than weird.

Grosvenor

road. Lush red marble, uncluttered geometric details and fine stained glass that almost shades into the Continental decadence of art nouveau make for a charming example of a building in Arts and Crafts style that may well be the work of celebrated pub architect Thomas Nowell Parr (see also Old Pack Horse p213).

Grosvenor (21)

Gastropub (Food and Fuel)
127 Oaklands Road W7 2DT
T (020) 8840 0007 🅵 🆈 grosvenorw7
www.thegrosvenorhanwell.co.uk
🕐 Mo-Sa 11.00-23.00, Su 11.00-22.30.
Children very welcome until 20.00.
Cask beers 4-6 (Sharp's, Truman's, Twickenham, Weird Beard), **Other beers** 4 keg 6+ bottles, **Also** 1 cider, 40 wines
🍴 Gastro menu **££**, 🪑 Back yard, ♿
Beer festivals, tastings, quiz (Mo), major big screen sport, functions

🚆 Hanwell 🚌 Grosvenor Road (various Ealing Broadway)
🚲 Link to Grand Union Canal towpath 🏃 Link to Capital Ring, Grand Union Canal Walk

A recent threat to turn this pretty corner pub into flats was met with a local outcry, and instead it was snapped up and restored as a beer-friendly gastropub, reopening in April 2014. The original mahogany bar is put to good use dispensing London beers, notably from nearby brewery Weird Beard, for whom the pub is pretty much a de facto brewery tap – look out for bottles too. The food menu changes daily and could include dishes like chicken liver parfait with spiced pear and ale chutney, ricotta gnocchi with tender stem broccoli, or rainbow trout with samphire and pink fir apples potatoes. And if that sounds precious, the atmosphere is relaxed and friendly and the prices good value, with a children's menu also available.

Pub trivia The pub was built in 1904 for Brentford's now defunct Royal Brewery, amid what were then newly developed residential streets just a short hop off the main

Magpie and Crown Top 25 (22)

Specialist, traditional pub
128 High Street, Brentford TW8 8EW
T (020) 8560 4570 🅵 MagpieAndCrown
🕐 Su-We 12.00-24.00, Th-Sa 12.00-01.00.
Cask beers 6 (local and unusual guests),
Other beers 5 keg, 50 bottles, **Also** 2 ciders/perries, malts, local spirits
🍴 Short imaginative pub grub menu **£**,
🪑 Small rear terrace
Occasional live music, DJs, pool

🚆 Brentford 🚲 Grand Union Canal towpath
🏃 Capital Ring, Grand Union Canal Walk, Thames Path

This imposing Brewer's Tudor high street pub has been a real ale stalwart since ending its Watney days in the 1990s, and since current licensee Tam arrived in 2010 a programme of continuous improvement has turned it into

Magpie and Crown

one of the best-stocked and friendliest beer pubs in London, with a well-scrubbed but cosily traditional interior. Local breweries like Brodie's, Cronx, Dark Star, Portobello, Redemption and Windsor & Eton regularly appear, on the cask pumps alongside Hardknott, Marble, Old Dairy or Thornbridge. There are often local 'craft kegs' too, while classic Belgian bottles like Rochefort are now outnumbered by English names including several more from London: Beavertown, By the Horns, Late Knights and Weird Beard among others. Simple home-made hot food might include Cumberland sausage and mash or sundried tomato and basil burger.

Pub trivia *The boat hull that now hangs incongruously from the ceiling was rescued when it washed up on the nearby riverbank.*

Masons Arms (23)
Traditional pub
51 Walpole Road, Teddington TW11 8PJ
T (020) 8977 6521
www.the-masons-arms.co.uk
⏲ *Mo-Th* 12.00-23.00, *Fr-Sa* 11.00-23.30, *Su* 11.00-22.30.
Cask beers 4 (Sambrook's, Tillingbourne, 2 unusual guests), **Other beers** 3 keg, 8 bottles ⓉⓁ Lunchtime rolls, cheeseboard *(Su)* **£**, 🪑 Small beer garden 🐾 ♿
Occasional quiz, live music, seasonal events, darts, rings, skittles, board games

⇌ Teddington 🚌 Teddington Memorial Hospital (281 285 Kingston, R68 Richmond) 🚲 Link to NCN4, Bushy Park paths ⚟ Link to London Loop, Thames Path, Bushy Park paths

Landlady Rae Williams had worked at this small corner pub for many years when she bought the freehold with a business partner in 2010, enabling her passion for real ale to flourish to discerning drinkers' benefit. The handpumps dispense Tillingbourne AONB and Sambrook's Junction, plus many guests rarely seen in London from the likes of Dorset, Empire, Green Jack, Tirril, Triple fff and Upham, usually including a dark choice. Lager is from Dortmunder and Hepworth, while bottled options include Coastal as well as solid English fare like Badger, Shepherd Neame and Wychwood. Fresh flowers offset a substantial collection of beer-related ephemera and

breweriana in a traditionally-styled and spotlessly-kept interior. Then there's the well-tended garden, in which old urinals have been recycled as planters. The modestly handsome building, with a fine tiled frontage now restored to its former glory, was once tied to the local Isleworth brewery.

Visitor note *Both Bushy Park, one of London's lesser known Royal Parks, and Teddington Lock, the upper limit of the tidal Thames, are within relatively easy walking distance.*

Mulberry Tree (24)
Contemporary pub
65 Richmond Road, Twickenham TW1 3AW
T (020) 8892 2427 🅕 🅨 mulberrytree_tw1
www.themulberrytreetwickenham.co.uk
⏲ *Mo-Fr* 16.00-23.00, *Sa-Su* 12.00-23.00.
    Children very welcome until early evening.
Cask beers 6 (unusual sometimes local guests), **Other beers** 6 keg, 24 bottles (UK, Belgium, international), **Also** 2 ciders/perries, wines ⓉⓁ Sharing plates, cooked bar snacks, enhanced pub grub **£-££**, 🪑 Large beer garden, ♿
Mother and child days, coffee days, acoustic music, summer barbecues, functions

⇌ Twickenham 🚌 Lebanon Court (numerous Richmond) ⚟ Link to Thames Path

This pub with a history dating back to the 1850s faced an uncertain future until rescued by the team behind the excellent Magpie and Crown in Brentford (p 220), reopening under its original name in October 2014 with a distinctive mulberry paint job. It's bigger and more contemporarily styled than the Magpie, with a wide main bar well lit from picture windows, a quirky and comfortable snug, and a family room at the back that by the time you read this should look out onto a pleasant garden. The changing cask range features a mix of strengths and styles from breweries like Ascot, East London, Hadrian Border (rarely seen in London), Marble, Thornbridge and Twickenham, with Belgian bottles from Brasserie de la Senne as well as more familiar choices like Chouffe, Rochefort and Tripel Karmeliet. There's also Erdinger wheat beer and Beavertown, Camden Town and Portobello beers in bottle and keg.

221

Noble Green Wines (25)

Shop

153 High Street, Hampton Hill TW12 1NL
T (020) 8979 1113
www.noblegreenwines.co.uk
f noblegreenwines y noblegreenbeer
⏲ *Mo-Fr* 11.00-20.00, *Sa* 10.00-20.00,
Su 11.00-18.00.
Cask beers Up to 6 (Dark Star, Twickenham,
unusual and local guests), **Other beers** 400
bottles, **Also** 5 ciders/perries, wines
Annual beer festival, tastings, meet the brewer

🚃 Fulwell 🚌 Parkside (R20 Fulwell) 🚲 Link to Bushy
Park paths 🏃 Link to London Loop

This shop opposite the Playhouse Theatre
was opened as its name suggests primarily as
a wine merchant but with a small corner of
bottled beers. Thanks to customer demand
the beers have expanded into a major selling
point, elbowing out some of the wines. Cask
ale is sold from gravity in a variety of packages
from two pints to whole firkins: suppliers
include Burning Sky, Dark Star, Hastings,
Redemption, Surrey Hills, Twickenham and
Windsor & Eton. The bottled range includes
locals like Beavertown, Belleville, Brixton, By
the Horns, Savour, Westerham and others
from the rest of the UK. Belgian choices
include limited availability beers from newer
and smaller breweries – Gaverhopke and Hof
ten Dormaal when I looked. Staff are helpful
and knowledgeable, the shop is spacious and
easy to browse, and steady improvements in
the range make this well worth a trip.

Real Ale (26)

Shop

371 Richmond Road, Twickenham TW1 2EF
T (020) 8892 3710   www.realale.com
f wwwrealalecom y RealAle_com
⏲ *Mo* 12.00-20.00, *Th-Sa* 10.00-21.00, *Su* 11.00-20.00.
Cask beers 3 (unusual sometimes local guests),
Other beers 270+ bottles, **Also** Bottled cider/
perry, 40+ fine wines, rare spirits and liqueurs
Tastings, meet the brewer

🚃 Richmond, St Margarets ⊖⊖ Richmond ⛴ Richmond
St Helens 🚌 Creswell Road (numerous Richmond) 🚲 Link to
Richmond Park paths, NCN4 🏃 Link to Capital Ring, Thames Path

Opened in 2005 as a shop window for online
retailer realale.com, this pleasantly appointed
corner shop just across Richmond Bridge was
named Independent Beer Retailer of the Year
in both the 2013 and 2014 Drinks Retailing
Awards. Focusing largely on small British
producers, it's been well placed to move with
changing times: "We used to have a wall full of
bitters," a staff member told me, "but it's a
different market now." Anspach & Hobday,
Brew by Numbers, Kernel, Partizan, Rocky
Head and Weird Beard get a good showing
alongside Arbor, Buxton, Celt, Oakham, Siren
and Wild, some of them poured from cask
into takeaway cartons. The international
range is solid but not especially adventurous
or exclusive: Founder's and North Coast from
the US, Belgium's Dolle Brouwers, European
gypsies Brewers & Union, Norway's Nøgne-Ø
and Japan's Hitachino Nest are typical.

Red Lion

Red Lion (27)

Traditional pub

92 Linkfield Road, Isleworth TW7 6QJ
T (020) 8560 1457   www.red-lion.info
f The Red Lion Isleworth y theredisleworth
⏲ *MoWe&Th* 12.00-23.30, *Tu&Su* 12.00-23.00,
Fr-Sa 12.00-24.00. Children until 19.00.
Cask beers 9 (Greene King, 8 unusual sometimes
local guests), **Other beers** 2 keg, **Also** 5 ciders/
perries, malts, gins, rums
🍴 Pub grub, baguettes £, 🌳 Beer garden, ♿
Beer festivals, jazz (Mo), jam session (We), quiz (Th),
live music (Sa-Su), amateur theatre, darts, pool

🚃 Isleworth 🏃 Link to River Crane Walk, Thames Path

A real hidden gem, the welcoming Red Lion has risen to the challenge of its location on an obscure suburban residential street by being both a great community local and a destination pub with a packed entertainment programme including performances by resident amateur theatre company Hiss and Boo. Casks feature Londoners like Belleville, Redemption and Twickenham alongside established names like Adnams, Butcombe and Timothy Taylor: styles lean towards the traditional but offer variety including milds and dark beers, and customers are invited to chalk up requests. If the old-style public bar with lino, benches and dartboard is too Spartan for you, look for a comfy corner done out as a 1950s living room complete with period TV.

Star and Anchor   (28)

Contemporary pub
94 Uxbridge Road W13 8RA
T (020) 8567 8747   🐦 starandanchor
www.starandanchor.com
🕐 *Mo-Th* 12.00-23.00, *Fr-Sa* 12.00-02.00, *Su*
    12.00-22.30. Children until 21.00.
Cask beers 2 (Brains, guests), *Other beers* 50+
bottles/cans, *Also* A few whiskies, cigars
🍴 Cooked bar snacks, upmarket pub grub **££**,
🪑 Rear beer garden, ♿
Tastings, monthly live music (Sa), quiz (Tu)

⊖ West Ealing

The two cask beers in this welcoming West Ealing pub are restricted to guests from the regular Heineken list, like Bath Ales and Brains. But much more mind-expanding are the fridges, packed with the work of local heroes Weird Beard, fellow Londoners Meantime and Tap East, and a solid international roster taking in Belgian classics and US and Scandinavian producers like Bear Republic, Mikkeller, Rogue and Sly Fox. Décor is solidly contemporary, but there are some cosy spaces and an inviting back yard with sheltered tables. Moderately priced upmarket pub grub might include smoked duck salad with orange and ale dressing, crispy pork belly with creamed savoy cabbage and caramelised apples, house made wild mushroom tortellini, sharing plates and imaginative cooked bar snacks.

Sussex Arms *Top 25*   (29)

Specialist, contemporary pub (Leisure & Catering)
15 Staines Road, Twickenham TW2 5BG
T (020) 8894 7468   🐦 TheSussexArms
www.thesussexarmstwickenham.co.uk
f thesussexarmstwickenham
🕐 *Mo-Sa* 12.00-23.00, *Su* 12.00-22.30.
    Children until 20.00.
Cask beers 10-12 (Twickenham, unusual
sometimes local guests), *Other beers* 6 keg,
30+ bottles, *Also* 6 ciders/perries
🍴 Pies and pub grub **££**, 🪑 Large beer garden,
front terrace ❀
*Acoustic/Irish music (Mo), quiz (We), jazz/blues
(alternate Th), summer hog roast/barbecue (Sa)*

⇌ Strawberry Hill   🚌 First Cross Road (110 Twickenham,
Hounslow, 490 Twickenham, Feltham) 🚶 Link to River Crane Walk

The transformation in July 2011 of this big Brewer's Tudor roadhouse just west of Twickenham Green from a sink boozer ("it wasn't a nice place," a regular once delicately told me) into a flourishing beer exhibition was sure evidence that the beer renaissance had reached the suburbs. A mouthwatering bank of handpumps focuses on small producers, including Twickenham, a few minutes walk away, and names like Arbor, Binghams, Magic Rock, Hardknott, Summer Wine and Tiny Rebel, in a notably wide range of styles and strengths. There's 'craft keg' from similar sources, and you might well find Brew by Numbers and Kernel among the bottles and cans besides imports from Oskar Blues and Stone and classics like Rochefort. The original dark wood and leaded windows have been restored, and there's a delightful little room at the back tiled in green and white. Beyond this, an old market barrow forms the centrepiece of a massive beer garden. The shortish menu highlights pies, local sausages, fishcakes and vegetarian options. Despite its fringe location the pub has rapidly become one of the best-loved beer venues in London, attracting customers in sufficient numbers to match its generous proportions.

223

Twickenham Fine Ales

Twickenham Fine Ales (30)

Taproom, shop

18 Mereway Road, Twickenham TW2 6RG

T (020) 8241 1825 TwickenhamAles

www.twickenham-fine-ales.co.uk

Shop *Mo-Fr* 09.00-18.00, *Sa* 10.00-13.00, *Su* closed *(no draught beer Mo-We)*; bar *Sa* rugby match days. Children welcome.

Cask beers 2-3 (Twickenham), ***Other beers*** 1 keg, 6 bottles (mainly Twickenham)

BBQ on rugby days only **£**,

Benches at front

Ticketed and bespoke brewery tours, occasional open days

Whitton, Twickenham First Cross Road (110 Twickenham, Hounslow, 490 Twickenham, Feltham) River Crane Walk

When the brewery expanded to a new site in the back streets north of Twickenham Green in December 2012, one objective was to become more welcoming to the public than previously possible. Visitor facilities have been gradually added, building on the connection between Twickenham, rugby union and real ale with a proper bar in the brewhouse itself that does a roaring trade when there's a Saturday match on, either at the main Twickenham stadium or Harlequins' Stoop ground. Aside from these, pre-booked brewery tours and other special events, it's off-sales only – in bottles all week, and on draught from Thursday onwards, in takeaway cartons or bigger containers to order.

TRY ALSO

Metro's **Grove** (1 Ealing Green W5 5QX, www.thegrovew5.co.uk), well-sited opposite Ealing Green, is a smartly refurbished place with a locally renowned menu, *al fresco* dining and six changing guest casks often from Sambrook's, Twickenham or Windsor and Eton. Not far away, the award-winning volunteer-run **Grapevine Bar** at Questors Theatre (12 Mattock Lane W5 5BQ, www.questors.org.uk/grapevine) is a long-standing real ale champion, with three guest casks from small and often local brewers, two annual festivals and a few bottles. It's open to CAMRA/EBCU members and guidebook carriers as well as theatregoers and is just opposite Walpole Park, home to the Ealing Beer Festival. The expansive **Ealing Park Tavern** (222 South Ealing Road W5 4RL, www.ealingparktavern.com) was reopened as a well-appointed brewpub by ETM, owners of the Gun (E14, p 118), early in 2015.

In Uxbridge town centre at the end of the District and Piccadilly lines, the unpretentious **Queens Head** (54 Windsor Street UB8 1AB, www.johnbarras.com) offers far more good guest beers than is usual for M&B's John Barras chain thanks to a keen manager. Just outside Harefield village, where the London boundary meets the Colne Valley Park, Brunning & Price's picturesque country house pub the **Old Orchard** (Park Lane UB9 6HJ, www.oldorchard-harefield.co.uk) has six casks including local guests plus over 150 whiskies. With an extensive terrace and garden overlooking the Grand Union Canal, it's well-placed for walkers and cyclists.

At Isleworth near where the Duke of Northumberland's River joins the Thames is famous historic riverside pub the **London Apprentice** (62 Church Street TW7 6BG, www.thelondonapprentice.co.uk), parts of which date from the 14th century. It's now one of the more beer-friendly venues in the Taylor Walker chain with several interesting, local and dark options among the six handpumps.

LONDON'S BREWING   Twickenham Fine Ales

Twickenham Fine Ales is now the fifth-oldest of all the London breweries and the oldest of the cask micros: it celebrated its first decade in grand style in September 2014 with a big party at the brewery and an anniversary IPA. When it opened it was the first brewery in Twickenham since Cole & Burrows closed in 1906. But drinkers outside its south-western heartland could be forgiven for assuming it's emerged out of nowhere in the last couple of years, because until very recently about 80% of production was sold within 5 miles (8 km) of the brewery. All that changed late in 2012 when a major expansion to long-sought new premises finally gave the rest of London the opportunity to enjoy its exceptionally well-made range of beers with contemporary flair but traditional heart.

Former IT professional and Twickenham resident Steve Brown used redundancy money to start the brewery in 2004 and intended from the first to give it that local identity, taking particular advantage of the area's association with rugby union, a sport where real ale, and not industrial lager, is the traditional tipple of choice. Back then, London's microbrewing scene was sparse and few entrants lasted long: his first head brewer, Tom Madeiros, joined from Grand Union, a failed Hillingdon micro. But Twickenham quietly thrived, developing not only admired cask beers but a sideline in interesting collaborations with Belgian and northern French brewers like Alvinne, St Germain and Struise. And when the beer scene in London exploded, it found itself struggling to cope.

"In the years before the move we were going sideways rather than up," recalls Steve, "and we realise now there was all this pent-up demand that we weren't able to meet. Now it's really taken off, and we've just gone through the 5,000 hl threshold for the lowest beer duty rate." Their kit has increased in size from 10 barrels (16 hl) to 25 (41 hl), with a major hike in fermentation capacity too.

Nine people now work for the brewery, with a brewing team headed by ex-WJ King brewer Stuart Medcalf and assistant brewer Dave Hall, formerly at Triple fff. The beer is in Metropolitan, Wetherspoon and many Enterprise pubs and the bottles, only available since 2013, are in Waitrose, Majestic and Oddbins. And Grandstand Bitter is due to be in Young's pubs during the Six Nations and Rugby World Cup tournaments in 2015.

The rugby connection pays off in other ways too: the bar at the brewery is open before every match at the main Twickenham stadium, home of the England team, or at local team Harlequins' Stoop ground nearby, and a visit has become a part of the match day ritual for many fans. They'll be open for longer hours during the tournaments, with a big screen in action, and aim to make the extended opening a permanent feature. And they're actively looking for a pub, although so much depends on finding the right site – in Twickenham, of course.

Further downstream, another classic and popular riverside pub, the **White Swan** (Riverside TW13DN, www.whiteswantwickenham.co.uk) at Twickenham, offers five often unusual guest beers and a few bottles in a lovely old split-level building. From here you can walk past Marble Hill Park to the pretty **Aleksander** (277 Richmond Road TW12NP, www.thealeksander.co.uk) to enjoy local guest casks and some interesting keykegs and bottles. The Mulberry Tree (p221) is between here and Twickenham town centre.

Twickenham is particularly rich in good pubs. In the town centre, the **Fox** (39 Church Street TW13NR, www.thefoxpubtwickenham.co.uk) occupies a well-restored mid-18th century building with a lovely old bar and an impressive modern atrium. Thanks to a tie, choice is more restricted than at sister pub the Sussex Arms (p223), but there's Twickenham beers and a few other interesting casks. Even the local Wetherspoon, the **William Webb Ellis** (24 London Road TW13BR, www.jdwetherspoon.co.uk), is a cut above: a well-styled remodelling of a former post office, it offers up to 10 cask beers.

Further south, the eye-catchingly crimson **Roebuck** (72 Hampton Road, Hampton Hill, Hampton TW121JN, www.roebuck-hamptonhill.co.uk) at Hampton Hill, not far from Noble Green Wines (p222), has guest casks from London and southeast brewers and the most bewildering collection of eccentric junk of any London pub: vending machines, fishing rods, a signed Henry Cooper boxing glove and a full-size wickerwork motorbike.

HEATHROW AIRPORT

A few years ago, no connoisseur would have expected to find good beer at a major international airport. So when JD Wetherspoon, known as a real ale champion on the high street, first dipped its toe into the airport trade in the 1990s, it was with low expectations: outlets were equipped with only a token handpump of Boddington's bitter. Then someone experimented with adding a few more cask lines, at which point everything, so to speak, took off. Since then other operators have arrived at the table, and although no British airport yet boasts a beer outlet of the seriousness to match, say, Stone's bars at San Diego International, it's surely only a matter of time. Meanwhile, beer loving air travellers who know where to look no longer have to resign themselves to industrial lager or a cup of tea.

This is particularly true at the vast London Heathrow Airport, or LHR as it's known to baggage handlers everywhere, just inside the far west edge of the capital. Even if it doesn't get to build its longed-for third runway (the decision may have been made by the time you read this), Heathrow is likely to remain the biggest airport in Britain. It's also currently the busiest airport in the world for transfer passengers and the fourth busiest of all airports, with 73 million passengers a year passing through its five terminals.

Heathrow is changing, in response not only to growing passenger numbers but also to rising expectations of the airport experience, including its catering outlets. Travellers are increasingly unprepared to put up with the same tired big brands flogging homogenised products at inflated prices to a captive audience. The management actively encourages operators with a more distinctive offer, from luxury brands like Bulgari and Gucci to innovative outlets for local and organic food. Good beer, particularly real ale, fits in well with this trend: it's an iconically British quality product that's equally valued by overseas visitors and British travellers.

Much of the retail action is focused on the newer terminals: giant Terminal 5, the British Airways hub, opened in 2008, and the completely rebuilt and uncannily similar-looking Terminal 2, the Queen's Terminal. The latter opened in June 2014 with the poshest Wetherspoon you've likely ever seen on one side of security, and an impressive airport debut from Fuller's on the other. All the airport bars sell food, and those on 'airside', after security checks, are obliged to offer 15-minute menus and 'grab-and-go' options like prepacked sandwiches, even the pub-type venues. The hours shown below are indicative: all are likely to stay open later in the event of major delays.

The bars on 'landside' tend to be quieter, mainly used by greeters, early arrivals and others in the know, including airport and airline staff, who aren't allowed to drink alcohol once airside. And with around 70,000 staff there's a signifi- cant market even without all the passengers and visitors. The top recommendation on this side is undoubtedly the aforementioned Wetherspoon, the **Flying Chariot**, which takes up nearly one whole side of the departures hall at T2, near check-in zone D.

This big, bright, open and stylish place is on two levels — three if you count the crow's nest rising from the upper floor, a popular spot for filming interviews thanks to its fine view of the tarmac. A long bar stocks London Pride, Doom Bar, a changing Adnams brand and two guests often from nearby brewers like Twickenham or Windsor & Eton, whose brewery most passengers will fly over within seconds of taking off. The bar also has the full range of Wetherspoon's 'craft' and world beers, including Devils Backbone, Erdinger, Goose Island, Meantime and Sixpoint. A special airport menu extends beyond the usual fare to dishes like peri peri chicken, Thai green curry and salmon fillets.

Also worth knowing about on landside are two bars run as part of Young's Geronimo chain. The **Three Bells**, a staff favourite tucked away upstairs at Terminal 3 above the Virgin check-in desks, is an enthusiastic supporter of the chain's beer festivals, installing a couple of extra casks on stillage behind the bar and offering three-thirds tasting paddles. The beers tend to be standard Wells & Young's products, with Meantime London Pale on keg and a few interesting bottles that include Special London. They've worked hard to create a cosy,

HEATHROW AIRPORT

comfortable space here with bookshelves, sofas and booths. A similar though slightly more basic offer is on hand at the **5 Tuns** at T5 (Heathrow Airport TW6 2GA, **www.geronimo-inns. co.uk/london-the-five-tuns**), by checkin zone G and Security South, sometimes including a Sambrook's beer.

Beyond security it's a busier and altogether glitzier world, as attested by Fuller's first airport bar, **London's Pride**

at T2, on the main departures concourse by gates A1 and A2. Much thought and investment has been put into this

handsome, white-tiled place: it has displays on the history of beer, a souvenir shop selling takeaways and merchandise, laptop-friendly charging points throughout and a library zone where you can both read and buy books. Well-kept Fuller's beers are served from cask and keg, including HSB and seasonals like Wild River, with bottled choices like 1845 and Bengal Lancer joined by beers from Meantime and Camden Town. As you'd expect, food is classic English pub grub fare — they average 130 plates of fish and chips a day, but there's also steak and ESB pie, slow cooked neck of lamb, veggie tagliatelle and children's menu. This is arguably the first and so far only bar at the airport you'd make an effort to visit if it was on the high street.

Wetherspoon's **Crown Rivers** at T5, downstairs

from security by domestic gate A7, has long struggled with an open site bisected by a busy public walkway, but is nonetheless hugely popular, expanding its space twice since opening and undergoing a major refurbishment early in 2015 to create a smarter bar of reclaimed wood on one side and an 'indoor garden' with five trees and a pergola on the other. An 18-gallon (82 l) cask of London Pride barely lasts a day here; the other regulars are Broadside, Exmoor Gold and Doom Bar, with at least six guests on every week, often from Windsor & Eton. The latter's Republika is a welcome feature on keg, and other Wetherspoon 'craft' lines are present and correct. Limited kitchen space necessitates a limited menu but they still offer plenty of pub classics, sandwiches and deli boards.

HEATHROW AIRPORT

Crown Rivers (31)

Contemporary pub (Wetherspoon)
Terminal 5 Airside, Heathrow Airport TW6 1EW
T (020) 8283 6208   🐦crownriverslhr
www.jdwetherspoon.co.uk
🕐 *Daily* 04.30-23.30. Children welcome.
Cask beers 5 (Adnams, Exmoor, Fuller's,
Sharp's, 1 often local guest), ***Other beers*** 5 keg,
10 bottles, ***Also*** A few gins and malts
🍴 Breakfasts, sandwiches, pub grub **£-££**, ♿
Beer festivals

🚉 🚇 Heathrow Terminal 5   🚲 Link to NCN6

London's Pride (33)

Contemporary pub (Fuller's)
Terminal 2 Airside, Heathrow Airport TW6 1EW
T (020) 3728 7978   www.londonspride.com
🕐 *Daily* 05.30-22.00. Children very welcome.
Cask beers 5 (Fuller's), ***Other beers*** 2 keg,
16 bottles (Fuller's, London), ***Also*** Wines,
specialist spirits
🍴 Breakfasts, sandwiches, enhanced pub
grub **££-£££**, ♿
Meetings, functions

🚉 🚇 Heathrow Terminals 1, 2, 3

Flying Chariot (32)

Bar (Wetherspoon)
Terminal 2 Landside, Heathrow Airport TW6 1EW
T (020) 8976 7540
www.jdwetherspoon.co.uk
🕐 *Daily* 05.00-23.00. Children welcome.
Cask beers 5-6 (Fuller's, Sharp's, Wells & Young's,
Windsor & Eton, guests), ***Other beers*** 5 keg,
9+ bottles/cans, ***Also*** A few gins and malts
🍴 Breakfasts, sandwiches, pub grub **£-££**, ♿
Beer festivals

🚉 🚇 Heathrow Terminals 1, 2, 3

Three Bells (34)

Contemporary pub (Geronimo)
Terminal 3 Landside, Heathrow Airport TW6 1AD
T (020) 8897 6755 www.geronimo-inns.co.uk/
london-the-three-bells
📘 TheThreeBellsPub   🐦 TheThreeBells
🕐 *Daily* 06.00-22.00. Children welcome.
Cask beers 3-5 (Sharp's, Wells & Young's,
occasional guests), ***Other beers*** 1 keg, 9 bottles
(mainly Meantime, Wells & Young's), ***Also*** Cocktails
🍴 Breakfasts, sandwiches, gastroish pub grub
£-££, ♿
Beer festivals, food promotions, seasonal events

🚉 🚇 Heathrow Terminals 1, 2, 3

OTHER PLACES
TO DRINK

Chains, pubcos & brewery pubs

Most London pubs and bars are ultimately owned by big groups, often either breweries or successors to breweries (see A short history of the London pub, p23). These divide broadly into two groups. **Managed houses** are essentially branches of the owning company, and their staff are on the company payroll. **Leaseholds** (sometimes called 'tenancies') are leased to independent businesses, in most cases at a lower-than-market rent in return for a contractual obligation to buy beer and sometimes other drinks from the owning company.

Managed houses are more likely to have obvious similarities to each other, and sometimes a strong common brand, though a few are deliberately unbranded and left to develop their own identity within a general framework. Leaseholds are much more varied. Brewery-owned ones will likely be brewery-branded and mainly feature the brewery's beer, perhaps with an occasional guest beer or two sourced through the brewery. Pubco ones will likely stock a range sourced by the pubco from several different breweries, which usually means better-known brands from bigger independents that can meet expectations on price and quantity.

Increasingly, though, pubco leaseholders are able to stock beers from smaller and more local breweries through the direct delivery scheme facilitated by the small brewers' trade organisation SIBA. Some licensees in managed chains have special dispensation to do this too and there are numerous examples in this book: both Fuller's and Greene King now operate pubs that mainly sell beer from other brewers. Some licensees have been able to negotiate lease-holds that are wholly or partly free of tie, paying a higher rent for the privilege of buying beer wherever they want, and such arrangements are likely to increase thanks to new legislation.

A minority of pubs, though a notably high proportion of those in this book, are **free houses** where the owners have no link to brewing. These may be purpose-built pubs that never belonged to breweries, or that have been abandoned by a brewery or pubco and sold on the open market, or buildings that weren't originally pubs. Some of them are genuinely independent while others belong to chains. The situation is further complicated by certain companies that manage small chains of pubs, some of them tied and some of them not – Antic is a good example.

Westow House

Below I list the main pubcos, brewery-owned pub groups and managed chains in London of interest to beer enthusiasts. Many of these offer something worth drinking in all or most of their outlets: big chains like Nicholson's and Wetherspoon, for example, are usually reliable standbys for a good guest cask or two in areas where there's little else. Use the web addresses shown to find out more; the numbers quoted are for Greater London.

Well and Bucket

Antic
www.anticlondon.com (37 outlets)

Founded by Anthony Thomas with a single pub, the East Dulwich Tavern, in 2000, Antic has become a major and very welcome presence on the scene, particularly in South London, where it's turned numerous neglected pubs and abandoned public buildings into valued community assets. It terms itself a 'pub collective' and there is no branding, but the venues are usually easily recognisable: large, decorated in shabby-chic style with eccentric collections of junk, a youthful but inclusive ambience, short but imaginative menus and at least a few interesting local cask beers and tasty bottles. A few are tied and more limited in range. A financial blip in a part of the business in 2013 resulted in several pubs being sold but this now seems to be behind them.

See Catford Constitutional Club (p168), Clapton Hart (p107), Hagen and Hyde (p193), Red Lion (p127), Royal Albert (p174), Westow House (p165).

Barworks
www.barworks.com (14 outlets)

Beginning with a spirits-led cocktail bar in the 1990s, Barworks has matured gracefully to yield some of London's best new beer-friendly bars, adept at promoting quality beer to new audiences, with links to Camden Town Brewery. Venues are varied and unbranded, though several boast a slightly unsettling fondness for surreal art. See also London Drinkers: Andreas Akerlund (p45).

See Black Heart (p133), Earl of Essex (p43), Electricity Showrooms (p87), Exmouth Arms (p75), Harrild and Sons (p70), Kings Arms (p119), Slaughtered Lamb (p76), Three Johns (p44), Well and Bucket (p88).

Belgo
www.belgo-restaurants.co.uk (4 outlets)

Founded by Québecois Denis Blais and Belgian André Plisnier in Camden in 1992, with what was then the far-sighted intention of introducing Londoners to Belgian beer and food, this small chain hasn't changed much since, though the rest of the beer world has moved on around it. It's cheerful and fun, the food is tasty, and there are still some old school classic beers on a list that errs towards multinational subsidiaries and bigger family brewers: don't expect to find cutting-edge newcomers. he original branch, Belgo Noord (p133), is representative of the others.

BrewDog
www.brewdog.com/bars (5 outlets)

The provocative and successful Scottish brewer now boasts a globetrotting chain including four bars and one bottle shop in London, all of them of sufficient interest to merit individual listings. Expect evangelical and knowledgeable staff, funky modern design, extensive keykegs from BrewDog, Mikkeller, the more cutting edge London brewers and others from around the world – and, perversely, no cask.

See BottleDog Kings Cross (p73) and BrewDogs Camden (p134), Clapham Junction (p183), Shepherds Bush (p209) and Shoreditch (p85).

BrewDog Shepherds Bush

231

Byron

www.byronhamburgers.com (36 outlets)

Not a pub group but a new generation gourmet burger chain with a notable and regularly changing bottled beer list. Byron Hoxton (p 86) is typical.

Camden Bars

www.camdenbars.com (10 outlets)

Built around places like the Lock Tavern in Camden (listed as a Try also p 138) and several other music-heavy pubs in North London, this group has since diversified into gastropubs and more community-focused boozers, picking up some venues from Antic. A few decent local and other cask beers can usually be relied upon.

See Beehive (p 148), Chequers (p 125).

Castle

www.mbplc.com/ourbrands/castle (100+ outlets)

Mitchells & Butlers' 'unbranded' chain includes numerous excellent pubs, usually with a more contemporary and individual ambience than their Nicholson's pubs, but the beer range seems to have got less interesting if anything over the past few years despite consumer trends. They usually have a few casks on offer and some imported quality kegs too, but lean too far towards bigger brewers and more mainstream brands, with little local identity. The legendary White Horse (p 214) is a notable exception.

Craft Beer Co

www.thecraftbeerco.com (6 outlets)

London's most important and cosmopolitan specialist chain, with an impressive range in all formats, including cask, though as so many London pubs now stock London brewers, they've recently tended to lean towards suppliers from outside the capital. The Cask has separate but related ownership arrangements but is the blueprint for the rest. See also London drinkers: Martin Hayes (p 77).

See Cask Pub and Kitchen (p 97), and Craft Beer Cos Brixton (p 184), Clapham (p 184), Clerkenwell (p 74), Covent Garden (p 78), Islington (p 43).

Draft House Westbridge

Draft House

www.drafthouse.co.uk (5 outlets)

Charlie McVeigh is a genuine pioneer of the current London beer renaissance, setting out to place a more contemporary and populist spin on quality world beer back in 2007 with the first Draft House in Battersea. The transatlantic influence is self-evident in the Webster's spelling, but these cheerful and smartly-run places have done a great job introducing a wide range of beer to a more diverse audience, including British beer with promotions like 'cask of the day', alongside straightforward but quality comfort food with much emphasis on meat. At one point they looked a little less on-the-ball than some more recent arrivals, but they've recovered impressively.

See Draft Houses Charlotte (p 93), Northcote (p 185), Seething (p 69), Tower Bridge (p 53), Westbridge (p 186).

Enterprise

www.enterpriseinns.com

Founded by Ted Tuppen in 1991, this has grown into Britain's biggest pubco, with 5,500 pubs UK-wide, almost all tied leaseholds, acquired by a variety of routes from the old Bass, Courage, Watney and Whitbread estates. Its founder, one of the most controversial figures in the industry, moved on in 2014. One of the main targets of criticism of the pubco model, it's been plagued by financial problems. Several of the pubs listed here are Enterprise lease-holds making full use of the direct delivery schemes that now give leaseholders access to a wider range of breweries, but as these are all otherwise independent businesses, each with its own approach, I haven't indexed them here.

Faucet Inn
www.faucetinn.com (17 outlets)

Try to ignore the naff pun in the name: most pubs in this smallish group founded by Steve Cox in 2001 are traditionally-styled, comfortable, characterful places with a few good cask ales, often including some from Westerham brewery. None has quite qualified for a full entry, but a couple are listed under Try also.

Fuller's
www.fullers.co.uk/pubs (126 outlets)

London's last surviving independent remains a vertically integrated regional brewery with an extensive pub estate including both managed houses and leaseholds. The balance is shifting more towards the former, now often big, smart places with an extensive food offer. You'll find the brewery's classic cask beers in practically all the pubs (with an active quality assurance

programme that includes a Cellarman of the Year award) and usually several bottled beers too. Other people's beers are increasingly served, particularly if they're from London, or from overseas brewers that Fuller's imports, including Chimay. For more about the brewery see p 212.

See Fuller's Brewery Shop (p 211), Harp (p 80, mainly guest beers),

London's Pride (p 228), Mad Bishop and Bear (p 98), Old Pack Horse (p 213), Olde Mitre (p 82), Parcel Yard (p 48), Red Lion (p 199), Star Tavern (p 100), Swift (p 194), Tap on the Line (p 200), Union Tavern (p 208, mainly guest beers).

Geronimo
See Young's

Greene King
www.findaproperpub.co.uk (91 outlets)

Based in Bury St Edmunds, Suffolk, and with a history dating back at least to 1799, this brewery was once a real ale icon. It emerged from the takeover wars of the 1990s a claimant to the title of Britain's biggest non-multinational brewery. It has earned the ire of beer campaigners for ruthlessly buying up and closing other independents, swelling its pub estate and cherry picking top brands that are then approximated in Bury. Unlike its predecessor national breweries, it's still committed to cask ale: its bestseller, IPA, has an historical right to the name but is now essentially a light and inoffensive bitter. In contrast, it's the only old-established British brewer to have retained the practice of 'staling' strong ale in big wooden vats and blending this with a 'running' beer to produce niche product Suffolk Strong.

Interestingly, the company itself seems to have realised its image and core products now have little appeal to certain consumers, and some of its outlets, including many in the Metropolitan chain (see below), stock almost none of its products. It owns both managed and leasehold pubs, and rents some of the latter free of tie, including to the Craft Beer Co (above). In 2014 GK also bought the Spirit group, once the managed division of Punch, in the process acquiring the Taylor Walker chain (below).

See George (p 53) and Metropolitan and Taylor Walker below.

Hall & Woodhouse
www.hall-woodhouse.co.uk/visit-our-pubs (7 outlets)

Founded in 1777 and once known for very traditional cask ale, this brewery in Blandford Forum, Dorset, is best known for its Badger trademark, and has oscillated between foregrounding this and its official name. It owns a

233

handful of London pubs, mainly traditionally styled and serving its straight-ahead cask beers and pasteurised bottles, including flavoured beers that are also popular in the supermarket trade.

See St Stephens Tavern (p 99).

Laine's
www.laines.london (8 outlets)

This Brighton-based company is expanding its London activities with a small estate of mainly big and characterful pubs, three of them with on-site breweries: see brewery entries p 294. The non-brewing pubs tend to stock at least a few cask and keykeg beers from the brewpubs, with a few interesting bottles as well. Its operations in the capital were previously branded Drink In London.

See Aeronaut (p 217), Four Thieves (p 187), Peoples Park Tavern (p 116).

Aeronaut

Marston's
www.marstonstaverns.co.uk (10 outlets)

Vying with Greene King for the title of Britain's biggest non-multinational brewer is this Burton upon Trent-based brewing group which, unlike its Suffolk-based rival, has kept many of its predecessor breweries as separate sites. As well as Marston's, well-known for Pedigree, the only pale ale still brewed using the historic Burton Union fermentation system, it encompasses Banks's, Brakspear, Jennings, Ringwood and Wychwood and still brews former London speciality Mann's Brown. Most of its pubs are outside London and in recent years it has reduced its holdings in the capital still further; none of those that remain have found their way into this book.

McMullen
www.mcmullens.co.uk/our-locals (21 outlets)

Established in Hertford in 1827, 'Macs', as it's known locally, is now the oldest brewery in Hertfordshire, though it downsized from an historic Victorian tower brewery to a new micro setup in 2006 to qualify for reduced beer duty. It brews several traditional cask beers, including a notable light mild, AK. Its London pubs are largely in the north and northeast, but it also has a couple in the West End, one of them in our Try alsos.

See Cricketers (p 125).

Metropolitan
www.metropolitanpubcompany.com
(40+ outlets)

This Greene King-owned chain has its roots in two small London-based groups, both of which specialised in modern, upmarket pubs with a strong food offer, often restored Victorian landmarks. The Capital Pub Company was launched by serial pub entrepreneur David Bruce in 2001, while Nick Pring and Malcolm Heap opened the first venue in the Realpubs chain the next year. GK bought both chains in 2011, eventually amalgamating them to form Metropolitan and converting some of its existing pubs to the format too. You'll have to look hard to spot signs of the Suffolk brewery's involvement and are unlikely to find its beers pushed heavily on the bar, though some of its 'craft' brands and beers from Scottish subsidiary Belhaven regularly pop up. Otherwise the beer is from a variety of brewers, including local suppliers, and some branches have a particularly impressive range. One even hosts Head in a Hat brewery (p 290).

See Florence (p 159), Hare and Billet (p 170), Williams Ale and Cider House (p 71).

Mitchells & Butlers
www.mbplc.com

Britain's biggest managed pub company is another Bass successor: it revives the name of a Birmingham brewery that merged with Bass in 1961 and was closed in 2002 when the remains of this world-famous Burton giant were carved up between the companies that are now AB InBev and MillerCoors. Its pubs are segmented into brands, including household names like All Bar One and O'Neill's. The ones of most interest to readers of this book are Castle and Nicholson's, which have separate entries, but Ember Inns – usually big, food-centred places – are sometimes worth a look too.

Nicholson's
www.nicholsonspubs.co.uk (45 outlets)

The most cask-friendly of the Mitchells & Butlers brands, appearing on traditionally-styled town centre pubs, often in heritage buildings. They usually have at least six casks on, including (in London branches) a Truman's beer and an own-brand pale ale commissioned from St Austell in Cornwall, and rotating guests from a seasonally-refreshed list, though some of the more enthusiastic branches source beyond this too. Each pub has a staff member other than the manager trained as a 'cask master' and there are regular cross-chain festivals.

See Blackfriar (p 68), De Hems (p 92), Falcon (p 187), Magpie (p 70), Swan (p 213).

Punch
www.punchtaverns.com

Britain's other major leasehold pub owner besides Enterprise, and almost equally controversial. It originated in 1997 with large tranches of former Bass and Allied Breweries pubs, both managed and leasehold, though the managed pubs were finally separated off into the Spirit group (see Greene King) in 2011. A few Punch leaseholders are included here: it offers its licensees a seasonally changing range of guest beers under the Finest Cask label (www.finestcask.co.uk) and also participates in the SIBA direct delivery scheme. It's recently dipped its toe into the managed house business again.

Remarkable Restaurants
www.remarkablerestaurants.co.uk
(14 outlets)

Despite its name, this small group run by Robert Thomas has some outstanding restored heritage pubs, including the celebrated Salisbury in Haringey, one of our Try alsos (p 154). It imports Litovel Czech lager into the UK, kegging it at Fuller's, whose beers the pubs

Magpie

often stock too, usually alongside good guests. It added a brewpub in 2014, with beers under the Dragonfly brand sold across the chain (see brewery listings p 286).

See George and Dragon (p 218), Shaftesbury Tavern (p 152).

Samuel Smith
(38 outlets)

Founded in 1758 in Tadcaster, this is the oldest brewery in Yorkshire, and rather like its home county is traditional, pragmatic and eccentric in equal measure. It owns a surprisingly large number of London pubs, including several meticulously cared-for heritage gems, known for their traditional atmosphere, lack of piped music and cheap prices. Everything on sale in them is own-brand, not just the single cask ale, Old Brewery Bitter, and the rather better specialist bottles, but the wines, spirits and soft drinks too. Needless to say, their notoriously publicity-shy owner doesn't bother with a website to tell you where they are, but such is their cult following that you can find numerous unofficial lists via Google.

See Princess Louise (p 83).

Shepherd Neame
www.shepherdneame.co.uk/pubs (44 outlets)

This family brewer on the edge of historic hop country in Faversham, Kent, is a strong claimant for the title of Britain's oldest brewery, with a documented history going back to 1698 and evidence of brewing on the site back to the 12th century. It began buying London pubs in the 1980s and now has quite an extensive estate of both managed pubs and leaseholds. All sell its traditional cask ales; the better ones sell bottled beers including an interesting new line in historic recreations.

See Eleanor Arms (p 115).

Crosse Keys

Star (Heineken)
www.starpubs.co.uk

Heineken is the only successor to Britain's former Big Six vertically-integrated brewers that still operates pubs: the 1,300-strong Star Pubs group is what remains of the former Scottish & Newcastle leased estate. If they sell cask, it's likely to be from Edinburgh subsidiary Caledonian, Theakston or another better-known independent. Occasionally you might spot an interesting import from the extremes of the Dutch giant's global business.

Taylor Walker
www.taylor-walker.co.uk

Bearing the name of a defunct East London brewery (see Yeast Enders p 123) to which it has only the most tenuous of connections, this branded chain of managed pubs is pitched in very much the same way as Nicholson's, concentrating on traditional décor, town centre and other prominent sites including several heritage pubs, and with cask beer an essential part of the package. At first the beer range played it safe but has notably improved recently, including commissioned beers from breweries like Westerham and the addition of interesting bottles, and some managers in particular have pushed the envelope. It was acquired in 2014 by Greene King as part of the Spirit package, so its future is now uncertain.

See Museum Tavern (p 48), Roebuck (p 199), Tabard (p 214).

J D Wetherspoon
www.jdwetherspoon.co.uk (150 outlets)

The only national pub group with no roots in the old brewery tied-house system, this was founded in 1979 with a single North London pub by outspoken entrepreneur Tim Martin, who named it after one of his former school teachers. The company now owns 900 outlets, all of them managed and free of tie, often in buildings not previously used as pubs. There's very much a set formula, with low prices, standard menus of pre-cooked food and identikit furniture, though the interior decorations have been getting more adventurous and individual recently. Cask ale is a major feature, with guests often sourced from small and local breweries, and the range of draught and bottled 'craft beer' expanded in 2014. Two beer festivals a year include such praiseworthy initiatives as inviting top brewers from abroad to recreate their beers in British breweries.

Wetherspoon is now a household name that's readily ridiculed, and while it's true that you're unlikely to visit the pubs for their character and atmosphere, much of the sneering is simple snobbery. A more serious criticism is that the aggressive pricing policy on specialist beer is challenging to brewers and undersells an artisanal product that should really merit a cost equivalent to its quality. On the plus side, besides stocking good beer the venues are devoid of piped

Hand in Hand

music, accessible, inclusive, family friendly, and sell food of consistently edible, though certainly not gourmet, quality from breakfast until late at night.

See Crosse Keys (p69), Crown Rivers (p228), Flying Chariot (p228), Fox on the Hill (p160), Knights Templar (p81), New Cross Turnpike (p177).

Young's

www.youngs.co.uk (150 outlets)

The former Wandsworth independent i s now just a pub company (see the Wandle Ram p196). Like most pub-owning successors of old breweries, it has both managed and leasehold pubs, the latter now rebranded as the Ram Pub Company (**www.rampubcompany.co.uk**). And like its arch-rival Fuller's, it's concentrated on large and lucrative managed pubs on good sites, known for their food as well as their drink. The pubs still sell Young's beer, now brewed under a rolling contract by Charles Wells in Bedford, including cask classics and bottled specialities, but you'll often find minority representation from others too, likely London brewers local to the pub (ELB in East London or Sambrook's in Southwest London, for example). In 2010 it bought another small London chain, Geronimo Inns, broadly similar in profile to Greene King's Metropolitan chain (above): these pubs retain their own branding though now also tend to stick mainly with Wells & Young's beers.

See Buckingham Arms (p96), Hand in Hand (p197), Lamb (p47), Old Sergeant (p194), Richard I (Tollys) (p173), Three Bells (p228).

Supermarkets & off-licences

Supermarkets did a sterling job in both making wine more accessible and raising our appreciation of it, but so far the beer revolution seems to have passed them by. You'll find one or two of the better-known favourites at keen prices, and some old school retro classics unlikely to get a look-in at more cutting-edge emporia, but otherwise you're better off seeking out one of the growing number of independent specialists, such as those featured in the main Places to Drink listings.

Indeed, in some ways things have gone backwards: both troubled giant Tesco (**www. tesco.com**) and its chief rival Sainsbury's (**www.sainsburys. co.uk**) have in the past sponsored innovative beer competitions and promotions, and the latter encouraged the fledgling Meantime brewery, but these initiatives have dwindled in favour of heavily discounted macro lager, indistinguishable pasteurised 'speciality ales' from bigger independents and obvious world beer brands from multinationals. 'Craft' beer has registered a little, though typically in the form of BrewDog's better known beers and new beers in trendy styles from old brewers. Asda (**www.asda.com**) and Morrisons (**www.morrisons.com**) aren't significantly different, though usually a bit cheaper. The best is undoubtedly more upmarket Waitrose (**www.waitrose.com**), with lots of Fuller's, Meantime, Sambrook's, Thornbridge and Twickenham and several bottle-conditioned imports, but they still try harder in many other categories and they don't seem to have noticed recent developments.

Austin, Texas-based aspirational grocery chain Whole Foods Market (**www. wholefoodsmarket.com**) has a presence in London, and while its stores haven't quite embraced speciality beer to the same extent as back home, it does much better than the home-grown chains, with a good local range as well as imports. The two biggest branches are listed as Try alsos, but smaller local stores are worth a glance too.

Branded off-licence chains are now a rare site on the British high street, but 1980s wine-glugging favourite Oddbins (**www.oddbins.com**) has enjoyed a welcome resurgence, with fine local beer part of the formula. A specialist beer shop in Blackheath opened too late for a full entry in the listings, but the London Bridge store is featured as a good example of a local branch (p58).

Mail order

Several of the specialist bottle shops listed as main entries offer mail order services: check their websites for details. Some breweries also sell direct by mail order, as indicated in the breweries listings (p 275). The following suppliers work by internet shopping and mail order only, with no walk-in sites, and typically stock a good range of London beers.

Ales by mail
www.alesbymail.co.uk

A keen promoter of London breweries that for several years has not only been offering a wide range of 'pick and mix' beers but some well-chosen curated cases. Aims to stock beer from every bottling London brewer by the end of 2015. Good beers from the rest of the UK and elsewhere too.

The Beer Seller
www.thebeerseller.com

Stocks almost exclusively London breweries, offering either pick-and-mix services or a variety of preselected cases based on both brewery and style. You can take out subscriptions to cases.

beermerchants
www.beermerchants.com

The public face of importers and distributors Cave Direct, this majors on Belgian, German and US beers, but includes numerous London brewers among its British selection, including themed mixed cases – not surprisingly as manager Phil Lowry is a founder of the London Brewers' Alliance.

DeskBeers
www.deskbeers.com

Specialises in delivering bottled beer selections to workplaces, with various quantity and frequency options, and with numerous London brewers on the list. It's been a hard week and you and your colleagues deserve it!

Eebria
www.eebria.com

A 'marketplace' providing online sales services to several of the key London breweries, as well as other UK brewers, and cider, gin and wine producers. Orders are despatched directly from the producer so stock is likely to be fresher, though delivery charges will be higher if you buy small quantities from several brewers. Access the service via participating breweries' sites or go to the main site to see all the producers.

Honest Brew
www.honestbrew.co.uk

Most proud of their monthly 'honesty boxes' containing selections hand-picked in accordance with the general preferences you specify. More conventional pick-and-mix and mixed case services are offered, featuring a range of London and other UK breweries. They also occasionally 'cuckoo' brew (p 292).

Outside the UK. Ales by Mail and Honest Brew will do their best to ship beer anywhere, and beermerchants regularly ships to mainland Europe. The Bottle Shop (p 66) has a Belgian-based partner (**www.bottle-shop.eu**) selling London and some other UK beers in Belgium, the Netherlands and some other countries.

Festivals & events

London now boasts a huge range of beer-related events, from giant festivals like the annual Great British Beer Festival (GBBF) to 'meet the brewer' nights in pubs, plus an increasing number of temporary pop-ups, markets and similar activities. Keeping track of all these is a challenge: the best source I've found, other than judicious use of Twitter, is the events diary at www.aletalk.co.uk. It's searchable by region and London events are included with others in Southeast England.

Beer festivals fall into two types: freestanding events in big venues not normally associated with selling specialist beer, and events in pubs and bars enhancing their regular range. The biggest organiser of the former kind is CAMRA: as well as the national GBBF, some London branches run their own festivals, and all are organised and staffed by volunteers. You pay an admission charge, reduced or sometimes free for CAMRA and EBCU members, and then pay for the beer as you go, at good value but not heavily discounted prices. Beer is mainly in cask; there's often also bottle-conditioned UK beers, draught and bottled imports and real cider and perry. Current details of CAMRA festivals throughout the UK are posted at www.camra.org.uk/events.

It's a sign of the increased interest in beer that there are now growing numbers of non-CAMRA events, including commercial initiatives: these usually feature 'craft keg' beer too, and work in a variety of different ways.

I've listed the major recurring events below. Details are based on recent examples but things can change from year to year so do check before making plans. Regularly recurring events in individual pubs and bars are referred to in the main Places to Drink section.

February

Battersea Beer Festival *2nd week,*
Battersea Arts Centre SW11
Organised by South West London CAMRA, with 180 casks plus draught and bottled imported beers, cider and perry. This may not take place in 2016 as the venue is being restored following a serious fire: check website for current information.
www.batterseabeerfestival.org.uk

Craft Beer Rising *3rd week, Old Truman Brewery E1*
This commercially-run event in an appropriate location features 70 or more breweries and beer importers from the UK and elsewhere, plus music and street food. Tickets, best booked in advance, include a number of beer tokens.
www.craftbeerrising.co.uk

London Beer Week *3rd week, across London*
Deliberately coinciding with Craft Beer Rising and organised by the people behind a similar wine week and cocktail week. Participating bars and pubs stock unusual beers and hold events, while drinkers find their own way around equipped with wristbands giving access to discounts and offers. First run in 2015 so no guarantee yet it will be repeated.

March

London Drinker Beer and Cider Festival
2nd week, Camden Centre WC1
Organised by North London CAMRA, this well-established and well-loved event has become something of an annual London beer showcase, but also includes beers from across the UK among its 150 casks, plus ciders, perries, imported and bottle-conditioned beers.
www.northlondon.camra.org.uk

London Brewers' Market *Last week,*
Old Spitalfields Market E1
This pop-up market organised through the
London Brewers Alliance, often alongside
the Independent Label Market music-based
event, is an excellent opportunity to track
down beer from numerous London brewers.
Also in July and November, and possibly at
other times too.
www.londonbrewersmarket.tumblr.com
🐦 londonbrewmkt

April

Wetherspoon International Real Ale Festival,
first two weeks, sometimes starting in late March,
J D Wetherspoon pubs across London
Branches stock more cask beers than usual
during this period from a long list of specials,
with some installing extra lines and stillages.
They're likely to include beers brewed by
overseas brewers in British breweries
and are also sold in flights of thirds.
www.jdwetherspoon.co.uk

Bexley Beer Festival *4th week,*
Old Dartfordians Association, Bexley DA5
75+ cask beers, ciders and perries at this
event organised by Bexley CAMRA.
www.camrabexleybranch.org.uk

May

Mild Month *all month, across London*
May is CAMRA's designated month to
support and promote mild ales, and a good
time to find examples in various pubs.

Kingston Beer Festival *2nd week,*
Kingston Workmen's Club KT2
50+ cask beers, mainly local, with ciders
and perries, organised by Kingston and
Leatherhead CAMRA.
www.camrasurrey.org.uk

June

Beer Day Britain *15 June, across London*
Newly launched in 2015, this is Britain's national
beer day, so look out for special events in a
variety of venues. It's led by beer advocate
and writer Jane Peyton (p 84) and supported
by CAMRA and various industry bodies.
www.beerdaybritain.co.uk

July

Ealing Beer Festival *2nd week, Walpole Park W5*
This open air event organised by West
Middlesex CAMRA is an excellent prelude to
GBBF, particularly in good weather, with 300+
cask beers, imported beers, cider and perry.
www.ealingbeerfestival.org.uk

London Brewers' Market *Last week,*
Old Spitalfields Market E1. See March.

August

Great British Beer Festival *2nd week,*
Olympia Exhibition Centre W14
With approaching 1,000 beers and 60,000
visitors, CAMRA's flagship national event is one
of the biggest of its kind in the world and a
must-do for every beer connoisseur. A huge
range of cask, bottle-conditioned beers and
one of the best international beer selections at
the *Bières sans frontières* bars, plus ciders and
perries, with rarities, special releases and tutored
tastings. Best to book tickets in advance.
www.gbbf.org.uk

The Great British Beer Festival at Olympia, London

London Beer City *2nd week, across London*
Organised by beer writer Will Hawkes in partnership with the London Brewers Alliance, this is a week-long collection of events around GBBF celebrating London's beer renaissance, from tap takeovers and dinners in pubs and bars to heritage walking tours led by your author.
www.londonbeercity.com

London Craft Beer Festival *End of 2nd week, Oval Space*
This more 'craft'-oriented, independently organised event follows on from GBBF, stocking keykeg beers as well as cask and bottled. Best to buy tickets in advance. The organisers run pop-up bars at other times of year too.
www.londoncraftbeerfestival.co.uk

September

Cask Ale Week *Last week, across London*
A national promotion celebrating Britain's national drink, supported by CAMRA and the brewing industry with numerous events and pub-based promotions.
www.caskaleweek.co.uk

London Oktoberfest *Last two weeks, and first two weeks of October, Kennington Park SE11 and Millwall Park E14*
In an authentic tent that moves between parks halfway through, with free admission except on Saturdays, and only one beer, a 5% festbier tanked from Bavaria, though they won't say who brews it. *Lederhosen* and *Dirndln* can be hired if you consider it necessary. London's German-themed bars and many other venues run additional Oktoberfest events.
www.london-oktoberfest.co.uk

Kent Green Hop Beer Fortnight *Last week, continuing into October, across London*
A fortnight dedicated to beer brewed with fresh Kent hops and supported by growers and brewers, concentrated on Kent but inevitably spilling into the capital as increasing numbers of London brewers create green hop beers.
www.kentgreenhopbeer.com

October

Wallington Beer Festival *2nd or 3rd week, Wallington Hall SM6*
Organised by Croydon and Sutton CAMRA, this has over 50 local cask beers plus ciders and perries.
www.wallingtonbeerfestival.org.uk

Wetherspoon Autumn Real Ale Festival
Last two weeks, usually continuing to early November, J D Wetherspoon pubs across London
Similar to the April event but usually with more beers from the UK and fewer from international brewers.

Twickenham Beer and Cider Festival
Last week, York House, Twickenham TW1
Around 75 cask beers including several from local breweries, plus ciders and perries, at this event organised by Richmond and Hounslow CAMRA.
www.rhcamra.org.uk

November

Nicholson's Autumn Beer Festival
First two weeks, Nicholson's pubs across London
Pubs in the chain stock a wide selection of autumnal cask ales including several specially commissioned beers.

Heathrow Beer Festival *Last week, Imperial College London Heston TW5*
A local but growing festival jointly organised by CAMRA members and the British Airways staff club, with around 50 seasonal cask ales, cider and perry.
wwwheathrowbeerfestival.co.uk

London Brewers' Market *Last week, see March.*

December

Pigs Ear Beer and Cider Festival *First week, Round Chapel E5*
This well-established event organised by East London and City CAMRA brightens the darkening evenings with well over 200 cask beers, plus imports, cider and perry. A good place to find dark beers, winter ales and East London brewers.
www.pigsear.org.uk

Other recommendations

I'm by no means the only chronicler of good beer, pubs and bars in London. For alternative recommendations, and a second opinion on some of the places listed here, consult the following sources.

Good Beer Guide

Published annually, this essential guide contains recommendations of top cask beer pubs across the UK as well as London, chosen by local CAMRA branches. It aims for a good spread of outlets so is particularly useful for recommendations in outlying areas not covered in this book. It's also available as a mobile app, a POI file and an e-book. www.camra.org.uk/gbg

Local CAMRA recommendations

The best resource for pub information updated by local CAMRA volunteers is now the UK-wide WhatPub database, www.whatpub. com. The London CAMRA website at www. london.camra.org.uk has a directory of all LocAle-accredited pubs stocking at least one cask beer from a local brewer (these days usually more). Free bimonthly magazine *London Drinker* is an invaluable source of news on openings and closures, new breweries and forthcoming events and many of London's beer specialists take out display ads. It's distributed free to pubs or can be read online at www.london.camra.org.uk/londondrinker. Some CAMRA branches still produce printed guides or have lists on their websites: see CAMRA in London (p 320).

Craft Beer London

Probably the most authoritative, thorough and critical source of information for the thinking London beer drinker after this book, this is a neat, low-cost and simple-to-use app for iPhone and Android maintained by beer writer Will Hawkes (p 243), who regularly overhauls its content. Great fun to sit on the bus watching the nearest recommended venues update in real time on your smartphone, and there's brewery information and news too. Find it on Google Play or the iTunes shop, or see www.craftbeerlondon.bluecrowmedia.com

A London Beer and Pub Guide

An independently-maintained and unapologetically personal online take on the London scene curated by self-confessed beer geeks Fred Waltman, based in Los Angeles but a regular visitor, and Jeremy aka bonsvoeux1 (p 215). Has one of the most up-to-date lists of London breweries too, highlighting those with taprooms. www.beerguidelondon.com

Ratebeer

One of the best-known and most widely-used crowd-sourced beer databases on the web, this includes a worldwide 'Places' section with extensive listings for London, all of them rated by users. The user base is big enough to lend the assessments some worth, though it's a little biased towards the most dedicated of enthusiasts. www.ratebeer.com

Londonist Best Pubs in London

A neatly-mapped selection based on regular polls of readers and contributors to this increasingly useful 'alternative' news and blogging site, which also regularly covers beer topics. www.londonist.com/pubs

Time Out

London's long-running and much-relied-upon weekly events and attractions guide is now a free publication, and widely distributed. Its annual pubs and bars guidebook has been discontinued, but there are numerous searchable reviews and recommendations on its website. www.timeout.com/london

Cask Marque

This is an industry-backed scheme for accrediting pubs on the basis of their ability to serve cask beer in good condition, based on regular inspection visits. There's a fee to participate, though, so plenty of pubs with first rate cellars aren't accredited, including a large number of smaller and independent operators. But it can be a useful way of finding reliable cask beer in an unfamiliar area, and there's an app too.
www.cask-marque.co.uk

London Pub Walks

Walking is a great way to discover London and its pubs and Bob Steel is an expert guide. His book, last revised in 2013, covers not just the well-known tourist areas but several more obscure but rewarding locations, including several cask beer outlets on each route.
www.camra.org.uk/camra-pub-walks

Heritage Pubs

Not every pub on the CAMRA and English Heritage inventories of historic pub interiors sells good beer, but many do, and all are worth visiting for their architectural interest. A full and regularly updated list, sorted by regions including London, is at www.heritagepubs. org.uk, which also has information about printed guidebooks.

London's Best Pubs

This handsome book by Peter Haydon and Tim Hampson features mainly traditional pubs, including heritage gems and other notable hostelries. Most of them serve at least some decent beer but the focus is mainly on appearance, atmosphere, siting and history. It was last updated in 2011 but these are largely the sorts of places that don't change very much.

Increasing activity on the beer scene has inevitably spurred even more people to write about it, so keep your eye open for other online or print publications, and expanded beer and bars sections in general guidebooks. Sadly it's also resulted in one or two tawdry and just shy of legally actionable cash-ins shamelessly recycling other people's research without great respect for accuracy (if you're reading this, you know who you are), so engage your critical faculties before you buy.

LONDON DRINKERS   Will Hawkes

Former Beer Writer of the Year, Will is the man behind authoritative app-based guide *Craft Beer London* (p242), and the organiser of London Beer City, a week of beer events in August (p241). He writes a monthly beer column for *The Independent*.

How do you rate London as a beer city, on a world scale?
One of the most interesting places in the world at the moment. There's so much energy here compared to other European cities: that's why we've got 70-odd breweries.

What's the single most exciting thing about beer in London at the moment?
The fact that good beer is popping up everywhere. Within 20 minutes'

walk of my home in Southeast London I can sample dozens of different beers at a variety of pubs. That wouldn't have been possible even 18 months ago.

What single thing would make things even better?
More places selling excellent food alongside excellent beer.

What are your top London beers right now?
Fuller's London Porter, The Kernel IPA Nelson Sauvin, Brew By Numbers 07|01 Witbier.

What's your top great beer night out?
A few beers at the Rake (p58) followed by dinner at Elliot's (12 Stoney Street SE1 9AD, www. elliotscafe.com), a tremendous restaurant that always has a couple

of decent beers on tap from people like Beavertown and Weird Beard.

Who's your London beer hero?
Andy Moffat of Redemption (p153). Impossible not to respect how he goes about his business.

Who will we be hearing a lot more from in future?
Hammerton (p147) have established themselves impressively quickly. I think they'll be an increasingly significant player.

Which are your other top beer cities?
I've had excellent beer in Philadelphia, New York City, Paris, Brussels, Prague, Düsseldorf, Cologne, Leeds and Manchester over the past 18 months: each of them is great in its own way.

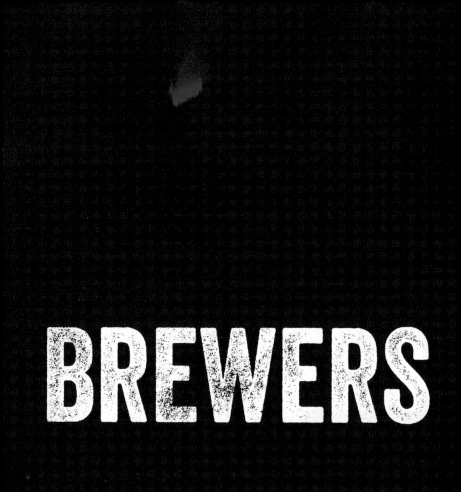

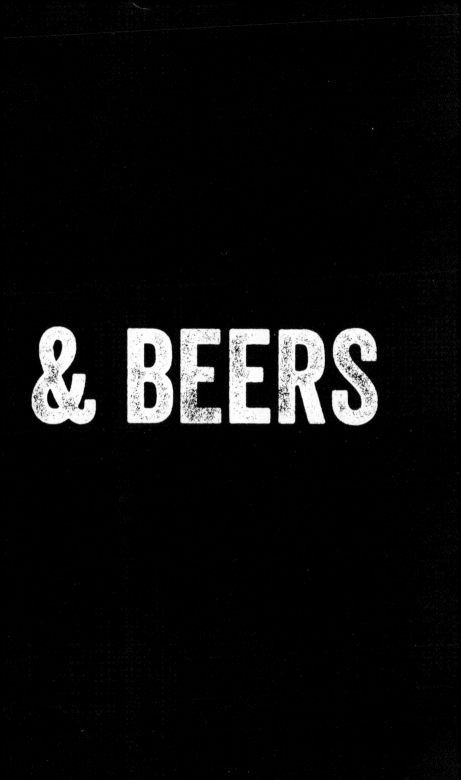

From grain to glass

What is beer?

Technically speaking, beer is a fermented alcoholic drink made from cereals. Fermentation is a natural process involving a microorganism called yeast, which grows by feeding on sugars dissolved in water, breaking them down in the process into alcohol and carbon dioxide. The source of the sugars is one factor determining the broad families of alcoholic drinks. Fruit sugars yield wine, cider and perry, while sugars derived from cereal starches yield beer. But beer is also a cultural artefact, the product of a certain tradition and practice of brewing that evolved through mediaeval Europe into the industrial age, eventually spreading across the known world.

Ingredients

Grains, malts and sugars

Grains in their raw state don't actually contain much sugar, but they are a good source of starch, another carbohydrate, which can be turned into sugar by the action of chemicals called enzymes. Malting the grain by steeping it in water to encourage it to germinate and then rapidly heating and drying it results in a sweeter, more enzyme-rich ingredient. One grain in particular, barley, has turned out to be ideally suited to malting and brewing. It's particularly rich in enzymes, and doesn't lose its husk during threshing so is less likely to turn to porridge and gum up the equipment. It also lends itself well to a range of different malting techniques, helping produce a wide range of flavours.

Most barley used in brewing is lightly kilned 'pale malt' or even lighter 'pilsner malt' but numerous speciality malts are often used alongside these to add character to different styles. Their variety is the result of different kilning times, temperatures and techniques.

Mild, Vienna, Munich and amber malts are progressively darker and toastier. Brown malt is darker still. Crystal and caramel malts ('cara-malts') have notable caramel and biscuity flavours. Chocolate and black ('patent') malts are highly kilned to give roasted and burnt flavours. Smoked and peated malts, the latter more normally used for whisky, lend distinctive notes to some beers. Roasted unmalted barley gives a classic bite to Irish stouts.

Barley malt is now so ubiquitous that you'll sometimes see it named as a defining ingredient of beer, and the term 'malt' on its own usually means malted barley. Beers can and have been made without it, but today they are little more than footnotes: gluten free beers, minor surviving ancient styles or occasional experiments by adventurous brewers. However other grains are regularly used alongside barley. Wheat is the next most important brewers' grain, used to give a unique character to wheat beers or in small quantities to aid head retention in more conventional styles. Rye and oats are also used in malted and unmalted form. More controversially, maize and rice, neither of which requires malting, add strength and smoothness to industrial lagers without troubling them with additional flavour; but maize has occasionally been employed for its own character.

Refined sugars can be added directly to beer, a practice frowned upon in some traditions but almost a defining characteristic of others, such as Belgian monastic-style brewing. Special crystallised sugars like candy and brewing sugar, liquid 'invert sugar', caramel, molasses and honey all find their way into beer. Pre-prepared malt extract is also occasionally used. Lactose, extracted from milk, is an unfermentable sugar that lends a milk gum chewiness to some sweet stouts.

Sacks of malted barley

Water

By far the highest proportion of the liquid in your beer glass is likely to be water, known as 'liquor' in the industry, where 'water' is the stuff you use for cooling and cleaning. Once, most breweries had access to their own springs or wells, and the liquor lent a *goût de terroir* to the beers. London, sitting on its basin of chalk, has water with a high mineral content including chlorides, which turned out to be perfect for porters and stouts. The local water in Burton upon Trent (and in several other historic brewing centres) is naturally richer in sulphates, better suited to hoppy pale ales, which is why many London brewers set up homes in Burton in the 19th century. Today, the chemistry is better understood, and most brewers are happy to purify and tweak the local mains water supply, known as 'town's liquor' in older breweries.

Hops and other flavourings

At one time in London and some other parts of England it was considered best practice to brew ale from grains and water alone. It's likely such beers relied for palatability on sourness and other flavours from wild yeast and bacterial fermentations, as otherwise they would have been cloyingly sweet and bland. Today's beers are balanced by additional ingredients with more interesting and aromatic flavours, most notably hops, cone-shaped clusters from a herbaceous climbing plant. As well as adding bitter, herbal and fruity flavours and spicy aromas to offset the malt, they help clarify and stabilise the beer and act as a natural preservative.

"Most working brewers love hops," wrote Michael Jackson in his *Beer Companion* in 1993, "and would use twice as much if the market researchers were not afraid of frightening the customer." In the last few years that taboo has been well and truly broken, led by the US craft brewing movement. Today, hops are brewing's equivalent of the wine industry's 'varietals', with a broad spectrum of varieties grown around the world. London brewers in particular have enthusiastically pushed hops into the spotlight.

Classic British hops like East Kent Goldings and Fuggles have an earthy, smooth character that contributes to both aroma and bitterness. Challenger, Northdown, Northern Brewer and dwarf hop First Gold are more recent varieties. Bramling Cross, a hybrid of Goldings and wild Canadian hops, has a distinctive blackcurrant flavour.

Traditional mainland European hops lend their grassy, lightly spicy notes to classic German and Czech lagers. Five varieties – Hallertauer, Hersbrucker, Spalt and Tettnang from Germany and Žatec (Saaz), originally from Bohemia – are sometimes known as 'noble hops'. Magnum and Perle are more recent German varieties, while Styrian Goldings is a Slovenian-grown substitute for English Goldings, though is actually derived from Fuggles.

Hop bines

caught some brewers' interest: they include fine aroma hops like Lublin and sturdy Styrian Golding derivatives like Celeia. But there are also signs that London brewers' passion for imported hops is cooling slightly, with more interest in both traditional and new English varieties and domesticated exotics like English-grown Cascade, some of it prompted by environmental concerns.

Hops are usually used in dried form, though some brewers make a point of commemorating the harvest with fresh hops in annual 'green hop' beers. With London's proximity to the traditional growing areas in Kent, and with various projects across the capital to encourage hop growing in private gardens and allotments, it's well worth keeping a lookout in late September and early October, after the harvest.

The finest hop flavour comes from whole cones, but some breweries find hop pellets, which take up less space and have a longer shelf life, easier to deal with. Liquid hop extract is an even more convenient but considerably less characterful alternative.

Like barley malt, hops are so ubiquitous in beer that according to some they're an essential ingredient, but they were once less prevalent and a variety of other herbs and spices can and have been used. Coriander, ginger, chocolate, coffee, dried citrus peel, cumin, mace, pepper, star anise, cloves, sweet gale, chilli, chamomile, nettles, tea, tobacco, juniper, spruce, seaweed, heather and even bacon and oysters find their way into contemporary beers – though almost always alongside rather than instead of hops. Fruit is another popular addition with a long historical precedent: cherries and raspberries are standard additions to some Belgian beers; apples, blueberries, gooseberries, damsons, peaches and grapes are just some examples of other species in the UK brewer's fruit bowl.

North American hops are almost always more exotic and distinctive, with grapefruit and pine flavours and plentiful bitter acids. The classic example is Cascade, which along with Centennial and Columbus forms the 'Three C's' group of assertively citric hops. Amarillo, Citra and the piney Chinook are popular for their exotic fruit flavours. More reserved entrants include Crystal and Liberty, which are closer to German hops, and Willamette, a fruitier form of Fuggles. Exotic hops from other places include New Zealand's Nelson Sauvin, its name referencing a resemblance in flavour to Sauvignon Blanc grapes, and blackberry-tinged Pacific Gem.

There are many more varieties and the choice is expanding all the time as breeding programmes seek to meet drinkers' new-found thirst for hoppy novelty. Hops from Poland, now the world's fifth biggest producer, have

Yeast and other microflora

The fermentation of beer must have started with airborne yeasts but over millennia, brewers empirically selected the best strains without really understanding what they were doing, by keeping back the residue of a particularly successful brew and adding it to the next. Today the vast majority of yeast used in brewing is cultured in laboratories.

Yeast can survive dormant for many years, and academic and commercial yeast 'libraries' retain thousands of cultures and strains.

Yeast is what distinguishes the two great beer families – ales and lagers. Ales are the older style, fermented with yeasts that work at relatively high temperatures of around 25°C over short periods and have a tendency to float to the top of the vessel, forming a foamy crust known as barm. Ale yeast cultures are often complex with numerous different strains mixed together, and produce correspondingly complex flavours with fruity notes.

Lagers developed from the practice in Bavaria of storing beer in cold caves – *lagern* means 'to store' in German – where brewers noticed it would ferment over long periods of time at much lower temperatures (5–9°C), with the yeast sinking to the bottom of closed vessels, producing a cleaner tasting and more stable result. Yeast cultures evolved that worked particularly well in these circumstances, and in 1883 brewing scientist Emil Hansen isolated the first single strain lager yeast at the Carlsberg brewery in Copenhagen, ushering in a new era of discipline for the previously unruly microorganism.

Ale yeasts and lager yeasts are sometimes labelled 'top fermenting' and 'bottom fermenting' respectively, for obvious reasons, but yeasts are no longer so neatly classified. Old-fashioned ale yeasts used in modern closed fermenting vessels are more likely to sink to the bottom while still producing beers that are characteristically ales. A better distinction is between 'warm fermenting' and 'cold fermenting'.

Yeast cultures can have a profound effect on the flavour of the finished beer – drinking two beers made to exactly the same recipe but with different yeasts side-by-side is a revealing experience. Old-established independent breweries usually maintain house yeast cultures which help give their beers a characteristic flavour – Fuller's yeast, for example, is known for its spicy orange notes. Newer breweries have been known to obtain yeast from more established colleagues, or even to cultivate it from the deposits in other people's bottle- conditioned beers. But most smaller brewers now buy their yeasts from a handful of international commercial suppliers, either dried or the usually preferred option of live liquid yeast. These suppliers maintain extensive catalogues of yeasts optimised for different styles, but inevitably some are more popular than others, which explains why beers brewed on different continents can taste so remarkably similar.

Conventional brewers' yeasts are members of the genus *Saccharomyces* ('sugar fungus'), but there are other yeasts, most famously *Bretannomyces* ('British fungus', as they were once endemic, though not entirely welcomed, in British breweries). 'Bret' ferments more thoroughly but more slowly, leaving behind distinctive funky, spicy, sweaty and farmyard notes traditionally described as "horse blanket", a sensory comparison that made more sense in the days when breweries kept stables of dray horses. Though usually seen as undesirable, these yeasts are more likely to express themselves in long-aged beers and are part of the flavour characteristic of certain Belgian styles. Now some brewers are seeking them out for a new breed of wild and wood-aged beers, and the yeast suppliers oblige by supplying cultured and more controllable versions.

Other naturally occurring microflora which are decidedly unwelcome in most fermenting vessels but have engaged the interest of more adventurous brewers include *Lactobacillus* bacteria. These produce lactic acid from sugar, creating the signature mild sourness of styles like lambic and Berliner Weisse and the new beers inspired by them.

Pitching yeast into wort

The brewing process

Malts and other cereals if used – the 'grist' – are mixed and milled. Then they're 'mashed': soaked in hot but not boiling water, releasing the enzymes that complete the conversion of starches into sugars. The sweet liquid, known as 'wort', is run off, usually with the help of additional hot water, and boiled with hops and perhaps other flavourings. Hops are often added in stages, with those towards the start of the boil contributing more to bitterness, and the 'late hops' near the end towards aroma. The hopped wort is cooled, put in a fermentation vessel, 'pitched' with the yeast culture and left to ferment. The fermentation time varies according to the yeast: typically 5–7 days for ales, up to two weeks for lagers.

During fermentation, the yeast feeds on the sugar, converting it to alcohol and carbon dioxide, giving the beer both strength and sparkle. The strength is dependent on the ratio of fermentable sugar in the original wort – the 'original gravity' – and the 'attenuation', the extent to which the yeast converts this to alcohol during fermentation. Highly attenuated beers are drier, with nearly all the sugar gone, while lower levels of attenuation leave more residual sugar to give a sweeter flavour. There are various ways of measuring alcohol content: the most common internationally is the percentage of Alcohol By Volume (ABV) which is used throughout this book.

After primary fermentation the yeast is separated off and the beer pumped to a separate conditioning tank for a further period of conditioning and maturation to round off the rough edges. For the best lagers this could take up to three months at temperatures just above freezing. One or two weeks is adequate for most modern ales. Additional hops can be added directly to the beer during conditioning, known as 'dry hopping'.

Up to this point, all beers, from macro lagers to the most artisanal limited edition from a nanobrewer, undergo the same basic processes – the differences will be in choice of ingredients and scale. There are some minority exceptions, notably spontaneously fermented lambic-style beers where the wort is left open to the air to become infected with wild yeasts and other microflora, and then undergoes a very lengthy and complex fermentation and conditioning in wooden vessels. A related technique is to condition more conventionally fermented beer further in wood, a technique once employed by porter breweries. Several London breweries have wood-ageing programmes, sometimes using casks that formerly contained wine or whisky to add additional layers of flavour.

Mashing at Gipsy Hill brewery

Packaging & dispense

All the way up to end of its conditioning, beer is a living liquid continuously evolving in flavour and character. By now most yeast activity will have ceased, the detritus sinking to the bottom of the vessel as sediment, but a few stray cells will still be nibbling away at the remaining sugars. What happens next has been the subject of discussion and controversy among brewers, consumer campaigners and interested drinkers for decades.

Most large scale commercial brewers seeking a uniform product that's easy to handle now filter and pasteurise the beer, heating it rapidly to kill off any remaining microbiological activity. This knocks most of the sparkle out of it too, so it's force-carbonated with additional carbon dioxide before packaging in sealed kegs, bottles or cans for distribution. When served on draught, this type of 'keg' beer is usually chilled and forced to the tap under pressure from further CO_2. All this may ensure a consistent and convenient result, but it can too easily result in a bland and lifeless one, with subtleties of flavour obliterated.

There are numerous alternatives. Beer can be filtered without being pasteurised, which will get rid of practically all active yeast without impacting so heavily on the flavour, though it will still likely need to be recarbonated. Or it can be left to 'drop bright' so clear beer can be drained from above the level of the sediment. The result is likely to be slightly hazy, and there will inevitably be a low level of fermentation still, but a skilled brewer can control for this.

For many connoisseurs, though – and in particular the Campaign for Real Ale – the ultimate in live, fresh beer is only achieved by encouraging a further fermentation in the vessel from which it's served, and then dispensing it without additional carbonation. This is the secret of cask beer, the unique style of draught beer for which British brewers

are so rightly renowned. But it also extends to bottle conditioned beer, and, increasingly, live beer in a number of other formats. Once again London brewers have led the field, and if there's a new way of serving great beer, you're likely to find it in the capital.

Cask beer

Cask is Britain's gift to the world of beer. Drinkers in parts of a few other countries, such as Germany, have also long enjoyed fresh unpressurised draught beer, and there's an increasing interest in cask techniques among specialist brewers and keen beer drinkers in the USA and elsewhere. But beer still fermenting in its cask remains an everyday drink only in the UK. The vast majority of outlets in this guide stock it, and I strongly recommend you take the opportunity to sample as much as you can responsibly drink.

A cask is a barrel-shaped container with a slightly bulging waist, once made from wood but now almost always from aluminium or plastic. Most are of a size known as a 'firkin' which holds 9 gallons (41 l), but there are also 'pins' of 4.5 gallons (20.5 l), 'kilderkins' or 'kils' of 18 gallons (82 l) and some obsolete larger sizes. Crucially, it has two openings: one near the rim of one of the heads, filled with a bung called a 'keystone', and the other at right angles to the first in the middle of the waist, filled with a bung called a 'shive'.

Casks are specifically designed to host a continuing fermentation. There may be enough residual sugar and yeast activity to ensure this simply by filling them with unfiltered and unpasteurised beer from the conditioning tank, but more likely the cask will be 'primed' with a little sugar or unfermented wort, and/or with additional yeast. Some breweries use a different strain for conditioning and might filter the beer before putting it into cask, though this is rare especially among smaller brewers.

Depending on the yeast strain, most of the solids will eventually settle. Casks are meant to be kept on their sides in a cradle called a 'stillage', so the sediment accumulates in the waist, enabling clearer beer to be drawn off above it through the keystone opening. The beer thus obtained is likely to be slightly hazy, so many brewers add 'finings', a tasteless gelatinous substance that slowly sinks through the liquid, taking suspended solid particles with it. Finings are often from fish sources, so some vegetarians and vegans avoid fined beers for this reason, but increasingly vegetable alternatives are used, and there's been a growth of interest in unfined beers as drinkers become more accepting of haze in specialist styles.

Prior to serving, the 'tut' which seals the hole in the shive is driven through and replaced with a peg called a 'spile', and a tap is driven through the keystone. If the beer is too lively at this point, a 'soft spile' of porous wood is placed in the shive so that much of the carbon dioxide can escape without too much air getting in. Contact with oxygen rapidly spoils beer, not to mention the danger of infection from airborne organisms: the blanket of carbon dioxide generated by fermenting beer will keep it at bay for a while. If there's too little carbonation, the cask is resealed with a 'hard spile' to let the fermentation develop further.

Once in optimum condition, the beer can be served direct from the cask via a tap in the keystone: this is the usual method at beer festivals and at some pubs, with beer either fetched from the cellar or kept in a cooled stillage behind the bar. But most likely the cask is hooked up via a tube to a hand-operated pump called a 'beer engine', and drawn into the drinker's glass using a distinctive pump handle on the bar, familiarly known as a 'handpump'. The spile helps restrict the flow of air into the cask as the liquid runs out, but the beer still needs to be consumed within a few days before it becomes flat, oxidised and vinegary.

Most cask beer is best served gently carbonated but certainly not flat, and cool but not chilled, at 'cellar temperature' of around 12°C. Handpumped beer is usually a little livelier than beer direct from the cask, with more of a

Racking fresh beer into casks

head, though in London and southern England in general, beer is traditionally served in glasses filled to the brim, with very little head. In the north of England, cask beer is typically served through a nozzle called a 'sparkler' with multiple narrow holes, aerating the beer to produce a bigger head. In recent years the use of sparklers has spread southwards and some London pubs use them indiscriminately, but they're arguably inappropriate for some beers, so the more conscientious places follow the brewer's recommendations.

The freshness and gentle carbonation afforded by cask beer delivers an incomparable drinking experience, and one particularly suited to the subtle, low-gravity session ales that became the norm in Britain in the 20th century. But it's not surprising that, given its complexities, expense, unpredictability and reliance on factors outside the brewer's direct control, the big brewing groups in the brave new world of the 1950s and 1960s were keen to jettison it as an unwanted anachronism. Their proposed replacements were keg ales, based on the simplest and cheapest cask bitters, unsympathetically overpasteurised, force-carbonated and chilled, obliterating any distinctive character or subtlety. These beers, and later even more egregious British-brewed keg lagers,

Secrets of the cellar

The cellar is the last link in the chain between the brewhouse and the glass on the bar, and what happens in it can radically affect the quality of that glass's contents, for better or worse. Yet, while most beer connoisseurs have visited a brewery or two, to almost all of us outside the licensed trade, the cellar remains a mystery. It's the place into which the bar staff annoyingly disappear when you're in a hurry to enjoy a last pint, muttering something about "changing the barrel."

The term 'cellar' implies an underground space but licensees still tend to talk about cellars if they're on the same level or even above the bar. In the days before temperature control they were underground because this was naturally the coolest place to keep the beer. These days their temperature is usually artificially regulated, and draught systems might have their own integral cooling.

As is evident from the description of cask beer above, a high level of cellar skills and best practice is absolutely vital in ensuring beer in this unique format is served at its best. Casks contain living beer: they must be treated gently, and their development carefully monitored with action taken accordingly. Good stock control is essential, and delivery, best before, spiling and tapping dates must be carefully and conscientiously tracked. Temperature, too, must be monitored and regulated. Some cellars are subdivided, with different sections kept at different temperatures.

Hygiene must be scrupulously observed, to reduce the risk of infections. A common problem area is the 'lines', the tubes running to the bar, usually bundled together into a 'python'. Depending on its length, a line itself could contain several pints of beer vulnerable to going stale and sour when the bar is closed or turnover is low. Beer that's been sitting for too long in the lines needs to be pulled through as 'ullage' (the industry term for beer waste that must be discarded), and regular, thorough line cleaning is essential.

It's not just cask beer that needs looking after. Kegs are less open to infection but dirty lines and poor general hygiene can still compromise the beer. The new generation of 'craft keg' beers all require their own kind of special treatment. Bottle conditioned beers must be kept still and cool, paying careful attention to their best before dates.

The venues listed in this book are reliable keepers of exemplary cellars. If you want to uncover more of the secrets of the cellar, a couple of featured pubs, the Hand in Hand (p197) and the Red Lion (p199), offer cellar tours. Another, the Finborough Arms (p206), has a glass-fronted cellar and if you ask nicely when it's not too busy, staff might oblige by pointing out the key features.

were forced on the public through aggressive marketing and the big brewers' control of the pub trade through the tied house system.

Consumer resistance to this led to the formation of the Campaign for Real Ale (CAMRA) in 1971, which has grown to become one of the most successful consumer organisations ever, also helping inspire the development of specialist brewing and beer appreciation internationally. It is largely thanks to CAMRA that cask beer, even though long since outsold by industrial lager, retains a major presence on the British beer scene: indeed, along with speciality beers in general, it's the only sector of the drinks industry in growth. CAMRA coined the term 'real ale' for cask beer, though it's since been extended to bottle-conditioned beer and live beer served from certain other containers (see below),

and isn't strictly accurate for all such beers as lagers as well as ales can continue to ferment after packaging.

A number of recent developments have contributed to reducing the hassle of cask. First, the bigger cask producers in particular have streamlined fermentation in various ways to reduce the time the beer spends in the cellar before it's ready to serve. Even so, some pubs are too hurried, and serve beer before it's ready. New systems for doing everything through the keystone enable casks to be kept upright in cellars with restricted space. 'Cask breathers' extend the shelf life by introducing a gentle blanket of sterile carbon dioxide as the beer runs out, but some devotees claim this inhibits natural fermentation, and CAMRA officially frowns on the practice.

Note too that casks can be filled with beer

that's 'racked bright' without enough live yeast for a significant fermentation. Such beer won't keep fresh for more than a day or two and needs to be drunk within a few hours once tapped. Bright beer is often supplied to temporary bars at events and private functions where there's no space or time for anything else and a rapid turnover can be expected. It isn't classed as real ale, though, and beer-specific events like beer festivals are planned and run so genuine cask can be served.

Beyond cask

When CAMRA was founded and for some time afterwards, pretty much the only beer worth drinking in Britain was cask beer. Aside from a tiny handful of bottle conditioned beers and a few other minor exceptions, all other beer was pasteurised and filtered into lifelessness. But in the past few years in particular, other ways of serving unpasteurised and unfiltered beers have proliferated, many of them following international practices. CAMRA now accepts that keg-conditioned beers served without additional gas, as well as bottle-conditioned beers, are real ale.

One thing all these systems have in common is that the resulting beer is almost invariably more carbonated than cask. Even if no gas is added artificially, without a shive and spile to control its release, the natural carbon dioxide produced by fermentation remains in the beer, producing a vigorous sparkle. I've met numerous dedicated cask drinkers who, though they appreciate that bottle conditioned beer is also real ale, don't like drinking it because it's "too fizzy."

Some of this is a matter of taste, and of style. The complexity of low-gravity English ale styles is undoubtedly enhanced by the gentle carbonation and cool serving temperatures of cask, and compromised by too much gas and chilling. Some brewers need to be told that their least assertive 3.8% bitters aren't the best candidates for bottle conditioning. But there's equally an argument that stronger and more robust styles, such as the new generation of hop-forward IPAs, require a different approach. Some of them can taste overpowering and cloying in cask, but sing when served with a livelier sparkle from a keykeg or bottle.

Tank beer, keykeg and other 'bag in box' systems

A variety of systems use double-layered containers to avoid contact between beer and air or gas. The liquid is sealed in a flexible inner layer, usually a large, tough polythene bag, protected by a rigid outer layer. When tapped, the beer either flows out under gravity as the inner layer collapses, or is pushed out by pressurising the space between the two layers.

'Tank beer' systems apply this principle on a grand scale using 1,000 l polythene-lined and integrally cooled and insulated steel tanks, often displayed in the bar as a talking point. On a more accessible scale are disposable recyclable plastic 20 l or 30 l 'keykegs', recognisable by their distinctive 10-sided outer cartons and popular with many smaller London brewers, and the alternative Ecofass system with disposable inner and reusable outer layers.

No-one would bother to use such systems for pasteurised products and most beer that goes into them is unfiltered too. Such beer likely contains at least some still-active yeast cells and with good yeast control it's even possible to encourage a further fermentation. In this case, the beer counts as real ale so long as no additional gas comes into direct contact with it.

More basic cardboard and polythene bag-in-box systems have long been familiar as 20 l 'polypins' and 10 l 'minipins' for enjoying draught beer at home, and several London brewers sell beer in this format, usually in bright form, though others now prefer minicasks and minikegs (below). Polypins are rarely used for beer in pubs and bars, though they're an accepted way of selling 'real' unpasteurised cider and perry.

Keg

Kegs are metal or plastic containers in a variety of shapes and sizes but generally designed to be used upright, with one opening in the top. Mainstream industrial pasteurised draught lager and stout are supplied in kegs, but more and more brewers are using them for specialist beers in more natural states, and even 'keg conditioned' beer. Additional gas pressure is needed to force beer out of the keg – usually carbon dioxide or a mix of CO_2 and nitrogen ('nitrokeg') – and some of this gas dissolves into the beer, one reason why keg dispense isn't regarded as 'real'. At CAMRA beer festivals where turnover is likely to be rapid, imported beer in kegs may be dispensed using air pressure, but this will cause spoilage if the beer isn't drunk within a few hours.

Minicask and minikeg

These neat little 5 l containers are currently the best way of enjoying draught beer at home. A minicask looks much like a miniature version of a real cask turned on its end, and even has two openings: a tap at the bottom and a vent at the top. This makes it ideal for cask-style refermenting beer, as the excess gas can be vented before serving, just like a real cask, and you can even practice cellar skills in miniature. A minikeg has only one opening and an integral CO_2 capsule to force the beer out: examples from small brewers are most likely to contain bright beer.

Bottle

Beer has been packaged in bottles for 400 years, and they're still the most popular format for beer at home. 'Bottle-conditioned' beer undergoes a further fermentation like cask beer and is classed by CAMRA as 'Real ale in a bottle'. This practice had almost died out in Britain in the 1970s, though it persisted in some other countries like Belgium. Today it's undergone a decisive revival, and most London brewers produce bottle-conditioned beer – hand bottling live beer is a practical, if labour-intensive, option for the smallest brewers without their own filtering equipment and bottling lines.

Depending on yeast, style and brewer's preference, the beer could be racked from conditioning tanks with residual live yeast, but is more likely to be primed and perhaps re-pitched with fresh yeast to ensure a vigorous secondary fermentation. Bottle conditioning generally works best with stronger beers (5% and up), and certain examples can be cellared, continuing to develop in complexity for many years. But most are intended to be drunk young – contemporary hop-forward beers in particular rapidly lose hop aroma with age, and some brewers mark them with a bottling date so you can identify the freshest bottles.

Successful bottle conditioning requires care, skill and scrupulous hygiene. Too little fermentation and the beer will be dull, flat and prone to infection. Too much and you'll end up with a 'gusher' that bursts from the bottle on opening, or, worse, an exploding bottle. Infections that weren't apparent when the beer was bottled have plenty of chance to establish themselves in the months spent on warehouse, shop and cellar shelves. By no means everyone gets it right all of the time, though success rates are improving.

All bottle-conditioned beer will contain at least some sediment and with a good yeast strain this should stick to the bottom of the bottle. Most brewers advise you to pour the beer carefully, leaving the sediment behind, but it's harmless and some drinkers are happy to pour it into the beer. German and Belgian-style wheat beers are intended to be served cloudy and brewers deliberately use yeasts that don't settle, or may advise you to agitate the bottle gently before pouring to achieve the desired cloudy appearance.

A few London brewers fill their bottles bright from the conditioning tank, unfiltered and unpasteurised but with no intention of provoking further fermentation. A few filter and recarbonate their bottled beers, while many mainstream bottled beers are pasteurised too.

Can

Of all the challenges to received wisdom mounted by the US craft brewing movement, one of the most dramatically successful has been the rehabilitation of the can, previously regarded as a receptacle worthy of only the very worst and most bland products of industrial brewing. Modern cans have resin coatings which prevent their contents picking up metallic flavours. Compared to bottles, cans are more effective at protecting beer from damaging light and oxygen, cheaper, lighter and easier to transport and store. There's an argument too that, though not reusable, they're more sustainable as they take less energy to produce and are easily recyclable.

London brewers like Beavertown, Camden Town and Fourpure have been early adopters of 'craft cans' in the UK. Most of their contents have been racked bright from conditioning tanks, though some of it is filtered. 'Can conditioning' is also possible though it requires careful yeast control to prevent exploding cans.

Cask or craft?

In the last edition of this book I liberally splashed around the term 'craft brewer' as an internationally applicable way of identifying someone who approaches brewing as a craft, using quality ingredients, skill, experience and imagination to produce beers of character and distinctiveness. But since then, there's been such controversy and confusion around this innocent term in the UK beer community that this time round I've found myself avoiding it or putting quotes around it, at least in connection with British brewing.

The term is in wide use in the USA where it has something like an official definition, at least as far as the Brewers Association, the trade body for independent brewers, is concerned. To summarise and paraphrase, a 'craft brewery' is an independent brewery below a certain size that doesn't concentrate on producing bland lagers from maize and rice. The definition is still open to criticism, though, not least because the size threshold is upped every time the biggest craft breweries get dangerously close to exceeding it.

Attempting to transplant this definition across the Atlantic is problematic. For one thing, breweries in Europe are on average considerably smaller than those in the United States. For another, unlike the US, in the UK and in certain other European countries like Belgium, Germany and the Czech Republic, we still have a significant indigenous traditional brewing industry using practices close to most people's understanding of the term 'craft' to produce distinctive local and regional styles. Indeed it's these cranky European styles and practices that largely inspired the US craft brewing movement in the first place, and still today even some of the most radical New World brewers regard the most old-fashioned Old World beers with great reverence.

Instead the term 'craft beer' in the UK seems to have been appropriated loosely to mean "those hoppy American-style beers with cool labels that are nothing like the brown bitter my grandad drinks." Or, depending on your point of view, "those new-fangled, overhyped, over-hopped and overpriced fizzy keg beers that my granddaughter drinks." Some even insist that craft beer specifically excludes cask beer, but if you push the self-declared craft drinkers on this, they usually make an exception for cask beers made by brewers they approve of. This is particularly odd at time when more and more US craft brewers are producing cask. CAMRA, however, is less confused and takes the straightforward view that all real ale is craft beer but not all craft beer is real ale.

At the same time, the established industry has scented a profitable trend, and set about identifying a 'craft beer sector' and a demographic it can target products at. The industry definition also seems to be based on fashionable novelty. Several of the established family breweries now have trendily-branded 'craft' beer ranges. In many cases this has been a good thing, unleashing the long-inhibited creativity of some of Britain's best and most experienced brewers. In a few cases it's been faintly embarrassing. But none of it has helped in clarifying what we mean by 'craft'.

London beer styles

When the late great beer writer Michael Jackson wrote *The World Guide to Beer*, the book that's usually acknowledged as introducing the modern concept of beer styles, in 1977, he could hardly have guessed that, less than 40 years later, interpretations of nearly all the styles he wrote about would be brewed commercially in his home city. Back then, the *Good Beer Guide* needed only three symbols to describe the cask repertoire of English breweries: one for mild, another for bitter, and an occasional third for "old ale or special".

It wasn't always so. Beer historian Ronald Pattinson once remarked to me that, at the beginning of the 20th century, "you could walk into a London pub and have a choice of five or six draught beers such as bitter, mild, Burton and porter, all completely different in character and with strengths ranging from 3% to 7 or 8% ABV". That diversity began to shrink exactly a century ago, during World War I, not only through shortage of ingredients but because of increasing taxation and regulation of the brewing industry – ostensibly in the name of the war effort but in reality largely driven by the same sort of ideological objections to alcohol consumption that gave rise to the USA's disastrous experiment with Prohibition from 1920–1933.

Heavy taxation based on a beer's gravity persisted into the interwar years, so beer strengths declined accordingly, and the industry responded to the challenges of the 1930s recession and of rebuilding after World War II by streamlining its output. By the time of the real ale revival in the 1970s, the idea that beer was all about low gravity session ales suitable for drinking in pints was firmly embedded in the British consciousness. The growth of microbreweries and the emergence of more discerning drinkers prompted a revival of interest in defunct styles like porter, and

new developments like golden and summer ales – but almost always at session strengths.

The current abundance is partly the legacy of Jackson himself. His work directly and indirectly inspired would-be brewers in countries like the USA, where big brewing had almost entirely obliterated older and more locally distinctive techniques and styles, to start rebuilding their beer culture from a blank sheet. The resulting enthusiastic eclecticism and cosmopolitan openness has now returned to the old European brewing heartlands to inspire a new generation of brewers. And nowhere is this more evident than London, a city with a long tradition of being open to exotic influences and new ideas.

All this makes it rather challenging to talk about specifically London beer styles. The beers with the deepest historical roots in the capital are porters and stouts, though, aside from a few wood-aged experiments, no contemporary London brewer makes porter in a way comparable to the 18th century methods of maturing strong porter for years in wooden vats. By the end of the 19th century, milds were a more typical London style, and in the early 20th century, the related sweetish style of bottled brown ale typified by Mann's Brown was regarded as an East End speciality. Today, hardly any London brewers offer a regular mild and none brews anything like Mann's Brown, which itself is still around but produced outside London.

Old school real ale drinkers associate the capital with the revered cask bitters brewed by Fuller's and Young's, the two independents that survived into the 1970s. While Young's is no longer brewed here, Fuller's is proud to remain a London brewer, though neither can really be said to brew beers in a distinctively London style. Instead they reflect a general southeast English preference for relatively dry and hoppy cask bitters, doubtless influenced by the proximity of the Kentish hop gardens, and drawn without sparklers with a low level of carbonation and a minimal head.

London can equally claim, alongside Wrexham and Glasgow, to be one of the UK's few genuine lager-brewing cities. In the 1930s, Barclay Perkins on Bankside became the first big British brewer to commit to lager production (see Southwark ale p 56). In the 1990s London was the birthplace of one of Britain's first 'craft lager' breweries, Freedom, and is still the home of one of its most successful, Meantime (p 172). And today the city can claim to be the UK's main centre for hop-forward US-inspired pale ales and IPAs: while a good few London breweries don't bother with standard bitter, pretty much all of them have at least one hoppy pale ale in their repertoire. Anyone tempted to express regret at this apparent departure from tradition should remind themselves that London originally gave the world not only porter, but India Pale Ale too.

Below I've tried to provide some basic navigation through the bewildering variety of beers now brewed in London, on a style-by-style basis, with tasting suggestions and notes. The suggestions aren't exhaustive and although I've picked what in my opinion are good examples, that certainly doesn't mean that nothing else is worth trying. There are now so many London-brewed beers I doubt any one person has tasted and assessed them all, and new ones are appearing all the time. The style categories, too, are pragmatic: beer styles are slippery things, and just when you think you have one pinned down, some pesky brewer insists on being creative and pushing the envelope.

BITTER

The signature style of English cask beer, and by far the most common, bitter evolved from the hoppy pale ales developed in the late 18th century: indeed brewers referred to it simply as 'pale ale' long after drinkers had taken to calling it 'bitter'. Thanks to the comparatively higher price of the pale malts needed to produce it, bitter was once a little more expensive than styles like porter and mild, and therefore seen as more upmarket and aspirational. Until very recently pretty much all English brewers made at least one bitter, and most likely more, and it's still easily the most prolific style brewed in the UK.

Because of its ubiquity and its perceived association with unadventurous real ale orthodoxy, it's sometimes vilified among the more extremist cliques of 'craft beer' enthusiasts as "boring brown bitter". But well-made cask bitter served in top condition is a marvellous thing, packing immense subtlety and complexity into a low gravity while remaining supremely refreshing and drinkable. Too much carbonation tends to mask this, so these beers really do work best in cask – the bottled versions, even if bottle conditioned, just aren't the same thing.

There's considerable variety – strengths range from 3% to 5.5% or more, though most cluster between 3.5–4.8%, while the colour is classically amber but can run from golden to nut-brown. In the days when brewers produced each basic beer style in a range of strengths, it was the usual practice to offer an ordinary bitter at about 3.5%, a best at around 4.4% and perhaps a special at 4.8% or more. Relics of this can still be traced, for example in Fuller's trio of Chiswick, London Pride and ESB. There's some grounds for identifying regional variations, but no distinctively London style, as noted above.

Classic bitters aim for a rounded flavour with a good balance between fruity, biscuity malt, often with crystal malt in the grist, sometimes giving a gently roasted crack in the finish, and a notable hop character achieved with earthy English varieties like Fuggles and Goldings. More recently some brewers have been including US hop varieties – not as novel as it might sound, as even in the 19th century British brewers used Oregon hops when domestic harvests were poor, though objected to their 'catty' flavours. Hop rates among the newer breed of bitters have notably increased too, but remember the term 'bitter' is relative, and by current world craft brewing standards, these are very polite beers.

Ordinary bitter

Dragonfly 2 O'Clock Ordinary (4%). Very tasty throughout with classic maltiness, berry fruit and a persistent hedgerow bitterness in the finish.

Fuller's Chiswick (3.5%). At its best a perfectly poised classic: a fine malty-fruity aroma with an earthy, sacky hop note from dry hopping, apple and blackcurrant fruit on the palate and a crisp, rounded finish with a bitter hint.

Sambrook's Wandle Ale (3.8%). Full-bodied, fruity and chewy with a slight artichoke note and a moderate soothing finish.

Best bitter

Hackney Best Bitter (4.4%). Orange on the aroma, an autumn fruit palate with a bitter edge, then some lettuce bitterness and a hint of roast on the finish.

Late Knights Morning Glory (4.4%). Traditionally malty-dry with blackcurrant, fudge, toasty notes and a refreshing berry finish.

Truman's Runner (4%). Dark amber with a slight whiff of fruity sulphur on a chestnut honey aroma, a good malt palate with

tangerine fruit and wine-like notes, with dark malt dryness and light hops on the finish.

Strong bitter

Fuller's ESB (Extra Special Bitter, 5.5%). Dark amber with a distinctive nutty, hoppy and liquorice-tinged aroma, rich malt, pine and generous orange fruit on the palate, and a long warm finish with malty weight and emerging pepper hops.

Dark bitter

This isn't a widely-recognised beer style, but a number of London brewers offer notably dark beers broadly in the bitter category that make for interesting comparisons when considered together.

East London ELB Nightwatchman (4.5%). Ruby brown with a berry and liquorice toffee aroma, rye bread and pine on an earthy palate, and a drying leafy finish with toffee hints.

Fuller's Gales HSB (Horndean Special Bitter, 4.8%). Brown with nuts and toffee, rich slightly syrupy malt and a slightly astringent finish with blackcurrant and roast notes.

Redemption Urban Dusk (4.6%). Chestnut-brown with fruit, chocolate and nutty, sappy malt, a bite of roast and a chewy finish with herbs and brown sugar.

throughout with a rosehip tartness, with hints of dark ginger on a nutty finish.

Tap East East End Mild (3.5%). Currently the only occasionally-brewed mild in London recognisable to the 1970s drinker, this dark ruby beer has notes of liquorice and straw with plenty of blackberry and apple fruit character and a lightly roasty bite.

MILD

Milds are usually assumed to be mild in terms of hop bitterness or strength, but originally mild meant 'fresh' and sweet, as opposed to matured acidic 'stale' beers like porter. Recognisably modern mild grew in popularity from the early 19th century but, as a cheaper beer with a downmarket 'flatcap' image, it later suffered in competition with bitter, particularly in upwardly mobile London. Mild retained a hold in the West Midlands and Northern England, where by the 1970s it was known as a low gravity, minimally hopped, malty, easy-drinking and usually dark beer optimised for refreshing factory workers.

Today mild is very much a niche drink and something of a threatened style. Promotions like CAMRA's Mild Month in May have helped sustain it, but it deserves to be more fully embraced by brewers and drinkers as a heritage beer that still has a lot to offer. No standalone London brewer currently brews a straightforward mild on a regular basis, though some have been reproduced from historic recipes. **Oscar Wilde**, with its Cockney rhyming slang name, is produced not that far outside London by Mighty Oak in Maldon, Essex, and is served in several East London outlets. See also under flavoured beers below for an interesting twist on the style.

Head in a Hat Trilby (4%). Not all milds were dark, as demonstrated by this orange-amber beer based on a 1935 London 'XX ale' recipe. Peach on the aroma, a thick nutty palate with vivid orange and other citric flavours and a subtle, lightly sweet finish.

Partizan X-Ale (6.1%). Another historic recreation, reflecting the former availability of mild in a variety of strengths. This dark brown beer has chocolate notes

GOLDEN ALE

Easy-drinking golden ales aren't a new invention – the original pale ales were golden in colour, though most of the draught bitters that developed from them took on a deeper, more amber appearance. By the 1990s, some British microbrewers were trying to wean drinkers off pale lager by brewing refreshingly crisp and clean lager-coloured ales, triggering a new proliferation of golden-hued cask ales. The trend has been further fuelled recently by the influence of US pale ales, which also tend to be lighter in colour, and it's become increasingly difficult to distinguish golden ales and pale-coloured bitters from the new breed of American Pale Ales (see below), particularly as many golden ales already contain US hops. The trio below are arguably more rooted in British beer culture than some, and work well from the cask.

Portobello VPA (4%). A yellow-golden, very easy-drinking beer with notes of elderflower, sweet grains and a refreshing lemon-grapefruit citrus character.

Redemption Trinity (3%). Three malts and three hops are used in this astoundingly flavoursome low gravity beer. Fresh grass,

citrus and a hint of rose on the floral aroma, then a chaffy palate with tropical fruit and even a note of smoke in a long, piny-bitter finish.

- **Twickenham Naked Ladies** (4.4%). A lovely grainy aroma with a note of tropical fruit, a crisp and tangy palate and assertive but balanced peppery bitterness in the finish.

PALE ALE

Pale-coloured beers have been around since the invention of coke in the 1640s made it easier to control the temperature at which malt was kilned. The best known pale ales are India Pale Ales, the robust, hoppy beers that dominated exports to India in the early 19th century, which originated in London (see Yeast Enders p122). These beers became popular in the domestic market too, though their strength and hop character were gradually whittled down. Some longstanding cask beers labelled IPA are still around today, though now indistinguishable from standard bitter, which itself is the result of a parallel evolution from 18th century pale ales. Some old-established breweries continued to refer to their bitters internally as pale ales until well into the second half of the 20th century.

Among the early successes of American craft brewers were beers based on English pale ales but using the more distinctive and assertive domestic hop varieties. Inspired by accounts of the original IPAs, brewers began boosting both strengths and hop additions to create distinctive 'hop-forward' beers that have since taken the international beer scene by storm. London now has the highest concentration of brewers in the country producing pale ales with liberal quantities of exotically-flavoured hops, not only from the US but from Australia and New Zealand.

Some London brewers are now making hop-focused pale ales with English and other European hops – both historical recreations using traditional varieties, and contemporary beers with more assertive local hops. And given the long-ingrained British habit of drinking in pints, it's not surprising that London brewers have been at the forefront of delivering hop impact in lower-strength beers. Some of these are designated 'Session IPAs', a term also used on the other side of the Atlantic where interest in flavoursome beers at lower gravities has been steadily growing. Others are simply developments of established UK styles like pale and golden ales.

Contemporary light ale

'Light ale' was historically the term used for the lowest strength pale ales. It could easily be reclaimed to describe a new wave of crisp, refreshing low-strength beers with well-defined hop character that are even lighter than Session IPAs.

Brodies Kiwi (3.8%) A delicately pale, summery beer focused on the character of New Zealand Nelson Sauvin hops, with a creamy aroma, vanilla, passion fruit and spicy grape flavours and a developing bitter tang.

The Kernel Table Beer (3%). A perfectly poised hazy golden beer with a light hoppy aroma, a crisp and cheerful pineapple-citrus palate, and a slightly peppery finish with lemon and mineral notes.

Weird Beard Little Things That Kill (3.5%). The hops in this beer change but it's always worth trying: a version with Citra, Summit and Mosaic had grapefruit, cleansing sharpness and just a hint of cattiness with a controlled bitterness.

Pale ale

These straightforward and refreshing
session pale ales lean equally towards
British cask traditions and a more
eclectic contemporary sensibility.

East London ELB Pale Ale (4%).
Surprisingly big, with orange on a
flowery and waxy aroma, a complex,
tangy and citric palate and grassy
bitterness on a slightly gritty finish.

Five Points Pale (4%). A golden beer
with rose, orange, grapefruit and
peach over crisp malt, and a lightly
bittering and spicy finish.
Southwark LPA (4%). A soft and very
drinkable pale gold beer with tasty
bready malt, plenty of lemon-citrus
character and quite a drying finish.

Amber ale

In the US, where most pale ales are golden,
'amber ale' indicates a contemporary-style ale
with a bit of coloured malt to deepen the
colour and malt character. In the UK, where
many standard session beers are amber-
coloured already, brewers tend to use the
term to mean a beer with the strength and
colour of a typical special bitter but with a
more assertive contemporary character.

Brixton Effra Ale (4.5%). Easy-drinking but
with plenty of character: a resinous
paraffin-tinged aroma, peach, orange and
a smear of hops on the palate, and an
earthy finish.
Moncada Notting Hill Amber (4.7%).
Grapefruit and exotic spice set up a full
cakey-malty palate that quickly turns
grapefruit-bitter, with a well-rounded
chewy finish.
Wild Card Jack of Clubs (4.5%). A flavoursome red-amber beer with fig roll biscuits,
marzipan and a dry, sappy finish reminiscent
of German Altbier.

India Pale Ale

Most new British-brewed IPAs use New World hops but a few brewers have either revived home-grown recipes from times before the hop content was reduced, or looked to new domestic hop varieties to add character without accumulating air miles.

Clarkshaws Phoenix Rising (4%). Not sold as an IPA but not far off pre-war specs for the style, this foregrounds the nutty, chocolate and lightly floral character of English Phoenix hops, with currant fruit, biscuit malt and a slightly oily, balanced bitterness.

Head in a Hat Tommy (4.2%). This 1914 London recipe demonstrates that even before World War I, IPAs were hoppier but not necessarily stronger than standard pale ales. Copious quantities of Whitbread Goldings Variety hops lend rich, burry spiced orange, hedgerow and lemon peel notes over creamy, honeyed malt.

Meantime India Pale Ale (7.4%). A strictly traditional IPA from one of London's pioneers of brewing innovation, with Kent Fuggles and Goldings hops. Brambly fruit, barley sugar, pineapple cubes and peaches with a powdery-dry finish.

Session IPA

Beavertown Neck Oil Session IPA (4.3%). Hazy yellow with grapefruit pith, pepper, pine, tobacco, earthy menthol and geranium notes and a superbly balanced finish.

Fourpure Session IPA (4.2%). Ripe mango and pine on the aroma, crushed pine kernels and lemon balm on a sweetish palate, with a lasting and perhaps just slightly too bitter finish.

American-style pale ale

I've included beers in a range of strengths here that display the intense aromas of New World hops while being a little less bitter than IPAs.

Beavertown Gamma Ray American Pale Ale (5.4%). This light amber beer with waxy pine, grapefruit, lemon marmalade and pineapple soothed by plenty of sweet malt has become a modern London classic.

Gipsy Hill Beatnik (3.8%). Hazy yellow with a grape and tropical fruit aroma, more exotic fruit on a full-bodied palate, and a lightly bitter lemon-jelly finish with black pepper, drinking particularly well from cask.

Kernel Pale Ale Centennial (5%). Geranium, peach and apple skins on the aroma herald a vividly fruity, citric palate with complex bitterness, and a tangerine hint in the finish.

Rocky Head Pale Ale (6.5%). An intoxicating burst of pineapple, passion fruit and grapefruit on the nose is followed by similarly fruity flavours over moussey pale malt, with a lightly dry roast touch on a long grapefruit finish.

American-style India Pale Ale

Brew by Numbers 05|01 India Pale Ale Amarillo & Citra (6.7%). A sulphur whiff over tangerine marmalade, notes of sweet onion and pepper on a richly malty palate and a slightly gritty, twiggy long-emerging bitterness on the finish.

Brixton Electric IPA (6.5%). Classic US-style with ripe apricot, pine, some toffee and full-on hops over slightly oily sweet malt on the palate, with a spicily hoppy finish.

Crate IPA (5.8%). Copper and more easy-going than most, including on cask, with muted fruit salad notes on the aroma, edgy hops on a rich, smooth and fruity palate, and a splash of lime in the finish.

Kernel India Pale Ale S C C A NS (6.8%). Earthy pine and passion fruit, a crisp and hoppy but controlled palate with more passion fruit and flowery notes and a peppery finish with biscuit malt showing through.

Black IPA

Some may baulk at the apparent contradiction of a black pale – indeed some brewers have tried to popularise the alternative term 'Cascadian Dark', without much success, and competition judging guidelines refer to it as 'American-style India Black Ale' – but once you taste one you'll understand exactly what is intended. It's an invented style, emerging from the USA in the last decade or so, combining the roast character of dark malts more familiar from dry stouts with the assertive aromas and flavours of contemporary hop varieties. It's a difficult balancing act, with a real danger of hop bitterness unpleasantly clashing with the dryness and acidity of the malts. But the best ones are tantalising if approached with an open mind. **Windsor & Eton Conqueror**, brewed just outside London, is another fine example.

Brodies Dalston Black IPA (7%). A beautiful balance of chocolate, dark cake and toffee with pine, citrus, liquorice and exotic fruit, and immaculately-controlled bitterness.

Bullfinch Notorious (7%). New Zealand hops add tropical and citrus flavours to this deep brown beer, with a fine bitter chocolate note in the finish.

Double IPA

The terms 'double', 'triple' and sometimes 'Imperial' indicate ever-stronger and hoppier pale ales, creating beers to approach with caution: the best are balanced and immensely complex, though definitely for contemplative sipping rather than swigging.

Weird Beard Holy Hoppin' Hell (9.6%). The hops in this change from brew to brew but always exhibit good judgement. A version with Green Bullet, Nelson Sauvin and Pacific Gem had a huge peach and tropical fruit aroma, with passion fruit, lemon and petrol on the palate and almost a coffee hint to the hop bitterness.

RED ALE

Another style name without too specific a
meaning other than to indicate a vaguely
reddish colour, this overlaps with amber ale.
Some London brewers add rye to the mix –
see also Rye beer below.

By the Horns Diamond Geezer (4.9%). An
aromatically malty aroma with hop notes,
a smooth and substantial palate with a
tangy bite, and a lightly nutty finish.

Five Points Hook Island Red (6%). Hints of
strawberry, chocolate, roast and a chewy,
lingering bitter grapefruit finish.

London Brewing Vista (4.5%). Plenty of fruit
cake malt supports citrus and floral hops
in this satisfyingly grainy dry-hopped ale.

SAISON

A few years ago, a section headed 'saison' in a
summary of London beer styles would have
been pointless – but that was before an unpretentious Belgian regional speciality became
the *style du jour* of the world's craft brewing
community. Originally, *saison* was a term
applied to golden ales brewed on farms in
Wallonia, the French-speaking part of Belgium,
for the refreshment of farm workers. Without
refrigeration it was impossible to brew successfully in the summer, so beers were made in
winter and laid down until summer – the term
simply means 'season'. The style was commer-
cialised from the end of the 19th century and
during the 20th century, in common with other
Belgian styles, strengths went up to compete
with cheaper spirits.

The generally accepted benchmark is
Saison Dupont, from Tourpes, actually quite a
clean-tasting, though beautifully balanced and
tasty, golden beer. Brewers in the USA were
inspired not just by imported Dupont but by
more eccentric interpretations, such as
Prignon Fantôme, often using flavourings and
exhibiting 'funky' wild yeast characteristics.
So saison has become a hard style to pin down
– it's usually golden, it's usually made with a
Belgian yeast, often derived from the Dupont
yeast, but there are numerous variations,
including examples made entirely with wild
yeast. The foremost London brewers of the
style are closer to Belgium and more directly
influenced by native saisons, but they're by
no means above a little creative license.

Brew by Numbers 01|07 Saison Citra (5.4%).
A gold beer with a pillowy white head, a
big citrus aroma and a slightly funky and
tart note on a lemon palate, with a lightly
bitter and refreshing finish.

Partizan Saison Grisette (4.8%). Inspired by
a related, amber-coloured style once
popular among Wallonian industrial
workers that all but disappeared in the
1950s, this delicious deep gold beer has
lemon thyme on the aroma, cracker malt,
rhubarb and custard on the palate and a
lingering spicy-malty finish.

Strawman Saison (3.9%). A pale straw beer
with a grassy, lime-splashed lagery aroma,
a crisp and lightly lemon-fruity palate and
cleansing, juicy finish with just a hint of
bitterness.

BROWN ALE

Beer historian Martyn Cornell calls brown ale one of the oldest beer styles, dating from a time when the only malts available produced brown-coloured beers. By the early 20th century, brown ales in London and southern England tended to be sweet, low alcohol bottled products like Mann's, related to dark milds, with a stronger, drier style popular in the northeast of England. Several Belgian brown ales are soured by long maturation in wooden vessels, rather like porter once was. Once again US brewers have found new ways of approaching all these beers, discovering that fruitier hops work particularly well against a sweet and biscuity darker malt base. The examples below take a contemporary rather than a traditional approach.

Brew by Numbers 09|02 Nut Brown Ale (6.3%). Faintly reminiscent of Yorkshire brown ales, this has generous chocolate and hazelnut malts, a firm dry palate and slightly minty and phenolic cranberry notes, with a fruit flourish on a long roast nut and coffee finish.

Pressure Drop Stokey Brown (4.9%). Tropical fruit, chocolate and smoky cedar twigs introduce soft fruit, grapefruit, coffee and hop resins in this satisfying and complex beer.

BARLEY WINE

'Barley wine' is used loosely as a general term for any ale, other than a porter or stout, with a strength approaching that of wine (7–11%). Strong beers have a long history in Britain, going back at least to the 16th century when the nobility cellared them in their homes. In the 19th century the strongest beers, often matured in the brewery for a year before release, were known as 'stock ales', and the current term dates only from the 1950s. Beers at this strength, if left unfiltered and unpasteurised, can go on maturing for a long time, developing a variety of complex flavours like a fine wine.

Fuller's Vintage Ale (8.5%). One of London's world class beers, this has been produced annually since 1997 in bottle conditioned form, with a recipe that changes slightly from year to year but is always simple and traditional and uses top quality ingredients. Big and mouth-numbing when young, with earthy and peppery hop flavours and the characteristic orange tang of the Fuller's yeast, it mellows beautifully after a few years, developing sherry and port notes over a smooth but complex mix of nuts, fruit and minerals.

Sambrook's No 5 Barley Wine (8.2%). First produced to mark the fifth anniversary of the brewery in 2014, this will also age grace-fully, with rich nutty malt, olive, cherry and orange notes and a lengthy chocolate truffle finish with rounded bitterness.

PORTER & STOUT

Porter was the first international beer style and the first industrial one, developed in London in the early 18th century (see City of Brewing p 12). It came in two forms – 'stale' porter matured for months and even years in oak vats, and a fresher 'mild' porter, with the two often mixed to customers' tastes by bar staff. As the 19th century progressed, 'stale' porter decreased in importance and more and more left the brewery gates as 'mild' beer.

Porter spread worldwide, proving equally popular in the cold Baltic and the warmer climes of the Caribbean and sub-Saharan Africa. Most famously it spread to Ireland, where the local variant flourished as its parent style declined towards the end of the 19th century, unable to meet the challenge from milds and bitters. The decline was a slow one but by 1958 porter brewing had ceased completely in Great Britain.

Porter came in a variety of strengths: 'plain' porter was weaker while 'stout' porter was stronger. The stronger version resisted the decline longer and eventually the term 'stout' came to be used in its own right. The original meaning of 'stout' as 'strong' was eventually forgotten, and as beer strengths in the British Isles declined overall, stout's original strength was forgotten too.

In 1978, partly inspired by Michael Jackson's musings on beer styles, a few British brewers started to experiment with approximations of old recipes, soon joined by colleagues in other countries. Porter has since comprehensively re-established itself as a modern specialist style though almost entirely in its 'mild' form.

Today, there's no consistent distinction between porters and stouts. Standard stouts are often inspired by the Irish variety – very dark brown, smooth, dry, with chocolate and coffee flavours, some of them with the bitter crack of roasted barley that's so distinctive in the versions brewed across the Irish Sea.

The term 'porter' tends to be used for beers that are broadly similar in character but where the brewer wants to avoid invoking a comparison with Irish stout. Some people argue that stouts should derive more of their bitterness from roast grains, while porters should present more hop bitterness, but this is by no means a generally accepted rule. There's a growing fashion, too, for adding raw or malted oats to the recipe, which lend a notably smooth texture. In this case, the resulting beer is usually known as an oatmeal or oat malt stout rather than a porter.

While most porters and stouts are now at relatively sessionable strengths of 4–5% ABV, more brewers, including a notable few in London, are once again ascending the scale of gravity, often using 19th century recipes. The most celebrated very strong, and notably hoppy, historic porter is Imperial stout at 9% or 10% ABV or more, originally developed in the late 18th century for export to Russia and the Baltic. Porters and stouts at slightly less daunting strengths of around 6–8% are sometimes termed 'Export'.

At the other end of the scale, low gravity (2–3%) sweet stouts, including milk stouts made with lactose, were popular in the early 20th century, and are now being reinvented by some adventurous brewers, though rarely at their original very low strengths. Baltic porters, another strand to the style, are porter-like beers brewed using lager yeasts, following the example of Baltic countries that adopted the style.

The thorough resuscitation of porter and stout is one of the great success stories of the brewing renaissance. Practically all London brewers have at least one example in their repertoire, often more, and the quality and diversity are remarkable. True, no-one has yet attempted staling porter in vats in 18th century fashion, though there have been some experiments with barrel ageing, and the idea has certainly crossed some brewers' ever-fertile minds. Porter has not only been brought back from the dead, it's come home.

Table porter

Anspach & Hobday The Table Porter (2.8%). Porter was once made both at very low as well as very high strengths so this modern low gravity version has a historical precedent. A remarkably flavoursome beer with subtle additions of fruity, flowery US hops alongside brown bread and lightly bitter, roasty flavours.

Session porter

These easy-drinking porters work particularly well from cask.

Brockley Porter (4.3%). Notably smoky with gravy hints, coffee, cake and a smooth finish with notes of chocolate and a late whiff of wood ash, full and balanced.

Gipsy Hill Dissident (4.8%). Caramel and liquorice aroma, cola and wood notes in a lightly burnt, toffeeish palate and apple and blackcurrant notes in the finish.

Redemption Fellowship Porter (5.1%). A substantial but soft example with tangy notes balancing the sweetness, chocolate and fruit and a lingering coffee finish.

Sambrook's Powerhouse Porter (4.7%). Dark chestnut with liquorice and sticky dark malt, blackcurrant notes and a slightly cindery finish, though not as roasty as some.

Strong porter

Anspach & Hobday The Porter (6.7%). A huge chocolate, malt loaf, vanilla and sultana aroma, a luxuriant chocolate palate and a complex finish with the bite of roast malt and returning vanilla notes.

Hop Stuff Gunners Porter (7.4%). Look out for aged versions, with wine and rum-like notes joining woody, nutty dark malt and chocolate marzipan, and a lightly warming finish.

Meantime London Porter (6.5%). Leather and roast chestnut on the aroma, a chocolate mousse palate with slightly peppery hops and light fruit and a sappy, very lightly acidic finish with salt and blackcurrant hints.

Session stout

Dragonfly Dark Matter (4.3%). A slightly dusty coffee-tinged aroma, a smooth palate with light roast notes and a stab of intense dryness on a chocolate-caramel finish.

Moncada Notting Hill Stout (5%). This oatmeal stout has a firm roasted character while remaining smooth and very drinkable, with chocolate, liquorice and light fruit.

Signature Black Vinyl Stout (4.2%). A relatively light-bodied interpretation with plenty of roasted malt, cocoa and fruity sweetness, turning notably roasty in the finish. Happily doesn't taste like vinyl.

Stronger stout

East London ELB Quadrant (5.8%). A collaboration with national homebrew competition winners, a silky and sweetish oatmeal stout with berry flavours and dry but controlled roast notes.

Redchurch Hoxton Stout (6%). Spicy liquorice aroma, piny hop notes on a brown bread and toffee palate and a long lingering coffee finish with more hops and a roasted barley bite.

Weird Beard Decadence (5.5%). A lusciously chocolately example made from a complex mix of grains, with plenty of tangy fruit, leady malt and almost a blue cheese note.

Speciality stout

Big Smoke Underworld Milk Stout (5%). Lactose adds toothiness and more of a milk chocolate note to this smooth but still dry stout.

Hammerton Oyster Stout (5.3%). Real Maldon oysters added to the boil are detectable but surprisingly successful in this briny, slightly minty stout that still has plenty of chocolate and coffee character.

Export stout

Brew by Numbers 08|01 Export Strength Stout* (7.4%). An intense mahogany beer with raisins and creamy coffee in the aroma, a perfumed palate and plain chocolate digestive notes in a superbly-balanced bittersweet finish.

The Kernel Export Stout London 1890 (7.8%). A cakey malt aroma with notes of tobacco and sulphur, with nettly, herbal flavours on a treacle and chocolate palate, and a beautiful roast dryness emerging in a long, rich and fruity finish.

Partizan Stout FES (8.7%). A thick and divinely fruity black stout: blackcurrant, soft fruit, tar and liquorice notes, balanced roast and a chewy, sticky burnt cake finish.

Imperial stout

Kernel Imperial Brown Stout London 1856 (10.1%). A dark brown beer leaving lots of lace, with aroma and palate rich in chocolate, prunes, caramel, liquorice, treacle and tingling alcohol. Charred notes emerge over rich malt in a long and elegant finish.

WHEAT BEER

Wheat has been used as a brewing grain since prehistory, but historically its use has often been regulated or prohibited to protect stocks for baking, and brewers have found barley more versatile and easier to work with. Wheat beer was once common in England, particularly in the southwest, only finally disappearing in the 1870s. By the 1960s it seemed in terminal decline elsewhere, limited to a few shrinking enclaves in Belgium and Germany. Then an obsolete style was revived in the village of Hoegaarden near Brussels and suddenly wheat beer was a young drink again.

Wheat beer is a warm-fermented ale style that's typically served unfiltered, unpasteurised and cloudy with suspended yeast. Belgian 'white beer' is made with unmalted wheat and spiced, typically with coriander and dried orange peel, giving a smooth milky quality with an orange tang. Bavarian Weißbier or Weizenbier is made with malted wheat and no spices, but has characteristic bubblegum, banana or clove flavours from the yeast. As well as the standard version, there are also dark and filtered variants. Brewers elsewhere, including in London, readily venture outside traditional boundaries, so you'll find wheat beers made with Bavarian yeast but with additional spicing, or hybrids with more traditional English ales.

Germany is also home to a couple of regional styles that were on the point of extinction before catching the imagination of the international craft brewing scene. Berliner Weisse is a low gravity wheat beer that undergoes a lactic fermentation, giving it a distinctive sourness. In the German capital it's usually sweetened with raspberry or woodruff syrup. A few London brewers now regularly produce beers inspired by the style, and some have further experimented with Gose, a wheat beer from Lower Saxony flavoured with coriander and salt.

Camden Town Gentlemen's Wit (4.3%). Belgian-inspired but flavoured with roast lemons and bergamot, this has a blossomy citrus aroma and a very crisp and clean palate, with perfumed tea and vanilla in the finish.

Pressure Drop Wu Gang Chops the Tree (3.8%). At base a Bavarian-style wheat but flavoured with foraged herbs, this is a delightfully moreish beer with notes of ginger, fennel, citrus and chamomile over a soft, wheaty backdrop with a delicate bitterness.

The Kernel London Sour (3.8%). Based on the Berlin style with a smacky lemon-tinged aroma, and notes of pomegranate and tobacco on a mildly soured palate. Hints of citrus and brown sugar on a refreshing finish.

RYE BEER

Alongside wheat, rye is one of several brewing grains eclipsed by the ubiquity of barley, though it continued in localised use, lending a distinctive spicy and oily note to Bavarian Roggenbier and the Finnish folk beer, sahti. More recently brewers have discovered it works well with certain hops, particularly in combination with deeper-hued barley malts that give a supporting biscuit body. Some brewers add rye to beers labelled 'red', so there's some overlap with this category.

Beavertown 8-Ball Rye IPA (6.2%).
A red-amber beer with a spicy overripe fruit aroma, a cracker-dry palate with confectionery notes and a mouth-filling soft malt finish with spreading hop bitterness.

Brewhouse & Kitchen Triple A Rye Beer (5%). Deep gold with varnished wood and nuts on the aroma, an almost whisky-like spicy cracker palate and a fruity, slightly stony finish.

Bullfinch RyPA (5.8%). Dark orange in colour, with vivid fruit and spice on a tea-like palate, and raisiny fruit in a balanced bitter finish.

SMOKED BEER

In the days when malt was still regularly dried over wood fires, smoky notes would have been common in beer. Brewing with smoked malt persisted into the modern era in a few isolated pockets, notably Bamberg in Upper Franconia, a rural and culturally distinct part of Bavaria where several idiosyncratic brewing styles and practices have survived. Here, smoked malt is deployed in lager styles like amber Märzen and dark Bockbier, but it's re-entered the international craft brewing lexicon in a variety of contexts, including brown ale and porter – appropriately as historically these beers would have included a proportion of smoky, wood-fired malts.

Anspach & Hobday The Smoked Brown (6%). A roast nut and smoky toffee aroma, then a full, rich and earthy palate with controlled smoky flavours and a dry, toasty finish.

Howling Hops Smoked Porter (5.2%). Piny hops blend surprisingly well with smoky malts in this toffee and liquorice beer that finishes moderately bitter.

WILD & SOUR BEERS

Beer probably originated when grain porridge or bread soaked in water or milk was fermented unintentionally by wild yeasts, perhaps drifting over from nearby fruit. Today most brewers strive to control fermentation as closely as possible with carefully nurtured yeast cultures – but in the lambic breweries in the Zenne valley to the west and south of Brussels and a couple of other pockets of Belgium, spontaneous fermentation has been retained as a commercial brewing practice. Here, wort is left out overnight to become infected with a complex mix of airborne yeasts and bacteria, then fermented and matured for anything up to three years in wooden vats and casks in which still more microflora have established themselves. Such beers are rarely drunk in their native form: they're sweetened with sugar, or blended, or steeped with fruit like sour cherries and raspberries.

Lambics and other sour traditional styles like Flemish brown ales, a distant relative of the original vatted porters, and Berliner Weisse (see above), have prompted great excitement among many contemporary brewers and more adventurous drinkers. The use of wild yeasts, lactic cultures and wood ageing is now one of the fastest growing phenomena on the international craft beer scene. Very few brewers outside Belgium have attempted genuine spontaneous fermentation (Elgood's in Wisbech, Cambridgeshire, is one exception). Most brewers use pre-prepared mixed cultures or rely on residual yeasts and bacteria in barrels working their magic on more conventional beers. The results tend to emerge in small quantities as one-offs and specials but the beers below are produced on a relatively regular basis and are consistently good.

Beavertown Appleation Barley Champagne (8.7%). A warm gold partly wild beer made with Bramley apples and refermented in a big 650 ml bottle, with apple, orange, lemon and funky notes, wafts of pear and fruit salad, then vanilla emerging on a smooth and creamy finish.

Rocky Head Hop Ditch (6%). A sweet blueberry custard aroma with tropical fruit and a hint of 'wet dog' funkiness, with cardamom, tobacco and pink pepper on a tannic palate and ripe peach and lemon on a lightly sour and citric finish.

FLAVOURED BEER

Before hops became ubiquitous, brewers deployed a huge variety of flavourings. There are records of fruit beers from ancient Egypt, and in the mediaeval Low Countries whole fortunes were made on closely-guarded herb and spice blends for beer, known as *gruut* or *gruit*. Fruit and spiced beers persisted in Belgium in particular to fire the imaginations of today's brewers, with flavourings now almost invariably used alongside, rather than instead of, hops. The results can be variable – flavours sometimes clash, or the additions overwhelm everything, but skilled hands can achieve great things. Spiced wheat beers are dealt with above, but here are some other good examples of the more adventurous side of London brewing.

East London ELB Orchid (3.6%). A dark mild infused with Madagascan vanilla pods, highlighting chocolate flavours on a gentle palate, with a flash of roast and light hops on the finish.

Head in a Hat Gin (4.1%). A golden ale with juniper and other 'botanicals' taken directly from the still at the City Of London distillery, with subtly perfumed bready malt and tart red berries.

Meantime Raspberry Wheat (5%). Taking its inspiration from both German and Belgian brewing, this cloudy pinkish beer is notably dry and refreshing, with defined but not overpowering raspberry perfume and drying almond on the finish.

Partizan Grisette Lemongrass Lychee (3.9%). An inspired pale yellow saison, with the added flavours complementing fruity New World hops on the aroma, saffron-like notes, and a smacky, refreshing finish with spiced lemon and vanilla.

Tap East Coffee in the Morning (5.2%).
With the roasted malts in porters and stouts already invoking coffee flavours, it's not surprising that several brewers have taken to adding real coffee, often in collaboration with specialist roasters. This example uses El Salvadorean beans from Grind to create a good blend of chocolate, black coffee, herbs and burnt cake notes, with a hint of rum.

Upstairs Arabian Nights (5.4%). This unusual milk stout 'cuckoo'-brewed at Clarence & Fredericks includes rye and lactose as well as black cardamons, subtly employed to add spiced tea notes to a rich, chocolate and treacle base.

LAGER

To many British drinkers, lager is a particular kind of gold, sparkling beer, invariably pasteurised, with a straightforward, clean, lightly malty, if not bland and boring, palate and a bit of grassy hop character. But the term lager designates a whole family of beers initially perfected in Bavaria, Austria and the Czech lands, fermented slowly at low temperatures using particular strains of yeast and then tank-conditioned at near-freezing for a notably smooth and clean-tasting result. Lagers can be gold, black, weak, strong and many other things, including unpasteurised, unfiltered and refermented.

Lager brewing in Britain goes back further than most people think, at least to the 1870s. But lager lagged far behind ale in popularity until the late 1960s when the big brewing groups began to throw their massive marketing weight behind characterless, low gravity golden lagers. Lager has outsold ale in Britain since 1989, but at the expense of discrediting itself in the eyes of discriminating British drinkers.

Commercial British lagers are invariably low-strength golden beers very loosely derived from the Pils and Helles styles, but elsewhere there are a large variety of alternative styles. Among others, Germany has unfiltered and unpasteurised lagers Kellerbier and Zoigl; stronger and sometimes deeper-coloured Märzen and Oktoberfest beers; lightly toasty and caramelly dark lager or Dunkel; very dark and roasty though rarely bitter Schwarzbier ('black beer'); and strong, malty and usually dark seasonal beers called Bock. The Czech Republic has an equally fine-grained range.

London has a history of pioneering the brewing of 'craft lager' in the UK using traditional methods and quality ingredients, and now a number of brewers in the capital are helping redeem the reputation of British lager. So far most attention is on the pale side, though darker and stronger beers are wont to appear as specials, and Zerodegrees brews a regular black lager. The examples listed below are not only made with appropriate ingredients and yeasts, but properly lagered for a reasonable time.

Pale lager

Camden Town Unfiltered Hells (4.6%).
A Helles that leans towards a Pils, with traditional German hop varieties, this is delicately pale with pollen, lemon and sacky notes, crisp hops and a slightly flowery finish, at its best a rival to many a German brew.

Meantime Brewery Fresh Lager (4.5%).
A blend of German and English ingredients gives a cereal aroma with grassy hops, a crisp and very lightly fruity and citric palate and a gentle vanilla wafer finish.

Redchurch London Lager (5%). Exotic hops lend passion fruit, citrus and lychee notes and big bittering resins o this crisp gold beer.

Pilsner

Pilsners are named after the West Bohemian city of Plzeň, or Pilsen in German, where this style of pale lager was first perfected in 1842. In the Czech Republic no-one would dream of applying the term to a beer from anywhere else, but in the rest of the world it's a designation that's become much debased. It should indicate a crisp, clean beer with a pronounced hop bite compared to more standard lagers.

Brick Peckham Pils (4.8%). An authentically grassy 'noble' hop aroma gets this off to a good start, with lime and vanilla notes on a grainy palate and a custardy finish with rooty bitterness.

Fourpure Pils (4.7%). This spicy beer is hopped more in accordance with modern tastes but with traditional varieties, with a grainy vanilla backdrop supporting a pronounced but balanced bitterness with lemon-drop notes.

Zerodegrees Pilsner (4.8%). Hazy and unfiltered, with a notably intense grassy hop aroma, a smooth palate with lime and resin notes and a gentler than expected finish.

Other styles

Brick Archway Steam California Common (4.5%). Steam beer, or California Common as it's now known in beer competitions, is a hybrid style that originated in Gold Rush-era San Francisco when immigrant German brewers were forced to use lager yeasts at warm temperatures as they had no access to refrigeration. The surviving historic example is Anchor Steam, which played a major role in the growth of the craft brewing movement. This Peckham-brewed example is biscuity with hints of orange, and an authentic peppery bitterness from Northern Brewer hops.

Head in a Hat Florence Stoat (5.8%). Before Burton upon Trent became associated with hoppy pale ales, it was famous for a deep amber, sweeter style which was imitated across the country, including in London, as Burton Ale. Burton survived well into the 20th century but then became almost completely forgotten, though Young's seasonal Winter Warmer, now brewed outside London, is a derivative. Among the historic recreations is this warming example, with a fruit pastille and raspberry aroma and a vinous quality with notes of whisky and dessert wine.

Orbit Neu (4.7%). Warm-fermented pale ales akin to British and Belgian styles are still brewed in the west of Germany, though they're now given a lengthy conditioning at low temperatures like lagers. They include delicate golden ale Kölsch in Cologne and dark amber, more malt-accented Altbier (literally 'old beer') in Düsseldorf. This is a decent rendering of the latter, named after a Krautrock band from the city that were an early spinoff from Kraftwerk. A biscuity aroma and palate have gentle pine and ginger notes and there's a fruit hint and a hum of crisp hops in the finish.

BREWERIES

Introduction

The following pages give details of all 70 London breweries active at the time this book went to press, alongside a few London-based beer firms without their own brewing kit, and breweries in development that are likely to be in operation by the time you read this.

By London breweries, I mean businesses with their own brewing equipment on its own site within the official boundaries of Greater London, producing beer for sale to the public. Separate brewing sites owned by the same company are counted separately; installations used by several different companies are counted only once.

By the time the book is published the situation is highly likely to have changed, so please check for updates at **www.desdemoor.co.uk/london**. Other good sources of information about London breweries are the London Brewers Alliance at **www.londonbrewers.org** and the independent site **www.beerguidelondon.co.uk**.

LocAle

LocAle is a CAMRA accreditation scheme with the praiseworthy aim of promoting pubs that sell locally-brewed cask beer, supporting consumer interest in local products and reducing the environmental impacts of transporting beers long distances. The CAMRA London branches recognise a pub as LocAle if it regularly stocks at least one cask beer brewed within 30 miles (48 km) of its front door, which for pubs on the edge of the Greater London boundary could include products from a significant distance outside London. Since there are now so many breweries *within* the boundary I've not attempted to list all these potential LocAle contenders, but I have appended details of three important breweries just outside the boundary whose beers regularly appear in London pubs. A full list of LocAle-accredited pubs can be found at **www.london.camra.org.uk**.

Brewery category

Brewpub. A brewery on the same premises as a pub or bar, principally brewing for in-house sales.

Microbrewery. An independently-owned small brewery (not part of a national or international group) established since the emergence of the modern beer consumer movement in the 1970s.

Independent. An independently-owned brewery established before the emergence of the modern beer consumer movement. London has only one such brewery.

Multinational. A subsidiary of a major multinational beer group. Again there's only one example left in London.

Beer firm. A company that develops and markets its own brands of beer, but doesn't own any kit on which to brew them. There are a variety of possible levels of engagement with the actual brewing, and brewers themselves increasingly make the distinction between 'contractors', who commission another brewery to brew to their specifications and leave them to get on with it, and 'cuckoo' or 'gypsy' brewers who temporarily take over someone else's brewing kit and do all the hands-on work themselves. Cuckoos work mainly in one brewery, while gypsies move between several, but the differences aren't precise and there are several shades in between.

Such arrangements are sometimes viewed with suspicion, but brewing kit and premises are expensive and taking advantage of someone else's facilities can be a good way for people with skills and ideas but little capital to establish themselves. Several London breweries have used cuckoo brewing or contracting as a stepping stone to owning their own kit, and so long as everyone is open and honest about where the beer is brewed, there's no reason to object to the practice.

Formats and facilities

I've used symbols to indicate the various ways in which the brewery conditions and packages its beer. For more background on this, see Packaging and dispense, p 251.

- ⊟ Cask beer
- ⊟ 'Craft keg' – unpasteurised and often unfiltered keg beer, keykeg etc
- ⊟ Standard pasteurised keg beer
- ⬩ Bottle conditioned beer
- ◌ Other bottled beer
- ⬩ 'Craft cans' – unpasteurised beer in cans

Facilities are shown as follows:

- 🛒 Shop selling beer to take away, and quite likely other products like branded merchandise
- 🍶 Taproom selling beer to drink on site
- ⬩ You can visit the brewery itself. This ranges from formal guided tours to the fact that the brewhouse is in the same space as the taproom and staff are happy to talk about it informally if they have time.
- ⊸ Beer is sold by mail order through the brewery website, either directly or via a customised link to a third party site

Don't assume all these facilities will be available at all times! Most taprooms are only open for limited hours and some brewery tours are booked up months in advance. Check the listings here and in the Places to Drink section for more details, and see the brewery website or call if necessary.

Location and contact details

The **London borough** (or other local authority outside London) where the brewery is located is given in brackets after the address.

Contact details for breweries use the same symbols and conventions as for Places to drink (p 32).

Most brewpubs, taprooms and brewery shops also have an entry in the Places to Drink section and **page references** direct you to it.

First sold beer. Some brewery reference sources quote start dates based on the first brew, but I prefer to show the date when the brewery first sold its beer to the public, as breweries are really only of interest to most drinkers once you can actually enjoy their work. Producing drinkable beer always takes at least a couple of weeks, or longer depending on the style, and teething troubles with new breweries can sometimes result in a significant gap between the first brew and the first beer that the brewer is happy to invite people to part with their money for.

Beer selection and rating

I've aimed to give a good idea of the beer on offer from each brewery, listing regular beers and mentioning significant seasonals and specials, with an indication of style, and the percentage of alcohol by volume in brackets where known. This is a challenge with some breweries that regularly change recipes, but I've done my best. Note, though, that these details are all highly likely to change: breweries are businesses and will adapt rapidly if a beer intended as a one-off proves particularly successful, or sales of an established regular are faltering.

- * Indicates a beer particularly worth trying
- ** Indicates an exceptional beer that all beer lovers should try at least once.

This doesn't mean that none of the brewery's other beers are worth trying. Though based on relatively extensive tasting experience and some expertise, these assessments are ultimately personal and subjective ones. You may disagree with me, or one of the brewery's other beers may suit you or your mood better. And though most London brewers now strive for consistency, they don't always achieve it. Sometimes a brewer can have a particularly good day with a normally underperforming recipe, and sometimes a recipe is tweaked with significantly improved results. The reverse can be the case too.

For more detailed tasting notes on selected beers, see the London beer styles section, p 257.

London breweries

AB InBev UK (Stag)
Multinational 📖 🍾
Lower Richmond Road SW14 7ET (Richmond upon Thames)   www.ab-inbev.co.uk
First sold beer: 1641

The last remnant of big brewing in London and one of only two active breweries in the capital dating from before the 21st century, though likely to close during the currency of this book. For more on its history see 'Roll out the red barrel' p 100.

Beers. Only mass-produced rice lager 'American' **Budweiser** (5%).

Aeronaut
See Laine Brewing (Acton)

Anspach and Hobday
Microbrewery 📖 🍺 🍴 | 🛒 🔪 🏭
118 Druid Street SE1 2HH (Southwark)
T (020) 8617 9510
www.anspachandhobday.com
🅵 Anspachandhobday 🐦 anspachhobday
First sold beer: February 2014   *See also* p 66

Jack Hobday and Paul Anspach are musicians and keen homebrewers who were inspired to take the next step when their porter was praised by beer and wine writer Oz Clarke. Tasting samples were available under the name Alements in summer 2012 but it wasn't until March 2014 that, with the help of crowd funding, they successfully launched their brewery and taproom in a Bermondsey arch. Bullfinch also regularly brews here.

Beers: Noted for dark beers: signature brew is **The Porter*** (6.7%). There's also a **Table Porter*** (2.8%) an **IPA** (6%) and an excellent **Smoked Brown*** (6%) plus various specials: this is possibly the first London brewery to attempt an American Cream Ale.

Antelope
See Big Smoke

Barnet Brewery
Brewpub 📖 🍺 | 🛒 🔪 🏭
92 Wood Street, Barnet EN5 4HY (Barnet)
See also Black Horse pub p 150
T (020) 8449 2230   🐦 TheBlackHorsePH
www.blackhorsebarnet.co.uk/brewery
🅵 The-Black-Horse-Barnet
First sold beer: March 2013

This Barnet brewpub has a refurbished 2.5 hl (1.5 barrel) brewhouse supplied by Iceni in Norfolk, with some vessels originally from the Federation Brewery in Newcastle, and draws on the experience of XT Brewery in Thame, Oxfordshire, in the same group.

Beers: Mainly session-strength (4%) golden ales and bitters for sale in the pub but there are occasional bottlings of strong and wood-aged beers such as old ale **Reluctant Prophet** (8%).

Bear Hug Brewery
Beer firm 📖 🍺
9 Gowlett Road SE15 4HX (Southwark)
T 07979 802433 www.bearhugbrewing.com
🅵 bearhugbrewing 🐦 BearHugBrewco
First sold beer: February 2014

After a fruitless search for premises and brewing on a pilot kit for festival sales, this Peckham-based team have settled on 'cuckoo' status for the time being, largely at Gadd's in Ramsgate, Kent, with the lager created at Schremser in Austria. They've also partnered with gourmet burger popup and occasional brewer BurgerBear to create a gourmet burger and craft beer bar, Stokey Bears, in Stoke Newington. A mead is planned, as well as a standalone brewery eventually. Some profits help support the Green Square scheme to preserve rain forest.

Beers: Mainly bottled, including pilsner **Bruno** (4.2%), **Spirit Pale Ale** (4.2%), **Himalayan Red Rye Ale** (5%) and the distinctively cloudy wheat beer-pale ale hybrid **Hibernation White IPA*** (5.2%).

Beavertown Brewery

Microbrewery
17 Lockwood Industrial Park, Mill Mead Road
N17 9QP (Haringey)   **T** (020) 3696 1441
www.beavertownbrewery.co.uk
BeavertownBeer
First sold beer: February 2012   *See also* p148

One of London's most admired and fastest-growing breweries, expanding twice in less than three years. See feature p149.

Beers: The core range of excellent contemporary beers are flagship American pale ale **Gamma Ray*** (5.4%), **Neck Oil Session IPA**** (4.3%), **Smog Rocket Smoked Porter***(5.4%), **8 Ball Rye IPA*** (6.2%) and **Black Betty Black IPA*** (7.4%). There are numerous seasonals, collaborations and specials including limited editions made on a pilot brewkit and often only sold through the brewery taproom and linked pub Dukes (p142). In summer the deliciously

refreshing **Quelle Dry-Hopped Saison** (4.4%) appears. Look too for extraordinary stuff in the Alpha series including **Appleation**** wood-aged "barley champagne" (8.7%).

Belleville Brewing

Microbrewery
36 Jaggard Way SW12 8SG (Wandsworth)
T 07712 298 273   bellevillebrew
www.bellevillebrewing.co.uk
First sold beer: March 2013

This 8 hl (5 barrel) brewery near Wandsworth Common was set up by 10 fathers with children at Belleville school, led by musician Adrian Thomas, and soon established a thriving local trade for its vaguely US-influenced beers. In June 2013 the brewery received a legal threat from AB InBev, alleging infringement of the trademark for its mass-produced sweetened Belgian lambic Belle Vue. Following national publicity, the threat was sensibly withdrawn.

Beers: The signature beer is the hard-to-categorise brownish session ale **Battersea Brownstone** (4.8%). Other regulars are **Northcote Blonde** (4.2%), **Chestnut Porter*** (4.9%), **Commonside Pale** (5%), **Thames Surfer** IPA (5.7%), and, unusually, a German-inspired black lager, **Balham Black** (4.6%), plus seasonals and specials.

Bexley Brewery

Microbrewery 🍺 🍴 🛒 🔨

18 Manford Industrial Estate, Manor Road,
Erith DA8 2AJ (Bexley)   **T** 01322 337368
www.bexleybrewery.co.uk
🔲 🐦 BexleyBrewery
First sold beer: September 2014

This cask-focused outfit, run by husband and
wife team Cliff and Jane Murphy on an Erith
industrial estate, is the first stand-alone
brewery in Bexley since Reffell's was closed
by Courage in 1956. The borough is known for
its colonies of feral ring-necked parakeets,
thus the logo. Monthly open days include a
brewery bar, off-sales and tours: check
website for details.

Beers are all cask: flagship **Bob Pale Ale**
(4.2%), a darker bitter called **Redhouse
Premium Ale** (4.2%), and various seasonals
including **Black Prince Porter** (4.6%).
The beers are often sold in southeast
London micropubs.

Big Smoke Brew Co

Brewpub 🍺 🍴 🥄 | 🗡

87 Maple Road, Surbiton KT6 4AW (Kingston
upon Thames) See also Antelope pub p197
T (020) 8339 9721 www.bigsmokebrew.co.uk
🔲 bigsmokebrewco   🐦 bigsmokebrew
First sold beer: September 2014

The first brewpub in the beer-focused
Catering & Leisure group of pubs, with an 8 hl
(5 barrel) brewhouse from Pallet Brew in
Horwich, producing very reliable and tasty
beers in the capable hands of Nick Blake and
the aptly-named Pete Brew.

Beers: Mainly on sale at the pub and others
within the group, but some beers are distrib-
uted outside it. Core beers include **Session
Pale** (3.8%), **Amber Ale*** (5%), **Dark Wave
Porter** (5%), **Electric Eye Pale Ale** (5%) and
the unusual **Underworld Milk Stout*** (5%).
Occasional beers include a very good
Bitter* (4.5%).

Black Horse

See Barnet Brewing

Bloomsbury Brewery

Brewpub 🍺 | 🥄

63 Lambs Conduit Street WC1N 3NB (Camden)
T (020) 7405 8278 www.the-perseverance.
moonfruit.com   🔲 theperseverancepub
First sold beer: August 2014

A small, occasional brewery in the cellar of
the Perseverance freehouse.

Beers are sold in the pub and vary in style.

Brew by Numbers (BBNo)

Microbrewery 🍺 🍴 🥄 | 🛒 🥄 🔨 ⌓🍴

79 Enid Street SE16 3RA (Southwark)
T (020) 7237 9794
www.brewbynumbers.com
🔲 Brew-By-Numbers   🐦 BrewByNumbers
First sold beer: December 2012   *See also* p66

Originally a very small, bottled beer operation
created by Tom Hutchings and David Seymour
in Southwark Bridge Road under the inspiration
of both Belgian styles and craft brewing in
Australia and New Zealand. Success prompted
a move to a Bermondsey railway arch where
the operation relaunched in June 2013 with
an 18 hl (12 barrel) kit hand-built from recycled
stainless steel vessels. The original equipment
has been retained for pilot runs.

Beers: A wide variety are made, all designated
by two numbers: the first indicates one of 15
basic styles, the second one of up to 13 variants

such as different hop varieties or extra flavour-ings. There's a range of saisons (usually*), barrel-aged brews, beers fermented with wild yeasts and lactic cultures, brown ales and imperial stout as well as more conventional contemporary-styled IPAs (some**) and pales. Standouts have included **01|02 Saison Amarillo & Orange*** (5.4%), **01|07 Saison Citra*** (5.4%), **03|01 Original Porter*** (6.1%), **04|02 Classic Berliner Weisse*** (3.7%), **05|01 India Pale Ale Amarillo & Citra*** (6.7%), **08|01 Export Strength Stout*** (7.4%) and **09|02 Nut Brown Ale*** (6.3%).

Brewhouse and Kitchen Highbury

Brewpub
2a Corsica Street N5 1JJ (Islington)
T (020) 7226 1026
www.brewhouseandkitchen.com/highbury

Brewhouse and Kitchen Islington

Brewpub
Torrens Street EC1V 1NG (Islington)
T (020) 7837 9421　　 BKIslington
www.brewhouseandkitchen.com/islington
First sold beer: October 2014　　*See also* p 42

Entrepreneur Kris Gumbrell's former Convivial pub chain ventured into brewing from 2011 with the Botanist on Kew Green and later the Lamb in Chiswick. This went on to inspire an entire brewpub chain, Brewhouse and Kitchen, created in partnership with former Mitchells & Butlers executive Simon Bunn. Convivial was later sold to M&B, who shut down brewing activities, but now the old brewing kits have popped up again in the first two London branches of the new chain. First to open was the branch near Angel station, with head brewer Pete Hughes in charge of the 4 hl (2.5 barrel) Botanist kit, and offering various brewing demonstrations and 'brewer for a day' packages. The similarly-sized former Lamb brewhouse should have reappeared on the other side of Islington by the time you read this.

Beers: The Angel pub produces mainly cask beers, the Highbury branch mainly 'craft keg' and lagers, with each supplying the other. Core cask beers, all named with local references, are **Arc Angel*** bitter (3.6%), **Spandau B** session IPA (4.4%), **Myddleton Blonde** (4.5%), **Watchmaker** strong bitter (5.5%) and **Chaplin American IPA** (6%). Seasonals and specials have included a tasty rye beer, **Triple A*** (5%). Core keg beers weren't confirmed at press time. Beers are also sold in minicasks.

Brick Brewery

Microbrewery 🍺 🍴 🛒 ⚓
209 Blenheim Grove SE15 4QL (Southwark)
T 07747 787636   www.brickbrewery.co.uk
🅕 Brick-Brewery-SE15 🐦 brick_brewery
First sold beer: November 2013 *See also* p 159

Founded by Ian Stewart in a railway arch at the back of Peckham Rye station, this brewery serves a mainly local market. The Chinese-built kit can brew 9 hl (5.5 barrels) and capacity was extended with new fermentation vessels late in 2014.

Beers: A range of international styles with local names, including a rare San Francisco-style steam beer, **Archway Steam California Common*** (4.8%) and a well-hopped lager, **Peckham Pils*** (4.8%). Other regulars are **Sir Thomas Gardyner** American Pale Ale (3.8%, named after the owner of a local orchard in the 1790s), **Kinsale Bitter** (4%), **Blenheim Black IPA** (5.1%) and **Pioneer IPA** (5.9%).

Brixton Brewery

Microbrewery 🍺 🍴 🛒 ⚓
547 Brixton Station Road SW9 8PF (Lambeth)
T 07761 436757   www.brixtonbrewery.com
🅕 🐦 BrixtonBrewery
First sold beer: October 2013   *See also* p 183

Conceived in March 2011 by homebrewing neighbours Jez Galaun and Mike Ross, who had also been involved in a local project to make beer from hops grown in local private gardens, this brewery was longer in the making than originally expected. It eventually opened with a 10 hl (6.5 barrel) brewhouse from Oban Ales in an arch not far from Brixton station, later expanding into a neighbouring arch. Appropriately for the area, the brewery has numerous local community ties, and names its beers with local references. The current head brewer is Dominic Hughes.

Beers: Most beers are produced in bottle-conditioned format, including **Reliance** Pale Ale (4.2%), tasty amber-coloured **Effra Ale*** (4.5%), **Windrush Stout** (5%), American pale ale **Atlantic** (5.4%), and **Electric IPA*** (6.5%). Specials have included a coffee stout in collaboration with a local roaster, and **Megawatt** Double IPA (8%) in 650 ml 'bomber' bottles.

Brockley Brewery

Microbrewery 🍺 🍴 🛒 ⚓
31 Harcourt Road SE4 2AJ (Lewisham)
T 07814 584338   🅕 🐦 brockleybrewery
www.brockleybrewery.co.uk
First sold beer: March 2013   *See also* p 167

A business founded by a group of six local residents, including head brewer Andy Rowland, in a small industrial unit not far from Brockley station, using an 8 hl (5 barrel) kit supplied by ABUK. As well as selling beer through local outlets, the brewery hosts a homebrew school.

Beers: Mainly cask, but some bottling off-site. Flagship **Pale Ale** (4%) is brewed alongside **Golden Ale** (3.8%), a good **Porter*** (4.3%) and **Red Ale** (4.8%).

Brodie's Beers

Microbrewery, brewpub 🍺 🍴 🛒 ⚓
William IV, 816A High Road E10 6AE (Waltham Forest). See also King William IV pub p 126
T 07828 498733
🅕 BrodiesFabulousBeers 🐦 BrodiesBeers
First sold beer: August 2008

The story of brewing at the Brodie family's Leyton pub, the King William IV, began in November 2000, when an 8 hl (5 barrel) kit designed by Pitfield's and Dark Star founder

Rob Jones started producing beer under the name Sweet William in a former stable building at the back. The venture failed in 2005 and the brewhouse was mothballed, only to be restored and relaunched under its current name in August 2008 by siblings James and Lizzie Brodie, originally as a point of interest to attract more customers to this very large pub. The initiative turned out to be one of the earliest shoots of a vigorous new crop of London brewers, and the Brodies have since established themselves among the scene's true mavericks, creating many hundreds of unusual and innovative beers in a vast range of styles. There's an long term plan to move to new premises, though the pub brewery will be retained, probably for wild and sour beers.

Beers: The focus remains on supplying the William, where intermittent festivals have been known to feature over 50 different house-brewed beers, and to a lesser extent the other Brodie's pubs in Soho (Old Coffee House p 93) and Covent Garden. The beers are sometimes seen in other outlets too. The variety is so great it's difficult to know where to start, and the results of such constant experimentation can vary from sublime to ill-advised. Recurring successes have included US-style beers like **Hackney Red IPA** (6.1%), **Hoxton Special IPA*** (6.6%) and **Dalston Black IPA*** (7%). Sessionable favourites are an easy-going single hop pale ale simply called **Citra*** (3.1%) and a comparable beer with New Zealand hops called **Kiwi*** (3.8%), alongside

Bethnal Green Bitter (4%) and **London Fields Pale Ale** (4%). As well as strong, dark options like **Smoked Rye Porter*** (7.3%) and **Superior London Porter*** (7.8%), there are fruit flavoured Berliner Weisse-style lactic wheat beers, Belgian-style brown ales and wood-aged imperial stouts which have been known to approach magnificence.

Bullfinch Brewery
Beer firm 🏠 🍴 | 🛒 🔖
118 Druid Street SE1 2HH (Southwark).
See also Anspach & Hobday p 66
T 07899 795823 www.thebullfinchbrewery.co.uk 🅵 BullfinchBrewery 🐦 Bullfinch_Ale
First sold beer: February 2014

Live sound engineer Ryan Mclean, who discovered international craft beer while travelling extensively for work with various bands, originally planned his own brewery but has ended up a part-time 'cuckoo' brewer working at Anspach & Hobday.

Beers: Supplies are limited, but the beers are always featured alongside Anspach & Hobday's own beers at the brewery's taproom, and occasionally elsewhere. Core beers include an approachable pale called **Rascal** (4.8%), tasty rye beer **RyPA*** (5%), hoppy pale ale **Hopocalypse** (6%), equally hop-forward dark ale **Notorious*** (7%) and a succession of specials and one-offs.

By the Horns Brewing

Microbrewery 🍺 🍶 🗑 🍴 | 🛒 🏷 🛠 🖱

25 Summerstown SW17 0BQ (Wandsworth)

T (020) 3417 7338 www.bythehorns.co.uk

🇫 🐦 bythehornsbrew

First sold beer: October 2011   *See also* p 192

Alex Bull and Chris Mills, then only three years out of university, started brewing at their base near Wimbledon greyhound stadium in September 2011, using a 9 hl (5.5 barrel) kit custom-built by John Trew of Oban Ales. They've proved one of the most successful of the new London breweries, combining traditional and contemporary appeal, and at the time of writing were stretched to capacity, frequently brewing twice a day to meet demand. Expansion into nearby units is likely.

Beers: Core beers sold in cask and bottle (unfiltered but not reconditioned) are pale ale **Stiff Upper Lip** (3.8%, also keg), best bitter **Mayor of Garrett** (4.3%), a distinctive red ale called **Diamond Geezer*** (4.9%) and **Lambeth Walk*** porter (5.1%). Other beers, like **Wolfie Smith*** amber ale (5.2%), dry-hopped **Crafty London Lager** (5.3%) and **Hopslinger** American IPA (5.7%) are usually only available in unfiltered keykeg or bottled. A programme of seasonals and specials includes more specialist styles like Black IPA, alongside occasional brews like bottle-conditioned Belgian ales.

Camden Town Brewery

Microbrewery 🍺 🍶 🍴 🗑 | 🛒 🏷 🛠

55 Wilkin Street Mews NW5 3NN (Camden)

T (020) 7485 1671   🇫 🐦 CamdenBrewery

www.camdentownbrewery.com

First sold beer: May 2006   *See also* p 135

Now one of London's biggest breweries, Camden Town began with a single vessel in the cellar of Hampstead pub the Horseshoe (p 136), with the first brews bearing the name McLaughlins, from a long-closed brewery in Rockhampton, Queensland, once owned by founder Jasper Cuppaidge's family. Struck by the popularity of his beer among pub customers, Jasper found investment to install a 20 hl computerised brewhouse from BrauKon, Germany, under railway arches, not in fact in Camden Town but in nearby Kentish Town. The expanded brewery was relaunched in June 2010 with a strategy of producing high quality, approachable, well-branded and consistent products, mainly in keg and bottle. Success has seen fermentation capacity expand several times, and the brewery now occupies an entire stretch of arches. In May 2013 it became the first new London brewery, and one of the first microbreweries in Britain, to invest in a canning line. In March 2015 the company exceeded its target of raising £1.5 million through crowd funding to finance a second brewhouse on a nearby site. The current brewing director is Alex Troncoso, the head brewer is Rob Topham, and the company is a London Living Wage employer. Look carefully at the logo and you can still see a horseshoe, a reminder of where it all began.

Beers: Mainly 'craft keg' and bottles inspired by US craft brewing and classic German and Belgian styles, widely available throughout London. Flagship beer **Hells** (4.6%), also in cans, is so-named as it's pitched halfwa y between a Helles and a pils; it's also sold as keg-only **Unfiltered Hells*** and in this form it's arguably London's best lager. A stronger, hoppier version is called **IHL** (India Hells Lager, 6.2%). Other year-round beers are a **Pale** (4%) which was one of the brewery's first beers, unfiltered spiced wheat beer **Gentleman's Wit*** (4.3%, also bottle conditioned and a World Beer Cup medallist), Irish-style 'nitro' stout **Ink** (4.4%) and a hoppy **Pils** (4.6%). There are seasonals,

collaborations under the Versus name, and annual special releases in 1 litre bottles – the 2014 example was a 9.5% wood-aged lager. Regular cask production was ended in 2012 though cask specials appear occasionally at the taproom and the Horseshoe. Currently some beer is contract-brewed in Belgium to meet demand but this will end when the second brewhouse is commissioned.

Canopy Beer Co

Microbrewery

Arch 1127 Bath Factory Estate, 41 Norwood Road SE24 9AJ (Lambeth)
T 07792 463386   www.canopybeer.com
 CanopyBeerCo
First sold beer: October 2014

A 6.5 hl (4 barrel) kit, bought from a brewery in Wakefield that never got off the ground, is fired up at least twice a week in a railway arch in Herne Hill by Matthew and Estelle Theobalds.

Beers: Mainly sold in cask and bottle are **Brockwell IPA** (5%), **Ruskin** Bavarian-style wheat beer (5.4%) and Belgian-style amber ale **Milkwood** (5.9%). An English-style pale ale, **1891 IPA** (4.6%), has been created for the Friends of Herne Hill Velodrome. More European-style beers are promised. Products are stocked by local outlets or can be pre-ordered for collection from the brewery.

Clarkshaws Brewing

Microbrewery

283 Belinda Road SW9 7DT (Lambeth)
T 07989 402687   www.clarkshaws.co.uk
 clarkshaws-brewing clarkshaws
First sold beer: September 2013

Started by the self-styled "beer imps", Ian Clark and Lucy Grimshaw, on a small industrial estate in East Dulwich, this expanded early in 2015 to its current railway arch site in Brixton. The 8 hl (5 barrel) kit is shared with London Beer Lab (below), though both brewers have their own fermenters and other equipment. Check the website for opening times.

Beers are not only Vegetarian Society-approved with no fish-based finings but contain only UK-sourced ingredients. With no exotic imported hops to play with, the brewery has become adept at seeking out new, unusual and flavoursome varieties from English growers to maintain its contemporary edge. Regulars among the cheerfully-labelled beers include **Gorgon's Alive** golden ale (4%), **Phoenix Rising*** (4%), a session ale with Phoenix hops, English pale ale **Strange Brew No 1** (4%) and **Hellhound IPA** (5.5%). There are changing specials too.

Crate Brewery

Brewpub

Queens Yard, White Post Lane E9 5EN (Tower Hamlets)
T 07834 275687   www.cratebrewery.com
 CrateBrewery
First sold beer: July 2012 See also p 114

Opened just in time for the Olympic and Paralympic Games by New Zealanders Tom and Jess Seaton, of the Counter Café nearby, and head brewer Neil Hinchley, this canalside brewpub and pizzeria is in a post-industrial arts and media colony on the western edge of the Queen Elizabeth Olympic Park. It's in the White Building, a former sweet factory redeveloped as an Olympic legacy project which also includes exhibition and performance spaces. Brewing originally took place on a small kit visible behind glass in the bar, but in summer 2014 the brewery upgraded to a new 16 hl (10 barrel) brewhouse plus a pilot kit in a

Crate Brewery

newly renovated location across the yard known as the Brew-Shed, which is regularly opened to the public as bar overspill or for special events. Further expansion is likely during 2015, with additional lagering tanks installed in a nearby warehouse so that all brewing can be brought in-house.

Beers: Cask regulars are also sold in bottled versions and include **Golden** (3.8%), **Pale** (4.5%), **Best** (4.3%), **Stout*** (5.7%) and an impressive **IPA*** (5.8%). There are various seasonals and specials, and Pale, IPA and Stout are also sold in keykeg. At the time of writing, the 'craft keg' **Lager** (4.8%) is contract-brewed at Alechemy in Edinburgh, though production should move to London during summer 2015.

The Cronx Brewery

Microbrewery
6 Vulcan Business Centre, Vulcan Way CR0 9UG (Croydon)   **T** 01689 809093
www.thecronx.com   TheCronxBrewery
First sold beer: August 2012

Drinks wholesaler Mark Russell and city worker-turned-brewer Simon Dale founded the Cronx. Operating from a 20hl (12 barrel) plant in an industrial estate in New Addington, it's the first stand-alone brewery in Croydon since Page and Overton closed in 1954. The name jokingly blends the name of an equally outlying New York City borough with Croydon's postcode.

Beers: Core lines are **Standard Bitter** (3.8%), easygoing blond ale **Kotchin** (3.9%: in case you're wondering, to kotch is to relax or enjoy doing nothing in particular), **Nektar** pale ale (4.5%) and **Entire** (5.2%), a porter inspired by Croydon's brewing history, also made in a chilli version. An **IPA*** (6%) features varying single hop varietals, and there are specials and seasonals too.

Dragonfly Brewery

Brewpub
183 High Street W3 9DJ (Ealing)
See also George and Dragon pub p 218
T (020) 8992 3712   DragonflyActon
www.dragonflybrewery.co.uk
First sold beer: May 2014

A fine-looking brewhouse with stacked fermentation vessels dominates the impressive main bar of this big Acton pub, operated by Remarkable Restaurants. Initial beers were developed by Conor Donoghue, formerly of the Botanist and Lamb brewpubs.

Beers: Mainly sold in the pub and others in the same group, in cask, keg or both depending on style. Core beers include a full and rich dark bitter, **2 O'Clock Ordinary*** (4%), **Dark Matter*** stout (4.3%), pale ale **Early Doors** (4.3%) and unfiltered Bavarian-style wheat beer **Achtung!** (5%, usually on keg). There are lots of specials in other styles and they've even tried their hand at a sour saison.

Earls Brewery

Brewpub 🍺 🍺 | 🥄
25 Danbury Street N1 8LE (Islington)
See also Earl of Essex pub p 43
T (020) 7424 5828   www.earlofessex.net
🐦 EarlsBrewery
First sold beer: April 2013

A brewery was installed in this excellent Islington beer venue, run by the Barworks group, in January 2013 but teething troubles delayed the sale of beer until April. Current head brewer is Matt Arens.

Beers: A very varied range of pale ales, IPAs, porters, saisons and other styles are sold in the pub and other Barworks venues, often well worth trying. **Farmhouse IPA** (7.5%), a hoppy beer with Belgian yeast, was one notable success. There are some unusual collaborations too, including with coffee roasters and other non-brewing businesses.

Ealing Park Tavern

Brewpub 🍺 🍶 🍺 | 🥄
222 South Ealing Road W5 4RL (Ealing)
T (020) 8758 1879   🔲 🐦 EalingTavern
www.ealingparktavern.com
First sold beer: March 2015

This gastropub, in a well-restored coaching inn, has its own 10 hl brewery from Oban Ales. The first brewery in the ETM group of pubs, it launched in February 2015 under the direction of head brewer Vladamir Schmidt.

Beers (not yet tasted) are sold in the pub and others in the group, as well as occasionally outside it. They include a **Pale Ale** (4%), a **Red Ale** (4.5%), an **IPA** (5%), a stout/porter and a monthly special. Production is initially all in cask but bottles and cans will be added later.

East London Brewing (ELB)

Microbrewery 🍺 🍶 | 🛒 🚂 🍺
45 Fairways Business Centre, Lammas Road
E10 7QB (Waltham Forest)
T (020) 8539 0805
www.eastlondonbrewing.com
🔲 eastlondonbrewing 🐦 eastlondbrew
First sold beer: September 2011

Former research and development chemist Stu Lascelles switched career paths as one of a wave of new East London brewers in the autumn of 2011. The brewery, in Leyton not far from the Lee Valley Park, has a 10 barrel (16 hl) plant installed by Dave Porter of PBC. Fermentation capacity was expanded in January and May 2013. Check website for opening times.

Beers: All the regular beers are sold in cask, bottle conditioned or in 'bag-in-a-box' format for draught at home. They include **Orchid*** vanilla-spiced mild (3.6%), the brewery's inaugural beer **Pale Ale*** (4%), contemporary-styled **Foundation Bitter** (4.2%), unusual dark bitter **Nighwatchman*** (4.5%), **Jamboree** golden ale (4.8%) and **Cowcatcher** American Pale Ale (4.8%). **Quadrant*** stout (5.8%) is a collaboration with homebrew competition winners, and there's a programme of seasonals.

Essex Street Brewing

Brewpub 🍺 | 🥄
Temple Brew House, 46 Essex Street WC2R 3JF
(Westminster)   **T** (020) 7936 2536
www.templebrewhouse.com/brewery
🔲 TheTempleBrewHouse
🐦 TempleBrewHouse
First sold beer: November 2014

Small chain the City Pub Co already had brew-pubs in Bath and Cambridge when it added this London branch near the Temple late in 2014. It has an 8 hl (5 barrel) kit under the supervision of head brewer Vanesa de Blas.

Beers: At least two cask beers are always on sale in the pub and in other venues in the group like the Lighthouse (p 188). Regular beers (not yet tasted) are **Temple Best Bitter** (3.8%) and **The Gavel** (7.1%), a strong American pale, with numerous specials and seasonals alongside.

Five Points Brewing

Microbrewery
3 Institute Place E8 1JE (Hackney)
T (020) 8533 7746　**fy** FivePointsBrew
www.fivepointsbrewing.co.uk
First sold beer: March 2013

For more on this popular Hackney brewery see feature p 109.

Beers: There are three core beers, sold in cask, keg and bottled forms: a Pacific pale ale named simply **Pale*** (4.4%), tasty **Railway Porter*** (4.8%) and the distinctive amber rye beer **Hook Island Red*** (6%). They're supplemented by specials and collaboration brews.

Florence

See Head in a Hat

Four Thieves

See Laine Brewing (Battersea)

Fourpure Brewing

Microbrewery
22 Bermondsey Trading Estate, Rotherhithe New Road SE16 3LL (Southwark)
www.fourpure.com
f fourpure　**y** fourpurebrewing
First sold beer: October 2013　*See also* p 66

At the southeast end of the Bermondsey strip, this is one of London's smartest and most ambitious new breweries, founded by former City technology firm executive Dan Lowe and

his brother Tom, both homebrewers. Head brewer John Driebergen, formerly of Meantime, commands a 30 hl (18 barrel) kit that was originally at Purity in Warwickshire, and there's a 1 hl pilot kit too.

Beers: Equipped with a canning line on opening, the brewery has been at the forefront of championing unfiltered and unpasteurised beer in 'craft cans' and its output is split roughly 50:50 between cans and kegkegs. Tasty but approachable and consistent beers are in broadly US- and mainland European-inspired styles. Core beers are **Session IPA*** (4.2%), **Pils*** (4.7%), **Pale** (5%) and **Amber Ale** (5.1%), and an occasional **Oatmeal Stout** (5.1%). Bottle-conditioned beers have included **Roux Brew*** (5.6%), a spiced wheat beer that won a competition to supply Michel Roux's restaurants within weeks of the brewery opening. There are numerous specials, some sold under the Outpost label, including exclusives only available in the taproom.

Fuller Smith & Turner

Independent 🍾 📋 🍴 🍶 🛒 🌾 ⚒ ☺
Chiswick Lane South W4 2QB (Hounslow)
T (020) 8996 2000
www.fullers.co.uk 📘 🐦 FullersBrewery
First sold beer: 1701   *See also* p 211

For more on London's last remaining historic
independent family brewery, see p 212.

Beers: Fuller's mainstay is its benchmark cask
ale, including a trio of classic bitters in ascending strength: delicate dry-hopped **Chiswick
Bitter**** (3.5%), flagship **London Pride*** (4.1%),
and Extra Special Bitter, better known as **ESB****
(5.5%), the last inspiring an entire beer style in
the US. These beers, which are stronger and
pasteurised in bottle and keg, are much better
appreciated from cask in prime condition.
Other regular cask beers include "crisp amber
ale" **Gales Seafarers** (3.6%), borrowing the
name of a Hampshire brewery Fuller's took
over and closed; a tasty new pale ale with US
hops, **Wild River*** (4.5%), also bottle conditioned; and **Gales HSB*** (4.8%), a distinctive
dark bitter that was originally Gales' flagship.
The very roasty **London Porter*** (5.4%) is
usually in keg or bottle but sometimes appears
in cask, as does contemporary IPA **Bengal
Lancer*** (5%, simply labelled IPA in the US),
originally created as a bottle-conditioned beer.
There are numerous other cask seasonals
and specials including autumnal fixture
Red Fox* (4.3%).

The brewery has ventured into 'craft keg'
with a contemporary lager-style beer,
Frontier* (4.5%), in reality made with the
standard ale yeast and lagered for six weeks
so technically more like a Kölsch. Nitrokeg and
bottled stout **Black Cab** (4.5%) also occasionally appears in cask. An outstanding range of
bottle-conditioned specials is led by the sublime
Vintage Ale** (8.5%), released annually with
a slightly different recipe and ageing magnifi-
cently. **1845*** (6.3%) is a deep, toasty and fruity
Victorian-style strong ale. The **Past Masters**
series (*–**) intermittently revives historic
recipes, while **Brewers Reserve*** is an annual
release of a strong (7.5%+) barrel-aged beer.
There's a new **Imperial Stout*** (10.7%), and
the brewery also retains a supply of vatted
old ale from Gales which is occasionally
blended with fresh beer and bottled as
Gales Prize Old Ale* (9%).

George and Dragon
See Dragonfly Brewery

Gipsy Hill Brewing

Microbrewery 🍾 📋 🍴 🛒 🌾 ⚒
11 Hamilton Road Industrial Estate SE27 9SF
(Lambeth)   **T** (020) 8761 9061
www.gipsyhillbrewing.com
📘 gipsyhillbrewing 🐦 gipsyhillbrew
First sold beer: July 2014   *See also* p 161

For more about this small brewery near Crystal
Palace, on the same industrial estate as London
Beer Factory (below), see feature p 162.

Beers: 70% of production is cask and the main
brief is to create sessionable beers at under
5% ABV, though some bottled versions and

specials may creep a little higher. Mainstays are the very drinkable **Beatnik Pale*** (3.8%), slightly more robust **Southpaw Amber** (4.2%) and **Dissident Porter*** (4.8%).

Hackney Brewery

Microbrewery 🍺 🍴 🍶
358 Laburnum Street E2 8BB (Hackney)
T (020) 3489 9595
www.hackneybrewery.co.uk
📘 Hackney-Brewery 🐦 HackneyBrewery
First sold beer: June 2012

Former homebrewers Peter Hills and Jon Swain both worked at Islington pub the Charles Lamb (p 42) when they decided to join the growing ranks of East London brewers in 2011. Their original brewhouse, under an arch of the Kingsland viaduct, produced only 9 hl (5.5 barrels) at a time but this was doubled to 18 hl (11 barrels) in summer 2014. The brewery became a London Living Wage employer the same year.

Beers: Most production is of lighter beers in cask, with some bottles, and, since the 2014 upgrade, 'craft keg'. Core cask beers are **Golden Ale** (4%), **Best Bitter*** (4.4%), **American Pale Ale** (4.5%) and **New Zealand Pale Ale** (4.5%). Kegs include a **Session IPA** (4.1%), hoppy pale **Citra-Amarillo** (5%) and **American IPA** (5.5%).

Hammerton Brewery

Microbrewery 🍺 🍴 🍶 | 🛒 🥡 🍻 🏷
8 Roman Way Industrial Estate, 149 Roman Way N7 8XH (Islington)
T (020) 3302 5880
www.hammertonbrewery.co.uk
📘 hammertonbrewery 🐦 hammertonbrew
First sold beer: April 2014

For more about this new brewery reviving a vanished brewing name, see feature p147. Usually open on the last Friday and Saturday of the month: check website for details.

Beers: **Pentonville Oyster Stout*** (4.2%), in cask, keg and bottle, uses oats as well as Maldon oysters. Other core beers include one of the few 'California Common' beers brewed regularly in London, **Islington Steam Lager** (4.7%), alongside **N1 Pale Ale** (4.1%) and stronger **N7 Pale Ale*** (5.2%). There are seasonals and specials too.

A Head in a Hat (Florence Brewery)

Microbrewery, brewpub 🍺 🍶 | 🥡
133 Dulwich Road SE24 0NG (Lambeth)
See also Florence pub p159
www.florencebrewery.co.uk
📘 FlorenceBrewery 🐦 AHeadInAHat
First sold beer: September 2007

Serial pub entrepreneur and brewer David Bruce, of Firkin fame (see Southwark ale p 56), dipped his toe into the brewpub concept again in April 2007 by installing a tiny brewery at the Cock and Hen pub in Fulham, then part of his Capital Pubs chain. The experiment was repeated in September with a slightly bigger 8 hl (5 barrel) brewery in a new Capital Pub in Herne Hill, formerly an Irish pub called Ganions and now renamed the Florence. Cock and Hen brewer Tony Lennon at first covered both sites, though the Cock was later sold to Young's and brewing discontinued. Tony moved on in November 2010, and the Florence brewhouse remained unused until the following February, when Peter Haydon (p291) moved in as brewer, initially on a profit share basis. The sale of Capital to new national Greene King later that year prompted fears for the brewery's future, which turned out to be unfounded when the new owner retained the pub's identity, and its brewing activities, as part of its Metropolitan chain. In April 2012 Peter bought the kit from Greene King and agreed to pay rent on the site – a unusual arrangement of one brewery operating from premises owned by another. He's since created his own brand, A Head in a Hat.

Beers: The cask beers originally created for the Florence are still brewed for sale in the pub and sometimes others in the chain, though they are rarely all on at once. They are dark, fruity **Bonobo** (4.3%), blond ale **Weasel** (4.5%), and flagship **Beaver** (4.8%), a wheaty golden ale with citrus zest. An unusual Burton-style ale, **Stoat*** (5.3%), has since been introduced.

A Head in a Hat beers are both cask and bottled and are largely historical recreations. They include a light pale ale, **Titfer Dinner Ale** (3.5%); mild **Trilby*** (4%); an English IPA from an early 20th century recipe, **Tommy*** (4.2%); and export porter **Topper** (4.8%). There have

been numerous specials and collaborations, notably **Gin*** (4.1%), a beer flavoured with gin botanicals made with the City of London Distillery, and **Prima Donna** made with hops grown by local residents as part of an urban garden project. Two beers are made exclusively for Cubitt House pubs, and some beers for Lost bars have also emerged.

LONDON DRINKERS **Peter Haydon**

Brewer, beer writer and pubs historian Peter ran the small breweries' trade organisation SIBA from his London office until 2002, helping persuade the government to reduce duty on beer for small producers. He then spent 10 years at Meantime before taking over the Florence Brewery near his home in Herne Hill. He specialises in recreating old recipes from long-gone London breweries under the brand A Head in a Hat.

How do you rate London as a beer city, on a world scale?
London was once the brewing capital of the world. While the number of breweries has grown exponentially in the last five years, we won't really re-enter the premier league until Londoners at large think about their city and their beer in the same way as the citizens of Munich, Brussels, Denver and Bamberg do.

What's the single most exciting thing about beer in London at the moment?
The can-do entrepreneurial spirit of so many recent startups and the speed with which they're changing the game. Look at Beavertown's cans, for example, or the scale of operation that Fourpure and Five Points started out with.

What single thing would make things even better?
Increased access to the market. There are still too many pubs that are not free to buy the beers they'd like to.

What are your top London beers right now (other than those from your own brewery)?
Beavertown Gamma Ray, Moncade Notting Hill Porter, Signature Session IPA.

What's your top great beer night out?
I've always been a huge fan of the Harp (p80). It's the archetypal London pub in the Victorian style

and it's great to see that new owners Fuller's are canny enough not to change a winning formula.

Who's your London beer hero?
Derek Prentice (p95). A lifetime's experience in London's greatest breweries has left him with undiminished enthusiasm for beer and brewing and a selfless generosity in sharing his wealth of knowledge with the new generation.

Who will we be hearing a lot more from in future?
Old Haydon's Almanac predicts that 2015 will be the sour beer year. There are a growing number of great sour beers out there and this year the drinking public will 'get' sour.

Which are your other top beer cities?
Munich and Brussels obviously, and Bamberg is very special. Denver, Seattle and Portland showcase the American take on modern beer. Top place to watch? São Paulo.

Hiver Beers

Beer firm 🍾 🍺 | 🛒
55 Stanworth Street SE1 3NY (Southwark) at
Maltby Street, see below
www.hiverbeers.com ⬛ ✖ HiverBeers
First sold beer: September 2013

Hiver Beers' smartly-branded honey beer was
the brainchild of Hannah Rhodes, formerly of
Meantime, who was inspired by London's urban
beekeepers. The beer itself is contract-brewed
by Hepworth in Horsham, though widely sold
in London, including at the firm's weekly stall
at the Maltby Street Ropewalk, near the
Modern Beer Co (p 66).

Beers: Currently a single golden ale, **Hiver** (5%),
made with organic malt and three honeys.

Honest Brew

Beer firm 🍾 🍺 | 🍷
21 Southey Street SE20 7JD (Bromley)
T (020) 3750 2366 ⬛ ✖ honestbrew
www.honestbrew.co.uk
First sold beer: September 2012

A trio of cuckoo brewers who have evolved
into a mail order business offering bespoke
beer cases, but still brew occasionally, sometimes in London at Late Knights and Signature
but more often at contract specialist RSM
Solutions in Durham.

Beers: Various beers in contemporary styles
have been brewed for bottle and occasionally
keg, notably the **Straight Up** series encompassing **Amber Ale** * (4.6%), **Pale Ale** (4.7%),
and a new stout.

Hop Stuff Brewery

Microbrewery 🍾 🍾 🍺 | 🛒 🍷 ⚗ 🍷
7 Gunnery Terrace SE18 6SW (Greenwich)
T (020) 8854 9509
www.hopstuffbrewery.com
⬛ hopstufflondon ✖ Hopstuffbrewery
First sold beer: November 2013   *See also* p 170

Created by ex-City boy James Yeomans, who
learned to brew at Grainstore in Rutland.
Crowd funding secured a 16 hl (10 barrel) kit
from Oban Ales in an industrial unit on the

newly redeveloped Woolwich Arsenal site,
and the beer names usually have local links.

Beers: Mainly cask, with some hand bottling,
keykeg and polypins, usually of sessionable
brews like **APA** (Arsenal Pale Ale 3.8%), best
bitter **Fusilier** (4.3%) and **Pale Ale** (4.5%).
More specialist are **Oatmeal Stout** (4.8%),
Renegade IPA * (5.6%) and the occasional
Gunners Porter * (7.4%), which might appear
in aged versions.

Hops and Glory

See Solvay Society p 304

Howling Hops

Brewpub 🍾 🍾 🍺 | ✏
315 Mare Street E8 1EJ (Hackney)
See also Cock Tavern p 107
T (020) 8533 6369 www.howlinghops.co.uk
⬛ Cock-Tavern ✖ HowlingHops
First sold beer: July 2012

Rescued Hackney beer champion the Cock
Tavern has boasted its own 6.5 hl (4 barrel)
brewery in the cellar since reopening, now
overseen by head brewer Gianmaria Ricciardi.
Expansion to a 25 hl (15 barrel) kit on a separate
site at Hackney Wick should take place in 2015,
with some brewing in the pub continuing.

Beers: A range of beers, some alluding to
historic recipes, is brewed on rotation for the
pub and its sister The Southampton Arms;
these do sometimes crop up elsewhere. Pale
ales in particular are brewed to multiple recipes

using old school brewery number practices, for example **Pale No 2** (3.8%) or **Pale XX Superior No 2*** (5.2%). Other favourites have included **Mild Ale** (3.3%), **Amber De Luxe*** (4.6%), **Smoked Porter*** (5.2%), **Chocolate Stout*** (5.5%) and **Domestic IPA** (5.9%), and as well as beers in inventive styles like a rye Gose.

Inkspot Brewery
Beer firm
42 Fox Hill SE19 2XE (Croydon)
T 07747 607803   inkspotbrewery
www.theinkspotbrewery.com
First sold beer: December 2012

A project launched by ex-Army officer Tom and restaurateur Bradley, initially to serve local outlets.

Beers: The first and flagship beer, **St. Reatham** (4.6%), is, unusually for London, a Munich-style amber lager. Other beers have included Bohemian-style *tmavý* **Czech Black** (4.6%), and an East India Pale Ale named after the calibre of an Army rifle, **5.56** (5.6%).

Kernel Brewery (The)
Microbrewery
11 Dockley Road Industrial Estate SE16 3SF (Southwark)   **T** (020) 7231 4516
www.thekernelbrewery.com
 The-Kernel-Brewery   KernelBrewery
First sold beer: December 2009 *See also* p 66

For more about arguably London's most renowned and influential new brewery, see feature p 63.

Beers: Most beer is bottle conditioned, with some keykeg and very occasional casks for beer festivals and other events. Numerous and often-changing beers mainly fall into two categories. First, there are fresh and hop-forward contemporary-styled pale ales and India pale ales with varying hop recipes: among the most noted of these have been **Pale Ales** with **Centennial*** (5%) and **Mosaic*** (5.4%); and **IPAs** with **Citra*** (6.7%), **Mosaic**** (7.2%), and the Scrabblishly-labelled **S C C A NS**** (Simcoe, Citra, Columbus, Apollo, Nelson Sauvin, 7%). Second, and in marked contrast, are often

strong and sturdy porters and stouts based on historic London recipes, notably **Export Stout London 1890**** (7.2%) and **Imperial Brown Stout London 1856**** (10.1%). Alongside these, an outstanding zesty light ale, **Table Beer**** (3%) is usually available, as well as a lactic **London Sour*** (around 2.3%) based on Berliner Weisse and sometimes sold in fruit-flavoured variants. Look out too for wood-aged specials and other unusual styles.

Kew Brewery

Microbrewery 🍺 🍴

477 Upper Richmond Road West SW14 7PU
(Richmond upon Thames) Check Facebook
for opening details

f KewBrewery 🐦 KewBrewery

Ex-Weird Beard brewer David Scott is striking
out on own with this new brewery, not far
from Kew Gardens, which should have opened
by the time you read this.

Beers (not yet tasted) use all-UK ingredients,
partly for sustainability reasons, and partly to
support Britain's hop industry, as David is from
Kent (the UK's predominant hop-growing area)
originally. They include session amber ale
Botanic (3.8%), hoppy golden ale
Sandycombe Gold (4.5%), a milk stout, a
porter with a chilli variant, a rye beer and the
Pagoda Pale series of single hop beers.

Laine Brewing (Acton)

Brewpub 🍺 | 🍴 ⚒

264 High Street W3 9BH (Ealing)
See also Aeronaut pub p 217

T (020) 8993 4242   www.aeronaut.pub

f 🐦 AeronautActon

First sold beer: November 2013

Laine Brewing (Battersea)

Brewpub 🍺 🍺 | 🍴 ⚒

51 Lavender Gardens SW11 1DJ (Wandsworth)
See also Four Thieves pub p 187

T (020) 7223 6927   www.fourthieves.pub

f 🐦 FourThievesPub

First sold beer: January 2015

Laine Brewing (People's Pints)

Brewpub 🍺 | 🍴 ⚒

360 Victoria Park Road E9 7BT (Hackney)
See also Peoples Park Tavern p 116

T (020) 8533 0040   f 🐦 peoplestavern
www.peoplesparktavern.pub

First sold beer: February 2014

Gavin George's small Brighton-based pub chain
InnBrighton first installed a brewery in October
2012 in its North Laine bar, in the celebrated
Brighton shopping area of the same name,
thus the beer brand Laine's. The first London
pub in the group to go the same way was the
Aeronaut in Acton, with an 8 hl (5 barrel)
brewery clearly visible behind the bar, overseen by head brewer Nic Donald, who even
persuaded brewing legend Derek Prentice (p95)
to brew a guest beer in July 2014. Another 8 hl
kit had by then appeared in the eastern wing
of the Peoples Park Tavern in Victoria Park,
with Jim Wilson, formerly of Brentwood

Brewery and Tap East, as head brewer, though he's since moved on. Interestingly this is actually the second brewery on the site: in 1986 the pub became the Flounder and Firkin, the sixth brewpub in David Bruce's pioneering Firkin chain (see Southwark Ale p 56). The most recent addition to the family is the Four Thieves, which has a distillery as well as an 8 hl brewery, with Nic dividing his time between there and Acton.

Beers: Most beer is sold in the brewpubs and in other Laine's houses. The Aeronaut brews session beer **Acton Ale** (3.8%) and **Porter** (4.7%), plus seasonals and specials, under the **Laine's** brand. The Victoria Park beers are branded **People's Pints** and include a **Best** (4%), an **ESB** (4.8%) and a cask-style **Pils** (4.8%). Specific beers for the Battersea site hadn't yet been developed at the time of writing, though there may well be some interchangeability with Acton. Unfiltered tank lager **Laine's Lager** (4.5%) and keg beers are currently commissioned from Hepworth in Sussex.

Late Knights Brewery

Microbrewery 🍶 🍺 🍷 | 🛒 🍺 ⌓
21 Southey Street SE20 7JD (Bromley)
www.lateknightsbrewery.co.uk
[f] LateKnightsBrewery [t] Late_Knights
First sold beer: May 2013

For more about this inventive South London brewery and mini-pub chain, see feature p 180. Details of intermittent openings are on the website.

Beers are sold through Late Knights' three London pubs and the free trade, mainly in cask and bottle with some keykeg. Regulars include pale ale **Crack of Dawn** (3.9%), American pale ale **Dawn's Early Light** (4%), **Hop o' the Morning*** stout (4.2%), impressive best bitter **Morning Glory*** (4.4%), red ale **Old Red Eyes** (4.5%) and **Worm Catcher** IPA (5%). There are numerous seasonals, specials, collaborations (often with pubs), historical recreations and oddities, such as a Polish IPA, and the facility has hosted several cuckoo brewers.

Left Bank Brewery

Microbrewery 🍶 🍺 🍷
1 Sutherland Road Path E17 6BX (Waltham Forest) **T** (020)
www.leftbankbrewery.co.uk
[f] [t] LeftBankBrewery
First sold beer: September 2014

"Probably London's smallest commercial brewery" is a licensed pilot kit working alongside bread and pickle maker the Fermentarium in Walthamstow's Black Horse workshop.

Beers (not yet tasted) are mainly bottled, and include **EKG Porter** (5%) and **Imperial Sorachi Saison** (7%) besides various pale ales.

London Beer Factory

Microbrewery 🍶 🍺 🍷 | 🛒 🍷 🍺
160 Hamilton Road SE27 9SF (Lambeth)
T (020) 8670 7054
www.thelondonbeerfactory.com
[f] londonbeerfactory [t] ldnbeerfactory
First sold beer: August 2014   *See also* p 164

An ambitious undertaking just across the yard from Gipsy Hill brewery (see above), this is the brainchild of brothers Sim and Ed Cotton – the latter spent several years in Australian vineyards before moving on to beer. Heriot-Watt trained brewer Archie Village commands a substantial 33 hl (20 barrel) kit.

Beers: All the core beers are sold in cask, with some kegging and bottling too. They include bitter **London Session*** (3.8%), popular contemporary-styled **Chelsea Blonde** (4.3%) and **Paxton Pale** (5%). A pilot brewery is used to produce specials and one-offs.

London Beer Lab

Beer firm 📦 🍺 | 🛒 🛍️ 🏭
283 Belinda Road SW9 7DT (Lambeth)
T (020) 8001 6552 www.londonbeerlab.com
📘 🐦 LondonBeerLab
First sold beer: December 2013

An interesting project begun by French-born homebrewer Bruno Alajouanine and Karl Durand O'Connor who met playing football when they both had jobs in the City. Initially the idea was to teach others how to brew, running courses in a Brixton railway arch on assorted very small kits including a 20l Speidel Braumeister, and packaging the results for their students to take away. But they also brewed some of their own beer for sale from an on-site shop (which also stocks other brewers' products) and a few local outlets, an arrangement that initially confused HMRC. They have now moved to sharing Clarkshaws' kit in a bigger arch nearby and although the courses continue, brewing their own beer is likely to become a more significant part of the business. Check website for opening times and courses.

Beers are mainly bottled: they include pale ales with varying hop recipes, historic porters and smoked stout.

LONDON'S BREWING London Amateur Brewers

Brewing is something people do for fun as well as profit, but while everyone accepts that, say, home cooks or gardeners can produce work of a quality that rivals and occasionally even exceeds that of professionals, homebrewing in Britain still struggles with a poor reputation. That is slowly changing, partly because, while earlier generations of British microbrewers largely migrated from the established industry, the current generation are more likely to come from a home-brewing background, much as in the US where for historical reasons there have always been close ties between the amateur and professional sectors.

London Amateur Brewers (LAB) is a case in point. It's an integral member of the London Brewers Alliance, and was the crucible from which several now highly-respected London breweries emerged, the Kernel and Weird Beard amongst them. But most of the 200 or so people on its books are happy to keep brewing as a hobby, vice-chair Ken Bazley tells me. For some it's admittedly a very serious hobby – a couple of members are more technologically advanced than some commercial breweries – though people who've never brewed at all are welcome, as are those with no more than a few big pots on the stove. And every so often, a particularly adept home-brewer is told by well-meaning friends that they should do this for a living, and an idea takes shape.

With no need to worry about sales, homebrewers brew what they like, motivated only by the urge to make it as well as possible. "The quality just gets better and better," says Ken. Homebrewers have not only helped popularise innovative contemporary styles, they've also been instrumental in resurrecting old ones. The publications of the august Durden Park Beer Circle provided the textbook for the Kernel's forays into porters and stouts, and three of its members regularly attend LAB. The London group has its own barrel ageing programme, as well as communal brewdays and competitions, with prizes often including the chance to work on a professional kit.

LAB was founded in 2008 by the late Ant Hayes, a legendary figure in homebrewing circles and an English brown ale enthusiast who set up numerous such groups both in the UK and his native South Africa. At that stage commercial brewing in London was at a low ebb but things were about to change dramatically, thanks in part to the homebrewing community. LAB has always been informally run, using electronic communications with no membership subscription or money changing hands.

Monthly meetings regularly attract 35–40 people. There's a talk or presentation, by a home-brewer or a professional, followed by a tasting session where members are encouraged to share their work, benefitting from mutual feedback and advice on improvements and dealing with technical faults. "In a way it's the most important part of the evening," says Ken. "Everyone's welcome, no-one looks down their nose at anyone, and it's a great way to socialise with your peers and get advice and ideas." You'd expect a certain amount of love in the air: the word 'amateur' is from an Old French root meaning 'lover of something' after all.

To get involved, see: www. londonamateurbrewers.co.uk

London Brewing (Highgate)

Brewpub 🍺 | 🖋

The Bull, 13 North Hill N6 4BX (Haringey)

T (020) 8341 0510   🔗 🐦 LondonBrewingCo

www.londonbrewing.com

First sold beer: September 2011   See also Bull pub p 151

London Brewing (North Finchley)

Brewpub 🍺 | 🛒 🖋

762 High Road N12 9QH (Barnet)

T (020) 8446 6661   🔗 🐦 LondonBrewingCo

www.londonbrewing.com

First sold beer: January 2015   See also Bohemia pub p 151

Dan Fox, former manager of the legendary beer pub the White Horse (p214), set up on his own in 2011 by reopening the Bull at Highgate as a brewpub with a 4 hl (2.5 barrel) kit. When Dan also took on notably larger pub the Bohemia in North Finchley in 2014, it was equipped with an appropriately larger 10.5 hl (6.5 barrel) kit. Head brewer Rich White looks after both sites, with the help of Jenna Dunseath.

Beers: The Highgate site brews cask beer including American pale ale **Highrise** (3.9%), distinctive bitter **Beer Street** (4%) and red ale **Vista** (4.5%) plus numerous specials. The North Finchley site focuses on 'craft keg' (not yet tasted) like **American Wheat** (4.5%), **Session IPA** (4.5%), **Stout** (4.5%) and **Rye IPA** (6.2%), Bottles may be added. Most beer is sold through the pubs, which stock each other's products.

London Fields Brewery

Beer firm 🍺 🍾 | 🛒 🖋 🍷

365 Warburton Street E8 3RR (Hackney)

T (020) 7254 7174

www.londonfieldsbrewery.co.uk

🔗 londonfieldsbrewery   🐦 LdnFldsBrewery

First sold beer: August 2011   See also p 111

The first new London brewery to be opened following publication of the first edition of this book, London Fields, just round the corner from the historic open space of the same name, heralded a brewing renaissance in East London in general and Hackney in particular. Launched with a heaving open weekend on August Bank Holiday Monday 2011 when locals and curious beer geeks drank the conditioning tanks dry, it's continued to pursue a policy of creating a direct relationship with its drinkers. The operation moved to a bigger arch at the present address in April 2012, with a 16 hl (10 barrel) kit from the former Ventnor brewery. A tasting room was later added though events continue to be held in the brewhouse itself. A newly recruited head brewer, German-born and -trained Ben Ott, significantly raised standards and consistency before moving on to the new Truman's. There was much speculation about the brewery's future at the end of 2014 following publicity around founder Jules Whiteway's past as a convicted drug dealer, shortly followed by his arrest for alleged VAT avoidance. Beer is now contract-brewed by Tom Wood in Lincolnshire

and others following the removal of the brewing equipment by early March 2015.

Beers include **Unfiltered Lager*** (4.1%), **Black Path Porter** (4.2%), Pacific-hopped pale ale **Hackney Hopster** (4.2%), bitter **Love Not War** (4.2%), **Wheat Beer** (4.7%), **Shoreditch Triangle*** IPA (6%) and numerous specials.

Meantime Brewing

Multinational subsidiary 🍴 🍺 🥂 🛒 🍾 ⚓ ⚓
4 Lawrence Trading Estate, Blackwall Lane SE10 0AR (Greenwich)
T (020) 3384 0582   🅵 🐦 MeantimeBrewing
www.meantimebrewing.com
First sold beer: April 2000

For more about London's second-largest and second-oldest independent brewery, see p172. A taproom and visitor centre have recently opened, with bookable tours: see website for details. See also Old Brewery below.

Beers: Meantime was the first British brewery to launch a Czech-inspired tank lager: **Brewery Fresh Lager*** (4.5%) is a version of its London Lager sold unfiltered and unpasteurised and without additional carbon dioxide from polythene-lined 1,000 l tanks. Other beers are generally brewery conditioned though unpasteurised, in conventional kegs and bottles, including sappy US-style **Yakima Red** (4.1%), **London Pale Ale** (4.3%), **Pilsner** (4.4%), the standard **London Lager** (4.5%), **London**

Stout (4.5%) and **Chocolate Porter*** (6.5%). Some beers are bottle conditioned including **Wheat Beer** (5%), **Raspberry Wheat*** (5%) and two superior products in 750 ml Champagne bottles, **India Pale Ale*** (7.4%) and **London Porter*** (6.5%). There are numerous special editions and seasonals – a **Festbier*** (5.6%) sometimes appears in the autumn. Meantime has never embraced cask beer: for a few years it commissioned a cask version of London Pale Ale from Adnams, but this was discontinued in 2012.

Moncada Brewery

Microbrewery 🍴 🍺 🍶
1 Buspace Studios, Conlan Street W10 5AP (Kensington and Chelsea)   **T** 0779 551 1505
www.moncadabrewery.co.uk
🅵 Moncada-Brewery 🐦 MoncadaBrewery
First sold beer: October 2011

Former chef Julio Moncada, originally from Argentina, was planning to open a specialist delicatessen but then realised that, while a deli requires supplies to be shipped from around the world, all the ingredients for brewing are available close to hand in Britain, so decided to create a brewery instead. A 10 hl (6 barrel) brewhouse from PBC was installed at the brewery's original site in the northern part of Kensington and Chelsea not far from the Grand Union Canal, in April 2011, but various setbacks delayed the launch until October

when the beers appeared at the first London Brewers Alliance showcase. Rising demand rapidly led to expansion, and since January 2013 the brewery has operated from bigger premises around the corner, with increased fermentation and storage capacity. Further expansion is likely.

Beers, all branded **Notting Hill**, are flavoursome and contemporary while working well in both cask- and bottle-conditioned forms. They include **Blonde** (4.2%), best bitter **Amber*** (4.7%), an oatmeal-slanted **Stout*** (5%), **Porter*** (5%) and **Ruby Rye** (5.2%). A recently added 'craft keg' beer is named **Red** (6%). Seasonals include a very light **Summer** beer (3.2%) and there are numerous specials.

Mondo Brewing

Microbrewery
86 Stewarts Road SW8 4UG (Wandsworth)
www.mondobrewingcompany.com
mondo.brewing mondobrewing
First sold beer: April 2015

The dream of US-craft-beer fans Tom Palmer and Todd Matteson, this new Battersea brewery uses a 10 hl kit from Zip Technologies in Hungary, with a taproom opening during the summer of 2015.

Beers (not yet tasted) include an Altbier, US-style pale, various IPAs and a brown ale, with lots of seasonal beers and one-offs, mainly in keg and bottle but with some limited edition cask releases.

Old Brewery Greenwich

Brewpub, multinational subsidiary
Pepys Building, Old Royal Naval College SE10 9LW (Greenwich) T (020) 3327 1280
www.oldbrewerygreenwich.com
OldBreweryGreenwich oldbrewery
First sold beer: February 2010 *See also* p 171

Meantime's plush pub-restaurant in the Royal Naval College, on the site of an institutional brewery operating between 1717 and 1858, is equipped with an automated brewhouse towering above diners. It's been used less than originally intended but should be up and running again in 2015.

Beers vary, and are usually exclusive to the pub. In the past, a lightly soured porter with the punning name Hospital Porter was among the more interesting products.

One Mile End

Brewpub
1 Mile End Road E1 4TP (Tower Hamlets)
See also White Hart pub p 121
T 07912 411147 OneMIleEnd
www.thewhitehartbrewpub.com
First sold beer: June 2013

Just across from the site of the old Mann brewery (see Yeast Enders p 121), this pub brewery was briefly known as Mulligans when it first opened. A small 4.5 hl (3 barrel) kit is used by head brewer Simon McCabe.

Beers: About a third of the output is drunk in the pub, the rest outside it, in cask and keykeg with some bottling. Core beers are **Salvation!** pale ale (4.4%), rye-tinged **Hospital Porter*** (its name alluding to the proximity of the Royal London Hospital, 5.3%) and **Snakecharmer IPA** (5.7%). Specials rotate through a repertoire of around 14 recipes including **Rye Mild** (3.8%). There's a modest barrel-aging programme with a Russian Imperial Stout planned.

Orbit Beers

Microbrewery
225 Fielding Street SE17 3HD (Southwark)
T (020) 7703 9092
www.orbitbeers.com OrbitBeers
First sold beer: August 2014 *See also* p 165

Robert Middleton worked in occupational pensions until a few years ago when he decided to take a career break travelling round his native Scotland visiting breweries, resulting in a book, *The Tea Leaf Paradox: Discovering Beer in the Land of Whisky*, and a keen interest in brewing. With the help of Stuart Medcalf of Twickenham Fine Ales, he set up this 16 hl (10 barrel) plant in a railway arch off Walworth Road. Robert's also a keen music fan, thus the strapline "Hi-Fidelity Brewing" and many of the beer names. The brewery supports the London Living Wage scheme.

Beers: Unusually for London, Orbit focuses on German-influenced beers which are lagered for up to four weeks then bottled or packed in keykegs. They include Alt-style **Neu*** (4.7%), Kölsch-style **Nico** (4.8%, namechecking the legendary Warhol superstar and sometime Velvet Underground *chanteuse*, who was born in Cologne: her family name, Päffgen, will be familiar to Kölsch devotees), and **Ivo*** pale ale (5.3%). Specials have included a smoked alt, **Leaf** (6.2%), and stout **Seven** (7%).

The Park Brewery

Microbrewery 🍺 🍺 🍶

95 Elm Road, Kingston-upon-Thames KT2 6HX (Kingston upon Thames)
T 07949 574618 ⓕ ⓨ TheParkBrewery
www.theparkbrewery.com
First sold beer: March 2014

This very small 1.5 hl (1 barrel) operation was founded by husband and wife team Josh and Frankie Kearns, originally to brew for the Jam Tree pubs in Clapham and Chelsea, but its activities have since diversified.

Beers: At first everything was bottled; cask and keykeg have since been added though availability remains relatively localised. Choices (not yet tasted) include **Killcat Pale** (3.7%) with Galaxy and Motueka hops, **Gallows Gold** (5%) with Simcoe and Galena hops, **Spankers IPA** (6%), **Dark Hill** (6.2%) and **Two Storm Ruby** (7.1%).

Partizan Brewing

Microbrewery 🍺 🍶 | 🍴 🥄 🍽 ⌁

8 Almond Road SE16 3LR (Southwark)
T (020) 8127 5053 ⓕ ⓨ PartizanBrewing
www.partizanbrewing.co.uk
First sold beer: November 2012 *See also p 67*

Former Redemption brewer Andy Smith (p 301) had the opportunity to create his own brewery when the Kernel upgraded and he was offered its old 6.5hl (4 barrel) kit. Another brewery in a Bermondsey railway arch, it's since become one of London's top performers for meticulously crafted artisanal beers. It's struggled to keep up with demand, and in April 2015 was at last able to expand fermentation capacity into a neighbouring arch. There are now two additional brewers, Chris Heaney and Josh Wheeler, but as at the Kernel, everyone is encouraged to do all the jobs.

Beers: A changing range of artisanal beers is mainly bottled, with some available in keykeg. The brewery is particularly strong on Belgian-inspired saison styles, notably the lighter-bodied **Saison Grisette**** (4.8%) and various **single hop saisons**, including **Citra*** and **Mosaic*** (both 7.4%). There are flavoured saisons too: **Grisette Lemongrass Lychee*** (3.8%) proved especially popular. More historically-slanted beers have included a strong mild, **X-Ale*** (6.1%), and a superb **Stout FES**** (Foreign Extra Stout, 8.7%). As at near neighbour the Kernel, the hops used in the pale ales vary: among the most celebrated have been **Centennial Citra*** (5.9%) and **IPA Citra Amarillo Simcoe*** (7%). Look out too for unexpected combinations, such as a black IPA with Czech Saaz hops. Pretty much everything is worth trying.

People's Pints

See Laine Brewing (People's Pints)

Perseverance

See Bloomsbury Brewing

LONDON DRINKERS | Andy Smith

Former chef and homebrewer Andy worked at Redemption before founding Partizan in Bermondsey, now one of the most highly-rated breweries in London. Andy brews the sorts of beers he'd like to drink himself, and is delighted he's able to share them with others.

How do you rate London as a beer city, on a world scale?
The UK scene in general is amazing at the moment and London is right at the top. It's unbeatable in terms of breweries and pubs.

What's the single most exciting thing about beer in London at the moment?
The rapid way things are changing, and the diversity, with new pubs opening all the time, new events

and great beer becoming more and more accessible.

What single thing would make things even better?
Quality. There are a few breweries out there that sometimes put out beer they shouldn't. And if those beers are drinkers' first experience of craft beer, it damages the whole industry.

What are your top London beers right now (other than those from your own brewery)?
The Kernel pale ales are still the best in London. Brew by Numbers Session IPA has got very, very good. And Fuller's Vintage Ale.

What's your top great beer night out?
I'd start with a tour of the Bermondsey breweries on a Saturday, maybe call in at the

Rake (p58) then head over to Hackney. There are now so many options over there but the Cock Tavern is one of the tops (p107).

Who's your London beer hero?
Derek Prentice (p95). I don't usually go in for heroes but he epitomises the term. Not only is he a great brewer, the scheme for training new apprentices he's now working on is enormously helpful.

Who will we be hearing a lot more from in future?
One Mile End at the White Hart (p121). I wasn't convinced when it started out but current head brewer Simon McCabe is now making some incredible beers.

Which are your other top beer cities?
Brussels is very high up there.

Portobello Brewing
Microbrewery 🍺🍴 🍶
6 Mitre Bridge Industrial Park, Mitre Way W10 6AU (Kensington and Chelsea)
T (020) 8969 2269 🔲 🐦 PortobelloBeer
www.portobellobrewing.com
First sold beer: December 2012

While most recent brewery startups in London are the work of enterprising homebrewers, this is an initiative from the established industry, set up by Glamorgan Beer Company's Richard Anstee and ex-Wells & Young's man Rob Jenkins, with Iain Masson, formerly of Greene King, as the first head brewer, since succeeded by Farooq Khalid. It's a sizeable operation with a target output of around 6,500 hl (4,000 barrels) a year, and investment in fermentation capacity has continued apace since opening.

Beers are among the most likely London brews to appear in chain pubs and on pubco guest lists. Regulars are **VPA*** (Very Pale Ale, 4%), easy drinking pale ale **Portobello Star** (4.3%) and **Market Porter** (4.6%), all in cask as well

as keg and bottle. **London Pilsner** (4.6%) is keg and bottled only. Occasional and seasonal beers have included an American pale ale.

Pressure Drop Brewing
Microbrewery 🍺 🍶 🔸
19 Bohemia Place E8 1DU (Hackney)
T (020) 8533 0614   🐦 PressureDropBrw
www.pressuredropbrewing.co.uk
First sold beer: January 2013

For more about this impressive Hackney brewer, see feature p109.

Beers are sold largely bottle conditioned or in keykeg, and only rarely in cask. Regulars are a superbly refreshing "foreaged herb Hefeweiss" named **Wu Gang Chops The Tree**** (3.8%) after a Chinese legend; **Pale Fire*** (4.8%), a pale ale with a newly developed hop variety; **Street Porter*** (4.9%); **Stokey Brown*** (5.1%), one of the inaugural beers and still deservedly popular;

Beers: Redchurch concentrated from the start on quality bottle-conditioned beer, but has since added some keykeg. Core lines include **Shoreditch Blonde** (4.5%), **Brick Lane Lager*** (5%), the brewery's inaugural beer **Bethnal Pale Ale** (5.5%), **Hackney Gold*** (5.5%, actually more of a US-style amber ale despite its name), **Hoxton Stout*** (6%), **Great Eastern IPA** (7.4%) and **Old Ford Export Stout*** (7.5%, sometimes available in a barrel aged version). Specials have included a low ABV **Black Pale*** (2.8%). More wild and wood-aged beers are likely to appear in future.

and **Bosko** IPA* (6.5%). Recurring specials include **Freimann's Dunkelweiss** (4.8%) and a very orangey Belgian-style wheat beer, **Wallbanger Wit** (4.7%) and there are various one-offs.

Queens Head
Brewpub 🍺 🍾 | 🔖
66 Acton Street WC1X 9NB (Camden)
T (020) 7713 5772   🐦 TheQueens_Head
www.queensheadlondon.com
First sold beer: March 2014   See also p 49

A very small 1 hl brewery in the cellar of a beer-friendly Kings Cross pub.

Beers: So far only a keg pale ale has been produced in small quantities for sale in the pub, though other styles and cask beers should appear in 2015.

Redchurch Brewery
Microbrewery 🍺 🍾 | 🛒 🔖 ⚗
275 Poyser Street E2 9RL (Tower Hamlets)
T (020) 3487 0255
www.theredchurchbrewery.com
📘 The-Redchurch-Brewery
🐦 TheRedchurchBrewery
First sold beer: September 2011 *See also* p 120

Former solicitor Gary Ward and partner Tracey Cleland named this brewery after their home street, launching the brand with a homebrewed trial batch in August 2011. The first commercial brew from their 13 hl (8 barrel) PBC kit in a Bethnal Green railway arch followed shortly afterwards.

Redemption Brewing
Microbrewery 🍺 🍾 | ⚗
2 Compass West Estate, West Road N17 0XL (Haringey)   **T** (020) 8885 5227
www.redemptionbrewing.co.uk
🐦 redemptionbrew
First sold beer: February 2010

For more about this stalwart of the new generation of London brewers, see feature p 153.

Beers: Redemption beers skilfully appeal to contemporary tastes without alienating traditional real ale drinkers. The core cask range includes masterful low gravity pale ale **Trinity*** (3%), **Pale Ale** (3.8%), stronger pale **Rock the Kazbek** (4%, with Czech Kazbek hops), award-winning hoppy amber ale **Hopspur*** (4.5%), curious hybrid dark bitter **Urban Dusk*** (4.6%), substantial porter **Fellowship*** (5.1%) and **Big Chief IPA** (5.5%). Stronger beers like Big Chief, Fellowship and Hopspur are bottled too. Numerous collaborations and specials have included a strong version of Urban Dusk aged on wood chips and called – you've guessed it – Bourbon Dusk.

Rocky Head Brewery

Microbrewery 🍺 🍴
16 Glenville Mews, Kimber Road SW18 4NJ
(Wandsworth)　**T** (020) 8875 9917
www.rockyheadbrewing.co.uk
📘 rockyheadbrewery 🐦 TheRockyHead
First sold beer: September 2012

This once claimed to be "possibly the most ramshackle brewery in the UK", with an 8 hl (5 barrel) kit pieced together by wine importer Steve Daniel and friends, from bits and pieces sourced with the help of former Roosters brewer Sean Franklin, including recycled components from the demolished Tetley brewery in Leeds. Despite the quality of its beers, the brewery remains a part-time business operating only at weekends.

Beers are mostly bottled conditioned, with some keykeg. The flagship is a superb contemporary **Pale Ale**** (6.5%), for some time the only product as the brewers sought to perfect it. Introduced since are **Session** (4%), American pale ale **Zen*** (4.8%), unusual sour ale **Hop Ditch*** (6%) and **Imitera** IPA (7.2%). During 2015 two others beers will be added to the core range, including a stout.

Sambrook's Brewery

Microbrewery 🍺 🍴 🍴 🍶 ｜ 🛒 🖌 ⚙
1 Yelverton Road SW11 3QG (Wandsworth)
T (020) 7228 0598
📘 🐦 SambrookAle
www.sambrooksbrewery.co.uk
First sold beer: November 2008　*See also* p 189

For more about one of the founders of the new wave of London breweries, see feature p 190.

Beers: Sambrook's has proved adept at reaching the established cask ale market. Mainstays, also available bottle conditioned in 500 ml bottles from the offsite bottling plant, are flagship 'ordinary' bitter **Wandle Ale*** (3.8%), **Pumphouse Pale Ale** (4.2%), special bitter **Junction*** (4.5%) and **Powerhouse Porter*** (4.9%), with a programme of seasonals including a mild. More recently it's added a range of beers aimed at a more contemporary market, sold in keg or 330 ml bottles: **London Pale Ale** (4.5%), **London Porter** (5%), **Battersea Rye*** (5.8%) and **Battersea IPA** (6.2%). **No 5 Barley Wine*** (8.2%) and **Imperial Stout** (10.4%) are produced occasionally in bottles only.

Signature Brew

Microbrewery 🍴 🍽 🍺 | 🖱
25 Leyton Business Centre, Etloe Road E10 7BT
(Waltham Forest) **T** (020) 3397 8878
www.signaturebrew.co.uk
f 🐦 SignatureBrew
First sold beer: January 2014

Music and beer fans Tom Bott, Sam McGregor and David Riley addressed their frustratoin at the way industrial beer brands dominate the music scene by bringing together musicians and brewers to create special edition brews. Their first beer, the General, created with the Rifles, was launched in September 2011, and since then collaborators have included Dry the River, Enter Shikari, Craig Finn, Professor Green, Ed Harcourt, dance label Hospital Records, Mastodon and Frank Turner. The first beers were developed at a pilot brewery in Hackney, then 'cuckoo'-brewed by Sam and Tom at Titanic in Stoke-on-Trent – Tom's father is the brewery's co-owner Dave Bott and his uncle veteran brewer and boss Keith Bott. Other breweries have since been used, including Londoners Hackney, Late Knights and London Fields. Late in 2013 the business moved into its current larger premises and launched a series of 'Originals' beers under its own name, still with music themes, with some trial commercial production on the pilot kit. In March 2015 a 16 hl (10 barrel) brewhouse formerly at Five Points was installed, and all brewing should have moved in-house by the time you read this.

Beers: The Originals range is sold mainly in cask, with some keykeg. It includes a bitter with New Zealand hops called **Session*** (4%), a US-style **Pale** (4.1%), **Black Vinyl Stout*** (4.2%), **Red Wedge** (4.7%), passion fruit ale **Candela Gold** (5%), **Lage**r (5%, not cask) and **IPA** (5.6%). The lager, IPA and pale are also bottled. The musical collaborations are predominantly bottled: among the most notable is a strong black IPA, **Black Tongue*** (8.3%), created with Mastodon.

Solvay Society (Hops and Glory)

Brewpub 🍴 🍽 🍺 | 🏷
382 Essex Road N1 3PF (Islington)
See also Hops and Glory pub p143
T (020) 7226 2277 🐦 SolvaySociety
www.solvaysociety.com
First sold beer: February 2014

Early in 2014, beer-friendly Canonbury pub the Hops and Glory started brewing occasionally for sale over the bar, using what was essentially a homebrew kit in the cellar. At about the same time, a brewing duo known as Solvay Society, comprising head brewer Roman Hochuli, who grew up in Brussels, and business partner JP Hussey, started working on a small 0.5 hl (0.3 barrel) Braumeister kit in the cellar of a Walthamstow pub, the Warrant Officer (which also had a role in the emergence of Wild Card), selling their first beer in March. They later transferred the kit to the Hops and Glory, resuming brewing in January 2015. The intention is to continue to perfect beers on a small scale and build a reputation while Roman completes postgraduate studies, then look to expand. The pub staff also occasionally use the kit, essentially 'cuckoo' brewing in their own nest.

Beers (not yet tasted) are mainly sold from keg in the pub, with some bottling. They include Belgian pale ale **Structure of Matter** (4.8%) and dry-hopped saison, **Coulomb** (5.2%), made with maize. Specials are likely to include a pink peppercorn rye tripel and a light ale. The pub's own beer is in varied styles.

Soul Rebel Brew Co

Beer firm 🍽 🍾
(Tower Hamlets) 🐦 SoulRebelBrewCo
First sold beer: November 2014

Ex-London Brewing and Weird Beard brewer Daniel Vane is currently working his way round the country creating collaboration brews at places like Hanging Bat, Mad Hatter and Northern Monk. He plans to preside at his own brewery somewhere in North London by the end of 2015.

Beers (not yet tasted): a variety of imaginative styles in keg and bottle, including a strawberry and white pepper wheat, a barrel-aged coconut imperial stout and brews with a breakfast theme like a tea and biscuit mild.

Beers (not tasted) are sold on cask in the pub, with two usually on at any time from a repertoire of Citra-hopped **Citrus Ale** (3.7%), **Blond** (4.1%), **English Pale** (4.3%) and **American Pale Ale** (4.5%). Other beers may be developed.

Strawman Brewery

Microbrewery
Arch 77, 876 Old Kent Road SE15 1NQ (Lewisham)
T (020) 7112 9102 ☐ ☑ strawmanbrewery
www.strawmanbrewery.com
First sold beer: June 2013

This very small brewery was originally in an arch near London Fields but soon outgrew the site and in December 2013 crossed the river to its current address, in another arch on the boundary of New Cross and Peckham.

Beers are bottle conditioned in limited quantities and include a notable **Saison*** (3.9%), amber lager **Munich** (4.5%), a **House Pale** with varying hop recipes (5%) and an **Amber** ale (5.3%).

Southwark Brewing

Microbrewery
46 Druid Street SE1 2EZ (Southwark)
T (020) 3302 4190
www.southwarkbrewing.co.uk
☐ southwarkbrewing ☑ southwarkbeer
First sold beer: October 2014   *See also* p 67

A new initiative from an industry veteran, the furthest northwest of the Bermondsey breweries was created by ex-Marston's brewer Peter Jackson. An 8 hl (5 barrel) kit is used though expansion is likely.

Beers: Untypically for Bermondsey breweries, the focus is mainly on cask session ales, including easy-drinking **LPA London Pale Ale*** (4%), English bitter **Best*** (4.4%) and hoppier **Gold** (5.2%). Beers are also bottled, and occasional brews include stronger bottle-conditioned stuff like **Peter's Stout** (8.9%), acknowledging Russian czar Peter the Great's incognito sojourn in southeast London.

Sultan Brewery

Brewpub
78 Norman Road SW19 1BT   *See also* p 200
T (020) 8542 4532
www.hopback.co.uk ☑ sultansw19

A microbrewery has been installed in an outhouse at the HopBack brewery's Wimbledon pub.
Beers: To be confirmed.

Stag

See AB InBev UK

Still and Star

Brewpub
1 Little Somerset Street E1 8AH (City of London)
T (020) 7488 3761   www.stillandstar.co.uk
First sold beer: December 2014

Pub landlord Michael Cox runs what's currently the only commercial brewery in the City using an automatic 0.8 hl (0.5 barrel) brewing kit with pre-programmed recipes.

Tankley's Brewery

Microbrewery
Sidcup (Bexley)
www.tankleysbrewery.com
☑ TankleysBrewery

Homebrewers Glenn Heinzel, originally from Australia, and Martin Hemmings plan to have a small 1.5 hl (1 barrel) brewery online in mid-2015.

Beers (not yet tasted) are likely to be "slightly off-centre" **Pale Ale** and **IPA**, with imaginative seasonals.

Tap East

Brewpub 🍺 🍺 🍶 | 🛒 🏷️

7 International Square, Westfield Stratford
City E20 1EE (Newham)   **T** (020) 8555 4467
www.tapeast.co.uk 🅵 Tap-East 🐦 TapEast
First sold beer: October 2011   *See also* p 117

This specialist beer bar in the Westfield
Stratford City shopping mall has its own 4 hl
(2.5 barrel) brewery visible behind glass.
Former Brentford brewer Jim Wilson helped
build up the range before moving on to the
Laine's brewery at Victoria Park (above):
his successor is Jonny Park.

Beers are in cask and keykeg, with occasional
bottlings, and are mainly sold in the pub and
connected outlets, such as the Rake and
Utobeer in Borough Market. Regular beers,
some of them based on historic recipes,
include low gravity **Tonic Ale** (3%), **East End
Mild*** (3.5%), **Jim Wilson Bitter** (3.8%),
American Pale Ale (4.4%), an **IPA** with
changing hop varieties (5.3%) and coffee stout
Coffee in the Morning* (5.5%). There are
numerous specials and collaborations, including an annual collaboration festival where a
horde of guest brewers is invited to use the kit.

Truman's Beer

Microbrewery 🍺 🍺 🍶 🍾 | 🏷️ ⚓ 🍷

2 Stour Road E3 2NT (Tower Hamlets)
See also Cygnet bar p 115
T (020) 8533 3575 **www.trumansbeer.co.uk**
🅵 🐦 trumansbeer
First sold beer: July 2013

For more on the history of this legendary name
in London brewing and how it was unexpectedly revived, see From Black Eagle to Dark
Star p 90.

Beers: Most beer is cask, with bottled versions.
Core beers include the first new beer to bear
the revived brand name, darkish best bitter
Runner* (4%). It's since been joined by **Swift**
golden ale (3.9%), and a 'craft keg' beer, **Pale**
(4.1%). There are various seasonals and specials,
including a good IPA, **Tom Ditto*** (4.9%) and
some brewed exclusively for Nicholson's pubs.
These beers are new recipes, but there have
been some bottle-conditioned heritage beers
too. **London Keeper*** (8%), a double export
stout from an 1880 recipe that was the first
brew in the new plant, can still be tracked down
and will keep on improving, while **Ben Truman
Pale Ale*** (6%) was recreated with the help of
former 'old' Truman brewer Derek Prentice.

Twickenham Fine Ales

Microbrewery ▤ ▤ ▯ | ▭ ✎ ⬛
18 Mereway Road, Twickenham TW2 6RG
(Richmond upon Thames) **T** (020) 8241 1825
www.twickenham-fine-ales.co.uk
🅕 TwickenhamBrewery 🐦 TwickenhamAles
First sold beer: November 2004   *See* p 224

For more about what's now London's second-oldest freestanding microbrewery, see feature p 225.

Beers: Most output is in cask, with core beers and some specials also bottled. The flagship is hoppyish golden ale **Naked Ladies*** (4.4%), a name I forgive as it's the local nickname for the sculptures on a landmark fountain at nearby

York House. A version of this beer, with the same recipe but with a different yeast and bottle conditioned, is intermittently brewed by Alvinne in West Flanders. Other regulars are crisp golden ale **Sundancer** (3.7%), full-bodied bitter **Grandstand*** (3.8%), and a newish amber beer, **Redhead** (4.1%), with roasted barley. There are four cask seasonals and 12 monthly specials, which have included **Black Eel*** (5%), a black IPA with English hops. A hoppy 'craft keg', **Tusk IPA** (4.7%), has recently been added. Occasional delights like a Belgian-style **Oud Bruin*** (8.1%), made in collaboration with Flemish colleagues Alvinne and Struise, are issued in very limited editions.

Ubrew

Microbrewery ▤ ▤ ▮ | ▭ ✎ ⬛
Abbey Street SE16 (Southwark)
www.ubrew.cc 🅕 🐦 ubrewcc

Expected to open amid the Bermondsey breweries during the first half of 2015, this crowd-funded venture isn't a conventional micro but a shared brewing kit aimed at homebrewers and small-scale 'cuckoos'. Would-be brewers can become members as individuals or groups, claim their own fermenting vessel and book space on a nanobrewery-sized kit, with training and courses also offered. It will be fronted by a bar stocking a wide range of beers besides house-brewed products.

Upstairs Brewing
Beer firm 🛢 🍾
London E17 (Waltham Forest)
www.upstairsbrewing.com
📘 🐦 UpstairsBrewing
First sold beer: June 2014

Homebrewer Michaela White went professional as assistant brewer at Clarence & Fredericks (see Volden Brewing below), and also 'cuckoo' brewed there in her own right as well as elsewhere. Eventually she aims to open a brewpub.

Beers: Best known for **Arabian Nights*** (5.4%), a milk stout spiced with black cardamon and using toasted rye malt. Other beers have included crisp pale **Aussie Breakfast Ale** (4.7%), a Belgian saison, and an autumn ale for a Wetherspoon festival made in collaboration with Tring brewery.

Volden Brewing
Microbrewery (Antic) 🛢
35 Neville Road, Croydon CR0 2DS (Croydon)
First sold beer: October 2012

Victoria Barlow and Duncan Woodhead moved into an industrial unit in Neville Road, Croydon in August 2012 to install a 20hl (12 barrel) kit, launching their first beers at the Wallington beer festival that October under the name Clarence & Fredericks. Assistant brewer Michaela White also brewed here in her own right under the name Upstairs Brewing (above). Despite success, Victoria and Duncan found they couldn't commit the investment in time and money needed to expand the business further, and in April 2015 they ceased brewing, selling the equipment to Volden Brewing, a subsidiary of the Antic pub group, who have long had aspirations to brew. The founders have retained the recipes and brands however so it's possible these might resurface in some form.

Beers: Currently only a golden ale, **Vim** (3.8%, not yet tasted), on sale exclusively in Antic pubs, with more to follow.

Weird Beard Brew Co
Microbrewery 🛢 🛢 🍴 🍾
5 Boston Business Park, Trumpers Way W7 2QA (Ealing) **T** (020) 3645 2711
www.weirdbeardbrewco.com
📘 weird.beard.798 🐦 WeirdBeard_Brew
First sold beer: March 2013

For more about one of London's most appreciated artisanal breweries, see feature p 219.

Beers appear in cask, keykeg, bottle conditioned or, now, in cans. Regulars are coffee stout **Black Perle*** (3.7%), American pale ale **Mariana Trench*** (5.3%), luscious stout **Decadence*** (5.5%), pilsner-style **Faithless Spreadsheet Ninja** (5.5%), a self-described "eccentric IPA" called **Hit the Lights** (5.8%), black IPA **Fade to Black*** (6.3%) and US-style IPA **Five O'Clock Shadow*** (7.3%). Several beers are made with changing hop varieties, including session pale ale **Little Things That Kill*** (around 3.5%) and the considerably bigger-boned Double IPA **Holy Hoppin' Hell***–** (around 9.5%). **K*ntish Town Beard** (5.5%) is an American pale specially brewed for BrewDog Camden: I'll diplomatically avoid repeating the story behind the name. There are numerous other single hop one-offs, collaborations and strong stuff: one particularly formidable brew is ironically labelled **Boring Brown Beer*** (8.2%).

White Hart
See One Mile End

Wild Card Brewery
Microbrewery 🛢 🍴 🍺 🏷 🍷
7 Ravenswood Industrial Estate, Shernhall Street E17 9HQ (Waltham Forest)
T (020) 8935 5560   📘 🐦 WildCardBrewery
www.wildcardbrewery.co.uk
First sold beer: February 2014   *See also* p 128

William John Harris and Andy Birkby, two old friends from Nottingham, originally developed their amber ale Jack of Clubs as homebrewers on homemade equipment in a garage. They then began commissioning it commercially from the Brentwood brewery, just outside London, in January 2013, working with another old friend, chemical engineer Jaega Wise (*below*), from the cellar of the Warrant Officer pub in Walthamstow (later also briefly home to Solvay Society). In May 2013 they installed a new 10 hl (6 barrel) kit from Oban Ales in an industrial estate on the edge of Walthamstow Village, with Jaega as head brewer. The brewery is a London Living Wage employer.

Beers are mainly cask and bottled. The original beer, distinctive amber ale **Jack of Clubs*** (4.5%) is still the flagship, now joined by blond ale **King of Hearts** (4.5%) and continuously hopped IPA **Queen of Diamonds** (5%), plus specials.

LONDON DRINKERS Jaega Wise

Jaega is head brewer at Wild Card in Walthamstow, an old friend of brewery founders Andrew and William, who has been involved in the project since the beginning. Her background is in chemical engineering – "I'm used to being one of the few women in my industry" – though she has a parallel career as a soul and R&B singer (www.facebook.com/jaegawisemusic). "Beer's got more fashionable since we started," she says, "but we're in it for the long haul. We like accessible beer with a broad appeal: when I'm developing a beer, I always ask myself, could I drink a pint of it?"

How do you rate London as a beer city, on a world scale?
A solid 9/10 for range and diversity, and good quality too, with some excellent beer from tiny breweries.

What's the single most exciting thing about beer in London at the moment?
The hop profiles. London brewers like Beavertown, Partizan and Pressure Drop have led the UK in developing very aromatic beers.

What single thing would make things even better?
Being able to get to drinkers more easily. It's still difficult for small producers to get their beers out there, and we need more outlets selling a diverse range, especially in central London.

What are your top London beers right now (other than those from your own brewery)?
Beavertown Gamma Ray, Five Points Pale and Hackney Dark Lager.

What's your top great beer night out?
I'd love to say the Wild Card brewery when we're open: it's a

great atmosphere with freshly brewed beer. But other than that, I like the Adam and Eve (p105): it's one of those places making good local beer accessible to a broader range of drinkers.

Who's your London beer hero?
Jane Peyton (p84). She's truly inspiring as well as knowledge-able and does great work introducing people to beer.

Who will we be hearing a lot more from in future?
The small pub chains that are doing such great work getting beer out there.

Which are your other top beer cities?
We're all from Nottingham and I always look forward to going back there. There's some fine breweries like Castle Rock and fantastic pubs like the Monkey Tree. And it's great to drink cask beer from sparklers!

Wimbledon Brewery

Microbrewery 🍺 🍺 🍴
8 Prince Georges Road SW19 2PX (Merton)
www.wimbledonbrewery.com
⬛ wimbledonbrewery 🐦 WimbledonBrew

A sizeable new project with a 50 hl kit near Merton Abbey Mills in the Wandle valley, helmed by veteran London brewer Derek Prentice (p 95) with Mark Gordon and Richard Coultart, rekindling a local tradition that lapsed when the original Wimbledon brewery burned down in 1889. Beers should be on sale by the time you read this, with a launch planned to coincide with 2015's Wimbledon tennis tournament.

Beers (not yet tasted): A traditional range with a contemporary slant, including session bitter **Common**, **Tower** special bitter, an IPA, a golden ale and a stout.

Zerodegrees Blackheath

Brewpub 🍺 | 🛒 🔖
29 Montpelier Vale SE3 0TJ (Lewisham)
T (020) 8852 5619   www.zerodegrees.co.uk
⬛ zerodegreesrestaurant 🐦 ZerodegreesBeer
First sold beer: August 2000   See also p 174

Currently London's longest serving brewpub, this minimalist bar-restaurant in Blackheath was also one of the first in the UK to draw its inspiration from the US craft-brewing scene, following a trip across the Atlantic by a member of a family of local restaurateurs. An automated 15 hl (9 barrel) kit was supplied by BTB in Germany and the regular beers were first devised by a head brewer from the US. There have been several changes of brewer since, with German-trained Janis Götte the most recent arrival. Branches with their own breweries have opened in Bristol, Cardiff and Reading, sharing the same name despite the fact that, unlike the original, they're considerably further from the prime meridian.

Beers: Most of the beer is sold on draught in the pub, unpasteurised and unfiltered from polythene-lined tanks using air pressure, though it's also available to take away in 5 l minikegs and is occasionally supplied in 50 l kegs to other outlets and private functions. The regular beers are **Black Lager** (4.6%), **Pale Ale** (4.6%) and a notably tasty **Pilsner*** (4.8%), plus a fruit beer and a wheat beer (both around 4.5%), the precise formulations of which regularly change. A sixth slot is reserved for a brewer's special, which can range far and wide though is often seasonally appropriate.

Breweries outside London

The following selected breweries are strictly speaking just outside Greater London but their products are regularly stocked as local beer in London outlets, particularly those relatively close to the breweries themselves.

Brentwood Brewing

Microbrewery ● ◊ ▮ | ⌂ ▲ ⌐

Calcott Hall Farm, Ongar Road, Brentwood CM15 9HS (Essex) **T** 01277 200483

www.brentwoodbrewing.co.uk

🐦 BrentwoodBeerCo

First sold beer: June 2006

Founded by Dave Holmes and Roland Kannor on a farm near Brentwood just beyond London's eastern edge, this award-winning brewery expanded significantly in 2013 to another farm site not far away, with a new 25 hl (15 barrel) kit. See the website for details of the on-site shop and visitor centre.

Beers: Brentwood supplies a wide range of cask ales, also available in polypins and bottle. The core beers are a remarkably flavoursome low-alcohol brown beer **BBC 2*** (2.5%), **IPA** (3.7%, actually a relatively lightly-hopped beer), maple syrup-dosed **Marvellous Maple Mild*** (3.7%), **Best** bitter (4.2%), **Gold** (4.3%), premium bitter **Hope and Glory** (4.5%), special bitter **Lumberjack** (5.2%) and unusual but successful orange-flavoured old ale **Chockwork Orange*** (6.5%). A wide variety of specials and seasonals have included a limited edition 'champagne' beer, **Van Kannor** (7.7%), in 750 ml bottles. The brewery hosts numerous cuckoo brewers and contractors: it produced the original Wild Card beers, has made own-brand beers for London's Antic pubs, and still brews Terry Pratchett-themed Discworld ales for mail-order retailer Ales by Mail.

Westerham Brewery

Microbrewery ● ◊ ▮ | ⌐

Grange Farm, Pootings Road, Crockham Hill, Edenbridge TN8 6SA (Kent)

T 01732 864427 🐦 WesterhamBrew

www.westerhambrewery.co.uk

First sold beer: June 2004

Not far south of the London boundary on a National Trust property in the Kent Downs Area of Outstanding Natural Beauty, this micro led by Robert Wicks took both name and yeast culture from the long-closed Black Eagle brewery in Westerham village, not far away.

Beers include a wide range of cask regulars, also in polypins and minicasks, often using hops from very local sources. They include session ale **Finchcocks Original*** (3.5%) with hops from Finchcocks hop garden, dark bitter **Grasshopper** (3.8%), golden ale **Spirit of Kent** (4%), premium bitter **British Bulldog*** (4.3%), **1965 Special Bitter Ale*** (4.8%), **Hop Rocket IPA** (robustly hopped with English hops, 4.8%) and strong speciality **Audit Ale*** (6.2%), inspired by a historical recipe. British Bulldog and Audit Ale are bottled too, alongside another heritage beer, **Double Stout*** (5.5%), and various pale ales, one of which, low gluten **Freedom Ale** (4.8%), celebrates anti-slavery campaigner William Wilberforce, who lived nearby. There's a low gluten bottled pilsner too, **Bohemian Rhapsody** (5%), and numerous cask seasonals and specials.

Windsor & Eton Brewery

Microbrewery 🍺 🍺 🍼 | 🍺
1 Vansittart Estate, Duke Street,
Windsor SL4 1SE (Windsor and Maidenhead)
T 01753 854075 www.webrew.co.uk
🅕 WindsorandEtonBrewery
🐦 WindsorEtonBrew
First sold beer: May 2010

Though outside the Greater London boundary to the west, Windsor & Eton is a founder member of the London Brewers Alliance and widely sold in London pubs: see feature p 313.

Beers are widely available in cask but also sold in minicask, polypin and bottle, the last sometimes at a slightly higher strength. Mainstays include light ale **Parklife** (3.2%), golden ale **Knight of the Garter** (3.8%), tasty New Zealand-hopped pale ale **Windsor Knot*** (4%), best bitter **Guardsman** (the brewery's inaugural beer, 4.2%), and black IPA **Conqueror*** (5%), also available in stronger bottle-conditioned form as **Conqueror 1075**** (7.4%). There's an authentic and excellent Czech-style lager, **Republika*** (4.8%), in keg and bottle, and various seasonals and specials. The brewery now hosts related project **Uprising**, brewing a contemporary-style IPA, **Treason*** (5.6%).

BEYOND LONDON'S BREWING   Windsor & Eton

Windsor & Eton Brewery holds the anomalous status of a London brewer outside London. It's in Windsor, a town which, despite sharing a river, royal residents and hordes of tourists with the capital, is technically beyond the London boundary to the west. The anomaly dates from a time, only a few short years ago, when London brewers were rather fewer than today. "It was spring 2010," recounts brewing director Paddy Johnson, "and we'd just got our first brew into the fermenters when we got a phone call from Phil Lowry, then at Brew Wharf. He invited us to this get-together of London brewers. There were eight breweries represented, and the evening went so well, we decided to found the London Brewers Alliance.

"We were a bit worried that night," he continues, "because we needed a new saccharometer [a device for measuring sugar content] to work out if the beer had fermented enough, and it hadn't yet been delivered. The very next day, Steve Schmidt from Meantime turned up on our doorstep with one in his hand. That sort of approach has epitomised the LBA ever since." Though the Alliance has since restricted its membership to brewers within the M25, Windsor & Eton retains 'grandfather rights' and is still an active member. "Going to that meeting was the best thing we ever did," reflects Paddy. "We've had so much business from London pubs because we're seen as a London brewer."

Paddy can also claim impeccable London brewing credentials. "I started in 1979 at Courage in Horsleydown," he recalls (see Southwark ale p56). "My first

brewday was Imperial Russian Stout – the head brewer said, 'You have to see this, we only do it once a year.'" Subsequently he worked across the country for Courage, Bass, and Scottish & Newcastle, then decided to set up on his own with his old friend Will Calvert, originally a Courage brewer who had moved on to work in confectionery, at Mars in Slough. The 17-barrel (28 hl) kit was fabricated at Malrex to

specifications devised by Paddy and another founding partner, Jim Morrison. "They loved us," Paddy remembers, "because Jim is an engineer and we knew exactly what we wanted."

The first beer was sold on St George's Day 2010 and the output has steadily built ever since: the brewery has since taken over two neighbouring units and now produces about 100 barrels (164 hl) a week, with a busy onsite shop and visitor centre. They're known for their impeccable cask beers, reflecting Paddy's lengthy experience, but they've also ventured into other styles. Czech brewer Tomáš Mikulica, of Pivovarský Dvůr Chýně near Prague, helped them develop a genuine long-matured Czech lager, Republika, which is still scrupulously produced to his specifications. "We even put copper bars into our stainless steel kettle," says Paddy, "as Tomáš insisted it should really be brewed in a copper one."

And now the next generation is firing up the mash tun. Paddy's son Kieran is currently being tutored by his father through his Diploma of Brewing, and is creating his own beers at the brewery under the Uprising brand. "We help, but all the decisions are down to him," says Paddy. Kieran's contemporary IPA has already caused heads to turn. Understandably given its location, Windsor & Eton regularly uses patriotic and royal references to name its beers, so it's interesting that, having previously added a beer called Republika, it now produces one called Treason. Let's be thankful for brewers who aren't afraid to stick their necks out.

Been & gone

Only two London breweries listed in the last edition of this book are not in this one. House-brewed beer had been sold at **Brew Wharf** (Southwark) since October 2005 but new owners discontinued brewing in May 2014. The bar still stocks a good beer range (p 51). **Ha'penny** (Redbridge), a part-time operation in rural surrounds at Aldborough Hatch in the East London suburbs, first sold beer in October 2009 but had ceased operations by the end of 2014.

Inevitably, given the dynamism of the scene in the four years since the book last appeared, some initiatives have bloomed only too briefly. **Adventure** in Chessington (Kingston upon Thames) unleashed a range of interesting bottled beers in June 2012 but little over a year later brewing was suspended and has not yet resumed. Crowd-funded **Brüpond** in Leyton (Waltham Forest) was launched in November 2012 by Colorado native David Brassfield, but folded in August 2013. The **Botanist** on Kew Green (Richmond

Meanwhile, on Gin Lane…

Beer isn't the limit of London's alcoholic heritage. While the city's vital role in brewing history is now little-known, for many people the word 'London' is firmly wedded to the word 'gin'. Once notorious as the obliterant of choice for the capital's underclass, London gin became an international jet set brand before almost disappearing from the city of its birth completely. In recent years a new crop of small distillers has started reclaiming the reputation of gin in London, buoyed by the same interest in all things local and 'craft' that's benefitted the microbrewing sector.

It's not surprising gin and beer come from the same places as they share a heritage and agricultural preconditions. Traditionally, gin begins life in the same way as beer, as a sugary liquid known to distillers as 'wash', obtained from grains, originally barley, which is then fermented. But while the alcohol in beer is purely the product of that first fermentation, gin, like other spirits, undergoes a concentration process known as distillation. Alcohol evaporates at lower temperatures than water, so the fermented liquid is gently heated

in a device called a still, and the alcohol fumes are captured and condensed to produce a much stronger drink – often so strong that it's diluted again before being sold. Today not all gins are grain-based: the spirit can derive from sugar beet or cane or even fruit, so long as it's legally of "agricultural origin".

Like beer, gin is flavoured with herbal matter, though not traditionally with hops and not before fermentation. Juniper berries are the signature 'botanical' but a range of other herbs and spices are also used, including some familiar to brewers past and present, like coriander, citrus peel, liquorice and anise. Today some gins are simply dosed with essences and concentrates, but legally London Gin must be re-distilled in an old-fashioned pot still, with the botanicals suspended in a basket above the vapours to produce a crystal-clear but aromatic result.

Gin first appeared in the 13th century in the Low Countries, another great brewing region, where it's known as *jenever* or *genever*, from *ginièvre*, the French word for juniper. Originally promoted as a medicinal

product, its popularity spread across the North Sea when Dutch *stadhouder* Willem van Oranje-Nassau ruled as William III of England between 1689–1702. Distillers could utilise poorer quality grain than brewers and didn't pay tax or require licenses, so the spirit was ridiculously cheap compared not only to heavily-taxed imported spirits from arch-enemy France but also domestic beer.

At the peak of the 'gin craze' in 1743, consumption stood at 10 l (2.2 gallons) per person per year, and the spirit was widely blamed for the poor health and degenerate behaviour of the urban poor. The view of gin as the dark side of alcohol consumption in Georgian England was eloquently illustrated in 1751 by engraver William Hogarth, who lived just across from what's now Fuller's brewery in Chiswick, in his famous diptych of Gin Lane and Beer Street. The former is a squalid hellhole of crime, stupor and madness where a syphilitic prostitute fails to notice her baby falling to its death. The latter is a paradise of social responsibility, good health and prosperity, where only the pawnbroker is on upon Thames) became a brewpub in September 2011, followed by sister pub the **Lamb** in Chiswick (Hounslow) a year later, but both ceased brewing by the end of 2013 after owning group Convivial was sold to Mitchells & Butlers: their kits are now in the Brewhouse and Kitchen venues.

Ellenberg's, run by former homebrewer Mike Ellenberg, shared a brewhouse in Hanwell (Ealing) with Weird Beard (p 219) when it opened in spring 2013 but a year later sold out to its sharing partner and folded as a separate entity. Travis Mooney's **Hoppy Collie** briefly sold beer from a pilot-sized kit in Hammersmith (Hammersmith and Fulham) from March 2013 but had disappeared before the end of that year. Another pilot-sized brewery that struggled was **Little Brew** (Camden): brewer Stu Small hand-delivered most of the beers around his Camden Town base from June 2012 but suspended brewing in October 2013, only to reappear with a bigger kit at a new location in July 2014 – in York, a long way beyond the horizons of this book.

a losing streak. A few years later, the gin craze had waned, following new legislation and the rising price of grain.

London distilleries established internationally-knowns gin brands in the 19th century, and gin gained its enduring association with tonic water in the British colonies where it was used to mask the taste of the quinine taken to combat malaria. But the capital never asserted an appellation and as a consequence 'London Gin' (or 'London Dry Gin' – the terms are interchangeable) can be made anywhere, so long as it conforms to the specifications. Burrough's **Beefeater** is the only surviving historic gin distillery in London, with roots going back to 1820s Chelsea, though it now occupies an anonymous site in a side street across from the Tesco on Kennington Lane. It's symptomatic of the increasing interest in gin that it finally opened a visitor centre in spring 2014 (www.beefeaterdistillery.com).

Undoubtedly key to this upsurge of interest is **Sipsmith**, opened in 2009 as the first new copper distillery in London since 1820 and the first of a new breed of small batch spirit makers (www.sipsmith.com). It began in Hammersmith but has since relocated to a larger site with a visitor centre in Chiswick, not far from Fuller's brewery, and, rather more ironically, Hogarth's house. You'll spot its products in numerous London pubs as well as supermarkets. Microdistillery **Sacred** opened in a Highgate back garden shortly after Sipsmith, originally working with brandy-style spirits but soon developing its own gin based on a historic recipe (www.sacredspiritscompany.com).

City of London, the first new distillery within the City for many centuries, followed in 2012. It has its own bar (www.cityoflondondistillery.com), and has collaborated with brewers including Head in a Hat. **Jensen's**, amid the Bermondsey breweries at Maltby Street Ropewalk (www.bermondseygin.com) and the **East London Liquor Company** in Bow (eastlondonliquorcompany.com) arrived in 2014, while the **Four Thieves** in Battersea (p187) is not only a brewpub but, from 2015, a distillery too.

City of London is also one of several London venues offering drinkers the opportunity to make their own gin by selecting their own botanicals; the punningly named **Ginstitute** in Notting Hill has a similar service (www.portobellostarbar.co.uk).

None of these companies, not even Beefeater, makes its own base spirit – instead neutral alcohol is bought in from 'agricultural sources', to be redistilled with signature blends of botanicals. But one notable addition to London's ever more diverse drinks industry is now making its own spirits from scratch using methods that in their initial stages very much resemble brewing. The **London Distillery Company**, established in Battersea late in 2013, is the first whisky distillery in London since the Lea Valley Distillery, on what's now the Olympic Park site, closed in the early 20th century. But as whisky can't legally be sold until it's at least three years old, don't expect to see a London single malt until at least 2017.

APPENDICES

More information

London

There are numerous **histories** of London. I've found these useful:

Peter Ackroyd, *London: the Biography*, Vintage 1991

Roy Porter, *London: a Social History*, Penguin 2000

Francis Sheppard, *London: a History*, Oxford University Press 1998

An essential visit for anyone interested in the city's history is the **Museum of London** (150 London Wall EC2Y 5HN, **www.museumoflondon.org.uk**) which as well as displays and events has an excellent bookshop.

Most big London bookshops have a range of **guidebooks** to contemporary London, including more specialist books on quirky and hidden features, and numerous walking guides. For a general guide I'd recommend *Time Out London* or the Lonely Planet guide, both of which are regularly updated. The official visitor guide at **www.visitlondon.com** is also useful and has lists of visitor information centres.

For **what's on information and latest news**, pick up a free copy of *Time Out*, check out **www.timeout.com/london**, or peruse insightful and increasingly comprehensive 'alternative' website www.londonist.com.

Transport information, a journey planner, walking routes and cycle maps are available from **www.tfl.gov.uk**. Though not perfect, the well-known A-Z series still has the best printed **mapping** (www.a-zmaps.co.uk), but you'll need the hefty Greater London edition to find all the places listed here.

Beer and brewing

For useful general reading on beer, including British beer, I'd recommend:

Stephen Beaumont and Tim Webb, *Pocket Beer Book 2nd edition*, Mitchell Beazley 2014: I declare an interest as I contributed the UK section, but this is a useful and impressively compact international survey. It's called the *Pocket Beer Guide* in the US.

Jeff Evans, *Beer Lover's Britain*, Inside Beer 2013 (e-book): An accessible and reliable introduction to British beer.

Randy Mosher, *Tasting Beer*, Storey Publishing 2009: A fascinating exploration of beer flavour from a renowned US author and homebrewing guru.

Garrett Oliver, *The Brewmaster's Table*, HarperPerennial 2005: The breakthrough guide to beer and food matching, now a decade old but still the definitive word on the subject.

Garrett Oliver (ed), *Oxford Companion to Beer*, Oxford University Press 2011: An encyclopaedic reference work for the dedicated enthusiast.

Roger Protz and Adrian Tierney-Jones, *Britain's Beer Revolution*, CAMRA Books 2014: An entertaining portrait of the UK's contemporary beer scene and the changes that have brought it about.

Tim Webb and Stephen Beaumont, *World Atlas of Beer*, Mitchell Beazley 2012: This large format introduction and guide is authoritative and unafraid to challenge received opinion.

For the historical accounts of beer and brewing here, I'm indebted in particular to:

Norman Barber, Mike Brown and Ken Smith, *Century Plus Plus of British Brewers 1890–2012*, Brewery History Society 2013

Jessica Boak & Ray Bailey, *Brew Britannia: The strange rebirth of British beer*, Aurum 2014

Geoff Brandwood and Jane Jephcote, *London Heritage Pubs: An inside story*, CAMRA Books 2008

Pete Brown, *Hops and Glory: One man's search for the beer that built the British Empire*, Macmillan 2010

Pete Brown, *Shakespeare's Local: Six centuries of history seen through one extraordinary pub*, Macmillan 2012

Martyn Cornell, *Amber Gold & Black: The history of Britain's great beers*, History Press 2010

Martyn Cornell, *Beer: The story of the pint*, Headline 2003

Peter Haydon, *The English Pub: A history*, Robert Hale 1995

Ian Mackey, *Twenty Five Years of New British Breweries*, self-published 1998

William Page (ed), 'Industries: Brewing' in *A History of the County of Middlesex*, 1911, accessed at **www.british-history.ac.uk**

Ronald Pattinson, *London!*, **www.barclayperkins.blogspot.com** 2010

John Spicer, Chris Thurman, John Walters and Simon Ward, *Intervention in the Modern UK Brewing Industry*, Palgrave Macmillan 2012

I've also made use of the comprehensive listings of British brewers at the independently-maintained website **www.quaffale.org.uk** and numerous pieces on Martyn Cornell's Zythophile blog at **www.zythophile.wordpress.com**.

Martyn's two books provide an excellent and approachable grounding in British brewing history, particularly *Amber Gold & Black* which also makes use of more up-to-date research. Pete Brown's *Shakespeare's Local* is a detailed but accessible history of the George (p 53), and so much more. Jessica and Ray's book is a meticulously researched and engaging account of the changing fortunes of beer in Britain in the last 50 years: their blog at **www.boakandbailey.com** has a wealth of great stuff too.

For those who really get the brewery history bug, there's the Brewery History Society, which publishes an always-engrossing journal as well as organising events. See **www.breweryhistory.com**.

Organisations

CAMRA in London

CAMRA has numerous branches in London running social activities for members as well as campaigning. Activities include pub and brewery visits, talks, tastings, maintaining pub information, running festivals, liaising with breweries, rating beer quality and researching listings for the *Good Beer Guide*. The London branches also jointly publish *London Drinker*, an excellent source of news and information about pubs, beer and beer-related events in the capital. All these activities are run by volunteers.

CAMRA's Greater London region now has a unified website at **www.london.camra.org.uk**. This has links to all 14 local branches and their websites, a diary of activities, lists of LocAle pubs, downloadable versions of *London Drinker* magazine, information about tasting panels and pub preservation and more.

Also active in London is CAMRA's national LGB group, LAGRAD (Lesbian and Gay Real Ale Drinkers) – the best source of information is the Facebook group **www.facebook.com/groups/lagrad**

To join CAMRA or get more information about the organisation nationally, see **www.camra.org.uk**
T (01727) 867201

London Brewers' Alliance

Founded in 2010, this is the trade organisation for breweries in London, and it's undoubtedly played a major role in the resurgence of London brewing, encouraging newcomers, championing London beer and improving quality. Full members must be commercial breweries operating within the M25 (with one exception: see Windsor & Eton p 312).

Its main object is to promote excellence in all aspects of brewing within London:

- by promoting the sale of beer brewed by its members
- by promoting its members
- by participating in any suitable event that promotes members' interests
- by cooperating with any other body that is deemed to have similar aims
- by supporting the improvement of brewing skills among the membership.

The website at **www.londonbrewers.org** has further contact details and information about member breweries, including links.

Places to drink by theme

Inside and out

Heritage pubs
On the national or regional inventories (see p32)
Beehive 148
Blackfriar 68
Blythe Hill Tavern 167
Express 218
Falcon 187
Fox *(Hanwell)* 218
George 53
Ivy House 163
Lamb *(Bloomsbury)* 47
Museum Tavern 48
Old Pack Horse 213
Olde Mitre 82
Pineapple 137
Princess Louise 83
St Stephens Tavern 99
Tabard 214

Interesting buildings
(not already covered above)
Bohemia 150
Café OTO 105
Catford Constitutional Club 168
Clapton Hart 107
Cock Tavern 107
Crate 114
Crosse Keys 69
Euston Tap 47
Exmouth Arms 75
Four Thieves 187
Fox on the Hill 160
George and Dragon 218
Gothique 193
Gun *(Docklands)* 118
Harrild and Sons 70
Holborn Whippet 80
Jerusalem Tavern 75

Katzenjammers 54
Kings Arms *(Waterloo)* 54
Knights Templar 81
Mahogany Bar 119
Old Brewery 171
Parcel Yard 48
Porterhouse 83
Sheaf 59
Sourced Market 49
St John 77
Swan 213
Tap on the Line 200
Understudy 61

Great gardens
Adam and Eve 105
Aeronaut 217
Beehive 148
Blythe Hill Tavern 167
Carpenters Arms *(Bethnal Green)* 86
Crown and Shuttle 86
Cygnet 115
Dalston Eastern Curve Garden Café 108
Express 218
Florence 159
Four Thieves 187
Gothique 193
Gun *(Docklands)* 118
Lighthouse 188
Masons Arms 221
Nags Head 126
Pelton Arms 173
Peoples Park Tavern 116
Pineapple 137
Red Lion *(Leytonstone)* 127
Smokehouse 145
Strongroom 88
Sussex Arms 223

On offer

Accommodation
King William IV 126
Sanctuary House Hotel (*Try also*) 101
St Christophers Inn 60

Arcade games (vintage)
Four Quarters 160

Art
Ask for Janice 73
Crate 114
Cygnet 115
Fox (*Hanwell*) 218
Old Pack Horse 213
Truscott Arms 207

Belgian-themed
Belgique Bistro 124
Belgo Noord 133
Brouge 217
Dove 110
Dovetail 74
Lowlander 82

Bermondsey breweries
See p64

Bottle shops
Bambuni 157
Beer Boutique 191
Beer Shop London 158
Bitter End 176
Bottle Shop 66
BottleDog Kings Cross 73
Brew Testament 114
Brockley Brewery 167
Clapton Craft 106
Craft Beer Shop 141
Dr.Ink of Fulham 209
Fuller's Brewery Shop 211
Good Taste 161
Hop Burns and Black 163
Modern Beer Co 66
Mother Kellys 120
Noble Green Wines 222
Oddbins London Bridge 58
Real Ale 222
Salusbury Wine Store 207
Sambrook's Brewery 189
Sourced Market 49

Utobeer 61
Wanstead Tap 127
We Brought Beer 195
Wine Cellar 179
Woodford Wine Room 128

Brewery showcases
See also Brewpubs, taprooms, and p230 for breweries with multiple pubs in London
Bridge House (Adnams) 52
Jerusalem Tavern (St Peter's) 75
Oaka (Oakham) 164
Porterhouse (Porterhouse) 83
Royal Oak (Harveys) 59
Sultan (Hopback) 200

Brewpubs
Aeronaut 217
Antelope 197
Black Horse 150
Bohemia 150
Brewhouse and Kitchen Islington 42
Bull 151
Cock Tavern 107
Crate 114
Earl of Essex 43
Florence 159
Four Thieves 187
George and Dragon 218
Hops and Glory 143
King William IV 126
Peoples Park Tavern 116
Queens Head (*Kings Cross*) 49
Sultan 200
Tap East 117
White Hart 121
Zerodegrees 174

Chain pubs
See p230

Child-friendly
Adam and Eve 105
Beehive 148
Belgique Bistro 124
Belgo Noord 133
Blythe Hill Tavern 167
Brouge 217
Bull 151
Dalston Eastern Curve Garden Café 108
Dukes Brew and Que 142
Exmouth Arms 75

Florence 159
Four Quarters 160
Fox *(Hanwell)* 218
Fox on the Hill 160
Gothique 193
Grafton 136
Grosvenor 220
Hand in Hand 197
Hope 198
Ivy House 163
Kernel Brewery 66
Lighthouse 188
London's Pride 228
Look Mum No Hands 112
Mad Bishop and Bear 98
Mulberry Tree 221
New Cross Turnpike 177
Old Brewery 171
Orpington Liberal Club 178
Peoples Park Tavern 116
Red Lion *(Leytonstone)* 127
Red Lion *(Barnes)* 199
Shaftesbury Tavern 152
Wanstead Tap 127
Whyte and Brown 94

Clubs
Leyton Orient Supporters Club 116
Orpington Liberal Club 178

Dutch-themed
De Hems 92

Food (exceptional)
Adam and Eve 105
Ask for Janice 73
Belgique Bistro 124
Bohemia 150
Bull 151
Bull and Last 135
Charles Lamb 42
Clapton Hart 107
Crate 114
Dean Swift 52
Dove 110
Dukes Brew and Que 142
Earl of Essex 43
Elgin 205
Gothique 193
Grosvenor 220
Gun *(Docklands)* 118
Hare and Billet 170

Harrild and Sons 70
Horseshoe 136
Lighthouse 188
London's Pride 228
Look Mum No Hands 112
Oaka 164
Old Brewery 171
Old Red Cow 76
Parcel Yard 48
Parlour 206
Powder Keg Diplomacy 188
Prince 145
Queens Head *(Piccadilly Circus)* 94
Quilon 98
Red Lion *(Barnes)* 199
Richard I 173
Smokehouse 145
Sourced Market 49
St John 77
Truscott Arms 207
White Horse 214
Whyte and Brown 94
Wright Brothers Oyster and Porter House 61

German-themed
Fest 210
Katzenjammers 54
Zeitgeist 62

Micropubs
Beer Shop London 158
Door Hinge 176
Long Pond 171
One Inn the Wood 178
Penny Farthing 178

Music
(Many more venues host live music occasionally but these places make it a major feature)
Aeronaut 217
Black Heart 133
Café OTO 105
Cygnet 115
Duke of Hamilton 136
Four Thieves 187
Grape and Grain 162
Ivy House 163
Lamb *(Highbury & Islington)* 144
Mahogany Bar 119
Orpington Liberal Club 178
Pelton Arms 173

Porterhouse 83
Queens Head (Kings Cross) 49
Red Lion (Isleworth) 222
Sebright Arms 120
Slaughtered Lamb 76
St Christophers Inn 60
Sussex Arms 223

Taprooms
Anspach and Hobday 66
Beavertown 148
Brew by Numbers 66
Brick Brewery 159
Brixton Brewery 183
By the Horns Brewing Co 192
Camden Town Brewery 135
Fourpure Brewing 66
Gipsy Hill Brewery 161
Hop Stuff Brewery 170
Kernel Brewery 66
London Beer Factory 164
London Fields Brewery 111
Orbit Beers 165
Partizan Brewing 67
Redchurch Brewery 120
Southwark Brewing Co 67
Twickenham Fine Ales 224
Wild Card Brewery 128

Theatre and comedy
Aeronaut 217
Black Heart 133
Duke of Hamilton 136
Exmouth Arms 75
Finborough Arms 206
Four Thieves 187
Horseshoe 136
Lyric 93
Mahogany Bar 119
Miller 55
Queens Head (Kings Cross) 49
Red Lion (Isleworth) 222
Tabard 214
Understudy 61

Nearby

Visitor attractions, landmarks, markets, arts and sport venues, parks, rivers and canals, transport terminals

Abney Park Cemetery
Jolly Butchers 143

Arcola Theatre
Café OTO 105

Arsenal FC Emirates Stadium
Lamb (Highbury & Islington) 144

artsdepot
Bohemia 150

Barbican Centre
Old Red Cow 76

Battersea Park
Lighthouse 188

Blackfriars station
Blackfriar 68

Blackheath
Hare and Billet 170
Zerodegrees 174

Borough Market
Brew Wharf 51
George 53
Katzenjammers 54
Market Porter 55
Rake 58
Sheaf 59

Brent River Park
Fox (Hanwell) 218

Brick Lane
BrewDog Shoreditch 85

British Library
Parcel Yard 48
Sourced Market 49

British Museum
Museum Tavern 48

Broadway Market
Dove 110

Broadway Theatre (Catford)
Catford Constitutional Club 168

Brompton Cemetery
Finborough Arms 206

Brockwell Park
Florence 159

Buckingham Palace
Buckingham Arms 96
Quilon 98

Bush Theatre/O₂ Shepherds Bush Empire
BrewDog Shepherds Bush 209

Bushy Park
Masons Arms 221
Noble Green Wines 222

Camden Lock
Belgo Noord 133
Black Heart 133

Cannon Street station
Pelt Trader 71

Chapel Market
Craft Beer Co Islington 43
Three Johns 44

Charing Cross station
Harp 80

Chelsea FC Stamford Bridge
Finborough Arms 206

Chinatown
De Hems 92

Chiswick Common
Old Pack Horse 213

Clapham Common
BrewDog Clapham Junction 183

Clapham Junction station/Clapham Grand
Falcon 187
Powder Keg Diplomacy 188

Corams Fields
Lamb *(Bloomsbury)* 47

Covent Garden Piazza
Harp 80
Lowlander 82
Porterhouse 83

Cray
Penny Farthing 178

Crystal Palace Park
Good Taste 161
Grape and Grain 162
Westow House 165

Epping Forest
Belgique Bistro 124
Cricketers 125

Eltham Park
Long Pond 171

Euston station
Euston Tap 47

Exmouth Market
Exmouth Arms 75

Fairfield Halls
Green Dragon 177

Fulham FC Craven Cottage
Dr.Ink of Fulham 209

Garage
Lamb *(Highbury & Islington)* 144

Geffrye Museum
Howl at the Moon 87

Gilette Square (Dalston)
Railway Tavern 145

Grand Union Canal
Fox *(Hanwell)* 218
Parlour 206
Truscott Arms 207
Union Tavern 208

Maritime Greenwich World Heritage Site
Old Brewery 171
Pelton Arms 173

Musical Museum
Express 218

National Gallery/National Portrait Gallery
Harp 80

New End Theatre
Duke of Hamilton 136

O₂ Academy Brixton
Craft Beer Co Brixton 184

Old Operating Theatre and Herb Garret
George 53

Old Spitalfields Market
Magpie 70
Williams Ale and Cider House 71

Paddington Recreation Ground
Elgin 205

Paddington station
Mad Bishop and Bear 98

Peckham Markets/Bellenden Road
Brick Brewery 159
Four Quarters 160

Peckham Rye
Flying Pig 160
Ivy House 163

Piccadilly Circus
Lyric 93
Queens Head (Piccadilly Circus) 94

Queen Elizabeth Olympic Park
Crate 114

Regents Canal
Belgo Noord 133
Black Heart 133
Charles Lamb 42
Dove 110
Fox (Dalston) 110
Wenlock Arms 44

Richmond Park
Roebuck 199

Richmond Theatre
Pigs Ears 198

Rivoli Ballroom
London Beer Dispensary 171

Roundhouse
Belgo Noord 133

Royal Arsenal Woolwich/Firepower
Hop Stuff Brewery 170

Royal Botanic Gardens Kew
Tap on the Line 200

Ruskin Park
Fox on the Hill 160

Shoreditch Park
North Pole 144

Smithfield Market
Ask for Janice 73
Old Red Cow 76
St John 77

Southbank Centre
Understudy 61

Spa Terminus
Kernel brewery 66

St Pancras International station
Parcel Yard 48
Sourced Market 49

St James's Park
Buckingham Arms 96
Quilon 98

Strutton Ground Market
Speaker 99

Tate Modern
Charles Dickens 52

Temple
Edgar Wallace 79

Places to drink index

Photo credits

The publisher would like to thank the pubs, bars, shops, restaurants, breweries and individuals who have kindly given permission for their photography to be printed in this publication. Specific thanks go to:

(Key: t = top, b = bottom, m = middle, l = left, r = right)

Steve Bainbridge 300
Doreen Joy Barber 109 (b), 265 (t), 288 (t)
www.beerguidelondon.com 128 (t), 206 (t)
Thomas Bowles 71
Dan Breckwoldt/Shutterstock.com 9
BrewDog 36 (b), 74, 85, 134, 183, 209, 231 (b)
Magnus Brunner 206 (b)
John Carey 98 (b)
Addie Chinn 111 (t)
Martyn Cornell 123, 130
Crate 19
Hollie Dent 121
Gillian Evans 69, 81 (b), 161 (b), 177, 227 (b), 228, 236
Mark Flisher 88, 254
Fourpure Brewing 65, 288 (b)
Phil Gammon 163 (t)
Elizabeth Grogan 74, 110
Mick Habgood 161
Cath Harries 4, 12, 15 (b), 17 (t), 23, 79 (t), 83, 99, 126, 154, 169, 173 (t), 174 (b), 176, 189, 249, 252, 268 (b), 272 (r), 298 (t), 310, 316
Paul Heneker 207 (b)
James Kendall 116, 187 (b), 217, 234, 294
Lisa Jane Photography 158
London Fields Brewery 111 (b), 297

Dan Marshall 60
Charlie McKay 107
Kris Menan 141
Des de Moor 17 (b), 37 (m), 38 (t), 108, 127, 140, 142, 222, 223, 258, 285, 286 (b)
Patricia Niven 77
Oddbins 58
James Perry 119
pisaphotography/Shutterstock.com 11
Chris Pollard 38 (bl), 82 (b), 214 (b)
Pres Panayotov/Shutterstock.com 318
Roger Protz 311
Robert Gunning Photography 153
Rupert Marlow Photography 250, 290
Southwark Brewing Company 305
Morgan Spencer 265 (b)
Bob Steel 82 (t), 214 (t), 220 (b)
Jamie Stewart 44
Claire-Michelle Taverner-Pearson 37 (t), 43, 46, 47, 48 (b), 49, 240
Paul Winch Furness 29, 62
Alastair Philip Wiper 63
Annick Wolfers 113
Wollertz/Shutterstock.com 274
Thomas Wootton 112

Acknowledgements

Many, many people participated in various ways in the making of this book, both wittingly and unwittingly.

First and foremost I'd like to thank the owners, managers and staff of all the beer outlets listed, not only for running great places and making a vital contribution to London's beer culture, but by being so courteous and helpful when I turned up unexpectedly with damn fool questions when they had customers to serve. I'm also extremely appreciative of the owners, managers and staff of all the London breweries, both for making great beer, and for taking time out from doing so to share their stories and views and, in many cases, some of their beers with me. Thanks also to the London Brewers' Alliance and John Cryne, Paddy Johnson and Steve Williams in particular.

Geoff Strawbridge, CAMRA's London Liaison Group and local branches have been extremely helpful in getting the word out there and keeping me in touch. The branches also deserve to be thanked for all the great work they've done over the years in protecting and promoting London's beer culture. Without them I suspect we wouldn't be enjoying the current abundance.

The following provided helpful additional suggestions and invaluable intelligence: John Paul Adams, Rachel Alcock, Ray Bailey, Stephen Beaumont, Jessica Boak, John Bratley, Ric Brown, Mark Chant, Melissa Cole, Jo Copestick, Colin Coyne, Liz Cronin, Simon Croome, the Deptford Dame, Mark Dredge, Stephen Eastwood, Charlie Gallagher, Eddie Gershon, Laura Goodman, Nick Goodwin, Jeremy Gray, John Gray, Will Hawkes, Tim Holt, Paul Kruzycki, Teresa Langston, Richard Larkin, Shea Luke, Thomas Marshall, Tim Martin, Siobhan McGinn, Charles Owens, Chris 'Podge' Pollard, Roger Protz, Evan Rail, Henri Reuchlin, Tony Roome, Steve Shapiro, Holly Simpson, Nathanial Southwood, Bob Steel, Julian Stone, Emma Stump, Roy Tunstall, Fred Waltman, Rex Ward, Tim Webb, Ian White and Gail Ann Williams. I raise a glass of Southwark ale to them all.

I'm further grateful to all the London Drinkers and other contributors named in the text, to Simon Hall, Julie Hudson and David Birkett at CAMRA Books, to designer Dale Tomlinson, to Emma Haines, Katie Hunt and Ian Midson who worked on the last edition, to the staff at the Deptford Lounge and their free wifi, and to Laura Hunt at Heathrow Airport for getting me from 'dirty' to 'clean' without a boarding pass. Thanks too to colleagues at the Ramblers who uncomplainingly covered for my absence.

As the original edition was my first book I also want to express my gratitude to the following: Tom and Jasper who first published my beer reviews on the Oxford Bottled Beer Database; Ted Bruning who gave me my first paid gig as a beer writer; and Sally Toms, Dominic Bates, Adrian Tierney-Jones and Tom Stainer who all supported my writing. My family clearly played an important role: Phyllis de Moor, Adèle de Moor and Sunil Sohanta de Moor. Thanks to them all.

Last but not least, there's my partner, Ian Harris, who as previously has been unfailingly patient and supportive despite not even liking beer. I've written a new edition of the bloody book, Ian. Bloody, bloody book.

Books for pub & beer lovers

CAMRA Books, the publishing arm of the Campaign for Real Ale,
is the leading publisher of books on beer and pubs. Key titles include:

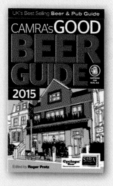

Good Beer Guide 2015

Edited by ROGER PROTZ

The original independent guide to good beer and good pubs.
You're never far from a great pint with the *Good Beer Guide* to hand.
Now in its 42nd edition, the fully revised and updated Guide
recommends pubs in England, Wales, Scotland, Northern Ireland
and offshore islands that serve the best real ale. From country inns
through urban style bars to backstreet boozers – if you love pubs,
don't leave home without the *Good Beer Guide*.

£15.99   ISBN 978 1 85249 320 2

Britain's Beer Revolution

ROGER PROTZ and ADRIAN TIERNEY-JONES

UK brewing has seen unprecedented growth in the last decade.
Breweries of all shapes and sizes are flourishing. Established brewers
applying generations of tradition in new ways rub shoulders at the bar
with new micro-brewers. Headed by real ale, a 'craft' beer revolution is
sweeping the country. In *Britain's Beer Revolution* Roger Protz and
Adrian Tierney-Jones look behind the beer labels and shine a
spotlight on what makes British beer so good.

£14.99   ISBN 978 1 85249 321 9

Good Bottled Beer Guide

JEFF EVANS

A pocket-sized guide for discerning drinkers looking to buy bottled real
ales and enjoy a fresh glass of their favourite beers at home. The 8th
edition of the *Good Bottled Beer Guide* is completely revised, updated
and redesigned to showcase the very best bottled British real ales now
being produced, and detail where they can be bought. Everything you
need to know about bottled beers; tasting notes, ingredients, brewery
details, and a glossary to help the reader understand more about them.

£12.99   ISBN 978 1 85249 309 7